From Discord to Harmony

From Discord to Harmony

Making Your Workplace Hum

edited by

LaVena Wilkin

Sullivan University

Tony Belak

University of Louisville

IAP

INFORMATION AGE PUBLISHING, INC.

Charlotte, NC • www.infoagepub.com

ACKNOWLEDGMENTS

We are so grateful our authors—whose expertise in scholarly writing, citations, and academic application—lightened our burden. Many are both scholars and practitioners, and they have a unique blend of understanding the research behind their topics and practicing the ideas they share with our readers. Several authors have or have had an affiliation with Sullivan University, whose early work in this field must be recognized.

Thank you, also, to Bob Wilkin (LaVena's husband) who is creating the website fromdiscordtoharmony.com—a place where we and our contributing authors can continue sharing perspectives, expertise, and supporting materials.

A special heartfelt "thank you" to Creighlynn Thoele, PhD. Dr. Thoele was our third set of eyes, and her insights, input, and perceptions strengthened the quality of our book.

From Discord to Harmony, page ix

SECTION I

FROM DISCORD

Toxic Leaders—Who They Are and What They Do

Whether they are labeled as *toxic leaders* (the typical term used in a military context) or *workplace bullies* (the common label used in a corporate environment), they are highly destructive. These types of leaders act aggressively toward their subordinates, are highly critical and dismissive, demand almost blind loyalty, frequently blame or take credit for the work of others, and play mind games strategically designed to keep people off-balance. They exert their dominance and exploit their power and authority by threatening, intimidating, yelling, or engaging in vicious and explosive verbal assaults intended to demean, undermine, and publicly humiliate those on the receiving end. Though rare, they sometimes also engage in physical attacks. Their subordinates generally hate or fear them (often both), and usually work very hard to stay out of their line of sight.

Why Should You Care?

Toxic leaders can (and often do) achieve extraordinary results, but the price is often sky-high given their destructive and often intolerable impact on people in the organization; however, they don't seem to care. They just want to get the job done as fast as humanly possible so that they can secure their next promotion and move on up. As a result of their short-term "take no prisoners" focus, they invariably leave their organizations in far worse shape than when they started.

Outcomes range from mutiny and death to an erosion of trust, increased turnover, domestic violence, higher absenteeism, increased alcohol and drug use, as well as reductions in employee health, motivation, productivity, happiness, and job satisfaction. As if all that were not enough, the organization is also often hit with related costs arising from increases in workers' compensation claims, plus marked spikes in both mental health and medical expenses (predominantly due to increased stress) incurred by both the target and sometimes also members of their family. In combination, these predictable outcomes seem like more than enough reason to want to do something about these destructive leaders.

There are some interesting distinctions between destructive leaders who operate within a military context from those operating in the corporate business world. These differences will be explored next.

The Toxic Military Leader: "It's All About Me"

According to a significant U.S. Army internal survey, an estimated 20% of American soldiers report having suffered under a toxic leader (Steele,

2011). So, what does it mean to be toxic? The term is generally applied to a leader who "appears driven by self-centered careerism at the expense of their subordinates and unit, and whose style is characterized by abusive and dictatorial behavior that promotes an unhealthy organizational climate" (Ulmer, 2012, p. 48). Similarly, others have characterized toxic leadership as "an apparent lack of concern for the well-being of subordinates," "a personality or interpersonal technique that negatively affects organizational climate," and "a conviction by subordinates that the leader is motivated primarily by self-interest" (Reed, 2004, p. 67).

Supported by a strong culture that considers mission accomplishment to be almost sacrosanct, toxic military leaders are intensely mission-focused which, of course, is entirely appropriate. It becomes a double-edged sword, though, when they fail to take into account *how* the results are attained. They tend to adopt a "results at any cost" strategy that does not factor in how working a rigorous and demanding work schedule (often including weekends) affects soldiers and their families.

The impact on people is similarly harsh when a toxic leader ambitiously overextends the unit on projects undertaken solely to enhance the leader's own standing in the eyes of his or her commander. In these situations, soldiers are often required to work for extended periods of time without adequate personnel or equipment on the off-chance that the toxic leader will get some extra benefit from his or her superiors by taking on the assignment. Consequently, the subordinates of toxic leaders feel that toxic leaders have no empathy for and simply do not care about them, resulting in high levels of organizational cynicism (Dobbs & Do, 2018). The result is that they either burn out and leave due to the relentless demands and harsh treatment or, perhaps worse yet, stay but feel angry and demoralized—not exactly the conditions to inspire or build a cohesive work unit.

Not only are toxic leaders results-driven to a fault, but they wholeheartedly embrace a "kiss up and kick down" style of operating. Their advanced interpersonal skills allow them to schmooze and get along well with senior leaders at the top echelon. This political savvy, coupled with their accomplishment of near-impossible missions, causes their superiors to hold them with high regard. Their solid reputation for being bright, personable, technically competent, and for getting things done overwhelms any suspicion by their boss that their means might not justify the ends (Ulmer, personal communication, March 30, 2015).

While toxic leaders are often revered by their superiors, their subordinates know all too well how abusive and excessively self-interested they can be. They are widely viewed as having little regard for people other than themselves. They are also perceived as being laser-focused on securing their next promotion or on the next opportunity to impress their superiors (but not necessarily on doing what is right for their subordinates or in the U.S.

Army's long-term best interest). In fact, they sometimes get involved in activities *only* if they believe that a senior leader will be available to impress.

This self-absorption causes subordinates to see the motive of their leader as being less about ensuring the Army's success, and more along the lines of "it's all about me, me... and me." Not surprisingly, toxic leaders do not tend to see themselves as arrogant, self-interested, destructive, or cruel. If they are aware at all of their impact on others, they rationalize their behavior as being "tough" and "mission-driven" while denigrating those who object to their operating style by calling them "whiners" and "crybabies."

The truth is their behavior is both tough and mission-driven; however, it goes far beyond that—their interactions with subordinates are widely perceived as harsh, abusive, intimidating, threatening, humiliating, and almost always demoralizing to those who work for them. For the rare toxic leaders who are actually aware of their negative impact on others, they don't seem to care as long as the mission is accomplished. The result is an excessive number of transfer requests or full resignations from the Army by soldiers under their command.

Developing and retaining talented subordinates is critical to the success of an all-volunteer Army; however, a toxic leader's failure to coach and inspire others may be the most lasting and destructive impact on the organization (Daniel & Metcalf, 2016b, 2015a, 2015b). Think about it: When individuals work for a corporation, they can quit and go to work for another company while remaining within the framework of their professions. However, when military personnel find their leaders to be so intolerable that they would prefer to leave the service, all they can do is resign and leave the military profession altogether, along with their pension. Dave Matsuda (2014) offered a disturbing synopsis of the problem as it occurs in the military, exclaiming, "Outside the wire, the enemy is the enemy; inside the wire, the command climate is the enemy" (para. 22).

Perplexingly, despite all of the devastation they leave in their wake, toxic leaders are usually successful—at least in the short-term. Why? Because they *do* get results. But by the time the damage they have caused to their unit is well understood, the toxic leaders are long gone, happily promoted and relocated to their next assignment—where they start the destructive cycle all over again.

The Toxic Corporate Leader: "I'm Gonna Get You—Whatever It Takes"

The U.S. Army most assuredly is not the only large organization with a toxic leader problem—the corporate sector also has its fair share of destructive leaders where they are generally referred to as workplace bullies. In a 2017

U.S. national survey on the phenomenon, about 19% of adult Americans reported that they have directly experienced bullying at work (defined in the survey as "repeated abusive conduct that is threatening, intimidating, humiliating, work sabotage, or work abuse"; Workplace Bullying Institute, 2017, para. 1).

Like toxic leaders, corporate bullies frequently misuse their power and authority, are excessively self-focused, prone to emotional outbursts, and often treat people unfairly (Daniel, 2009). But there is one key difference: Unlike the toxic military leader whose actions tend to negatively affect the command climate of the entire unit, toxic corporate types typically single out a single employee to torment, humiliate, or intimidate for a period of time—until they move on to their next target.

A corporate bully's motive is described as, "I'm gonna get you—whatever it takes." Some targets describe the experience as being "an all-out personal attack" (Daniel, 2009, 2012). Indeed, findings support these sentiments by showing that toxic corporate leaders act with *malice*—defined as the "desire to cause pain, injury, or distress to another" ("Malice," n.d.). What this means is that their behavior is intentionally abusive and purposefully targeted toward specific individuals, usually with the intent to drive the person out of the organization (Daniel, 2009, 2012).

Tough Bosses Everywhere: "Tough but Fair"

Although there are some differences between toxic leaders based on whether they are operating in a military or corporate context, studies have shown that tough bosses are virtually the same in both environments (Daniel, 2009, 2012; Daniel & Metcalf, 2015a, 2015b, 2016a). Think of tough bosses as almost the polar opposite of toxic leaders. While toxic leaders are almost universally bad for an organization, tough bosses—people who both get things done and care for their people—are essential for success.

The profile of a tough boss most often looks like this: professional, self-controlled, highly self-aware, emotionally mature, results-oriented, and striving to make long-term decisions that are good for both the people and the organization. Like toxic leaders, tough bosses are also passionate about getting results; in fact, they are sometimes perceived as nearly *maniacal* in their efforts to meet their goals.

As a result, tough bosses are by no means "soft" or easy to work for. A key differentiator is that tough bosses make sure to show that they really care about their people—by taking time to mentor and coach, by getting to know their people on a personal level through frequent two-way communications, by recognizing and celebrating performance, by taking personal responsibility for mistakes in their department, and by acting quickly to resolve interpersonal conflicts or address other work-related concerns. This more humane approach results in a generally positive work climate (at least most days). People who work for tough bosses consistently characterize them as "tough but fair"—and generally feel a great deal of loyalty and respect for them.

Lest the picture seem too rosy, though, the challenge of working for a tough boss should not be minimized. They are usually intense and highly driven individuals. Their demanding (and sometimes perfectionistic) expectations undoubtedly create a fair amount of tension and stress for those who work for them. The difference is that employees understand that their drive for results is not personal or mean-spirited but is meant to benefit both them and the organization.

It is important to note that tough bosses place a heavy emphasis on employee development, and spend a great deal of time mentoring and coaching their subordinates. This focus, coupled with their adherence to high standards, helps to ensure that their organizations are continuously building a pipeline of strong, well-trained future leaders. Ultimately, this may be their greatest legacy to the long-term success and sustainability of their organizations.

While it should come as no surprise, participants in studies that my colleagues and I previously conducted were adamant that tough bosses should not be admonished or cautioned to "tone it down" simply because they set the bar high for their subordinates and are not necessarily easy to work for. In fact, they made a very strong case that tough, demanding, and results-oriented leaders are absolutely *essential* for organizational success—and we could not agree with them more.

Assessing Toxic Leader Behaviors

Some of you are by now probably thinking to yourself: Is my boss a toxic leader? Or, hitting a little closer to home, you might be asking yourself: What about me? Am I toxic or just tough? To get a handle on either answer, here are the most common toxic behaviors identified and "grounded" directly in research findings to-date (Daniel, 2009, 2012; Daniel & Metcalf, 2015a, 2015b, 2016b). Check "yes" to any and all that seem to apply.

 # *Toxic Leader Behaviors*

Do you (or someone you know)

1. care about achieving results so much that you fail to consider the impact of the work and schedule on employees and their families?
2. excessively focus on your own pay and promotions?

3. take credit for the work of others?
4. always think you are right and that your ideas are the best ones?
5. fail to get to know your employees on a personal level?
6. unconcerned about or oblivious to employee morale?
7. fail to allow discussion or debate because you consider it a threat to your authority?
8. often make short-term decisions that make you look good but that are likely to be detrimental to the organization in the long run?
9. appear charming and personable to your boss but treat your employees badly?
10. engage in angry tirades and/or attack people verbally or physically?
11. intentionally seek to threaten, intimidate, or humiliate people?
12. treat people unfairly, inconsistently, and with a lack of respect?
13. blame others for mistakes but take no personal responsibility?
14. have an inflated sense of self-importance?
15. commit to meeting goals without securing the proper funding, resources, or personnel?
16. fail to mentor or develop your employees?
17. create a climate of fear, anxiety, or mistrust at work?

Getting a Handle on Your Own Toxic Tendencies

It is sometimes easy to identify someone else as a toxic leader, but harder to be objective when assessing your own behaviors. As a result, it is a good idea to invite other people to weigh-in. You must risk being vulnerable and ask for direct and candid opinions about your effect on others. You will get the most benefit from talking with colleagues and friends who you know will be brutally frank with you (although it will undoubtedly be hard to hear).

Get an executive coach who can help you critically examine yourself and who can also provide you with strategies and tools to support you as you make adjustments to your way of operating at work. Take time to listen and pay closer attention to your impact on others. If you have not yet explored the Myers-Briggs Type Inventory (MBTI®), consider taking this assessment (or something similar) to learn more about your preferences and personality style. Participate in your company's system of 360-degree feedback assessment to see how you are coming across to your boss, peers, and subordinates at work.

Work on improving your self-awareness, self-regulation, motivation, empathy, and social skills—all of which make up your emotional intelligence. The data showing that emotional intelligence is a key differentiator between star performers and others is irrefutable (Wilkins, 2014). Above all, though, refrain from making excuses to yourself or others about your use of power and authority in ways that are motivated, at least in part, by ego and self-interest. After all, these are your negative behaviors—own them. Any change is tough, but until you decide that changing yourself is absolutely required and you begin the hard work that it will take to get there, leading with a toxic twist will remain your default modus operandi—and history suggests that it will ultimately derail your career.

Assessing Tough Boss Behaviors

Now that you have some idea about toxic tendencies, here are the most common tough boss behaviors that we uncovered in previous studies (Daniel, 2009, 2012; Daniel & Metcalf, 2015a, 2015b, 2016a). Check "yes" to any and all that seem to apply.

 # Tough Boss Behaviors.

Do you (or someone you know)

1. care about achieving results but also consider the impact of the work and schedule on your employees and their families?
2. have tough and demanding expectations for yourself and your subordinates about achieving results?
3. have a high level of self-awareness, empathy, and emotional maturity?
4. show care and concern for your people?
5. act professionally and with self-control at work?
6. seek to resolve conflicts fairly and quickly?
7. give credit and recognition to others?
8. celebrate and reward the successful efforts of your subordinates?
9. treat people fairly, consistently, and with respect?
10. take time to mentor, coach, and develop your subordinates?
11. take personal responsibility for mistakes in your unit or department?
12. make decisions that are in the long-term best interest of the organization?
13. seek to develop a positive and respectful work climate?

If you determine that you have a significant number of these attributes, kudos to you for exhibiting the type of leadership that creates a positive and respectful work environment—one that is associated with long-term positive outcomes both for employees, as well as for your organization. Although employees may feel pushed and challenged (as noted earlier, it is not necessarily easy for an employee to work for a tough boss), they are also likely to be highly productive, feel that they are being mentored and are expanding their skills, while also feeling respected and appreciated at work.

So What?

Hopefully these checklists have provided a quick way for you to assess your own behaviors (or those of your boss, and maybe both). Why is this important? Armed with this knowledge, on an individual level, you can decide to proactively change some of your less desirable behaviors in order to stay on a positive leadership track at work.

For organizations, clearer distinctions between toxic leaders and tough bosses can help with quicker identification of both. This means that tough bosses can be more quickly recognized and rewarded for their constructive leadership style, and toxic leaders can be paired with a coach or mentor in an attempt to get a handle on their destructive tendencies; however, if they cannot or will not change, the sad truth is that the best option is to hold them accountable and fairly quickly show them the door.

What You and Your Organization Can Do About a Toxic Leader

What You Can Do

Recommendations from previous study participants about how *individuals* can most effectively respond to a situation involving a toxic leader include (Daniel, 2009, 2012; Daniel & Metcalf, 2015a, 2015b, 2016a):

- Just "wait it out" knowing that the individual is likely to be promoted or transferred soon.
- Use your chain of command to report the abusive behavior.
- Avoid the toxic leader.
- Identify a person the toxic leader trusts and work through that individual.
- Make it a point to learn what *not* to do from the toxic leader.
- Communicate regularly and provide feedback intended to help the toxic leader become more self-aware of his impact on others.
- Check your organization's policies to see if the toxic leader's actions are improper or illegal and approach the problem from that angle.
- Provide "cover" for your subordinates in order to protect them.
- Teach subordinates what "good leadership" looks like and regularly practice it to ensure that toxic behaviors are not imitated and do not inadvertently become part of your organization's culture.
- File a complaint with HR or senior leaders in your company (but there is generally little confidence that HR will actually step in to resolve the problem).

Other research has suggested that it is essential for subordinates to accept the fact that they cannot change their boss. According to Shufelt and Longenecker (2017),

> This observation is not fatalistic, but rather realistic . . . subordinates must adjust their own behaviors and adopt new methods of interacting to accommodate the shortcomings and "bad boss" tendencies of their superiors. . . . When a follower is faced with a toxic leader, his or her potential response options are "much more than just suffering in silence or quitting. (p. 4, 9)

There are numerous potential practical responses that can assist a suffering subordinate, used either individually or in combination. Shufelt and Longenecker (2017) suggested that proactive implementation of some (or all) of these strategies are viable ways to respond to a toxic leader:

- Put yourself in your boss's shoes.
- Get on the same page as your boss.
- Work hard to know and understand your boss's strengths and weaknesses.
- Conduct regular assessments of the overall quality of your current relationship with your boss and conduct an annual strengths, weaknesses, opportunities, and threats analysis.
- Communicate using your boss's rules.
- Be proactive and stay aligned with your boss.
- Establish your "brand" and make it a practice to under-promise and over-deliver.
- Be a problem solver.
- Always show respect for your boss (even if he or she might not deserve it).
- Know when it's time to leave the situation behind.

What** Your **Organization Can Do

Paradoxically, the organization itself may inadvertently create an environment where toxic leaders and bullies run rampant due to well-intentioned pay, bonus, and promotion practices that drive unintended behaviors that negatively impact the workforce (Daniel, 2013; Daniel & Metcalf, 2015a, 2015b, 2017). In previous research studies, participants identified a number of potential leverage points—changes to an organization's current culture, systems, policies, and processes that are most likely to minimize the potential for or eliminate toxic leadership entirely (Daniel & Metcalf, 2015a, 2015b, 2016b, 2017). These include:

- Revise your policies, mission statement, and other important corporate documents to ensure that they explicitly state the company's expectations that interactions with all employees should be handled in a respectful and civil manner (even during times of disagreement), and that disrespectful or abusive behavior will not be tolerated.

- Increase leader emphasis on and accountability for leader selection and development (e.g., deep vetting before making key hires, more mentoring and coaching, more one-on-one conversations, regular feedback on performance, and the development of reward and recognition mechanisms for senior leaders who excel in subordinate development and consequences for those who do not).
- Consider changes to the performance evaluation process (e.g., to include input from not only the individual's boss, but also a random sampling of his or her peers and subordinates, plus a review and consideration of the organization's most recent employee engagement survey data, with specific emphasis on those units or departments he or she supervises).
- Consider changes to the promotion process (e.g., include input from multiple levels, examine the results of employee engagement and climate surveys, and solicit input from prior senior leaders).
- Make changes to the bonus system to negate awards to leaders who do not live up to the company's norms of civility.
- Increase emphasis on and accountability for the regular use of climate and/or employee engagement surveys (e.g., require surveys to be conducted on a regular basis, act on the data to ensure accountability and improve trust, and increase the frequency of on-site visits to units by senior leaders so that they can personally observe the climate and talk with employees).
- Consider expanding the organization's emotional intelligence training to include officers and managers at all levels.

Hopeful Signs for the Future

The evidence is overwhelming that toxic leaders permeate the highest levels of most organizations in fairly large numbers; they are destructive and they cause significant damage to both their people and their organizations—but there is still reason to be optimistic about the future, and here are just some recent examples of progress.

The U.S. Army has focused on the problem, relieving a number of high-ranking toxic officers for creating negative toxic command climates in recent years (Forsling, 2017; Zwerdling, 2014). Moreover, the #MeToo movement, a movement focused on ending sexual misconduct at work, is also gaining momentum and has received significant funding from the TIMES UP Legal Defense Fund to assist affected women in their legal efforts to bring their complaints forward (see https://metoomvmt.org/ and https://www.timesupnow.com/). Conversations are occurring with increasing regularity on social media about what constitutes appropriate workplace conduct (Daniel, 2017b; Daniel & Metcalf, 2013, 2015b).

Numerous corporations have similarly terminated high-flying senior executives for their abusive behavior at work—despite their high-profile status or the fact that they were getting results (Almukhtar, Gold, & Buchanan, 2018). In addition, the *Healthy Workplace Bill*— legislation that would provide legal redress for health-harming mistreatment occurring at work—has been considered (but not yet adopted) by legislatures in more than two dozen states (see http://healthyworkplacebill.org/). In combination, these recent events suggest that employees will no longer tolerate abusive behavior of any kind at work. The days of complicit silence and of ignoring the "elephant in the room" appear to be ending.

Wrapping It Up

Really smart organizations have already figured out that they will not be able to attract and retain really great people by allowing them to be abused or disrespected. Toxic leaders are uninspiring, demoralizing, and always destructive—which is why, thankfully, that style of leadership is rapidly going the way of the dinosaur.

Enlightened companies understand that employees work at their best when they are treated with trust, respect, and fairness—timeless values that really matter to people and which will never go out of style. At the same time, organizations are waking up to the fact that abusive leaders drive away talent, making them simply too expensive to keep—regardless of their ability to deliver results.

HR managers and leaders who understand this can significantly help to shape the company's culture, policies, and practices, as well as its employee communications, training, and related prevention efforts (Daniel, 2018). The new organizational strategy emerging when it comes to dealing with toxic leaders is sharply focused on accountability and goes something like this: "Find them, fix them, or fire them" (Owens, 2014, para. 19).

So, here's a word to the wise: It's a new day. Toxic leaders are increasingly being viewed as irrelevant relics of a long-ago past—the workplace equivalent of dinosaur fossils. The choice for toxic leaders is now clear: change or become extinct.

ACKNOWLEDGMENTS

The author would like to express her sincere appreciation to her husband and colleague, Dr. Gary Metcalf, who has been her chief collaborator and thought partner on many of the research studies, books, and articles mentioned in this chapter; however, any errors or omissions are hers alone.

REFERENCES

Almukhtar, S., Gold, M., & Buchanan, L. (2018, January 11). After Weinstein: 71 men accused of sexual misconduct and their fall from power. *The New York Times.* Retrieved from https://www.nytimes.com/interactive/2017/11/10/us/men-accused-sexual-misconduct-weinstein.html?_r=0

Daniel, T. A. (2009). *"Tough boss" or workplace bully?: A grounded theory study of insights from human resource professionals* (Doctoral dissertation). Fielding Graduate University, Santa Barbara, CA.

Daniel, T. A. (2012, Spring). Caught in the crossfire: When HR practitioners become targets of bullying. *Employment Relations Today, 39*(1), 9–16. Retrieved from http://onlinelibrary.wiley.com/doi/10.1002/ert.21349/abstract

Daniel, T. A. (2013, July). Executive success and the increased potential for ethical failure. *SHRM Quarterly Legal Report.* Retrieved from https://www.researchgate.net/publication/258032251_Executive_Success_and_the_Increased_Risk_of_Ethical_Failure

Daniel, T. A. (2017a, Winter). Managing toxic emotions at work: An examination of HR's unique role as the "organizational shock absorber." *Employment Relations Today, 43*(4), 13–19.

Daniel, T. A. (2017b, November). A not-so-radical workplace manifesto. LinkedIn *Pulse.* Retrieved from https://www.linkedin.com/pulse/not-so-radical-workplace-manifesto-teresa-a-daniel-jd-Ph.D./

Daniel, T. A. (2018). The role of human resources in the prevention of workplace bullying and mobbing. In M. Duffy & D. C. Yamada (Eds.), *Workplace bullying and mobbing in the United States* (pp. 235–264). Santa Barbara, CA: ABC-CLIO.

Daniel, T. A., & Metcalf, G. S. (2013). NFL case shows how hazing can devolve into bullying. *Lexington Herald Leader.* Retrieved from http://www.kentucky.com/opinion/op-ed/article44453499.html

Daniel, T. A., & Metcalf, G. S. (2015a). *Crossing the line: An examination of toxic leadership in the U.S. Army.* Retrieved from https://www.researchgate.net/publication/274252085_Crossing_the_Line_An_Examination_of_Toxic_Leadership_in_the_U.S._Army

Daniel, T. A., & Metcalf, G. S. (2015b). Are you a toxic leader or just a tough boss? *SHRM HR Magazine, 60*(6). Retrieved from https://www.shrm.org/hr-today/news/hr-magazine/Pages/070815-toxic-leader-or-tough-boss.aspx

Daniel, T. A., & Metcalf, G. S. (2016a). *Stop bullying at work: Strategies and tools for HR, legal & risk management professionals.* Alexandria, VA: SHRM Books.

Daniel, T. A., & Metcalf, G. S. (2016b, November 4). *Crossing the line: An examination of toxic leadership in the U.S. Army.* International Leadership Association Conference presentation. Retrieved from_https://convention2.allacademic.com/one/ila/ila16/index.php?PHPSESSID=gjot95i5u79qb8vikc1383dov2&cmd=Online+Program+Search&program_focus=fulltext_search&search_mode=content&offset=0&search_text=teresa+daniel

Daniel, T. A., & Metcalf, G. S. (2017, Spring). How some companies unwittingly make bullying a rational choice. *Employment Relations Today, 44*(1), 15–24.

Dobbs, J. M., & Do, J. J. (2018, January 11). The impact of perceived toxic leadership on cynicism in officer candidates. *Armed Forces & Society, 45*(1), 3–26. Retrieved from http://journals.sagepub.com/doi/full/10.1177/0095327X17747204

Forsling, C. (2017, August 23). The military has a toxic leadership problem. *Task & Purpose.* Retrieved from https://taskandpurpose.com/military-toxic-leadership-problem/

Malice. (n.d.). In Merriam-Webster Dictionary. Retrieved from http://www.merriam-webster.com/dictionary/malice

Matsuda, D. (2014, May 24). *A study of Army suicides in Iraq: A 2010 in 2014 context.* Retrieved from https://www.linkedin.com/pulse/20140524145604-76082895-a-study-of-army-suicides-in-iraq-a-2010-study-in-2014-context

Owens, D. M. (2014, March 1). Dr. David Posen's prescription for work stress. *SHRM HR Magazine, 59*(3), 44.

Reed, G. E. (2004). Toxic leaders. *Military Review, 84*(4), 67–71.

Shufelt Jr., J. W., & Longenecker, C. O. (2017, November). Practical lessons learned for dealing with toxic leaders and bad bosses. *Military Review Online Exclusive.* Retrieved from http://www.armyupress.army.mil/Journals/Military-Review/Online-Exclusive/2017-Online-Exclusive-Articles/Practical-Lessons/

Steele, J. P. (2011). *Antecedents and consequences of toxic leadership in the U.S. Army: A two-year review and recommended solutions* (*Technical Report 2011-3*). Ft. Leavenworth, KS: Center for Army Leadership.

Ulmer, W. F. (2012, June). Toxic leadership. *Army,* 47–52 at 48.

Wilkins, M. M. (2014, December 31). Signs that you lack emotional intelligence. *Harvard Business Review.* Retrieved from https://hbr.org/2014/12/signs-that-you-lack-emotional-intelligence

Workplace Bullying Institute. (2017). *2017 U.S. workplace bullying survey.* Retrieved from http://www.workplacebullying.org/wbiresearch/wbi-2017-survey/

Zwerdling, D. (2014, January 6). Army takes on its own toxic leaders. *National Public Radio.* Retrieved from https://www.npr.org/2014/01/06/259422776/army-takes-on-its-own-toxic-leaders

CHAPTER 2

RECOGNIZING AND RESPONDING TO WORKPLACE BULLYING AND MOBBING

Guidelines for Business Leaders

Maureen Duffy

The workplace is all about relationships. These relationships include those between supervisors and subordinates, coworkers with each other, and workers with customers and people served. Work relationships also include the relationship between a particular worker and the tasks and actions that need to be accomplished in order to fulfill the mission of the organization, however large or small that mission may be. Organizational leaders set the tone in their organizations, for good or for bad, and their attitudes and actions will either foster or discourage workplace bullying and mobbing.

There is a strong ethical case and a strong business case to be made for building workplaces around the core value of respect for the dignity of each and every worker. In this chapter, why leaders should pay attention to both the ethical and business cases for preventing workplace bullying and mobbing will be discussed. The following key sets of information will be

From Discord to Harmony, pages 17–33

reviewed: (a) what workplace bullying and mobbing are and are not; (b) the devastating effects of bullying and mobbing both on individual workers and on their organizations; and (c) strategies leaders can take to prevent bullying and mobbing.

Leaders who are successful in implementing the value of dignity at work will cultivate workplaces that are resistant to bullying and mobbing. Valcour (2014), citing the work of researcher Andrew Sayer, stated:

> Dignity is a fundamentally social phenomenon that arises through interaction, and therefore it depends on a mix of both independence and interdependence.... In dignified work relations, people carefully avoid taking advantage of the inherent vulnerability of the employment relationship and power differentials in organizations. (para. 4)

The social phenomenon that Valcour (2014) described as dignity at work is, at its heart, relational. It is about how people are treated and how they treat each other. She also asserted that "dignity exists when people are listened to and taken seriously regardless of their position—and feel they can disagree respectfully and be heard, without fear of reprisal" (Valcour, 2014, para. 4). Because how people treat each other at work represents a combination of beliefs, attitudes, and behaviors that arise from a person's background and personality, influencing workplace behavior can be challenging. Yet that is precisely what organizational leaders must do in their efforts to eliminate and prevent workplace bullying and mobbing.

DEFINING WORKPLACE BULLYING AND MOBBING

Conflict is an inescapable part of human interactions and is as normal as cooperation. Not all conflict at work is bullying. Much of it is normal, predictable behavior. Indeed, conflict that is well managed and openly acknowledged and addressed can be the source of creativity and innovation in human relationships and in the establishment of workplace goals and strategies. Conflict and cooperation are two sides of the same coin of human interactions. However, conflict that devolves into disrespectful and aggressive behavior can become a triggering event for the development of workplace bullying and mobbing in which an individual is targeted for abuse that continues and intensifies over time.

In the 1990s in the United States, Ruth and Gary Namie spearheaded a campaign against workplace bullying, and have spent their lives working to eliminate and prevent it. They have been leaders in putting the topic of workplace bullying before American workers and organizational leaders and demanding that real measures be implemented to stop it. They define workplace bullying as "repeated, health-harming mistreatment of a person by one or more workers that takes the form of verbal abuse; conduct or behaviors that are threatening, intimidating, or humiliating; sabotage that prevents work from getting done; or some combination of the three" (Namie & Namie, 2009, p. 1).

Scholars and practitioners have spent a lot of time considering what the appropriate term should be to describe workplace abuse. In the United States, workplace bullying is the most widely used term with workplace mobbing increasingly in use as well. Other terms such as emotional abuse, workplace abuse, abusive supervision, workplace incivility, harassment, and hostile workplace environment are also used (Yamada, Duffy, & Berry, 2018). Each term has a slightly different emphasis, but what the terms have in common is their focus on the mistreatment of others in the workplace. Workplace mobbing emphasizes the group and ganging up nature of workplace abuse in which others are either recruited or imitatively join in the targeting of a worker for mistreatment. Workplace mobbing scholars, Maureen Duffy and Len Sperry (2012) defined workplace mobbing as follows:

> Workplace mobbing is nonsexual harassment of a coworker by a group of members of an organization for the purpose of removing the targeted individual(s) from the organization or at least a particular unit of the organization. Mobbing involves individual, group, and organizational dynamics. It predictably results in humiliation, devaluation, discrediting, and degradation; loss of professional reputation; and, often, removal of the victim from the organization through termination, extended medical leave, or quitting. The results of this typically protracted traumatizing experience are significant financial, career, health, and psychosocial losses or other negative consequences. (p. 52)

It is important to understand that while most bullying and mobbing originates from supervisor to subordinate that it is by no means the only direction in which bullying and mobbing can happen. Coworkers can bully and mob one another and those in lower levels of the organizational hierarchy can target and gang up on someone higher up, even at the top of the organization.

Bullying and Mobbing as Forms of Scapegoating

In the workplace, bullying and mobbing are forms of scapegoating—ways of blaming a worker for problems in the workplace and targeting that worker for abuse, often with the goal of driving that worker from the job or organization. Scapegoating, as a solution attempt that ultimately fails, has been around for a long time and is recorded in the Old Testament in the Book of Leviticus. As an ancient practice, scapegoating bears remarkable resemblance to bullying and mobbing today. In ancient times, scapegoating involved procuring an animal, originally a goat (hence the name), and projecting onto that goat or another animal all the sins and misfortunes of the community.

The literal scapegoat would then be driven out of town by the community, often to the edge of a cliff or precipice over which the goat would have no choice but to fall to its death. Over the centuries, we have become very good at scapegoating, even sophisticated as in workplace bullying and mobbing. However, it seems we have failed to learn the central lesson from it—that scapegoating doesn't work and that it only provides temporary, illusory relief before the need to find another scapegoat to blame arises again and the whole process repeats itself.

Risk Factors for Becoming a Target of Bullying and Mobbing

The study of scapegoating sheds some light on who is likely to become a target of bullying and mobbing in the workplace. Rene Girard, a French historian and philosopher of social science, is the preeminent scholar of studies of scapegoating. Girard (1986) clearly identified scapegoats as victims, indeed as arbitrary victims. But scapegoats have some characteristics in common that allow them to be studied more as a group. Girard sees victims, who are ultimately selected as scapegoats, as individuals who occupy liminal space on the fringes or margins of a community—they are not fully a part of the community but not fully outside of it either. In particular, Girard stated that those more likely than others to become scapegoats are women, children, the elderly, those with physical abnormalities or disabilities, members of ethnic or racial minorities, the poor, and, interestingly, those with natural gifts or characteristics like beauty, intelligence, charm, or status like wealth or position that set them apart as exceptional.

Workplace bullying and mobbing research regarding who is likely to become a target (or victim), while not yet extensive, gives us some tantalizing leads about who is more likely than others to become a target. At this stage of our knowledge about targethood (or victimhood) from workplace bullying or mobbing, the following categories of people seem to be at higher risk than others: those who are different from the cultural norm within the organization (which could include a whole range of differences from the dominant organizational norm), including those with differing communication styles like first-generation immigrants; those who speak out or challenge organizational practices; those who expose workplace corruption or wrongdoing; and those who are hardworking and conscientious (Duffy & Sperry, 2012, 2014; Friedenberg, 2008; Namie & Namie, 2018). These risk factors for becoming a target of workplace bullying and mobbing bear an uncanny resemblance to the risk factors identified by Girard (1986) for becoming a scapegoat.

Examples of Workplace Bullying and Mobbing

Keashley (2018) reminded us that workplace bullying and mobbing, types of workplace aggression and abuse, are not single events but rather ongoing patterns of relationship with others at work. Workplace bullying and mobbing are patterns of hostile interactions. For business and organizational leaders, preventing workplace bullying and mobbing requires the ability to recognize the pattern of negative acts indicative of workplace abuse. The following recognizable types of aggressive and abusive workplace behaviors (shown in the list below), when repeated over time within patterns of relationship to a target, are indicators of workplace bullying and mobbing. Only a very small number of such behaviors, when repeated over time, are required to qualify as evidence of workplace bullying or mobbing. What is common to all of these behaviors is flagrant lack of care and respect for the dignity of the worker.

The following examples are derived from the pioneering work of Heinz Leymann (2010) in the area of workplace mobbing during the 1980s, and from the work of Einarsen and Hoel (2001). In the list below, the designation *a worker* refers to anyone employed at any level of the organizational hierarchy from senior management down.

Negative Acts Related to Unethical Communication

- gossip and rumors of a negative nature about a worker or failure to correct such gossip or rumors;
- insulting, ridiculing, humiliating, or otherwise, offensive remarks made publicly or privately about a worker;
- false allegations of a personal or professional nature about a worker;
- excessive teasing or sarcasm toward a worker;
- yelling, screaming, or other expressions of rage toward a worker;
- ignoring, shunning, exclusion, or other types of isolation of a worker, such as relocation of office or work area to outside of the area of normal workflow;
- failure to impart information essential to adequate performance of a worker's job; for example, failure to notify a worker of an important meeting or change in policy or strategy;
- holding meetings about a worker without the worker's knowledge or presence;

- intimidating or threatening remarks and/or behavior toward the worker, including remarks suggesting the worker shouldn't stay in the organization any longer or should find another job;
- excessive criticism and fault-finding of a worker's work product and efforts;
- excessive monitoring and supervision of the worker; and
- improper use of performance reviews to negatively characterize a worker, either personally or occupationally, in order to "paper trail" for the purpose of removal from the workplace.

Negative Acts Related to Workload and Work Resources

- excessive and unmanageable workload assignment;
- unreasonable or impossible timelines and targets;
- inadequate resources to do a job coupled with full accountability for outcome;
- assignment of work below one's level of skill, competence, and experience; for example, assignment of trivial or busywork;
- taking away of meaningful and satisfying work assignments;
- demotion within the context of workplace harassment or abuse;
- sabotage of work product; and
- failing to give credit for work product and contributions or improperly taking credit for work done by another.

In order to reduce and ultimately prevent workplace bullying and mobbing, business leaders need to know what these forms of interpersonal abuse are and how to recognize them when they see them in the workplace. As the examples of bullying and mobbing behaviors described above illustrate, some negative acts are more overt than others, making them easier to identify, and some are more hidden, requiring close attention to the patterns of interaction and relationship within which they occur.

The definitions of workplace bullying and mobbing provided earlier in this section include the fact that damage to health is a central feature of exposure to workplace bullying and mobbing. Damage to health occurs across a continuum and includes damage to physical, psychological, and psychosocial health. The negative health consequences of workplace bullying and mobbing are so important that they will be considered separately in the following section.

HEALTH CONSEQUENCES OF EXPOSURE TO WORKPLACE BULLYING AND MOBBING

When considering the fairly extensive body of research that has been collected to date about the negative health outcomes of workplace bullying and mobbing, business leaders might be surprised to learn that these negative health outcomes can be considered workplace injuries rather than discrete illnesses or disorders arising from within the individual (Davenport, Schwartz, & Elliott, 1999; Duffy & Sperry, 2012, 2014). As more and stronger associations between workplace bullying and mobbing and the subsequent development of physical and psychological ill-health emerge, the risk of liability for organizations and managers correspondingly increases. Increased recognition of the negative health consequences associated with bullying and mobbing as injuries rather than illnesses would increase liability for organizations in which bullying and mobbing occur, and is part of the business case for doing something to stop it.

The business case for addressing and preventing workplace bullying and mobbing centers on mitigation of liability risk and mitigation of direct and indirect losses. Workplace bullying and mobbing exposes companies to reputational damage, increased employee turnover since a company where bullying and mobbing happens is not a desirable place to work, low morale, increased absenteeism, and increased use of medical benefits and health insurance that could result in higher premiums for companies. Increased litigation and the costs of defending lawsuits from targets and even potentially from witnesses add to the burden for companies where bullying and mobbing are allowed to go unchecked. While the cost of workplace bullying and mobbing to organizations can be measured in dollars, reputational damage, and reduced morale, the cost to targets can be life-altering in terms of a wide range of negative physical, psychological, and psychosocial health consequences.

Anyone interested in cultivating values-centered workplaces, where care, respect, and dignity are afforded to every worker, needs to appreciate the high price of these negative health consequences paid by bullied and mobbed workers. Given the sizable number of Americans who identify as having been bullied or mobbed in the workplace, the damage to their collective health cannot, in justice, be ignored. Using the Bureau of Labor non-farm labor statistics from 2014, Keashley (2018) stated that "9.8 million workers are currently being bullied or mobbed, 35–40 million have experienced bullying and mobbing in their working careers, and 35–45 million have witnessed the bullying and mobbing of others" (p. 46). Those numbers reflect a huge number of people exposed to the health-damaging stressors of bullying and mobbing who are at risk for the development of physical, psychological, and/or psychosocial health consequences.

Physical Health Consequences

Most people know from personal experience that when they are under acute and, especially, chronic or long-term stress their physical health often suffers as well. Bullying and mobbing fall under the category of chronic stress since these abusive processes last from months to years. From a common-sense perspective, it isn't at all surprising that a bullied or mobbed person would experience physical health problems like stomach aches and other gastrointestinal disturbances, sleep problems, generalized aches and pains, and an overall increased susceptibility to viruses and whatever else is going around in the community.

In the case of workplace bullying and mobbing, the research on health consequences backs up this common sense perspective that chronic stress causes physical health problems. Coronary heart disease, both onset of new disease and exacerbation of existing disease, gastrointestinal problems, headaches, sleep disturbances, generalized fatigue and exhaustion, and impaired immune functioning that increases one's susceptibility to a whole host of other diseases are all negative health effects of bullying and mobbing documented in the professional literature (Cassitto & Gilioli, 2003; De Vogli, Ferrie, Chandola, Kivimäki, & Marmot, 2007; Punzi, Cassito, Castellini, Costa, & Gilioli, 2007; Yildirim & Yildirim, 2007).

Psychological Health Consequences

Victims of workplace bullying and mobbing go through a series of emotional responses, over time, as they come to realize what has been happening to them. Initially, they are often confused and bewildered—at a loss as to understand their new pariah status within their workplace. Bullying and mobbing are public workplace events and coworkers soon understand that it's probably in their best interests to keep their distance from their bullied coworker who is now on the outs with supervisors and others. Very few coworker witnesses intervene on behalf of a bullied or mobbed colleague. The ensuing social distance between a bullied or mobbed target and his or her coworkers is often interpreted as betrayal by the target.

Fulfilling the mission of a workplace requires trust and coordinated action among coworkers for tasks to be completed and goals to be accomplished. Feeling that one has been betrayed by coworkers or supervisors destroys workplace trust and further isolates the target of workplace bullying or mobbing. The end result for most bullied or mobbed targets is an overwhelming sense of violation and injustice—a sense that they have been treated unfairly and that the inherent wrong of their unfair treatment must be corrected. The powerful emotions surrounding the realization that one has been bullied or mobbed and the sense of powerlessness to change the situation that often goes along with these powerful emotions sets the stage for the development of psychological disorders.

As well as studying the social process of workplace mobbing, Leymann and colleagues also examined the health consequences of having been a victim of mobbing (Leymann & Gustafsson, 1996). What they found was sobering; namely, that in Sweden at the time of their research, 15% of suicides could be associated with recent victimization from workplace mobbing. In a different study by different researchers, the first of its kind to assess suicide risk after exposure to mobbing (i.e., being a target or victim of mobbing), the results were similarly stark. Fifty-two percentof those exposed to mobbing were assessed as posing some suicide risk, and over 20% were assessed as posing a medium to high suicide risk (Pompili et al., 2008). Such findings in the professional research literature that connect workplace mobbing to suicide and increased suicide risk are the kind of findings that should keep business leaders awake at night. Workplace bullying and mobbing happen in the context of abuse-tolerant organizations, and responsibility for changing abuse-tolerant organizations rests with business leaders.

Suicide and increased suicide risk certainly point to the experience of clinical depression. The psychological disorders most associated with workplace bullying and mobbing are depression, anxiety, post-traumatic stress disorder, and symptoms of post-traumatic stress disorder (PTSD) in the absence of a full-fledged PTSD diagnosis (Duffy & Sperry, 2012, 2014; Duffy & Yamada, 2018). It should be noted, as in the research about suicide and suicide risk mentioned above, not everyone who is exposed to bullying or mobbing develops these psychological disorders just as not everyone exposed to a carcinogen develops cancer. That fact, however, does not mitigate the toxicity of the exposure either to workplace bullying or mobbing or to cancer.

All of these psychological disorders associated with exposure to workplace bullying and mobbing can significantly affect a person's ability to function and to cope with the demands and challenges of day to day living. They can interfere with memory, thinking, and decision-making, and impact feelings about oneself, others, and the future. Post-traumatic stress disorder and symptoms of post-traumatic stress disorder can also rob a person of the sense of safety and trust in the world needed to move forward and accomplish life goals.

The experience of trauma happens after exposure to a stressor that threatens a person's life or bodily or psychological integrity, especially in a situation in which the person is absolutely or relatively powerless to protect or defend oneself. Natural disasters, vehicular accidents, attempted murders and assaults, torture, and imprisonment are all examples of the kinds of stressors commonly associated with the subsequent development of post-traumatic stress disorder or symptoms. Other types of stressors are also associated with the development of post-traumatic stress symptoms and workplace bullying and mobbing is one of those stressors. Workplace bullying and mobbing is a threat to one's livelihood and ability to provide for oneself and one's family and is also a threat to personal and professional/occupational identity. This dual threat to livelihood and identity combined with little or no power to protect oneself or effectively fight back renders a bullying and mobbing victim vulnerable to the development of post-traumatic stress disorder or a cluster of its symptoms, and the professional literature bears this out.

The psychological health consequences of workplace bullying and mobbing are potentially severe as this section describes. Depression, anxiety, post-traumatic stress disorder, and post-traumatic stress symptoms without the full-fledged diagnosis of PTSD are potentially life-altering conditions that can affect a person's ability to function across a wide range of life activities and domains.

Psychosocial Health Consequences

How we act in the world and relate to other people relies on many taken-for-granted assumptions and beliefs about how the world works. If we were required to examine our beliefs and attitudes about the world in advance of making each and every decision or taking a particular action, our effectiveness as actors in the world would be greatly impeded. For targets of workplace bullying and mobbing, that's exactly what happens. When trust in others and belief in the world as fair and just are shattered, business as usual doesn't happen anymore. Decisions about whom to trust become complicated and exhausting, and beliefs about likely outcomes of plans become marred by pessimism.

The negative acts that are the core feature of bullying and mobbing are fundamentally abusive, and targets experience them as morally wrong, unfair, unprovoked, and unjust. Not surprisingly for targets, supervisors and coworkers who participated in the bullying and mobbing of them can no longer be trusted even if the targets liked and counted on them before. If these same supervisors and coworkers had friendly and cooperative relationships with the targets before the bullying and mobbing, the loss to the targets is compounded because these friendships and social relationships are effectively over. The net effect to targets is a loss of trust, loneliness and isolation, and the sense that the world is unjust and unfair.

As one can easily imagine, the feelings of isolation, mistrust, betrayal, and injustice do not remain confined to the workplace in which the bullying and mobbing happened. The sense of mistrust, suspicion, and newly acquired belief that the world is unjust and unfair tend to quickly get generalized to other relationships and situations outside of the workplace, undermining the personal and relationship resources that a target used in the past to get through difficult times. These losses are long-lasting, maybe lifelong, and certainly affect a target's health and well-being indirectly, if not directly. Unfortunately, that's not the end of the story of psychosocial losses.

These psychosocial losses are made worse by the practical complications that also accompany bullying and mobbing for many targets. Damage to reputation, self-doubt, loss of professional or occupational identity, financial problems associated with job problems, trouble getting job references, issues of re-employability in the case of actual job loss, and lack of confidence in one's ability to perform well in another job setting all can rear their ugly and destructive heads following workplace bullying and mobbing.

These negative health consequences should give pause to anyone inclined to trivialize the experience of bullying or mobbing or to brush it off as something that happens only to weak people. Targets of workplace bullying and mobbing can be anyone, but, as discussed above, are often those with particular talents and a willingness to speak out and up for principles and for people. Business leaders, in particular, need to understand the dimensions of documented harm that can and do accrue to victims of workplace bullying and mobbing. It would be reasonable to assume that no one wants these kinds of negative experiences in their workplaces, and certainly not these kinds of damaging effects to health and personhood. Knowledge of these potential harms to person and health in the wake of workplace bullying and mobbing makes it all the more urgent to do something about the problem and to lead effective action to reduce and prevent it. Strategies for business leaders committed to eliminating and preventing workplace bullying and mobbing are the focus of the next section.

RESPONDING TO THE PROBLEM OF BULLYING AND MOBBING

In this section, some frameworks and strategies for thinking about how to actively foster workplace cultures that center on the values of care, dignity, and respect will be provided. To do this, let me start with a quick story from personal experience.

Over the years, I have done many presentations about workplace bullying and mobbing for community groups in addition to my academic and clinical work in the area. It didn't take long for me to notice a common theme in the kinds of questions and comments I got from community group members, most of whom were employees and managers or business owners. The gist of the comments and questions were about how, in particular cases, we could know for sure that bullying and mobbing were real and not just exaggerations of discontented workers who wanted to get something out of their employers or who were troublemakers and exaggerators by nature. People seemed to have no trouble acknowledging that the bullying and mobbing behaviors and their damaging effects that I described in detail in the talk were real and harmful. Their difficulties with the ideas from my talk arose when they started to think about what they themselves would do in the face of a bullying or mobbing claim, and how they would determine if it was "real." A kind of knee-jerk defensiveness and denial seemed to take over at this point in the discussion—quickly followed by appeals on behalf of management and ownership to look at the problem from their side because they have businesses to run and important, sometimes difficult, decisions to make about personnel and how best to get the job of the organization done.

Here is the key point. Talking about bullying and mobbing in terms of the social processes involved, the negative behaviors targeted towards victims, and the damaging and often long-term effects on victims is implicitly to talk from a victim or target-centric position. We are not used to doing this. We are much more accustomed, and until very recently, much more comfortable I would dare to say, talking about a social problem from the perspective of those in positions of power—that is, from the perspective of managers and owners in the case of the workplace. To pay serious and careful attention to the experience of the one with minimal or no power is not something we are used to doing.

We don't have far to look to know that this is the case. The #MeToo movement really only gathered momentum this year with the exposé about Harvey Weinstein and his alleged serial abuse of women. It has taken decades for the accounts of victims of sexual harassment and abuse to be taken seriously and with respect. Workplace bullying and mobbing accounts are victim accounts. We don't have offenders (bullies and mobbers) standing in line to tell their stories. Victim accounts of interpersonal abuse seem to make people uncomfortable and defensive until a critical mass is reached that forces a cultural shift. It seems like that critical mass has been reached in the area of sexual abuse of women, but we are still a ways off from reaching a critical mass of victim accounts of bullying and mobbing that compel societal acknowledgment and corrective action. But that time will come and, most likely, sooner rather than later. Business leaders with foresight and wisdom can also be cultural leaders by initiating serious efforts to prevent workplace bullying and mobbing now before a cultural shift forces attention and action and before lawsuits for bullying and mobbing become everyday fare.

ACTION STRATEGIES FOR LEADERS TO ADDRESS WORKPLACE BULLYING AND MOBBING

1. *Learn about the problem.* As an organizational leader, you can do little that is effective to combat workplace bullying and mobbing if you

have not bothered to learn about the nature of the problem and its effects on targets and on businesses. The topics that are covered in this chapter, namely what workplace bullying and mobbing are and are not and the nature of the effects of bullying and mobbing on both targets and organizations, are starting points in developing a usable knowledge base for prevention efforts. The nature of the problem of workplace bullying and mobbing, its scope, and its effects are surprising to those who know little about the topic. In the absence of accurate information, workplace bullying and mobbing are more likely to be dismissed as occasional problems without serious consequences. Grappling with the full extent of the problem requires accurate information and solid data.

2. *Acknowledge that workplace bullying and mobbing could happen in your organization or workplace.* Denying the possibility that workplace bullying or mobbing could happen in your workplace or organization only increases the likelihood that it might happen. Workplace bullying and mobbing can happen in any organization even though some are considerably more abuse-prone than others. Accepting and acknowledging the possibility that your organization could, in fact, experience instances of workplace bullying or mobbing increases leadership alertness to the problem and promotes more continuous efforts to combat it. Denying that it could happen implies that the problem is solved and doesn't really need to be addressed in an official and serious way.
3. *Be clear about the values that organize the mission and strategy of your organization.* If the core values of dignity, care, and respect are not central to your organization's functioning consider a core values overhaul. An organization's core values reflect what leadership thinks is important. Dignity and mutual respect are the building blocks of an abuse-resistant organizational culture. Of course, just saying that important values matter isn't enough. Monitoring the degree of alignment between espoused values and actual values in practice is key to developing and maintaining a values-centered workplace.
4. *Collaborate with key stakeholders at all levels of the organization to develop and implement anti-bullying and anti-mobbing policies.* Policy development is a critical step in creating workplaces that are safe, humane, and free from bullying and mobbing. Including key organizational stakeholders in thinking through and drafting anti-bullying and anti-mobbing policies increases ultimate buy-in to those policies. Management and staff alike need to have confidence in anti-bullying and anti-mobbing policies and to see them as protective rather than as bothersome or punitive. Clear steps for policy implementation also need to be spelled out. Special care needs to be taken with

the development of reporting procedures so that all organization members can feel safe from harm or reprisal if they have a need to file a bullying or mobbing complaint. Duffy (2009) has drafted detailed information and steps to facilitate effective anti-bullying and anti-mobbing policy development.

5. *Incorporate continuous training and education about workplace bullying and mobbing into your package of workplace training programs.* Training and education about workplace bullying and mobbing needs to include a variety of training formats (face-to-face, panel discussion, guest speaker, video, and online), and be offered on an ongoing basis not just during onboarding of new hires. Watching an online video during the onboarding process and checking a box indicating completion of the task is a woefully inadequate way to educate workers about bullying and mobbing, and doesn't begin to scratch the surface of what is needed. Workers need to understand that everyone in the organization, including each and every one of them, has a personal share in the responsibility of creating a psychologically safe, humane, and abuse-resistant culture. Leaders might usefully ponder how to inspire their organizational members to take on this responsibility of creating a work culture marked by dignity and respect, and how they might lead from the top in this effort.
6. *Take every complaint of bullying, mobbing, and other forms of interpersonal aggression seriously.* Procedures need to be in place for handling workplace complaints of bullying and mobbing. Every organizational member needs to be assured that any complaint of bullying and mobbing will be taken seriously. As difficult and sensitive as such complaints may be to handle, turning a blind eye is not an option. Additionally, it is essential that procedures for handling and following through on complaints are fair to everyone involved—the complainant, alleged offender, and witnesses. Organizations that don't have procedures in place for handling complaints of bullying and mobbing are the ones that will be caught off guard and vulnerable to runaway escalation of the initiating problem.
7. *Restore a worker harmed from workplace bullying or mobbing to full membership in the workplace.* In every situation of workplace bullying and mobbing the target is singled out for mistreatment, and is isolated and becomes ostracized. Isolation, shunning, and ostracism are among the most difficult of social experiences for people to endure, and neuroscientists tell us that these experiences actually cause physical pain. By definition, workplace bullying and mobbing are forms of interpersonal abuse. Acknowledgment that a harm has been done is an important restorative practice that validates a target's sense that an injustice has been perpetrated. Acknowledg-

ment of harm done is a beginning restorative practice. One of the most powerful ways an organization can communicate its stand against bullying and mobbing is to restore a targeted worker to full membership and respect within the organization. This level of restorative practice requires enlightened leadership and can only be accomplished by those in leadership positions.

8. *Remember that solutions to workplace bullying and mobbing must be systemic in nature.* The process of scapegoating is a process of blaming an individual for the problems of a group or community. When examining scapegoating, it's obvious that group and community interactions are an essential part of how scapegoating gets underway—no different than in the case of workplace bullying and mobbing. Bullying and mobbing don't happen in isolation from the rest of the workplace. How workgroups interact and the culture of the workplace all play critical roles in the development of instances of bullying and mobbing. Bullying and mobbing do not happen in isolation from the rest of the workplace and are not individual events between individual people. Bullying and mobbing are nested within larger patterns of interaction in a particular workplace or organization. As such, the problem of workplace bullying and mobbing can never be solved by only looking at individuals and individual action and behavior. To solve the problem of workplace bullying and mobbing requires a systemic view that includes looking at individual behavior, but that also looks at workgroup and organizational behavior and culture. The larger workplace context greatly influences whether workplace bullying and mobbing occur, and must be included as a unit of analysis in all efforts to address and prevent workplace bullying and mobbing. Efforts to address workplace bullying and mobbing that do not include a systemic view are doomed to failure.

CONCLUSION

It is difficult to dismiss workplace bullying and mobbing as a minor problem in modern workplace life even after only a cursory look at its scope, its impact on individual target-victims, and on the cost to the bottom line of organizations in which it occurs. Workplace bullying and mobbing is not a minor problem. It is a serious problem with substantial negative impact for everyone affected. However, it's a problem that can be meaningfully addressed by the committed actions, in particular, of business leaders who set the tone for what happens within their organizations. Hopefully, this chapter has provided a knowledge base that you, as business leaders, can use to increase your understanding of the problem, along with guidelines for developing effective action strategies to counter and prevent workplace bullying and mobbing. The action strategies presented here, while they may not always be easy to do, are not simplistic, but are grounded in a systemic understanding of workplace bullying and mobbing that places care, respect, and dignity as the central values organizing effective responses.

REFERENCES

Cassitto, M. G., & Gilioli, R. (2003). Emerging aspects of occupational stress. *La Medicina del Lavoro [Workplace Medicine]. 94*(1), 108–113.

Davenport, N. Z., Schwartz, R. D., & Elliott, G. P. (1999). *Mobbing: Emotional abuse in the American workplace.* Collins, IA: Civil Society.

De Vogli, R., Ferrie, J. E., Chandola, T., Kivimäki, M., & Marmot, M. G. (2007). Unfairness and health: Evidence from the Whitehall II Study. *Journal of Epidemiology and Community Health, 61*(3), 513–518.

Duffy, M. (2009). Preventing workplace mobbing and bullying with effective organizational consultation, policies and legislation. *Consulting Psychology Journal: Practice and Research, 61*(3), 242–262.

Duffy, M., & Sperry, L. (2012). *Mobbing: Causes, consequences, and solutions.* New York, NY: Oxford University Press.

Duffy, M., & Sperry, L. (2014). *Overcoming mobbing: A recovery guide for workplace aggression and bullying.* New York, NY: Oxford University Press.

Duffy, M., & Yamada, D. C. (Eds.). (2018). *Workplace bullying and mobbing in the United States* (Vols. 1 & 2). Santa Barbara, CA: Praeger.

Einarsen, S., & Hoel, H. (2001, May). *The negative acts questionnaire: Development, validation and revision of a measure of bullying at work.* Paper presented at the 10th European Congress on Work and Organisational Psychology, Prague, Czech Republic.

Friedenberg, J. E. (2008, April 11). *The anatomy of an academic mobbing. The First Hector Hammerly Memorial Lecture on Academic Mobbing.* The University of Waterloo, Ontario, Canada.

Girard, R. (1986). *The scapegoat* (Y. Freccero, Trans.). Baltimore, MD: Johns Hopkins University Press.

Keashley, L. (2018). Prevalence of workplace bullying and mobbing among U.S. working adults: What do the numbers mean? In M. Duffy & D. C. Yamada (Eds.), *Workplace bullying and mobbing in the United States* (Vols. 1 & 2; pp. 25–51). Santa Barbara, CA: Praeger.

Leymann, H. (2010). *Workplace mobbing as psychological terrorism: How groups eliminate unwanted members* (S. Baxter, trans.). Lewiston, NY: Edwin.

Leymann, H., & Gustafsson, A. (1996). Mobbing at work and the development of post traumatic stress disorders. *European Journal of Work and Organizational Psychology, 5*(2), 251–275.

Namie, G., & Namie, R. (2009). *The bully at work.* Naperville, IL: Sourcebooks.

Namie, G., & Namie, R. (2018). Risk factors for becoming a target of workplace bullying and mobbing. In M. Duffy & D. C. Yamada (Eds.), *Workplace bullying and mobbing in the United States* (Vols. 1 & 2; pp. 53–74). Santa Barbara, CA: Praeger.

Pompili, M., Lester, D., Innamorati, M., De Pisa, E., Iliceto, P., Puccinno, M., & Girardi, P. (2008). Suicide risk and exposure to mobbing. *Work, 31*(2), 237–243.

Punzi, S., Cassito, M. G., Castellini, G., Costa, G., & Gilioli, R. (2007). Mobbing and its effects on health: The experience of the "Clinica del Lavoro Luigi Devoto" in Milan. *La Medicina del Lavoro [Workplace Medicine], 98*(4), 267–283.

Valcour, M. (2014, April 28). The power of dignity in the workplace. *The Harvard Business Review.* Retrieved from https://hbr.org/2014/04/the-power-of-dignity-in-the-workplace

Yamada, D. C., Duffy, M., & Berry, P. A. (2018). Workplace bullying and mobbing: Definitions, terms and when they matter. In M. Duffy & D. C. Yamada (Eds.), *Workplace bullying and mobbing in the United States,* (Vols. 1 & 2; pp. 3–23). Santa Barbara, CA: Praeger.

Yildirim, A., & Yildirim, D. (2007). Mobbing in the workplace by peers and managers: Mobbing experienced by nurses working in healthcare facilities in Turkey and its effect on nurses. *Journal of Clinical Nursing, 16*(8), 1444–1453.

CHAPTER 3

WORKPLACE INCIVILITY

Implications and Solutions

Helen MacLennan

WHAT IS INCIVILITY?

What differentiates incivility from other forms of misbehavior is its low intensity and the absence of a clear intent to harm anyone. According to Andersson and Pearson (1999), incivility is "low-intensity deviant behavior with ambiguous intent to harm the target, in violation of workplace norms for mutual respect" (p. 457). In other words, incivility is simply the act of behaving in a manner that is considered disrespectful, rude, or uncivil. In fact, it is often a result of thoughtlessness rather than intentional malice (Porath & Pearson, 2013). Some examples of incivility might include:

- using rude hand gestures,
- interrupting coworkers during conversation,
- not allowing coworkers to express their opinions,
- taking credit for the work of others,
- failing to acknowledge the work of others,
- excluding others from communications or activities,

From Discord to Harmony, pages 35–47

- ignoring emails from others,
- sending curt or harsh email messages,
- neglecting to say thank you,
- using condescending remarks,
- abruptly ending conversations,
- neglecting to acknowledge the presence of another,
- leaving unpleasant tasks for others, and
- the use of unkind words.

Unfortunately, incivility doesn't get the same attention as violence and aggressive behavior at work as it is less intense and less transparent in intent; however, it's much more prevalent (Pearson, Andersson, & Porath, 2000). Because of its low intensity, incivility is often perceived as being inconsequential. For instance, you may not think much about the fact that Robert in the sales department frequently interrupts or hangs up on his coworkers, or that Mary in operations tends to take credit for the work of her subordinates, but these behaviors are generally a pattern of behaviors rather than isolated incidents. An uncivil pattern of behavior can erode coworker and customer relations and can result in serious consequences for an organization.

INCIVILITY AT WORK

The workplace has the potential to be largely an incivility-free zone or refuge from the harsh incivility that has taken root in our public squares"

—Weber Shandwick, 2017, para. 3)

Incivility can strain workplace relationships, reduce employee job satisfaction, and impact job performance in many ways. It has been liked to racial and gender discrimination (Cortina, 2008), sexual harassment (Lim & Cortina, 2005), abuse of power (Foulk, Lanaj, Tu, Erez, & Archambeau, 2018), feelings of demoralization (Miner & Smittick, 2016), organizational commitment (Kabat-Farr, Cortina, & Marchiondo, 2018), and workplace aggression (Andersson & Pearson, 1999; Walker, Van Jaarsveld, & Skarlicki, 2017). Employees confronting incivility at work may also use more sick days or may even opt to leave the organization.

Cyber Incivility

Antoci, Delfino, Paglieri, Panebianco, and Sabatini (2016) defined online incivility as a "manner of offensive interaction that can range from aggressive commenting in threads, incensed discussion and rude critiques, to outrageous claims, hate speech and harassment" (para. 1). When compared to face-to-face communication, there are several qualities that make the internet ripe for uncivil behavior. Suler (2004) described what is known as the *Online Disinhibition Effect,* which explains how individuals say and do things in a cyber environment that they wouldn't typically do otherwise, based on:

- *Anonymity*—Individuals using online communications may be able to mask, perhaps only partially, their identity, which allows them to deviate from typical and more socially acceptable behavior.
- *Invisibility*—The lack of instant feedback in the form of body language can increase the possibility of perceived incivility, whether intentional or not. When individuals' identities are masked, they may not feel the need to conform to the social norms for courteous behavior.
- *Asynchronicity*—Because online communication usually does not happen in real-time, it allows individuals to opt out of conversations or delay responding. This delay, whether it is intentional or not, can be perceived as incivility.
- *Power equality*—The internet can blur or eliminate power hierarchies that exist elsewhere. As a result, individuals may be more willing to share their thoughts, without fear of retribution.

Customer Incivility

Incivility doesn't only happen inside the organization. It can come from customers, vendors, and service providers. Customer service employees are likely to encounter incivility from customers and are just as likely to reciprocate (Walker et al., 2017). Over time, those employees who receive consistent uncivil treatment from customers have been shown to have decreased task performance quality, increased counterproductive work behaviors (Mao, Change, Johnson, & Sun, 2017), and emotional exhaustion (Hershcovis, Gervais, Cameron, & Bozeman, 2018).

CAUSES OF WORKPLACE INCIVILITY

Rude and uncivil behaviors are rampant in our society, and those behaviors can either stem from or spread into the workplace. Research indicates that some of the antecedents to workplace incivility are:

- perceived exhaustion (Blau & Andersson, 2005),
- experienced incivility (Torkelson, Holm, Backstrom, & Schad, 2016),

- organizational change (Pearson et al., 2005),
- high demands at work (Pearson et al., 2005),
- lack of job autonomy (Jex, Burnfield-Geimer, Clark, Guidroz, & Yugo, 2010),
- poor leadership (Pearson et al., 2005),
- passive leadership (Harold & Holtz, 2015),
- disorganized or dirty physical environment (Sliter & Jones, 2015), and
- lack of coworker solidarity (Itzkovich & Heilbrunn, 2016).

Power Differentials

Feelings of power can lead to a sense of superiority and an attitude that condones the mistreatment or degradation of individuals who are perceived to hold an inferior status (Scott, 2007). Unfortunately, because kindness can be perceived as weakness, incivility can be used as a display of strength and power over others. This explains why uncivil behaviors are more likely to come from individuals with greater personal power and be directed to those below them (Boyd, 2006; Callahan, 2011; Caza & Cortina, 2007; Clark, 2008; Pearson & Porath, 2005, 2009). Rude behaviors from the supervisor may seem to be perfectly acceptable when directed at peers or subordinates but unacceptable when directed at the president of the organization.

Leader Behaviors

Leadership dictates the norms of acceptable behavior within an organization. Leaders who model or tolerate incivility may foster additional, and possibly more intense, forms of mistreatment in retaliation (Cortina & Magley, 2003). Because the attitudes and actions that form the organizational culture are likely to start at the top, a sense of superior power and the resulting perceived justification for incivility may become the norm in an organization, particularly if it stems from management.

Interestingly, doing nothing may also contribute to the problem of incivility. Research indicates that employees who work for a passive manager are more likely to experience and propagate workplace incivility (Harold & Holtz, 2015). After all, uncivil behaviors have the tendency to multiply, particularly when there is little chance of negative consequences.

Retaliation

The targets of incivility may respond at the time of the incident or may retaliate later. Regardless of the timing, retaliation can occur at the individual level, where retaliation is directed to the agent, or at the organization level, where the organization itself suffers the consequences. Responses at the individual level are likely to include reciprocal incivility, but it may also take a more ambiguous form, such as failure to share important information, neglecting to give appropriate credit, or purposely excluding the agent from activities. Responses to incivility may also escalate in intensity, to include verbal aggression, physical aggression, and physical violence, perpetuating and expanding a cycle of negative behaviors.

Targets of incivility often respond in the form of retaliation to the organization (Itzkovish & Heilbrunn, 2016). These responses may be unintentional, such as increased absenteeism, reduced level of performance, employee turnover, and decreased job satisfaction and productivity. Responses can also include intentional misconduct, including unethical behaviors such as employee theft, or may take the form of decreased interest in job performance quality, including customer service.

THE DANGER OF IGNORING WORKPLACE INCIVILITY

The Spread of Incivility

Allowing incivility to go unchecked within an organization increases the likelihood that the use of uncivil behaviors will eventually spread throughout the entire organization, creating a culture of incivility. Once that happens, it becomes very difficult to change. Consider that existing employees will likely mirror behaviors that are accepted within their organization, particularly if those behaviors come from the top of the organizational hierarchy. New hires will also likely assimilate into the organization by conforming to those existing behaviors. Those who can't conform will likely struggle and eventually leave. Over time, the organization is left only with those employees who contribute to or ignore the problem.

Covert Discrimination

The idea that certain individuals are considered "inferior" by "superior" members of either an organizational or socially constructed hierarchy will increase the likelihood of inequitable treatment to those at the bottom. However, because inequitable treatment and overt discrimination are unacceptable, and often illegal, workplace incivility may be used instead as an ambiguous and covert form of discrimination against those in undervalued social classes (Cortina, 2008).

Abuse of Power

Because power gives rise to the acceptance of incivility toward "inferiors," those in higher positions of power may be likely to perpetuate other detrimental forms of unequal treatment to those who exist below them on the social hierarchy. As a result, incivility can result in abuse of power, and subtle and ambiguous forms of mistreatment. It can even result in unintentional racial and gender discrimination, placing the organization at risk for costly litigation.

Power is also related to the expectations of how one should be treated. For instance, powerful leaders will likely have high expectations about the respect that they deserve and how they should be treated by subordinates. As a result, they may perceive incivility from others more frequently, and respond with reciprocal incivility or aggression to garner the respect that they feel they deserve (Foulk et al., 2018).

Spillover

Incivility at work can also spill over into customer relationships, reducing customer service quality during in-person, telephone, and web-based interactions. In addition, employees who are targets of incivility at work tend not to leave it at the office, but instead take it home, where it can negatively impact sleep (Demsky, Fritz, Hammer, & Black, 2018), family relationships (Pichler, Livingston, Ruggs, & Varma, 2016), and marital satisfaction (Ferguson, 2012).

Monetary Costs of Incivility

Table 3.1 is adapted from Pearson and Porath's (2009) research and estimates the financial impact of incivility. The estimates are based on an organization with 10,000 employees and an annualized revenue of $100,000 per employee.

CREATING A CULTURE OF CIVILITY

Creating a culture of civility offers a way for every organization to improve performance, increase employee job satisfaction, improve team performance, and improve customer service. But, changing an existing organizational culture takes time, and leadership will need to take an active role. To begin managing incivility in the workplace, leaders need to bring

TABLE 3.1 Financial Costs of Organizational Incivility

Effect of Incivility	Percentage of Employees Affected	Organizational Cost per Hour	Estimated Annual Financial Cost to Organization w/10,000 Employees
Lost time due to worry	53%	$2,650	$63,693.75
Lost time avoiding offender	28%	$1,400	$33,649.00
Weakened commitment	37%	$1,850	$5,549,200.80
Reduced work effort	22%	$1,100	$528,770.00
Decreased time at work	10%	$500	$312,455.00
Employee replacement cost	12%	$600	$60,000,000.00
Think about changing jobs	46%	$2,300	$221,122.00
Legal costs			$35,000.00
Witnesses to incivility			$961,400.00
Cost of managing incivility			$262,500.00
Absenteeism			$1,443,600.00
Stress/healthcare costs			$1,500,000.00
Total Estimated Annual Cost of Incivility			**$70,911,390.55**

Source: Pearson & Porath, 2009

awareness of the issue to the entire organization and set clear expectations of expected behaviors. Research shows that employees who feel that their organization supports a culture of civility will have a more positive view of the organization overall (Tarraf, 2017).

Organizations should be proactive and strategic in their attempts to create a culture of civility through the development and implementation of policies and practices designed to encourage mutual respect and civil behavior. With input from a variety of stakeholders, leaders should work to develop policies and procedures that will serve as the foundation for a civil workplace. Workplace civility policies will need to consider employee free speech rights under the National Labor Relations Board, a code of conduct that includes basic standards for acceptable behavior in the workplace (Office of Public Affairs, 2017).

Pay Attention

Changing the organizational culture will take vigilance. Spend time watching and listening to the interactions in the workplace. While employees may be on their best behavior when they know they're being watched, pay attention to workplace cliques, individuals who others seem to avoid, and so on. Identify employees who display signs of emotional exhaustion, high levels of stress, or low levels of tolerance.

Leadership

Leadership will serve as the example and should understand their roles and responsibilities regarding modeling and reporting uncivil behavior. According to a Weber Shandwick (2018) case study, approximately half of all employees surveyed indicated a belief that leadership is responsible for enforcing civility in the workplace. Enlist the help of leadership by training them to be civility coaches for your employees. They should understand the importance of consistently modeling civil behavior in interactions with subordinates, peers, and stakeholders outside of the organization.

Because poor or ineffective leadership contributes to the problem of workplace incivility, a great deal of attention should be paid to continuous leader development. Leadership training should also focus on communicating with diverse populations, conflict management and negotiation, and tolerance.

Responsibility Structures

Assigning responsibility for compliance to civility taskforces, managers, departments, or committees has been shown to be very effective in organizational change initiatives (Kalev, Dobbin, & Kelly, 2006). Findings show that training and mentoring may be more successful when used in combination with these responsibility structures (Kalev et al., 2006).

Team Building

Strengthen workplace relationships with team-building exercises that your employees may even enjoy. Employee solidarity, or the feeling of belonging to a group, has been shown to be positively related to workplace civility (Itzkovich & Heilbrunn, 2016). In fact, it's suggested that not only will coworker solidarity decrease incivility, it can also serve to provide support to targets and witnesses of incivility as well as increase the likelihood of reporting unacceptable manager behaviors (Itzkovich & Heilbrunn, 2016).

Training

Because research indicates that people generally prefer, and are better positioned, to interact with and serve those from the same social identity group, experience and practice in engaging and communicating with people representing a wide range of perspectives can reduce in-group favoritism and incivility toward out-group members (King, Dawson, West, Gilrane, Peddie, & Bastin, 2011). Remember, one size does not fit all when communicating with a diverse group of employees and/or customers.

There are a large number of civility training programs available that include elements related to diversity, inclusion, cultural sensitivity, communication, and conflict management. While conflict management training may prove helpful in reducing retaliatory incivility, there are mixed feelings about mandatory training focused solely on diversity and inclusion. Weber Shandwick (2018) indicated that about 66% of employees believe that diversity and inclusion training should be mandatory. However, diversity training alone is unlikely to correct deep-rooted biases, and may even serve to elicit negative reactions from employees and exaggerate stereotyping (Kalev et al., 2006). It should be used as part of a comprehensive initiative.

Customer Service Focus Groups

Allowing employees to create and participate in focus groups comprised of individuals who perform customer service functions can serve several purposes. First, connecting and sharing with others and building a network of relationships can help to combat emotional exhaustion and decrease employee stress (Jantz, 2017). As we know, stress is a leading cause of incivility at work. Second, focus groups will allow employees to share best and worst practices for dealing with customer incivility.

Feedback and Reporting

Solicit feedback from employees and customers that specifically asks about the organization's performance regarding civil interactions. Keep in mind that, although it takes more time and effort, customers are usually more willing to provide detailed information by phone rather than through a written or online survey.

Eliciting employee feedback may be more difficult. Many employees are reluctant to speak up about mistreatment that they suffer or witness at work, particularly if it stems from their coworkers or supervisors. Weber Shandwick (2018) indicated that only 33% of employees feel safe reporting incivility or harassment at work, and approximately 48% of employees don't trust management to handle their complaints about incivility or harassment. Thus, help ensure that employees are encouraged to report inappropriate behaviors. Also, employees may be more likely to share information, particularly about negative behaviors, when their identity is protected. Create a way for employees to share information anonymously. This can be accomplished using online survey software or an old-fashioned suggestion box. Employees may also be willing to share information when leaving the organization. Ask specific questions about patterns of incivility during employee exit interviews.

Rewards

Promote civility by recognizing employees who exemplify the culture you are attempting to create. There are many ways to reward your employees, and it doesn't need to cost much. For instance, a designated parking spot, lunch with the boss, or even time off are good examples of employee rewards. For additional ideas, ask employees to brainstorm potential rewards. They will appreciate being included in the process. The most important thing about rewards is that the recipient and the reason for the award should be communicated to everyone. Create a repository for employees to nominate others who they deem worthy of recognition.

Hire for Civility

New hires have the potential to negatively influence your company culture. Focus on personality rather than just skills in making hiring decisions. Pearson and Porath (2013) indicated that only about 11% of organizations report considering civility during the hiring process. Also, because of the importance of coworker solidarity, include potential coworkers in the interview process. It's important that new hires fit in and be able to conform to the culture.

During the interview process, ask situational questions that may indicate how a prospect will react to stressful situations, including customer incivility, and how well they work within a team. Ask about previous employment situations. A prospect who talks over you, interrupts, or complains about anything during the interview will probably not be the best candidate for your organization.

CONCLUSION

Taken alone, incivility in the workplace may seem to be of no great cause for concern. However, because incivility is typically a pattern of behaviors, uncivil behaviors are not likely to be isolated incidents. Each act of incivility has at least one instigator and one target, both with their own complex network of individuals with whom they interact, both inside and outside of the organization, who can all be affected. When you consider the potential impact of just one uncivil act, you may begin to understand how easily workplace incivility can spread throughout the organization and potentially escalate to aggression or violence.

Changing an existing organizational culture will take a concerted effort, and it will not happen overnight; however, bringing a norm of civility to your workplace can reduce employee stress and turnover, while increasing productivity and customer satisfaction.

REFERENCES

Andersson, L., & Pearson, C. (1999). Tit for tat? The spiraling effect of incivility in the workplace. *Academy of Management Review, 24*(3), 452–471.

Antoci, A., Delfino, A., Paglieri, F., Panebianco, F., & Sabatini, F. (2016). Civility vs. incivility in online social interactions: An evolutionary approach. *PLoS One, 11*(11). https://doi.org/10.1371/journal.pone.0164286

Blau G., & Andersson, L. (2005). Testing a measure of instigated workplace incivility. *Journal of Occupational and Organizational Psychology, 78*(4), 595–614. https://doi.org/10.1348/096317905x26822

Boyd, R. (2006). The value of civility. *Urban Studies, 43*(5/6), 863–878.

Callahan, J. (2011). Incivility as an instrument of oppression: Exploring the role of power in constructions of civility. *Advances in Developing Human Resources, 13*(1), 10–21. https://doi.org/10.1177/1523422311410644

Caza, B., & Cortina, L. (2007). From insult to injury: Explaining the impact of incivility. *Basic and Applied Social Psychology, 29*(4), 335–350.

Clark, C. (2008). Student perspectives on faculty incivility in nursing education: An application of the concept of rankism. *Nursing Outlook, 56*(1), 4–8.

Cortina, L. (2008). Unseen injustice: Incivility as modern discrimination in organizations. *Academy of Management Review, 33*(1), 55–75.

Cortina, L., & Magley, V. (2003). Raising voice, risking retaliation: Events following interpersonal mistreatment in the workplace. *Journal of Occupational Health Psychology, 8*(4), 247–265. https://doi.org/10.1037/1076-8998.8.4.247

Demsky, C., Fritz, C., Hammer, L., & Black, A. (2018, April 23). Workplace incivility and employee sleep: The role of rumination and recovery experiences. *Journal of Occupational Health Psychology, 24*(2), 228–240. https://doi.org/10.1037/ocp0000116

Ferguson, M. (2012). You cannot leave it at the office: Spillover and crossover of coworker incivility. *Journal of Organizational Behavior, 33*(4), 571–588. https://doi.org/10.1002/job.774

Foulk, T., Lanaj, K., Tu, M., Erez, A., & Archambeau, L. (2018). Heavy is the head that wears the crown: An actor-centric approach to daily psychological power, abusive leader behavior, and perceived incivility. *Academy of Management Journal, 1*(2), 661–684.

Harold, C., & Holtz, B. (2015). The effects of passive leadership on workplace incivility. *Journal of Organizational Behavior, 36*(1), 16–38.

Hershcovis, M. S., Gervais, L., Cameron, A., & Bozeman, J. (2018). The effects of confrontation and avoidance coping in response to workplace incivility. *Journal of Occupational Health Psychology, 23*(2), 163–174.

Itzkovich, Y., & Heilbrunn, S. (2016). The role of co-workers' solidarity as an antecedent of incivility and deviant behavior in organizations. *Deviant Behavior, 37*(8), 861–876.

Jantz, G. L. (2017, February 6). Say farewell to emotional exhaustion. *Psychology Today.* Retrieved from https://www.psychologytoday.com/us/blog/hope-relationships/201702/say-farewell-emotional-exhaustion

Jex, S. M., Burnfield-Geimer, J. L., Clark, O., Guidroz, A. M., & Yugo J. E. (2010). Challenges and recommendations in the measurement of workplace incivility. In J. Greenberg (Ed.), *Insidious workplace behavior* (pp. 239–271). New York, NY: Taylor & Francis.

Kabat-Farr, D., Cortina, L., & Marchiondo, L. (2018). The emotional aftermath of incivility: Anger, guilt, and the role of organizational commitment. *International Journal of Stress Management, 25*(2), 109–128.

Kalev, A., Dobbin, F., & Kelly, E. (2006). Best practices or best guesses? Assessing the efficacy of corporate affirmative action and diversity policies. *American Sociological Review, 71,* 589–617. Retrieved from https://www.cfa.harvard.edu/cfawis/Dobbin_best_practices.pdf

King, E. B., Dawson, J. F., West, M. A., Gilrane, V. L., Peddie, C. I., & Bastin, L. (2011). Why organizational and community diversity matter: Representativeness and the emergence of incivility and organizational performance. *Academy of Management Journal, 54*(6), 1103–1118.

Lim, S., & Cortina, L. (2005). Interpersonal mistreatment in the workplace: The interface and impact of general incivility and sexual harassment. *Journal of Applied Psychology, 90*(3), 483–496.

Mao, C., Chang, C., Johnson, R., & Sun, J. (2017, December 28). Incivility and employee performance, citizenship, and counterproductive behaviors: Implications of the social context. *Journal of Occupational Health Psychology, 24*(2), 213–227. Retrieved from http://dx.doi.org/10.1037/ocp0000108

Miner, K., & Smittick, A. (2016). Workplace incivility, culture of honor, and aggression: Precarious manhood and the demoralized male. *Culture, Society, and Masculinities, 8*(1), 20–38.

Office of Public Affairs. (2017, December 14). *NLRB establishes new standard governing workplace policies and upholds no-camera policy in Boeing.* Retrieved from https://www.nlrb.gov/news-outreach/news-story/nlrb-establishes-new-standard-governing-workplace-policies-and-upholds-no

Pearson, C., Andersson, L., & Porath, C. (2000). Assessing and attacking workplace incivility. *Organizational Dynamics, 29*(2), 123–137.

Pearson C. M., Andersson L. M., & Porath C. L. (2005). Workplace incivility. In S. Fox & P. E. Spector (Eds.), *Counterproductive work behaviour: Investigations of actors and targets* (pp. 177–200). Washington, DC: American Psychological Association.

Pearson, C., & Porath, C. (2005). On the nature, consequences and remedies of workplace incivility: No time for "nice"? Think again. *Academy of Management Executive, 19*(1), 7–18.

Pearson, C., & Porath, C. (2009). *The cost of bad behavior: How incivility ruins your business and what you can do about it.* New York, NY: Portfolio.

Pichler, S., Livingston, B., Ruggs, E., & Varma, A. (2016). *Understanding the high performance workplace: The line between motivation and abuse.* Abingdon, England: Taylor and Francis.

Porath, C., & Pearson, C. (2013, January 1). The price of incivility. *Harvard Business Review.* Retrieved from https://hbr.org/2013/01/the-price-of-incivility

Scott, J. (2007). Power, domination, and stratification: Towards a conceptual synthesis. *Sociologia, Problemas E Practicas, 55,* 25–39.

Sliter, M., & Jones, M. (2015). A qualitative and quantitative examination of the antecedents of customer incivility. *Journal of Occupational Health Psychology, 21*(2), 208–219.

Suler, J. (2004). The online disinhibition effect. *Cyber Psychology and Behavior, 7*(3), 321–326.

Tarraf, R. C. (2017). *Understanding workplace incivility experiences and the moderating role of mindfulness* (Doctoral dissertation). Available from Electronic Thesis and Dissertation Repository, 4757. Retrieved from https://ir.lib.uwo.ca/etd/4757

Torkelson, E., Holm, K., Backstrom, M., & Schad, E. (2016). Factors contributing to the perpetration of workplace incivility: The importance of organizational aspects and experiencing incivility from others. *Work and Stress, 30*(2), 115–131. https://doi.org/10.1080/02678373.2016.1175524

Weber Shandwick. (2017, June 13). *In an increasingly uncivil society, the workplace is becoming a sanctuary for many Americans* [Press Release]. Retrieved from https://www.webershandwick.com/news/in-an-increasingly-uncivil-society-the-workplace-is-becoming-a-sanctuary-fo/

Weber Shandwick. (2018). *Civility in America 2018: Civility at work and in our public squares.* Retrieved from https://www.webershandwick.com/wp-content/uploads/2018/06/Civility-in-America-VII-FINAL.pdf

Walker, D., Van Jaarsveld, D., & Skarlicki, D. (2017). Stick and stones can break my bones but words can also hurt me: The relationship between customer verbal aggression and employee incivility. *Journal of Applied Psychology, 102*(2), 163–179.

CHAPTER 4

RESTORATIVE JUSTICE

Principles and Inclusive Applications in Organizations

Nancy Geist Giacomini and Monica Valentine

This chapter draws from the collaborative insights of two higher education thought leaders with theory to practice expertise across both student conduct and conflict management, and strategic human resource and diversity management. Together we advocate for the incorporation and expansion of restorative principles and practices in education and business to help people better manage and resolve disputes. We believe in the power of early prevention and appropriate conflict intervention at the lowest and most effective levels, in ways that build stronger relationships and more inclusive communities. Our shared perspectives on restorative justice are inspired by our commitment to helping organizations give everyone a voice while achieving common goals.

Whether on campus or in the workplace, conflict occurs when people with different backgrounds and priorities come together. Conflict often begins with personality differences, perceived inequities, poor communication, and unmet needs, which can quickly escalate if not managed. When

From Discord to Harmony, pages 49–80

conflicts erupt, organizations of all types are challenged to help those who violate cultural expectations, norms, and rules take accountability for their mistakes, make amends for their actions, and refrain from repeat offenses; all while empowering harmed individuals and communities to be heard and to play a central role in resolving the harm.

This two-part chapter provides a restorative framework for building inclusive cultures. Our goal is to create a nexus between student resource management and human resource management as it relates to applications of organizational justice that are inclusive, restorative, and centered in learning over control without trading on compliance and risk management requirements. We draw from our diverse lenses as practitioners, parents, and educators privileged to teach and develop humans-as-resources in ways that optimize individual and organizational accountability, community, and civility. In short, we hope to amplify the message that to be inclusively excellent in conflict and conduct management, schools and organizations must "break out of the false dichotomy of doing the right thing versus doing the thing right" (Taylor & Varner, 2009, p. 24).

PART ONE: A JUSTICE PRIMER FOR ORGANIZATIONS STRIVING TOWARDS INCLUSIVE EXCELLENCE

Centering Dichotomy

To center what it means to do the right thing and the thing right all at the same time in conduct and conflict management, we first need to identify the thing as justice rather than restorative justice. We do not stay strictly in the restorative justice (RJ) lane for a couple of reasons. The first is that RJ is not ours as non-indigenous people. Our perspectives are shaped by Western culture. We respect the time-honored traditions of RJ and focus this chapter on how to evolve and incorporate restorative principles in organizations in ways that authentically support the unique relationships and communities found there. The second is that being inclusive extends to systemic inclusion. Existing retributive systems of justice and calls for transformative justice, as found in criminal justice reform and on college campuses in search of better ways to manage sexual harassment and misconduct, are instructive. Philosophical differences that inform institutionalized practices belong in this inquiry and have helped prompt openness among RJ practitioners to create hybrid approaches that incorporate RJ values and applications alongside existing systems. Lastly, RJ is not a panacea. Even as it gains renewed attention as a promising approach, RJ can fall short of inclusive aims, just like any other institutionalized application of justice. Concerns include the perception that RJ lacks the transformative capacity needed to mitigate identity-based inequity. Another barrier is that RJ requires that those who have caused harm are safe to acknowledge that harm and are willing to be held accountable. This does not play well within traditional progressive-discipline models that use sanctions, like those that escalate from warnings through school suspension, expulsion, and job termination, for violations of community rules and expectations. Here, disincentives are two-fold: (a) Acknowledging a mistake or wrongdoing carries the real risk of separation from community, and (b) disciplinary action requires heavy documentation and record retention that may further compromise a person's future place in community with others.

It is for these reasons that we take a comprehensive approach to RJ in ways that invite deeper reflection about wholesale justice and challenge structural inequality. Whether focused on the contractual agreements between employee and organization or between student and school, we are each obligated to one another to behave in ways that keep our communities humming along. Simply put, inequity and injustice gums up the works and must, therefore, be part of the dialogue.

What Makes Justice Retributive, Restorative, and/or Transformative?

There are a variety of theories and models that inform systems of justice. Fundamentally, they differ in terms of how we perceive and respond to violations of shared cultural rules and norms, as well as how we use that system to hold people accountable. The values and beliefs we hold about justice and discipline are rooted in our upbringing. It is our families of origin, our schools, our religious communities, social groups, and so on that instill a sense of right and wrong, guilt, shame, and responsibility. We absorb clear messages about what accountability looks like based on the versions of punishment, restitution, and forgiveness we are used to. In turn, these play out in formalized systems of justice with roots in retribution, restoration, and transformation, each with different underlying goals, assumptions, strategies, and consequences. Because we are not all raised nor oriented to justice in the same ways, defining what it means to be "just" is not as straightforward as we might think.

Today's U.S. systems of justice that inform community, campus, and organizational due process interpretations are by and large retributive, even if we don't mean for them to be. Retributive justice rests in the value of punishment befitting a clearly stated violation of a community standard, law, or rule. Prevention and rehabilitation are often in the mix, but secondary to meting out what can be defended as fair and consistent sanctions per policy. The codes and rules we live by at home, work, and school travel with personal values and "thou shalt not" prohibitions against acts that could compromise one's good standing in a safe and well-functioning community. When rules are violated, there are consequences. These consequences are designed to punish the offender and discourage recidivism while sending a message to others not to take the same risk. What many may take for granted is the restorative or rehabilitative value of a retributive approach to justice. The truth is that institutionalized punishment of this sort typically stops short of holistic or hybrid approaches that act to repair harm and restore community as it reforms the wrongdoer. After years of public outcry, together with the added weight of recent celebrity star power, the federal criminal justice reform bill dubbed "The First Step Act" has been put forward to the U.S. Senate to remediate these justice shortfalls, and is in political motion as we write. Similarly, campus Title IX guidance on how to apply this federal statute against sex and gender discrimination, including sexual misconduct, is in play. Changes introduced during the Obama administration, and perceived by some to favor victims and survivors over those they report for wrongdoing, are gone. New changes under contentious review purportedly seek to protect both reporting parties and respondents more equitably in investigation and due process responses. Moreover, mediation and restorative options are back on the table to address harms through less formal and more remedial processes than full adjudication.

Retributive justice has not always been the law of the land. Restorative justice (RJ) is rooted in thousands of years of successful peacemaking practices by indigenous peoples, including First Nation peoples of North America, the Maori of New Zealand, and the Inuit of Canada, Greenland, and Alaska. Worldwide restorative practices still flourish and are gaining renewed mainstream attention as a way to counter systemic power exploitation and address identity-based inequities in present retributive justice practices. Restorative approaches in practice today are often found as alternative or companion responses to violations managed within traditional U.S. juvenile and criminal justice systems, as well as in K–12 schools, special education dispute management offerings, and higher education conduct and conflict resolution programs. Over the past several decades, RJ has gained popularity on college campuses as a way to address student misconduct and to help build and maintain responsible student communities. Similarly, RJ practices are gaining popularity with corporate human resource leaders interested in leveraging inclusiveness to address harm and conflict in the workplace. It stands to reason that RJ's growing popularity in schools and communities will continue to drive restorative approaches in the workplace too.

Part of RJ's growing appeal is that it reprioritizes attention more equitably across victims, offenders, and their communities than is found in criminal justice style approaches. Restorative principles and practices can also address early and escalating conflict and conduct before it prompts formal and often more punitive disciplinary responses. A skilled facilitator can work with stakeholders to address everything from small community violations of shared expectations (think noise, privacy, use of shared space, etc.) to domestic abuse, violent crime, and even death so long as all parties are willing, equally empowered, and protected. In this way, RJ is seen by advocates to better align with values of diversity and inclusion than retributive practices that position people against one another and often privilege one party over the other while excluding the community altogether.

Like conflict management, what is compelling about RJ is the idea that people and communities can be empowered to hold one another accountable in constructive ways with satisfying and effective results. Embracing RJ requires a shift from framing misbehavior as rule-breaking that requires third party intervention and punishment to regarding the same behavior as violations of people, relationships, and community. The idea is that if there is a harm created between people it creates an obligation—that is, to identify and repair the harm and restore the relationship and community. In this paradigm shift, there are essentially three central questions as developed by RJ pioneer Howard Zehr (2015, p. 31):

- "Who has been harmed?" rather than "What laws have been broken?"
- "What are their needs?" rather than "Who did it?"
- "Whose obligations are these?" rather than "What do they deserve?"

Common RJ practices used to repair harm include victim-offender mediation, circles, and conferencing. Each process is unique and requires specific facilitator skill sets, but all are designed to safely and voluntarily bring those harmed and those who have harmed together. Once together in mediation, or in circles and conferences that invite broader stakeholder participation, victims and those who have caused their harm are helped to explore what has happened, the impact, and a future vision for making things right. Forgiveness and reconciliation are sometimes but not always part of this personal journey of healing. Restorative-based victim-offender panels and victim assistance programs as found in the criminal justice system help support and repair harm experienced by victims/survivors. Similarly, ex-offender assistance programs offer restorative support services to offenders once held accountable for a crime and help offenders reintegrate back into a community that they have harmed. The Centre for Justice & Reconciliation: A program of Prison Fellowship International (www.restorativejustice.org), provides additional details about each of these programs, with applications transferable to organizations and schools.

While these process options are each distinct and tailored to specific community needs and interests, all are premised on restorative principles that provide the foundations needed to more deeply explore justice. Foundations include restorative interest- and relationship-based principles of repairing harm, rebuilding trust, and restoring community and have broad appeal as a way to move from cultures of punishment and retribution to cultures that embrace accountability, forgiveness, reconciliation, and restoration.

Restorative justice is gaining momentum at the same time that transformative justice advocacy is on the rise, and while there may be some areas of overlap in principle, these justice models and the theories that inform them are not the same. Transformative justice does not seek to revamp existing punitive models or encourage hybrid versions of justice. Rather, it advances an entirely new system of criminal justice (and justice systems that draw from punishment-based retributive models) based on social justice theory. Transformative justice seeks to put an end to things like inequitable incarceration rates and penalties, including life imprisonment and death sentences, based on identity. Nocella's (2011) "Overview of the History and Theory of Transformation Justice" (www.review.upeace.org) and the work of the Equal Justice Initiative (eji.org) under the leadership of Bryan Stevenson provide compelling content for readers wishing to learn more.

Transformative justice advocacy begs the question of how we conceptualize expressions of injustice, from a modest interpersonal slight to full betrayals that act to dehumanize, discount and destroy people and relationships. A sense of injustice is further interpreted through our own identities and past experiences; like justice, how we perceive injustice, is personal. Unchecked, it can trigger escalated conflict, violence, and prolonged litigation, often regardless of the physical, emotional, and financial costs (Deutsch, 2014). Considering injustice in context to how we practice justice is necessary if we hope to transform broken systems and break out of Taylor and Varner's (2009) false dichotomy; that is, we can both design policies and practices that align with standards of compliance and risk management (doing the thing right), while at the same time demonstrate an ethic of care, equity, and fairness (doing the right thing). Simply standing behind established policies is seldom restorative or transformative, and does little to address real and perceived injustice and repair harm.

Finding common ground agreement about justice and injustice can present challenges. We know all too well that these concepts are conflated with values and beliefs which tend to divide people along philosophical, religious, and political lines. This is true globally, nationally, and in our more local communities as found in education and at work. Our different orientations to the human experience, like we find in dichotomies of control vs. learning, relationships vs. results, optimist vs. pessimistic, change vs. status quo and so on, impact what we believe to be true about justice and the human condition. They further color how we conceptualize justice that leans retributive or restorative and muddy inclusive dialogue necessary for shared meaning making. Still, there are common denominators within the work of justice that can bring us closer together.

Coming closer together around everyday justice requires that we name and operationalize some shared core values. Deutsch (2014) synthesized these core values to include: nonviolence, human equality, shared community, fallibility, and reciprocity (pp. 18–19). In other words, we might fundamentally agree that in order to live and work together in relative physical and psychic safety we must invest ourselves in acts that do no harm. This includes obvious macro-level harm as well as the more nuanced micro-level aggressions that act to hurt the well-being of others. Making good on the pledge that all people are created equal and should be treated as such "does not imply that people necessarily have the same status, privileges, power, needs, or wealth. It does imply that such differences are not the consequence of one's violation of the other's entitlements" (Deutsch, 2014, p. 18).

Shared community at work and school supports constructive conflict and conduct management through a mutual commitment to cultural values and norms without devaluing human rights and individual differences. Within this context, fallibility speaks to our imperfections, unique and differing perceptions and orientations to the world, and our willingness to forgo judgment and extend forgiveness. Reciprocity in the workplace speaks to how we treat one another, and the expectation that I will be fair to you and you to me. Living into the full meaning of these core commitments is tested from time to time in ways that expose the raw alternatives of violence, inequality, condemnation, and injustice. These test our sense of community, and how we meet these challenges ultimately signals whether a community will carry on in safety together. Few of us are international players in the work of peacebuilding, but all of us contribute to community justice at home, school, and work. Deconstructing justice down to culturally common ground invites individuals and organizations to take a fresh look at accountability practices and policies, constructively challenge those that have fallen out of alignment with shared cultural missions that speak to diversification and inclusive excellence, and in turn evolve better practices, protocol, and messaging about who we are and what we aspire to be (Deutsch, 2014).

Finding Common Ground for More Restorative Principles, Practices, and Policies

Better restorative practices and policies start with a broad look at what it fundamentally means to engage others through a restorative lens while staying grounded in Deutsch's (2014) core commitments to nonviolence, equality, community, fallibility, and reciprocity. Appendix IV in *The Little Book of Restorative Justice* (Zehr, 2015) offers a list of 10 essential ways to live more restoratively, together with a breakdown of RJ principles and how they align with applications of criminal justice and restorative justice. Central across restorative justice teachings is hope and a future-oriented vision that tomorrow can be better than today. We synthesize Zehr's (2015) reproduced list with footnote credit to http://emu.edu/now/restorative-justice/2009/11/27/10-ways-to-live-restoratively/ through our own lenses of student and human resource conflict management expertise for transferability to campus and workplace applications of justice. Each pair of assertions is interconnected and equally important in different ways.

1. *Access and Inclusion:* There are few universal truths and ways of being in the world. Decentering our own priority experiences and working against identity-based and unearned privilege opens us up to that expanded moral universe of those we choose to understand, learn from, and care about. Grounding our definition of justice in values that support the full and equitable expression of diversity framed as social justice and inclusive excellence requires that we authentically confront injustice and work against "isms" that act to exclude, discount, and harm others, even as we are doing our own individual work to further personal multicultural awareness.
2. *Relationships and Results:* Interpersonal and intergroup relationships with one another and extended out into our systems and physical community matter. To live restoratively means that we must strive to build strong respectful relationships and aspire to achieve inclusive, constructive, common interests. These are the key ingredients of collaborative processes that lead to equitable, sustainable, win-win outcomes in conflict and problem-solving.
3. *Collaboration and Empowerment:* Restorative justice embraces a shift from control-centered decision making to that centered on collaboration and learning. In this way, decision making that reflects restorative qualities necessarily involves those impacted by the decision itself and seeks to empower parties equally and equitably, to embrace hope and view conflict as an opportunity for positive change as they work to create their own inclusive version of a better future.
4. *Responsibility and Respect:* Living restoratively requires that when we hurt someone we acknowledge that harm and work to make it right. Our primary investment is in the other person's experience at our hands, and in making our relationship and shared community whole again. Ownership does not wait until we are proven wrong in ways defined by formal laws and rules; neither does it mean that we forgo our own perceived and real harms. To accept restorative justice in principle means to "do the right thing even when no one is watching" (with credit to Charles Marshall's work in Shattering

the Glass Slipper). Respect and responsibility to one another are not conditional.

5. *Listening and Dialogue:* We are often conditioned to prioritize our own thoughts over listening deeply to the experiences of others. In restorative justice, the priority is to listen in ways that promote learning, understanding, and empathy, with a focus on relationship building over an end result that might be personally rewarding. RJ embraces vulnerable dialogue with others to advance learning and mutual meaning making.
6. *Intent and Impact:* Becoming increasingly conscious of human and environmental justice through a restorative lens means that we must care not only about what we intend in our words and deeds but how what we do impacts others and our common world. Social justice style exercises that promote a journey of self-awareness related to identity-based power, privilege, and oppression help us "stand in the shoes" of others who may be oriented differently and help decenter our own lived experiences to care about what it feels like to live another identity and set of unique experiences. With credit to the wise Maya Angelou, when we know better, we tend to do better. In turn, when our impact does not match a good faith intent, RJ invites us to do the work needed to try again, do-over, and/or work to set things right going forward.

Control and punishment versus learning and reconciliation, as orientations to applied justice, figures prominently in the U.S. retributive model of criminal justice and provides an imperfect model for systems of redress in schools and places of work. The idea is that when rules are broken, punishment is not only deserved but necessary. The punishment is meant not only to keep someone from repeating a violation but to discourage others from doing the same thing. Schools and organizations have taken their contextual cue and shaped student and human resource policies over time to similarly name rules and apply largely punitive sanctions when violations occur. In school, retributive responses look like separating students from the community with warnings, detentions or probationary statuses, suspensions, and expulsions. At work, employee retribution might take the form of poor evaluations, loss of pay, or job termination. Other consequences might also be applied to educate, restore, and reform, but the priority response in retributive style justice is punishment.

The trouble is that these foundations in control do not align with aspirations of inclusive excellence or social justice, nor do they embrace an alternative learning orientation to interpersonal and intergroup conflict management and problem-solving in the communities we create together.

TABLE 4.1 Orientation to Problem Solving

	Control Orientation	Learning Orientation
Goals	• To assert sufficient control to ensure that my own definition of a problem is solved in ways I see fit	• To maximize my opportunity to create alternatives and test whether they work or not
Assumptions	• Other people can't be influenced • Problems can't be solved unless they are solved "my way"	• Other people can be influenced • I can be influenced/constraints can be altered
Strategies	• Unilaterally impose my solutions and act as though I am not doing so • Do not request feedback about my own ideas • Shoot down others and don't share reasons why • Reflect privately on results	• Identify shared responsibility for problem definitions and for solutions • Encourage others to react to my plans, and do the same for others • Experiment off-line with alternatives • Discuss results publicly
Consequences	• Low team commitment and responsibility • Public "group think" • Private politicking and subterfuge • Polarized group dynamics • High risk to raise difficult problems	• Increased team participation • Higher team commitment and responsibility • Increased willingness to raise problems • More resources to tackle them • More creativity and better solutions

Note: Revised from the adaptation of Diana Smith's "Working Paper" found in Cloke & Goldsmith, 2011, p. 178.

Consider orientations of control and learning as they play out in terms of goals, assumptions, strategies, and consequences in community with others.

Conflict Scenarios That Contrast Control/Punishment and Learning/Restoration

Dichotomies like those expressed as orientations of learning versus control or identified by Taylor and Varner (2009) as doing the right thing versus doing the thing right present simplistic versions of our lived experiences. While it is rare to find a pure application of these orientations, they are instructive to the dialogue of conflict management for students and other humans as resources. Organizational culture can be shown to tip one direction or the other along a range of expressions that imply control or learning as the norm. In turn, these orientations influence how justice is served.

These orientations evolve a meaningful discussion about justice, and how to help transform organizational and institutional cultures that embrace control and punishment toward cultures of learning and restoration. The generalized case study offered here draws from trending conflict themes to help us explore the impact of these orientations, as we imagine the what, why, and how of justice, transformed.

CASE STUDY

A group in a shared community reacts to the U.S. #MeToo movement with growing accusations that existing policies and processes meant to address and manage gender inequity, including discrimination, unlawful access and inclusion practices, harassment, and assault, are systemically unfair, chilling, and tipped in favor of those who offend. They demand that the community #BelieveSurvivors and take immediate action when an incident is reported that causes harm based on gender identity. Some fear that this clashes with established due process rights, and perceive rising criticism and activism as a new and unfair "war on men." On the day of a high profile, widely broadcast decision related to claims of sexual assault against someone who identifies as a heterosexual man of power, someone enters the main public restroom designated for men and scrolls #TIMES UP . . . HE IS GOING DOWN AND YOU ARE NEXT! in red lipstick across the full wall mirror. Those who see the message make a formal report and demand that the incident be investigated. They also demand that those responsible for the threatening vandalism be held accountable in the same way the process would be used if roles were reversed and the women's restroom had been similarly vandalized.

* * *

Reflect on this scenario through lenses of control/punishment versus learning/restoration outlined in Table 4.1. How do these perspectives differently inform your personal reaction and anticipated responses? How do these align with the approach your existing community might take? What does that tell you about the culture, justice orientations, and alignment of values between you and your organization?

This activity helps explore some often unconscious personal and organizational convictions about accountability and justice while gauging the cultural norms, values, and expectations at work or school. The more out of alignment our personal convictions are with the overall workplace culture the more discomfort we might expect to feel, particularly when we sense an inability to effect change. This strained alignment shows up in everything from rates of attrition and sick days to mental health challenges and failed or lackluster individual and team goal achievement. It also impacts the bottom line of a place and calls a stated mission of diversity and inclusion into question. In short, we feel this sort of strained alignment even when we cannot name it directly. A colleague once described her experience moving from a destructive control-oriented place of work to one invested in constructive collaboration to be as visceral as the difference between breathing smog and pure oxygen (Schrage, personal communication, n.d.). It is literally hard to breathe in a culture that does not reflect our own sense of right and wrong related to justice. Valentine's (2018) research presented later in the chapter expands on the importance of alignment and authenticity.

Fortunately, taking a closer look at justice as an orientation and cultural expression can open dialogue, flush out intention in context to impact, and influence changes big and small. Airing out our approaches to justice, with the goal of doing inclusive, restorative justice better invites individual and systemic changes big and small. It is a journey much like that we take to build multicultural competence, and allowances can be made for incremental steps found in hybrid approaches that incorporate theories and practices that advance authentic values of diversity and inclusion within accountability practices.

Expanded Approaches That Center Learning and Restoration as Inclusive Excellence

There are expanded conflict and conduct management models currently in use to inform schools, communities, and organizations wishing to move in the direction of more restorative, inclusive justice applications. We explore several in this section.

Schrage and Thompson (2009) introduced the groundbreaking Spectrum of Resolution Options with foundations in social and restorative justice 10 years ago drawing from their collaborative work at the University of Michigan, where the model is in use today (www.oscr.umich.edu). The Association for Student Conduct Administration (www.theasca.org) has also drawn from this model to teach expanded conflict and conduct management options to international practitioners. The visual in Figure 4.1 helps conceptualize resolution pathways that balance organizational commitments to access and inclusion, community restoration, learning and development, risk management, and legal compliance. Foundations in restorative and social justice embody principles of "inclusive excellence," endorsed by the Association of American Colleges and Universities (www.aacu.org) and adopted by many colleges and universities to give further institutionalized meaning of diversity and inclusion initiatives across identities at every organizational level.

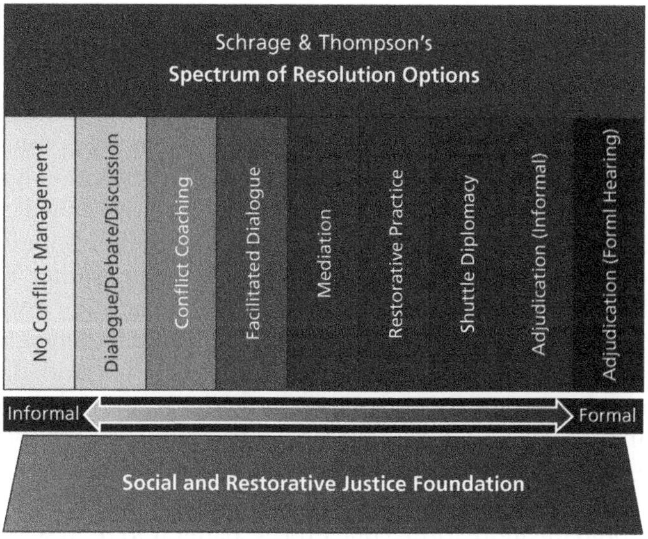

Figure 4.1 Figure developed by Schrage and Thompson (2008); published in Schrage and Thompson (2009).

The Schrage and Thompson (2009) model is applicable within school conduct processes that inform or overlap those used to investigate and resolve allegations under Title IX (gender equity). The PRISM (Promoting Restorative Initiatives for Sexual Misconduct) Project, a project centered on restorative justice (RJ) on college campuses is a leading example of how RJ is being advanced to address gender-based human rights protections, with transferable lessons for the broader workplace community (https://www.skidmore.edu/campusrj/prism.php). Even as we write, Google just announced an overhaul of sexual harassment and misconduct policies in response to a New York Times report and employee walkout some 20,000 strong over a failed systemic response to gender-based harassment and abuse. In addition to Google's added transparency and training, arbitration will reportedly be added as an option of redress in cases of alleged misconduct to put an end to protecting offenders (Wakabayashi & Benner, 2018). This is happening at the same time the Office for Civil Rights and Department of Education move into the later stages of overhauling guidelines for investigating, adjudicating, and managing student sexual harassment and assault on campus, after revoking Obama-era guidance related to gender inequity and violence against women. Anticipated guidelines make room for RJ and mediation across both education and human resource management. How well they support inclusive excellence remains to be seen. Concerns include the perception that changes meant to recalibrate the accommodations and rights of accused students equally with those who identify as survivors will negatively impact hard-won victims' rights and compromise #movements that have helped break silence related to sexual violence and systemic misogyny.

Another integrated spectrum style approach in place to help manage and resolve conflict unique to an identified community is found across K–12 special education programs. Here, a range of resolution options are in place at a state level and under the overall jurisdiction of the Federal Department of Education as part of compliance requirements under the Individuals with Disabilities Act (IDEA) and Free and Appropriate Education (FAPE) legislation. In brief, state departments of education are required to provide impartial mediators to help resolve disputes between families and schools over the education plans of identified students with disabilities. Over time, required mediation services in model states have expanded to include Individualized Education Plan (IEP) facilitation, conflict coaching, and resolution conferences as ways to empower families and schools to jointly negotiate and resolve disputes together in ways that de-escalate conflict, and forgo the more formal due process pathway to redress. Additional information can be found on state department of education websites and from CADRE: The Center for Appropriate Dispute Resolution in Special Education (www.cadreworks.org).

Within and beyond the field of education, organizational human resource management practices share similar investments in expanded process options to resolve workplace conduct and conflict. Integrated conflict management systems (ICMS) offer expanded process options and may be administrated out of offices that support customer service or human resource access and inclusion operations, and/or led by confidential ombudspersons who serve as neutrals with an impartial role helping manage and resolve interpersonal organizational complaints (www.ombudsassociation.org).

These offices can come under scrutiny in times of crisis and organizational change, necessitating added collaboration with public relations and communications offices, legal counsel, and leadership by chief executive officers. American Airlines, for instance, faced pressure from the National Association for the Advancement of Colored People (NAACP) and widespread negative press in 2018 after a high profile series of reported racially biased incidents against African-American passengers. In response the airline CEO met with key stakeholders including complainants/victims, NAACP leaders and civil rights representatives. What resulted were change initiatives released in a NAACP press release to include (a) an independently led "diversity and inclusion gap analysis" and "action plan"; (b) "company-wide implicit bias training"; (c) an "overhaul [in] its existing customer discrimination claims process" and the addition of a "new customer resolution team"; and (d) "increasing awareness of work environment policies and the process to report concerns and improve its internal oversight and resolution of team member discrimination claims" (Press Release: NAACP Commends American Airlines on Plan for Change, December 1, 2017, www.naacp.org).

Starbucks recently found themselves in similar hot water after videos went viral showing escalating confrontations between staff and customers of color over apparent inequitable customer prohibitions against loitering and use of restrooms (see YouTube examples from Philadelphia and Los Angeles). These high profile incidents prompted among other initiatives, a public apology and newsworthy nationwide half-day store shut down in May 2018 for mandatory staff racial bias training. Ongoing institutionalized efforts to address implicit racial bias among staff and repair the harm caused while preventing future incidents remain to be seen.

Although formalized interpersonal and intergroup RJ applications are not widespread in the United States, companies often navigate these sorts of escalated public conflicts and exposed individual harms with apology and promises for constructive transparent steps forward for greater future actions and accountability. These responses flirt with RJ principles, but typically prioritize results-oriented public relations and risk management over the more person-centered restorative work of repairing harm and rebuilding trust. Models and theories asserting a similar dual concern approach are largely outgrowths of the pioneering 1970s work of Kenneth W. Thomas and Ralph H. Kilmann. The Thomas-Kilmann Conflict Mode Instrument (TKI) is a useful way to assess personal conflict styles of collaborating, compromising, avoiding, competing, and accommodating that align with a two-dimensional model measuring assertiveness (results) and cooperativeness (relationships) in conflict (www.kilmanndiagnostics.com). Related, the conflict dynamics profile (www.conflictdynamics.org) administrated out of Eckerd College offers a second online individual and 360 assessment that identifies individual hot buttons in conflict together with information to help tame triggers.

Award-winning authors Bill Eddy and L. Georgi DiStefano provide additional de-escalation techniques, presented as the CARS method (connect-analyze-respond-set limits), that fundamentally help those in conflict focus on de-escalation techniques meant to calm and redirect while moving toward a future-oriented focus on choices and consequences (2015). Interested readers might take a look at *It's All Your Fault at Work: Managing Narcissist and Other High-Conflict People* (Eddy & DiStefano, 2015) or visit the High Conflict Institute website: www.highconflictinstitute.com. And while our experience and focus in this chapter is largely U.S. based, some cutting edge employment work on the topic is being published in the United Kingdom, including "There's More Than One Way to Solve a Dispute" published July 25, 2017 by Jane Simms. Mayvin's (2016) *Restorative HR Practice Toolkit* that coins RHR as restorative human resource management, described as "a pioneering field of practice that brings together HR and OD with restorative justice to help solve HR problems for themselves" (p. 1).

Many organizations employ mediation as an alternative to litigation in resolving disputes between employees and management or in cases of company and customer/vendor disputes. Some companies have mediation or arbitration as a policy and first line of defense in hopes of preventing conflict from escalating into costly, embarrassing, and damaging court cases. Employee assistance programs (EAP) also provide services for dispute resolution. For instance, an employee can be referred to meet with a neutral third-party mediator by management, HR, or EAP to reconcile a conflict, or can voluntarily seek these services without a referral. Some employees are resistant to using mediation, due to perceived concerns that going to mediation suggests an inability to handle conflict on their own. Others may fear that conflict resolution and restorative processes, particularly those done in house, share proximity to disciplinary steps and may be detrimental to job advancement or success. Still, there is widespread agreement that mediated resolution processes can be uniquely equipped to help people in conflict equitably manage and resolve their own conflicts in effective and sustainable ways.

Let's revisit the case study introduced a few pages ago to move our more conceptual inquiry and presentation of models into real-life application. Recall that in this scenario a community is faced with a perceived clash between #MeToo and #BelieveSurvivors movements, and fear that these movements clash with established due process rights and signal a "war on men." Against this backdrop comes a high profile public proceeding which seems to prompt the bathroom post: #TIMES UP . . . HE IS GOING DOWN AND YOU ARE NEXT!

Common organizational responses and integrated conflict management systems may be visually represented to range from less to more formal process options like those found in the Schrage and Thompson Spectrum Model (2009). These approaches align with interest-based and rights-based response options across a continuum. Communities that operate from a control/punishment framework will likely respond with more formal rights-based investigation and process options. Limited third-party due process adjudication and shuttle style negotiation and resolution options may be introduced under the heavy influence of legal and/or union representation and guidance. In these cases, due process and individual privacy rights trump community process and restorative interests. Responses aimed at supporting the harmed community are often limited or absent altogether.

Cultures that embrace learning/restoration as an orientation will more often make room for less formal, independent, or hybrid interest-based process options that act to balance process with personal empowerment. These communities are better positioned to introduce mediation, victim-offender conferences, and restorative justice circles that bring impacted people together voluntarily in facilitated ways. These are also communities that may model successful un-facilitated approaches to conflict in ways that de-escalate and mitigate more formal responses without burying systemic issues that need collaborative and sustained attention. Whether as a stand-alone or companion process to more formal options, the goals, assumptions, strategies, and consequences are different. Working theory-based foundations that rest on inclusion and restoration, and orientations to control and learning, are predominant players in whether and how we make room for a fuller range of responses.

Applied to our case study, we anticipate that many readers were tempted to approach the incident from the familiar framework of control and punishment. Gut-check questions likely centered on things such as: "What happened?"; "Who did it?"; "Has a rule been broken?"; and "What should the consequences be?" Quite possibly, the incident would be escalated to a person charged to administrate such incidents, and should the vandal(s) be found, a confidential investigation and adjudication process would ensue. The person empowered to manage the incident would hold the power to solve the problem distinct from the community harmed. If no vandal was identified, the incident would remain unresolved, and in many cases, there would be nothing left to do but for the community to move forward without resolution. Returning to the dichotomy of doing the right thing versus the thing right (Taylor & Varner, 2009), the organization would take heart that they followed their own policies and did the thing right in ways that prioritized process over people. In this way, unilateral solutions would have excluded the opportunity for transparent collaboration, creativity, feedback, or evaluation. In other words, case closed is often good enough even if harm remains.

But what if the approach was different? Readers who allowed themselves to look past a fixed pie perception of this situation, in which artificial limits check our natural ability to be curious, collaborative, and interpersonally engaged, might have found themselves asking different questions. In turn, these questions might lead to different outcomes. Here, through lenses of learning and restoration, questions might center on: "What is the harm?" and "Who is responsible and how can it be repaired?" Rather than relying on one right or wrong way to resolve the incident, the opportunity exists to prioritize people in ways that don't compromise process but rather expand options for resolution. This version of doing the right thing invites communities to come together around a problem, and share responsibility with others to define and resolve the issue in a collaborative transparent process.

Version one of our case study might move toward two distinct outcomes. In one scenario, the culprit(s) is caught and punished. In the other, the culprit is never identified and the case is closed. In terms of inclusive justice, neither is particularly satisfying. Version two of our case study lends itself to near limitless alternative outcomes. In one scenario, perhaps the vandal is caught, accepts responsibility, has a chance to explain their intent, comes to understand the harmful impact of their action, and atones to the community in a restorative conference or circle and apologizes. This restorative approach can occur with or without a companion punitive approach as called for by the culture of the community and legal obligations of the organization. Perhaps mediation or a victim-offender conference would be in order to mitigate the harm caused to direct stakeholders. Facilitated dialogue might be offered to help the community process the act, the incentive behind the act, and the bigger context of the behavior. This, in turn, might prompt additional community action and/or shed light on structural concerns in the organization that need attention and go well beyond some representative words on a mirror. The point is that the more capacity a community has to embrace learning and restoration over control and punishment, the more inclusive, collaborative, and restorative it can be when responding to harm between people in their community without trading on safety, legal, and risk management requirements.

A fair question at this point is "Why"? Why evolve policies and practices that have been carefully crafted and vetted? The answer is embodied in the humanness of people themselves. Consider the fictitious actor responsible for writing "#TIMES UP... HE IS GOING DOWN AND YOU ARE NEXT!" Let's say they are a community member that identifies as female. An investigation ensues and she admits responsibility to the person who administrates these matters, explains that she was motivated to act by a deep sense of despair and hopelessness about the current U.S. climate and perceived state of gender inequity and victim blaming, and identities herself as a sexual assault survivor. She adds that she was triggered to write her message because she felt there was no other way to be heard. Traditional lines of support seemed unavailable. Past training focused on escalating harassment reports rather than empowering her to safely and effectively confront unwanted low-level conduct herself. In her case, she discloses that her supervisor engages in inappropriate conduct, making it all but impossible to escalate concerns without fear of job consequences. She further recounts stories in which female colleagues who raised concerns were met with insensitive investigators without trauma-informed protocol. Others were held at arm's length by male colleagues fearful of false accusations, resulting in fewer mentorship and sponsorship opportunities that hindered networking and job advancement. In yet another case, a male colleague responded to a sexual harassment grievance by a female colleague by filing an equal grievance about her.

We could go on. The bottom line is this: The organization's zero-tolerance policy states that gendered threats and postings that create a hostile environment are punishable by suspension from the community. With this and alternative scenarios in mind (i.e., the offender identifies as . . . with their own reasons and story) consider again what you would do and why you would do it.

Asking the question "why" encourages organizations to move thoughtfully in the direction of expanded resolution options and restorative practices as an expression of a legitimate commitment to inclusion and diversity. Further, we know that control and punishment chills collaboration, creativity, buy in, and outcomes. It can readily create a culture of "every person for themselves" in which people will sooner duck and cover than speak up. An orientation to learning and restoration, on the other hand, yields cultures of resilience and promotes constructive risk and responsibility taking. It also helps establish environments where people can be confident participating in an inclusive accessible process of interpersonal resolution and change management, and be able to make mistakes without fear of punitive consequence without regard to identity.

Organizations are in the unenviable position of finessing risk management, public relations, human resource management, and legal requirements all at the same time. In short, encouraging and requiring that all instances of a possible violation be escalated and investigated into the most formal processes of redress may look good on paper, but for many it does not resonate; it is the antithesis of interpersonal communication, conflict de-escalation and resolution, learning, restorative justice and inclusion. While it is vital that people who feel harmed and violated are not re-traumatized by the processes meant to support them, people in community can be afforded the opportunity to hold one another accountable in safe and effective ways that stop the unwanted behavior, mitigate the harm, and allow for learning, apology, amends and accountability going forward.

As a side note of interest before turning from this case study, a lesser known movement to the #MeToo movement is #HowIWillChange, in which men vow to break the status quo and hold one another accountable for inappropriate behavior in order to stop future harm. As the movement gains momentum, it offers a model approach to addressing behavior interpersonally in ways that move people forward instead of focusing on what can't be undone, no matter the process. Sexual harassment is acknowledged as a source of low employee morale, low productivity, and high employee turnover. Similar climate consequences are seen in schools and on college campuses as low student satisfaction and retention rates. Organizations cannot effectively take on sexual harassment and misconduct without investing in a culture of diversity and inclusion at all levels, in which transparent expectations and rules are equitable and applied faithfully across identity. These expectations and the processes used when there is harm must also be collaboratively shaped, sustained, and evaluated by those with a first-hand stake in the community if buy in and interpersonal accountability is to occur.

We explore related cautions and readiness tests in the content to follow. Readers who would value seeing real-life restorative and mediated process options in action will find a great many examples with a simple YouTube search. One particularly noteworthy restorative justice clip that we use in graduate courses draws from an incident of community vandalism in Bucks County, Pennsylvania. The 35-minute free resource is published by the International Institute for Restorative Practices (https://youtu.be/tBMIEManHoA).

Amplifying Restorative Principles and Inclusive Values as Process Options Grow

Ours is not an exhaustive review of available resources and applications across fields. Still, it is safe to say from our own experiences that while interest continues to grow, fully expressed restorative justice applications and training is uneven. The examples provided present successful and evolving ways to expand conflict and conduct management practices that rest on restorative and inclusive foundations. At the same time, they introduce the importance of theory to practice clarity and capacity building. Without an authentic and sustainable commitment to the "why" and "how" of expanding restorative justice and conflict resolution options, the "what" can fall short of inclusive excellence; worse, ill-conceived efforts may cause harm. Precautions include:

- Both mediation and restorative justice applications like victim/offender conferences and community circles cannot be a forced choice. They risk being ineffective, even unsafe, when an alleged wrongdoer is not ready or able to accept accountability. This is particularly true when stakeholders are experiencing trauma related to the harm.
- A sense of injustice may expose the need for a bigger picture transparent dialogue before conflict resolution or a restorative justice practices can be entertained. These processes must never be used to minimize, hide, or perpetuate systemic injustice. Restoring justice is certainly different from masking injustice.
- Processes and the people administering them must demonstrate equitable responsiveness across those harmed and those who may have caused harm. While efforts to de-escalate conflict and repair harm can head off institutional liability, they are not shortcut fixes

and can't just look good on paper. They must demonstrate a sincere and lasting ethic of care and commitment to inclusion.

- Resolution and restoration are works in progress. If what really happened remains in dispute, new issues arise, or parties remain dissatisfied and unheard, process participants can rightly feel isolated and unsupported.
- Facilitated processes and the policies that support them should be done with rather than done for; this means that if done well they will teach and empower people to resolve future disputes and restore relationships more effectively and constructively on their own. This may help counter concerns about process privacy, record keeping, retaliation, and misperceptions that discount reporting parties are troublemakers.

PART TWO: A PRACTITIONER'S GUIDE FOR MORE INCLUSIVE, RESTORATIVE ACCOUNTABILITY PRACTICES

Assessing Risk and Readiness for Change

Reimagining justice in community takes care and authentic capacity. It is vulnerable and important work that stands to expose deeply held individual and organizational convictions about the nature of right and wrong, and challenge how we operationalize justice. Taylor and Varner (2009) published a comprehensive set of transferable questions applicable across higher education and the workforce at large to help gauge constructive readiness for this work (Table 4.2). These questions assess staff and organizational capacity and help guide work meant to align learning and law in authentic and skillful ways, while mitigating possible individual and organizational harm. Adapted into a worksheet exercise, Taylor and Varner's (2009) content is useful for teams seeking to encourage constructive dialogue, decision making, and action planning related to expanding more inclusive and restorative process options.

Completed worksheets can help organizations operationalize the nuanced meanings behind justice, and establish how well conduct and conflict management policies and practices align with institutionalized values as they relate to restorative and inclusive values. An authentic inquiry can also help identify individual and team training needs and readiness for change. At their core, reflecting on these things "challenge the premise that fairness requires sameness. Fairness is not about everyone being treated the same, but rather it is about everyone getting what they need. This is the foundational principle of social justice" (Taylor and Varner, 2009, p. 34). A popular cartoon, originally introduced in 2012 as "Illustrating Equality

TABLE 4.2 Readiness for Inclusive Change: A Capacity Building Assessment

Reframing organizational conflict and transforming human resource management principles and practices is strategic thoughtful work. It must be done responsibly and in ways that invite inclusive ongoing stakeholder engagement at all organizational levels and across functional areas throughout each stage of the planning, decision making, implementation, and evaluation process. Use this Assessment Worksheet individually and in teams to consider organizational capacity for inclusive change management in ways that balance learning, restoration, and employee development with organizational harm and risk management priorities. Answers will help gauge readiness for inclusive change and identify areas of strength and those that require added capacity building. Place an "X" along the provided continuum in answer to each of the first three sets of question.

Are you/your staff:	
1. Educated in current theory and research regarding learning processes and outcomes, as well as moral and ethical development?	Yes Somewhat Not yet
2. Advanced in their own development of internal foundations to instill reasoned, ethical, and principled decision making in their work?	Yes Somewhat Not yet
3. At a level of professional maturity to deal with the ambiguity and messiness inherent in nontraditional models of practice grounded in inclusion?	Yes Somewhat Not yet
4. Supported by bench strength, motivation, creativity, and diversity to employ a range of resolution strategies and work meaningfully with employees?	Yes Somewhat Not yet
5. Competent in assessment to measure impact?	Yes Somewhat Not yet
6. Ready with a demonstrated track record of making sound judgments?	Yes Somewhat Not yet
Does your functional unit:	
7. Employ best practices in its current work?	Yes Somewhat Not yet
8. Have a mission, vision, strategic plan, and evaluation methods that can support an inclusive approach to the work?	Yes Somewhat Not yet
9. Have educated and experienced staff to carry out an inclusive approach?	Yes Somewhat Not yet
10. Have sufficiently strong relationships with key partners and leaders to build partnerships for this work?	Yes Somewhat Not yet
11. Demonstrate functioning in a status quo or change management phase, assuming the current work is being done well within its established framework?	Yes Somewhat Not yet
12. Resourced at a level that can accommodate approaches that may bring greater effectiveness but perhaps not greater efficiency?	Yes Somewhat Not yet

(continued)

TABLE 4.2 Readiness for Inclusive Change: A Capacity Building Assessment (continued)			
In divisional work:			
13. Informed by the most current theory, research, and best practices?	Yes	Somewhat	Not yet
14. Conceptually and tangibly supportive of an inclusive learning approach to its work rather than a more activities/services-oriented approach?	Yes	Somewhat	Not yet
15. Articulated and measured as learning outcomes?	Yes	Somewhat	Not yet
16. Grounded in valuing active learning interventions?	Yes	Somewhat	Not yet
17. In a phase that supports reframing inquiry and efforts (i.e., are they in a status quo or change management phase and how will this impact dialogue around change)?	Yes	Somewhat	Not yet
At the organizational level (make brief notes in answer to provided questions):			
18. What is the organization's culture and approach to learning, conflict and conduct management?			
19. What is the scope of conflict resolution and conduct management services currently offered?/ How broad or narrow is conflict work defined?			
20. How is the current approach perceived as effective in achieving desired learning outcomes?			
21. What behavioral challenges may be more suited to expanded conflict resolution process options?			
22. Which groups present unique opportunities to expand process options and practices?			
23. Where are potential partners, colleagues, competitors, and naysayers?			
24. Is the organization in a status quo or change management phase?			
25. Does the organization have the capacity to withstand scrutiny and support its educational aims?			
26. Do the current policies and practices of key partners support or undermine active learning interventions?			
27. What is the current scope and capacity of the organization's support services to sustain a broad range of conflict resolution?			

Note: Worksheet by Taylor, S. H., Varner, D. T. & Giacomini, N.G. adapted from the published work of Taylor, S. H. & Varner, D. T. (2020). Reconciling Legal Obligations with Education Goals: Revisiting Foundations of Student Conflict Work. In J. M. Schrage & N. G. Giacomini (Eds.), *Reframing Campus Conflict: Student Conduct Practice through the Lens of Inclusive Excellence.*

vs. Equity" by Craig Froehle, simplifies some important related distinctions, and has inspired dozens of memes. Figure 4.2 is borrowed from a Facebook post courtesy of fb.com/wokefolks. Others have found expression in organizations from NYU's Stern School of Business, Huffington Post, United Way, and the Association of American Colleges and Universities (for an interesting read, find "The Evolution of an Accidental Meme" at https://medium.com/@CRA1G/the-evolution-of-an-accidental-meme-ddc4e139e0e4).

The version illustrated in Figure 4.2 updates Froehle's original with a frame to show the difference between equality, equity, and justice. Equality is shown to treat everyone the same; yet, give each kid the same-sized box to stand on without accounting for the impact of differing heights, it still causes one to be left out and another to enjoy height as an advantage. Equity tailors how we treat people based on what they need by providing boxes of different heights to help everyone see over the fence. Justice removes the wall as a structural barrier so that each spectator can experience common ground without any advantages or disadvantages.

If organizations are authentically committed to equity and restoration, they will create cultures in which people are willing to be like the children who give up their positions of advantage so that others can be raised up. Justice, in turn, requires us to be the kids who recognize the presence of the fence as a barrier and are courageous enough to take it down. If we were better artists, we might add a fourth restorative justice frame in which the children might be seen in dialogue acknowledging past harm while

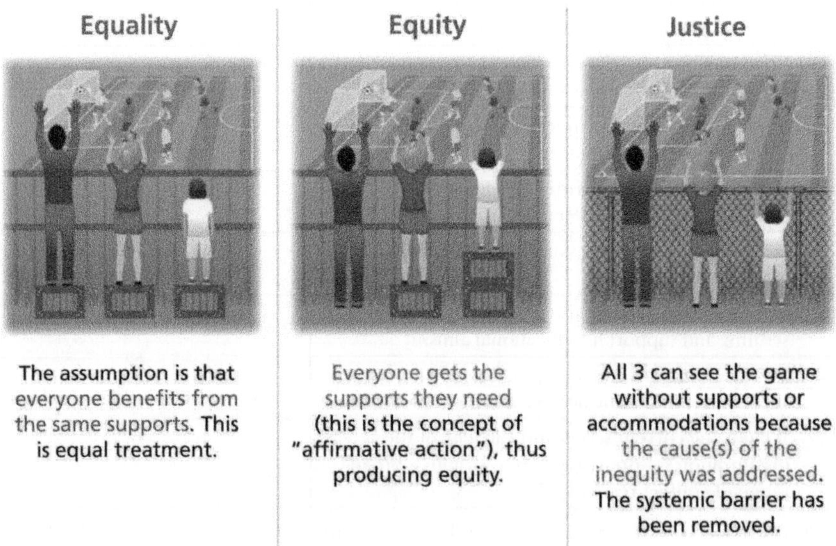

Figure 4.2 The difference between equality, equity, and justice (image obtained from fb.com/wokefolks).

apologizing for and forgiving one another. Perhaps content would include them collaborating for added solutions that include everyone's thoughts, needs, and interests about enjoying the game. The players might even pause to join the dialogue, invite the kids to play too, and so on.

Capacity Building, Legitimacy, and Authenticity in the Work of Inclusive Excellence

An understanding of how organizations legitimatize diversity and inclusion messages helps shed additional light on the importance of capacity building and inclusive excellence. As seen in the literature on organization and diversity management, diversity and inclusion are parallels to justice and restorative justice. For example, Valentine's (2018) research which decoded corporate mission and diversity statements culled from organizations making the 2015 Diversity, Inc. Top 50 Companies for Diversity list, shows that compliance alone is not a strong legitimating expression of equity, fairness, diversity, and inclusion. In other words, it is not enough to use familiar/common words associated with diversity on corporate landing pages to comply with legal requirements and expect that they will be perceived as authentic (Valentine, 2018).

If the institutional structures fail to legitimatize the message, cognizant stakeholders will notice. In other words, it becomes obvious when organizations "talk the talk" but do not "walk the walk." The same authenticity is required in our personal work related to deeply informed attempts at inclusive justice and helps demonstrate the nexus between learning and justice. Inclusion positively correlates with learning and effectiveness as a measure of legitimacy in organizational discourse. This theme focuses on increasing the representation of traditionally underrepresented groups to learn from diversity, integrating cultural differences and bringing about positive change, and incorporating diversity throughout work processes to yield innovation (Valentine, 2018). It also runs parallel to restorative principles that express inclusion as a full community commitment to supporting those who have been harmed while also helping offenders confront and learn from the impact of their wrongdoing. This is especially meaningful if an offense is due to some degree of cross-cultural misunderstanding that might be clarified and healed while bringing people closer together.

An organization that embodies learning as a cultural value and structural orientation for internal stakeholders and elevates social justice sensitivity into expressions of corporate social responsibility into the larger community is also one that demonstrates a higher authentic commitment to diversity and inclusion. On the flip side, those that lean into more control-centered goals, assumptions, and strategies likely bear the consequences found from Table 4.1, to include reduced rates of learning and knowledge acquisition; less diversity in perspective sharing necessary for more creativity, commitment, collaboration, and constructive change; lower commitment and higher polarization; and difficulty in solving problems and sustaining solutions and the like. And while inclusively excellent organizations may not name what they are doing as "justice" outright, the cited research shows that they demonstrate authentic justice bearing efforts that help people feel valued, respected, and equally cared for across identity. These efforts are identified through statements that speak to paradigms across discrimination and fairness, access, and legitimacy to prove that they are being good corporate citizens, while being moral, ethical, just, and equitable. Diversity leaders are those organizations that learn from diversity and convey social justice sensitivity in word and deed; this is what sets these organizations apart from the competition (Valentine, 2018).

Building a Restorative Toolkit Framed on Inclusive Excellence

Being just, and institutionalizing what that means, travels with how we make sense of equity, privilege, power, and fairness. These truths are deeply rooted in a common culture, yet are as diverse as our lived experiences. The things that once made justice a for-granted and even taboo concept might also be said to have reached a tipping point within the context of an agitated national and global community. Activism against inequality continues to escalate, silos that previously separated experiences and knowledge between people and fields are being bridged, and silences broken. In short, deconstructing justice to its roots as viewed through goals, assumptions, strategies, and consequences is the only way to reclaim the most basic of American principles—justice for all.

So, to the original focus of this chapter: What do we do when a difference, conflict, violation, or harm occurs? How do we treat each other, teach each other, and hold one another accountable in a diverse community at school and work? What does it say about us? And, can we/how can we do better? We present some working thoughts to close out this two-part chapter that draw from our unique, collaborative experiences across fields of education and human resources and intersect in expertise related to inclusive conflict, conduct, and diversity management.

Restorative HR Practices: A Toolkit to Drive Inclusive Excellence and Diversity Branding

Before building a practical application toolkit to further goals of expanding inclusive justice in theory and practice, we need to have a working understanding of the unique climate and culture of a place. We also need to check how committed internal and external stakeholders are to doing the work, and how tolerant they are to being vulnerable and resilient. To be good at advancing justice, we need to first lay strong foundations supported by theories and models that speak to principles of inclusive excellence across holistic restorative approaches to conduct and conflict management. These foundations then support authentic application skills, processes and know-how. Simply broadening the scope of conflict resolution and conduct management services currently offered in the organization is not enough. The system as a whole must be able to sustain both the vision and broad institutionalized range of conflict resolution pathways across divisions in ways that empower parties and shape more inclusive processes and policies. Investing in expanded options requires full collaboration by inclusive stakeholders. Rather than mere breadth of services, we need depth.

Justice deserves a deep dive. We cannot stop at reform that camps out in restorative or transformative models any more than we can rest in the crime and punishment mindset of a control- and rights-based retributive model. Those that take on this work must ask questions and drill down to the common ground values, goals, assumptions, strategies, and consequences that inform how we exercise justice. We must wrestle with the underpinnings in order to build up from solid foundation, work alongside people, and bring them with us. As justice administrators, advocates, organizational leaders, and community members alike, we are responsible for holding people accountable and being accountable ourselves, in ways that are premised in an ethic of care, equity, and justice. Finally, our toolbox must include ongoing ways to sustain the vision, mission, and strategic plan invested in evolving inclusive, restorative justice. We must be ready and willing to evaluate the investment and weigh the impact against intent to gauge whether current approaches are effective in achieving desired results in real and perceived ways. All this must be done in ways that respect the organization's past, current, and future tolerance for public exposure, push back, and risk. Once we have done this intentional groundwork, we are ready to build the toolbox. What follows are broad workplace examples with transferable content for other diverse communities in which people invest in a common culture and aspire to become more restorative and just as an expression of inclusive excellence.

Justice as Equitable Hiring

Justice can take the form of transparent and targeted recruitment activities and hiring practices that advance underrepresented populations as a visible commitment to diversity and inclusion. At the same time, these initiatives must mitigate the sense that "when you are consciously or unconsciously accustomed to some level of unearned privilege, measures that further equality and diversity initiatives can feel like oppression" (https://www.huffingtonpost.com/chris-boeskool/when-youre-accustomed-to-privilege_b_9460662.html). A similar expression is found in the popular unattributed notion that "equal rights for others does not mean less rights for you. It's not pie." Still, even when everyone is aligned with the process and goals of inclusive excellence, moving in that direction can feel uncomfortable, even threatening. Conflict management practitioners often talk about expanding the pie to help move people in conflict away from the idea that their resources are limited. Creative collaboration and buy-in, with both internal and external stakeholders, together with ongoing evaluation of impact and intent, will help everyone feel included and informed in the process of transformation and change.

How do we do it?

- Update job descriptions, applications, and other forms to eliminate problematic phrasing or wording that can promote bias, as well as unnecessary requirements that could prevent certain groups from applying.
- Highlight the existing diversity and inclusion within your company—include actual photos and video testimonials of diverse employees to reflect visible diversity and to showcase a commitment to employing and retaining diverse populations (not just race and ethnicity, but also sexual orientation, gender identity, religious affiliation, cognitive diversity, etc.).
- Include affirmative action policy or equal employment opportunity (EEO) statements in advertisements, and talk about your employee resource groups (ERGs) where employees come together based on shared characteristics and common interests to establish a "safe space" and support system that gives a sense of belonging, understanding, and collective success.
- Partner with local organizations that serve primarily underrepresented populations in the community to develop effective recruitment plans, such as the Urban League, the National Association for the Advancement of Colored People (NAACP), American Association of Retired Persons (AARP), Veteran's Employment and Training Services (VETS), etc. Support their events and conferences, and encourage your employees to participate in these organizations.
- Provide opportunities for potential candidates to learn more about the diversity in your company. Share your diversity goals publicly, talk about the culture of transparency that you live by, and integrate diversity recruiting into your employment brand through social media to promote corporate commitment to diversity.
- Assemble a diverse interview panel with a wide range of backgrounds to help decrease unconscious bias in the hiring process.
- Educate hiring managers on unconscious bias and the implications of making judgments on a person's character, experiences, or back-

ground based on observations that are unrelated to potential job skill, performance, and work ethic.
- Personalize recruitment by developing relationships with potential candidates, engaging them, and building a strong talent pipeline. Involve visibly diverse senior managers in outreach efforts.

Justice as Job Satisfaction

Inclusive recruitment and hiring removes barriers and gets qualified, diversely talented people in the door. Effective retention strategies (such as formal mentoring programs, ERGs, mandatory D&I training for all employees, stay interviews, etc.) keeps employees there in ways that are satisfying and productive all around. Promoting equality, equity, and justice in community with others is necessary for a healthy expression of culture, rich in trust, learning, individual and shared achievement and celebration, and authentic expressions of access and inclusion. It is the metaphoric stuff previously referenced to as pure oxygen versus smog. While umbrella terms have evolved over the years from tolerance of difference to social justice, followed by diversity and inclusion (D&I) to the present day expressions of inclusive excellence, there are some common practices that promote inclusive wellbeing, mutual respect, community, and civility as they relate to justice.

How do we do it?

- Eliminate a culture of systemic gender and racial discrimination that prevents qualified people from obtaining full-employment and current talent from contributing to the fullest of their abilities.
- Support the "ban the box" campaign, and consider hiring ex-convicts who have served their sentences and paid their debt to society—provided that the crime is unrelated to the duties of the position.
- Be effective environmental stewards, protect human rights, and be a good corporate citizen—recognize employee social consciousness by providing employee resource or affinity groups, offering paid time-off for civil engagements. Motivate employees with incentives to do their part in maintaining social responsibility by explaining how their choices affect company costs and the environment in which they live.
- Question entry-level compensation that is well below the market pay rate for the position, because it limits diversity and reduces inclusiveness and transparency based on socioeconomic status.
- Facilitate a well-run employee feedback program that builds trust and loyalty with management—train mangers to listen, ask open-ended questions, and respond with a "no-fault feedback" approach.

Justice as Learning and Restoration

Sometimes, we mess up. Stripping justice down to common ground in ways that re-prioritize learning over control allows us to counterbalance human fallibility with humanity, where "each of us is more than the worst thing we've ever done" (Stevenson, 2014, pp. 17–18), and our culture makes space for the opportunity to repair harm, rebuild trust, and restore community. Traditional institutionalized risk management and accountability protocol prioritize the idea that equates "same" processes and outcomes with "fair" processes (Taylor and Varner, 2009). But as we have learned, we are not cutting up pie. Hybrid versions of justice that tailor and expand process and accountability options can be restorative, educational, and even retributive (punitive) as required by relevant legislation and precedent, all at the same time.

How do we do it?

- Expand process options along a continuum that empowers people to resolve incidents of conflict and conduct at the lowest and most effective levels, borrowing from models already widely in use across K–12, higher education and special education, as well as juvenile and criminal justice practices that incorporate deferment options into restorative justice practices like victim offender conferences and circles.
- Institutionalize accessible basic and advanced conflict management and restorative justice training that incorporates theories on identity and social justice. Even if employees do not actively facilitate mediation and RJ practices themselves, training will introduce them to the foundations of conflict resolution and community while promoting the shared language needed to nurture a culture of inclusion, learning, collaboration, resilience, and peacemaking.
- Partner with external community members already doing the work of restorative and transformation justice. Facilitators from outside the organization are often viewed as more impartial/multi-partial, as well as private/confidential. Who will facilitate must not be a barrier to entering a restorative process.
- Embrace mistakes and violations as part of the process of growth and learning. Most mistakes and missteps can readily be used one-on-one, in teams, and across the organization as lessons to improve how things are done in the future, all while validating that the culture supports learning over control.
- Avoid zero tolerance policies in favor of those that make room for human fallibility and redemption. When strict policies and sanctions are deemed culturally necessary, couple them with clear value-driven explanations that rest on community safety and civility. Remember that institutionalized systems of justice are our way of keeping communities together safely. If someone is expelled from the community, find a way to express why without compromising a person's privacy rights.

- Support opportunities for those who have caused harm to take accountability, seek rehabilitation, ask forgiveness, make repairs, and ask for restoration back into the community.
- Equally support those who identify as victims and survivors. Harm can carry trauma, and often times, due process and even restorative justice can feel tipped in favor of those who cause harm over those who have experienced harm. It is not mutually exclusive to #believesurvivors with expressions of care, accommodation, support, gentle listening, steady communication, and a just process while at the very same time providing equal access, care, and process to those who are alleged to have caused harm.

Concluding Remarks

We are advocates for restorative justice in context to the more inclusive inquiry needed to transform justice and mitigate injustice. To be done authentically, restorative justice must be more than a trending theme in conflict and conduct management. It invites us back to the root foundations of how we decide who we care about, how we hold one another accountable, and what we do to keep ourselves and others safe while working to stay together. Communities are part of the human condition, just like the conflict, misdeeds, harms, and injustice we find there. Understanding these things and managing them in principled effective ways that take everyone's voices and experiences into consideration takes more than a good set of policies. Theory to practice applications must be institutionalized and evaluated ongoing. They must be legitimate, authentic, and transparent while balancing results and relationships. They must center learning and restoration over control and punishment. If not, unmanaged conflict, harm, and injustice together take a toll on individuals and organizations alike.

Defining justice is challenging. As a concept it can be complex and nuanced, interwoven with cultural meaning and largely taken for granted, at least until there is perceived injustice, big or small. Feelings of injustice and inequity that expose systemic power exploitation and identity-based discounting, exclusion, harassment, and physical harm, present both challenges and opportunities for change. Do we listen and learn in times of conflict and change, or control and punish? What do we do when a difference, conflict, violation, or harm occurs? How do we treat each other, teach each other, and hold one another accountable in a diverse community and what does it say about us? Can we/how can we do better? How is the moral universe of who we care about and who we care less about reflected in our institutionalized culture and expressed when it comes to managing conduct and conflict? While we wrestle with the broader meaning of justice, we are all presented with the opportunity to move towards a working agreement that the cost of injustice is high, and then commit to the capacity building needed to advocate for inclusive excellence and equitable restorative applications of justice across identities and communities.

REFERENCES

Cloke, K., & Goldsmith, J. (2011). *Resolving conflicts at work: Ten strategies for everyone on the job* (3rd ed.). San Francisco, CA: Jossey-Bass.

Deutsch, M. (2014). Cooperation, competition, and conflict. In P. T. Coleman, M. Deutsch, & E. C. Marcus (Eds.), *The handbook of conflict resolution: Theory and practice* (3rd ed., pp. 3–28). San Francisco, CA: Jossey-Bass.

Eddy, B., & DiStefano, L. G. (2015). *It's all your fault at work: Managing narcissist and other high-conflict people.* Scottsdale, AZ: Unhooked Books.

Mayvin. (2016, May). *Restorative HR practice: A toolkit.* Retrieved from https://mayvin.co.uk/wp-content/uploads/2016/09/RHR-Toolkit-v.May-2016.pdf

Nocella, A. J., II. (2011). An overview of the history and theory of transformative justice. *Peace & Conflict Review, 6*(1), 1–10. Retrieved from http://www.review.upeace.org/pdf.cfm?articulo=124&ejemplar=23

Schrage, J. M., & Thompson, M. C. (2008, June). *Using a social justice model for conflict resolution to ensure access for all students.* Paper presented at the Donald D. Gehring Academy for Student Conduct Administration, Salt Lake City, UT.

Schrage, J. M., & Thompson, M. C. (2009). Providing a spectrum of resolution options. In J. M. Schrage & N. G. Giacomini (Eds.), *Reframing campus conflict: Student conduct practice through a social justice lens* (pp. 65–84). Sterling, VA: Stylus.

Simms, J. (2017, July 25). *There's more than one way to solve a dispute.* Retrieved from https://www.peoplemanagement.co.uk/experts/advice/more-than-one-way-solve-dispute

Stevenson, B. (2014). *Just mercy: A story of justice and redemption.* New York, NY: Spiegel & Grau.

Taylor, S. H., & Varner, D. T. (2009). When student learning and law merge to create educational student conflict resolution and effective conduct management programs. In J. M. Schrage & N. G. Giacomini (Eds.), *Reframing campus conflict: Student conduct practice through a social justice lens* (pp. 22–49). Sterling, VA: Stylus.

Taylor, S. H., & Varner, D. T. (in press). Reconciling legal obligations with education goals: Revisiting foundations of student conflict work. In J.M. Schrage & N. G. Giacomini (Eds.), *Reframing campus conflict: Student conduct practice through the lens of inclusive excellence.* Sterling, VA: Stylus.

Valentine, M. M. (2018). *Corporate success in a diverse world: Analyzing corporate discourse for legitimacy of profitable U.S. companies* (Doctoral dissertation). Available from ProQuest Dissertations & Theses database. (10932686).

Wakabayashi, D., & Benner, K. (2018, October 25). How Google protected Andy Rubin, the 'father of Android.' *The New York Times.* Retrieved from https://www.nytimes.com

Zehr, H. (2015). *The little book of restorative justice* (2nd ed.). New York, NY: Good Books.

CHAPTER 5

MAINTAINING HARMONY IN IRISH WORKPLACES

A View of Workplace Dispute Resolution Practice in Ireland

Gerry Rooney

Ireland is home to many multinational American companies. The Irish workplace, with its attendant rules and regulations, provides a stable environment for productive organizations. It has contributed to Ireland's economic growth where its economy grew by 7.3% in 2017, three times faster than the wider Euro area, according to new European Union (EU) Commission estimates (Raidió Teilifís Éireann, 2018). The surge, driven by the activities of multinational companies operating in Ireland, made it the fastest-growing country in the EU.

This chapter looks at the developments in Ireland regarding workplace dispute resolution, and what can be gained from the interventions and innovations that are emerging as best practices, as well as contributing to Ireland's attractiveness as a center for foreign direct investment. This chapter

From Discord to Harmony, pages 81–102

focuses on the perspectives of the author as a mediator, adjudicator, investigator, and trainer in interpersonal conflict matters and situations.

THE BENEFITS OF BUILDING COLLABORATIVE WORKPLACE RELATIONSHIPS

Ireland, as Europe's largest green space (Discover Ireland, 2018), is renowned for its hospitality, scenery, unique culture, and "craic." Many of those who visit the Emerald Isle recount the friendly nature of its people, and despite the occasional rainy day, visitors are not dampened by their experience. For a small island nestled off the west coast of Europe, Ireland is world-renowned. The total population of Ireland (to include Northern Ireland) is estimated at 6.6 million citizens, of which 4.8 million live in the Republic of Ireland. It is also estimated that a further 60–80 million people make up the diaspora worldwide. Always willing to share our heritage, the largest St. Patrick's Day parade in the world is celebrated in New York City, with Savannah, Georgia, also hosting one of the world's biggest St. Patrick's Day parades.

Following an enjoyable 18-year career in the Irish Naval Service, which forms an important element of the Permanent Defence Forces in Ireland, my own career navigated its way into workplace dispute resolution. After my military career, I worked with the employer's agency for the local government sector in the late 1990s. At that time, significant investment was being made into labor relations within the Irish public sector to build capacity in order to manage and deliver on organizational change in a fast-growing economy. The efforts paid dividends as it cemented industrial peace between management and the trade unions. The parties invested significantly in building collaborative relationships to change the culture of industrial relations between management and staff representatives, and the work I was involved in provided rich material for my research that I conducted while earning my Master of Science degree in human resource development. The building of collaborative processes between management and the unions was focused on staff engagement practices. This work aligned with the academic learnings from my master's studies and convinced me that an organization's human resources will develop better and will more likely embrace change when shared interests are the focus of the relationship. Little did I know then that the concept of shared interests would become core to my current work as a mediator and workplace facilitator.

The investment in building collaborative approaches between management and the trade unions at that time delivered on a sustained period for low-level adversarial industrial relations, whilst change was facilitated across the public sector. The trend, which was influenced by the social partnership model (Baccaro & Simoni M. International Institute for Labour Studies, 2004), saw a remarkable drop in days lost due to collective disputes. For example, during the 1980s some 50 working days lost per 100 employees were lost in the public sector on collective disputes, but by the early years of the millennium this had dropped to approximately 5 working days per 100 employees (Wallace, McMahon, & Gunnigle, 2004; Murphy & Roche, 1997).

By the mid-2000s, the Irish economy was booming. Full employment and the dizzy heights of a successful economy contributed to the Celtic Tiger, but the tiger was soon to look like it was becoming extinct with the financial challenges that emerged from 2008. We say in Ireland that when the American economy gets a cold, Ireland gets a flu, and the American credit crunch became Ireland's financial crash and a national crisis. While America's economy sneezed and coughed, Ireland's economic condition looked terminal! The symptoms were also to have an impact on workplace harmony.

From 2008 to 2014, during and in the aftermath of the global economic crisis, an increase in the days lost due to collective disputes in the Irish public sector was experienced. However, the trend of days lost was recorded at approximately 8 days per 100 employees, much lower than the previous recession during the 1980s (Teague, Roche, Gormley, & Currie, 2015). Despite the post-2008 austerity measures which significantly impacted public sector employees, Ireland's dispute resolution procedures appeared less adversarial and destructive than heretofore. Significant hardship was visited upon public sector employees with pay cuts, increased working hours, and recruitment moratoriums. Similarly, many job losses occurred in the private sector.

Currently, the private sector is recovering and Ireland is nearing full-employment levels again. Meanwhile, the public sector, with high levels of trade union membership amongst its workforce, is experiencing a period of renegotiation of the austerity measures and pay restoration. What is emerging is a return to harder approaches in collective bargaining compared to that which had been experienced prior to the economic crash. However, to date, the public sector has not experienced destructive strikes or polarized adversarial relationships that would have been more typical of previous generations. So, this led me to ask the following questions: What innovations have likely influenced workplace dispute resolution trends in Ireland? And, what can we learn from this that can contribute to more harmonious workplace relations at an individual level?

EMERGING TRENDS IN THE NATURE OF WORKPLACE CONFLICT

The Irish industrial relations model is built on a pluralist approach (Calveley, Allsop, Rocha Lawton, & Huesmann, 2017) where it is acknowledged that many legitimate interests influence the collective relationship that develops between an employer and its staff. In general, the political framework in Ireland, where the pendulum swings slightly left or right of the center, supports a voluntarist model. The voluntarist principle (Wallace et al., 2004) is based on good faith and enables trade unions and employees to regulate their own relations without interference from public authorities. That is, the state provides support for dispute resolution but does not get directly involved in the dispute resolution outcomes unless in its role as an employer.

Notwithstanding, Ireland has introduced a plethora of legislation supporting the rights of employees and, as a member of the European Union, these rights have grown significantly over the past 30 years. The enhanced floor of employee rights has perhaps challenged the traditional collective bargaining approaches, whereby, employees can now individually seek the protection of their rights without recourse to a collective approach. This situation has most likely influenced the general decline in trade union membership which is now approximately 24% of the workforce (Organisation for Economic Cooperation and Development, 2018). It is recognized that for many of the U.S. corporations based in Ireland, trade union membership is significantly lower or nonexistent, and wherein most U.S. corporations there is no union recognition.

An analysis of how stable industrial relations are in Ireland can be shown by the significant drop in days lost due to workplace disputes over the past 30 years. The experiences of workdays lost in the private sector in Ireland depicts a very strong downward trend since the 1980s. From 2000, the days lost in the private sector are relatively insignificant compared to those lost in the public sector. The trend of a low record of collective conflict and collective disputes, therefore, presents a reassuring trend, with general stability being noted. (Teague et al., 2015).

Another interesting shift can be seen when a review of the issues that influenced collective disputes from the 1970s to 2010 is compared to the type of disputes that are currently reported. By 2010, there had been a shift from disputes relating to pay issues to conflict relating to employee engagement, dismissal, and redundancies (Teague et al., 2015). This development reflects a change in the focus of disputes. With reference to Maslow's hierarchy of needs (Maslow, 1943), it appears employees' concerns have moved up the pyramid of motivational interest from safety issues relating to pay and conditions to social and more intrinsic matters, including self-actualization associated with engagement and how organizational change impacts individuals at the workplace. Whilst pay and conditions will always create potential for workplace disputes, in general, the issues in focus in the modern workplace appear to be more associated with the perceptions and realities of the relationship employees have with their employer and vice versa. Indeed, the heightened awareness of individual rights, and a growing focus regarding the equity in the employment relationship between employer and employee, that go beyond the basic terms and conditions of an employment contract is becoming a feature in our workplaces.

This shift is perhaps reflected with the uncovering of inappropriate behavior at an individual level, as highlighted in the #MeToo campaign, and more recently with a call to remove confidential and binding arbitration agreements typified in workplace contracts (Tippet, 2019) such as those operated by the high-tech businesses from the Silicon Valley and beyond. It is evident that the focus of workplace disputes and the approaches to dispute management are certainly going through a change from the collective to the individual, with an increased focus on issues that can negatively impact personal and interpersonal relationships at work.

WORKPLACE DISPUTE RESOLUTION SYSTEMS IN IRELAND

This shift in the pattern of conflict at work is reflected in the systems established in Ireland to assist in an early resolution of workplace conflict. Over 70 years ago, the Irish State recognized a need to create an independent third-party process to assist in workplace dispute resolution. Realizing the need to support ongoing relationships in the workplace, a Labour Xourt was established in 1946 under the Industrial Relations Act, 1946. The mission statement of the Labour Court is: "To provide high quality, fair and impartial arrangements for the resolution of industrial disputes and the determination of appeals in disputes based on employment law" ("The Labour Court," n.d.). The functions of the court have been altered and extended by subsequent legislation, including the Workplace Relations Act of 2015 which provided the most profound changes since the 1946 act. Under the provisions of the 2015 act, the Labour Court now has sole appellate jurisdiction in all disputes under employment rights enactments, and a newly formed Workplace Relations Commission deals with disputes of first instance, including individual complaints against employers. Indeed, even the language is changing in how the legislation is titled—a focus on relations in the workplace being a cornerstone influencing the architecture that underpins what needs to be sustained in the modern workplace. Perhaps this should come as no surprise, for over 20 years ago it was Daniel Goleman (1998) who postulated, "The rules for work are changing. We're being judged by a new yardstick: not just by how smart we are, or by training and expertise, but also by how well we handle ourselves and each other" (p. 3). Now it appears we are not just being judged by this yardstick, but being measured and made accountable for it.

The long-established Labour Court in Ireland is not a court of law. It operates as an industrial relations tribunal, hearing both sides in a case and then issuing a recommendation (or determination/decision/order, depending on the type of case), setting out its opinion on the dispute and the terms on which it should be settled. Recommendations made by the court concerning the investigation of disputes under the Industrial Relations Acts 1946–2015 are not binding on the parties concerned; however, the parties are expected to give serious consideration to the court's recommendation. Ultimately, the Labour Court recognizes that responsibility for the settlement of a dispute rests with the parties, and this is a significant ethos in influencing the culture of workplace conflict resolution in Ireland. Notwithstanding, the court's determinations under the employment rights enactment are legally binding (The Labour Court, n.d.). The court's functions can be divided between those matters relating to industrial relations issues, typically collective disputes, and those relating to the determination of appeals in issues relating to employment rights that have been dealt with by a newly formed, state-funded independent Workplace Relations Commission (WRC). The Labour Court continues to play a significant role in supporting workplace dispute resolution measures in Ireland, receiving 1,093 referrals in the year 2017 alone ("The Labour Court," n.d.).

In 1969, the state recognized the need to have a forum to address individual employment rights and established the Rights Commissioner Service to investigate disputes, grievances, and claims for small groups of employees and individuals (Law Reform Commission, 2008). The aim of the Rights Commissioner Service was to "provide people with access to justice without undergoing an excessively legalistic process" (Mulvey, 2008, para. 69). A review of the activity trends of the Rights Commissioner Service (Teague et al., 2015) showed an average of 2 employees per thousand referring cases to the service since the early 1970s. However, the service experienced a dramatic increase in the number of referrals during the first decade of the millennium with complaints being referred to the service growing to 10 employees per thousand by the year 2010.

Under the 1990 Industrial Relations Act, the Rights Commissioner Service was subsumed into a newly formed Labour Relations Commission (LRC). This further reflected developments of the state's interest in supporting businesses in their efforts to build a capacity in dispute resolution. It also underpinned the voluntarist concept wherein, with the appropriate assistance, the responsibility for the settlement of a dispute rests with the parties. In addition to providing a forum for individual dispute resolution, which continued under the Rights Commissioner Service, the LRC also established an Advisory Service to assist workplaces with informally exploring and resolving disputes before they became damaging to the relationships and business entities involved. This Advisory Service provided a successful avenue to informal conflict resolution, and where unresolved cases could progress to the Labour Court as "a court of last resort." The Advisory Service division also offered innovative developments, particularly in the area of facilitation of dispute resolution/avoidance/structures in private enterprises and public service organizations.

Another service provided by the LRC was a conciliation service, described as a voluntary mediation process that facilitated a search for agreement between disputing parties (Law Reform Commission, 2008). The aim of conciliation, which was provided free of charge, was to bring about a timely and effective settlement of industrial disputes without resort to strikes or lockouts, and to hasten the termination of work stoppages or industrial action where these have occurred. In 2005, the LRC established a workplace mediation service in response to a perceived demand for an informal and confidential dispute resolution service, focusing on disputes involving individuals or small groups of employees (Law Reform Commission, 2008). This mediation service created a stronger awareness amongst human resource (HR) practitioners of informal conflict management procedures that are less costly and timelier in resolving workplace disputes.

A further role of the LRC was to issue codes of practice on industrial relations matters as empowered under Section 42 of the Industrial Relations Act of 1990. These codes of practice are written in consultation with employers, trade unions, and other interested parties, and were issued by the minister for enterprise, trade, and employment under a declaration order. Although not binding, the codes provide a guide for the use of employers, trade unions, and others to highlight and encourage the adoption of good industrial relations practice. Courts, industrial relations tribunals, and institutions do take the codes of practice into account, and deem them to be relevant as admissible evidence in determining any proceedings before them. Fifteen codes of practice have been issued to date, including a code for dealing with grievances and discipline in the workplace and a code of practice detailing procedures for addressing bullying in the workplace (Workplace Relations Commission, 2017).

Two further developments also occurred in building support to assist in workplace dispute resolution. In 1977, the former Redundancy Appeals Tribunal, which was established in 1967, became the Employment Appeals Tribunal (EAT). The EAT was an independent body bound to *act judicially* and was established to provide a speedy, fair, inexpensive, and informal means for individual workers to seek remedies for alleged infringements of their statutory rights (Law Reform Commission, 2008). The EAT dealt with cases or claims involving unfair dismissal, constructive dismissal, redundancy, minimum notice of termination of employment, terms of employment, holidays, payment of wages, and deductions from wages. Then, in 1998, the Equality Tribunal was established under the Employment Equality Act of 1998 to ensure proper compliance with the increasingly complex body of equality legislation (Teague, 2005). Its core function was to investigate and/or mediate complaints of unlawful discrimination, and its services were free of charge. The Equality Tribunal had competence to act on nine prohibited grounds of discrimination (gender, civil status, family status, sexual orientation, religion, age, disability, race, and membership of the Traveller community). Its mediation service reported a 56% success rate.

Reflecting the changing nature of work, a major reform of the workplace dispute resolution structures occurred in 2015 under the Workplace Relations Act 2015. The 2015 act has made provisions with respect to the resolution, mediation, and adjudication of disputes and complaints relating to contraventions of, or entitlements under, legislation governing the employment relationship between employers and employees. The 2015 act also dissolved the LRC, the EAT, and the Equality Tribunal, and established the WRC to deal with all employment complaints in the first instance, with the Labour Court empowered to be the Court of Appeal.

Since 2015, the access to dispute resolution services for workplace issues in Ireland has been simplified, with the WRC as the first point of contact for dealing with workplace disputes in the event that they cannot be resolved locally. The WRC provides a mediation service, an adjudication service (where complaints that were formally raised under the EAT, the Equality Tribunal, and the Rights Commissioner Service are subject to adjudication decisions and recommendations), and an inspection service.

Accordingly, Ireland has established a transparent, accessible, and independent third-party support system to workplaces to assist and decide upon a range of disputes that can occur in the workplace. This support is placed on a statutory footing under the WRC and the Labour Court. According to the WRC strategy statement, its central policy and activities are primarily concerned with accommodating competing interests in facilitating and assisting workplace change (Workplace Relations Commission, 2016). It is also concerned with creating an environment of equity and fairness in employment, which plays a key role in contributing to the overall architecture of economic and social investments. Specifically, the collective and specialized services of the WRC all play a vital role in contributing toward industrial peace, maintaining and sustaining enterprise productivity, and engaging with employers and trade unions on issues of employee pay and rewards. Securing fair, impartial, and effective employment rights, adjudication services, and appropriate and essential employment standards and enforcement are vital and important components of the strategic operations of the WRC (Workplace Relations Commission, 2016).

A FOCUS FOR BUILDING TRUST IN THE EMPLOYEE–EMPLOYER RELATIONSHIP

Based on my own experience of being involved in public sector industrial relations, and in building the management/labor partnership approach from 1998 to 2003 in the local government sector (which employed approximately 33,000 people), it became clear to me that when relationships are built on trust significant levels of cooperation can be created that facilitate a win–win outcome. I have observed that this shared approach creates a more harmonious workplace when compared to the traditional adversarial tactics in collective bargaining of win–lose or win-some–lose-some approaches to disputes. A shared approach or interest-based focus further inculcates appropriate levels of respect at a human level, and this underpins the stances parties can take when negotiating. A very obvious outcome of an approach built on mutual interest in Ireland is reflected in the significant decline of workdays lost due to unresolved conflict; as identified earlier, from in excess of 70 (50) days lost per 100 employees in the public sector (private sector) during the 1970s to approximately 8 days lost (almost no days lost) per 100 employees in the public sector (private sector) during the first decade of the new millennium. Equally significant are my observations that during and post the severe challenges brought about by the economic crisis, I noted a less adversarial approach being adopted to the significant decline in public service conditions of employment relating to pay and career progression from 2008 to 2014. This is not to say that the trade unions had weakened their approach or concern for their members' rights. However, I do believe the skills developed for building a collaborative/partnership approach has helped develop an environment where trade union leaders and senior management are better prepared to adapt an approach where the interests of both parties are recognized.

Another significant shift that I have observed is a changing priority in interests from trade union members. This, I believe, has perhaps influenced dispute resolution approaches in the workplace. Data collected between 2001 and 2005 indicated that union members prefer to be represented on a cooperative basis, or through partnership with employers, than through collective bargaining of a more conventional and adversarial character (Geary, 2007). Supported by the growing body of employment rights, employees are now more confident in enforcing their individual rights across a widened range of work and employment. This is reflected in the growth of individual claims presented to the WRC (some 14,000 individual cases during 2017) when compared to the weighting toward collective disputes up to the 1990s (Workplace Relations Commission, 2018). It is, therefore, safe to conclude that Ireland's comprehensive set of statutory bodies that are responsible for the resolution of employment grievances and disputes, and which were consolidated with the Workplace Relations Act of 2015, has influenced the approach to workplace conflict resolution in Ireland. Indeed, having reviewed this matter, there is an important distinction that can be made in employment disputes between conflicts of interest and conflict of rights. Conflicts of interest are normally associated with disputes between employers and employees over aspects of pay and working conditions, such as changes to reward systems or proposed changes to the working environment. Conflicts of rights are more concerned with alleged violations of legally enforceable employment rights (Teague, 2006).

RESOLVING INTERPERSONAL WORKPLACE CONFLICT AND DISPUTES

Conflict, whether based on conflict of interest or conflict of rights, is an inevitable part of everyday working life. I am of the view that an important issue is the need to resolve any such conflict quickly as unresolved conflicts generally become disputes—and disputes gather stories, entrench positions of the disputants, and can become more costly to resolve. As identified in the Gibbons Report (Gibbons, 2007),

> When a dispute arises in the workplace, it is the interests of all parties to resolve it as soon as possible. There is a window of opportunity for early resolution. Delay increases the likelihood of positions becoming entrenched and the dispute leading to formal processes, with significant natural costs to both parties... And a serious impact on employers and employees in terms of lost time, stress and the likely breakdown of the employment relationship. (p. 23)

Unwinding the stories that have contributed to a dispute can be the most challenging element of dispute resolution. It is within these stories that the memories and hurt are stored, and where each party needs to be provided with the opportunity to feel heard and feel understood before trusting any rebuilding of the relationship. When I act as a workplace adjudicator for an employment dispute, I am required to hear the stories, adduce evidence, and decide on balance, whether an employee was wronged or not. The outcome generally is at least one dissatisfied party as the adjudication focus is to make a decision on the matter. At times, the parties remain adversarial toward each other throughout the hearing and can leave in that fractured state of mind as they wait for a decision, hoping they or their representatives/advocates have influenced an adjudicator sufficiently to find in their favor. I often wonder how much more of a challenge it must be for the party who has not won a favorable decision when an ongoing employment relationship is still required after the conclusion of a hearing. Adversarial processes contribute to adversarial relationships.

On the other hand, when I facilitate a mediation process with parties in a dispute, the storytelling has a completely different dynamic. In a mediation process, the parties acknowledge that their mutual interest is to have a lasting resolution to the dispute. It's about making things better, not perfect. And better relationships and workplaces have a better chance of becoming closer to being perfect, productive, and more harmonious.

At a recent mediation I facilitated, two colleagues in senior sales roles had a very difficult relationship with each other. They had fallen out and both were complaining to their managers about each other, each vying for the other to be moved or dismissed. When they met in the mediation process and shared their positions, it seemed to me that it was more like an adjudication than a mediation—both expressing the other was at fault and how the other party was damaging the company. In fact, as I listened it became difficult to see where things had gone wrong and who was at fault. I began to think I was glad I did not have to make a decision about who was more right or more to blame than the other! My dad's attitude would have been to bang their two heads together and tell them to grow up—it seemed like a good strategy to try! But once they heard each other and I reflected back the stories, and they listened to me as I paraphrased and summarized what they had been doing to each other, I suspect it all began to sound a little bit embarrassing to each of them. But with their heels dug in, neither of them was prepared to compromise. However, there was a common interest emerging. Both of them wanted what was happening to stop, both of them knew the sales were being impacted, and when I began getting them to reflect on what would happen if it continued, neither of them liked that story line. So once that was acknowledged and with a little bit of refocusing, I encouraged them to start talking about what needed to change, and if matters were resolved, what the workplace would look like and how their sales figures might improve. Clearly, they agreed they would not like management to make a decision that one or the other had to leave the business—both expressed how that would impact them personally, and both seemed to be surprised that their feelings of hurt were similar and not a good place to be. The conversation was now becoming one based on mutual interest, and they even began to reflect on when they did work well together. The outcome was an agreement to change their behavior toward each other, and they even came up with a code of conduct they could agree to. Whilst they did not leave the process as buddies, they gave each other a meaningful handshake and an apology for what they had done. The HR manager who had asked me to provide the service was hugely appreciative of the change she had observed following the mediation. Though they agreed I would come back a few weeks later to review the agreement, when I checked in they confirmed I was not needed yet asking that the opportunity to review issues be kept open. I doubt they will be calling me. As ever,

I wondered why they had not taken the opportunity to talk together earlier when they knew matters were not going well instead of allowing the dispute to fester for almost a year. Not engaging to resolve issues early on is a common thread I have observed in many interpersonal conflicts.

In the spirit of seeking an early resolution of a workplace dispute, the established structures in Ireland require that most workplace complaints under the relevant employment legislation be submitted within 6 months of the last occurrence of a breach (with some exceptions to extend the submission of a complaint to 12 months). This can assist in avoiding the evolution of a toxic workplace, particularly with rights-based issues. However, a particularly difficult challenge when dealing with workplace conflict is a breach in an interpersonal relationship at a human level, specifically because it may not always be evident as to what rights have been breached. Many HR practitioners are challenged with how best to deal with highly subjective interpersonal conflicts. There is no doubt that when interpersonal conflict emerges in the workplace it can evolve into an intractable situation and develop into a difficult dispute.

We all experience interpersonal conflict from time to time, perhaps on a daily basis, and in many cases we have coping strategies which enable us to deal adequately with such conflict. Our innate skills and habits enable us to prevent such conflicts from becoming damaging disputes. Nonetheless, there are few, if any, workplaces that have not had to deal with a breakdown of an interpersonal relationship that leads to an uncomfortable environment for those that experience it. The collateral damage also impacts workplace productivity and harmony. Furthermore, it is well established that unresolved stressful situations lead to physical and psychological harm. So, whilst an organization may find it challenging to deal with interpersonal conflict at work, it has a duty of care to address any reasonable causes that may impact an employee's health, safety, and welfare at work. In this regard, workplace bullying (defined, in part, as repeated inappropriate behavior that, if continued could reasonably be regarded as undermining a person's dignity and respect at work) is a serious problem and, where it remains unresolved, is a source of considerable individual suffering which impacts the performance of organizations. The two sales managers mentioned earlier had described each other's behavior as bullying, yet they were appalled to think the other thought they were a bully.

We are aware of the negative outcomes associated with bullying and of the significant wider costs to the working environment and potentially to human life that unaddressed bullying behavior can cause. Surveys in Ireland indicate that around 8% of people who attend work report either experiencing or observing inappropriate human behavior (Health and Safety Authority, 2001). These trends are higher in public sectors and educational and health sector environments.

In attempting to address the tenuous nature of workplace bullying, a code of practice was issued by the then LRC in Ireland in 2002 ("Procedures for Addressing Bullying in the Workplace," 2002), which identified bullying as:

> [The] repeated inappropriate behaviour, direct or indirect, whether verbal, physical or otherwise, conducted by one or more persons against another or others, at the place of work and/or in the course of employment, which could reasonably be regarded as undermining the individual's right to dignity at work. (Department of Enterprise, Trade and Employment, 2002, p. 2)

Recognizing that unresolved bullying behavior is a health and safety issue, the Health and Safety Authority in Ireland also published a code of practice in 2007 (Health and Safety Authority, 2007). Both these codes are issued as guidance for employers, employees, and their representatives to implement and adhere to effective procedures for addressing allegations or instances of workplace bullying. It is recognized that both informal and formal procedures should be set up in workplaces to assist in resolving bullying-related disputes. Recognizing the significantly personal nature of bullying, the codes of practice suggest mediation as an informal process that can be used between the parties when dealing with complaints of bullying. The policy also identifies that when matters remain unresolved they should be investigated under a process that adheres to fair procedures within the principles of natural justice.

A substantial body of research literature is emerging on bullying behavior, and on incivility in the workplace. Incivility, as identified by ACAS,[1]

> manifests as a low level negative behaviour such as rudeness, disregard for others, or treating others with disrespect—but which may not be considered "extreme" enough to constitute bullying. However, research finds that these negative behaviours often overlap with bullying and, where left unchecked and unmanaged, contribute to the creation of cultures that tactically accepted bullying. (Evesson, Oxenbridge, & Daylor, 2015, p. 4)

Organizations with poor workplace climates tend to ignore the behavior, or worse still, see it as positive (Evesson et al., 2015). Whilst bullying is not necessarily a top-down trait, research indicates that an organization's climate both influences, and are strongly influenced by, behaviors and values of managers and their commitment to supporting or not the well-being of their staff. Management and organizational leaders are, therefore, the role models for setting the culture and for championing a positive working environment.

The courts in Ireland have established that unresolved bullying in the workplace can lead to physical and psychological injury, and that employers may be held liable for such injury if they have failed to put in place reasonable safeguards to prevent the behaviors that can cause the injury. Awards of six-figure sums have been granted to plaintiffs where employers have not met their responsibilities to maintain a safe working environment with regard to bullying behavior. Specifically, the courts identified (with reference to the code of practice on bullying) that the behaviors need to be objectively measured, with specific focus of measurement on: (a) whether what occurred was appropriate under the circumstances, (b) was repeated in that there was a reasonable proximity to the alleged harmful events, and (c) whether the behaviors could be reasonably regarded as undermining a person's dignity at work (*Quigley v. Complex Tooling & Moulding Ltd*, 2009). The courts have upheld that disciplinary procedures and performance management, whilst unwelcome to the plaintiff, do not necessarily meet the threshold of bullying (*Ruffley v. The Board of Management of Saint Anne's School*, 2017). The courts have, therefore, set a reasonably high bar with regard to the measurement of bullying behavior, and whether such behavior will be regarded as undermining a person's dignity at work to the extent that it could be deemed to be harmful and injurious.

With regard to a model for understanding dignity at work, I find that Dr. Donna Hicks' (2011) work on dignity provides a helpful model and accessible language around what behaviors, or lack of awareness, can impact a person's dignity at work, irrespective of cultural, gender, age, or other differences. Hicks (2011) concluded that what stands in the way when people are trying to negotiate a resolution to a dispute is when there are unacknowledged and unaddressed violations of their dignity. The dignity model was, therefore, developed to address this underlying human desire to be treated with dignity, and the equally powerful desire to be acknowledged for the indignities one has suffered. It created an acceptable language for discussing the emotional injuries all human beings endure in conflict but are reluctant to talk about for fear of appearing weak. Hicks (2011) identified the 10 essential elements to dignity (Box 5.1).

As a practicing mediator, I encourage the disputing parties to reflect on these elements and to identify where they believe the other party has breached them. Then, a narrative can be created around where the hurt is actually occurring in order to create a mutual understanding of the nature of the dispute rather than to purely focus directly on the behaviors that occurred. Whilst this approach takes some time with the parties, it does enable parties who wish to take ownership of how the matter can be resolved to find a resolution that addresses the violation of their dignity—which, after all, is a central definition of bullying, but not easily understood in the heat of the conflict.

I have used this model successfully. For example, I mediated two managers that had not spoken civilly to each other for a number of years, and

BOX 5.1
10 ESSENTIAL ELEMENTS OF DIGNITY

- *Acceptance of Identity*: Approach people as neither inferior nor superior to you; give others the freedom to express their authentic selves without fear of being negatively judged; interact without prejudice or bias, accepting how race, religion, gender, class, sexual orientation, age, disability, and so on, are at the core of their identities; and assume they have integrity.
- *Recognition*: Validate others for their talents, hard work, thoughtfulness, and help; be generous with praise; and give credit to others for their contributions, ideas, and experience.
- *Acknowledgment*: Give people your full attention by listening, hearing, validating, and responding to their concerns and what they have been through.
- *Inclusion*: Make others feel that they belong at all levels of relationship (family, community, organization, nation).
- *Safety*: Put people at ease at two levels: physically, where they feel free of bodily harm; and psychologically, where they feel free of concern about being shamed or humiliated, so that they feel free to speak without fear of retribution.
- *Fairness*: Treat people justly, with equality, and in an even-handed way, according to agreed upon laws and rules.
- *Independence*: Empower people to act on their own behalf so that they feel in control of their lives and experience a sense of hope and possibility.
- *Understanding*: Believe that what others think matters; give them the chance to explain their perspectives, express their points of view, and actively listen in order to understand them.
- *Benefit of the Doubt*: Treat people as trustworthy; start with the premise that others have good motives and are acting with integrity.
- *Accountability*: Take responsibility for your actions; if you have violated the dignity of another, apologize and make a commitment to change hurtful behaviors.

whose CEO quite frankly had enough and was of the view that one or both had to go. After a day in mediation, which was held on a wet Friday the 13th in winter, both managers had gained a full understanding of how their behaviors had impacted each other and perhaps their colleagues. They wholeheartedly apologized, shook hands, and left the meeting together stepping out into the rainy evening and sharing the same umbrella that I gave them—which I never got back! But, such is the power of mediation; it can even overcome a suspicious Friday the 13th! I also find when I'm investigating cases of workplace bullying that reference to the Dr. Hicks model and the behaviors that have occurred enables an objective assessment of the complaint, and grounds a decision as to whether somebody has in fact behaved in a manner that amounts to a breach of the definition of bullying.

A MESSAGE FOR HR PRACTITIONERS

If the underpinning approach to workplace dispute resolution in Ireland is that the responsibility for the settlement of a dispute rests with the parties, as professed by the Labour Court, then surely the obligation of HR practitioners is to create an environment where the parties can successfully engage in conflict resolution. Yet, I have observed that despite HR practitioners being aware of the situation, a high level of workplace bullying related conflicts are allowed to fester and develop, grow their own stories, create camps and divisions in the workplace, and blatantly disregard the fundamentals of dignity and respect in the relationship. In such circumstances, the emotions held by the parties have become fueled with hurt, the parties become blinded with anger, and the approach to resolve matters becomes focused on self-interest and win-at-all-cost rather than an appropriate regard for the other party.

The message to be learnt from this is a need for organizations not only to have a policy and procedure for dealing with bullying behavior, but also to build a competency in conflict management and conflict resolution. The old adage of "what gets measured gets managed" runs true here—few organizations identify conflict management as a core competency that should be recognized and measured as a key performance indicator. Yet the cost of conflict is real, not only in the risk to the health, safety, and well-being to those living through an interpersonal dispute in the workplace, but also on lost productivity.

It had been estimated that the cost of conflict for U.S. businesses is $389 billion in paid hours or the equivalent of 385 million working days lost each year (CPP Global, 2008). Interestingly, the Joint Commission, which is a U.S.-based organization that accredits more than 21,000 U.S. health-care organizations and programs, identified conflict management as a leadership accreditation standard (Joint Commission, 2009). Perhaps this concept is worthy of replication in performance management metrics for managers in any workplace. How many productive hours a month are lost due to work colleagues spending time with petty conflicts? Based on an average hourly wage, what is this costing the business, not to mention the cost it may take when lawyers become involved?

My firm belief is that workplaces need to build awareness amongst staff at all levels about what amounts to inappropriate behavior, and what incivility looks like. In addition, a workplace that has implemented policies and procedures to deal with inappropriate behaviors will help inculcate the right level of civility and respect amongst its members. Whilst external reinforcements such as legislation and third-party bodies that are established to assist in the resolution of disputes, as evidenced in Ireland, do provide the impetus for organizations to be less tolerant of disrespectful behaviors, I hold the view that building internal competencies amongst management and staff will also go a long way to support a workplace culture that does not accept incivility.

THE OPPORTUNITY OF WORKPLACE MEDIATION PROGRAMS

Indeed, building internal processes to encourage parties to resolve their own disputes as close to the source of the dispute as possible can help encourage a cultural shift toward better interactions at a human level. This is particularly true when dealing with the highly subjective nature of bullying behavior. In seeking to resolve acts of inappropriate behavior in the workplace, the option for the recipient to engage directly with the perpetrator rather than being encouraged to seek a resolution through some third-party body creates a better opportunity for restorative justice and a positive cultural shift. It creates the opportunity for the parties to build on the principles of respect at a human level, an essential element for any civil society.

Internal mediation programs provide this option, and, with a skilled mediator, the parties can be afforded a safe environment to explore their differences and take ownership of the resolution. The process is especially suitable when the perpetrators may not have been fully aware of the impact of their behaviors on their work colleagues. It allows for a space and a confidential process to explore and resolve matters, and it is a process that does not prejudice the opportunity to bring a more formal complaint forward in the event a mutually agreeable resolution is not possible.

From my perspective, this creates a different dynamic within the organizational culture because parties will be aware that they will have to be accountable for their behavior to those they offend, and the citizens within the organization will learn to resolve their own disputes and behave in a more respectful way toward each other. As stated by Judge Barry Stuart, former Chief Judge of the Territorial Court of Yukon, Canada,

> The health of a community improves when its members participate in conflict resolution. When they leave the task to others the quality of community life declines. Gone is the collective sense of belonging. Gone as well is the community's natural capacity to prevent crime, redress the underlying causes, and rebuild the broken lives and relationships. (Church Council on Justice and Corrections, 1996, p. XII)

The message is strong; HR practitioners need to build capacity within their organizations for dealing with conflict. In failing to do that they contribute to a culture where unresolved conflict festers and contaminates the potential to create a positive working environment.

Mediation is increasingly being used to resolve disputes in many areas of life. As an alternative dispute resolution (ADR) process, it involves a neutral third party bringing two or more sides together with the aim of reaching a mutual agreement. Policy-makers and organizations are increasingly recognizing that mediation, and other forms of ADR, have a particular place in the workplace. As postulated by ACAS and the Chartered Institute of Personnel and Development (CIPD), "People are the key to organisational success and productivity, and negative conflict between individuals or groups of individuals can severely hamper an organisation's drive for competitive advantage and damage employee well-being" (Podro & Suff, 2013, p. 3).

As mentioned earlier, mediation is a service offered by the WRC in Ireland as part of its dispute resolution suite of services. Ireland has also enacted a Mediation Act in late 2017, thus recognizing the benefits that the process can provide to disputants, reducing costs, and providing a speedier resolution for the disputants that is focused on a mutually agreeable outcome. When the parties want to resolve matters, I find that workplace mediation can provide a successful outcome where, in my practice, the disputing parties are satisfied with a settlement in over 80% of cases associated with interpersonal and relationship matters. Furthermore, in some of the cases that are not resolved in the mediation process, the parties have decided not to progress to a formal process or have moved on, sometimes deciding to move or change career. Indeed, the parties can also come up with creative solutions in the mediation process and take ownership of those solutions.

The WRC mediation service, which is typically focused on rights-based issues, reported 46% success rate in 2017, and the conciliation of some 942 rights-based disputes reported an 84% success rate (WRC, 2018). The message is, therefore, clear; when parties are provided with the opportunity to have an input into the resolution of their dispute using ADR processes, then a mutually agreeable outcome is more likely, and relationships are less likely to be terminally damaged. A properly implemented ADR process can provide an insurance against a more toxic culture and creates a culture where parties learn to behave more reasonably when in conflict.

CONCLUSION

So, what does all of this mean for the Irish workplace? In 2018, Ireland was ranked the 14th happiest country in the world (Helliwell, Layard, & Jeffrey, 2018). An earlier survey in 2016 identified that workers in Ireland are the fourth happiest in the world, and the happiest in the European Union (Indeed, 2016). The study reviewed 35 countries and was based on an analysis of five different elements contributing to job happiness, which included work–life balance, quality of management, office culture, job security and advancement, and compensation and benefits. Workers' ages also appeared to impact the survey's readings, with countries with older workers unhappier at work, perhaps due to the fact that their responsibilities make work/life balance harder to achieve.

In addition, a recent survey reported that 73% of Irish professionals work beyond their contracted hours (O'Flaherty, 2016). The survey also identified that almost three-quarters of all Irish employees work longer than their contracted hours. One in five employees works 10 additional hours per week, which adds up to an extra 3 months per year. More than 40% said they were more productive during that time. The survey was conducted across a variety of professional sectors, including accounting and finance, financial services, technology, engineering, science, and office support. So, we appear to be happier and work harder.

I am convinced that the state's support in the provision of free dispute resolution services for the workplace, through the WRC, has contributed to this. So too has the jurisprudence from the courts that have established that employers have a responsibility for their employees' psychological health and well-being, and that unchecked and unreasonable bullying behavior will be punished by the courts. Anecdotally, I also believe that it is in the Irish culture to maintain relationships, least of all because we believe we will always find a connection with those we meet. This regard for maintaining a relationship underpins an innate level of respect. During the development of the Good Friday agreement to resolve the bitter cross-community dispute in Northern Ireland, we have learnt that understanding differences whilst focusing on mutual interest can help rebuild and sustain relationships. And when we value the importance of having a relationship, conflicts become less destructive, even if our differences are obvious. Senator George Mitchell had the insight to recognize this when he successfully contributed to the Northern Irish peace talks. Where others had failed over the years, Senator Mitchell recognized the power of building relationships on areas of mutual interest rather than trying to resolve the differences. It is still far from perfect in Northern Ireland, but it's better than it was before Senator Mitchell's insights energized the process.

It should, therefore, be no surprise that Ireland has become an attractive location for many U.S. multinational corporations. There are many reasons why companies locate themselves in Ireland, but it all starts with positive leadership and policies (IDA Ireland, 2020). Successive Irish governments have developed an open economy which has attracted over 700 U.S. firms in Ireland, directly employing some 155,000 people. U.S. firms indirectly support a further 100,000 jobs in the Irish economy. In total, this accounts for 20% of employment in Ireland. Collectively, U.S. investment in Ireland amounts to $387 billion. U.S. investment in 2017 accounted for 67% of all foreign direct investment in Ireland. U.S. firms in Ireland form a critical part of Ireland's cutting edge, internationally traded goods and services economy in industries, such as information and communications technology, biotechnology, pharmaceuticals, medical technologies, and financial services ("The American Chamber," n.d.).

NOTE

1. The Advisory, Conciliation and Arbitration Service (ACAS) is a Crown non-departmental public body of the Government of the United Kingdom. Its purpose is to improve organisations and working life through the promotion and facilitation of strong industrial relations practice.

REFERENCES

Baccaro L., & Simoni M. International Institute for Labour Studies. (2004). *The Irish social partnership and the "Celtic Tiger" phenomenon.* Geneva, Switzerland: International Institute for Labour Studies.

Calveley, M., Allsop, D., Rocha Lawton, N., & Huesmann, M. (2017). Managing the employment relationship. In G. Rees & P. Smith (Eds.), *Strategic human resource management: An international perspective* (2nd ed., pp. 281–323). London, England: SAGE.

Church Council on Justice and Corrections. (1996, July). *Satisfying justice: Safe community options that attempt to repair harm from crime and reduce the use or length of imprisonment.* Ottawa, Canada: Author.

CPP Global. (2008, July). *Workplace conflict and how businesses can harness it to thrive* (Human Capital Report). Retrieved from https://shop.themyersbriggs.com/Pdfs/CPP_Global_Human_Capital_Report_Workplace_Conflict.pdf

Discover Ireland. (2018). *Irish tourist board.* Retrieved from https://www.discoverireland.ie/

Evesson, J., Oxenbridge, S., & Daylor, D. (2015, November). *Seeking better solutions: Tackling bullying and ill-treatment in Britain's workplaces* [ACAS Policy Discussion Paper]. Retrieved from http://docplayer.net/16622026-Policy-discussion-paper-seeking-better-solutions-tackling-bullying-and-ill-treatment-in-britain-s-workplaces.html

Geary, J. (2007). Employee voice in the Irish workplace: Status and prospect. In R. Freeman, P. Boxall, & P. Haynes (Eds.), *What do workers say? Employee voice in the Anglo-American world.* Ithaca, NY: Cornell University Press. Retrieved from https://www.researchgate.net/publication/264481825_Employee_Voice_in_the_Irish_Workplace_Status_and_Prospect

Gibbons, M. (2007, March). *Better dispute resolution: A review of employment dispute resolution in Great Britain.* Retrieved from https://webarchive.nationalarchives.gov.uk/20090609022048/http://www.berr.gov.uk/files/file38516.pdf

Goleman, D. (1998). *Working with emotional intelligence.* New York, NY: Bantam Books.

Health and Safety Authority. (2001). *Dignity at work: The challenge of workplace bullying. Report of the task force on the prevention of workplace bullying.* Dublin, Ireland: Stationery Office. Retrieved from https://www.drugsandalcohol.ie/5751/

Health and Safety Authority. (2007, March). *Code of practice for employers and employees on the prevention and resolution of bullying at work.* Retrieved from https://www.hsa.ie/eng/Publications_and_Forms/Publications/Occupational_Health/CoP_Bullying.pdf

Helliwell, J., Layard, R., & Sachs, J. (2018). *World happiness report 2018.* New York, NY: Sustainable Development Solutions Network.

Hicks, D. (2011). *Dignity: Its essential role in resolving conflict.* New Haven, CT: Yale University Press.

IDA Ireland. (2020). *Ireland, right place right time.* Retrieved from https://www.idaireland.com

Indeed. (2016). *Job happiness index.* Retrieved from http://blog.indeed.com/hiring-lab/indeed-job-happiness-index-2016/

Joint Commission. (2009, November 19). *Leadership in healthcare organizations: A guide to Joint Commission leadership standards* [White Paper]. San Diego, CA: The Governance Institute. Retrieved from https://www.jointcommission.org/assets/1/18/WP_Leadership_Standards.pdf

Law Reform Commission. (2008, July). Alternative dispute resolution consultation paper, LRC CP 50-2008. Dublin, Ireland: Government Stationary Office.

Maslow, A. (1943). A theory of human motivation. *Psychological Review, 50(4),* 370–396.

Murphy, J., & Roche, W. (Eds.). (1997). *Irish industrial relations practice.* Dublin, Ireland: Dublin Oak Tree Press.

Mulvey, K. (2008, March 5). *Annual report 2006 and statement of strategy 2005–2007: Discussion with LRC.* Joint Committee on Enterprise, Trade and Employment debate. Retrieved from https://www.oireachtas.ie/en/debates/debate/joint_committee_on_enterprise_trade_and_employment/2008-03-05

O'Flaherty, K. (2016). *Infographic: The Irish working hours survey 2016 results.* Retrieved from https://www.morganmckinley.ie/article/morgan-mckinleys-working-hours-survey-2016-results

Organisation for Economic Co-Operation and Development. (2018). Trade union [data set]. Retrieved from https://stats.oecd.org/Index.aspx?DataSetCode=TUD

Podro, S., & Suff, R. (2013, February). *Mediation: An approach to resolving workplace issues.* Retrieved from http://m.acas.org.uk/media/pdf/n/n/Mediation-an-approach-to-resolving-workplace-issues.pdf

Procedures for Addressing Bullying in the Workplace (Declaration) Order. (2002). S.I. No. 17 of 2002, Industrial Relations Act 1990 Code of Practice: Ireland.

Quigley v. Complex Tooling & Moulding Ltd, [2009] 1 IR 349. (2009). The Supreme Court, Ireland.

Raidió Teilifís Éireann. (2018, February 7). *Commission eyes Irish GDP growth of 7.3% in 2017, fastest in European Union.* Retrieved from https://www.rte.ie/news/business/2018/0207/938985-economy-growth-forecasts/

Ruffley v. The Board of Management of Saint Anne's School [2017] IESC 33 (2017). The Supreme Court, Ireland.

S.I. No. 17/2002–Industrial Relations Act 1990 (Code of practice detailing procedures for addressing bullying in the workplace) (declaration) Order 2002. (n.d.). Retrieved from http://www.irishstatutebook.ie/eli/2002/si/17/made/en/print

Teague, P. (2005). *Towards flexible workplace governance: Employment rights, dispute resolution and social partnership in the Irish Republic.* Dublin, Ireland: The Policy Institute, Trinity College Dublin.

Teague, P. (2006). New employment times and the changing dynamics of conflict resolution at work: The case of Ireland. *Comparative Labor Law & Policy Journal, 28*(1), 57–89.

Teague, P., Roche, W., Gormley, W., & Currie, D. (2015). *Managing workplace conflict: Alternative dispute resolution in Ireland.* Dublin, Ireland: Institute of Public Administration.

The American Chamber. (n.d.). Retrieved from https://www.amcham.ie/about-us/about-the-american-chamber.aspx

The Labour Court. (n.d.). Retrieved from www.workplacerelations.ie/en/WR_Bodies/Labour_Court

Tippett, E. (2019). Non-disclosure agreements and the #MeToo Movement what do we do now? *Dispute Resolution Magazine.* Retrieved from https://www.americanbar.org/groups/dispute_resolution/publications/dispute_resolution_magazine/2019/winter-2019-me-too/non-disclosure-agreements-and-the-metoo-movement/

Wallace, J., McMahon, G., & Gunnigle, P. (2004). *Industrial relations in Ireland* (3rd ed.). Dublin, Ireland: Gill & Macmillan.

Workplace Relations Commission. (2016). *Statement of strategy 2016–2018.* Retrieved from https://www.workplacerelations.ie/en/Publications_Forms/WRC-Statement-of-Strategy-2016-2018.pdf

Workplace Relations Commission. (2017). *Annual Report.* Retrieved from https://www.workplacerelations.ie/en/news-media/workplace_relations_notices/workplace_relations_commission_publishes_2017_annual_report.html

CHAPTER 6

WHAT SHOULD YOUR ORGANIZATION KNOW BEFORE EMBARKING ON THE EXPLORATION–EXPLOITATION JOURNEY?

The Exploration–Exploitation Paradox: Insights, Considerations, and Managerial Implications

Shalom Charles Malka

Whether you are a student of business administration or a practitioner in the field of management, the twin orientations of exploration and exploitation should be of interest to you. The dual concepts occupy a central place in strategic management thought and practice as evidenced by the rich literature that deals with both. You don't have to necessarily be part of "big business" to grasp their importance for the future of any organization in

From Discord to Harmony, pages 103–119

times of accelerating change. Learning about them is as vital for small business as it is for large firms.

Equally as pertinent, such learning should help you understand the paradoxical existence at the roots of exploring and exploiting activities, and their relevance to conflict management in theory and practice. Being cognizant of the conflict-ridden nature of the relationships associated with both orientations, as well as recognizing their relevancy to conflict management, is a necessity that should be pursued. When conflict abounds, recognizing forces that trigger escalation and de-escalation of conflict is vital. We identify such forces within the context of exploration–exploitation activities and assert that firm managers should be familiar with those igniters and diffusers of conflict.

Consider this brief chapter to be an appetizer of sorts, aimed at whetting your appetite for your own self-exploration and study of the concepts. As such, the next pages will provide some answers to "why" and "how" questions that run through your head. However, it is also likely that other questions will be left unanswered. My hope is that your curiosity is ignited enough to propel you to dig deeper into the "mechanics" of exploring and exploiting, and how they can be applied in your organization.

Before we begin, here are several related aspects of exploration and exploitation that we will touch on. We explore their importance and merits, their paradoxical state, the dilemma they present to organizations, and key practical solutions for balancing both orientations and for adequately addressing related constraints. We address the critical role of top managers in coordinating and reconciling conflicting activities that are part of exploration and exploitation, and conclude with a set of recommendations for you as a manager as well as for your organization.

You may notice a common thread that runs through our discussion: The critical role that negotiation and collaboration play as mediums for ensuring that a discord that can potentially arise from these twin constructs is diffused. And, the ways such discord can be converted to a more harmonious existence between these two equally important drivers of firm growth.

EXPLORATION AND EXPLOITATION—WHAT ARE THEY? WHY ARE THEY IMPORTANT?

An early work offered distinct characteristics associated with each orientation: Exploration is associated with discovery and with risk-taking, variance-enhancing, and experimentation whereas exploitation is associated with refinement, efficiency, routinization, and variance-reduction (March, 1991). A more recent work further emphasizes their distinctions: Whereas explorative activities seek divergence of information, processes, and experience, exploitative activities are characterized by the converging of information, processes, and experience (de Visser & Faems, 2015).

Hopefully, a picture is forming in your mind as to their distinct nature and importance. Consider some additional characteristics encapsulating the unique flavor of each orientation. Exploration involves search and play, and calls for a decentralized organizational architecture coupled with a loose culture. It seeks little or no formalization of procedures and routines, and involves radical-revolutionary innovation (i.e., new and novel products and services). Its prime efforts are directed at exploring new technologies as well as new knowledge and learning. On the other hand, exploitation is driven by formalized procedures and practices involving production and control, and calls for a centralized architecture with a tight culture in support of a high degree of routinization. Exploitation quests involve incremental-evolutionary innovation (i.e., improving and leveraging existing products and services). Its efforts are directed at exploiting current technologies, and on utilizing existing knowledge and learning.

Both orientations appear critical to a firm's survival and continued growth, as exploring and exploiting affect both the current operations of a firm and its future viability. The list of studies in support of such argument is long. Let me capture in a sentence the essence of recent findings: Engaging in both orientations is essential for firm adaptation, particularly in times of rapid change that affects resource allocation and turns current technology and existing knowledge into a state of obsolescence (e.g., Lisboa, Skarmeas, & Lages, 2013; Maleti, Maleti, Dahlgaard, Dahlgaard-Park, & Gomiscek, 2014).

Think about it this way: An organization must leverage what it has and knows (exploit) in order to sustain its current operations. It must also engage in new discoveries (explore) to enlarge its knowledge base for future growth. In essence, exploring and exploiting activities reach across a multitude of business operations, including technology innovation and product development, knowledge extraction, and organizational learning. Put differently, exploration and exploitation are designed to ensure firm adaptation and survival, and competitive advantage and sustainability.

You may conclude that since they are of paramount importance, organizations ought to pursue them both. My intention is not to overwhelm you but rather to acquaint you with the complexity emanating from the pursuit of such a premature conclusion. Therefore, here are additional questions that should be considered before drawing conclusions: For instance, are exploration and exploitation two opposite ends of a continuum? Are they two independent orthogonal orientations? Should they be viewed as complementary, or in competition with one another? Furthermore, should a firm strive for a balance between exploration and exploitation? And if so, should this be done through ambidexterity (i.e., the simultaneous pursuit of both via a structural separation of units that specialize in either exploring or exploiting), or through a punctuated equilibrium (i.e., continuously alternating between periods of exploration and exploitation)?

Complex questions indeed. But before attempting to address them, let me discuss the apparent contradictions that exist between our dual orientations. Once you grasp their paradoxical existence, you will develop a better understanding of the dilemma they present organizations with, and the challenges managers face when attempting to pursue either one, or both.

EXPLORATION AND EXPLOITATION—WHAT SHOULD YOU KNOW ABOUT THEIR PARADOXICAL EXISTENCE?

Exploring and exploiting activities are essential for firm survival, but they also create paradoxical challenges that compel firm managers to be adaptive and engage in two seemingly contradictory but indivisible learning activities. For instance, exploiting existing knowledge and refining current products, while concurrently exploring new knowledge and developing novel products. Execution of these activities are largely driven by contradictory mindsets and guided by opposing objectives. Furthermore, they call for inconsistent architectures and require conflicting competencies. Also, consider that exploitation utilizes processes that reduce variability and enhance productivity and efficiency, while using existing technological trajectories. Exploration, on the other hand, utilizes processes that increase variation and foster an autonomous environment and culture, while pursuing experimentation with new technological trajectories.

Here are some additional contradictions for you to consider: While exploitation calls for a defined resource commitment, as well as for the deployment of available competencies, and is guided by a pre-calculated and predictable rate of return, exploration calls for larger investment, tends to consume more resources, and involves a return on investment that is unclear and less certain as reported by some studies (e.g., Cui, Walsh & Zou, 2014). Contrary to exploration, exploitation follows a predictable low-risk path with limited operational deviations, and lower production costs by efficiently deploying existing resources, and by refining the value of existing products through incremental innovation (Vos & Vos, 2013).

Since explorative effort is aimed at radical innovation, it requires time and investment, as well as risk-taking and failure tolerance. Radical innovation also involves search for new knowledge within the firm and outside; hence, it involves knowledge transfer and knowledge sharing with external parties. And contrary to the exploitative effort, calculating with certainty the time it takes to convert new ideas to new products, and the returns from the commercialization of such radical products, tends to be difficult to estimate.

Unlike exploration, exploitative effort that is driven by evolutionary innovation exploits feedback from current customers and chain suppliers about existing products and services. These products allow for a more accurate estimation of returns, but are easy to imitate by competitors. However, overdependence on existing products, regardless of the improvements introduced through incremental innovation, can lead to obsolescence in the absence of new knowledge and new products.

Exploitation strives to shore up existing capabilities and current resources for meeting the firm's present goals, and for gaining the upper hand relative to the current competition. Exploration seeks to develop new capabilities and gain an upper hand relative to future competitors. And, whereas exploitation activities target the survival needs of the firm, exploration activities address the firm's sustainability needs and future growth (Sinha, 2015).

Bear in mind that while exploratory innovation is necessary to reduce risk of obsolescence, the intent is to generate abnormal returns by exploring new markets, new offerings, and new customers. As such, it is riskier and more complex, and calls for relatively heavy funding and new knowledge. Furthermore, market opportunities for such innovation are not clearly marked, and competition is uncertain.

You realize that such characteristics of explorative innovation results in increased interdependence as well as in an increase in information exchange, information sharing, and knowledge sharing. And while exploitation related innovation seeks improvements in current products, caters to existing customers, and uses current technology, it cannot sustain itself for long. In a word, an organization cannot rely on one leg, and one leg only!

By now, you are probably cognizant of the sharp differences and contradictions between the dual concepts. To help you better reflect on their key distinctions, I captured them succinctly in a summary table provided in Figure 6.1. Reflect on its content before you move on to the next sections!

You may rightly ask: What message does Figure 6.1 convey to us? Is there a clear take away? The answer is a straightforward one: Exploration and exploitation share a contradictory existence, as well as incompatible goals under the same organizational umbrella. Bartos and Wehr (2008) pointed to incompatible goals as a key driver of conflict and proposed three possible causes of goal incompatibility: contested resources, incompatible roles due to the division between those who tend to protect the interests of the firm versus those who protect the interests of their immediate unit, and incompatible values that bond a group together due to a separation between groups and/or organizations. I contend that all three causes of goal incompatibility hold true in the case of exploration–exploitation, and present top managers with difficult trade-offs as they attempt to bridge the gap between

Key Features	Exploration	Exploitation
Associated Terms	Search, discovery, play, flexibility, variance-increasing, loose culture.	Refinement, efficiency, routinization, variance-decreasing, tight culture.
Strategic Intent	Breakthrough technology, loose-coupling client, and passion.	Profit, tight-coupling customer, and discipline.
Preferred Structure	Decentralized systems. Organic organizational principles.	Centralized systems. Mechanical organizational principles.
Type of Innovation	Radical. Development of novel products and new competencies. Leveraging new technologies.	Incremental. Improvements of current products. Exploiting existing competencies and leveraging current technologies.
Targets	New products, new customers, and future markets.	Existing products, current customers, and existing markets.
Time Perspective	Long-term benefits. Future growth.	Immediate benefits. Current growth.
Risk and Returns	Risk-taking. Uncertain returns on investment.	Risk-averse. Predictable returns on investment.
Knowledge and Learning	Explore new knowledge and new learning.	Exploit existing knowledge and current learning.
Trap Susceptibility	Failure trap. Failure in search, leads to more search, and possibly to more failure.	Success trap. Current success reduces incentive for doing things differently.

Figure 6.1 A paradoxical existence: The contradictory nature of exploration and exploitation.

their related activities. It is these difficult trade-offs that lead managers to designate the management of conflict as a top priority.

Conflict, as a dynamic force, is amenable and can be tamed for the benefit of the parties involved. However, left unattended, the tensions emanating from exploration and exploitation can fuel discord at the workplace and expose the firm to harmful internal conflict. Recognizing some of the contradictions that exploration and exploitation share is but an initial first step. Ultimately, it helps managers define related dilemmas and adopt proper solutions for reconciling such tensions and conflicts.

I trust that you are aware that the effective undertaking of such issues bears heavily on decision-makers in any organization. For top managers, such activities present supreme challenges that necessitate the mastering of effective negotiation skills and the utilization of appropriate conflict management practices. A manager's ability to negotiate tensions and resolve contradictions that emanate from exploration and exploitation also determines the ability of the firm to adapt to changing market conditions and withstand the competition. Notwithstanding their paradoxical dynamics, firms must be proficient in both exploring and exploiting. How well a firm can explore and exploit determines its growth trajectory and viability, or, on the other hand, its decline and ultimate demise.

EXPLORATION AND EXPLOITATION—WHAT SHOULD YOU KNOW ABOUT THE DILEMMA THEY CREATE? ARE THERE TRADEOFFS TO BE CONSIDERED?

F. Scott Fitzgerald once exclaimed, "The test of a first-rate intelligence is the ability to hold two opposing ideas in mind at the same time and still retain the ability to function." I argue that this quote encapsulates the dilemma organizations face when contemplating and executing exploration and exploitation activities. March (1991) stated succinctly that the basic dilemma confronting an organization is "to engage in sufficient exploitation to ensure its current viability, and, at the same time, devote enough energy to exploration to ensure its future viability" (p. 105).

While pursuing both is vital, doing so is difficult given the fundamental differences between these twin orientations, as well as the natural tendency among firms to gravitate toward exploitation at the expense of exploration (Benner & Tushman, 2015; Gupta, Smith, & Shalley, 2006). Here is the core issue to consider: Organizations and their key decision-makers pursue what they are comfortable with and what they already know; they tend to follow what is certain and within reach—all of which are features characteristic of exploitation. Exploration, on the other hand, is radically different as it involves a high degree of unpredictability, with outcomes that are often costly and risky, and returns that are distant and uncertain as we discussed earlier.

This natural tilt toward exploitation, while understandable, is detrimental to the firm's long-term survival. It may well yield some positive short-term results, but it exposes the firm to technological and product obsolescence, and is taxing for customers in the long-run. Engaging less in exploration, or ignoring it altogether, exposes the firm to vulnerabilities vis-à-vis the competition, particularly when facing technological changes and market turbulence.

In addition, as you may realize, the natural tilt toward exploitation also involves over reliance on process management approaches (e.g., Lean Six Sigma, Just-in-Time, Balanced Scorecard, and TQM) that further inhibit exploration. Increased process management tends to be associated with an increase in exploitative innovation, and a decrease in exploratory innovation. Support for this assertion is reported by several works. For instance, Benner and Tushman (2015) found that efficiency and variance reduction associated with exploitation appear to have a dampening effect on exploration activities. Interestingly, the authors found support for their argument in the poor long-term performance of several renowned companies following the adoption of process management practices, and their continued struggle to reinvigorate (Benner & Tushman, 2015). One such firm is Motorola, the inventor of Six Sigma, which succeeded in its pursuit of efficiency and reliability, but failed to gain any long-term success in the mobile phone industry. Such failure was attributed to its preoccupation with incremental innovation, coupled with process management, at the expense of exploration activities, thereby reducing its ability to adapt to a changing landscape in the cellular industry (Benner & Tushman, 2015).

Motorola's failure magnifies the dilemma that many large and small firms face regarding exploration and exploitation. You may ask: What about trade-offs? Well, one can ultimately argue that attention and resources must be devoted to both orientations, and follow a more symmetric trajectory that equally benefit exploring and exploiting activities. To paraphrase F. Scott Fitzgerald, a firm must pursue two opposing orientations at the same time, and still retain the ability to function and prosper well into the future. In sum, ambidexterity attainment is at the heart of the challenge, but the more desirable goal to pursue.

EXPLORATION AND EXPLOITATION—FACED WITH SUCH A DILEMMA, WHAT CAN BE DONE? IS THERE A SUPPORTED SOLUTION TO CONSIDER?

The answer is yes! In fact, the literature suggests not just one, but several practical solutions for addressing the dilemma at the core of the exploration–exploitation debate. Four such solutions deserve a closer look: structural separation, sequential punctuated equilibria, organizational context, and behavioral integration.

Structural Separation

Structural separation, also known as structural ambidexterity, is a mechanism that enables a firm to engage in exploration and exploitation activities simultaneously by creating distinct, loosely coupled organizations with experimenting units that are separated from the exploiting units. The exploratory units are small and decentralized, and are characterized by loose culture and processes. The exploitation units are larger and centralized, with tight culture and processes. The former units succeed through experimentation and increased variation; the latter units succeed through variability reduction and increased efficiency and control.

Benner and Tushman (2003) argued in their seminal paper that these contrasting units must be physically and culturally separated, and should have distinct incentives and managerial teams. As critical, these differentiated units must be strategically integrated by the firm's most senior team. To be effective in an ambidextrous dual-structure, "the senior team must develop techniques that permit them to be consistently inconsistent, as they steer a balance between the need to be small and large, centralized and decentralized, and focused both on the short term and long term simultaneously" (Benner & Tushman, 2003, p. 248). Being able to negotiate tensions and form strategic alliances between the subunits, and between the subunits and partners outside the firm, determines the success of the top management team in balancing the synchronous pursuit of exploration and exploitation.

Sequential Punctuated Equilibria

Sequential punctuated equilibria, also known as sequential ambidexterity, argues against organizational disintegration and related coordination costs that are part of a physical separation of two mutually exclusive modes of innovation and learning (Burgelman, 2002; Lavie, Stettner, & Tushman, 2010). Alternatively, the firm should sequentially pursue each activity. Punctuated equilibrium is a related concept that is being used by proponents of sequential ambidexterity. Accordingly, exploration and exploitation activities alternate between convergent and reorientation phases that are triggered by stress and conflicts within and outside the firm. From a relatively long convergent period of exploitation, the firm transitions to a relatively short reorientation period of exploration that follows again with a convergent period of exploitation.

Organizational Context

Organizational context, also known as contextual ambidexterity, refers to the ability of the firm to simultaneously exhibit adaptability and alignment across business units. As is the case with any decision capable of impacting firm survival, management's role is paramount. Within the context of ambidexterity and firm management, Gibson and Birkinshaw (2004) asserted that intellectual faculties and behavioral capacities of top executives to negotiate tensions, reconcile contradictions, and manage conflicting demands are essential for alignment in support of exploitation, and adaptability in support of exploration.

Adaptability involves activities designed to meet changing demands in the firm's environment for the long run, while alignment reflects coherence amongst all activities across a business unit for the short term. Gibson and Birkinshaw (2004) found support for their assertion that an organizational context characterized by a combination of stretch, discipline, support, and trust is superior in achieving contextual ambidexterity. The authors' findings also suggest that a manager's faculties and capacities complement the firm's structural arrangements relative to the way exploration and exploitation are pursued and executed (Gibson & Birkinshaw, 2004).

Behavioral Integration

Following in a similar vein and building on the concept of behavioral integration, Lubatkin, Simsek, Ling, and Veiga (2006) proposed another link between a firm's top managers' social and tasks characteristics, primarily their collaborative behavior, and ambidexterity attainment. The authors' main argument is that a structural separation of exploration and exploitation activities, while necessary, is not sufficient for achieving ambidexterity (Lubatkin et al., 2006). Additional factors that rest with the firm's top managers influence their ability to pursue both orientations and, therefore, must be considered as well.

Lubatkin et al.'s (2006) assertion is that top managers' behavioral integration—a term coined by Hambrick (1994), referring to the degree of collaborative behavior as well as the quality-quantity of information exchanged and degree of a joint decision making—determines the firm's ability to deal with the contradictory knowledge processes emanating from exploration and exploitation. The greater the integration, the higher the likelihood of concurrently attaining ambidexterity.

Specifically, an elevated behavioral integration amongst top management teams means a better synchronization of social and task processes that are associated with collaborative behavior amongst its members. Absent behavioral integration, top managers' collaboration is diluted and the quality of interactions is largely reduced.

WHAT SHOULD YOU AND YOUR ORGANIZATION CONSIDER?

Cutting across these solutions, and reflecting on the proposed options, some related drawbacks are worth mentioning. While structural separation may work well for relatively large companies with sufficient resources in support of exploration and exploitation activities, it may be too taxing for small firms given operational and coordination costs. And while temporal sequencing may be a viable option for smaller firms, it is an insufficient mechanism in times of fast environmental turbulence and change that requires quick alignments.

Unlike structural separation, contextual ambidexterity does not require a dual-structure. Instead, it calls for top managers to create administrative mechanisms that foster certain behaviors from members of a business unit who are engaged in both exploration and exploitation. Contextual ambidexterity is considered a higher-order approach capable of generating long-term benefits, given its focus on organizational culture.

Culture as a context refers to the dominant set of values, beliefs, and principles capable of influencing individual and collective behaviors toward ambidexterity, thereby reconciling tensions between what Andriopoulos and Lewis (2009) termed discipline and passion. Discipline calls for conformity with the firm's existing objectives, thus aligning with exploitation (Andriopoulos & Lewis, 2009). Passion stresses engagement with search and creativity, and with challenging new radical discoveries, thus associating more with exploration.

Viewing the four proposed solutions from a conflict management perspective yields a few implications. Structural separation eliminates the proximity between the exploring and exploiting teams, and with it the potential for conflict between autonomous entities. However, conflict may migrate up the ladder and affect top managers that are tasked with coordinating the exploration–exploitation activities, and the very work of the autonomous units.

No structural separation exists under temporal sequencing, thus exacerbating the conditions that may lead to inter-intra conflict during and following each activity rotation. Top managers' role in diffusing friction and managing destructive conflict is more pressing and more critical under the temporal sequencing. Both contextual ambidexterity and behavioral integration, with their emphasis on culture and collaborative behavior, respectively, highlight the role of managers in diffusing conflict while utilizing proper strategies for that purpose.

You may well conclude that top managers that employ either contextual ambidexterity practices, or behavioral integration principles, are better equipped to manage conflict under both structural separation and temporal sequencing.

EXPLORATION AND EXPLOITATION—WHAT IS YOUR OWN ROLE AS A MANAGER? WHAT SHOULD YOU AND YOUR ORGANIZATION KNOW?

The strategic management literature supports the centrality of the firm's leadership in ensuring the successful execution of either structural or contextual ambidexterity (e.g., Lubatkin et al., 2006; Simsek, Heavey, Veiga, & Souder, 2009). Top firm managers establish and nurture appropriate context that fosters ambidexterity.

You may be interested to know that firm leadership characteristics, processes, composition, and behavioral integration are reported to play an essential role in ensuring a balance between exploration and exploitation activities. Upper echelon theory (Hambrick, 2007), for instance, links top firm managers' decisions and actions with their experiences, personal characteristics, values, and personalities. This theory establishes that top managers' processes and composition influence firm outcomes and performance.

An interesting finding, in this respect, suggested that top managers with long affiliation with their firm tend to engage more with exploitative activities, while "outsiders" with shorter affiliation with their current firm tend to engage more with exploratory activities (Beckman, 2006). The argument is that sharing the same values and frame of reference prevents affiliated managers from thinking differently, thus making the composition and diversity of the firm's top managers more critical.

In addition to context and leaders' characteristics, the degree of behavioral integration being fostered by the firm's top managers is just as critical for achieving and maintaining ambidexterity. A high degree of integration leads to, and is facilitated by, a high degree of collaborative behavior, joint decision-making, and sufficient flow of information amongst top managers. More specifically, the ability of top managers to excel in ambidextrous firms depends on three team attributes: their shared vision, the level of their social integration, and their contingency rewards (Siegal & Hambrick, 2005; Smith & Tushman, 2005). Shared goals and values shift members' attention from a potentially narrow and harmful preoccupation with self-maintenance toward a greater goal that is centered on the firm's viability and future. Common goals and values propounds a shared vision. A higher level of top team social integration is found to be linked to negotiation and compromise as well as increased collaboration across units (Jansen, George, van den Bosch, &Volberda, 2008).

Social integration and collaboration also lead to enhanced social interaction, cooperation, and trust among top firm managers. Finally, top team contingency rewards act as the glue that bonds the first two attributes; rewards foster collaboration and create commitment to organizational goals. Team contingency rewards encourage top managers to consider both exploration and exploitation for resource allocation, reduce damaging interpersonal competition, and facilitate negotiation and collaboration (Govindarajan & Trimble, 2005).

If you are the CEO of your organization, note that your role in an ambidextrous firm is no less critical. Championing shared goals and values and emphasizing a shared vision amongst top managers helps set the stage for collaborative action. CEOs, as transformational leaders, are cheerleaders that help extract distinct value from units with conflicting agendas, and serve as an anchor for harmonious relationships across the firm (Vera & Crossan, 2004).

Given the empirically supported benefits inherent in ambidexterity and its determinants, you may ask as to the conditions under which ambidexterity is likely to succeed. O'Reilly and Tushman (2008) offered five such conditions that rest largely with the firm's top leadership. A sound ambidexterity requires a firm to have in place "a clear strategic intent, an overarching vision and set of values, an aligned senior team, an appropriate organizational architecture with targeted integration, and the ability of the senior team to manage the inevitable trade-offs and conflict" (O'Reilly & Tushman, 2008, p. 200).

Finally, exploration and exploitation may compel you as a top manager to develop ambidextrous capabilities since the mindset, skills, and processes required for exploitation are radically different than those required for exploration. These capabilities stem from cognitions and behaviors of top firm managers that ensure coordination and learning, innovation, and knowledge sharing, and involve product improvement and new product development, alliances, and joint ventures beyond firm boundaries.

By now, I'm certain that you realize that these top managers' capabilities must also include skills in conflict management, integrative negotiation, and collaboration. A collaborative management culture produces the most favorable outcomes compared with other conflict management approaches (Todaro & Stirpe, 2017). In establishing such a conflict management system, the individuals within and across subunits are given an equal opportunity to present their suggestions and opinions to the conflict. The final solution is a result of clear communication and cooperation between the conflicted parties.

EXPLORATION AND EXPLOITATION—WHAT ARE SOME RECOMMENDATIONS FOR YOUR ORGANIZATION TO FOLLOW? WHAT ARE SOME IMPLICATIONS FOR YOU TO CONSIDER?

Whether a large firm with research and development capabilities, or a small firm with a distinct team tasked with exploration activities, such as new business development, a few recommendations appear applicable and vital to either organization type. I consider the following to be of paramount importance to your organization, as well as to you as a manager.

1. Pursuing exploration and exploitation simultaneously requires the articulation of a shared vision, coupled with all-embracing goals, and the ability of top managers to skillfully negotiate inherent tensions that emanate from the contradictory nature of exploitation and exploration. Employing principles of integrative negotiation, using persuasion, and encouraging collaboration between teams from differentiated units are necessary activities capable of fostering firm harmony. Effective conflict management and a proper reconciliation of contradictions may well determine the degree of coexistence between exploration and exploitation.
2. The widespread adoption of process management as a means for ensuring current customer satisfaction and near-term returns, while favorable to exploitation, tends to be less conducive to exploration. Process management techniques—such as Six Sigma, TQM, Just-in-Time, Balanced Scorecard, and ISO 9000—seek efficiency and control, much like exploitation and its related activities. Therefore, they should be kept out of explorative activities as they inhibit creativity, impede variability, and suppress change.
3. Relying on existing knowledge alone is insufficient for the development of new products. Exploiting new knowledge that may well reside outside your organization requires the formation of alliances, and calls for collaboration with external partners as well as for the transfer of information between parties. Such exchanges are guided by shared interests and mutual benefits, and involve tradeoffs that must be carefully negotiated. Distributive negotiation, with its narrow zero-sum game mindset, is least desired, and is counterproductive when seeking partnerships that involve the exchange of knowledge and new learning. Instead, an integrative negotiation approach that seeks to enhance value for all parties involved via enhanced collaboration and interaction is the appropriate path to follow. Consider the pursuit and benefit of a win–win strategy!
4. Organizational context and behavioral integration with their focus on characteristics of firm top leaders cannot be ignored. A consideration must be given to the relationship between characteristics of top managers, such as their cognitive style and organizational contexts. Such attention should be extended during transitional periods, both following the departure of a top executive as well as during the rehiring process, and when a firm transitions into a different strategic configuration. In addition, your organization's stakeholders, particularly its investors, as well as external entities, such as change agents and fund managers, should be cognizant of the collective cognitive competence of top managers as this may

furnish valuable insights on a focal firm's future innovative strategy and viability.

5. Direct implications for the firm itself must also be considered, especially for a small firm. Small firms that are in an early phase of the innovation cycle—with products in an exploratory phase—may benefit more from a leader who is intuitive in approach. Small firms that are in later phases of the innovation cycle may benefit from top executives who are more analytical.
6. Top leaders are champions of the firm's learning capability. Developing learning capability proved effective in pursuing ambidexterity and in managing the paradoxical existence between exploration and exploitation (Lin, McDonough, Lin, & Lin, 2013). Learning capability is established through the combined effects of internal learning and external partnering, coupled with an open culture that fosters knowledge sharing and collaboration. These practices generate a follow-up effect of concurrently stimulating exploration and exploitation activities.
7. An observation made by Benner and Tushman (2015) carries a fundamental implication for the way firms' explorative activities have been conducted. Exploration today is likely to reside outside the boundaries of the firm given that open innovation enjoys a dominant trajectory (Benner & Tushman, 2015). Aligning community-centered innovation with the firm's exploration activities requires awareness on your part as a top manager. Such a path is worthy of consideration as a viable alternative to an exclusive reliance on costly in-house innovation practices.

A WRAP-UP AND A FINAL WORD

Pursuing exploration and exploitation is a necessity for any organization that wishes to thrive in a landscape shaped by accelerated change. Doing so within the same organization challenges managers on two key fronts. Managers must be cognizant and aware of simmering tensions and conflicts that characterize exploration and exploitation paradoxical coexistence. As critical, it requires skill and knowledge as to the best strategies for negotiating conflicts and reconciling differences. And not least, one must recognize the importance of collaboration and consensus-building as an essential strategy for minimizing destructive tensions. While goal incongruence, divergent strategic objectives, and cultural differences increase tensions between exploration and exploitation units, mutual dependence increases the likelihood and incentives for managers to collaborate.

A final comment is worth considering. Firm managers at all levels are primarily recognized for their technical expertise and hard skills. In today's workplace, hard skills alone are insufficient for ensuring individual and team success, and ought to be complemented by a set of soft skills. Given the challenges exploration-exploitation presents to managers, acquiring and fine-tuning managers' soft skills is vital. Emphasis should be put on key areas, such as personal communication and interpersonal relationships, conflict management and negotiation, consensus building, and collaboration.

As you seek symmetry and balance between exploration and exploitation—not over-tilting toward one or the other—so you should seek symmetry between soft and hard skills. Both are necessary for your own continued growth and effectiveness, as well as for your organization's continued competitive advantage and sustainability.

REFERENCES

Andriopoulos, C., & Lewis, M. W. (2009). Exploitation-exploration tensions and organizational ambidexterity: Managing paradoxes of innovation. *Organization Science, 20*(4), 696–717.

Bartos, O., & Wehr, P. (2008). *Using conflict theory.* New York, NY: Cambridge University Press.

Beckman, C. (2006). The influence of founding team company affiliations on firm behavior. *Academy of Management Journal, 49*(4), 741–758.

Benner, M. J., & Tushman, M. L. (2003). Exploitation, exploration, and process management: The productivity dilemma revisited. *Academy of Management Review, 28*(2), 238–256.

Benner, M. J., & Tushman, M. L. (2015). Reflections on the 2013-decade award – "exploitation, exploration, and process management: The productivity dilemma revisited" ten years later. *Academy of Management Review, 40*(4), 497–514.

Burgelman, R. A. (2002). Strategy as a vector and the inertia of coevolutionary lock-in. *Administrative Science Quarterly, 47*(2), 325–357.

Cui, A. P., Walsh, M. F., & Zou, S. (2014). The importance of strategic fit between host-home country similarity and exploration exploitation strategies on small and medium-sized enterprises' performance: A contingency perspective. *Journal of International Marketing, 22*(4), 67–85.

de Visser, M., & Faems, D. (2015). Exploration and exploitation within firms: The impact of CEO's cognitive style on incremental and radical innovation performance. *Creativity and Innovation Management, 24*(3), 359–372.

Gibson, C. B., & Birkinshaw, J. (2004). The antecedents, consequences, and mediating role of organizational ambidexterity. *Academy of Management Journal, 47*(2), 209–226.

Govindarajan, V., & Trimble, C. (2005, May). Building breakthrough businesses within established organizations. *Harvard Business Review, 83*(5), 58–68.

Gupta, A. K., Smith, K. G., & Shalley, C. E. (2006). The interplay between exploration and exploitation. *Academy of Management Journal, 49*(4), 693–706.

Hambrick, D. (1994). Top management groups: A conceptual integration and reconsideration of the "team" label. In B. Staw & L. Cummings (Eds.), *Research in organizational behavior* (pp. 171–214). Greenwich, CT: JAI Press.

Hambrick, D. (2007). Upper echelon theory: An update. *Academy of Management Review, 32*(2), 334–343.

Jansen, J. P., George, G., van den Bosch, F. J., & Volberda, H. W. (2008). Senior team attributes and organizational ambidexterity: A moderating role of transformational leadership. *Journal of Management Studies, 45*(5), 982–1007.

Lavie, D., Stettner, U., & Tushman, M. L. (2010). Exploration and exploitation within and across organizations. *Academy of Management Annals, 4*(1), 109–155.

Lin, H.-E., McDonough III, E. F., Lin, S.-H., & Lin, C. Y.-Y. (2013). Managing the exploitation/exploration paradox: The role of a learning capability and innovation ambidexterity. *Journal of Product Innovation Management, 30*(2), 262–278.

Lisboa, A., Skarmeas, D., & Lages, C. (2013). Export market exploitation and exploration performance linear, moderated, complementary and non-linear effects. *International Marketing Review,* 30(3), 211–230.

Lubatkin, M. H., Simsek, Z., Ling, Y., & Veiga, J. F. (2006). Ambidexterity and performance in small- to medium-sized firms: The pivotal role of top management team behavioral integration. *Journal of Management, 32*(5), 646–672.

Maleti, M., Maleti, D., Dahlgaard, J., Dahlgaard-Park, S. M., & Gomiscek, B. (2014). Sustainability exploration and sustainability exploitation: From a literature review towards a conceptual framework. *Journal of Cleaner Production, 79*(15), 182–194.

March, J. G. (1991). Exploration and exploitation in organizational learning. *Organization Science, 2*(1), 71–87.

O'Reilly III, C. H., & Tushman, M. L. (2008). Ambidexterity as a dynamic capability: Resolving the innovator's dilemma. *Research in Organizational Behavior, 28,* 185–206.

Siegal P. A., & Hambrick, D. (2005). Pay disparities within top management groups: Evidence of harmful effects on performance of high-technology firms. *Organization Science, 16,* 259–274.

Simsek, Z., Heavey, C., Veiga, J. F., & Souder, D. (2009). A typology for aligning organizational ambidexterity's conceptualizations, antecedents, and outcomes. *Journal of Management Studies, 46*(5), 864–894.

Smith, W., & Tushman, M. L. (2005). Managing strategic contradictions: A top management model for managing innovation streams. *Organization Science, 16*(5), 522–536.

Sinha, S. (2015). The exploration-exploitation dilemma: A review in the context of managing growth of new ventures. *Vikalpa, 40*(3), 313–323.

Todaro, M. C., & Stirpe, L. (2017). Teams in small technology-based firms: The roles of diversity and conflict management. *Journal of Technology Management & Innovation, 12*(2), 11–17.

Vera, D., & Crossan, M. M. (2004). Strategic leadership and organizational learning. *Academy of Management Review, 29,* 222–240.

Vos, G. B., & Vos, Z. G. (2013). Strategic ambidexterity in small and medium-sized enterprises: Implementing exploration and exploitation in product and market domains. *Organization Science, 24*(5), 1459–1477.

CHAPTER 7

EXCHANGING CACOPHONY FOR CONGRUENCE

Lessons From the Public Sector

Angie Lewis, Kyle Werner, and Sandy Zehr

You arrive to work early today, stop by the break room to start a fresh pot of coffee, say good morning to Paul, who also arrived early, and hit the lights as you get to your cubicle. Getting to the office early allows you to pick back up the project you were working on yesterday so that you can finish a few details before giving the customer a call to let them know that not only are you finishing ahead of schedule, but you are able to solve the issue related to integration of the new performance enhancement they requested. In addition to speed of delivery and a capability upgrade, you and your team negotiated tremendous supplier contract rates that will result in the entire project coming in at a cost much lower than expected. Yes, today is going to be a great day, and getting in early allows you to take the time necessary to thank your teammates, complete the delivery notification information, and check in with the boss to find out about the next project in the queue for you and your team to begin.

From Discord to Harmony, pages 121–140

Isn't this how we all begin our day at the office, where everything is going right and with a sense of harmony and accord? The title of this chapter introduces an uncommon term to describe and an all too common state within the workplace—discord. *Cacophony* is the harsh result of the mixture of multiple chaotic sounds, or the opposite of a perfectly choreographed harmony. In the world of work there are deadlines, problems, personalities, rules, agendas, politics, and any number of other variables that work against a state of harmony. In addition to a multitude of variables, the nature of the work and the size and complexity of the environment are considerations that can impact the level of natural accord as well.

Within this chapter, we will examine a workplace environment that is highly technical in purpose and both large and bureaucratic by structure. Each of these descriptors is an indicator of the potential for discord. Yet, within the organization described exists a sense of harmony that is rare and unique. The leaders of this organization invest heavily in leadership development and continually emphasize the importance of leadership principles and behaviors; there is a focus on people that cultivates and rewards high levels of engagement amongst the workforce. The criticality of the products and services provided by the organizational team is understood by all, and there is broad recognition that out-of-the-box thinking and innovative solutions are paramount to near-term operational success and long-term mission relevancy. In addition to cultural elements, the organization also proactively and intentionally manages conflict through formalized mechanisms. Although the sense of harmony that has been described is rare and unique, the building blocks for its existence are within reach and available to all. As you read about this organization and the elements that contribute to its highly productive and harmonious environment, we challenge you to develop your own ideas and strategies to exchange cacophony for congruence.

INHERENT CACOPHONY

Intellectual capital has become the premier source of strategic competitive advantage for organizations in the 21st century as the rate of technological change continues to accelerate within a globalized marketplace. It is often the intent of an organization's leadership to cultivate a workplace environment that is harmonious in nature, where each individual employee and the collective group of employees maximizes their fullest potential, and the organization achieves record accomplishments year after year. While the aforementioned strategy sounds admirable, the known reality for most organizational leaders is that the workplace often presents a myriad of situationally dependent challenges, constantly emerging crises, and unexpected daily issues that are best addressed through active management techniques.

The ability of an organization to create an environment that fosters congruence within the workplace presents a significant challenge and a strategic opportunity within both private and public sector organizations. This chapter includes views from a management practitioner perspective within a public sector organization whose purpose is to provide scientific and technological solutions for national defense warfighting systems. In this organization, there is no question that the energy, passion, and commitment of employees and their intellectual contributions are integral to organizational performance and overall business success. To that end, what are the mechanisms to best cultivate and realize the most return from the investment in human capital, and how can organizations ensure institutionalization of these mechanisms to drive predictable levels of performance and success?

In order to institute a culture within this organization that consistently yields exceptional products and services, there exists basic fundamental priorities that are transferrable from one sector to another and across functional disciplines. The relationship between leadership philosophy, priorities, and action, combined with an employee engagement focus and intention, has resulted in a culture that incentivizes and rewards problem-solving and other forms of innovation outcomes. Although not implemented as an intentional and well-developed strategy from the outset, there is certainly value in a reflective look at these elements in the context of the current academic literature and with examples of their practical applicability within the organization.

INTRODUCING NSWC CRANE

Observations, best practices, and lessons learned for this chapter are sourced from evaluation of the Naval Surface Warfare Center Crane Division (NSWC Crane) organization. NSWC Crane is a naval laboratory located in southwest Indiana that provides the American warfighter with solutions to their toughest technical challenges in order to better equip sailors, marines, soldiers, and airmen with a decisive advantage over potential adversaries. This is achieved through design, development, acquisition, and sustainment of warfighting systems utilized throughout the armed services within the Department of Defense (DoD). Origins of NSWC Crane date back to 1941 when the organization was commissioned originally as a Naval Ammunition Depot, responsible for the production, storage, and demolition of conventional ammunition. Since its commissioning 7 decades ago, the purpose of NSWC Crane has evolved and grown, resulting in recognition worldwide as a modern and sophisticated leader in the highly technical mission areas of strategic missions, electronic warfare, and expeditionary warfare.

Today, NSWC Crane is responsible for multi-domain, multispectral, full-life cycle support of technologies and systems enhancing capabilities of the nation's warfighter. This work is accomplished by a highly technical workforce, comprised primarily of scientists, engineers, and electronics technicians. There is also a corporate business structure in place that supports the laboratory through workload and workforce planning, financial management, safety, security, information technology, human resources, contracts, supply, and other traditional overhead functions. Structurally, this naval laboratory is one of many unique federal laboratories across the country, each with its own specific set of functional and technology-based mission areas.

Over the past decade NSWC Crane has experienced a significant and deep transformational change to align itself exclusively to the three mission areas of strategic missions, electronic warfare, and expeditionary warfare. In addition to the transformation associated with the workload of the organization, a cultural evolution has also taken place over this timeframe. These changes in NSWC Crane were preceded by a near closure of the facility through a DoD initiative to realign and close bases in an effort to realign work, develop technology centers of excellence, and reduce overhead and infrastructure costs. When the leaders of NSWC Crane recognized how close the organization was to closure, it became a strategic imperative to ensure stronger brand identity, align workload to national priorities, and provide even higher levels of service and support associated with the organization's products amongst the workforce.

In order to promote a sense of urgency around the importance of workplace culture, the executive leaders published guiding principles that explicitly communicate to all employees and to management the importance of placing a priority focus on the creation of an innovation culture that values leadership and employee engagement. The guiding principles are shared broadly with employees beginning in the first week of employment during the organization's standard onboarding program. The principles are also reinforced in multiple ways, including through their display on posters that are prominent within the workspaces, through inclusion in internal training courses, and within messages shared by senior executives on a recurring basis. Clarity and unity surrounding the guiding principles are elements of the strategy that were not left to chance. It is with much effort and intention that these concepts are shared broadly and explicitly so that their value is understood and known to all within the organization.

Due to their understanding of the value of employees, NSWC Crane's leaders aspire to attract, develop, and retain a world-class workforce. Within the culture, there is an emphasis on leadership behaviors and skills, which are encouraged and cultivated at all levels of the organization. They have adopted a leadership philosophy to teach transformational leadership principles in a systematic manner, and that is valued as an enabler to employee engagement.

Within NSWC Crane, leaders are investing energy in establishing expected leadership norms and behaviors, and are working to instill them within the workforce through a systematic leadership development program.

The development of a harmonious workplace was not a stated objective of NSWC Crane's transformation from the onset. However, through this chapter we will explore elements of the organization's transformation and how each element may have contributed to its current environment of highly functioning work teams. In the sections that follow, the role of leadership through leadership development and culture is discussed. Two leadership-focused academic studies that examine NSWC Crane are cited: one quantitative and one qualitative. Additionally, two quantitative studies based on this organization are presented: one focused on employee engagement and the other on an innovative culture. We will also discuss the mechanisms in place within NSWC Crane that focus on proactive conflict management. Observations, lessons learned, and best practices related to NSWC Crane's transformational change serve as the principal source of contributions to the remainder of this chapter.

LEADERSHIP

To provide a focus on leadership within an organization's culture, specific efforts to develop the common attributes amongst successful leaders are needed (Paarlberg & Lavigna, 2010). In addition to recruiting personnel with leadership potential, organizations should ensure that career planning, broad assignment selection, and challenging leadership tasks are utilized as mechanisms to further develop a culture of leadership (Kotter, 1990). A United States Office of Personnel Management (OPM; 2015) report emphasized the importance of leaders at all levels of the organization, specifically because of the influence leaders have on the daily experience of the workforce and the impact they have on shaping the perception of the organization's culture in the view of its employees.

There have been two academic studies focused on the leadership development program at NSWC Crane. The first, a quantitative analysis, found statistical significance in the relationship between participation in the leadership development program and both organizational performance and personal outcomes, such as promotion and performance pay rates (Seidle, 2010). A recent qualitative study of NSWC Crane's leadership development approach also found that the leadership strategies and cultural objectives, which inform the leadership development approach, resulted in strong levels of employee engagement and buy-in (Lewis, 2018). NSWC Crane's leadership development program focuses on leadership attributes, elements of a leadership-centric culture, and the importance of leaders and their influence within the organization. It is this focus that contributes to leadership behaviors that cultivate and promote a harmonious work environment.

Leadership Development

NSWC Crane invests energy, time, and resources in establishing expected leadership norms and behaviors, and works to instill these norms and behaviors within the workforce through a systematic leadership development program. The executives of NSWC Crane chose the leadership challenge model, authored by Kouzes and Posner (2012), as the cornerstone for the organization's program and designed course content and curriculum around the model that teaches practical application of the behaviors and actions of successful leadership specific to their organization's mission and culture. They have demonstrated commitment to this program through more than 10 years of consistent investment and participation in these leadership workshops by sending more than 450 employee-leaders through the program.

The leadership challenge is considered a transformational leadership model which is defined as "leadership performance that occurs when leaders broaden and elevate the interests of their employees and inspire followers to look beyond their own self-interests for the good of the group" (Ölçer, Florescu, & Năstase, 2014, p. 385). This inherent focus on employees and their interests is in alignment with the cultural imperative and the guiding principles that govern behaviors and interactions within NSWC Crane.

NSWC Crane's leadership development program includes workshops that focus on the five leader practices outlined in the leadership challenge model, specifically model the way, inspire a shared vision, enable others to act, challenge the process, and encourage the heart (Kouzes & Posner, 2012). How each of these practices is applicable within NSWC Crane and their relevancy to harmonious work teams is summarized below:

1. *Model the Way*—Participants discover the importance of their own voice and values, and learn about the criticality of the example they set for others. Discussions within this workshop emphasize accountability, brand, and personal work reputations. These focal points lead to a higher standard within the workplace that becomes the benchmark for all employees to observe and emulate.
2. *Inspire a Shared Vision*—This leader practice stresses the importance of evolution, change, strategy, and future focus for the employees of NSWC Crane. Participants are required to envision the future for their role or their unit within the organization and are taught how to use passion, imagery, and other forms of communication

to enlist others to share in their vision. Possibility thinking and forward-looking behaviors have contributed to unity and alignment at various levels throughout the organization, and have improved communication skills amongst the staff.

3. *Enable Others to Act*—Through the program's workshops, participants spend time together learning about the attributes of leadership and practicing the behaviors in a safe learning environment. The practice of enabling others is intended to foster collaboration and demonstrate the value of strengthening and supporting others. Personal agendas, competition, and hoarding information are all elements that are counter to harmony and accord. Within the program, challenges are presented to the participants that demonstrate performance, and success with task completion are elevated when disparate individuals come together to work collectively and rely upon the unique and individual talents of those around them and on their teams.
4. *Challenge the Process*—An element of organizational performance and success is the ability of an organization's leaders to innovate new approaches and continually improve processes and outcomes. Participants of the leadership development program identify a specific leadership challenge facing their work unit or team and then complete assignments outside of the classroom to overcome and manage through the challenge. The importance of this practice is emphasized to the employee-leaders so that within the workplace each of them becomes equipped to search for improvement opportunities and demonstrate willingness to experiment and take risks.
5. *Encourage the Heart*—One of the program's workshops focuses on appreciation for individual contributions, demonstration of leadership attributes, and other regular workplace activities. The pace of work and the busyness of everyone's lives sometimes result in overlooking accomplishments and successful contributions. Within NSWC Crane, there is a lot of pressure for high levels of performance so focusing on this leader practice stresses the importance and value of recognizing the contributions of others and taking time to celebrate achievements.

The five leader practices described above are rooted in scholarly research. When Kouzes and Posner (1993) described *model the way* in their leadership challenge model, the underlying components of the practice were integrity, personal example, and trust in competence. The importance of integrity to leadership is well established within the literature (Covey, 1996; Kouzes & Posner, 1993; Nair, 1994; Rinehart, 1998). Integrity is inextricably linked to a leader's character and credibility and incorporates four essential values according to Russell and Stone (2002), specifically, "truth-telling, promise-keeping, fairness, and respect" (p. 148).

The importance of *inspiring a shared vision* is also echoed within leadership literature. It is sometimes described as pioneering, or the act of developing or preparing a way. Ulrich (1996) spoke to the importance of leaders that create and shape the future through their problem-solving approaches and risk-taking behaviors. Similarly, Yukl (1998) discussed the value of leadership to drive change behaviors within organizations and to utilize the power of influence to lead others into the unknown.

Servant leadership is foundational to the third practice: *Enable others to act.* From the early description offered by Greenleaf (1977), the notion that service to others is a primary motivation for leadership has been the subject of much research. This theory of leadership places the leader as the servant to employees and establishes a primary function of leadership to focus on the needs of others (Covey, 1990; Greenleaf, 1977; Kouzes & Posner, 1993; Rinehart, 1998). The heart of this practice requires that leaders provide the information, resources, and training needed for employees to be successful within their task and role assignments.

Challenge the process is the fourth practice of this model. Persuasion, competence, and willingness to take risk are required for this leadership practice. Bass (1990), Greenleaf (1977), and Yukl (1998) each identified persuasion as a critical leadership skill and tied its use to opportunities to enhance the organization through positive change rather than selfish motives. Competence is essential for multiple reasons, but in relation to this practice, it is an enabler to trust in the leader's ability to initiate change in the right areas at the right times. Having knowledge and ability is a precursor to appropriate risk-taking behaviors.

The final practice is *encourage the heart.* Demonstration of appreciation of others through care and encouragement are hallmark leadership traits (Covey, 1990; Greenleaf, 1977; Kouzes & Posner, 1993). Empathy, involvement, and enrichment of others represent traits of leaders that are effective in showing appreciation.

Within this transformational leadership model, there are guidelines established for creating leadership best moments and the importance of communication for teaching, motivating, inspiring, and investing in others is explicit. NSWC Crane's leadership development program was developed to include not only the content and principles of the Leadership Challenge model, but also to reinforce the leadership attributes that are expected and desired within the organization's culture.

Leadership Culture

Instituting a clear philosophy of leadership and working to develop an organizational culture based on consistent goals, priorities, and behaviors are efforts predicted to result in an engaged workforce. "Leadership is the most important competency for ensuring success and long-term sustainability during organizational transformation" (Cherry, Davis, & Thorndyke, 2010, p. 38). In an examination of NSWC Crane's strategic planning efforts, we identified people, knowledge management, and leadership as critical to the organization's success.

Within NSWC Crane, the leadership strategies associated with organizational culture, guiding principles, and organizational values serve to establish workplace norms and expectations that are descriptive of the environment that is desired for the entire workforce. In addition to descriptors, executives have worked to align rewards and incentives in a way that reinforces the organization's cultural objectives. Tangible examples of this alignment include opportunities for leadership development available to all employees, allocation of funding to promote continuous personal and professional education, and policies that promote respect and inclusion of all employees.

An employee focus within the culture is an explicit objective of NSWC Crane's executive leadership. The association of mission, vision, and values with the concept of putting people first has created a sense of importance for the work and the workforce. Within this public sector organization, the importance of the work and the association of the workforce with something they view as larger than themselves and important to the nation is another motivation for high levels of performance. There is recognition throughout the organization that agility, effectiveness, and competitive advantage are necessary for the long-term success and relevancy of the laboratory.

EMPLOYEE ENGAGEMENT

One clear source of differentiation for an organization is an engaged workforce. Engagement has been positively linked to employee morale, job performance, willingness to take on additional assignments, and organizational success (Bailey, Madden, Alfes, & Fletcher, 2017). Employee engagement can lead to opportunities to differentiate organizations, promote strong leadership, and create positive organizational cultures. According to the United States Office of Personnel Management (2015), the federal government has not been known for stimulating engagement among its expansive workforce. The measures of an engaged workforce include positive implications on organizational culture, such as goal alignment, innovation outcomes, and increased productivity (Bailey et al., 2017). Since this is not something inherent within the federal workplace, let's explore the activities and strategies employed at NSWC Crane that lead to high levels of buy-in and engagement, and result in a transition from cacophony to congruence.

Within NSWC Crane, employees take pride in their mission and assignments and increased buy-in results from the level of commitment that materializes through a sense of unity and congruence. Although not an objective put in place for the result of creating harmony and reducing conflict, the alignment demonstrated by this workforce is certainly a great example of the contribution strategic clarity can make toward employee engagement and workplace accord. We previously asserted that one outcome associated with NSWC Crane's leadership approach is engaged employees.

Leadership at NSWC Crane demonstrates awareness of the vast potential of an engaged workforce through establishment of the organization's guiding principles. One of three NSWC Crane's guiding principles is *ethos*, or the organizational aspiration to create a culture of innovation that values leadership and employee engagement. When considered in light of the other two NSWC Crane guiding principles, *execution* and *excellence*, perhaps it can be extrapolated that the benefits resulting from employee engagement associated with ethos serve to enable the other two principles, leading to strong organizational performance and resulting in superior quality products and services.

Employee engagement is a term generally considered to have originated with Kahn (1990), who defined the concept as, "The harnessing of organizational members' selves to their work roles" (p. 694). Kahn's (1990) research identified three necessary elements for an employee to become engaged: psychological meaningfulness, psychological availability, and psychological safety. When employees feel that their work is useful and valued by the organization, they will experience increased levels of psychological meaningfulness. In cases where employees are afforded physical, emotional, and cognitive resources, they possess increased psychological availability. When employees feel that they can speak up in the workplace and be themselves without risk of negative career consequences, they can be considered psychologically safe.

At NSWC Crane, the focus on people and the teaching of the leadership development program provide contributions to each of these three elements. The association with the United States' national defense and the relevancy of NSWC Crane's mission provide employees a clear connection to the importance and meaningfulness of their work and value of their assignments. Efforts to recognize and reward team and individual contributions occur routinely as another mechanism to demonstrate and create meaningfulness. Work teams operate in highly autonomous settings and are well-resourced to achieve operational results. Employees are encouraged to be collaborative and are challenged to explore innovative and new approaches to accomplishing work. Multi-disciplined teams promote diversity of thought in arriving at solutions, and respectful and healthy debate is encouraged amongst these teams.

Increased levels of employee engagement provide numerous benefits to the organization, including increased performance, satisfied customers, and decreased voluntary employee turnover (Harter, Schmidt, & Hayes, 2002). Engaged employees are passionate and committed to the organization (Schaufeli, 2012; Shuck, Rocco, & Albornoz, 2011) and can become a source of competitive advantage (Christian, Garza, & Slaughter, 2011).

While there are many beneficial aspects to an engaged workforce, it is important to note that negative effects exist when employees are not engaged. Disengaged employees negatively impact the organization through decreased performance, increased costs, and employee turnover (Frank, Finnegan, & Taylor, 2004). In some cases, disengaged employees may even act in such a manner as to demoralize those who are engaged (Endres & Mancheno-Smoak, 2008). Research published in 2011 suggested that disengaged employees cost United States organizations $343 billion each year (Rivera & Flinck, 2011, p. 487).

Although NSWC Crane is a public sector organization, with somewhat different operating precepts as those in the private sector, employee engagement is an important topic within the organization. Federal agencies with higher levels of employee engagement experience enhanced efficiency, improved levels of client satisfaction, increased innovation, and less voluntary employee turnover (Marrelli, 2011; U.S. Office of Personnel Management, 2015). As such, NSWC Crane leadership has been intentional about creating an organizational culture characterized by employee engagement.

NSWC Crane Case Study

An empirical research study which focused on employee engagement at NSWC Crane produced important results in support of the cultural evolution within the organization (Zehr, 2017). The study placed emphasis on the role of psychological safety in employee engagement and vice versa. Levels of NSWC Crane employee engagement and the three psychological conditions (psychological meaningfulness, psychological availability, and psychological safety) described as necessary for employee engagement by Kahn (1990) were collected for further examination.

Results of the study pointed to psychological safety as a predictor of employee engagement (Zehr, 2017). As one's psychological safety increases, so does employee engagement. Additionally, the reciprocal condition was found to be predictive. As one's employee engagement increases, so does one's psychological safety. In both directions of the relationship between employee engagement and psychological safety, the study results suggested that psychological meaningfulness was positively correlated. As a result, one could assert that within NSWC Crane the elements of employee engagement, psychological safety, and psychological meaningfulness work together to create a virtuous value-chain cycle of sorts. When one of the three traits increases, so do the other two.

For the organizational leader within the public sector, and perhaps the private sector as well, a greater understanding and application of the results can be a powerful tool in the quest for organizational evolution and cultural transformation. Based on leadership's continual focus on ethos as one of the organization's guiding principles, the results of Zehr's (2017) recent study, and personal observations and experiences, we have derived a set of NSWC Crane's best practices for potential application within other organizations. In general, these best practices can be categorized into three broad concepts: embrace social exchange, focus on the compound nature of employee engagement, and regularly measure and monitor progress.

Embrace Social Exchange

An organization's leadership is uniquely positioned to effect positive cultural change. As part of the exchange process, employees continuously evaluate the balance of what is being given to the organization with what they receive in return, which is the essence of social exchange theory (Homans, 1958). The perceptive leader understands the "give and take" nature of the exchange relationship and works to create conditions conducive for positive social exchange. For example, the NSWC Crane leadership team has placed a renewed emphasis on the establishment of trust and transparency. Leaders are focused on demonstrating principles of authentic and transformational leadership to ensure congruence between leadership words and actions. This initiative is illustrative of an understanding of favorable social exchange as a basis for employee engagement. Other factors that are conducive to employee engagement include diversity, inclusiveness, beneficial coworker relationships, goal clarity, comfort with risk-taking, and opportunities for individual development.

Compound Nature of Employee Engagement

As a federal laboratory, NSWC Crane regularly utilizes systems engineering concepts to manage systems throughout their life cycle, from early conceptual design through sustainment and maintenance phases. A systems approach can be applied to leverage the compound nature of employee engagement. As previously noted, employee engagement is a compound construct consisting of components that include psychological meaningfulness, psychological safety, and psychological availability. By viewing employee engagement as a system, NSWC Crane leadership is able to initiate a variety of actions to effect increases. For example, an employee experiences psychological meaningfulness when he or she is engaged in work that matters and is appreciated by organizational leaders. By helping employees become involved with impactful work, NSWC Crane leadership increases psychological meaningfulness which, in turn, increases employee engagement. Likewise, activities that are designed to create an environment in which employees can speak up without concern for career repercussions lead to increased levels of psychological safety which then lead to employee engagement. By intentionally addressing the various elements of the system that encompasses employee engagement, leadership at NSWC Crane develops an enthusiastic, committed, and engaged workforce.

Regularly Measure and Monitor Progress

Research examining employee engagement at NSWC Crane measured levels of employee engagement (Zehr, 2017). In an effort to better understand progress of intentional efforts to create an engaged workforce, NSWC Crane leadership recently committed to annual measurement of employee engagement. In this manner, leaders will be able to track the effectiveness of efforts to increase employee engagement and have year-to-year comparative data available. It is important that management practitioners, whether in the public sector or private sector, regularly measure and track employee engagement within the workforce. In doing so, the effectiveness of strategic efforts to increase employee engagement can be monitored and evaluated.

INNOVATION

As the pace of global change continues to accelerate, an organization's ability to innovate has become, and will continue to be, a competitive advantage for organizational success. NSWC Crane is striving to create an organizational culture of innovation that values leadership and employee engagement. Creating the proper culture can improve organizational performance by empowering employees to act quickly, communicate regularly, and, perhaps most importantly, be highly innovative. The ability of an organization to create a culture of innovation is a significant challenge in any situation but is particularly difficult within public sector organizations (Borins, 2006). In public sector organizations, such as NSWC Crane, regulatory policies essentially define the boundaries for the organization to operate within and stifle innovation (Cozzens, 2011). However, organizations can implement specific actions that are known to increase innovation and influence cultural attributes that contribute toward the creation of a culture of innovation.

A quantitative research study was conducted to empirically examine the support for an innovative culture within the bureaucratic climate of NSWC Crane (Werner, 2017). The study was designed to increase the understanding of the relationships between key factors that influence support for an innovative culture within a United States DoD federal research laboratory. The researcher examined the relationship of five factors on the organization's support for an innovative culture. The five factors were collaboration, workforce autonomy, resource supply for innovation, managerial trust and workforce enthusiasm, and transformational leadership. Outcomes of the study demonstrated that the five factors account for 75% of the variance in support for an innovative culture within the laboratory, and revealed collaboration and workforce autonomy as the two most significant opportunities for increasing the organization's support for an innovative culture.

So, what are practical management implications and specific actions that can be implemented by an executive team interested in improving an organization's innovative culture? Werner's (2017) study results concluded that executive leaders and mid-level managers can increase an organization's support for an innovative culture through two primary courses of action: increase collaboration and increase workforce autonomy. Each will be discussed in the sections that follow.

Increase Collaboration

According to Werner's (2017) findings, collaboration has the highest predictive power, predicting 54.5% of the model's predictive power, and represents the opportunity area to most significantly impact support for an innovative culture. Examples of actions to increase collaboration to support an innovative culture within NSWC Crane include: (a) formally recognize collaboration as an organizational value through creation of published material that clearly defines collaboration and identifies the significance of collaboration's importance to organizational performance, personal job satisfaction, and continued strategic growth for the laboratory's mission; (b) create tangible ways to measure collaboration, internal and external to the organization; (c) align internal incentives that recognize collaboration as an organizational value; (d) create central innovation centers within the organization that will increase interaction among employees from across all parts of the organization; and (e) use technology to create a space for employees to use digital collaboration tools to provide advice to one another, share stories, and volunteer to join initiatives where they have considerable passion.

Increase Workforce Autonomy

Werner's (2017) study results also showed that workforce autonomy has the second-highest predictive power, predicting 11.4% of the model's outcome. Based on Werner's findings, suggestions for increasing workforce autonomy to support an innovative culture within NSWC Crane include: (a) build a more risk-tolerant culture from the top down through the creation of a formalized approach to innovation, which will in turn elevate employee creativity; (b) establish an organizational climate where leaders at all levels have relationships where they personally connect and empower employees through trust; (c) challenge and incentivize the organization's leaders to transition from *doing* to *teaching*, *mentoring*, and *inspiring* their employees; and (d) create a task force to both identify and remove barriers that prevent innovation and empower employees.

CONFLICT MANAGEMENT

In today's society, there is an emphasis on conflict resolution in the workplace due to routine employee interactions, human resource systems, organizational structure issues, competition for resources, and the need for increased collaboration and interdependence (Arnold & Pulich, 2003; Katz & Flynn, 2013). The importance of dealing with organizational conflict is underscored through the proclamation that "the means by which organizations manage conflict might very well be one of the most significant factors they currently face in regard to costs, efficiency, effectiveness and employee retention" (Dana, 2001, p. 397). According to Katz and Flynn (2013), "How conflicts are managed [is] the critical element in determining if they have a negative or positive effect on the workplace environment" (p. 396). There are multiple areas of organizational conflict within NSWC Crane worthy of acknowledgement, such as labor and management disputes, cross-organization disagreements, and role conflicts throughout the organization. Thus, NSWC Crane has adopted an integrated approach to conflict management that utilizes various techniques and tools to ensure avenues for addressing multiple types of issues are available to all employees. Several of the tools and techniques utilized within the organization include formalized administrative and union grievance procedures, regulatory-based equal employment processes, traditional supervisor to employee resolution, and peer-to-peer discussions.

Alternative dispute resolution (ADR) refers to methods and techniques used to facilitate the resolution of conflict and disputes without resorting to formal litigation or court proceedings (Mackie, 1991). Lipsky and Avgar (2008) presented a case for a holistic approach to ADR programs and conflict management within the workplace. They described traditional ADR as a management-driven activity and highlighted the utility of such systems for solving issues across a wide range of organizational settings and various types of conflict (Lipsky & Avgar, 2008). Their strategic theory of conflict management asserts that organizations focused on the prevention and active management of disputes are generally interested in the impacts of such efforts on the attainment of strategic goals and objectives.

One source of conflict within NSWC Crane and many organizations is the relationship between the labor union and management. Recognizing this relationship as a possible source of conflict, NSWC Crane implemented an ADR technique to address, manage, and resolve disputes in an effort to mitigate the need for formal litigation. For nearly two decades, NSWC Crane has engaged in a labor-management forum for the purpose of discussing workplace policies, conditions, and other issues of interest to employees. The labor-management forum is comprised of senior management officials and senior union officers, and the team is responsible for adjudicating grievances, implementing policies, negotiating agreements, and discussing workforce relevant topics. Within the labor-management forum, both parties have a common interest in the overall welfare and well-being of the workforce as well as an interest in the effective execution of the organization's mission to support the nation's warfighters. In light of the natural opposition that generally characterizes union and management, the labor-management forum was formed specifically with a purpose to maintain open lines of communication and to emphasize the importance of effective relationships for the overall good of the organization. As discussed by St-Pierre and Holmes (2010), management has a responsibility and role to influence employee perceptions of fairness and to instill a sense of trust in the organization. In this regard, NSWC Crane has a model forum that is predicated on employee voice, cooperative relationships, and mutual commitment to interest-based outcomes.

Executives of NSWC Crane conduct an annual climate survey of all employees with the intent to understand the employees' perceptions of the culture within their workplace. In addition to receiving a comprehensive report of the results, a small team is convened to analyze the information. This team also hosts employee focus groups to gain additional insight into areas of concern or opportunities for improvement that emerge from the data. Additionally, during times of significant organizational change there is an increased emphasis placed on face-to-face communication and opportunities for questions and answers. These mechanisms result in feedback that is acted on and incorporated into larger strategic improvement efforts.

Effective conflict management tools and techniques are essential to NSWC Crane's success due to the criticality of the laboratory's strategic planning process and the established corporate priority to create a culture that attracts, develops, and retains a world-class workforce. Integral to this strategy is the emphasis on transformational leadership for the purpose of promoting innovation and employee engagement as has been discussed. Managing conflict within this employee-focused organizational culture allows for avenues to correct and alter situations that do not live up to the high standards that have been established.

SUMMARY

Within this chapter, we examined a workplace environment that is highly technical in purpose, and both large and bureaucratic by structure with much potential for discord. Within NSWC Crane, there exists a sense of harmony that is rare and unique, and we offered insight into the culture through the lens of leadership development, employee engagement, and innovation. We concluded with a description of an intentional approach to conflict management.

Recall the opening description of arriving to work full of energy and excitement over the day ahead and ready to face the challenges of the next project in the queue. This is a reality at NSWC Crane. The leaders of NSWC Crane invest heavily in leadership development and continually emphasize the importance of leadership principles and behaviors. Additionally, there is a focus on people that cultivates and rewards high levels of engagement amongst the workforce. And finally, the criticality of the products and services provided by this team is understood by all, and there is broad recognition that out-of-the-box thinking and innovative solutions are paramount to near-term operational success and long-term mission relevancy.

The sense of harmony and accord that has been described is rare and unique; however, it is also intentional and the result of strategic clarity, leadership commitment, and proactive workforce management techniques. The building blocks for this type of workplace culture are within reach and available to all. As you read about NSWC Crane and the elements that contribute to its highly productive and harmonious environment, we hope you developed your own ideas and strategies to exchange cacophony for congruence within your organization.

REFERENCES

Arnold, E., & Pulich, M. (2003). Personality conflicts and objectivity in appraising performance. *The Health Care Manager, 22*(3), 227–232.

Bailey, C., Madden, A., Alfes, K., & Fletcher, L. (2017). The meaning, antecedents, and outcomes of employee engagement: A narrative synthesis. *International Journal of Management Reviews, 19*(1), 31–53. https://doi.org/10.1111/ijmr.12077

Bass, B. M. (1990). From transactional to transformational leadership: Learning to share vision. *Organizational Dynamics, 18*(3), 19–31.

Borins, S. (2006). *The challenge of innovating in government.* IBM Center for the Business of Government. Retrieved from http://www.businessofgovernment.org/report/challenge-innovating-government

Cherry, R. A., Davis, D. C., & Thorndyke, L. (2010). Transforming culture through physician leadership development. *Physician Executive, 36*(3), 38–44.

Christian, M. S., Garza, A. S., & Slaughter, J. E. (2011). Work engagement: A quantitative review and test of its relations with task and contextual performance. *Personnel Psychology, 64*(1), 89–136.

Covey, S. R. (1990). *Principle-centered leadership.* New York, NY: Fireside Books.

Covey, S. R. (1996). Three roles of the leader in the new paradigm. In F. Hesselbein, M. Goldsmith, & R. Beckhard, (Eds.), *The leader of the future: New visions, strategies, and practices for the next era* (pp. 149–159). San Francisco, CA: Jossey-Bass.

Cozzens, S. E. (2011). End of empire: External and internal transitions in US policies for science, technology, and innovation. *Prometheus, 29*(4), 393–409.

Dana, D. (2001). *Conflict resolution: Mediation tools for everyday worklife.* New York, NY: McGraw-Hill.

Endres, G. M., & Mancheno-Smoak, L. (2008). The human resource craze: Human performance improvement and employee engagement. *Organization Development Journal, 26*(1), 69–78.

Frank, F. D., Finnegan, R. P., & Taylor, C. R. (2004). The race for talent: Retaining and engaging workers in the 21st century. *People and Strategy, 27*(3), 12–25.

Greenleaf, R. K. (1977). *Servant leadership: A journey into the nature of legitimate power and greatness.* New York, NY: Paulist Press.

Harter, J. K., Schmidt, F. L., & Hayes, T. L. (2002). Business-unit-level relationship between employee satisfaction, employee engagement, and business outcomes: A meta-analysis. *Journal of Applied Psychology, 87*(2), 268–279. https://doi.org/10.1037/0021-9010.87.2.268

Homans, G. C. (1958). Social behavior as exchange. *American Journal of Sociology, 63*(2), 597–606.

Kahn, W. A. (1990). Psychological conditions of personal engagement and disengagement at work. *Academy of Management Journal, 33*(4), 692–724.

Katz, N. H., & Flynn, L. T. (2013). Understanding conflict management systems and strategies in the workplace: A pilot study. *Conflict Resolution Quarterly, 30*(4), 393–410.

Kotter, J. P. (1990, May). What leaders really do. *Harvard Business Review, 68*(3), 103–111.

Kouzes, J. M., & Posner, B. Z. (1993). *Credibility: How leaders gain and lose it and why people demand it.* San Francisco, CA: Jossey-Bass.

Kouzes, J. M., & Posner, B. Z. (2012). *The leadership challenge* (5th ed.). San Francisco, CA: Jossey-Bass.

Lewis, A. D. (2018). *Employee engagement in a public-sector environment: A grounded theory study of leadership development and organizational culture* (Doctoral dissertation). Available from ProQuest Dissertations and Theses database. (Accession No. 10749536)

Lipsky, D. B., & Avgar, A. C. (2008). Toward a strategic theory of workplace conflict management. *Ohio State Journal on Dispute Resolution, 24,* 143–190.

Mackie, K. J. (1991). Dispute resolution: The new wave. In K. J. Mackie (Ed.), *A handbook of dispute resolution: ADR in action* (pp. 1–7). New York, NY: Routledge.

Marrelli, A. F. (2011). Employee engagement and performance management in the federal sector. *Performance Improvement, 50*(5), 5–13. https://doi.org/10.1002/pfi.20216

Nair, K. (1994). *A higher standard of leadership: Lessons from the life of Gandhi.* San Francisco, CA: Berrett-Koehler.

Ölçer, F., Florescu, M. S., & Năstase, M. (2014, October). The effects of transformational leadership and emotional intelligence of managers on organizational citizenship behaviors of employees. *Review of International Comparative Management,* 15(4), 385–401.

Paarlberg, L. E., & Lavigna, B. (2010, September–October). Transformational leadership and public service motivation: Driving individual and organizational performance. *Public Administration Review, 70*(5), 710–718.

Rinehart, S. T. (1998). *Upside down: The paradox of servant leadership.* Colorado Springs, CO: NavPress.

Rivera, A., & Flinck, J. (2011). Employee-led, employee engagement in the federal government: SAMHSA People First. *Advances in Developing Human Resources, 13*(4), 479–493.

Russell, R. F., & Stone, A. G. (2002). A review of servant leadership attributes: Developing a practical model. *Leadership & Organization Development Journal, 23*(3), 145–157.

Schaufeli, W. B. (2012). Work engagement: What do we know and where do we go. *Romanian Journal of Applied Psychology, 14*(1), 3–10.

Seidle, B. (2010). *An examination of leadership training and development in the public sector: Impact on leader and organizational effectiveness* (Doctoral dissertation). Available from ProQuest Dissertations and Theses database. (Accesssion No. 3439300)

Shuck, B., Rocco, T. S., & Albornoz, C. A. (2011). Exploring employee engagement from the employee perspective: Implications for HRD. *Journal of European Industrial Training, 35*(4), 300–325. https://doi.org/10.1108/03090591111128306

St-Pierre, I., & Holmes, D. (2010). The relationship between organizational justice and workplace aggression. *Journal of Advanced Nursing, 66*(5), 1169–1182.

Ulrich, D. (1996). Credibility X capability. In F. Hesselbein, M. Goldsmith, & R. Beckhard (Eds.), *The leader of the future* (pp. 209–220). San Francisco, CA: Jossey-Bass.

United States Office of Personnel Management. (2015). *Engaging the federal workforce: How to do it & prove it.* Retrieved from https://admin.govexec.com/media/gbc/docs/pdfs_edit/engaging_the_federal_workforce_white_paper.pdf

Werner, K. R. (2017). *An examination of support for an innovative culture at a United States Department of defense federal research laboratory* (Doctoral dissertation). Available from ProQuest Dissertations and Theses database. (Accesssion No. 10689251)

Yukl, G. (1999, Summer). An evaluation of conceptual weaknesses in transformational and charismatic leadership theories. *Leadership Quarterly, 10*(2), 285–306.

Zehr, S. L. (2017). *Safe to be engaged or engaged to be safe? A quantitative examination of the relationship between employee engagement and psychological safety within the federal workforce* (Doctoral dissertation). Available from ProQuest Dissertations and Theses database. (Accesssion No. 10742930)

CHAPTER 8

MANAGE ANGER SPECTRUM PITFALLS TO WORK IN YOUR FAVOR

Kimberly Castle

We all have strong feelings about anger. Those opinions are based upon our own lived experiences in and out of the workplace regarding anger. My doctoral research focused on the motivations of a workplace bully and the bad behaviors they utilize. My work in the academic community has centered upon conflict management in the workplace, while my work in personal consulting has focused on domestic violence offenders and parents who are needing to learn discipline and cooperative parenting techniques. As a mediator helping parties settle all kinds of issues over a broad range of conflicts, I have seen that anger is an ever-present force. As someone also certified in restorative justice, I practice a transformative approach to work and life, constantly asking myself and others, "How do we move forward from here?" Anger is certainly a piece of this body of work—it can be utilized constructively, and there are some tools to help that process. I believe it can empower us, and help us accept change and grow, if handled positively. This chapter lends to the reality that we spend lots of time working,

From Discord to Harmony, pages 141–150

and emotions are a big part of the workplace, like it or not. Workplaces are more and more competitive and challenging; therefore, addressing subjects out of our comfort zone is important in the concept of making our workplaces more peaceful and compassionate.

WHAT IS ANGER?

Anger is one of those emotions that is both natural and uncomfortable at the same time. We all experience anger, and we all have a different description of such. Anger is not the enemy—it is what we do with our anger that often creates a mess of things. Learning to manage our anger, use it to our advantage, and overcome the impulses surrounding our anger will make our workplaces truly hum.

Anger makes us feel bad and it also fuels us—sounds like an oxymoron. It sometimes grabs us by surprise, and we are swept up in its path. The best course of action is to manage our thoughts and control it. That happens as we understand its tenacity. By understanding what anger truly is, we are embarking on the first step to overcoming its pitfalls. There are many types of anger—here are a few:

- action anger—usually aggressive in nature;
- hidden anger—holding it in at all costs;
- verbal anger—counter attacking anyone who offends them;
- self-harming anger—when the issue seems so big, it turns inward;
- anpredictable anger (comes seemingly out of nowhere)—didn't see it coming;
- habitual anger—something agitates them all the time;
- judgmental anger—when the anger is seemingly justified;
- overwhelming anger—it controls everything;
- revenge anger—it is planned;
- manipulative anger—to devise a certain outcome;
- anger for a cause—it consumes us and is fueled by the greater good (morally just);
- pouting anger—just let me be and I will get over it;
- rage—no rhyme or reason for the out of control actions—blackout possible;
- planned anger—allowing designated time to be angry and recover; and
- black-out anger—like a drunk experience, there is an anger that is so strong, we do not remember the episode. (IED: Intermittent Explosive Disorder)

Anger makes some individuals uncomfortable, and it causes others to be mad. Some of us avoid those feelings by burying them in our soul and then we may be prone to an explosion; others are set off down the angry path easily. We all know someone like that. When we work around a coworker who flies off the handle easily, we walk on eggshells and may develop anxiety over such folks. Others have no problem counter-attacking such individuals. The first step to managing anger at work is understanding it.

Geddes and Stickney (2012) studied a phenomenon in the workplace called muted anger, wherein anger is hidden from management and those seemingly responsible for the anger. An employee feels, perhaps out of fear to speak up or voice concern, that to voice their anger might do themselves harm. The study found that communication moves forward about anger incidents based upon intensity of feelings, and colleagues with high organizational commitment will more likely advocate for their angry colleague when a problematic situation occurs. In some sense, when colleagues confide in one another, trust is invoked. When anger is shared, bonding may even occur. But the outcome of choosing not to communicate feelings with management seems negative and unproductive. The best outcome is produced when employees practice expression of feelings, even if anger is present.

While we might recognize the types of anger and those we harbor, understanding each term will provide a deeper look into our own triggers and thought patterns and present the best course of action to help us overcome negative behaviors. For example, if we feel strongly that we are passed over for a promotion long overdue, we might seek revenge or we might just need to pout. Both of those thought patterns are unproductive and both could be considered common practice, unfortunately. If we do not work on our thought patterns to correct negativity, workplaces may suffer. Another reaction to the feeling of anger is the invocation of rage; however, if that is the case, seek help because that thought pattern is unhealthy. While these types of anger give title to the feelings, to begin to solve any issues around our anger we must first accept that we are responsible for ourselves. Anger is a choice, and we can choose to let it go. That process takes practice.

THE ANGER CYCLE

Events happen every day that are out of our control, and the *thoughts* (based upon our lived experiences) we have about such events cause us to have *feelings* (physical ones) which leads us to take *action* (thus causing a new event) and the cycle continues.

EVENT → THOUGHTS → FEELINGS → ACTION → and on and on . . .

Since events are out of our control, and feelings are physical in nature, we cannot really change that, but by managing our thoughts and being deliberately cautious in our actions, we can curtail our anger events. Because our thoughts are a product of our lived and learned experiences, recognizing them for what they are enables us to create new reactions deliberate in nature. For example, when someone criticizes us, do not picture a sibling or your parents; think of it as a coaching moment and learn from it. By managing our thoughts, we control our feelings. By controlling our feelings, we make better choices and our actions will cause better results. This will lend to positive outcomes, even when we feel anger. Anger management training encompasses techniques to improve reactions.

Anger is a strong emotional response to conflict; some of the main causes are frustration, hurt, annoyance, and disappointment. Some of the most common reactions to anger include being passive-aggressive and responding in sarcasm or never directly responding to the source of our anger. Another reaction is to feel as if everyone is out to get us (paranoia). One study by Kassinove and Tafrate (2002) found that people with high trait anger have reactions more frequent, intense, and enduring. They also found that aggression could be physical, verbal, and include substance abuse. In general, this type of anger affects our relationships, our health, and our jobs. Kassinove et al. (1997) found that 58% of anger episodes include yelling and screaming. If, at any time, anger disrupts normal living as we are accustomed to, obtain therapy, seek training, and resist the urge to give in to bad behavior. Self-recognition and ownership of our bad behaviors is the first step to changing the anger cycle.

WHY IS THIS IMPORTANT?

Sometimes anger is useful and other times it is destructive. Two things we might ask ourselves to be sure if anger may help or hinder the situation are, "Is our anger directed toward someone who has knowingly, intentionally, and unnecessarily acted in a hurtful manner?" and "Is our anger useful? Does it help us achieve a desired goal, or does it simply defeat us?" (Newman & Newman, 2008). Our anger is most often caused by a belief that someone is acting or is treated unfairly, or that some event is unjust. My doctoral research on bad behavior motivations was fueled by the dramatic sense of justification and resulted in the generation of the self-motivation justification theory (Castle, 2014) which explains the bad behaviors of a workplace bully. Each subject of my research justified their bad behavior; many people justify their anger in a similar manner. Justification is like playing the blame game and/or minimizing our own responsibility to anger. Justification is defined as the act of validating or rationalizing unethical behavior, as in when a person engages in detrimental conduct but makes that conduct personally and socially acceptable by somehow portraying it as serving a value norm (Bandura, Barbaranelli, Caprara, & Pastorelli, 1996; Sykes & Matza, 1957). This condition enables people to rationalize their behaviors no matter how bad those behaviors are. The problem is that we then expect others to act according to our morals and values, which negates others' morals and values. Putting ourselves in another's shoes may sound cliché, but it is the best way to rectify and control our thoughts.

WHAT SHOULD WE DO?

Remember, everyone gets angry and it is perfectly natural. However, bad behaviors are not normal behavior, and the workplace is no place to display poor actions. To combat those uncomfortable feelings of anger, take the following steps:

- Count to 10 (it works).
- Be firm but professional (do not insult).
- Find humor (but do not laugh inappropriately).
- Walk, run, or work out to get the adrenaline out.
- Get a hobby to relax.
- Use imagery.
- Close your eyes for a minute and breathe.
- Find logical thoughts about our anger that are not misplaced because of our lived experiences.

When we are angry, our body feels it by the heartbeat, the sickness in our stomach, the sweaty palms, the red face, and the anxiety. When we have the "where with all" to breath, we fill our muscles with oxygen versus adrenaline. Another chemical produced by anger is cortisol, known to contribute to all sorts of ailments. Regular exercise combats these unhealthy tendencies. When we bury our anger without healthy releases, it may even cause illness, such as an ulcer, a heart condition, or other stressful condition.

Some other important techniques include:

- Use the STOP method (Stop, think, pause, then act).
- Practice difficult discussions with a friend.
- Don't make your anger public.
- Count to 10 or a hundred—whatever it takes.
- Drink water; it calms our bodies.
- *Breathe* slowly and deeply.
- Devote time to meditate and be grateful.
- *Choose* to react calmly to events.
- Think positive.

- Try to take things less seriously. Everything is not a crisis.
- Laugh more (It really is the best medicine).
- Ask yourself, "How would my mentor handle this?"
- Avoid tensing your muscles.
- Repeat a calming phrase to yourself.
- Listen to your favorite music.
- Get plenty of sleep.
- Avoid alcohol when feeling angry.
- Use empathy to try and understand other parties' perspectives.
- Don't hold grudges.
- Take a timeout.
- Use "I" statements and refrain from beginning a sentence with "you."

Realistically, others should not be able to affect our mood or alter our work practices. But, when things do not go our way or proceed according to plans, be adaptable, flexible, and as some say, "Go with the flow." It seems cliché, but it works and helps change our inner attitude. Learning to calm ourselves and our restless thoughts helps us gain peace of mind. This is the most effective tool to overcome anger and achieve peace of mind. Development of an attitude that helps us detach and separate ourselves from negativity will make for a calmer inner self, therefore, transcending a calmer workplace.

Remember, emotion is our body's response to our thoughts, which is triggered by those events out of our control. This is seen through our own interpretations, and our mind is cluttered by the mental images that are unique to us, like good versus bad, just versus unjust, or our own sense of right or wrong. If we did not think different from others we would be one large group think tank, and group think is not good for workplaces. Rather, it is the differences that we have which generate creativity, change, and, therefore, growth.

Quite often, anger is considered a negative emotion, but it is arguably also an inspiring emotion that sparks change and motivation. When we do not allow it to interfere with our objectives, we can direct anger's energy to inspire changes. After all, anger can cloud our judgment, cause us pain, and make us ill, so redirecting that energy is worth the cause. If we are conscious of directing our behaviors to positive outcomes, what can go wrong?

The three ways we can interrupt negativity are to change our thoughts, change our language, and change our physical location. We change our thoughts by learning new habits; we change our language by consciously speaking positively; and we change our physical location by taking a step back and looking up—the sky is filled with calmness. If you are sitting, stand and head to a window. In my own graduate classrooms, I will sometimes ask students to stand beside their chairs and look around, then I ask them to step up on to their chair seat and take another look around. It is always amazing to see their expressions as they are amazed at the difference in their perspectives.

A friend of mine once said, "Can't never could." If we don't try, we will not experience the positiveness that leads to peace in the workplace. Each time we utter the word "can't," we predetermine a negative result in most cases. Instead, change the word "can't" to "won't"—it implies choice and ownership, therefore, empowering the decision. Taking control of anger is empowering.

MINDFULNESS

One of the new management science buzz words that helps us maintain peace is mindfulness. Mindfulness is "a method of shifting one's attention inward to observe our thoughts, feelings, and actions without interpretation or judgement" (Goleman & Lippincott, 2017, para. 2) in the moment we are in. It began over 2,500 years ago as a part of Buddhism, according to *Psychology Today* (Henrique, 2015). Stay mindful of the things that lead to negativity and steer clear—when negative thoughts enter our minds, change course. It is okay to be angry, just change how it is perceived and make it work for you. Surrender the need to win or be "right"—separate thoughts from you, the person. When the group at work gets negative, find one that thinks positive. Be grateful. It sounds simple, but the realization that there are bigger things than us keeps us grounded and removes that need to control.

And do not hold on to grudges. Forgiveness does not come easy for us, but allow others that have upset our day to start over the next time we encounter them in the workplace. Just the thought changing process that allows others to start over at each encounter helps us manage the negativity.

Most of us know our triggers and if we avoid them, things are more peaceful. When we allow a person that we work with every day to be a trigger, we may allow that to control us—by giving them a "do over" opportunity each time we encounter them, there is not an opportunity for them to be our trigger any longer. It is all in our mind-set.

Being mindful means that we take active steps to solve problems and we do not give in to the need to win or the need to control—we just try to remain neutral, proactive, and thoughtful at each turn. Seek closure and positivity.

Another technique that may work for the angry disposition is to practice imagination. We all have one at times. Visualize how it would feel not to be angry, mad, or frustrated. Imagine how freeing it would be. Keep your thoughts positive; the law of attraction teaches us that positiveness breeds positivity and negative thoughts breed negativity.

A therapist in my building speaks of "visualization out of the problem"—imagine how that would feel and pretty soon the problem is diminished. By picturing yourself out of the conflict you can imagine the possibility. Being mindful and purposeful in changing our thought process ensures that we will control our reactions when anger is presented. Creating a peaceful attitude improves our lives in the workplace.

Recently, I had an exchange with a colleague about kindness and the lack of it in the world—it was pointed out to me that we seem to have forgotten that being kind does not make us weak. That is a misnomer. Kindness and a peaceful heart are signs of strength—it means we use mindfulness to be deliberate and helpful rather than disagreeable and negative. That act of changing our angry thoughts, and therefore, changing our reactions, fosters better communication, better relationships, and ultimately, better workplaces.

Being mindful prevents us from holding on to anger, because if we are mindful to our feelings we will take all options to solve the conflict into account. When our mind chooses to be unconscious of anger and we bury it, it will come out in an inappropriate manner. Strike a healthy balance of picturing positive outcomes and practicing good communication so we do not bury negativity.

We should distinguish between anger and attack when thinking mindfully. In our society where tablets, cell phones, and email are used more often than verbal communication, choosing our words in a mindful and deliberate manner is wise; however, all too often people feel attacked as their communication techniques get rusty with all the electronic ways to communicate taking the lead. Don't let that deter your efforts to be mindful and purposeful when trying to solve conflict where anger may be present. Remember that anger can be positive in business and relationships, but attack is not.

A good way to improve our techniques to communicate when we are angry is to be on top of our game in anger management overall. Managing anger is a choice. Anger is an emotion, not a behavior.

EMOTIONAL INTELLIGENCE

According to Psychology Today ("Emotional Intelligence," 2018), emotional intelligence (EQ) refers to the ability to manage one's emotions. It consists of three skills: emotional awareness of our own emotions, problem solving skills, and managing our emotions that we understand. EQ is also thought to include our management of others' emotions when we understand if someone needs to be cheered up, comforted, or coached. Understanding how the world looks through a coworkers' lens adds to our EQ. We discussed this earlier in empathy as a tool for addressing anger. There are no real valid tests to derive an EQ score, but the Myers-Briggs personality assessment and DISC are both used in organizations to consider EQ to solve problems or conflicts as both of these assessments consider compatibility and behavior tendencies. People who are good at reading emotional cues know when they are angry and how to express themselves without violating norms, thus implying a high EQ (Robbins & Judge, 2018). The art of intuition may additionally hold a place in EQ because trusting our gut enables us to use tools like empathy, forgiveness, and leadership. It is widely assumed that those with high EQ tend to have fulfilling relationships, make better leaders, and listen well (Robbins & Judge, 2018). People with high EQ are self-aware, conscious of others' feelings, straightforward, have life balance in work and personal lives, and put others at ease. It is also assumed that EQ can be learned. In an angry situation, drawing from our EQ is a reasonable tool to expand upon. Working with an anger management specialist may be necessary to truly benefit at the highest levels.

SUMMARY

There is an old Cherokee Indian legend about a wise grandfather and his grandson and the tale of two wolves. As the legend goes, the boy tells the grandfather that he feels as if there are two wolves wrestling inside of him. One is "bad" and one is "good." He asked the grandfather what that meant.

The grandfather who is anxious to teach the young boy about life tells him that the bad wolf and the good wolf are fighting to survive. The bad wolf is made up of evil, greed, arrogance, self-pity, anger, resentment, inferiority, lies, false pride, superiority, and ego. The good wolf is made up of joy, peace, love, hope, serenity, humility, kindness, benevolence, empathy, generosity, truth, compassion, and faith. Further, the grandfather tells the boy that the same fight goes on in all of us.

The boy thought for a moment and considered all he had learned, and then he asked his grandfather, "Which one survives?" The grandfather merely replied, "The one we feed."

That legend summarizes quickly how important it is to consider how we want to be thought of in and out of our workplaces. Being mindful about anger and our presentation is a way of life and an important tool when confronted with conflicts. The choices we make will determine which wolf in us survives.

REFERENCES

Bandura, A., Barbaranelli, C., Caprara, G. V., & Pastorelli, C. (1996). Mechanisms of moral disengagement in the exercise of moral agency. *Journal of Personality and Social Psychology, 71*(2), 364–374.

Castle, K. (2014). *The workplace bully: A grounded theory study exploring motivational influences of bullying behavior at work* (Doctoral dissertation). Available from ProQuest Dissertations and Theses database. (UMI No. 3636399)

Emotional Intelligence. (n.d.). Retrieved from https://www.psychologytoday.com/intl/basics/emotional-intelligence

Geddes, D., & Stickney, L. (2012). Muted anger in the workplace: Changing the sound of employee emotion through social sharing. In N. Ashkanasy, C. Hartel, & J. Wilfred (Eds.), *Experiencing and managing emotions in the workplace research on emotion in organizations* (Vol. 8; pp. 85–103). Bingley, England: Emerald Group.

Goleman, D., & Lippincott, M. (2017, September 8). Without emotional intelligence, mindfulness doesn't work. *Harvard Business Review.* Retrieved from https://hbr.org/2017/09/sgc-what-really-makes-mindfulness-work

Henrique, G. (2015, February 6). *What is mindfulness and how does it work?* Retrieved from https://www.psychologytoday.com/us/blog/theory-knowledge/201502/What-is-mindfulness-and-how-does-it-work

Kassinove, H., Sudhodolsky, D., Tsytsarev, S., & Soloyyova, S. (1997). Self-reported constructions of anger episodes in Russia and America. *Journal of Social Behavior and Personality, 12*(2), 301–324.

Kassinove, H., & Tafrate, R. (2002). *Anger management: The complete treatment guidebook for practitioners.* Atascadero, CA: Impact.

Newman, W., & Newman, E. (2008). *Domestic violence: Causes and cures and anger management.* Lexington, KY: Newman International.

Robbins, S., & Judge, T. (2018). *Essentials of organizational behavior.* Boston, MA: Pearson.

Sykes, G., & Matza, D. (1957). Techniques of neutralization: A theory of delinquency. *American Sociological Review, 22*(6), 664–670.

CHAPTER 9

THE ERA OF #METOO AND TIME'S UP

A Spotlight on Sexual Harassment at Work

Teresa A. Daniel

Recent high-level terminations suggest that sexual harassment and misconduct continue to be rampant in our workplaces, and it is a serious issue—one that has been persistent and pervasive in organizations throughout the United States for many years. However, the national dialogue about the problem took on a new urgency during the fall of 2017 with the firing of movie mogul Harvey Weinstein ("Harvey Weinstein Timeline," 2019). The magnitude of the problem was confirmed quickly after this news was reported. In fact, in the first 24 hours after actress Alyssa Milano suggested that victims of harassment reply "me too" to a tweet she made in October of 2017, 12 million women made #MeToo posts on Facebook (Harvard Business Review Staff, 2018).

It is not just the entertainment industry that has had a wake-up call. Similar allegations (with similar consequences) have been made about nearly

From Discord to Harmony, pages 151–169

100 other powerful people in fields including media, technology, religious organizations, the military, sports, universities, hospitality, finance, and politics—and they seem to keep falling (Berkowitz, 2017). This pernicious issue crosses industries, income levels, occupations, and educational levels.

How did we get to this moment where an old issue has taken on such a new sense of urgency? In the past, victims of harassment typically failed to mention it to their friends or family out of shame, fear, or legitimate concerns about losing their job. Bystanders who witnessed the abuse were often reluctant to get involved. This combination of inaction is how perpetrators have gotten away with it for so long—a situation that has been referred to as the *complicity of silence.* However, as more women have risen into positions of leadership, there is less tolerance for behavior that is now widely viewed as unprofessional—and unacceptable. The era of silence or inaction as a response to bad behavior appears to be over.

The national Society for Human Resource Management (SHRM) has published a chronology of many of the events which have collided to create this heightened demand for action and accountability—and the end of the silence (Gurchiek, 2018). The sheer volume of terminations due to harassment, along with the relentless media coverage of the issue, has made it more culturally acceptable to talk about sexual harassment than ever before.

As an employment lawyer and HR practitioner, I have been working on this issue for nearly 30 years. With 3 decades of laws, training, and media coverage, you would think that the problem would have been solved by now but, sadly, as recent events suggest, it has not. The ubiquity of sexual misconduct at work is especially surprising given the huge amount of money that organizations spend on their compliance efforts—the training programs, hotlines, and other systems designed to prevent and detect violations of laws, regulations, and company policies. Any estimate of a company's annual cost of compliance is underestimated, though, because the thousands of valuable employee hours consumed every year by training and other compliance activities are not generally taken into account.

There is good news, though. Women who come forward with allegations of sexual assault or misconduct are now being heard and, more importantly, believed. It appears that we are at what author Malcolm Gladwell (2002) refers to as a *tipping point*—"that magic moment when an idea, trend, or social behavior crosses a threshold, tips, and spreads like wildfire" (n.p.). Other social scientists refer to these seismic shifts in social mores as a "*norms cascade*" (Harvard Business Review Staff, 2018). Initiatives such as the #MeToo movement (https://metoomvmt.org/) and the Time's Up Now (https://www.timesupnow.com/) legal defense fund are also gaining momentum and showing no signs of stopping.

This chapter will examine the issue of sexual harassment in this era of #MeToo and Time's Up, and seek to provide candid and practical recommendations for both individuals and employers about how to deal with these issues at work. First, though, we will examine the legal definition of the problem, its prevalence, plus its impact on targets in order to set the context for the recommendations which will follow.

DEFINITION OF THE PROBLEM

Federal regulation 29 CFR § 1604.11 (2009) defines sexual harassment as follows:

> (a) Harassment on the basis of sex is a violation of section 703 of title VII. Unwelcome sexual advances, requests for sexual favors, and other verbal or physical conduct of a sexual nature constitute sexual harassment when (1) submission to such conduct is made either explicitly or implicitly a term or condition of an individual's employment, (2) submission to or rejection of such conduct by an individual is used as the basis for employment decisions affecting such individual, or (3) such conduct has the purpose or effect of unreasonably interfering with an individual's work performance or creating an intimidating, hostile, or offensive working environment.
>
> (b) In determining whether alleged conduct constitutes sexual harassment, the Commission will look at the record as a whole and at the totality of the circumstances, such as the nature of the sexual advances and the context in which the alleged incidents occurred. The determination of the legality of a particular action will be made from the facts, on a case by case basis.
>
> (c) [Reserved]
>
> (d) With respect to conduct between fellow employees, an employer is responsible for acts of sexual harassment in the workplace where the employer (or its agents or supervisory employees) knows or should have known of the conduct, unless it can show that it took immediate and appropriate corrective action.
>
> (e) An employer may also be responsible for the acts of non-employees, with respect to sexual harassment of employees in the workplace, where the employer (or its agents or supervisory employees) knows or should have known of the conduct and fails to take immediate and appropriate corrective action. In reviewing these cases the Commission will consider the extent of the employer's control and any other legal responsibility which the employer may have with respect to the conduct of such non-employees.
>
> (f) Prevention is the best tool for the elimination of sexual harassment. An employer should take all steps necessary to prevent sexual harassment from occurring, such as affirmatively raising the subject, expressing strong disap-

> proval, developing appropriate sanctions, informing employees of their right to raise and how to raise the issue of harassment under title VII, and developing methods to sensitize all concerned.
>
> (g) Other related practices: Where employment opportunities or benefits are granted because of an individual's submission to the employer's sexual advances or requests for sexual favors, the employer may be held liable for unlawful sex discrimination against other persons who were qualified for but denied that employment opportunity or benefit. (p. 198)

Courts and employers generally use the definition of sexual harassment contained in these guidelines. Moreover, this language has also formed the basis for most state laws prohibiting sexual harassment. It is important to note that a key part of the definition is the use of the word *unwelcome.* Unwelcome or uninvited conduct or communication of a sexual nature is prohibited. Conversely, welcome or invited actions or words are not unlawful. Sexual or romantic interaction between consenting people at work may be offensive to observe and may even violate company policy, but it is not sexual harassment.

The courts have generally concluded that a victim need not say or do a particular thing to indicate unwelcomeness. Courts will review all of the facts to make this determination and recognize that some victims may legitimately be afraid to complain (especially if the harasser is his or her boss or is acting physically intimidating in other ways).

Victims may be coerced into going along with sexual talk or activities because they believe they will be punished or fired if they protest. Consent can be given to a relationship and then withdrawn when the relationship ends. Once withdrawn, any continued romantic or sexual words or actions are not protected by the past consenting relationship, and may be considered sexual harassment.

The law prohibits unwelcome "sexual" conduct and words or actions "of a sexual nature." Some conduct, such as kissing, hugging, pinching, grabbing, blocking the victim's path, leering or staring, or standing very close to the victim may be either sexual or nonsexual, and must be evaluated in light of all relevant facts in order to make a determination of unlawfulness.

Another important part of the legal definition is that the conduct must be, among other things, *severe* and *pervasive.* A single uncomfortable incident will not generally rise to the level of actionable sexual harassment (although it could, depending on the circumstances). However, your company should not wait until conduct is unlawful before responding to it. The goal should be to prevent and remedy harassing behavior before it becomes so pervasive and severe that an employee is actually harmed by it.

PREVALENCE OF THE PROBLEM

It is useful to examine the prevalent statistics in order to understand just how many people are impacted by harassment at work. In January 2018, the nonprofit organization Stop Street Harassment commissioned a 2,000-person, nationally representative survey on sexual harassment and assault in the United States (Stop Street Harassment, 2018). This survey asked 1,000 women and 1,000 men about verbal harassment, sexual touching, cyber sexual harassment, being followed on the street, genital flashing, and sexual assault. Among its key findings:

> 81% of women and 43% of men reported experiencing some form of sexual harassment and/or assault in their lifetime, and 38% of women said they had experienced sexual harassment in the workplace. While verbal sexual harassment was the most common form (77% of women and 34% of men), an alarming 51% of women and 17% of men had been touched or groped in an unwelcome way. 41% of women and 22% of men said they were sexually harassed online. One-third of women and one in 10 men reported being physically followed, while 30% of women and 12% of men experienced genital flashing. 27% of women and 7% of men reported experiencing sexual assaults. (Stop Street Harassment, 2018)

The largest continuing study available to date, the *National Intimate Partner and Sexual Violence Survey* (conducted by the Centers for Disease Control and Prevention), focuses on physical harassment more than verbal. Its latest report indicated that 1 in 2 women and 1 in 5 men have experienced sexual violence other than rape during their lifetime; and, 1 in 5 women and 1 in 67 men reported rapes or attempted rapes (Black et al., 2011).

Another poll, from "*The Washington Post*/ABC News Poll" (2017), reported that more than half of American women had experienced "unwanted sexual advances" (n.p.). This 2017 poll used a broader catchall term rather than the specific behaviors outlined in the more recent Stop Street Harassment survey, which may account for the lower incidence rates (given that studies that ask about specific behaviors or that cover longer periods of time tend to report more harassment).

In 2016, the U.S. Equal Employment Opportunity Commission (EEOC) released a comprehensive study of workplace harassment in the United States. This study concluded that "anywhere from 25% to 85% of women report having experienced sexual harassment in the workplace" (Feldblum & Lipnic, 2016, p. 8). While it was noted in the report that this is a "strikingly wide gap," the EEOC concluded that the problem is very substantial even by its most conservative estimate—actually, they statistically predict that 1 in 4 people is affected by workplace sexual harassment. It is important to also note that some victims of sexual harassment are men. In fact, men filed nearly 17% of the sexual harassment complaints submitted to the EEOC in 2016 (Feldblum & Lipnic, 2016).

HOW HARASSMENT IMPACTS THE TARGETS

One of the most recent studies to report the impact of sexual harassment was published in May of 2017. This study found that women who were sexually harassed were 6.5 times more likely to change jobs than those who were not harassed (McLaughlin, Uggen, & Blackstone, 2017). In addition to the trauma of ending one's employment and the impact of such an early exit on one's future promotional opportunities, the next most obvious and immediate effect is that each departure diminishes the individual's lifetime earning power every time they must start over. In addition, an early exit diminishes the impact that the individual could have had on the organization through the continued contribution of their ideas—a loss not only to the individual's growth and development (and future promotional opportunities), but also a loss both to society and to our economy.

The study also found that women who experienced unwanted touching or multiple harassing behaviors reported "significantly greater financial stress" in the subsequent 2 years after the harassment ended (McLaughlin et al., 2017). The study highlighted how unwanted, unwelcomed sexual harassment can disrupt the career path of its innocent victims, and potentially leave them worse off financially. It also underscored the desperate measures that targets of harassment are forced to take in order to escape abusive workplaces.

Individuals who are harassed report stress-related conditions, such as anxiety and depression, trouble sleeping, a higher incidence of medical problems, and even pose a higher risk for suicide (Stop Street Harassment, 2018). Those who elect to file a complaint against their harassers often find it difficult to continue working within the same organization or may find it harder to land a new job due to being branded within their industry as a "troublemaker."

In a candid chronology in *The Atlantic* magazine about her personal experience of losing her job due to sexual harassment, writer Deborah Copaken (2018) stated:

> Sexual harassment, you would like to tell everyone, is not about sex. It's about a person in power systematically leveraging that power to lure you into his orbit and either proffer or take away your money, work, healthcare, and financial stability, depending on your positive or negative response to his sexual overtures. Respond in the affirmative, and you've prostituted yourself. Respond negatively, do not respond at all, or get a lawyer involved, and there goes your career. (para. 33)

Women who speak up are frequently blamed and retaliated against. They are often legitimately concerned about whether or not they will be believed or whether their organization will discount the issue as a "personality conflict" or feel that the harasser is a "star" and, therefore, too valuable to the organization for them to sideline or lose. In addition, even though retaliation is illegal, those who formally bring a charge frequently end up receiving poor performance evaluations after making a complaint (often resulting in the loss of their job), or they are marginalized within either their company or industry, or both.

If you consider what an ordeal it is (both emotionally and physically), and take into consideration what a poor career move it is, and how costly in terms of legal expenses it generally turns out to be for those who do elect to confront their harasser publicly, it is highly unlikely that a person would willingly put themselves under that microscope if they did not truly feel that they had somehow been wronged. In combination, shame, fear, high legal expenses, and cultural norms all conspire to allow sexual harassment to either not be reported at all, or to be underreported. It is important to consider that while men clearly have a strong motive to harass and then lie about it, women really do not have much of a motive to fabricate the truth or to bring false allegations. This is another way to assess a person's credibility when they decide to file a complaint.

COUNSEL FOR INDIVIDUALS

Recent events have provided an incredible foundation for the development of some basic rules of conduct—what I am referring to here as a *Not-So-Radical Workplace Manifesto*—10 suggestions for having a successful career (and for avoiding termination). Although these proposed rules are absurdly self-evident, recent scandals at workplaces throughout the nation suggest that they are not so well understood (or, if they are understood, they are not well-practiced).

Be forewarned, though: The rules contain some sexually charged language. It seems that some people need guidance about how to act at work that is crystal clear and unequivocal—what I think of as "knock you over the head" and extremely explicit kind of work rules. These suggestions are drawn directly from the shocking and sometimes jaw-dropping facts reported in the coverage of numerous recent high-level terminations (Berkowitz, 2017).

So, here it goes:

1. You should not harass or assault your coworkers or subordinates, regardless of your job title or rank. No one gets a free pass to treat others abusively.

2. Keep your hands to yourself. Other than a professional handshake or a friendly hug with a colleague who is also a friend, you should not physically touch your coworkers or subordinates, and you should definitely not have sex with them on your office desk or, to be clear, anywhere else at work.
3. Keep your private areas covered at work.
   - What this means for men is that you should keep your penis in your pants at all times, and you should never drop your pants to expose your underwear (or other body parts) to anyone at work.
   - For women, this means that you should not wear clothing that shows your cleavage or breasts, that is too tight or too short, or clothing that is best suited for after hours in a bar or on a date. If you dress like a sex object, don't feign surprise if you are viewed as one and treated accordingly. Ladies, you can't have it both ways. In a word, dress professionally for work and however you want to at home or on a date.
4. Do not masturbate in front of anyone at work. Comedian Samantha Bee, in her inimitable way, recently provided some memorable (but somewhat raunchy) counsel in this regard (Ramos, 2017)—and it's worth a look.
5. Do not text pictures of your genitalia to anyone, even upon request. People go to prison for this kind of stuff.
6. Do not text provocative photos of yourself to anyone. Even vacation photos of yourself in swimwear, underwear, or similar minimalist clothing (aka pictures suitable for a spread in *Victoria's Secret* catalog or the swimsuit edition of *Sports Illustrated* magazine) should not be sent to your boss or colleagues. If you are "friends" with people you work with on social media, do not post these types of picture there either.
7. Do not enter into a romantic relationship with your boss. Based on the disastrous situations that I have seen occur at work, be assured that these types of situations almost never end well.
8. Do not date or enter into a personal relationship with anyone that you supervise. If the relationship becomes more important to you than your work, take action. Find a new job or ask for a transfer.
9. Unless it is an invitation to a group gathering, do not ask employees or colleagues to come to your home. If there is a situation that requires such a visit, have the decency to greet them at the door fully clothed (and do not come out of your shower naked or appear in your underwear).
10. And, finally, if you feel that you are being sexually harassed at work (or witness someone else being harassed), report it immediately. The days of complicit silence are over.

Men and women will always be attracted to each other, and work is a great place to meet similarly minded people. However, it is important to act professionally at all times and draw appropriate and inviolable boundaries about work and play. Although it is still acceptable to compliment your colleagues at work, there is a big difference between "that's a nice dress" and "you look hot in that dress." Show up at the office each day focused on the work you are being paid by your employer to do—not on finding a date.

It's really not that hard. Work is work and play is play. Take great care to observe those boundaries and do not confuse the two. Remember that when most people go to work, they really just want to work.

Now that we have covered the individual perspective, we will turn our attention to the employer perspective and discuss what organizations can and should be doing in the wake of #MeToo and Time's Up.

RECOMMENDATIONS FOR EMPLOYERS

Although the laws and regulations have not changed, there has clearly been a seismic shift in the way we as a society have collectively begun to think about sexual assault, harassment, and other forms of similar misconduct at work. This recent spotlight on the problem suggests that employers are likely to experience an increase in formal complaints, or at least more inquiries from employees about their policies and processes. As a result, employers should revisit their internal practices to ensure that they are providing appropriate safeguards to protect all employees from abuse at work. At the same time, such a review should also focus on ensuring that safeguards are in place to protect the company from potential legal liability.

No industry and no employer is immune from the potential for a costly, embarrassing, and egregious harassment situation; as a result, the focus of all employer efforts should be on *prevention*—creating the processes and systems needed to help create a culture of respect and accountability where harassment is simply not a viable option.

Here are some ideas you and your company may want to internally discuss and consider (in conjunction with both your legal counsel and HR team). In addition, there are some potential problem areas that you may want to audit and questions that you may want to strategically ask in order to be sure your company's strategy is comprehensively designed to both prevent and effectively respond to potential claims of sexual harassment if (and when) they happen:

1. ***Do you have an effective anti-harassment policy and complaint procedure?***

At a minimum, a comprehensive policy and complaint procedure should include the following elements:

- a clear explanation of the prohibited conduct (This should include a prohibition about sexual harassment [and that it specifically includes contact that is both physical and/or verbal, and through email, texts, and social media postings] *and* that also prohibits any other forms of harassment based on a protected status [including race, ethnicity, and religion]. It should specify that the policy applies to both employees and nonemployees, both on the job and at company-sponsored social events);
- an unequivocal statement that those who complain will be protected from retaliation;
- a clearly described complaint process that provides accessible avenues of complaint (and preferably several different ways to make the complaint);
- assurance that the employer will protect the confidentiality of the complainant—*to the extent possible*;
- a process that provides for a fast, thorough, and impartial investigation by an experienced investigator; and
- assurance that the employer will take immediate and appropriate corrective action if it determines that harassment has occurred.

Importantly, it should be noted that the U.S. EEOC has recently issued guidance about promising practices to prevent harassment ("Promising Practices for Preventing Harassment," n.d.). These guidelines provide clear recommendations about what constitutes a comprehensive and effective harassment policy and complaint system, guidance about leadership and accountability, as well as suggestions about effective training and communication practices. Employers are advised to review all of the laws, regulations, and information on the EEOC's website (https://www.eeoc.gov/laws/types/sexual_harassment.cfm), and consider implementing their detailed recommendations to the maximum extent practicable.

2. ***Do you require those who witness sexual harassment to notify the company of its occurrence and, if so, do you train them about what to do?***

An emerging best practice is to include in your policy and training a requirement for "bystanders" (e.g., those who may witness the bad behavior but not be directly involved in the situation) to affirmatively notify the company of the potential problem and to intervene as may be appropriate given the facts of the situation (e.g., by disrupting the situation, asking the victim to meet in the break room to extract them from an uncomfortable moment and/or to tell them that you noticed the problem, by asking questions after the incident to explore the person's intent and/or to let them know that what they did or said was inappropriate, or simply by saying something like "that joke wasn't funny").

This strategy has reportedly shown promise in the military, on college campuses, and by nonprofits (Miller, 2017). Including this requirement in your policy will ensure that *all* employees are accountable for ensuring that sexual harassment is not permitted to exist in your organization—at least not for long.

3. ***Do you broadly and regularly disseminate the harassment policy and conduct expectations to employees?***

Employers should provide every employee with a copy of the policy and complaint procedures and redistribute it periodically. Companies should also post it in central locations (e.g., bulletin boards, Intranet, etc.), and incorporate the policy into their code of business conduct as well as their employee and manager handbooks. It is advisable to also require employees to sign an acknowledgment that they have read, understand, and agree to abide by the policy's terms at the time of their initial hire and annually thereafter (or at least every other year at a minimum).

In addition, communications to employees should also stress the company's expectation that employees will notify management or human resources immediately if they witness any behavior that even *may* be in violation of the company's policy against harassment. A common way to communicate this expectation to employees is this: "If you see something, say something; otherwise, your silence makes you complicit in perpetuating the problem." Or in the words of Mahatma Gandhi (n.d.), "Silence becomes cowardice when occasion demands speaking out the whole truth and acting accordingly" (para. 1).

4. ***Are senior leaders actively involved in setting the tone and a "culture of respect" for the organization?***

Senior leaders must be actively viewed as serious about enforcing not only a "culture of compliance" (e.g., simply putting out a policy in an attempt to comply with the law and minimize litigation expenses), but, more importantly, a "culture of respect" that includes treating all employees fairly and with dignity (Daniel, 2003). If management fails to allocate appropriate time and resources for training and communication, does not attend training sessions, or are seen as joking about the policy and the seriousness of the issue (or worse yet, are actually seen engaging in the harassment of an employee or customer), it will seriously undermine the company's efforts to ensure a harassment-free workplace.

It is also helpful for executives to be kick-off speakers for annual training sessions, and to be involved in activities such as sending letters to employees, broadcasting video messages, making personal appearances at department meetings, writing in company newsletters, and so on. Most importantly, senior executives must model the expected behavior, and quickly intervene if they see a colleague treating another employee in an inappropriate manner. A respectful culture starts at the top. If employees begin to believe that they can get away with mistreating their coworkers, not only are the victims demoralized and harassed, but witnesses and bystanders (including men) are likely to begin to mistrust senior leaders and view them as out of touch or simply uncaring about how employees are being treated.

5. Do you conduct quick and thorough investigations upon receipt of a complaint?

An independent, fact-finding investigation by a neutral party should be launched immediately upon receipt of a complaint. It may also be necessary to take immediate action to ensure that further harassment does not occur while the investigation is taking place (e.g., by making scheduling changes, transferring the alleged harasser, or placing the alleged harasser on non-disciplinary leave with pay pending the conclusion of the investigation). If employees do not believe that issues of sexual harassment are being treated seriously by the company and its senior leaders, they are more likely to escalate their complaints by going outside of their company's reporting procedures. Employers should make it clear that investigations will be thorough, and that the punishment will fit the seriousness of the offense, regardless of the offender's status or role within the organization.

6. Do you implement prompt corrective action at the conclusion of an investigation, if warranted?

Remedial measures should be designed to:

- *Stop the harassment* (e.g., oral or written warning, transfer or reassignment, demotion, reduction of wages, suspension, discharge, training or counseling, and post-event monitoring to ensure that there is no retaliation and that the harassment has stopped).
- *Correct its effects on the employee* (e.g., restoration of leave taken by the employee because of the harassment, expungement of any negative evaluations that are unmerited, reinstatement, an apology by the harasser, monitoring treatment of the employee to ensure no retaliation occurs in the future, and other appropriate "make whole" actions appropriate to the circumstances).

- *Ensure that the harassment does not recur* (e.g., the discipline imposed on the harasser should be proportional to the seriousness of the offense, up to and including termination).

Importantly, for those who choose to violate obvious standards of appropriate workplace conduct, the consequences should be swift. Accountability has to be tough to be real.

7. Do you provide counseling and assistance for targets of harassment?

Sexual harassment can have serious and long-lasting consequences for the individual who has been victimized. As a result, organizations should offer immediate access to qualified counselors who have been trained to diagnose and treat these types of issues in order to minimize the longer-term emotional impact that the sexual harassing incident may have on the individual.

8. Do you hold frequent and mandatory anti-harassment training sessions?

Periodic, interactive training about sexual harassment, the company's policy against it, and the complaint and response process can help to ensure that all employees and managers understand what it is and how to identify it (with examples), as well as their responsibility to act if they see it happening (e.g., notify their supervisor, HR, or senior management of the potential problem). Training should be provided to employees at every level and every location of your organization. Ideally, it should include role-playing exercises and active discussions about real-life scenarios so that employees can "practice" how to respond.

9. Do you hold expanded training sessions for supervisors and managers?

Because supervisors and managers have additional responsibilities, and are generally held to a higher standard of expected conduct, there should be special training for them to make sure that they are fully aware of their duties and responsibilities to act under the company's policy and complaint procedures. Employers who demonstrate that they have fully informed all employees and managers about the policy and procedures are far more likely to avoid potential liability as well.

10. Do you communicate your company's expectations about expected workplace conduct at regular intervals?

In addition to reaffirming the company's harassment policy and complaint procedure, it is also recommended that regular communications to employees also reinforce the company's expectations that employees will engage in civil and respectful interactions with their coworkers—at all times and regardless of level.

11. Do you evaluate your anti-harassment policy and practices regularly?

It is advisable to undertake an annual audit of your policies and practices to ensure that they continue to comply with current laws, and EEOC guidelines and recommended best practices ("Sexual Harassment," n.d.), updating them as necessary. It is essential that training is conducted in a serious and regular manner, and that employees feel empowered to report harassment if they personally experience it or see it happening to others. This means that they must trust their leaders and the company's system to be fair and to protect them.

12. Do you take proactive steps to prevent harassment that go beyond the minimum required by law?

Comprehensive policies and complaint procedures are absolutely critical components of a strong anti-harassment effort. But taking action that goes beyond simply what is mandated by law is essential to ensure that your company's efforts are not perceived as mere response to meet legal requirements and to protect the company from litigation. Companies who approach the problem from that perspective will not affect organizational culture.

Periodic employee surveys, training that encourages workplace civility and a respectful workplace, bystander intervention training, inclusion of the way an individual treats subordinates and/or coworkers in performance evaluations, and reviews of internal metrics (e.g., complaints, increases in workers' compensation, absenteeism, etc.) are examples of proactive ways to do more than just perfunctorily issue a policy, require employees to attend an annual training session, and call it "good."

In addition, companies with more gender equity tend to have fewer complaints of sexual harassment (Cooper, 2017). Why? Because harassment tends to flourish when men are in power and women are in less senior roles. Importantly, then, paying and promoting men and women equally, and including both genders on teams, can go a long way toward minimizing the risk of harassment in your workplace (Miller, 2017).

In addition to these policy-related considerations, here are a few other ideas that employers may wish to consider in order to strengthen internal practices and further protect their companies:

13. Do you regularly review the number of complaints and lawsuits, both cumulatively and among specific departments, in an effort to spot emerging patterns or problems?

Data related to complaints, lawsuits, workers compensation, attendance, and medical costs should be regularly reviewed to spot potential problems in certain divisions or departments that may be developing so that preventive measures can be quickly employed

14. Do you conduct appropriate due diligence prior to hiring a new employee?

Due diligence should be conducted prior to making an offer to most new hires, not only to ensure organizational "fit" but also to determine if the candidate has a record of bad behavior. Conducting background investigations and mining the candidate's social media to uncover offensive photos or postings can be a rich source of information that can protect the company from making an inadvisable hiring decision.

15. Do you include provisions within your employment contracts to protect the company if an executive engages in misconduct?

If an executive is terminated for misconduct, the last thing you want is for them to walk away with a golden parachute that could be viewed as a "reward" for their bad behavior. Instead, it is advisable to include what is often referred to as a *clawback* provision in your employment contracts that clearly states that if an individual's employment is terminated for cause (e.g., confirmed violation of company policy, sexual misconduct, financial fraud, embezzlement, etc.), then the agreement is automatically terminated, and no further payments are due.

16. Do you regularly advise senior management and your board of directors about policy changes, and provide them with data about internal complaints and significant lawsuit filings?

It is suggested that both senior leaders and your board be notified about significant changes to your policy and procedures, as well as data regarding complaints and lawsuits. This will allow them to be informed and vigilant about identifying trends so that they can ensure that preventive measures are implemented and regulatory disclosures are timely made.

17. Do you have procedures and an internal team in place that will help you to determine whether or not a public disclosure is required?

Some significant terminations, resignations, or complaints (e.g., against an executive officer or board member) trigger obligations which require the company to file specific documents with the Securities and Exchange Commission (e.g., Form 8-K, proxy, etc.). Moreover, in certain cases, a public company may have an obligation to publicly disclose harassment claims, lawsuits, or investigations to the extent that the matter is likely to have a quantitatively or qualitatively material impact on the company.

18. Are you prepared to respond quickly if a full-blown crisis happens within your company?

It is important to be prepared to respond quickly in the event of a significant harassment complaint or termination event, especially when it involves a senior executive or member of your board of directors. Take steps to identify the appropriate team of experts who should be involved before a problem surfaces in your organization. Retention of a public relations and/or crisis management firm in advance is useful so that you can agree on a preliminary response protocol.

It is also highly recommended that you retain experienced outside counsel now so that they will be ready to help you sort through the complicated issues that a high-level event will likely trigger. In addition, auditing your practices and procedures and proactively reviewing employment agreements to determine relevant termination provisions on a regular basis will ensure that you are ready to appropriately respond to any significant issue that may come your way.

CONCLUSIONS

Recent events have demonstrated that harassment at work is still a huge and pervasive problem. Anti-harassment laws have been in place now for nearly 3 decades, yet there have still been more than 12,000 harassment claims filed with the Equal Employment Opportunity Commission each year since 2010 ("Charges Alleging Sex-Based Harassment (FY 2010–FY 2017)," n.d.). It must be noted, though, that there has never been a #MeToo or Time's Up movement—until now. Together, these initiatives are likely to be a catalyst for real and lasting change by shining a bright light on what we, as a civil society, will and will not tolerate as acceptable workplace behavior going forward.

It is important to understand that this renewed sense of urgency to combat sexual harassment is not a fight between men and women. As the issue was further explained in a 2018 *Harvard Business Review* article: "It's a fight over whether a small subgroup of predatory men should be allowed to interfere with the ability of employees to show up and do what they signed up for: work" (*Harvard Business Review* Staff, 2018, para. 5).

Although the standards for accountability may be in flux, this much is clear: Eradicating sexual harassment from our workplaces can no longer be relegated to a company's HR department. It is everyone's job—and it will take all of us working together to have even a remote chance of really fixing the problem.

The #MeToo movement has begun to shift social attitudes, and has inspired widespread calls for change. It has also resulted in unprecedented accountability. Harassment is increasingly being viewed by major corporations and their boards of directors not just as a potential legal liability, but also as an issue carrying the potential for serious reputational and business risk (Kantor, 2018). Its persistence and prevalence, coupled with our collective inability to stop it, though, suggests that it will be tough to eradicate from our organizations. However, it is critical that we not only *try*, but that companies take action to move more women into positions of power (perhaps the ultimate solution to ending sexual harassment), and change corporate cultures across the United States to finally get the job done.

It is way beyond the time to say farewell to the world where men can treat the workplace like a fraternity house or a pornography shoot. As stated on the Time's Up (n.d.) website:

> The clock has run out on sexual assault, harassment and inequality in the workplace. It's time to do something about it... No more silence. No more waiting. No more tolerance for discrimination, harassment or abuse. TIME'S UP™. (n.p.)

DISCLAIMER

The information contained in this article is for informational purposes only and not for the purpose of providing legal advice. You should contact your attorney to obtain advice with respect to any particular issue or problem, including making revisions or updates to your sexual harassment policies and procedures. Use of and access to this article does not create an attorney–client relationship between the author and the user. And lastly, the opinions expressed in this article are the opinions of the author and may or may not reflect the opinions of the university.

REFERENCES

Berkowitz, J. (2017, November 1). Here's the complete list of men accused of sexual harassment since Harvey Weinstein. *Fast Company*. Retrieved from https://www.fastcompany.com/40489989/heres-the-ever-growing-list-of-men-accused-of-sexual-harassment-since-weinstein

Black, M. C., Basile, K. C., Breiding, M. J., Smith, S. G., Walters, M. L., Merrick, M. T., ... Stevens, M. R. (2011). *The national intimate partner and sexual violence survey (NISVS): 2010 summary report*. Atlanta, GA: National Center for Injury Prevention and Control, Centers for Disease Control and Prevention.

Cooper, M. (2017, November 27). *The 3 things that make organizations more prone to sexual harassment*. The Atlantic. Retrieved from https://www.theatlantic.com/business/archive/2017/11/organizations-sexual-harassment/546707/

Daniel, T. A. (2003, Fall). Developing a "culture of compliance" to prevent sexual harassment. *Employment Relations Today, 30*(3), 33–42.

Harvey Weinstein Timeline: How the Scandal Unfolded. (2019, January 10). Retrieved from http://www.bbc.com/news/entertainment-arts-41594672

Charges Alleging Sex-Based Harassment (FY 2010–FY 2017). (n.d.). Retrieved from https://www.eeoc.gov/eeoc/statistics/enforcement/sexual_harassment_new.cfm

Copaken, D. (2018, March 9). How to lose your job from sexual harassment in 33 easy steps. *The Atlantic.* Retrieved from https://www.theatlantic.com/entertainment/archive/2018/03/how-to-lose-your-job-from-sexual-harassment-in-33-easy-steps/555197/?utm_source=newsletter&utm_medium=email&utm_campaign=atlantic-weekly-newsletter&utm_content=2018030

Feldblum, C. R., & Lipnic, V. A. (2016, June). *U. S. equal employment opportunity commission, select task force on the study of harassment in the workplace.* Retrieved from https://www.eeoc.gov/eeoc/task_force/harassment/upload/report.pdf

Gandhi, M. (n.d.). *Quotable quotes by Mahatma Gandhi.* Retrieved from https://www.goodreads.com/quotes/51203-silence-becomes-cowardice-when-occasion-demands-speaking-out-the-whole

Gladwell, M. (2002). *The tipping point: How little things can make a big difference.* Boston, MA: Little.

Gurchiek, K. (2018, March 7). *Timeline: Sexual harassment allegations and the workplace.* Retrieved from https://www.shrm.org/hr-today/news/hr-news/pages/timeline-sexual-harassment-allegations-swamp-the-workplace.aspx

Harvard Business Review Staff. (2018, February 22). *Work after #MeToo, your questions answered.* Retrieved from https://hbr.org/2018/02/work-after-metoo-your-questions-answered

Kantor, J. (2018, March 23). #MeToo called for an overhaul. Are workplaces really changing? *The New York Times.* Retrieved from https://www.nytimes.com/2018/03/23/us/sexual-harassment-workplace-response.html

McLaughlin, H., Uggen, C., & Blackstone, A. (2017, May 10). The economic and career effects of sexual harassment on working women. *Gender & Society, 31*(3), 333–358. Retrieved from http://journals.sagepub.com/doi/pdf/10.1177/0891243217704631

Miller, C. C. (2017, December 11). Sexual harassment training doesn't work. But some things do. *The New York Times.* Retrieved from https://www.nytimes.com/2017/12/11/upshot/sexual-harassment-workplace-prevention-effective.html

Promising Practices for Preventing Harassment. (n.d.). Retrieved from https://www.eeoc.gov/eeoc/publications/promising-practices.cfm

Ramos, D. R. (2017, October 11). *Samantha Bee shares "penis PSA" in wake of Hollywood's sexual harassment scandals* [Video file]. Retrieved from https://deadline.com/2017/10/samantha-bee-penis-psa-harvey-weinstein-scandal-1202186895/

Sexual Harassment. (n.d.). Retrieved from https://www.eeoc.gov/laws/types/sexual_harassment.cfm

Sexual Harassment, 29 C.F.R. § 1604.11 (2009, July 1).

Stop Street Harassment. (2018, February). *The facts behind the #MeToo movement: A national study on sexual harassment and assault.* Retrieved from http://www.stopstreetharassment.org/wp-content/uploads/2018/01/Full-Report-2018-National-Study-on-Sexual-Harassment-and-Assault.pdf

Time's Up. (n.d.). Retrieved from https://www.timesupnow.com/
Washington Post/ABC News Poll. (2017, October 11–15). Retrieved from http://apps.washingtonpost.com/g/page/politics/washington-post-abc-news-poll-oct-11-15-2017/2249/

CHAPTER 10

JOIN THE PEACE TRAIN

Incorporating Peace-Building Principles and Practices in Your Organization

Christina Murtaugh

On October 5, 2017, the *New York Times* outlined egregious and violent behavior by entertainment mogul Harvey Weinstein—decades-long patterns of rape, harassment, intimidation, and retaliation (Kantor & Twohey, 2017). In subsequent reports, the role of other leaders within the organization and the industry as a whole demonstrated that this individual behavior was supported by the system and culture of the entertainment industry (Farrow, 2017). These reports also concluded that the dynamics of phenomena—the direct actions of Mr. Weinstein, the systems' omission to hold Mr. Weinstein accountable, and the mentality within the culture—were harmful to the victims' survival, well-being, freedom, and identity. Mr. Weinstein was the center of multidimensional violence within his company and the entertainment industry more broadly.

This is a blatant example of the three types of causes of violence that people can face in their professions: direct, structural, and cultural. This chapter aims to help you understand these causes and results of violence in our

From Discord to Harmony, pages 171–187

professional lives as well as how the practices to build peace can facilitate the development of positive, productive work environments.[1] Past efforts on workplace violence have largely focused on blatant, direct causes—physical safety, homicide and suicide, and sexual and physical assault (including threats). Other business administration efforts look at structural and cultural violence through the lens of bad behavior and workplace satisfaction. This chapter will utilize peace and conflict principles to break down these traditional silos to help understand the full scope of violence within our work life. As readers consider how violence and harm is occurring in their teams, organizations, and industries, the chapter will then leverage peacebuilding approaches—honed over the past 50 years around the world—to provide practical approaches and activities to reduce violence and support the constructive management of conflicts.

WHY CARE ABOUT PEACE AT WORK

My journey to see organizations through peace and conflict paradigms sparked through a single conversation with a human resources specialist who worked for an organization with a mission to build peaceful societies. In discussing patterns within the organization, I made the comment, "I don't understand why we aren't listening to the advice we give governments and organizations around the world." This human resource expert posited back, "This is a job. It is a transaction. We pay you, and in return you carry out your job duties. We aren't the work we do." I was frustrated and crushed—both because this human resource person didn't understand the work we actually did building peace around the world, and that her transactional mentality was informing a host of policies and actions across the organization. I was also able to reflect and recognize that I—as a mid-level professional within the organization—had agency and power to reduce the harm and facilitate a positive work environment. This chapter aims to capture how I came to understand both the principles and practices of developing peaceful organizations.

While I have bought into the positive role peace-building can play within our work life, why should you, as the executive, mid-level manager, or support staff? In short, you, your team, and your organization will be happier, healthier, and more successful. There is a strong correlation between satisfaction and engagement at work with productivity and profitability for organizations (Fulmer, Gerhart, & Scott, 2003; Harter, Schmidt, Agrawal, Plowman, & Blue, 2016). Peaceful workplaces will manifest in both the attitudes and behaviors of employees. Consider the alternative to peace in the workplace. Violence in the workplace is both on the rise and costly. In 2016, violence-related fatalities at work were the highest since 2010, while suicide was the highest since 1992, when data was first collected (Bureau of Labor Statistics, 2017). Studies from the 2000s put the cost of workplace injuries from violence around $202 billion per year (Cartwright, 2013; Hoobler & Swarberg, 2006). These numbers are only capturing one piece of the overall violence at the workplace, as only direct forms of violence are even tracked and studied.

Before diving into the principles of peace, violence, and conflict, it is also important to note what this chapter is not about. There is ample evidence that corporations contribute to peace and violence within the broader society. Consider, for example, the assaults and deaths of community members perpetrated by private security forces of corporations mining for natural resources, the environmental degradation from oil spills, or the psychological trauma inflicted by human traffickers. These are all important forms of violence to study and prevent. This chapter, however, is focused on the violence within organizations rather than between organizations and society more broadly.

What Violence Happens at Work

Peace is infused in cultures across the globe. Peace train. Peace out. Peace be upon you. You can hear the term espoused by religious leaders, read it in social media feeds, see its symbol at protests. Yet, few people take the time to understand the meaning and application of peace in our work lives. This section will first consider the definition of peace and the related terms of violence and conflict. It will then discuss their importance to organizations.

Definitions of peace fall into two broad categories: negative and positive. Negative peace is the absence of direct harm to people. Positive peace is when every person has his or her needs met. Both terms can also be defined by the absence of violence. Negative peace is the absence of direct violence. In addition to direct violence, positive peace is also the absence of structural and cultural violence. Given the interconnectedness of peace and violence, understanding the definition of violence is also critical.

At its most basic level, violence is the cause of harm to someone. Johan Galtung provided the most holistic definitions of both the causes and the harms, referenced in Table 10.1 (Galtung, 1996; Galtung & Fischer, 2013). Each cause can contribute to a harm, with cultural violence manifesting across a myriad of mediums (Galtung, 1990).

Building negative peace is focused on barriers to direct survival—for example, killing and assault. Building positive peace, conversely, is focused on eliminating barriers to all causes and harms. Each cause also may lead to varying levels of harm. For example, both murder and assault are direct violence on a person's survival—just different degrees of harm. In addition

TABLE 10.1 The Causes and Harms of Violence

Cause	Harm
Direct Acts of Commission	*Survival* Ability to Live
Structural Acts of Omission	*Wellness* Ability to Decent Life
Cultural Justification for Direct and Structural	*Freedom* Liberty and Ability to Make Choices
	Identity Ability to Maintain Humanity

to the potential for varying degrees of harm, some causes of violence may harm multiple human needs (see Table 10.2). Racism, for example, is structural violence that can harm all four core human needs.

This chapter uses the term *violence* throughout to highlight the various forms of harm that are often ignored or discounted within organizations. While some research and practice have explored negative peace within organizations—especially criminal forms of violence and suicide—language used for other forms of violence, such as bad behavior, incivility, and toxic culture connotes less harm that other forms of violence. In reality, the results of direct, structural, and cultural violence can be equally harmful.

How do harms emerge? Harms are formed from conflict, a natural part of living that occurs when two or more people pursue incompatible goals (Snodderly, 2011). Conflicts are not always violent—they can create positive transformation and innovation. The key is ensuring that individuals, structures, and cultures constructively manage conflicts to limit harm. So, in the workplace, consider how you can continue to support all employees' needs while managing and transforming the conflicts. This chapter primarily

TABLE 10.2 Causes of Violence in Relation to Harm to the Core Human Needs

	Harm			
Cause	**Survival**	**Wellness**	**Freedom**	**Identity**
Direct	Death	Assault Misery	Repression Expulsion	Desocialization Dehumanization
Structural	Exploitation	Exploitation	Division Segmentation	Marginalization
Cultural	Religion, Ideology, Language, Art, Education, Sciences			

Source: Galtung, 1990, p. 292

focuses on how to react to the violence that emerges from destructive conflicts. The final part of the chapter will also include examples of how organizations can work strategically to constructively harness conflicts within the workplace before destructive violence takes place.

> **IS THERE WORKPLACE VIOLENCE?**
>
> A manager in a small media company refuses to address an intimate relationship between two employees. From the manager's vantage point, this relationship was a private matter and, therefore, didn't impact the workplace. Now, one might ask why an intimate relationship between two people is violence. Where is the harm? Harm is context specific. So, consider an additional piece of information: One of the partners had previously had relationships with other members of the team. If the manager ignores the issue, the manager could potentially foster structural violence—omitting to understand the full context of the intimate relationship and its impact within the workplace.
>
> In the above circumstance, all those engaged in the intimate relationship have a new, sexualized identity in addition to their identity as a professional. Is there workplace violence? The manager will assess whether direct acts, structural omissions, or workplace culture are harming these identities. Gossip within the workplace may inculcate negative, demeaning names for those having the intimate relationship—for example, homewrecker or slut. A manager refusing to address workplace culture then creates a harmful structure. At that point, two forms of workplace violence exist. As will be discussed in the section on applying peace-building practices, there are a number of approaches the manager could take in this situation to support the needs of all the members—including the two in a new relationship. The point here is that ignoring single events contributes to workplace violence.

When Violence Happens at Work

Understanding what violence and conflict mean to the workplace is a great step toward fostering a positive-peace organization. Next, you will want to consider when violence is occurring. Research from the peace-building field demonstrates that violence is often cyclical—"every civil war that began since 2003 was a resumption of a previous civil war" (World Bank, 2011, p. 57). The United States is not an exception to these cycles either (Turchin, 2016). When root issues of the violence are not addressed, violent symptoms can also morph from one cause to another, and change the human needs they are impacting. In considering the temporality of violence at work, inherent conflicts can play a role. Consider a business' life cycle from start-up to decline (see Figure 10.1).

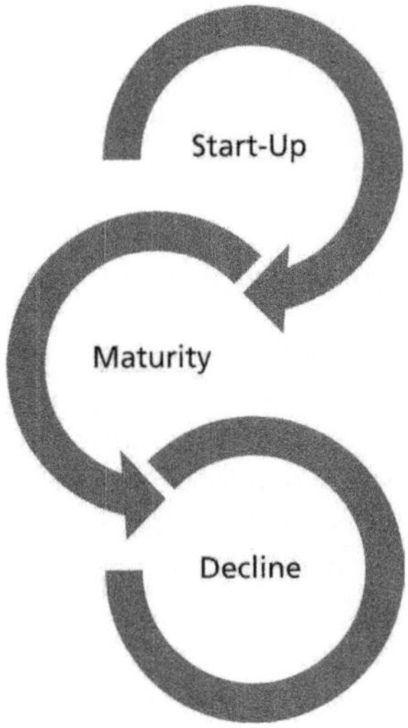

Figure 10.1 The life cycle of a business.

In the start-up phase, organizations are faced with a number of conflicts within the process of founding—defining the brand position, creating revenue out of product and service ideas, establishing a legal structure, and deciding which human and technical resources to invest in, to name a few. Conflicts may come from different visions among founders, diverse priorities of investors, or changes in the global marketplace. It is also in this phase that the organization is setting the foundation to manage these conflicts. Constructive processes can set up the organization for a peaceful workplace, while destructive processes may lay roots of violence that will mutate throughout the company's lifecycle.

CONFLICT DURING START-UP: LYFT VERSUS UBER

The contrasting year Uber and Lyft faced in 2017 demonstrates how managing conflicts during the start-up phase of a company is essential in determining the level of direct, structural, and cultural violence within the workplace. Uber's internal workplace conditions publicly surfaced in 2017, lifting a curtain that revealed a violent workplace that was inculcated as the company moved from start-up to maturity. Several reports simultaneously highlighted the difference in Lyft, Uber's smaller competitor, in transforming the transportation and delivery industries.

Uber's workplace conditions reportedly included sexual harassment and groping, homophobic slurs, and incentives that prioritized revenue and growth metrics over and above treatment of colleagues, to name a few (Isaac,

2017). These direct actions were either ignored or mismanaged by leadership and human resources (Fowler, 2017). These symptoms were rooted in a culture that manifested conflicts and then mismanaged them. Values focused on achieving growth and revenue above the acts people took or the structure and culture that developed. The fallout from the publicity of the violent workplace were measured in loss of monetary value and the shedding of the CEO and dozens of executives (Carson & Gould, 2017).

In comparison, Lyft focused on inclusion and authenticity. Research groups built support systems for employees within the company, and leadership routinely carried out roles of customers to experience their company's culture in action, focusing on the relationship between driver and rider rather than the transaction (Morgan, 2017; Peretez, 2018). In 2017, Lyft grew geographically, in number of customers and in monetary investments.

Companies that successfully manage conflicts during the start-up phase may not be out of the woods. As new conflicts emerge—particularly transitioning from start-up to maturity, and then during successive phases of growth, rebranding, or decline—the potential for destructiveness exists. However, companies can create processes to assess the degree of direct, structural, and cultural violence (and positive peace) throughout the life cycle of the organization.

In addition to the business cycle, each organization is an interconnected system; therefore, where violence occurs within the organization is also important.

Where Violence Happens at Work

The workplace is an ecosystem that, at its core, is a series of structured relationships between individual people. Those structures may be laid out by organizational structure or developed informally through shared experiences or identities. The ecosystem also expands beyond the formal workplace hierarchy—partners, beneficiaries, and competitors impact your organization.

When considering whether violence exists—and consequently how to transform the system into a peaceful organization—understanding where violence occurs within the ecosystem is critical. Moreover, intentionally or not, violence by one individual or within one team will often have consequences elsewhere within the organization. Developing a map of your organizations' ecosystem can assist in the process of understanding where violence exists and how it might be interconnected (see Figure 10.2). With the understanding of the entire ecosystem, capturing where violence may

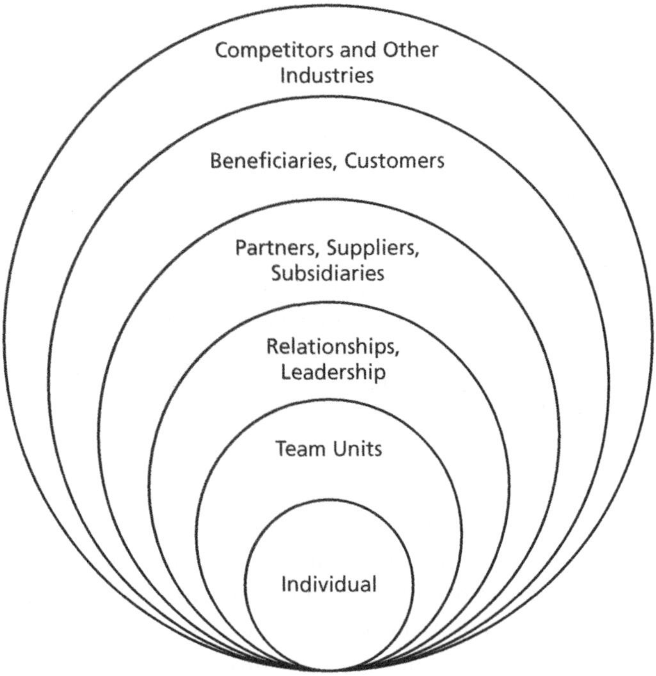

Figure 10.2 An organization's ecosystem.

be occurring can help move you from reacting to single events to proactively changing structures and cultures.

HOW TO LIMIT VIOLENCE AND FACILITATE PEACE

The previous section focused on understanding the potential violence within workplaces: what types of violence, when that violence may take place, and where it may occur. Common to all this is that violence within organizations is dynamic—it could have many causes and consequences, it could build off of existing forms or spur new forms of violence, and violence that appears unrelated could be connected. No individual can eradicate this complex problem. So, where do you fit into the change?

This section will focus on what individuals in the organization can do to cultivate positive peace. It will begin by discussing sources of power that individuals can utilize in leveraging agency in the process of change. It will then discuss the basics of change processes. Finally, it will outline dialogic and nonviolent action approaches to building positive peace within an organization.

Finding Your Agency

Everyone within a workplace has agency to desire and, therefore, launch change processes. The agency in change is borne from individual and collective power—the ability to act or influence others' actions. As you consider how to cultivate power for change, the first step is to assess your own power within the work place. The following are examples of sources of power to consider:[2]

- *Decision-Making*—This power includes the decisions inherent in your role and your influence on others with decision-making power;
- *Financial*—This power focuses on the amount of money you control, such as the size of your team's budget or the amount of revenue your team brings to your business. You can also assess your influence on internal revenue, such as your control over salary and bonuses.
- *Moral*—This power focuses on the degree others perceive you as ethical, honest, and principled.
- *Intrinsic*—This power focuses on your knowledge, skills, and abilities.

Once you have considered your own sources of power, you will want to strategize on both what sources of power are needed and the level of power needed to create transformative change. As will be discussed below, you can utilize both dialogic and nonviolent action to increase the sources of power.

Managing Change

Peace-building aims to create an environment where systems can change—and within those systems individuals spearhead that change. The key for developing systems change is for people within the organization to understand where the organization is in comparison to where the organization wants to be (see Figure 10.3; Leroux-Martin & O'Connor, 2017; Senge, 2006; Stroh, 2015).

The process of changing systems is rarely linear. Thus, most change processes will require flexibility and adaptation to the changes as they occur. This will bring about its own set of conflicts—both to the individuals being asked to change attitudes, behaviors, and conduct, and to the relationships between people and teams. Organizations may want to assess and supplement their capacity to manage flexible change.

The adaptive change required may also raise questions regarding accountability. Throughout many segments of American society, individualism is prioritized over collectivism. Our solutions to workplace violence and misconduct likewise prioritize individual accountability over system accountability.

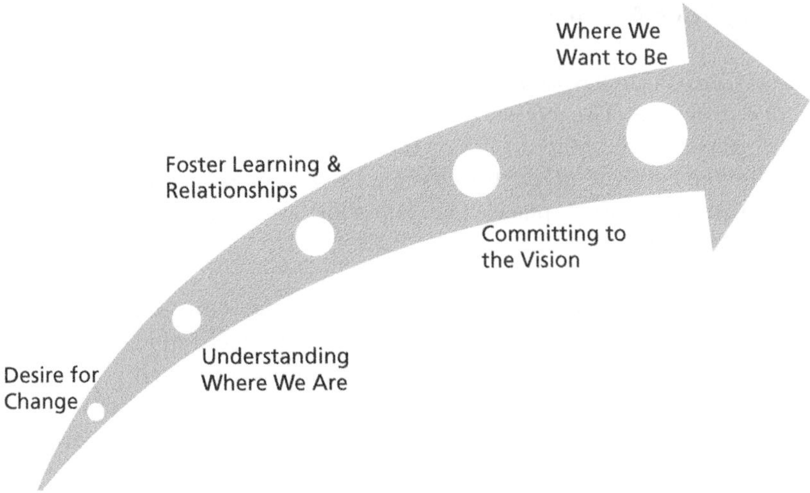

Figure 10.3 The process of changing systems.

In practice, organizations may resort to a demotion, transfer, or firing, depending on the degree of violence involved. Individual action may be a symptom, rather that the cause, of violence. Therefore, simply removing someone from the organization will not lead to sustained change.

THE ASIA FOUNDATION'S INNOVATION: STRATEGY TESTING TO MONITOR SYSTEMS CHANGE

Consider the role systems-thinking and adaptive change principles might play in leveraging information on single events into identifying patterns as well as into an understanding of the structures and culture at play. The traditional mechanisms used to monitor program performance in the peacebuilding field are logic frameworks, indicator targets, and assessing success to targets. The process assumes a level of certainty in how the change will occur, which is deficient when changing power and relationships in violent systems. The Asia Foundation, a nonprofit organization focused on development in Asia, developed an approach rooted in mapping experiences from diverse constituencies throughout the change process (Ladner, 2015).

Their monitoring begins with articulating a hypothesis on what change will occur—their strategy—based on existing knowledge of the problem and barriers to change. At iterative points—every few months—the team carries out a testing workshop. They each identify events, changes in context, and internal decisions since their previous check-in. Through this timeline, they analyze how this information changes their understanding of the problem and barriers to change. These dialogues could be externally or internally facilitated, depending on the team's context. They finally make adjustments to their strategy, as needed.

Taking this approach to monitoring change within a society, organizations, and teams can move beyond yearly workplace assessments and utilize this mapping approach to understand their own internal direct acts, structures, and cultures that may be causing violence. Each individual can keep an ongoing account of events they have experienced and observed. At specific intervals throughout the year, individuals and teams can discuss these events, analyze how these events change their understanding of direct, structural, and cultural forms of violence in their workplace and modify what changes would be useful to developing a positive peace environment.

How can organizations harness collective accountability? The next section will outline tactics that can be utilized to create shared understanding of the violence and empower the collective to identify actions that can lead to a desired workplace.

Dialogic and Action Approaches

This final section outlines key practices from the peace-building field that can be harnessed within your organizational change process. With the conflict transformation field, practitioners are harnessing dialogic traditions alongside nonviolent action traditions to change violent systems into peaceful systems. What do the terms dialogic and action mean in this context? Dialogic approaches focus on engaging different individuals and groups to cultivate mutual exchange. Nonviolent action approaches focus on realigning power from those supporting violence toward those supporting peace. Table 10.3 provides

TABLE 10.3 Dialogic and Nonviolent Action Approaches

Dialogic	Nonviolent Action
Facilitation Surfacing subconscious assumptions through face-to-face exploration of issues	*Non-Cooperation* Actively not taking part in social, economic, legal, or political activity (boycotts, strikes, civil disobedience)
Negotiation & Mediation Bargaining to solve conflicting goals and problems	*Intervention* Actively inserting oneself into a conflict to change the power dynamics
Learning Leveraging participant's experience to share and learn new knowledge and skills	*Protest and Persuasion* Aims to raise broader awareness and galvanize support for desired systems change (community building, petitions, marches)

Source: Miller & King, 2005

key practices within each approach.[3] These tactics are not mutually exclusive—the type of change may require community building with those impacted as well as facilitated dialogue to foster new cultural values within the organization.

THE UNITED STATES INSTITUTE OF PEACE: USING FACILITATION TO REFORM JUSTICE AND SECURITY

Communities in many parts of the world face high levels of direct, structural, and cultural violence. Few programs had demonstrated sustainable strategies to transform justice and security systems to foster positive peace within these communities. The United States Institute of Peace cultivated the Justice and Security Dialogue program that harnessed a number of different peacebuilding approaches. The program was grounded in facilitated dialogue, which created a space for a cross-section of the community and government to convene (The United States Institute of Peace, n.d.). This gave participants an opportunity to legitimize one another's violent experiences. Through the facilitation process, these different groups created shared understanding to build more trusting relationships: The dialogic approaches created a new common identity for participants. From there, participants identified activities to achieve common goals. For example, some communities used civil servant participants to influence a local government's trash collection services. Through their collaborative effort, the trash removed an enormous security threat—a place terrorists used to hide improvised explosive devices. In another community, police participants asked nonprofit leaders to carry out and publish research on the drivers of crime, as the first step of a strategy to increase the willingness of politicians to carry out legal reforms.

While not many organizations will be focused on improvised explosive devices or the drivers of crime, you can use the fundamentals: combining dialogic and nonviolent action approaches to transform your organization's systems.

Several factors can be weighed to determine which tactics to start with:

- *What is the level of power of those requesting change in comparison to the degree of violence you are trying to change?*

  Dialogic tactics are most effective when the people who are leading or supporting the process have the power to change the violence. For example, if the issue is direct violence by a new hire toward an existing team, the team members have enough formal and informal authority to initiate facilitated dialogue with the new employee about team members' experiences. In comparison, a workplace that has deep-rooted racism will need executive leadership to buy into the process. The people with power to change the structures and cultures will need to not only be present during the process, but also open to the problem and willing to initiate reforms. If people don't have that buy-in, groups will want to consider nonviolent action approaches to change the level of power invested in the change.

USING COMMUNITY BUILDING WITHIN THE ORGANIZATION: WOMEN AT NIKE

Women at Nike, Inc., utilized nonviolent action approaches to galvanize support to end the direct, structural, and cultural violence against women in the organization (Creswell, Draper, & Abrams, 2018). A cohort of women began building a knowledge base of the violence through informal surveys. This tactic cultivated a broader group of women willing to highlight the organization's violent workplace. Through these actions, they were able to persuade Nike's CEO to make needed changes within the organization's leadership. This tactic operated outside of existing processes, which had failed to address individual events of harassment, bullying, and barriers to professional growth. Other tactics can similarly be utilized with organizations to cultivate a positive-peace workplace and limit sources of violence.

- *Are those leading the change process perceived as neutral?*
  Dialogic approaches are more effective when the individual or unit leading the change is trusted and perceived as neutral—that they are not perceived as having a specific interest in the change needed. A manager could mediate conflicts between two team members. Human resources could facilitate a dialogue between staff members and their manager. But, in many situations, these individuals are not perceived to be neutral or may not be trusted. Without trust or neutrality, identifying a third party is crucial. Moreover, consider who the third party is accountable to, as their accountability structure may erode trust over time. If the violence is company-wide, an ad hoc working group consisting of people from across the organization—including those harmed—and the board could inculcate the third party from mistrust.

ARE HUMAN RESOURCES NEUTRAL?

Key takeaways from a yearly culture scan found that junior-level staff are far unhappier, less engaged, and dissatisfied than mid- and senior-level staff, as well as in comparison to levels in previous years. Concerned with what led to these divergences, human resources requested all junior staff to attend a discussion on the culture scan results. Human resources was unprepared for the discussion. While junior staff outlined a number of issues with the direct relationship with their supervisors and team members, a fundamental issue was the lack of action by human resources and a belief that human resources was concerned with managing external and board perceptions of the workplace rather than addressing junior staff concerns.

This exemplifies a fatal error by human resources—they held a subconscious assumption that they were not a part of the workplace conditions. In short, single events become larger structural violence due to the lack of action by human resources. What can human resources do? Bringing in a third-party facilitator and convening a dialogue can lead to exploration of the workplace conditions and unearth human resources' own assumptions.

- *Should you create a new process or utilize existing processes?*
  Addressing internal workplace conditions can add a significant burden to all employees, on top of existing roles and responsibilities. Organizations can assess their existing process—for example, dispute resolution, recruitment, and continuing learning—and consider integrating dialogic approaches. Or, ad hoc change processes may be created—for example, topical working groups or healing workshops.

STARBUCKS AD HOC RACIAL HEALING TRAININGS

In April 2018, two Black men were arrested for sitting at a Philadelphia Starbucks table awaiting a meeting. Starbucks identified two key forms of violence—cultural violence in the form of unconscious bias of employees and structural violence in the form of policies and procedures that omitted protections from the cultural violence (Rose, 2018). Solutions to addressing these root forms of violence would come from changing the mindsets of employees and policies and procedures of the company, not from removing one symptom (the employee in question) from a single store. Implicit in Starbuck's assessment of the violence was that their organizational violence was also a symptom of broader violence within society. No amount of recruitment or firing of individuals would change the existence of racism at Starbucks.

To address this issue, Starbucks announced an ad hoc, employee-wide workshop on unconscious bias. The company has noted this ad hoc event will be a part of a longer, more widespread set of changes. Companies can similarly consider launching an ad hoc event in an effort to galvanize internal energy toward addressing the issue, and then initiating a longer process of integrating peace-building approaches into existing processes.

- *Within the change process, when are peace-building approaches most effective?* The change process, as noted above, requires moving from where the organization is to where it wants to be. Organizations can use peace-building approaches in developing a vision for where they want to be, in preparing staff for change, and in fostering a commitment to the new vision. Peace-building approaches require resources—time, people, and money—so organizations may need to prioritize the critical parts of the process. High levels of violence may result in prioritizing facilitated dialogue in developing the new vision. A lack of awareness of violence may result in prioritizing community building to prepare staff for change.

CONCLUSION

This chapter provided an introduction to the principles of peace, violence, and conflict in order to expand our awareness and understanding of potential destructive workplace environments. Through this expanded knowledge, we then have the opportunity to develop more peaceful organizations. To that end, the final section of this chapter outlined both dialogic and nonviolent action approaches that can help you transform your organization from harmful to peaceful systems. These examples are not exhaustive, but provide you with a launching off point.

NOTES

1. Unless otherwise cited, illustrative examples used in this chapter are taken from individual conversations the author has had with people of varying age, gender, race, and ethnicity, working in a number of industries. The majority of conversations focus on experiences within the United States.
2. A final form of power is coercion. This form of power is a source of direct harm, and therefore isn't included in assessing power to foster a peaceful vision.
3. For a more robust discussion on the complementarity of dialogic and nonviolent action to transforming violent systems, refer to "Powering to Peace: Integrated Civil Resistance and Peace-building Strategies," by V. Dudouet, 2017, International Center on Nonviolent Conflicts.

REFERENCES

Bureau of Labor Statistics. (2017, December 19). *Census of fatal occupational injuries summary, 2016* [News release]. Retrieved from https://www.bls.gov/news.release/cfoi.nr0.htm

Carson, B., & Gould, S. (2017, June 26). Uber's bad year: The stunning string of blows that upended the world's most valuable startup. *Business Insider*. Retrieved from http://www.businessinsider.com/uber-scandal-crisis-complete-timeline-2017-6

Cartwright, G. (2013, August 6). Perspective: The phenomena of workplace violence. *Law Enforcement Bulletin*. Retrieved from https://leb.fbi.gov/articles/perspective/perspective-the-phenomena-of-workplace-violence

Creswell, J., Draper, K., & Abrams, R. (2018, April 28). At Nike, revolt led by women leads to exodus of male executives. *The New York Times*. Retrieved from https://www.nytimes.com/2018/04/28/business/nike-women.html

Farrow, R. (2017, October 10). From aggressive overtures to sexual assault: Harvey Weinstein's accusers tell their stories. *The New Yorker*. Retrieved from https://www.newyorker.com/news/news-desk/from-aggressive-overtures-to-sexual-assault-harvey-weinsteins-accusers-tell-their-stories

Fowler, S. (2017, February 19). Reflecting on one very, very strange year at Uber [Web log post]. Retrieved from https://www.susanjfowler.com/blog/2017/2/19/reflecting-on-one-very-strange-year-at-uber

Fulmer, I., Gerhart, B., & Scott, K. (2003). Are the 100 best better? An empirical investigation of the relationship between being a "great place to work" and firm performance. *Personnel Psychology, 56*(4), 965–993.

Galtung, J. (1990, August). Cultural violence. *Journal of Peace Research, 27*(3), 291–305.

Galtung, J. (1996). *Peace by peaceful means: Peace and conflict, development and civilization*. London, England: SAGE.

Galtung, J., & Fischer, D. (2013). *Springer briefs on pioneers in science and practice 5. Johan Galtung: Pioneer of peace research*. Heidelberg, Germany: Springer.

Harter, J. K., Schmidt, F. L., Agrawal, S., Plowman, S. K., & Blue, A. (2016, April). *The relationship between engagement at work and organizational outcomes: 2016 Q12 meta-analysis* (Report, 9th ed.). Washington, DC: Gallup. Retrieved from http://www.workcompprofessionals.com/advisory/2016L5/august/MetaAnalysis_Q12_ResearchPaper_0416_v5_sz.pdf

Hoobler, J., & Swarberg, J. (2006). The enemy is not us: Unexpected workplace violence trends. *Public Personnel Management, 53*(3), 229–246.

Isaac, M. (2017, February 22). Inside Uber's aggressive, unrestrained workplace culture. *The New York Times*. Retrieved from https://www.nytimes.com/2017/02/22/technology/uber-workplace-culture.html?smid=tw-share&_r=0

Kantor, J., & Twohey, M. (2017, October 6). Harvey Weinstein paid off sexual harassment accusers for decades. *The New York Times*. Retrieved from https://www.nytimes.com/2017/10/05/us/harvey-weinstein-harassment-allegations.html?_r=0

Ladner, D. (2015, September). *Working politically in practice series, case study no. 3. Strategy testing: An innovative approach to monitoring highly flexible aid programs.* San Francisco, CA: The Asia Foundation.

Leroux-Martin, P., & O'Connor, V. (2017, October, 23). Systems thinking for peacebuilding and rule of law: Supporting complex reforms in conflict-affected environments. *Peaceworks.* Retreived from https://www.usip.org/sites/default/files/2017-11/pw133-systems-thinking-for-peacebuilding-and-rule-of-law-v2.pdf

Miller, C. E., & King, M. E. (Ed.). (2005). *A glossary of terms and concepts in peace and conflict studies* (2nd ed.). Addis Ababa, Ethiopia: University for Peace.

Morgan, B. (2017, November 1). Culture is the customer experience Lyft you need. *Forbes.* Retrieved from https://www.forbes.com/sites/blakemorgan/2017/11/01/culture-is-the-customer-experience-lyft-you-need/#6982bff81528

Peretez, M. (2018, March 18). The secrets behind Lyft's dynamic culture. *Forbes.* Retrieved from https://www.forbes.com/sites/marissaperetz/2018/05/16/the-secrets-behind-lyfts-dynamic-culture/#24c3a7588ee5

Rose, J. (2018, May 29). *'I'm not aware of that': Starbucks employees receive racial bias training* [Audio file]. Retrieved from https://www.npr.org/programs/all-things-considered/2018/05/29/615081646

Senge, P. M. (2006). *The fifth discipline: The art & practice of the learning organization.* New York, NY: Doubleday.

Snodderly, D. (Ed.). (2011). *Peace terms: Glossary of terms for conflict management and peace building.* Washington, DC: United States Institute of Peace.

Stroh, D. P. (2015). *Systems thinking for social change.* White River Junction, VT: Chelsea Green.

Turchin, P. (2016). *Ages of discord: A structural-demographic analysis of American history.* Chaplin, CT: Beresta Books LLC.

United States Institute of Peace. (n.d.). *Justice and security dialogues: USIP brings communities together to strengthen the rule of law.* Retrieved fromhttps://www.usip.org/programs/justice-and-security-dialogues

World Bank. (2011). *World development report 2011: Conflict, security, and development.* Washington, DC: World Bank.

CHAPTER 11

A WORKPLACE BULLYING PERSPECTIVE

Blending the Melodies of Ballads (the Story) and Classical (the Research)

William Hymes and LaVena Wilkin

Why do some people feel the need to humiliate, ridicule, or sabotage their employees or their coworkers? Why do people become the targets of a workplace bully? If you recognize yourself as a bully or a target, what can you do to change? This chapter seeks to answer those questions through the eyes of research conducted by LaVena, and more importantly, by Bill's story. Bill has been on both sides of the divide, as a workplace bully and as a target of workplace bullying. Although he believes his story is unremarkable, it provides an eye-opening perspective about workplace bullying through the bully's lens. It is not often that one has an opportunity to see inside the mind of a workplace bully and understand the viewpoints and motivations of that person. Much of this chapter is open, honest, and brutal; it is shared by Bill in his own words. While the research supports certain aspects of his story, his candid story provides a wealth of ideas for future studies to help scholars understand workplace bullying on an even deeper level.

From Discord to Harmony, pages 189–199

One reason he believes his story is unremarkable is that workplace bullying occurs so frequently. It is becoming a commonplace occurrence that has become normalized. Indeed, according to a survey conducted by Zogby for the Workplace Bullying Institute, 37% of American workers have been affected by workplace bullying (Workplace Bullying Institute, 2017). Another interesting statistic from the Zogby survey is that the highest percentage of workplace bullies are employed in the healthcare industry. Bill has had a career as an exceptionally skilled thoracic surgeon.

WHAT IS WORKPLACE BULLYING?

The Research

A generally accepted academic definition of workplace bullying is that it involves behaviors that are harassing or offending; those behaviors may include socially excluding someone, or they may negatively affect someone's work tasks. In order for the label bullying to be applied to a particular activity, interaction, or process, it has to occur repeatedly and regularly (such as weekly) and over a period of time (such as 6 months). Bullying is an escalating process in the course of which the person confronted ends up in an inferior power position and becomes the target of systematic negative social acts (Einarsen, Zapf, & Cooper, 2003).

Specifically, workplace bullies use a variety of antisocial and hostile tactics to intimidate their targets, and these behaviors lie on a continuum from mild to extreme. Milder more covert behaviors include giving the target the silent treatment, gossiping or spreading rumors, and socially isolating the target (Salin, 2003). More extreme and blatant behaviors include altering work tasks, intimidating physical gestures, ridiculing, insulting and gossiping, making verbal threats, and threatening physical violence (Zapf, 1999). As shown in Table 11.1, these behaviors are summed up in three broad categories (Rayner & Hoel, 1997).

TABLE 11.1 Categories of Workplace Bullying Behaviors

Threats to Professional Standing	Threats to Personal Standing	Isolation
Verbally insulting the target	Withholding vital information	Isolating the target
Intimidating the target	Taking credit for the target's work	Ostracizing the target
Humiliating and ridiculing the target	Denying access to training	
Spreading rumors and gossip	Assigning impossible tasks or workloads	
Giving the silent treatment	Sabotaging the target's work	

TABLE 11.2 Comparison of Workplace Bullies and Tough Managers

Workplace Bullies	Tough Managers
Abuse of Power	Objective and Fair
Personally Focused	Organizationally Focused
Emotional Outbursts	Unemotional
Unfair/Inconsistent Actions	Objective

Rude behavior is not necessarily workplace bullying. In fact, there is no law against being a jerk. So, when does rude and uncivil behavior cross over into workplace bullying? Sometimes, the continuum of behaviors blurs that line. Moreover, often times, tough management is confused with workplace bullying. Daniel's (2009) research determined that the overarching factor that sets the workplace bullying apart from tough managers is the bully acts with malice, and the tough manager values humanity. Table 11.2 shows a comparison of a tough manager and a workplace bully (Daniel, 2009).

Bill's Experience

A tough manager will be attentive to performance indicators and enforce tough standards. This benefits the group as a whole by elevating everyone's performance. The tough manager's goal is improvement of the group as a whole, and while negative reinforcements are in their tool kits, generally rewards and sincere praise are more effective with people who are already aware of their elite status and have already demonstrated their desire to contribute to the group. Tough managers will put the group's accomplishments before their own, and will favor objectivity, fairness, and consistency. In contrast, a bully will frequently favor some people over others, and subordinates are often pitted against one another.

Bill's Story

As a surgeon, Bill says he used his power in unhealthy ways to achieve goals and get others to do what he wanted. He viewed power as the most expedient path to an end result. According to him, authoritarian behavior has utility; it has a valid position in both hierarchical structures and in more equal environments where there is insufficient time for deliberation and collaboration. From Bill's perspective, tough bosses, the ones who enforce standards and do not tolerate substandard performance, benefit the organization. They cultivate elite talent, foster high levels of commitment, support high wages for their charges, and improve morale by enforcing standards among the group. However, there is a fine line beyond which the enforcement is more for the self-interest of the supervisor than service to the company at large and to the manager's subordinates. This is the line in the sand between tough management and workplace bullying.

THE LINKAGE BETWEEN POWER AND WORKPLACE BULLYING

The Research

Both Bill's experiences and his perceptions are supported by the scholarly literature on the connection between power and workplace bullying. According to Dahl (1986) power is necessary to control behaviors and to encourage necessary changes. Without power, social systems would not function efficiently (Boulding, 1990). However, power becomes destructive when it is abused. Losing sight of what is good for the organization and focusing on one's own self-interest may be the beginning of destructive abuse of power (Boulding, 1990).

ANTECEDENTS OF WORKPLACE BULLYING

Why do working adults bully their coworkers? There is not one overarching reason people bully (Einarsen, 1999). In fact, the root causes include both organizational (Salin, 2003) and individual factors (Zapf & Einarsen, 2003). Bill sums them up with three words: pushes, pulls, and permissions. The pushes (similar to pressure) are:

- personality,
- personal history,
- entitlement and grievance,
- personal ambition or quest for status, and
- threats to values or authority.

The pulls (similar to rationalization) are:

- ease and expedience,
- time pressure and limitation of alternatives,
- past successes,
- institutional culture,
- habit, and
- fear of being taken advantage of.

The permissions (similar to opportunity) are:

- power differential,
- insufficient monitoring and control,
- discounting and deferral of costs, and
- target's role.

Often, destructive power is associated with threatening behavior that can be acted upon when one person has control over something the other person values, such as economic power. Additionally, individuals may turn to destructive power when they believe they are losing control or when behaviors are legitimized (Boulding, 1990). In fact, Bill believed that if something was to be done correctly and expediently, bullying behaviors needed to be used to control the process.

In Bill's Words

Of considerably less importance, but nevertheless worth mentioning, is the target's role in the abuse of power. Bullies are skilled at exploiting their targets' conscientiousness, perfectionism, desire to please, and general good nature. Targets are exquisitely sensitive. Targets often question their culpability in the conflict and empathize with the bully. They endlessly question their role in provoking the behavior. Ironically, this is never productive and only causes the target more pain.

This is not meant to be a discouragement of these commendable qualities, but more to serve as a warning to increase awareness of their potential exploitation. It seems as though I should come forth with some brilliant suggestion for how to arrest this behavior and set things right. Unfortunately, my experience has led me to no such epiphany. Appeasement, avoidance, neglect, and counter-aggression seem to work or not work with no readily apparent pattern. I have found ways to arrive at disappointing outcomes using all of them. Obviously, this is a nonscientific data analysis; my sample is skewed, since the times it has failed stand out to me much more readily than the much more forgettable times damaging conflict was avoided.

The Research

There is not one overarching reason people bully (Einarsen, 1999; Zapf, 1999). In fact, the root causes include both organizational and individual factors (Salin, 2003; Zapf & Einarsen, 2003). People who are perceived as different, have low self-esteem, or are overachievers may become targets

(Baron & Neuman, 1998; Harvey, Heames, Richey, & Leonard, 2006; Zapf & Einarsen, 2003). Bullies may feel a need to boost their own self-esteem, they may lack social competencies, or they make decisions that protect their position at the expense of the target (Zapf & Einarsen 2003). A more recent study also found that people bully because they have a self-righteous attitude and believe if they do not bully, the job will not be completed properly (Castle, 2014).

THE SENSE OF ENTITLEMENT

In Bill's Words: A Glimpse Into the Mind of a Bully

The bully typically works from a deeply held belief of entitlement. It is a very difficult behavior pattern to break, given its simplicity, expedience, and deferral of costs. There is a huge opportunity for self-deception here. If we can idealize a hierarchy to be a true meritocracy, it becomes apparent that the superordinate superiority is validated by their status. It is legitimate for the most educated, the most informed person, to act in the group's interest, even if it is in an authoritarian manner. It becomes easy to justify the exercise of power as appropriate and proper in the name of benevolence. In that construct, it becomes completely natural and reasonable that any disagreement is a threat to outcomes, and thus to the group. Conflict must be suppressed or overcome. I can tell you that there is not a shred of self-consciousness or doubt. Convenient excuses for suppressing dissent include time pressure, too many and too varied opinions, and a deeply held belief that one's own point of view is the one true path.

Earning sufficient trust from subordinates to identify their individual needs and desires is laborious and often fraught with awkwardness and discomfort. Negotiation is not a controllable process; its course is not predictable. Not only is it far easier and faster to exert one's authority, but is also much more likely, in the short term to yield the desired outcome. "Shut up and do it" leaves little room for nuance and interpretation; the choice for the employee is binary, and the consequences of a negative response are obvious. For the superordinate, the long-term consequences are clouds on a distant horizon that can be safely ignored. Self-awareness comes late in this game, if at all.

Speaking for myself, I have been surprised more than once when I have seen a threat to someone's sense of entitlement being viewed as a threat to their very existence and how often it engenders behavior that is collectively destructive in response. I am not sure if this has been due to a lack of empathy or insight on my part; however, it is nevertheless true more often than I care to think about. This entitlement all too frequently becomes habitual and is prone to rationalization. Frequently bullies find justification for their behavior in allegiance to patriotism, spirituality, excellence, or any number of altruistic and lofty ideals. This reinforces the threat sensitivity. And, that threat to entitlement becomes an assault on the bully's entire belief and value system.

An example

I am divorced. I have a 13-year-old son who lives with his mother. During the short times I get to see him, if I give him any adverse feedback, he withdraws, ignores me, and goes back home. If I ask him to do something he does not want to do, such as set the table, take out the garbage, or hang up his clothes, he is gone. I am his father; he should do as I say. Right? No. He has free will. He has good alternatives, and I am grateful that he has good alternatives. Denying him his alternatives is not making him more obedient, and it is not going to make him happy. I have not respected his right to decide. I can say, "When you are in my home, these are the expectations" and enforce them consistently. This respects his autonomy and my home at the same time. If being with me does not bring value to him, that is my problem, not his, and he is free to go. How much more time and effort on my part does it take to treat a 13-year-old as autonomous and worthy of dignity and respect? In all honesty, it takes a lot of time and effort. But I would venture that the outcomes I want will be more likely with this approach than an autocratic one. But it is a very different model than the one I was raised to believe in. It definitely involves giving up some ground in the short run in exchange for the hope of an improved relationship and the long term gain.

THE LEADER'S ROLE IN WORKPLACE BULLYING

The Research

Often organizational leaders either do not know how to deal with bullying behaviors, or they do not understand the costs involved with avoiding or mismanaging them (Georgakopoulos, Kent, & Wilkin, 2011; Salin, 2003; Wilkin, 2010). The negative impact for the target can be exacerbated when allegations of bullying are discounted, considered tough management, or labeled as personality conflicts. Additionally, since many workplace bullies are supervisors, when bullying behavior is condoned, it becomes part of the organizational culture (Tepper, Duffy, Henle, & Lambert; 2006), and employees may begin to emulate that behavior. This trickle-down effect magnifies the problem. In addition, increased diversity, globalization, lack of organizational education and training, and poor interpersonal and social skills are antecedents of workplace bullying (Georgakopoulos, Kent, & Wilkin, 2011).

In Bill's Words

Monitoring is problematic. All the incentives for detection are reversed. What qualifies as abuse is hard to distinguish from poor leadership. It is nearly impossible to detect until the abuse becomes obvious, and even then, the temptation is to deny the problem and avoid discussion. The bully is usually empowered in some way, and confrontation of the behavior is often daunting and invites retaliation and little is to be gained politically in a hierarchy for standing up for the unempowered. Power over others is a fringe benefit. No financial incentives are available to reward supervisors who exercise power conservatively and judiciously. Given that supervisors have a measure of legitimate power over their employees, removing the opportunity is generally not an option.

A word needs to be said here about leadership and how poorly it is understood, how poorly we are prepared for it, and how easy it is to fall prey to the illusion that we are much better leaders in our minds than in reality. Being the leader means there's no one to tell us we are not doing a stellar job. How many among us are willing to seek out adverse feedback without being defensive? How long does it take to develop a trusting and mutually beneficial relationship with someone who can safely offer candid, meaningful, and constructive feedback, or even better, listen to unconstructive feedback and be able to separate the anger and the chaff from the nugget of identifiable improvement that is buried within? Here's a test: Do you feel ready to give and receive adverse information to and from sub and superordinates? Can you agree that it is both very important and not well taught?

The experience of giving adverse feedback is, at best, very uncomfortable. Consider that the work relationship can be as important as the spousal relationship, and for the most part, we spend more time and energy at work than with our spouses. Our livelihoods and even our identities are tied up in our jobs. There is so much on the table all at once that it is no wonder that these conversations are fraught with emotions. And defensiveness. I can honestly say that my personal preference for honesty and directness is not shared widely among the population, and my failure in this vital aspect of leadership has been instrumental in making me want to re-evaluate my approach. In fact, I would go as far as saying that initially, my belief was that humiliation was the desired outcome. Thinking if I can humiliate people for their mistakes, they will make special effort to do better, and I failed to understand the harm I inflicted. Having been on both sides of that approach, I can attest to its inadequacy in achieving a positive outcome.

BILL'S JOURNEY (IN HIS OWN WORDS)

I have been on both sides of the bullying equation. I have good reason to believe I have been insufferable. I have watched bullies blindly paint themselves into a corner as this strategy isolates them and makes their workplace intolerable and ultimately unsuccessful. And I would be less than honest if I said I did not derive a certain amount of satisfaction and inner peace from seeing them struggle and fail as a result.

Perhaps, because I have been on both sides of the divide, perhaps getting to the point in life where I felt like I could no longer continue being the person I was forced me to rethink many of my relationships and my interactions and question if, maybe I could be happier and more fulfilled if reconsidered some of my strategies. Perhaps, this can be illustrative and informative in the everyday, common life experience. Perhaps, here too are some lessons learned from mistakes made, from doing it the wrong way first, and perhaps, it may make one less apology necessary and alleviate some small degree of guilt and regret. A humble goal, to be sure, but one that may be more realistic and achievable than one that is overly ambitious. And, being honest with oneself is where it all starts.

I have been a bully. Or put a little more precisely, I have used power in unhealthy ways to achieve my goals and to get others to do what I wanted. We all have. It takes less thought, engenders less angst and uncertainty, and it cuts out unnecessary discussion. Its attractiveness as a strategy is undeniable, particularly when there is an established pattern of it being used successfully in the past.

Similarly, it is relatively easy to look at an egregious example of abuse of power, identify its abject moral failure, display its targets, quantify its costs, and revile its practice. Thus, having identified the two extreme ends of the spectrum, we can define a continuum, extending from effective leadership practice, through the spectrum of less and less benevolent and appropriate leadership behaviors into varying degrees of abuse of power extending to exploitation and cruelty. The point is that while strict definitions are necessary tools, identifying the exact location along a continuum is a futile exercise, and one in which more than one of the parts is moving. At what point does a drive for excellence cross over into obsession and be used as, or considered, a weapon? What is a forgivable slight, and what is abuse that is intolerable?

As a gag gift one Christmas, I was given a set of CDs from the Great Courses series on conflict management. I actually listened to all 30 hours and came to the conclusion that there are alternative ways to achieve my goals other than imposition of my power or authority. Maybe it's because I have been a bully and I need to see myself as being a moral person, one who is not evil, but one who has succumbed to forces greater than his contemporaneous moral sense should have allowed. Maybe it's because I have regrets and am troubled with looking at my behavior in retrospect. Maybe I am embarrassed and should have known better. Perhaps that's true for many of us.

What it has led me to is the realization that there are great strengths among us. These strengths have the potential to accomplish much. While we chafe and are frustrated by limitations of our strengths, the damage potential and destructiveness inherent in unrestrained strengths is more costly than we generally appreciate. Our limitations, frustrating as they are, are not our enemy. And patience, kindness, and tolerance have rewards, though perhaps not immediately.

Full disclosure: Change is hard. There is comfort in a model of authority and control; there is uncertainty and work involved in a model that respects free will and autonomy of others, and requires careful analysis and a search for areas where interests can align instead of just giving orders. People do not naturally gravitate towards diversity; no one instinctively wants to make the extra effort and take on the risk of making friends with the person with the strange accent or who dresses differently. But the truth is, as any human resource professional of any of our large customer service corporations will admit, there is strength derived from making this effort. So, while the metamorphosis we are discussing requires an acceptance of uncertainty, a loss of control, and an initial decrease in efficiency that comes with having to obtain consensus rather than just giving orders, in the long run, there is benefit.

My advice is this: Expect bullying to happen. Do not take it personally. The line between what is tolerable and what is intolerable is very subtle and develops incrementally. Be aware of your gut feeling that the cost of the bullying is more than the expected benefits. If there is an opportunity to negotiate, consider taking the time to phrase the issue diplomatically and in terms that demonstrate benefit for the other party. Proactively seek alternatives if a confrontation seems likely. There are always alternatives. Do not take it personally; do not dwell; forgive and move on. Do not be afraid to be the person you think you should be for fear of being taken advantage of. This will happen no matter what, so let the person you want to be endure, rather than letting an act of random maliciousness define you.

REFERENCES

Baron, R. A., & Neuman, J. H. (1998). Workplace aggression–The iceberg beneath the tip of workplace violence: Evidence of its forms, frequency, and targets. *Public Administration Quarterly, 21*(4), 446–464.

Boulding, K. E. (1990). *Three faces of power.* Newbury Park, CA: SAGE.

Castle, K. M. (2014). The workplace bully: A grounded theory study exploring motivational influences of bullying at work. Retrieved from ProQuest Dissertations and Thesis. (Accession Order No. AAT 3636399)

Dahl, R. (1986). Power as the control of behavior. In S. Lukes (Eds.), *Power: Reading in social and political theory* (pp. 37–58). New York, NY: New York Press.

Daniel, T. (2009). *Stop bullying at work: Strategies and tools for HR and legal professions.* Alexandria, VA: SHRM.

Einarsen, S. (1999). The nature and causes of bullying at work. *International Journal of Manpower, 20*(1/2), 16–27.

Einarsen, S., Hoel, H., Zapf, D., & Cooper, C. (2003). The concept of bullying at work. In S. Einarsen, H. Hoel, D. Zapf, & C. Cooper (Eds.), Bullying and emotional abuse in the workplace: International perspectives in research and practice (pp. 3–30). New York, NY: Taylor & Francis.

Georgakopoulos, A., Wilkin, L., & Kent, B. (2011). Workplace bullying: A complex problem in contemporary organizations. *International Journal of Business and Social Sciences, 2*(3), 1–20.

Harvey, M. G., Heames, J. T., Richey, R. G., & Leonard, N. (2006). Bullying: From the playground to the boardroom. *Journal of Leadership & Organizational Studies, 12*(4), 1–11.

Rayner, C., & Hoel, H. (1997). A summary of literature relating to workplace bullying. *Journal of Community & Applied Social Psychology, 7*(7), 181–191.

Salin, D. (2003). Ways of explaining workplace bullying: A review of enabling, motivating and precipitating structures and processes in the work environment. *Human Relations, 56*(10), 1213–1232.

Tepper, B. J., Duffy, M. K., Henle, C. A., & Lambert, L. S. (2006). Procedural injustice, victim, precipitation, and abusive supervision. *Personnel Psychology, 59*(1), 101–123.

Workplace Bullying Institute. (2017). *2017 WBI U.S. Workplace Bullying Survey.* Retrieved from https://www.workplacebullying.org/wbiresearch/wbi-2017-survey/

Wilkin, L. (2010). *Workplace bullying in academe: A grounded theory study exploring how faculty cope with the experience of being bullied.* Retrieved from ProQuest Dissertations and Thesis. (Accession Order No. AAT 3447190)

Zapf, D. (1999). Organisational, work group related and personal causes of mobbing/bullying at work. *International Journal of Manpower, 20*(1/2), 57–69. https://doi.org/10.1108/01437729910268669

Zapf, D., & Einarsen, S. (2003). Individual antecedents of bullying: Victims and perpetrators. In S. Einarsen, H. Hoel, D. Zapf, & C. Cooper (Eds.), Bullying and emotional abuse in the workplace: International perspectives in research and practice (pp. 165–185). New York, NY: Taylor & Francis.

SECTION II

TO HARMONY

CHAPTER 12

COACHING YOUR PEOPLE THROUGH TOUGH SITUATIONS

Barbara J. Lassiter

Hopefully, you are the type of leader your staff *gets* to follow rather than one they *have* to follow. Assuming you are a good leader, helping your people through episodes of workplace bullying (WB) or workplace intimate partner violence (WIPV) will be easier when your people trust you. Neither WB nor WIPV are situations that anyone wants to occur; however, they do happen, and in the case of WB, they happen too often.

WORKPLACE BULLYING

In 1970, the Occupational Safety and Health Act (OSH Act) was enacted into law, and it required employers in the United States to provide employees with a hazard-free workplace to avoid serious harm or death to their employees (Occupational Safety & Health Administration [OSHA], n.d.). While some employers may consider *hazard-free* to mean a workplace free

From Discord to Harmony, pages 203–218

of physical obstacles, working in a toxic environment where employees feel emotionally unsafe or devalued can be just as dangerous, if not worse. The organization best known for researching and exposing the dangers of WB is the Workplace Bullying Institute (the Institute). The Institute has defined WB as, "Repeated mistreatment of an employee by one or more employees; abusive conduct that is: threatening, humiliating, or intimidating, work sabotage, or verbal abuse" (Namie, 2017, para. 1).

According to a 2017 national survey, using a sample size of 1,008 people across the United States the Institute found the following: 19% of employees are bullied at work while another 19% of their coworkers (bystanders) see it happening, and 61% of employees are aware bullying is occurring (Namie, 2017). Thus, with a U.S. population of 326,474,013 in 2017, approximately 62,030,062 employees experienced WB or saw it happening, and 293,826,117 employees were aware WB was occurring in their workplace. In total, 60.4 million employees in the United States are affected by WB (Namie, 2017). Even more concerning, 61% of the workplace bullies hold positions of power: In other words, workplace bullies are often bosses, managers, or supervisors, and of these, 70% of the bullies are men and 65% of the targets (victims) of the bullying are women.

In spite of the adverse health effects experienced by 40% of bullied employees, 29% of them do not say anything about their abusive treatment (Namie, 2017). If the bullied employee *does* say something, 71% of employers and 60% of their coworkers react harmfully toward the bullied employee, with an end result being that 65% of targets lose their jobs. Even more interesting was a 2012 study by Namie that indicated 88.4% of employers refused to accept responsibility for WB by acting to stop it when incidents occurred (sample size 250).

Legally, WB behaviors are separated into three areas: (a) types of negative behaviors, (b) frequency and continuation of behavior occurrences, and (c) the harm the behavior does to the victim, whether psychological or physical (Saunders, Huynh, & Goodman-Delahunty, 2007). Signals that WB may be occurring include overt or covert negative treatment by the perpetrator, overt or covert negative language against the target, or a blend of those behaviors, and the bullying may be either subtle or aggressive (Saunders et al., 2007). Other types of WB are clarified as follows: (a) Abuse of power is called *authoritative bullying*; (b) escalating interpersonal disagreements causes *dispute-related bullying*; (c) when the real target is too dangerous to bully and aggression is used against someone other than the actual target, it is called *scapegoating* or *displaced bullying*; (d) picking on someone based on prejudice of some type is *discriminatory bullying*; and (e) bullying that is used for oppressive practices or for exploiting employees is *organizational bullying* (Lutgen-Sandvik, Namie, & Namie, 2009).

Oftentimes, the targets of WB experience feelings of helplessness and believe they are powerless to stop the abuse. Targets also tend to feel vulnerable and unable to protect themselves from the bullying (Saunders et al., 2007). Surprising to some is the fact that WB can happen to anyone no matter what stage of their career they are in (Lutgen-Sandvik & Tracy, 2012). Not surprising, however, is that men are not the only bullies in the workplace; women bully others as well.

While women who bully in the workplace may direct their attention to men at a rate of 33%, they are most likely to bully other women (67% of women are bullied by other women; Namie, 2017). Women who bully tend to prefer using passive-aggressive tactics and like to bully using *relational aggression*. In relational aggression, women bullies may ignore the target, gossip, harm the target's reputation, or steal the target's friends, romantic partner, or spouse (Crothers, Lipinski, & Minutolo, 2009). Women bullies may also make sure the target knows that she is not welcome to join a group or activity; this leaves the target feeling ostracized and increases job dissatisfaction; physical, emotional, and psychological health problems; higher stress levels at work; impaired problem-solving skills; and lower functioning overall (Crothers et al., 2009). So, who are the most likely targets of WB? Are they the weak and vulnerable who go unnoticed at work?

WHO ARE THE TARGETS OF BULLIES?

According to the Workplace Bullying Institute (2018), the most likely targets are the most competent employees and those who have been there the longest. Targets are often autonomous and refuse to be acquiescent yet they are nonconfrontational and avoid exchanging aggressive tactics with the bully; they are also more competent than the bullies who harass them (Namie, 2018). Targets are likely to demonstrate better social skills, possess higher degrees of emotional intelligence, and are perceived as warm and caring toward others and are well-liked in return. Targets demonstrate ethical behavior: They are honest and tend to be transparent as well. People who are empathetic and want to support and nurture others are the most likely to become targets because they appear weak to the workplace bully (Namie, 2017). Furthermore, those who are Hispanic or African American are overly represented as targets of WB.

Consider this true story where names have been changed and locations excluded for privacy:

> A highly competent investigator, Kevin, was hired by a state government agency to investigate welfare fraud. The new investigator had years of experience,

was professionally groomed, well educated, and he happened to have dark skin inherited from his father's southern Egyptian heritage. The management team hiring him was very excited to have Kevin on board, and they encouraged others in the department to make him feel welcome.

In addition to the two hiring managers, Reid and Tim, the department consisted of four women investigators and two men—one of whom was an investigator and one who worked as an analyst. Everyone seemed to be affable and reasonably friendly. Thus, Kevin was pleased with the reception he received from his superiors, and believed he might have found a place he could make a positive impact with his training and experience. Kevin was feeling optimistic and did his best to fit into the department culture by participating in department activities and offering to help his coworkers.

Within a short time, Kevin was tackling cases that could not be resolved by the other investigators in the department, and he began closing a number of cases that brought in a substantial amount of money to the state. In contrast, the women investigators were slow to get any investigations completed, and frequently complained that their department budget for the year was too high for them to meet. The new budget goal for the department was set at $600,000 in closed welfare fraud cases for that fiscal year.

As Kevin settled in, the director of the agency made two key changes in the department. He reassigned both Reid and Tim, the two hiring supervisors, to other areas in the department, and promoted one of his protégés, Sam, to take over as the new supervisor. Unfortunately, Sam had little or no experience either doing investigations or supervising staff members. He was floundering in his decision-making abilities, and his lack of competence showed. Within a very short time, the work environment shifted, and the staff could sense the difference. Some of the women investigators saw Sam's weakness as an opening and began currying favor with their new boss. Sam, in turn, responded positively to their compliments and fawning requests for less work and more favors. The women wanting favors made sure to act like they looked up to him, so it bolstered his self-confidence.

The women, who had been pleasant and respectful before now, began criticizing Kevin and making snide comments about him either directly or loudly enough for him to overhear. When Sam asked one of the female investigators to go with Kevin to work on a case in the field, she responded, "I would *never* go anywhere with him!" She was allowed to stay in the office while Kevin went to the appointment by himself. Even worse, no one commented on her offensive statement.

Once started, the abusive behavior by the women in the office quickly escalated. When the department was having a barbeque as an employee activity, Kevin asked what they wanted him to bring. To his surprise, when Kevin arrived with the soda and chips as requested, no one touched either one, and one of the women intentionally threw the unopened foods into the trash in front of him, letting him know they would never eat anything he touched.

Kevin quickly got their message: He was not wanted, and he avoided such employee functions in the future.

As the abuse continued unabated, Kevin requested a meeting with his former supervisor, Reid, and asked what he could do to reduce the animosity. Reid suggested that Kevin stay out in the field completing his investigations as much as possible, and start applying for a transfer to another department when openings became available. Reid told Kevin that the women in the department had gotten rid of another woman in the past because they disliked her color. She was African American. Kevin took Reid's advice and stayed in the field as much as possible, but one afternoon, when he was in the office working, the department was having their monthly birthday cake celebration.

One of Kevin's biggest tormentors went around to each cubicle asking if the person wanted a piece of cake. When she came to Kevin's cube, however, she simply glared at him, stuck her nose in the air, and walked away; she never asked if he wanted cake. Another time, Kevin overheard the women joking about one of their past supervisors. One of the women quipped, "He used to be a good guy until he went over to the *dark* side," and the women laughed as they turned and looked at Kevin. On another occasion, one of the women commented, "We need to get rid of him (meaning Kevin) and get someone who fits better and who looks like us." In the meantime, Kevin kept his thoughts to himself and continued to work on his caseload, solving more cases, and applying for jobs in other departments where he hoped to face less hostility.

Ultimately, as too often happens with targets of WB, Kevin was discharged from his job based on false allegations made by his female coworkers; this happened only a few weeks before he would have become a tenured employee who could not be fired easily. During the 10 months of his employment, Kevin closed over $606,000 in welfare fraud cases—more than the entire department budget by himself. He received no praise and no credit for his hard work; instead, he was humiliated and denied unemployment compensation.

After a costly appeal, Kevin won his claim and finally received his unemployment compensation, but his work record was tarnished for being dismissed with no cause, and it continued to follow him when he applied for other jobs in law enforcement. Over time, Kevin was able to overcome the unjustified blemish on his stellar record, and eventually ended up promoted at another law enforcement agency in a different state where his experience and integrity mattered.

Workplace bullying is able to exist because employers fail to create an environment that has zero tolerance of such behaviors, and when WB does occur, the perpetrator is unlikely to be punished for his or her actions (Lassiter, 2017a; Namie, 2017). As already noted, oftentimes, the workplace bully is someone in management—the boss, manager, supervisor, or crew chief, so this makes the work environment even *more* likely to remain toxic. One might wonder why targets of WB are not protected under the law since this is such a prevalent problem across the country, but, as of the date of this chapter, there is no federal law to prevent WB and protect the victims thereof in spite of continuing efforts by the Institute to get such a law passed.

What may be even more concerning is the response of employers to WB. The Institute reported that 22% of the abuse never came to the attention of the employer, and 34% claimed they were unsure of whether WB occurred in their organization or not (Namie, 2017). Of the WB occurrences where a complaint *was* filed, 26% of employers did nothing while 46% completed a cursory investigation, yet nothing changed as a result. When employers *did* take allegations of WB seriously and followed up with an investigation that provided proof of the allegations, 23% of the targets found positive change occurring for themselves while 6% of the workplace bullies experienced negative consequences.

Another true story with names and locations omitted may serve to emphasize results of WB further.

Ruth was hired as an executive assistant to the CEO of a small regional medical facility. In addition to supporting the CEO, she was tasked with supporting the CFO and the director of marketing. Todd, the CEO; Matt, the CFO; and Jayne, the director of marketing, all seemed very pleased with their choice of the new executive assistant, and they did their best to make her feel welcome. During her final interview prior to being hired, Ruth had asked what the CEO considered to be the top three things he wanted done in the first 90 days, and once hired, Ruth set about working on the contracts that were Todd's top concern. She learned her job as quickly as possible to make sure she was being productive and providing value to Todd and his team, and her efforts were not going unnoticed. Todd began telling everyone in the office and those who came to meet with him that Ruth was doing an excellent job and how pleased he was with her diligence and competence.

In the beginning, Jayne, the marketing director, took it upon herself to take Ruth around the entire facility and introduce her to everyone. While Jayne seemed friendly enough, as the two women made their way from department to department, Ruth noticed that Jayne would make both critical and snide remarks about different people she was meeting behind their backs. Jayne also seemed to want Ruth to side with her disparaging opinions about the other staff members when Ruth did not know them. Ruth could hear alarm bells in her head as she realized that Jayne could be someone dangerous to disappoint. Thus, while Ruth continued to be both friendly and professional, she was very careful about what she said to Jayne.

As Ruth continued to get things done, Todd's praise grew more effusive, and the more Todd complimented Ruth, the more distance and wariness

Jayne began to display. One day when Todd and Jayne were going to a luncheon together, Jayne made it a point to stop at Ruth's desk to demand a contract Ruth had completed. As Todd and Jayne waited, Ruth went through her files to her contract folder and found it empty. Perplexed, Ruth said she had completed the contract several days before and filed it, but it was not there. Todd did not seem especially concerned as Ruth checked several other locations on her desk where the contract may have been, but Jayne made a cutting remark about Ruth losing a critically important contract before leaving with Todd for the luncheon.

After they left, Ruth went back through all the file folders in case the contract was misfiled, but it had vanished. Several days later, Jayne told Ruth she wanted some papers off her desk for a meeting, and when Ruth went to retrieve the paperwork, she uncovered the missing contract hidden under another file on Jayne's desk. Ruth quietly returned the contract to its rightful location and never said anything about it to either Jayne or Todd. From that point on, Ruth began locking her desk every night when leaving, and she hid the key so Jayne could not gain access to her work. The assistant to the director of nursing, who had a desk next to Ruth's, told her that Jayne had tried to get into Ruth's desk several times and was furious when she found it locked and could not find the key. The other assistant's comment reassured Ruth that she had made a prudent decision. Interestingly, Jayne never said anything to Ruth about trying to access her desk, and Ruth acted like she did not know about Jayne's attempts.

As the days went on, Todd continued to praise Ruth's competence, and the more he did, the more work projects would disappear off Ruth's desk when she was asked to run errands for Jayne. Ruth finally created a spreadsheet and tracked every single letter, contract, and project by date, last location, and who had the paperwork. While constantly updating the spreadsheet doubled her workload, Ruth knew she needed to keep her job because she had a family to support, and the spreadsheet helped her track the mysterious disappearance of her work. Several weeks after Ruth began her spreadsheet, Todd left for his annual 2-week vacation. He left Matt and Jayne in charge of the office, at which point Jayne began to abuse Ruth on a daily basis.

Jayne would order Ruth to do something and then claim she never told Ruth to do it. She wrote scathing emails questioning Ruth's intelligence, and subtly suggested Ruth's job was on the line. Jayne's verbal abuse escalated when other people were not in the office, and eventually, Ruth was at wits end. She printed out the emails and took them to HR to find out what could be done to help her.

The head of human resources (HR) listened to Ruth's concerns, read the emails, and he agreed they were abusive. He also warned Ruth that Jayne had a substantial amount of power with Todd, and told Ruth that Jayne had turned her sites on other employees she disliked in the past and had gotten them fired. The head of HR told Ruth she could file a complaint with corporate headquarters, but that by the time they got around to looking into things, Jayne would have heard about it, and Ruth would be fired. Instead, he suggested that Ruth wait for Todd to return from vacation, schedule time for a private meeting, and share her concerns with him. Discouraged, Ruth returned to work, counting the days until Todd returned. Jayne's attitude and abuse were so wearing that Ruth felt ill coming into work each day, and she dreaded returning after a weekend.

When the day of Ruth's meeting with Todd finally arrived, she gathered the documented proof of her treatment and entered his office. He was in a good mood after his vacation and asked Ruth what was on her mind. Ruth addressed her concerns as tactfully as possible and offered the emails to Todd, but he refused to even look at them. He suggested that Ruth do her best to smooth things over with Jayne, and then ended the meeting. Ruth left the room feeling ill: she had no idea how she could resolve Jayne's dislike of her, but she tried again. She continued being professional, courteous, and friendly toward Jayne, and Ruth offered to do extra things to help her, but Jayne continued to treat Ruth poorly.

About a week after Ruth's meeting with Todd, he asked her to come to his office at the end of the workday. Ruth showed up on time, and Todd invited her in and invited her to sit. Ruth had taken her notebook and pen to jot down notes of what Todd might need done since they often had brief start or end of day meetings. Todd began by saying he wanted Ruth to know she was the best executive assistant he had ever had, but he was letting her go. Since Todd, Matt, and Jayne were a team, Ruth had to please all three of them, or she was not pleasing any of them, and Jayne was not pleased with Ruth at all.

Ruth was shocked! She had never been fired before. Ruth was still reeling when Todd offered to give her a personal letter of recommendation and be a good reference on her behalf. Todd also told Ruth she was welcome to be re-hired at another facility in the corporate chain if she wanted to stay with the company, and he said that although Ruth had not been with the facility long enough to qualify for her vacation pay, he was willing to give it to her if she signed a waiver promising not to take any further action against the facility or Jayne. Todd's final remark let Ruth know she might have some type of legal action against the facility, but as much as she wanted to refuse to sign the waiver, she needed the money to support her family while she found other work, so Ruth reluctantly signed the waiver and received the small amount of vacation pay due her after only 3 months on the job.

HEALTH IMPLICATIONS FROM WORKPLACE BULLYING

In 2017, the Institute found that 40% of targets (sample size, 1,008) experienced impacts to their health from working in toxic environments where they were bullied (Namie, 2017). In fact, health consequences are common results of both WB and workplace intimate partner violence (WIPV). A longitudinal study of 1,084 hospital employees showed that long-term bullying affected the stress levels of the study participants for a clinical diagnosis of depression, and suggested there might be a likelihood that WB could contribute to cardiovascular disease if obesity was not involved (Kivimaki et al., 2003). Another study of 22 bullied employees indicated that many of the targets felt the experience was a traumatic event or a life crisis that caused them to feel internally wounded and vulnerable (Hallberg & Strandmark, 2006). Hallberg and Strandmark (2016) uncovered a number of health issues related to WB.

For example, bullied targets complained of insomnia, an inability to focus, anxiety, mood swings, depression, fear, and feelings of despair. Other symptoms of WB included memory loss, gastric problems, headaches, respiratory problems, cardiac problems, pain, and hypertension; in addition, study participants with preexisting chronic health concerns such as diabetes or asthma experienced exacerbated symptoms from the bullying. Targets of WB also experienced thoughs of suicide; and both women and men had a higher likelihood of PTSD when bullied, with women experiencing higher levels of PTSD when compared to men. (Hallberg & Strandmark, as cited in Lassiter, 2017a).

WORKPLACE INTIMATE PARTNER VIOLENCE

As with many things, the definition of physical, mental, and emotional abuse has changed over the years. Today, the term *domestic violence* has broadened to cover anyone living in a domestic situation that abuses or is abused by another person in the household; so, this means a son who abuses his parents or an aunt who abuses her cousin's children is committing domestic violence. In contrast, *intimate partner violence* (IPV) specifically relates to abuse between intimate partners, whether they are the opposite sex or the same sex, and whether they are cohabiting, married, or dating. In this chapter workplace intimate partner violence will be known as WIPV, and it may be male on female (the most common form of IPV), female on male, or same sex partners against each other. IPV is no respecter of persons. Not only does it happen to women and men, IPV happens in all socioeconomic classes, at all educational levels, in any job or profession, and it happens to people of any skin color and any ethnicity.

> IPV takes many forms: verbal insults, emotional maltreatment, psychological cruelty, physical violence, and sexual assault... Emotional and psychological abuse includes threats or actions of withdrawing affection, withholding financial support, stalking, public or private humiliation, or devaluing the intimate partner's self-esteem or self-confidence. Physical violence encompasses strik-

> ing, kicking, biting, punching, hair-yanking, suffocating, or using some form of weapon to cause bodily injury or death to the partner; and sexual abuse includes forced sexual intercourse, unwanted touching, and rape including sodomy, anal or oral sexual contact. (Lassiter, 2017a, pp. 44–45)

The most recent National Intimate Partner and Sexual Violence Survey in 2010 found the following, after interviewing 16,507 adults (9,086 women and 7,421 men): Nearly 1 in 10 women in the United States (9.4%) has been raped by an intimate partner in her lifetime, including completed forced penetration, attempted forced penetration, or alcohol/drug facilitated completed penetration. Approximately 1 in 45 men (2.2%) has been made to penetrate an intimate partner during his lifetime. An estimated 16.9% of women and 8.0% of men have experienced sexual violence other than rape (being made to penetrate an intimate partner, sexual coercion, unwanted sexual contact, and non-contact unwanted sexual experiences) by an intimate partner in their lifetime. Women and men experienced many types of physical violence ranging from being slapped to having a knife or gun used against them. Women had a significantly higher lifetime prevalence of severe physical violence by an intimate partner (24.3%) compared to men (13.8%). Women had a significantly higher lifetime prevalence of stalking by an intimate partner (10.7%) compared to men (2.1%). Nearly half of U.S. women (48.4%) and half of U.S. men (48.8%) have experienced at least one psychologically aggressive behavior by an intimate partner during their lifetime (Breiding, Chen, & Black, 2014, pp. 1–2).

What you may be surprised to learn is the reasons people give for committing IPV against their partner. Flynn and Graham (2010) completed a study on the justifications for IPV, and the results were as follows:

> IPV [was used] to show love, or IPV [was] necessary because of the partner's character flaws. IPV [was committed due to] an inability to communicate, or IPV [was] caused by stress over everyday living situations such as job loss, stress from child rearing or family situations, marital challenges, financial problems, health issues, or a variety of stressors. In fact, any pressure rated highly as being the reason for IPV. Additional reported reasons for IPV included perceived aggression, threats to a relationship or threats of harm to the individual. Arguments, refusing sex, being insensitive, or disrespectful, or lying were all reasons given for justifying IPV. Alcohol abuse was cited several times as being the cause of IPV with intoxicated men being the most common perpetrators; drugs were mentioned less often as contributing to IPV. Women were more likely to commit IPV for emotional reasons such as punishment or anger while men were more likely to perpetrate IPV to inflict pain. Attempting to stop a partner from doing something rated relatively high as a reason for IPV as did gaining a sense of control. (Flynn & Graham, as cited in Lassiter, 2017a, pp. 50–51)

"Additional causes of IPV [were] related to mental health problems such as post-traumatic stress disorder (PTSD), depression, or anxiety, and these conditions linked back to alcohol and substance abuse as well" (Reingle, Jennings, Connell, Businelle, & Chartier, 2014, as cited in Lassiter, 2017a, p. 52).

HEALTH EFFECTS OF INTIMATE PARTNER VIOLENCE

It should be obvious that the results of recurring IPV will erode the victim's health over time. "A World Health Organization (WHO) study found that there may be internal injuries as well as physical injuries like bruising, fractures, concussions, wounds, bite marks, eye or ear injuries, sprains, burns, signs of forced sexual violence and other visible symptoms" (García-Moreno, Jansen, Ellsberg, Heise, & Watts, 2005, as cited in Lassiter, 2017a, p. 57). Cardiovascular problems, chronic pain, central nervous system complications, a greater probability of sexually transmitted disease, unwanted pregnancy, miscarriage, or birth problems are also possible (García-Moreno, Jansen, Ellsberg, Heise, & Watts, 2005; Ghanbarpour, 2011). IPV victims often develop memory problems or display mental health issues like PTSD, anxiety, psychosomatic disorders, depression, and attempted suicide (Dutton et al., 2006; García-Moreno et al., 2005; Ghanbarpour, 2011). There is an additional risk of IPV victims becoming substance abusers as well (Dutton et al., 2006).

WORKPLACE INTIMATE PARTNER VIOLENCE

Currently, WIPV costs employers an average of $1.8 billion in reduced productivity and nearly 8 million workdays each year, and this fails to account for the health care costs charged to employers that are caused by injuries, counseling services, or crisis intervention (Giga, Hoel, & Lewis, 2008; Rice, Finkelstein, Bardwell, & Leadbetter, 2004). The aforementioned numbers neglect to include indirect costs such as legal issues or the organization's reputation (Bryant, 2010). A study by Corso, Mercy, Simon, Finkelstein, and Miller (2007) found that there are 2.2 million medical injuries from WIPV annually in the United States at the cost of $4 billion, and the cost of lost productivity from those injuries amounted to $33 billion—these were only from injuries reported by the victims of WIPV; many injuries were not. Of these costs, the National Center for Injury Prevention and Control found that employers cover 52% of the costs of WIPV (Doll & Binder, 2004).

Even more surprising are the findings from a 2012 nationwide study by Tiesman, Gurka, Konda, Coben, and Amandus (2012) on female homicides (known as *femicides*) between the years of 2003 and 2008. In total, 142 women were murdered in their workplace, and most of these were in private organizations rather than public agencies. "[A total of] 78% of women were murdered by IPV; 51% of the victims died in an accessible building or a parking lot, and the perpetrators were most often current or past husbands or boyfriends" (Tiesman et al., 2012, as cited in Lassiter, 2017a, p. 59).

Moreover, many employers are either unaware, discount, or ignore the fact that many of the perpetrators of WIPV may actually work for their companies or organizations, and many of these perpetrators have been found to use company time to commit crimes against their intimate partners (Lim, Rioux, & Ridley, 2004). Lim et al. (2004) study of 152 convicted heterosexual IPV abusers indicated that almost 75% of the abusers had easy access to their partners at work; 75% used their employer's resources whether it was phones, email, or company vehicles to intimidate, threaten, check up on, or pressure their partner; and, nearly 25% of the abusers contacted their partner despite a restraining order that was in place. Lim et al. (2004) also found that 11% of the abusers took weapons with them to work.

Surprisingly, employers often supported the abusers, and the abusers were often allowed to make required court appearances while using paid work time or being provided with paid leaves of absence (Lim et al., 2004). Even more unsettling was the fact that some of the employers were supportive of employees who were convicted of abuse, and 10% of those employers even posted bail for abusive employees (Lim et al., 2004). (Remember, these abusers were already convicted of their crime, so it was not simply a matter of *he said, she said.*)

The key point of all this information on WIPV is that your organization and you, as a leader, have a responsibility to provide safety at work for employees or run afoul of the Occupational Safety and Health Act (OSH Act). If one of your employees is severely harmed by WIPV, your organization may be required to allow the victim time off through the Family Medical Leave Act (FMLA) or through the Americans with Disability Act (ADA; Meinert, 2011). "By 2011, more than 40 state laws existed that offered some form of protection for victims of WIPV; further[more, and] depending on the circumstances, a number of states provided unemployment insurance for the victims of WIPV" (Meinert, 2011, as cited in Lassiter, 2017a, p. 63).

COACHING YOUR PEOPLE

Now that you have the background on both WB and WIPV, how do you, as a leader, handle such situations? The first, and the most important, thing you can do is actually *lead.* It is the leadership of an organization that sets the tone for the rest of the company. If you are not part of the senior management team, meet with them and encourage the creation of an atmosphere of *zero tolerance* for any type of workplace violence, then make sure your people are aware of the policy. Clearly define what each type of workplace violence is and post the definitions throughout your business location along with posters indicating the zero-tolerance policy for WB and WIPV. Include definitions for WB and WIPV in the employee handbook, be sure to have a discussion on the topic with your people, and provide training at least once a year so all employees are clear about both forms of workplace violence. Staff needs to understand what WB and WIPV are, how to recognize them, what to do about it if they see them occurring or are happening to them, and how and when to report these forms of workplace violence to management (immediately).

Encourage senior management to create a threat assessment team, including an expert in security to help your organization keep your work environment safe from intruders. Ensure that doors are kept locked where appropriate, and use security badges or other staff IDs that have current photos so employees are clearly recognizable. Establish emergency procedures for a time when intruders gain access, and be sure every employee knows what to do, where to go, how to get there, and ways of staying safe when possible. Again, this can be part of your annual training on workplace violence in general.

Make sure that employees have confidence that they will be heard and anything they report will remain confidential. Encourage bystanders (who are usually coworkers) to come forward and report abuse as well, and ensure their confidentiality so they feel safe and protected. Furthermore, be sure there is *no* retaliation against your people if and when they step up and report abuse in any form. Unless and until your people believe they can trust you (and any management team member), it is unlikely you may hear about workplace violence until it escalates into a serious, if not deadly, situation. Support for the targeted victim is [also] critical if the [organizational] culture is going to change enough to reduce the incidence of violence and bullying in the future (Lassiter, 2017b).

Additional steps to take include the following:

> Train supervisors on identifying/defining workplace violence, de-escalating conflict, seeking out support and resources to prevent/respond to violence, understand workplace policies and use of policies when appropriate. Provide confidential reporting options for all levels of employees with a clear escalation plan. [Investigate] suspected or reported incidents of workplace violence [and take] administrative or disciplinary actions including termination [when appropriate]. Build teamwork and develop trust, so prevention and intervention are possible, accepted and expected. (Lassiter, 2017b, pp. 4–5)

- Be sure your people can identify precursors to violence, and make sure they understand that threats to injure a coworker should be considered as having the same consequences as an actual action (Lassiter, 2017b). Moreover, provide access to an Employee Assistance Program (EAP) if your organization is able to do so. Employee Assistance Programs can provide short-term counseling and other solutions as well as referrals to other resources to help employees who have been victimized or who are the perpetrators of workplace violence and request help to end their actions (Lassiter, 2017a).
- Finally, there is a saying in coaching: "People don't care how much you know until they know how much you care" (Theodore Roosevelt, n.d.). Doing your best to live by these words will help you to establish and develop open and honest communication with your people and build a bond of trust. Where there is trust and open communication, there is less likely to be subversive behavior that undermines your ability to lead, and it is more likely to create a work environment that is healthy and safer with mutual respect among your team. Foster a high-quality workplace where you are a leader that your people *get to follow,* and your life as a leader will be one that is emulated by others.

REFERENCES

Breiding, M. J., Chen J., & Black, M. C. (2014). *Intimate partner violence in the United States—2010.* Atlanta, GA: National Center for Injury Prevention and Control, Centers for Disease Control and Prevention. Retrieved from https://www.cdc.gov/violenceprevention/pdf/cdc_nisvs_ipv_report_2013_v17_single_a.pdf

Bryant, M. R. (2010). *Dealing with violence in the workplace.* Retrieved from http://www.shrm.org/india/hr-topics-and-strategy/employee-advocacy-relations-and-engagement/pages/dealing%20with%20violence%20in%20the%20workplace.aspx

Corso, P. S., Mercy, J. A., Simon, T. R., Finkelstein, E. A., & Miller, T. R. (2007). Medical costs and productivity losses due to interpersonal violence and self-directed violence. *American Journal of Preventive Medicine, 32*(6), 474–482. https://doi.org/10.1016/j.amepre.2007.02.010

Crothers, L. M., Lipinski, J., & Minutolo, M. C. (2009). Cliques, rumors, and gossip by the water cooler: Female bullying in the workplace. *The Psychologist-Manager Journal, 12*(2), 97–110. https://doi.org/10.1080/10887150902886423

Doll, L., & Binder, S. (2004). Injury prevention research at the Centers for Disease Control and Prevention. *American Journal of Public Health, 94*(4), 522–524. Retrieved from https://www.ncbi.nlm.nih.gov/pmc/articles/PMC1448287

Dutton, M. A., Green, B. L., Kaltman, S. I., Roesch, D. M., Zeffiro, T. A., & Krause, E. D. (2006). Intimate partner violence, PTSD, and adverse health outcomes.

Journal of Interpersonal Violence, 21, 955–968. https://doi.org/10.1177/0886260506289178

Flynn, A., & Graham, K. (2010). "Why did it happen?" A review and conceptual framework for research on perpetrators' and victims' explanation for intimate partner violence. *Aggressive Violent Behavior, 15*(3), 239–251. https://doi.org/10.1016/j.avb.2010.01.002

García-Moreno, C., Jansen, H., Ellsberg, M., Heise, L., & Watts, C. (2005). *WHO multi-country study on women's health and domestic violence against women: Initial results on prevalence, health outcomes and women's responses*. Geneva, Switzerland: WHO Press. Retrieved from https://www.who.int/reproductivehealth/publications/violence/24159358X/en/

Ghanbarpour, S. A. (2011). *Understanding factors that influence the practice of safety strategies by victims of intimate partner violence* (Doctoral dissertation). Available from ProQuest Dissertations and Theses database. (UMI No. 3528556)

Giga, S. I., Hoel, H., & Lewis, D. (2008). *The costs of workplace bullying*. London, England: Unite the Union.

Hallberg, L. R., & Strandmark, M. K. (2006). Health consequences of workplace bullying: Experiences from the perspective of employees in the public service sector. *International Journal of Qualitative Studies on Health and Well-Being, 1*(2), 109–119. https://doi.org/10.1080/17482620600555664

Kivimaki, M., Virtanen, M., Vartia, M., Elovainio, M., Vahtera, J., & Keltikangas-Järvinen, L. (2003). Workplace bullying and the risk of cardiovascular disease and depression. *Occupational Environmental Medicine*, 779–783. https://doi.org/10.1136/oem.60.10.779

Lassiter, B. J. (2017a). *Workplace intimate partner violence and workplace bullying: Best practices for early bystander intervention training* (Doctoral Dissertation). Available from ProQuest Dissertations and Theses database. (UMI No. 10641416)

Lassiter, B. J. (2017b). *Bystanders: The secret to ending workplace intimate partner violence and workplace bullying*. Unpublished White Paper.

Lim, K. C., Rioux, J., & Ridley, E. (2004). *Impact of domestic violence offenders on occupational safety & health: A pilot study*. Maine Department of Labor and Family Crisis Services. Retrieved from http://www.state.me.us/labor/labor_stats/publications/dvreports/domesticoffendersreport.pdf

Lutgen-Sandvik, P., Namie, G., & Namie, R. (2009). Workplace bullying: Causes, consequences, and corrections. In P. Lutgen-Sandvik & B. D. Sypher (Eds.), *Destructive organizational communication* (pp. 27–52). New York, NY: Routledge Press.

Maurer, R. (2014). *When domestic violence comes to work*. Retrieved from https://www.shrm.org/resourcesandtools/hr-topics/risk-management/pages/domestic-violence-workplace-nfl-ray-rice.aspx

Meinert, D. (2011, October 1). Out of the shadows. *HR Magazine*, 50–55.

Namie, G. (2017). *2017 Workplace Bullying Institute U.S. workplace bullying survey* (Survey Report). Retrieved from https://workplacebullying.org/multi/pdf/2017/2017-WBI-US-Survey.pdf

Occupational Safety & Health Administration. (n.d.). *Enforcement*. Retrieved from https://www.osha.gov/SLTC/workplaceviolence/standards.html

Reingle, J. M., Jennings, W. G., Connell, N. M., Businelle, M. S., & Chartier, K. (2014). On the pervasiveness of event-specific alcohol use, general substance use, and mental health problems as risk factors for intimate partner violence. *Journal of Interpersonal Violence 29,* 2951–2970. https://doi.org/10.1177/0886260514527172

Rice, M. W., Finkelstein, E., Bardwell, R. A., & Leadbetter, S. (2004). The economic toll of intimate partner violence against women in the United States. *Violence and Victims, 19*(3), 259–272. https://doi.org/10.1891/vivi.19.3.259.65767

Roosevelt, T. (n.d). “People don’t care how much you know until they know how much you care.” Retrieved from https://www.goodreads.com/quotes/34690

Saunders, P., Huynh, A., & Goodman-Delahunty, J. (2007). Defining workplace bullying behaviour professional lay definitions of workplace bullying. *International Journal of Law and Psychiatry, 30*(4–5), 340–354. https://doi.org/10.1016/j.ijlp.2007.06.007

Tiesman, H. M., Gurka, K. K., Konda, S., Coben, J. H., & Amandus, H. E. (2012). Workplace homicides among U.S. women: The role of intimate partner violence. *Annals of Epidemiology, 22*(4), 277–284. https://doi.org/10.1016/j.annepidem.2012.02.009

Workplace Bullying Institute. (2018). *Who gets targeted: Why me?* Retrieved from https://www.workplacebullying.org/individuals/problem/who-gets-targeted/

CHAPTER 13

CONFLICT COACHING MODEL TECHNIQUES FOR WORKPLACE MANAGERS, LEADERS, AND PRACTITIONERS

Gary Boettcher

Managers who help their people resolve conflict through a self-determined learning experience will find themselves leading a highly effective organization humming along with decisively competitive productivity.

—Gary Boettcher

Some people always seem to be arguing, fighting, or entrenched in negative activity that angers others or creates rifts among friends, coworkers, and even family members. Keep reading and you will learn more about how to manage troubled workplace relationships driven by these ostensibly difficult personalities through conflict-coaching techniques.

Coaching methodologies are deeply personal and require a high degree of trust in order to build a constructive coach–client relationship. This chapter is written in the first person because conflict coaching is such a deeply personal experience. Discussing processes and techniques from a

From Discord to Harmony, pages 219–243

personal perspective will help readers embrace the topics of coaching conflict and conflict coaching (two separate experiences), especially for managers overseeing workplace disputes where relationships matter.

This chapter will focus on how the comprehensive conflict coaching model and CINERGY™ model of conflict coaching can be applied along with other conflict management principles to generate consensus-based durable outcomes (Jones and Brinkert, 2008; Noble, 2012). When properly applied, these techniques can be practical at all organizational levels, with organized labor, and in personal life settings.

What makes me qualified to write on this topic and why use conflict-coaching principles instead of other alternative dispute resolution processes such as arbitration and mediation? After earning a master's degree in dispute resolution/conflict management, I earned Virginia Supreme Court mediator certifications in all four Virginia courts and completed the Federal Mediation and Conciliation Service (FMCS) labor arbitrator-training program, which granted me membership to panels of FMCS labor arbitrators around the country. My Myers-Briggs type is INTP, and I have a highly innovative cognitive style based on Kirton A-I theory (Kirton, 2011), thus I am forever trying to learn "why" and ultimately help folks improve their personal performance, especially when it comes to workplace dynamics.

Also, as a high-ranking member of organized labor and later as president of an international trade organization (Coalition of Airline Pilots Associations [CAPA]), with access to top-level government cabinet and executive officials, I spent two decades helping people and organizations manage disputes through collaborative and integrative processes. Later in my career, I sat as a neutral on more than 100 cases when I realized that my efforts to help resolve intractable disputes were taking place too late in the process. People and organizations trapped at the impasse barricade were so entrenched in destructive behaviors and negative emotions that I could do little to heal broken relationships and restore trust.

In 2009 I began providing third-party neutral facilitation services that helped people and organizations achieve successful resolutions *before* relationships soured. Coaching consultations became a mainstay of my practice. Eventually I learned how to implement techniques that address differences in personality (Myers, McCaulley, Quenk, & Hammer, 2003), cognitive style (Kirton, 2011), and perspective-taking so as to capture the value of diverse thought. In that journey I discovered two conflict coaching models: (a) the Jones and Brinkert (2008) model of conflict coaching and (b) the CINERGY model (Noble, 2012), and have since used both models to help clients manage workplace and life conflicts.

Conflict is a complex concept found in all facets of our lives, from family relationships to international politics. Unresolved and unmanaged conflict is more than toxic to the workplace environment. Dana (2006) suggests that unmanaged employee conflict may be the largest manageable cost in today's modern organizations. Furthermore, Dana (2006) claims that 65% of performance problems are a result of stressed employee relationships and that managers spend up to 42% of their time managing team conflict instead of organizational agendas (Dana, 2006; Hessel, 2003). Unmanaged workplace conflict results in wasted time, reduced quality in decision-making, loss of skilled and talented workers, increased training costs, unnecessary restructuring, sabotage/theft/damage to workplace assets, lower job motivation and reduced satisfaction, lost work time, increased health costs, poorer customer relations, and overall lost productivity (Dana, 2006).

Conflict is too knotty and intricate to be managed by any one theoretical perspective. As Edward Deming said, "All models are wrong, but some are useful" (1997). Techniques can be applied across all dimensions of society and within the workplace to mitigate situations that threaten to fragment relationships and diminish organizational productivity. Based on my extensive experience coaching workplace conflict and applying conflict coaching techniques, when combined effectively, I found these processes to be highly useful to my clients (Jones & Brinkert, 2008; Noble, 2012).

First, it is important to recognize that conflict tension is a necessary part of optimal creativity. Conflict is neither good nor bad, and it would be a grave error to try to eradicate it entirely. However, unmanaged conflict can be harmful. Your goal as a supervisor/practitioner should be to manage tension at an effective level so as to extract the highest value attainable from any such situation.

Your inability to manage conflict could result in destructive behaviors. But if you do it right, you can capture the value of a diversity of thought and increase workplace efficiencies. Which would you prefer to achieve?

COACHING VERSUS THERAPY, COUNSELING, AND CONSULTING

Let us start by defining some key concepts and identifying some misconceptions and misused terms. I will begin with the differences between counseling, consulting, therapy, and coaching.

According to the *Farlex Partner Medical Dictionary*, a *psychotherapist* (or therapist) is a generic term for the person who treats mental illness or emotional disturbances through both verbal and nonverbal communication in the field of clinical psychology. Therapists help those with mental and emotional challenges. The terms therapist and psychotherapist are widely accepted as interchangeable in the field of medicine ("Psychotherapist," n.d.). People often mistakenly say "I am seeing a therapist" when in reality they are visiting with a counselor or a coach.

A *counselor* is a professional "trained in providing information, guidance, and recommendations to individual clients or families to support their decision-making and development of coping skills" ("Counselor," n.d.). Counselors help people manage past difficulties.

Whitmore (2002) explains, "Coaching is unlocking a person's potential to maximize their own performance. It is helping them to learn rather than teaching them" (p. 8). Furthermore, Hudson (1999) writes, "A coach is someone trained and devoted to guiding others into increased competence, commitment, and confidence.... A coach is a person who facilitates experiential learning that results in future-oriented abilities" (p. 6). The excellent coach helps the client to heuristically grow and make constructive changes that positively affect the client's future. Coaches often ask questions like, "What can *you* do differently next time to improve the outcome?" It is a process of self-discovery and self-determination.

Goldsmith, Lyons, and McArthur (2012) cite another profession commonly confused with the pedagogies of coaching, counseling, and therapy; that is, consulting. Goldsmith, et al., (2012) notes that the coaching consultant "Helps the client to develop a new way of seeing, feeling about, and behaving in situations that are defined by the client as problematic" (p. 37). Even though many consulting gigs contain some aspect of coaching, there is a need to clearly define the three roles that differentiate consulting from coaching. A consultant is: (a) an expert on specific topics, (b) a diagnostician and fixer of processes and organizational factors, and (c) a process expert that helps the client improve, manage, and create ways to better manage the organization or self (Goldsmith, et al., 2012). The consultant generally focuses on fixing processes versus people.

A common way of differentiating the four professions is that therapists strive to fix what is broken; counselors try to heal the past, consultants fix or improve processes, and coaches endeavor to help their clients manage a better personal future. Therapies, counseling, consulting, and coaching are distinct professions that help people manage their lives. But with coaching, there is one significant difference.

Counseling and therapy professions are highly regulated and require education and training for certification and/or licensure in nearly every state. Certification in one state often is not transferable to another. Coaching and consulting do not require certification or licensure. Anyone can hang a shingle and call himself or herself a coach or consultant. Literally dozens of kinds of coaching and process consultants exist. Coaching is an unregulated profession with dozens of organizations offering pseudo-certifications.

Two primary organizations are striving to bring order and excellence to the profession: The International Association of Coaching (IAC®), and The International Coach Federation (ICF®). These two organizations do not compete with each other because one focuses on coaching methodology while the other grants credentials based on coach performance.

ICF (n.d.) website specifically claims, "The International Coach Federation strives to advance the art, science and practice of professional coaching and exists to lead the global advancement of the coaching profession (Learn More, para. 1)." The ICF also seeks to ensure that training meets ICF standards, with a focus on how well the coach knows the methodology and science behind a specific style of coaching as opposed to how well the coach can effectively implement it. Accredited training programs can be found at the website http://becomea.coach

Alternatively, The International Association of Coaching, IAC, focuses on mastery of the coach's performance versus focus on specific knowledge of a coaching process. The IAC claims the organization: "is an independent, global professional association of coaches dedicated to the ongoing pursuit of coaching mastery in order to effectively support clients toward achieving their goals—wherever the client may be on their personal or professional path" (Overview, para. 8). The IAC claims a specific mission different from the ICF.

> Part of what makes the IAC® different from other coaching organizations is the way we assess coaching mastery, and our belief that attending coach training or graduating from any specific program is not sufficient evidence that a coach can, in fact, coach. (IAC Overview, para. 1)

Clearly, IAC credential emphasis is on coaching performance versus coaching methodology.

The coaching profession is maturing with credentialing balance brought by the IAC and ICF. Largely, coaching models and frameworks draw from academic research, introspective assessments, and the psychological and social sciences. A good coach is incredibly helpful to his or her client and can coach successfully using either or both IAC and ICF perspectives.

COACHING WORKPLACE CONFLICT VERSUS THE COMPREHENSIVE CONFLICT COACHING MODEL

Many coaching frameworks and models can help organizational leaders and supervisors manage workplace conflict. Most coaching models directly involve the client/worker using these steps:

- client-based diagnostics (sometimes using storytelling),
- involving the right stakeholders needed to make necessary changes,
- feedback/assessment processing,

- identification of behaviors that need to change to effect change,
- envisioning of what new relationships would look like,
- review of what has been learned so an action plan can be designed,
- design an introspective plan to evaluate future behaviors to manage change on a continuing basis, and
- development of a timeline to review ongoing/future behaviors and re-evaluations to manage ongoing change (Goldsmith et al., 2012; Jones & Brinkert, 2008).

Generally to make effective change the manager/leader should use all of the aforementioned steps when managing conflict in the workplace or when coaching workers to constructively deal with peer-to-peer conflict.

A major purpose of this chapter is to focus specifically on both the Jones and Brinkert (2008) model of conflict coaching (also known as the comprehensive conflict coaching [CCC] model) and the CINERGY model of conflict management coaching. Additionally, I will address specific conflict management techniques that can be applied by the workplace manager to effectively address workplace conflicts and preserve good working relationships. Before delving into the CCC model, we need to define a couple of more terms.

Exactly what is conflict? The *New Oxford American Dictionary* defines the term conflict as a serious and typically protracted dispute, war, or clash, and identifies 35 more synonymous words within their English thesaurus aligned with the singular word *conflict* (McKean, 2005). For the purpose of this work, conflict means more than a mere difference in opinion. Throughout this chapter I will simply define conflict as "competition for a limited resource." The way folks compete for the limited resource will determine whether the conflict outcome is positive or negative and/or good or bad. How people address the conflict event is a choice. Disputants can approach a conflict event constructively or destructively, therefore, each person must purposely decide what kind of outcome they want and then choose behavior that will result in the desired outcome. Constructive conflict management generally will yield the highest valued outcomes.

A workplace example may help you more clearly understand the definition.

Sally, Jane, and Sam are friends who work in separate parts of the organization. Sally and Jane frequently work together on projects and both like to listen to music while working. Sam is introverted and likes things quiet so he can concentrate. The boss assigns Sam and Sally to work together while Jane is out on medical leave. Sally always has music playing at her desk, and the constant noise is driving Sam crazy. A department policy allows music at a reasonable volume as long as it does not negatively disrupt others' performance. Sam complains to the boss and Sally is eventually called into the boss' office. What happens next? The manager can resolve the issue without worker input or alternatively, the workplace manager can use either the CCC model or CINERGY model to resolve the conflict issue and restore the peer-to-peer relationship to regain workplace efficiencies.

In the above example, Sally's tunes and Sam's quiet world are only preferred differences of opinion/behavior. There was not a conflict until there was a change in the limited resource of "work environment" which disrupted Sam's ability to produce quality work. The supervisor's ability to manage this conflict event could result in restoration of workplace productivity. But if handled improperly, the manager-oriented solution could also anger the person who is not appeased, create an irrevocable split between Sally and Sam, and potentially initiate a department-wide rift.

"The prescriptive approach, in its pure form, assumes that the expert knows what the participants need" (Lederach, 1996, p. 48). Lederach (1995) also notes, "A constructionist view suggests that people act on the basis of the meaning things have for them" (p. 10). In other words, the manager with a prescriptive-constructionist approach would view or create manager-based solutions, without disputant input, based on the manager's personal perspectives. In this case, if the manager is also introverted, he or she may agree with Sam and ask Sally to turn off the music app, not realizing that Sally's music is actually a behavioral motivator that helps her keep her energy up throughout the day (Myers et al., 2003).

The manager coach must not assume he/she will define a satisfactory or fair resolution on behalf of the disputants based solely on the manager's perspective. A therapist may be able to prescribe a course of action in the best interest of a client's mental health resultant of many hours of training and science. But a manager acting as a conflict coach cannot assume, infer, or presume to know what is best for the disputants. Alternatively, the manager must help the clients co-create a self-determined and satisfying resolution. Moreover, manager-based solutions also risk the loss of leadership neutrality and can create a milieu of bias. The disputants must be empowered and allowed the opportunity to resolve the dispute as seen through their respective viewpoints—results based on the parties' collaborative and consensus-based solutions.

The manager can achieve co-created consensus-based results if he/she leads them through the CCC or CINERGY models of conflict coaching. The previous simple example does not need the workers to go through the entire CCC model in eight to 12 1-hour sessions, over the course of a 2–3 month period (a normal timeframe for the CCC model). However, the precepts of the CCC model may provide a framework for the manager to help the disputants amicably resolve their differences with a durable solution that restores the relationship, and thereby preserves workplace harmony and productivity through interest-based processes.

The fundamental cornerstone of coaching excellence is that the clients must freely self-determine a solution-based resolution. Coaches and managers must be careful not to coerce or persuade the coachee(s) to accept a manager-generated outcome (Noble, 2012). Instead, the manager must lead the disputants to a consensus-based resolution that disputants create together in a mutually beneficial effort. Let us closely examine the CCC model and see how it can be used to manage workplace conflict.

OVERVIEW OF THE COMPREHENSIVE CONFLICT COACHING MODEL

Jones and Brinkert (2008) write, "Conflict coaching is a process in which a coach and client communicate one-on-one for the purpose of developing the client's conflict-related understanding, interaction strategies, and interaction skills." (pp. 4–5). Although not specified in the definition, contextual issues such as organizational culture, social culture systems, interpersonal issues, and communication behaviors, affect any coaching dynamic. Although coaching is generally thought of as *problem solving for one,* the CCC model can be used with multiple employees individually, and even simultaneously with an entire group or team (Noble, 2012). Consider that each workplace group has a cognitive and behavioral style (Kirton, 2011; Myers et al., 2003), which in turn generates a group identity. The group can apply the CCC model principles and create a group resolution through a consensus-based process as led by the department or organizational manager.

The basic CCC model is comprised of three distinct segments: (a) preparation for coaching and a determination if coaching is appropriate, (b) a four-step process of coach-client interactions, and (c) a parallel learning model comprised of assessment, establishing benchmarks of success, re-evaluation, and continued feedback.

The CCC model is a basic "rock and roll" model where what is discovered in the current stage may fundamentally change a discovered perception in a previous stage. That means the client will rock forward, make new discoveries, and then roll backwards modifying and validating past perspectives, and then rock forward again to progress to the next stage with new viewpoints.

Centric to the CCC model is the core four-step process:

1. Discovering the initial story, refining the story, and testing the story
2. Exploring three perspectives that define relationships:
    a. identity
    b. emotion
    c. power

3. Crafting the best story—imagining what the best outcome could look like
4. Enacting the best story—identifying behaviors needed to achieve success

Following successful completion of these four stages, the coach and client must work to assess the level of the client's learning experience and then create a timeline of implementation actions to complete the success strategy.

Jones and Brinkert stress that the length of the coaching process is determined by the depth of the conflict, the ability of the client to envision and move forward, and the time it takes to manage the respective degree of *lost face* by the aggrieved. Jones and Brinkert (2008) suggest that a moderately extensive conflict-coaching relationship could take about 10 1-hour sessions over the course of 2–3 months. A complicated situation might require multiple sessions in each of the four steps before the client can move forward with confidence. In lesser disputes, a 1-hour session may suffice. But the value and richness of a deep coach–client relationship should not be sacrificed merely to save time or money.

PLANNING FOR THE COACHING EXPERIENCE

The first step in every neutral third-party intervention is an initial conversation to determine whether the coach and client are a fit. The manager may determine that he/she should not act as conflict coach so as not to risk the chance of losing office-place neutrality or be seen as biased by one of the disputants. Instead, the manager would have an outside party conduct the coaching sessions. After all, the goal is to achieve workplace synergy where the entire staff is humming the same tune. Bias or favoritism will destroy trust and ultimately disrupt work.

Noble and Jones and Brinkert both recommend that the coach determine whether there are any reasons for recusal (bias, conflict of interest, or strong philosophical differences) from the prospective coach–client relationship. Second, the coach must decide whether they have the experience and skills to meet the client's needs. Third, the coach must determine whether the client is of the right frame of mind to benefit from a coaching process or whether there are mental competency issues. Is there credible potential for the client to engage in self-evaluation, determination, and focus to make any necessary changes? Fourth, the coach must determine whether the client has the time and motivation to meet and fully engage in the process. Finally, the coach must help ground the client's expectations. Frisch (2005) also suggests that if there are issues of substance abuse or psychological impairment, the coach should refer the client candidate to a therapist group instead of coaching.

IMPARTIALITY AND NEUTRALITY

Based on my extensive experience as a neutral third-party practitioner, clients too often are looking for justification and retribution and expect the neutral coach to legitimize the client's feelings and retribution-seeking expectations. Every coach/manager coach must strive to be impartial and neutral.

Impartiality and neutrality are separate concepts, but not mutually exclusive. *Impartiality* is the absence of bias or preference for an interest, person, process, or outcome (Moore, 2003). *Neutrality* is the absence of a preference for a specific type of relationship or behavior between disputants and or the third-party neutral and/or the absence of expectation of favor for behaving or acting a certain way when sitting as a neutral consultant (Moore, 2003). No person is without bias because we all have opinions. Being neutral means you have the self-control to not allow your personal opinion to influence your coach–client relationship or the client's right to self-determine of an outcome resultant of the coaching event (Moore, 2003).

Lesko (2018) wisely notes that often the notion of "perception is reality" leads to jaded bias in the workplace and could be the core factor of a workplace dispute. What others think and "hear" truly matters. Lesko identifies nine common workplace biases that affect how people feel, ultimately act, or react in the workplace. All nine of the Lesko-identified biases identified below can be resolved by seeking balanced perspectives from other cohorts. Coaches need to be aware of and prepared to address these nine biases with clients and insure their own biases do not affect the neutral coach–client relationship:

1. *Self-fulfilling bias or prophecy:* You expect it so subconsciously you help it happen.
2. *Escalation of commitment:* You consciously commit to a known failing effort.
3. *Randomness error:* Haphazard commitment to a hope instead of facts.
4. *Risk aversion:* Failure to take reasoned and measured steps for fear of failure to achieve a task . . . avoiding all risk unnecessarily.
5. *Hindsight bias:* Falsely predicting an outcome after the event has occurred.
6. *Fundamental attribution error:* Blaming yourself for failure when the blame actually rests on external factors beyond your control.

7. *Self-serving:* This is an external bias where others take credit for what the coachee may have accomplished. The client will feel cheated in that others took credit for a job well done that should have been attributed to the client.
8. *Selective perception:* Also known as unfair or unmerited favoritism. It can be unfairly given or taken. The client may be hurt or may unconsciously hurt others, not realizing they have unmerited favor toward someone or a process.
9. *Halo effect:* It is a result of looking at a good part of the bigger view with a failure to fairly and objectively view the entirety of the person, event, or process.

These specific Lesko identified workplace biases are not the only biases that affect people in dispute or neutrals. Although bias can be an important factor in dispute resolution, further discussion is beyond the scope of this chapter. For more information on bias in conflict and dispute resolution settings, see Livingood (2007).

THE COACHING PROCESS: STAGE 1—DETERMINING THE STORY

The coach begins Stage 1, or the *discovery process,* by having the disputant share their *initial story* about the conflict event (Jones & Brinkert, 2008). Stage 1 is multistep in that the coachee shares initial memories, feelings, and activities that took place throughout the conflict event from a variety of perspectives achieved through a series of coaching questions. The coach has the client tell the story several times using a variety of question-based strategies. The overarching goal is to help the coachee discover the complete story from a fact-based perspective in a coherent narrative and in accurate context (Jones & Brinkert, 2008). This is accomplished through client-reflective analysis as led by the coach.

After sharing the initial story, the coach then encourages the client to go beyond the initial description of the conflict event and encourages the client to *refine the story* by asking perspective-taking questions that uncover the counterpart's version of the event. The coach asks the client to tell the story from the client's perspective, "What happened to me, from my viewpoint?" The coach also asks the client to role-play the counterpart's actions and share the possible narratives the counterpart may have felt and/or experienced and may ask a question like, "What happened to me from my counterpart's perspective?" The goal of the coach is to have the coachee chronicle the complete story from a vantage point that represents both disputants' viewpoints (Jones & Brinkert, 2008).

During story refinement, the coach does not challenge, pressure, or persuade the client to draw any conclusions. Rather, this stage is about helping the coachee reach an accurate, coherent, and comprehensive version of the conflict event. The coach will continue to ask questions from a variety of angles until the client's version no longer adds new facts, information, or context to the storyline.

Once the coach thinks the client has shared an accurate historical perspective of the conflict event, the coach then becomes more assertive to test the client's understanding of the event from a fact-based perspective. Generally the coach will challenge any hostile attributions the client has placed on the counterpart to see whether the client can draw any alternative conclusions as to why the counterpart might have acted out in the conflict event. The end of Stage 1 is an opportunity for the coach to help the client become grounded in reality if previous storytelling exercises have not helped the client make more sense out of the conflict event. This end stage is where the coach helps the client validate unsubstantiated assumptions, inferences, and presumptions about the counterpart's behavior and motives. Testing does not always reveal the complete truth or accurately represent all the facts, however, at the end of Stage 1, the coach and client should have a better foundation and understanding of the whole event so further analysis and action can be taken in future stages (Jones & Brinkert, 2008).

STAGE 2: EXPLORING THREE PERSPECTIVES—IDENTITY, EMOTION, AND POWER

Identity, emotion, and power are dominant factors that influence every relationship. In Stage 2, the manager coach will strive to help the client view these three factors as lenses through which the client should comprehensively see the conflict event. The coach can help the client move on to "next actions" only after the client fully understands the influences of identity, emotion, and power. These three factors are inextricably linked, which means they must be treated with the understanding that any specific action that affects one factor will also affect the other two. Thus the manager coach must take the time to ensure that the client has a holistic understanding of how these factors have influenced the conflict event and what role they may play in achieving a solution (Jones & Brinkert, 2008).

Identity

Jones and Brinkert (2008) never clearly define the term identity, yet they closely examine many factors that affect identity. Identity answers the question, "Who am I?" Identity is situational and must be defined in context. In an organizational setting, the identify framework lens is multidimensional, and often these factors are linear:

- Personal: exists beyond the work setting in regard to gender, race, ethnicity, age, origin, and religion
- Professional: credentials, education, and formality (doctor, lawyer, CEO)
- Situational: positional hierarchy within the organization
- Relational: horizontal, lateral, co-worker, and direct report
- Organizational: identity of the organization also identifies the person
- Cultural: impacts both local and broad-based cultural categories, such as a particular race or ethnicity, socioeconomic status, gender, and sexual orientation

Jones and Brinkert (2008) liken identity to facework, which further personalizes identity. If one loses face, they have lost their identity. If they lose their face (identity), their emotions are directly affected, and they likely also lose power. There are four face-saving actions coaches should cover with their clients:

- Never do anything that would diminish someone's face (including the client's). Do not diminish others' faces and do not weaken your own face.
- If you do cause loss of face, do not minimize your role by shifting blame and attention to others. Do not make excuses and do not make counterclaims. Explain why the action was taken, especially if it was meant to minimize further loss of face.
- Take personal responsibility for the behavior: Be accountable, which generally requires an apology without trying to justify the action. Make the conversational repair, and offer up a remedy if one is available.
- If another causes your client face-loss, seek the counterpart's admission and ask them to take responsibility through a specific course of action that is genuine and made in a face-restoring manner.

Emotion

Our memories are generated in the amygdala, and since people feel feelings before they think thoughts (Rusk & Miller, 1993), what we remember about a dispute is generally driven by our feelings and not rational thought. Myers et al., (2003) also notes that *feeling* decision makers often shut down in a feedback conversation when *thinking* decision makers make constructive critical comments that interrupt the feeling decision maker's preference for harmony in workplace relationships. In other words, feeling decision makers personalize critical comments, even if the comments are process based. Disengagement generally results in frustration and further stresses the relationship for both parties.

Myers' National Representative Sample for distribution of types and preferences indicates that 75.5% of women and 43.5% of men are feeling decision makers. Myers et al. (2003) research further specifies that about 68% of managers have a MBTI type preference for sensing, thinking, and judging and are considered thinking decision makers oriented toward linking ideas together through logical connections based on the laws of reason. These combined research facts mean that on average, nearly 60% of organizational employees are feeling decision makers. So managers must not only learn what to say constructively, they must also learn how to say it so the employee receives the feedback well (see Boettcher, 2019, this volume, Chapter 19 or Stone and Heen's [2015] discussion on feedback). Managers need to know their own behavior typology preferences (Myers et al., 2003) so they can appropriately coach/counsel those employees with opposite-behavior typology using language that engages and empowers employees instead of conversationally "shutting them down" (Myers et al., 2003).

Jones and Brinkert (2008) further note, "When a coach clarifies a client's emotions, the coach also narrows the possible resolutions that will be most effective. Emotion also involves a physiological component—a physical sensation and a physical reaction" (p. 93). A rush of emotions that flood the body can make it difficult for the client to think clearly. The ability for either party to rationally continue the conversation due to unmanaged emotions nearly always results in destructive outcomes, either in the present or in the future.

Emotion management is a choice. The first step in constructively managing emotions is for the party to acknowledge the behavior and then take a purposed action that results in a constructive next step. Sometimes a simple pause in the conversation is required so the party can make the next step a constructive and positive event. Do not try to move forward while the client is angry. Acknowledge the anger and then come back to the discussion when the client can move forward with positive emotions (Fisher & Shapiro, 2006).

What and how we value people, places, and things can trigger emotions. Ultimately, ethics, morals, and values drive how clients frame conflict issues and the options they will choose to resolve the event. Action items that are fair, just, and good or bad may also drive the client's outcome expectations. "That is just not right!" can and often is directly connected to emotion and identity, and probably will affect how face is restored. Moreover, a client's conflict style (see Thomas and Kilmann's work on conflict styles at the website http://www.kilmanndiagnostics.com) or in Thomas and Kilmann

(2007) may drive the client to avoidance where shame, anger, frustration, and disappointment are withdrawn and internally buried until the next time when the client may seemingly irrationally explode.

It is important to note that conflict style and emotion-management techniques work only for people with normal and healthy personalities. If a manager or coach suspects there may be mental health issues, he or she should notify Human Resources and get them the help they need. Do not try to be a therapist or psychologist if you are not.

Fisher and Shapiro (2006) suggest five core concerns that build a framework to help people better manage emotions in practically every type of relationship. The core concerns must be met with appropriate actions measured by fairness, honesty, and consistency. Fisher and Shapiro (2006) claim, "The difference between having a core concern ignored or met can be as important as having your nose underwater or above it" (p. 17). The four Fisher and Shapiro core concerns that apply to conflict coaching dynamics are:

- *Appreciation:* Find merit in what others think, feel, or do—show it.
  - Listen beyond the words. Hear the music too.
  - Hear the meta-message buried within the message. Closely examine words that may often come across as noise.
  - Ask questions in your own words to validate and demonstrate that you "heard" what the other person said and meant.
- *Build Affiliation:* Turn your adversary into your colleague by connecting at a personal level.
  - Create a new link by doing your counterpart a favor. Plan joint activities, and execute them with care.
  - Keep contact, meet in person, hold unofficial private meetings, and circle back, but beware of attempts at manipulation.
- *Autonomy:* Respect theirs without impinging on it, and simultaneously expand yours.
  - Expand your autonomy by brainstorming, making recommendations, and creating options with your counterpart before decisions are made.
  - Inform, consult, and then decide together.
- *Acknowledge Status:* Personal, organizational, and social.
  - Proper status-recognition can enhance influence and esteem. So recognize their status, and acknowledge yours.
  - Demeaning a person's status may result in negative emotions such as embarrassment, resentment, shame, or frustration.

Emotions are often thought of as obstacles, yet when managed properly they can become a great asset in dispute-resolution processes. In my experience as a practitioner, humans tend to mirror one another's emotions. If you are positive and upbeat and your counterpart is frustrated and angry, keep an even and upbeat disposition. Eventually your counterpart will move toward neutral and then exhibit positive emotions. Positive emotions mitigate fear and suspicion and can move the relationship from adversarial to cooperative (Fisher & Shapiro, 2006). Be aware that the brain generates chemicals that affect emotions. Chemical generation is initiated by the subconscious state—a state the client cannot control (Rusk and Miller, 1993). More discussion on the effects of brain chemistry and subsequent effect on emotions are addressed in Boettcher (2019, this volume, Chapter 19) on the topic of conversational intelligence (Glaser, 2014).

"Emotions are powerful, always present, and hard to handle" (Fisher & Shapiro, 2006, p. 3). There are three myths or errors about emotions that if mismanaged, will result in more harm to the relationship. First, people cannot just stop having emotions. If someone is angry, they need time to work through the anger. Sometimes a pause with resumption the next day is necessary. The golden rule about anger is: *It is okay for someone to become angry. However, only one person at a time should get angry* (Fisher & Shapiro, 2006). Second, you cannot ignore emotions because emotions affect the body, thinking, and behavior (Fisher & Shapiro, 2006; Rusk & Miller, 1993). If you find yourself having to manage negative emotions, suggest a pause and resume the meeting/discussion at a later date. But always set the date and identify a purpose for the meeting before you leave the current meeting. Third, an attitude of "Just deal with it!" is unrealistic and dangerous. Dealing directly with emotions when on the negative side of the emotion continuum, even for professionals, increases the risk that both parties end up escalating the conversation into a destructive zone and may further erode the relationship (Fisher & Shapiro, 2006). In a confrontation, the stronger the emotions, the higher the risk will be that one or both parties will lose emotional control. Take a pause and begin future discussions with positive emotions. As a manager coach, always strive to determine the parties' relative emotion on the constructive–destructive emotion continuum. What is it? Why is it? How should you manage the moment? Also, people hold or hide meta-emotions that may be covered by another emotion (Jones & Brinkert, 2008). For example, Sally might be angry about having to turn off her music, but the feelings of hurt and disappointment because Sam did not directly share his problem with Sally, could be driving Sally's anger. An apology by Sam and a Sally/Sam co-creation of a solution to manage Sally's music, might restore the empty trust bank, reset the relationship, and get the team humming along again.

Power Perspectives

Much research has been done and many opinions expressed on power dynamics. Whether it is physical size, strength, intelligence, wealth, or social or organizational status, some people have more power than others

(Boettcher, this volume, Chapter 19). In workplace disputes, the manager coach will likely find that compliance, control, dominance, empowerment, and influence factors are commonplace (Jones & Brinkert, 2008). Rusk and Miller (1993) bifurcate power into acts of coercion or persuasion. Coercion forces behavioral change and often leaves a string of destructive emotions in the wake, such as frustration, anger, disappointment, apathy, dissatisfaction, and so on. Persuasion, on the other hand, if managed in a collaborative milieu, generally results in consensus-based decision-making with buy-in and commitment. Persuasion preserves identity and invokes positive emotions, whereas coercion threatens identity and generally fosters hidden negative emotions that can escalate to destructive behaviors over time (Rusk & Miller, 1993).

Social and Cultural Influences on Workplace Relationships

Given the vast amount of diversity in the workplace, social, cultural, and organizational power also play roles in workplace relationships. Hofstede and Hofstede (2005) claim that the individualism index and the collectivist index in regard to power distance-index are negatively correlated. The power distance index (PDI) indicates the degree to which the people are willing to accept these power differences; that is, the higher the number, the more accepting a society is of differences in power between its members. Thus in a large PDI culture (a collectivist region such as Central America), subordinates are highly dependent on their superiors and readily accept power differences built into the hierarchy of the organizational structure. It is also likely that the emotional distance between superior-to-subordinate is great—subordinates are not likely going to challenge their boss' decision. Conversely, in a small PDI culture, such as the United States, workers are more likely to challenge power differences both laterally and horizontally. In a multicultural organization, employees from cultures with a small PDI are likely to challenge others in the workplace, yet those employees from collectivist cultures are generally loath to rock the boat. Peer-to-peer stress may result because cultural differences drive perspectives and expectations of workplace power dynamics, dynamics that are often not clearly understood.

For example, Sally's family came from Panama (high PDI culture) a few years ago. Sally is a family-oriented person and considers her department to be part of her extended family. Sam's family tree dates back to the pre-Revolution time period (low PDI culture). Sam is always respectfully challenging the boss and organizational policies. This open practice of challenging leaders tends to embarrass Sally, and over time she has become resentful of Sam's behavior toward executives and supervisors. Sally hides her resentment and dissatisfaction with Sam's behavior, yet those meta-emotions, resultant from power dynamics that are not culturally understood, helped escalate the music conflict. As the manager coach strives to resolve the dispute between Sally and Sam, the manager needs to ensure that all the three lenses of identity, emotion, and power are adequately addressed.

STAGE 3: CRAFTING THE BEST STORY

Appreciative inquiry is a strength-based process that focuses on what is good or accomplished well (Jones & Brinkert, 2008). Instead of the manager coach asking, "What is wrong?" the focus should be on what is working well and how those dynamics can be used to improve other processes. *Our focus becomes our reality,* so we must identify what the problematic issue(s) may be and then shift our focus to solution-creation. In other words, *craft the best story.* As the manager coach helps the client do so, he or she must be careful to only bring what is best about the past to the present/future. Jones and Brinkert suggest that our models of appreciative inquiry and problem solving look like this:

- *Appreciative Inquiry*: (a) Appreciate and value the best of what is, (b) envision and co-create opportunities of what *might be,* (c) hold a collaborative discussion on what *should be,* and (d) co-create what *will be.*
- *Problem-Solving*: (a) Identify the problem, (b) determine the causes, (c) co-create solutions, and (d) plan and execute an implementation strategy.

Often, to attain the best outcomes the parties must jointly brainstorm ideas, even provocative, grandiose, or unrealistic propositions. Visioning with appropriate tension helps the parties create a consensus-built and durable solution that adds value to the relationship or process. Use phraseology such as, "What does wild success look like?"; "Describe the new world if…"; "Imagine if we could…"; and so on. Learn to ask questions effectively to promote self-discovery (Noble, 2014).

After envisioning the best story, the parties must responsibly test the plan of action for soundness and achievability, especially if the story was subjectively created in lieu of using objective fact-based processes. The client(s) may not have the education or skill set to achieve objective evaluations and might need help from the manager coach. Thus, during the testing phase, it is not uncommon for the story to be modified or for intervening steps to be added. Education, knowledge, skills, and training may also be needed to achieve ultimate success. If the manager coach must change roles to instructor/teacher, that transition must be clearly defined and acknowledged by all parties or the manager coach may risk the loss of neutrality (Jones and Brinkert, 2008).

STAGE 4: COMMUNICATION SKILLS, CONFLICT STYLES, AND NEGOTIATION OPPORTUNITIES

Thompson (2000) states, "Communication is a dynamic process of *listening, processing,* and *expressing* information and meaning... a circular process of transferring information *and* meaning from one person to another person or group, involving a sender, a message, and a receiver" (p. 1). Boettcher (2014) notes that even in a focused communication situation such as the dialogue between commercial airline pilots and air traffic controllers, the three most common mistakes made between these highly trained professionals are readback, hearback, and erroneous information. People simply do not always hear what was said or correctly understand the intended content, even when they are required to repeat back the message and are trained to use precise language. Boettcher (2013) also noted that flawed communication often occurs between organized labor and management, where specific language is used to create complex negotiated contracts. If communication can fail in such circumstances, what is the likelihood that it can fail between two emotionally charged coworkers? The forthcoming discussion will offer strategies the manager coach can use to improve communication between disputants and the workplace in general.

Manager coaches should strive to create a communication model within their departments/organizations such that the sender encodes a message, the receiver decodes the message and recodes the message back to the sender in the form of feedback to create two types of validation: (a) the sender's message was framed so it could be understood, and (b) the receiver correctly understood the intent of the sender's message (Thompson, 2000). The receiver validates the sent message by asking questions for understanding. The receiver can also restate the sender's message by using the receiver's respective language followed up by the question, "Did I understand you correctly?" Do not merely parrot or mirror the same words, you must use your own words or language for accurate validation on the sender's meaning. Using your own language and *getting it right* also helps the sender feel heard.

Confrontation, Confirmation, and Comprehension

Jones and Brinkert (2008) approach communication skills with a focus on confrontation, confirmation, and comprehension. Even minor miscommunications can lead to confrontation. When confrontation occurs, the manager coach must address issues of respect and identity (confirmation) and ensure that both parties can understand and hear the perspectives of their counterparts (comprehension).

Effective communication begins with acknowledging that a conflict event is active, then continues with communication about the conflict issue in a way that respects both clients' identities in a cooperative and non-defensive manner. In other words, people need to "feel heard." When they feel heard they decisively feel like the other party understands their perspective without passing judgment—their identity remains intact, and empathy ensues. This leads to positive emotions, and a continuity of useful power is shaped to balance the relationship.

Disputants must eventually implement any resolution or solution created by the parties to ameliorate the dispute. Even with consensus-based solutions there will likely be some problematic issue during implementation. Development of sound communication practices, feedback processes, and prestructuring other alternative dispute resolution processes is a must to avoid future misunderstandings and unnecessary problematic issues. Alternative dispute resolution processes and conversational intelligence (C-IQ®) are discussed in Boettcher (2019, this volume, Chapters 17 and 19) and Glaser (2014).

CINERGY MODEL OF CONFLICT MANAGEMENT COACHING

In 1999, Connie Noble, a practicing ADR attorney in Canada, began research with a diverse group of adults in a variety of workplace settings to determine why they would engage in one-on-one workplace coaching sessions and what outcomes they expected. In a private conversation and with permission, Noble disclosed that the groups' needs were not "necessarily about resolving matters or delivering hard messages nicely," rather individuals needed to preserve their ability to "be" (to preserve their identity) during a conflict with another human. Subsequently, based on her extensive research, core coaching competencies, a code of conduct, and through certification processes, Noble created the CINERGY model of *conflict management coaching* and practiced the model from 2000 to 2004 in Canada, Ireland, and Australia. She then developed a peer-to-peer workplace coaching model for the Transportation Security Administration and managed the conflict-coaching model from 2004 to 2011. Today she continues her private practice as a coach, educator, and trainer, with clients around the world and is an exemplar within the coaching industry.

The CINERGY model (Noble, 2012) has seven linear stages:

- C: Clarify the goal to help the client determine what he/she might want to achieve during the coaching experience. Goals can and do change during the process. The coach should not make any assumptions or presumptions about the meaning behind the goals first identified by the client. The coach must ask the right kind of questions to validate the meaning of the client's words to facilitate client's self-discovery (Noble, 2014). Sometimes the client simply needs to vent and get the words out before they can move forward, so let them vent without judgment (Noble, 2012).
- I: Inquire about the situation to learn what original interaction(s) precipitated the dispute or conflict event. Focus on the words that drive the client's emotions. Inquiry is not a fact-finding endeavor. Strive to identify whether the client is in conflict with a person, a behavior, or a process.
- N: Name the elements of the conflict event through a deconstruction process so the client can a) increase their own personal awareness and b) consider the counterpart's viewpoint. The N-stage drills down into the concepts first identified in the I-stage. This is also the time to use introspection to identify and acknowledge any new awareness issues, insights, and perspectives from a holistic vantage point. The N-stage is a time to reflect on original goals and make appropriate changes as necessary.
- E: Explore the options and possibilities for achieving the newest goals. It is also a good time to do a SWOT (strengths, weaknesses, opportunities, and threats) analysis on the possible choices. The coach may need to help the client understand that solutions must meet mutually beneficial needs of all concerned parties.
- R: Reconstruct the conflict event to help the client constructively envision a viable and durable plan of action. The coach should confirm the client's plan to ensure that the plan will successfully achieve the client's goals. Reconstruction is a good time to test assumptions, presumptions, and inferences in order to validate the veracity of desired outcome(s). This coaching stage focuses not only on what to do, but also on what should not be done. It is a time for the client to envision how they "want to be" (Noble, 2012). It is a time to solidify future intentions.
- G: Ground the challenges that may preclude the client from achieving a successful outcome. The goal of the coach is to help clients remain constructive, positive, and future-focused as they overcome barriers that would block them from achieving their goals. Grounding happens only after the client constructs a plan of action.

- Y: Yes, the commitment to move forward for the next step. Each coaching session concludes with this step—a positive affirmation to remain future-focused as they move through each stage. Clients often find it is useful to keep a journal that documents emotions, thoughts, and progress. The journal is also a meaningful way to capture introspection and takeaways the client learned throughout the process. It is an excellent way to acknowledge the client's positive progress throughout the CINERGY journey.

Noble claims that the CINERGY model can be used in more than traditional one-on-one coaching sessions. The model can be used with family disputes, estate planning and settlement, or boards of directors and is a useful framework for group-conflict coaching. Additionally the model can be used before, during, and after mediation, during and after conflict events, in education and training sessions, and to generally strengthen an individual's conflict management competence. In other words, the CINERGY model is not dispute-specific.

Core to the CINERGY model is the proper use of questions. Noble (2014) notes, "As with other forms of coaching, asking powerful questions is a core competency that is meant to facilitate client's self-discovery—an integral step in any effort to make positive changes in our lives" (p. 3). The model is grounded in future-focused and goal-orients results based on clients' self-determination. In other words, coaches should not ask leading questions to manipulate a response or action from the client. Neither should the coach make suggestions or tell the client what to do. Coaches frame powerful questions that guide clients through a transformative introspective journey through which they learn about themselves and identify constructive ways to manage future conflict events with confidence to be who they are.

CONCLUDING THOUGHTS

To summarize: Conflict is a complex and multidimensional concept found in all facets of our lives. Conflict is neither good nor bad. However, how people manage conflict is a choice that produces either constructive or destructive outcomes. Rarely is the outcome of conflict neutral, and even if the outcome is neutral, the likelihood is that latent value was left uncovered and unclaimed by the disputants.

The phenomenon of conflict is too knotty and intricate to be managed by any one theoretical perspective or model. Effective conflict managers and dispute-resolution practitioners use a variety of models and techniques.

The comprehensive conflict coaching model and CINERGY model, when managed with effective communication, conflict-resolution strategies, and principled negotiation techniques, are powerful processes for manager coaches and practitioners (see Boettcher, 2019, this volume, Chapter 17, for more on negotiation techniques).

Effective conflict-resolution processes always include telling the story to identify the issues and to reveal the holistic perspectives of the parties. Repair and control of identity (face), emotions, and power, can then lead to more meaningful and respectful conversations as the parties strive to identify the interests and concerns often hidden in a conflict event. Once a deep-dive into the why behind the wants is achieved, the parties can then focus forward and move into creating a meaningful consensus-based resolution that fulfills the criteria of the newly discovered "best story" and preserves the client's desire "to be" (Boettcher, 2019, this volume, Chapter 17; Noble, 2012).

Appreciative inquiry leaves the bad behind and brings the good forward to help the parties co-create mutually beneficial and satisfying solutions that are then implemented through intelligent conversations techniques (Jones & Brinkert, 2008). Enacting the best story through consensus-based problem-solving results in durable resolutions. The durable journey will be interrupted with some problems because complications do occur requiring a newly negotiated modification to move forward again. The constant learning-feedback cycle repeats and is most effectively managed when the parties share a relationship that is filled with trust and transparency. Solutions can be elegant or thorny. Conflict counts, so every coach, leader, and manager should supervise conflict events wisely. If disputants do not constructively manage conflict events and co-create solutions, the outcome may be forced upon the disputant(s) through binding arbitration or litigation processes, which may result in highly unsatisfactory outcomes for all parties.

REFERENCES

Boettcher, G. W. (2013). Analysis of a labor union's organizational structure: Capturing the synergies of constructive conflict in an organizational redesign. *Journal of Conflict Management, 1*(1), 41–57.

Boettcher, G. W. (2014). Underperformance during crisis decision-making situations: A qualitative theory on the role distractions play in pilot performance. *PQDT Open*: ProQuest LLC.

Counselor. (n.d.). *In MegaLexica medical dictionary online.* Retrieved from https://www.online-medical-dictionary.org/definitions-c/counselors.html

Dana, D. (2006). *Managing differences.* Prairie Village, KS: MTI.

Deming, E. (1997). The Deming system of profound knowledge. [Review of the DVD *How are we doing?* Produced by The W. Edwards Deming Institute, 1997].

Fisher, R., & Shapiro, D. (2006). *Beyond reason: Using emotions as you negotiate.* New York, NY: Viking-Penguin Group.

Frisch, M. H. (2005). Coaching caveats. *Human Resource Planning, 28*(3), 14–16.

Glaser, J. E. (2014). *Conversational intelligence.* Brookline, MA: Bibliomotion.

Goldsmith, M., Lyons, L. S., & McArthur, S. (2012). *Coaching for leadership* (3rd ed.). San Francisco, CA: Pfeiffer.

Hessel, G. (2003). The cost and management of organizational conflict. *New Hampshire Business Review, 25*(15), 9A.

Hofstede, G., & Hofstede, G. J. (2005). *Cultures and Organizations: Software of the mind.* New York, NY: McGraw-Hill.

Hudson, F. M. (1999). *The Handbook of coaching: A comprehensive resource guide for managers, executives, consultants, and human resource professionals.* San Francisco, CA: Jossey-Bass.

IAC Overview. (n.d.). International Association of Coaching. *About: Overview.* Retrieved from https://certifiedcoach.org/about/

ICF. (n.d.). *International Coach Federation. Learn more.* Retrieved from http://becomea.coach

Jones, T. S., & Brinkert, R. (2008). *Conflict coaching: Conflict management strategies and skills for the individual.* Los Angeles, CA: SAGE.

Kirton, M. J. (2011). *Adaption-innovation in the context of diversity and change.* New York, NY: Routledge.

Lederach, J. P. (1996). *Preparing for peace: Conflict transformations across cultures.* Syracuse, NY: Syracuse University Press.

Lesko, A. P. (2018). *Go beyond the job description.* Alexandria, VA: SHRM.

Livingood, J. (2008). Addressing bias in conflict and dispute resolution settings. *Dispute Resolution Journal, 62*(4), 52–61.

McKean, E. (2005). *The new Oxford American dictionary.* New York, NY: Oxford University Press.

Moore, C. W. (2003). *The mediation process: Practical strategies for resolving conflict* (3rd ed.). San Francisco, CA: Jossey-Bass.

Myers, I. B., McCaulley, M. H., Quenk, N. L., & Hammer, A. L. (2003). *MBTI Manual: A guide to the development and use of the Myers-Briggs Type Indicator®* (3rd ed.). Mountain View, CA: CPP.

Noble, C. (2012). *Conflict management coaching: The Cinergy model.* Canada: Cinergy.

Noble, C. (2014). *Conflict mastery: Questions to guide you.* Canada: Cinergy.

Psychotherapist. (n.d.). In *Farlex Partner Medical Dictionary.* Retrieved from https://medical-dictionary.thefreedictionary.com/psychotherapist

Rusk, T., & Miller, D. P., (1993). *The Power of ethical persuasion: From conflict to partnership at work and in private life.* New York, NY: Viking Adult.

Stone, D., & Heen, S. (2015). *Thanks for the feedback: The science and art of receiving feedback well.* New York, NY: Penguin Books.

Thomas, K. W., & Kilmann, R. H. (2007). *Thomas-Kilmann Conflict Mode instrument.* Sunnyvale, CA: CPP.

Thompson, H. L. (2000). *The CommunicationWheel [sic] workbook.* Watkinsville, GA: Wormhole.

Whitmore, J. (2002). *Coaching for performance: A practical guide to growing your own skills.* Boston, MA: Nicholas Brealey.

CHAPTER 14

MANAGING CONFLICT IN THE LOCAL CHURCH

Tony Rose

Finding a chapter in this book on conflict in the church may bring a wry smile to your face. I am not sure the reason for your smile, but I do know some not so pleasant experiences that might be the cause. It could be an experience at a church that soured your mind on church for the rest of your life. You may presently be part of a church that is embroiled in a seemingly senseless conflict. There is also the chance that you have been puzzled for years at the inability of many church members to simply admit their church not only has conflicts but handles them terribly.

I have been in church ministry for over 37 years. My last 25 years have been spent as senior pastor in the same church. I would like to be able to tell you that churches are the model to study for properly handling conflict, but I cannot. What I can say is that studying conflict management processes in the church can provide material for developing a uniquely discerning lens for understanding some of the finer details of relational conflict within most any organization.

The subject of conflict management in the church is worthy of a book-length treatment. My aim in this chapter is to offer a few broad categories

From Discord to Harmony, pages 245–257

accompanied by specific insights to help readers better understand the nature of conflicts in the church. There are a couple of limitations I need to set out so that what I write can be properly understood. When I refer to the church, I am addressing a broad spectrum. My aim is to write with enough specificity to provide actionable application for managing conflict in the church. However, due to the limitations of one chapter, I will also write with a generality in hopes that my thoughts can apply to most any church across the broad spectrum of orthodox Christianity. I will not address other faiths because to do so would be writing out of ignorance. The second limitation is that when addressing the church I am addressing church in the culture of the United States. Some of the points I make could possibly cross cultures, but I am not equipped to accurately say whether they could or not.

A FAULTY SYSTEM FOR UNDERSTANDING AND MANAGING CONFLICT IN THE CHURCH

For the last 10 years, alongside my own pastoral ministry, I have had the privilege to serve other churches by helping them work through conflicts and crises. Through the process of this work, I discovered that most of the churches for which I have served had a conflict management system. However, these systems were well camouflaged and hidden deep in the DNA of each church. Conducting individual interviews proved invaluable in discovering each church's process for handling conflicts. The interview process was demanding, though. It is important to note that in order to gain candid answers from church members the consultant needs a good understanding of church life and a respectful demeanor. Church members are often uncomfortable answering direct questions about their church's problems. The skillful use of "humble inquiry" is indispensable for gathering helpful data (Schein, 2013). The information learned from the interviews is necessary to helping the church accurately define their problem.

Conducting interviews in multiple churches led to a fascinating discovery. I learned that many individuals could describe the conflict in their church, detail the path it was taking, and name the people directly involved in it. The fascination occurred when I asked if the church had a defined system for managing conflicts. Almost everyone said, "No." The oddity of this mismatched data opened a window to better understand why many churches handle conflict the way they do. Or, should I say mishandle.

Typically, conflict management systems in a church develop and evolve over time. Though the conflict managing process is not written down anywhere, it tends to become part of the church's very nature. The system may be faulty and ineffective, but it has become part of "the way we do church here." Strange as it may seem, churches tend to cling to these evolved patterns of handling conflict. It is likely the church is actually aware of the ineffectiveness of its process. But, that is not enough to make them change it. Why? There is an accumulated value to this treasured process because it has produced a strange but cherished fruit. The evolved system of handling conflict may seldom produce good outcomes, but it almost always produces predictable outcomes. Predictable outcomes remove uncertainty which, in turn, lessens fear. The root of fear is anything that threatens the felt sense of stability found in the comfortable familiarity of "church as we know it." Churches and their leaders tend to cherish stability. Predictable outcomes for conflicts provide the church with a sense of stability. Sadly, that sense of stability is an ungrounded false sense.

Consultants may make the unpleasant discovery that they have a problem to solve before they can even effectively address the current conflict. They may need to demonstrate that the church has a faulty and ineffective means of handling conflict. Doing that without creating an offense is a difficult task. If the church agrees that they have a faulty system, the next task is to design and implement a new effective one. Strangely, changing the way a church handles conflict tends to produce a lot of conflict. Doesn't all this make church consulting sound fun?

HELPING THE CHURCH GAIN WISDOM FROM PROBLEMS ROOTED IN THE PAST

You may be thinking, "This mess is too messy to mess with." I would like to convince you otherwise. I use a statement often in counseling individuals. It is equally true in consulting with a church. What is it? *The past is to be learned from, never lived in.* The disastrous manner in which some churches handle conflict can convince you their case is hopeless. I think it should pique our interest as to why and how the church of Christ, in which his peace is to rule, can experience conflicts and handle them so poorly. Twenty-five years of shepherding the same flock through many good times, and not just a few bad times, has taught me that hidden under the piles of past mistakes lies a precious fuel for future growth. For a little perspective on the worth of digging through the piles of past mistakes, the church where I am a pastor was founded in 1802. When I became a pastor in 1993, the church was still worshiping in the same sanctuary it had been in since 1895. We had a virtual mountain of past mistakes, and I helped to add to it. However, it is my 25 years with these people that have convinced me to face the past and learn from it, but never live in it. Treasures of great value are buried in those piles.

For a church to learn from the mistakes in its past, the church members, its leaders, and the consultant working with them must be convinced that God has enough grace, and they have enough grit to face the past, admit mistakes, and use the precious findings of honest inquiry to build a better future.

THE UNDETECTED DEVELOPMENT OF A FAULTY UNDERSTANDING

How does a church develop a faulty pattern for handling conflict? How does that faulty pattern become accepted as the norm? Many factors contribute to the patterns of conflict management developed in each church. No two churches are exactly the same, but I think it is possible to name some significant factors that tend to have some effect on most churches' attitudes toward conflict and their managing of it. Helping the church identify these factors can be a part of moving them toward a healthier ideology and process of managing conflict.

We will consider three factors affecting the contemporary church's manner of handling conflict: maintaining a strong but hidden resistance to change, having a false conception of conflict in the church, and a societal decline of relational skills. We will consider each issue in the order they are mentioned. The order is simply for organization of thought. It does not represent any form of priority or hierarchy.

MAINTAINING A RESISTANCE TO CHANGE

The church's reputation for resisting change is legendary, but the reason for her resistance to change may not be so well understood. Some things the church never intends to change because they are part of the church's doctrine and confession of faith. There are other things in the church, however, that should change if it is going to remain effective at communicating an unchanging message to a changing world. What causes a church body to become protective of practices that are out of date, no longer productive, and quite faulty in operation? We caught a hint of this problem earlier.

Individuals and organizations are quite odd when it comes to change. When considering making certain changes we might experience a surge of energy that increases a positive sense of adventure about making the change. But, when we begin to implement the first steps of making the chosen change its real costs come into view. Our sense of adventure can turn into a considerable fear. Once an experience of change moves above the inviting sense of novelty our resistance factor quickly rises. Some churches operate by structures and processes that have developed over a long period of time. The congregation can unwittingly enshrine its way of doing church with a strong layer of protective gold. A church will aggressively protect a revered part of church life not because they believe it is right, helpful, or necessary: The church protects its valued traditions because threatening such treasured practices feels like the very life of the church is being threatened.

I was called in to help a church at the crossroads of change and conflict. The church was experiencing a surge of growth in its membership. Church life was experiencing unexpected change. The pastor and some of the new lay leadership could see a bright future, but they realized some organizational and operational adjustments needed to be made if the church was going to sustain its growth. Two opposing ideologies arose in the church. One was the new vision of a changed structure to facilitate present and future growth. The second one was to not mess with "what has always worked for us here." By the time I was called in the tension level was high. The church had been at this juncture before with other pastors and the outcomes were not good. When the time for change had come, second power structures in the church were revealed. The first power structure was the one on paper. It basically consisted of the pastor, the pastoral staff, the deacons, and the committee chairpersons. The second power structure would only come to life when the core of the church felt threatened. It consisted of a handful of people that by default of historical precedent had been the real decision-making body in the church for years.

After several weeks of work involving one-on-one interviews, small group meetings, and a full church body meeting, it appeared the pastor and the newer leaders in the church were ready to take the challenge; to lovingly face the opposition of "the old guard" and make the necessary changes. There was still some evident tension, but the excitement and motivation were high enough to overcome it. When it was time to take the first step of implementation the imbedded functional value system of the church took over. The enthusiastic new leadership lost their courage. The long-term controlling members of the church came out into the open for confrontation. The accumulated value of safety through sameness over years of challenged but cherished practices far outweighed the hope of a far greater future. The church chose to turn down all the proposed changes. In doing so the congregation preserved its sense of stability but lost its pastor, some of its new leaders, and the opportunity for a different future. The congregation succeeded in maintaining stability. But was that really a success?

The underlying reason for many church conflicts is the placing of eternal value on temporary things in the church. The church deals with the great things of human life. It addresses not only time but eternity. It is no easy thing to keep one's value system balanced in such serious matters. Conflict in the church is usually over some type of personal or corporate value. These conflicts are difficult when our value systems are healthy. But an imbalanced value system created by placing undue worth on past practices creates an environment for nearly unmanageable conflicts. Needless resistance to change easily converts into rocket fuel for conflict in the church.

A FALSE CONCEPTION OF CONFLICT IN THE CHURCH

In 1653, British pastor Richard Baxter wrote, our "affections follow the understanding's conceptions" (Baxter, 1653/1830, p. 27). To say the same thing today would sound a bit like, "the way we feel toward someone is based on the picture of him or her that we have developed in our minds." Baxter's statement represents an issue of the ages in human relationships. It is common for us to develop our feelings (affections) about people based upon what we have conceived them to be in our own minds, not upon who they actually are. Though it is common, it is also potentially lethal to relationship development.

We also develop our feelings about things and experiences in life based upon our mental conceptions of them. How do you conceive of relational conflict in the church? It is not natural for anyone to enjoy relational conflict. Conflict disturbs our emotions, raises our blood pressure, and, at times, ends relationships. Therefore, a prominent conception is that conflict is a bad thing. Church congregations tend to have a shared concept that conflict is a bad thing. Conflict, and its usually untidy fallout, is on the church's "not allowed here" list. The plainest way to say it is that the church conceives conflict as a sin. Thinking conflict is sinful breeds a seriously unhealthy denial and avoidance of interpersonal conflict. Having a false conception of conflict has crippled the church in its abilities to properly manage conflict. The church has been blinded to the fact that conflict, properly managed, can produce good results.

Peacemaker Ministries is a fine organization that helps churches face and manage their conflicts. The organization defines conflict as "a difference of opinion or purpose that frustrates someone's goals or desires. This definition allows for the fact that not all conflict is bad" (Barthel, & Edling, 2012, p. 16). It is an odd thing that the church has conceived conflict as a sin. The Scriptures are a deep well of ancient wisdom for facing conflict in the church. The mental concept that conflict is a sin has clouded the church's interpretation of its own Scriptures. A well-known passage in the Bible's Gospel According to Matthew speaks metaphorically but directly to the issue of interpersonal conflict.

> Why do you see the speck that is in your brother's eye, but do not notice the log that is in your own eye? 4Or how can you say to your brother, 'Let me take the speck out of your eye,' when there is the log in your own eye? 5You hypocrite, first take the log out of your own eye, and then you will see clearly to take the speck out of your brother's eye. (Matthew 7:3–5, KJV)

Many church members have mistakenly taken this passage to mean they are not supposed to confront others about their faults. Obviously, this is a clouded view of the text, obscured by an ill-conceived mindset concerning conflict. The passage simply "forbids premature and improper confrontation. Before you talk to others about their faults . . . you need to face up to yours" (Sande, 2004, p. 79).

Centuries of experience and the church's Scriptures teach us that conflict is a normal part of life on this earth. The church has been given the tools to become an example to the world for handling conflict properly. Too many times it has been a demonstration of how to royally mishandle conflict. Much improvement could be made by gaining a healthy conception of conflict. Denying conflict is defeating relational development. Avoiding conflict atrophies the strength of relationships. The church has been blinded to the Scripture's counsel for handling conflict to her own peril. The Bible is a book of stunning transparency concerning human character and behavior. Some people are caught off guard with the raw nature of how the Scriptures report the stories of human relationships. I am quite content to not have lived when the Bible was being written. I would be facing many embarrassments if God decided to tell my relational blunders to the whole world. However, that is exactly what the Scriptures do. Some of God's finest servants are found in the middle of messy conflicts. This is not the place to explain them all, but pointing out a few might help you realize the church should not be surprised by conflict.

One great conflict recorded in the New Testament was between Paul, the great apostolic missionary, and his coworker and dear friend Barnabas. The conflict is recorded in Acts 15:36–41. Barnabas' cousin Mark had traveled with Paul and Barnabas on their first mission journey, but he abandoned them before the journey was completed. When it was time to start out on a second trip, Barnabas wanted to take Mark with them again but Paul did not. Their disagreement was so intense these two great men parted company and went their separate ways. For some reason, the writers of Scripture did not tell us how Paul and Barnabas reconciled. However, New Testament letters written after their conflict provide strong evidence that Paul reconciled with both Barnabas and Mark.

The New Testament also reports that the church experienced conflicts over money, status, spiritual experiences, and relational difficulties. In Paul's letter to the church at Philippi, he addressed a specific conflict in their church. He called the two ladies in conflict by name and urged them to come to an agreement. Instead of treating them and their conflict as sinful, Paul enlisted the help of a third party to guide them to reconciliation. When he spoke of the two women in conflict, he described them in gracious and encouraging terms. He did not condemn them for being in conflict.

A brief but honest reading of Scripture reveals that conflict was indeed a part of church life. It can also be seen that conflict was not necessarily viewed as a sin, but was approached as an opportunity to grow in personal and relational maturity. In his letter to Colossae, the Apostle Paul gave clear instruction concerning the development of peace and unity in the church. Fulfilling his instructions on relationship building in the church would have been no easy task. He taught them that unity in the church could only come if they were to bear with one another, to forgive one another, and to seek harmony in the church through genuine love. The friction produced by being in relationships can dull our love for others. Or, it can be the instrument that hones our relational skills.

This quick glance points to a small portion of the New Testament's teaching about conflict. From years of studying the Scriptures and working in the church, I find myself astonished that the church has such a poor conception of conflict. I am convinced if a local church would be willing to take what the Scriptures teach about conflict at face value and adopt a more biblically informed conception of conflict, it could become an example of excellence in conflict management.

UNHEALTHY UNDERSTANDING OF THE INDIVIDUAL SELF AND A SOCIETAL DECLINE IN RELATIONAL SKILLS

The two issues of having an unhealthy understanding of the individual self and the societal decline in relational skills could be dealt with separately, but they are so closely related it is suitable to combine them here. The limits of a single chapter may be a blessing in disguise. You should probably give thanks for such a limit. I have two fears concerning a book length treatment of conflict in the local church: One is that it would drone on so long no one would ever finish the book. Secondly, if I told too many actually stories of church conflicts I might prevent you from ever going to church. The individual self and a societal decline in relational skills are newer to the playing field of catalysts for church conflict than the first two subjects. I have chosen these two issues because I think the church is inadequately informed about each of them. A failure to recognize the catalytic power they possess for creating and sustaining church conflict will be costly to the church's future.

The Bible, when rightly understood, teaches a healthy concept of the individual self and the practice of self-denial. The biblical perspective is that healthy self-development chiefly occurs in the context of relationships with others. Relationships provide the mirror in which we can see a reflection of our relational and emotional maturity. Without relationships we have no means to take or be offered helpful measurements of our true self. The biblical perspective is that relational conflict is one of the chief components necessary for developing a healthy, mature self. Denying and avoiding conflict are a sure way to emotional and relational immaturity. Insulating ourselves from the friction of relationships removes "the conditions for the possibility of achieving a coherent self" (Crawford, 2015, p. 22). Our current cultural understanding of the self is rooted in the Enlightenment. We have held on to the concept of autonomy developed during the Enlightenment without the context of that time. Autonomy from inordinate and infringing power structures was a chief causal element in the concept of the self which developed during the Enlightenment. "Understood literally, autonomy means giving a law to oneself. The opposite of autonomy thus understood is heteronomy: being ruled by something alien to oneself" (Crawford, 2015, p. 24). The contemporary cultural idea of the sovereign self has become unruly. The unhealthy idea of an unchallengeable self has crept deep into the church. We have grown comfortable with autonomy—being a law unto ourselves. The trouble with this is that "everything located beyond your head is regarded as a potential source of heteronomy, and therefore a threat to the self" (Crawford, 2015, p. 24). It does not take sophisticated mental processing to see the disastrous relational consequences that would come from such an idea of the self. Two fundamental falsehoods are perpetrated by such a position. The first mistaken ideal coming from the concept of a sovereign self is that truth is determined within the self apart from the influence of others. Inevitably, then, the second falsehood is that anything that contradicts my conception of reality is a threat to be feared and opposed, not an opportunity to develop a more mature self. A mere glance at our own nation, which has grown up with this conception of the self, will reveal that it is an explosive catalyst for creating division through undefinable conflicts. I am convinced the ideology of the autonomous self is a relatively new, but heavy, contributor to the difficulties of managing conflict in the church.

It is inviting to imagine that a strong individual self is developed in the disciplined environment of chosen isolation. Daily reality and the Scriptures teach the church the opposite. The demands placed upon us by the things and people surrounding us do not keep the self from developing. Such demands are the very ground of healthy self-development. "We find ourselves *situated* in a world that is not of our making, and this 'situatedness' is fundamental to what a human being is" (Crawford, 2015, p. 26). There are times where our situation is more than uncomfortable. Yet, it is the very discomfort that provides the key refining elements for the development of a mature and healthy person. We may not like conflict, but it is one of those necessary forming factors in becoming a healthy individual able to productively function in the relational constraints of the local church. We avoid conflict because of the pain it can cause. But we also avoid conflict because it has a unique ability to reveal the true self. When we are in conflict, our words and behaviors are responses or, more accurately, reactions, to the person we are in conflict with. Conflict has a way of removing the public persona we show to people in comfortable circumstances and revealing the raw nature of our true self. We find such revealing to be embarrassing. Conflict, like no other interaction, provides the opportunity to look deep inside ourselves. Conflict opens the door for us to make real change deep in the core of our character. Such exposure and development are about as pleasant as major surgery. However, if we intend to reach lasting relational maturity we must be willing to face the temporary pain. The opportunity for personal transformation is one of the highest values of conflict. The second great double benefit from properly engaging in conflict is learning to learn from our opposition and presenting the church with higher quality outcomes from a combined perspective.

Walking right beside the ideology of the autonomous self is an observable societal decline in relational skills. I will only be able to open a window through which we can take a look at this problem. The church is already feeling the effects of this decline, but I do not know if it is aware of the decline or of where it is coming from. My concern is that the decline in relational skills and its causes will become a greater problem for the church than any of the other issues I have mentioned. Personal and corporate relational deficits will obviously present serious difficulties for the healthy management of conflicts. Relationships are the DNA of the local church: relationships to God and to other people. What will happen to church life if there is a serious decline in our relational skills?

If a healthy self is dependent upon interaction with other people then we must become skilled at receiving and applying the feedback we receive from them. Without other people our "experiences are partial, and may sediment as idiosyncratic bad habits" (Crawford, 2015, p. 63). "Feedback in relationships is rarely the story of you *or* me. It's more often the story of you *and* me" (Stone & Heen, 2015, p. 23). Interaction with other people includes conversation, disagreement, encouragement, and conflict. For most of us, it takes hard work and a lot of practice to become skilled at healthy relational interaction. Matthew Crawford (2015) wrote,

> I call this an "art" because it requires both tact and doggedness. And I call it a moral accomplishment because to be good at this kind of conversation you have to love the truth more than you love your own current state of understanding. (p. 63)

So, if there is an actual societal decline in relational skills, what is fueling it? In a phrase, our mediated existence. Church life was designed by God to always have a geographic location, a cultural setting, and face-to-face interaction with one another. Though I hate to admit it, Gutenberg's printing press cracked open the door to our modern day mediated existence. You and I are experiencing a mediated life anytime we have an interaction through a medium: a telephone call, an email, a text. A mediated existence is partially actual and partially virtual. The church was never meant to be a virtual experience. It is to always be actual. The thought of experiencing church as virtual reality is everything but virtuous. The practices of the church and the individual Christian are to take place in the real world or there is no need for their existence.

Technology has presented us with many wonderful tools and conveniences in life. It would be unwise to stop using our technological gadgets just because the use of them can create new problems. Anything in this life can be misused. I am not blaming technology for the erosion in relational skills. I am, however, placing some blame at the feet of our unfiltered acceptance of a technologically mediated life. Mediated virtual relationships do not have all the necessary ingredients to develop into healthy personal relationships. Without the friction of face-to-face interaction with one another we have no way of registering the quality of our relationships or of our relational skills. And when it comes to the most serious matters the church deals with, life and death, there is not an ounce of virtual reality about facing either of these.

The world is still populated with a large number of people who grew up with two main mediums of communication other than face-to-face conversation. We wrote letters and made phone calls. Even then, we all knew that we could represent ourselves through the medium of a letter or a phone call in a manner quite different from our true selves. If you are a parent, have you tried to call your teenager on his or her cell phone lately? Did they answer? No, they didn't. You have probably learned that using some form of texting or instant messaging is the only way to get a response. In addition to that, we no longer have to use words to communicate. Our phones provide us with an unlimited supply of emoji's to say what we need to with pictures. Would it be unfair to say that we have digressed in our communication skills all the way back to caveman days?

Though the issue of a mediated life is complex and will probably be with us in ever-evolving forms, it is not terribly difficult to see it presents considerable problems for healthy relationship building. This means it also creates new challenges in developing abilities to handle conflict well. Having multiple forms of media to connect with other people rather than face-to-face relationships, combined with the idea of an autonomous self, has led to a kind of keen self-protective instinct. According to Crawford (2015),

> We increasingly deal with others through representations of *them* that we have. This results in interactions that are more contained, less open-ended,

> than a face-to-face encounter or a telephone call, giving us more control. In this domain we have a frictionless array of weak ties to other people who can be summoned according to our own needs. (p. 176)

If you have ever wondered what real purpose the church can have in the contemporary world, I hope you can see one here. What else is so well designed for regular personal interactions? Where else can we find an organization that has an ancient, timeless manual for understanding human nature? Are there other places that truly encourage the tedious process of letting others have access to your inner person so that they may both point out faults and offer tender correction? I am very aware that few churches may come anywhere close to these lofty ideals, but that is indeed part of its core purpose. The world would be a better place if the church fulfills it.

CONCLUSION

I have no claims to being prophetic, but I do think that if the church does not educate itself about living in a mediated world it will face many surprises being completely unprepared. It is certainly no time for the church to retreat behind its protective walls of "that's not how we do church here." The opportunities for the church to have impact in our culture are actually greater than ever due to the development of a mediated, virtual world. Deep in the human heart is the need and longing for serious, engaging, supporting human relationships. With most organizations chasing the tail of technological advancement and removing more and more opportunities for face-to-face interaction, the church can actually offer what people truly need and long for. The growing opportunity for the church to be "the" place that helps people meet their need of healthy personal interaction is a gift. If the church is going to rise to the challenge and meet this need, it must choose to recognize both the difficulties of doing so and the demands of getting prepared to meet it with actual excellence. A new and surprising door has been opened to the church. It remains to be seen if we will walk through it.

REFERENCES

Barthel, T. K., & Edling, D. V. (2012). *Redeeming church conflicts.* Grand Rapids, MI: Baker Books.

Baxter, R. (1830). The right method for a settled peace of conscience and spiritual comfort. In W. Orme (Ed.), *The practical works of the Rev. Richard Baxter* (Vol. 9; pp. 1–287). London, England: James Duncan, 37, Paternoster Row. (Original work published 1653)

Crawford, M. B. (2015). *The world beyond your head.* New York, NY: Farrar, Straus and Giroux.

Sande, K. (2004). *The peacemaker: A biblical guide to resolving personal conflict* (3rd ed.). Grand Rapids, MI: Baker Books.

Schein, E. H. (2013). *Humble inquiry.* San Francisco, CA: Berrett-Koehler.

Stone, D., & Heen, S. (2015). *Thanks for the feedback: The science and art of receiving feedback well.* New York, NY: Penguin Group.

CHAPTER 15

BRAIN FUNCTION'S ROLE IN CONFLICT

How the Lizard and the Puppy Effect Decision-Making

Peggy McNeive

Most people experience situations after which, upon reflection, they do not understand why they reacted in a certain way. You may meet someone for the first time and immediately like them or, on the other hand, dislike them. A sense of foreboding may overtake you when you are walking down the street, even in broad daylight; often times this leads to speeding up your step, crossing to the other side of the road, or going into a nearby shop.

In the 1960s, Dr. Paul McLean forwarded a theory concerning why people react in different types of situations. The "triune brain" theory proposes that an individual's brain reacts to experiences in a systematic way. These automatic responses may prevent an individual from effectively and productively dealing with conflict. In order to assist individuals in resolving conflict, a person acting as a neutral can utilize methods to work through the automatic responses; this may assist the individuals in conflict to consider options to resolve their differences.

From Discord to Harmony, pages 259–275

THE TRIUNE BRAIN THEORY

Paul MacLean, a neurologist, first introduced the theory of the "triune brain" in the 1960s; the concept is discussed in his book *The Triune Brain in Evolution: Role in Paleocerebral Functions* (MacLean, 1990). MacLean's basic concept is that the brain has three distinct areas which are used to analyze situations and react to them. Each part of the brain views circumstances differently because they developed at a distinct evolutionary time period. Prior to MacLean's triune brain concept, it was believed the neocortex controlled the other two parts of the brain. MacLean's theory is a drastic departure from this belief.

The three areas of the brain, as described by MacLean (1983), are the amygdala, the hippocampus, and the neocortex. All of our senses are involved in the functions of the brain —seeing, hearing, smelling, tasting, and feeling. The functions of these three parts of the brain are shown in Figure 15.1 and discussed below.

The Amygdala or Reptilian Brain

The amygdala portion of the brain is often referred to as the *reptilian brain*; it is the oldest and least developed (MacLean, 1983). Reptiles and mammals experience the same type of reactions humans experience when the reptilian part of the brain is in control of the situation. The reptilian part of the brain reacts in three different ways: flight, fight, or freeze. These reactions are commonly known as the three "Fs." All three reactions are designed to ensure survival of the person experiencing the reaction, but exhibit themselves differently.

As discussed earlier, many people have experienced walking down the street and suddenly feeling like they needed to flee from the area as soon as

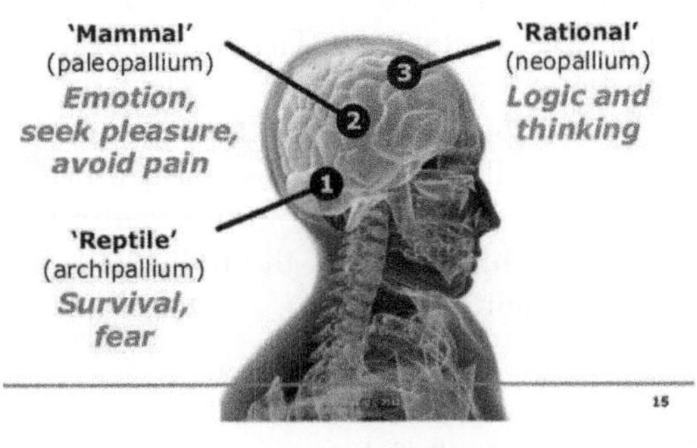

Figure 15.1 The triune brain. *Source:* Hawaii Naturopathic Retreat, 2017.

possible. Individuals usually do not know why they have this reaction; however, in most circumstances your reptilian brain has detected something wrong and is encouraging you to leave a potentially dangerous situation. Perhaps you caught something out of your peripheral vision, or you felt someone watching you, or the unfamiliar surroundings "spooked" you. No matter what the trigger was, your reaction will probably be the same; you need to get out of the area. This is the *flight* reaction.

On the other hand, if your reaction is to push back and confront what you believe to be the enemy, you are experiencing the *fight* reaction. An example that exemplifies this fight reaction is a union attorney's story concerning her client's (referred to as the business agent) reaction to a proposed settlement agreement. The union's attorney worked with the management's attorney to reach an agreement resolving a grievance. When the union attorney described the proposal to the business agent, he had a volatile reaction to it; he immediately rejected the settlement, saying it was not acceptable because it did not meet the needs of the union. The union attorney stated that when she called the next day to see if the business agent would accept the offer on behalf of the union, he agreed to it. The original fight reaction dissipated when the business agent had the time to think about the offer rationally.

The *freeze* reaction occurs when you are caught on the spot, for example, when someone asks you a question and you can't come up with the answer, or when someone chastises or insults you and you do not respond. Often, after such an encounter, we think about what we should have done or how we should have responded. We could not think of the answer or decide on a comeback when we were in the moment because our brains did not have the ability to react quickly. The least attention is paid to the freeze response because flight and fright are the most common reactions.

These reactions come into play when we are facing a conflict that invokes an immediate response; they are subconscious. The reptilian brain is active even in deep sleep. If we have some time, even a short time, we may utilize a different part of our brain to determine our response. One of the keys to resolving conflict is to get past an individual's initial reaction and work toward a more rational response.

The Hippocampus or Limbic System

According to MacLean's (1983) theory, the hippocampus portion of the brain was the next to evolve. This part of the brain, sometimes referred to as the *puppy* or *mammalian*, is designed to determine if a situation the individual is entering is safe or not. Our brains store an enormous amount of prior experience. The longer we live the more experiences we have in our storeroom. The *limbic system* as a whole is the primary seat of emotion, attention, and emotionally charged memories. These memories develop patterns in the brain, which a person relies on to determine the safety level of later situations.

Our brains look for patterns or paths when entering a situation. These include a quick analysis of whether you have experienced this situation before, what the experience means to you, what you have done in the past in the same situation, and how it turned out. If the situation is familiar, we feel safe and enter into the situation without apprehension because we can put them into the pathways we have already established. If the situation is less familiar, most often, the brain responds by deferring to the reptilian response. The puppy brain will defer to the reptilian brain quickly if there are sufficient signs that the situation is not safe. The amygdala is more likely to categorize the situation as a threat because it is designed to detect everything as a threat.

Making new pathways in our brains, which establish a situation of "safe," is more difficult as we age because we are used to following the pathways we have already established. These pathways may be responsible for the "first reaction" we so often rely upon to assess a new person. If we sense something in the person that makes us feel safe, or reminds us of others we know, we tend to warm to them immediately. If the individual has traits or characteristics unfamiliar to our past experience, we tend to keep our distance and are more cautious in our approach to them. This is also known as intuition. According to Amthor (2016),

> There are good things and bad things about intuition. Intuition is good to the extent that certain aspects of a situation may generate useful warnings with your needing to consciously remember the circumstance... On the other hand, intuition can lead to stereotypes and rigidity of behavior. You may then have to use reason to overcome stereotypes or take reasonable risks to accomplish things even if they entail situations having some danger. (pp. 270–271)

It is the job of the neocortex to help you through the sense of danger and make an informed decision about the appropriate action.

The Neocortex

The third part of the brain discussed in McLean's (1983) theory is the *neocortex*, also known as the "rationale" part of the brain. This is the most recently developed part of the brain. It distinguishes man from other animals. Although animals have a neocortex, it is much smaller and less developed. The neocortex is divided into the right and left hemispheres, also known as right- and left-sided brain. Carter's (2014) description of the difference between the right and left sides of the brain is provided below:

> Speech and language, stepwise reasoning and analysis, and certain communicating actions are based mainly on the left side in most people. Since nerve fibers cross from left to right at the base of the brain, this dominant left side receives sensory information from and sends messages to, muscles in the right side of the brain... the right hemisphere is more concerned with sensory inputs, auditory and visual awareness, creative abilities and spatial-temporal awareness. (p. 57)

Our ability to think critically and analyze situations is centered in the neocortex. It can take new experiences and ambiguous information and determine how to interpret it in order to react appropriately.

Although most experiences do not need extensive analysis (i.e., we instinctively walk, talk, or cook a meal without too much thought), we need to pay attention to even these everyday activities. If we do not pay enough attention to these "rote" activities it may result in accidents. For example, when a person texts when they are driving attention is diverted from the rational part of the brain and may result in a car accident. The same type of diversion in the kitchen may result in burns when we are baking.

Accepted Aspects of the Triune Theory

Though neuroscientists have concerns with the triune theory (these will be discussed in the next section), some aspects of the theory are accepted by the neuroscience community. According to Carter (2014), "The amygdala is involved in learning to approach or avoid things and hence with emotion" (p. 24). It is the portion of the brain that triggers the fight, flight, or freeze reaction. Amthor (2016) also asserted that "the amygdala appears to be a different part of the memory circuit. It has the same structural similarities to the hippocampus, but its inputs and outputs are associated with stimuli that have emotional salience" (p. 226). Emotions controlled by the amygdala include, but are not limited to, anger and fear. This also supports the triune brain theory since these are the reactions involved in deciding whether to stay and fight or flee a situation.

Research shows that the hippocampus plays a "crucial function in the creation of memory.... The kinds of memories that the hippocampus are involved in creating are explicit, knowledge-based memories, such as associating the west end of a water hole with danger from a predator" (Amthor, 2016, p. 35). According to Carter (2014), "Some of the experiences we have change brain cells in such a way that the pattern of neural activity that produced the original experience can be replicated later in time" (p. 38).

She continued, stating that "this process gives rise to recall, or memory, which enables us to use past experience as a guide to how to behave in the present" (Carter, 2014, p. 38).

The amygdala and the hippocampus work together to determine how we should react. McEwen (1999) provided a good explanation of the symbiotic relationship between these two parts of the brain.

The amygdala is essentially the first structure to be activated in our fear response, and it contributes the emotional flavor to memories, especially fear-related memories. The hippocampus works closely with the amygdala and is involved in our memory of events and also in spatial orientation. The amygdala is concerned with the emotion of the event; the hippocampus takes care of the so-called contextual, or episodic, memory—the who, what, when, where parts of the story—in effect (McEwen, 1999, pp. 94–95).

By working together, these two parts of the brain determine what our initial reaction will be to any given event. When we are in a dispute situation, our initial reaction is, generally, an emotional response. These tend to be accelerated when the atmosphere or the physical setting are foreign or uncomfortable for us. In these situations, the hippocampus concedes to the amygdala and our fight, flight, or freeze instincts take over.

Criticisms of the Triune Theory

As with all scientific theories, the basic premise of the triune brain is not accepted by a number of neuroscientists. One of the main concerns is that the concept is too simplistic and/or does not consider other scientific concepts (Keys, 1999). Some scientists accept the fundamental theory as a basis for understanding how brain functions can affect the way individuals react to situations, but question its inability to recognize the cooperation that takes place between different parts of the brain. Neuroscientists believe that, although the triune brain theory provides a clear view of assessing and analyzing sensory information, it does not fully take into account a human's intellectual capacity (Komninos, 2018).

One of the simplistic aspects of the triune brain theory rests with the proposal that an individual's reactions will go through the three stages of assessing and acting on a situation in a linear fashion, and will not regress to the prior stages once the individual has begun to process the information rationally. Although this may be the case in some circumstances, it is not always the case. Some individuals may move quickly through the first two stages to the rational thinking stage only to transgress at some point to the fight, flight, or freeze stage.

One example of a dramatic change in a person's reaction to a situation from rational to emotional was relayed by a mediator concerning a contract negotiation in which he was involved (Federal Mediation and Conciliation Service, n.d.).[1] Contract negotiations between the company and a union had taken place for a number of months; the parties were making slow but steady progress. After meeting with the union in a separate caucus, the mediator went into the company's caucus room. When the mediator entered the room he noticed the company's attorney was looking at a brochure about labor management cooperation and seemed agitated. Immediately after the mediator came into the room, the attorney picked up the brochure, threw it at the mediator, and said, "We don't want to hear anything about labor management cooperation. We are in contract negotiations and there is no place for cooperation." The mediator did not respond to the violent outburst of the attorney. Instead, he suggested that he leave the room so the management team could take a break and talk about its response to the union's proposal. The mediator did not know what precipitated the attorney's response, but did know reasoning with him would be difficult when he was agitated.

Parties may also use the "fight" reaction as a way of achieving a better negotiating position or to give themselves some breathing room. One situation in which this happened was during a grievance mediation. A union representing power plant employees filed a grievance when the company decided to eliminate a classification of employees and layoff the employees in the classification. Employees in this classification, on the whole, had a great deal of seniority. The union took the position that the employees were entitled to bid into other positions and, if layoffs were necessary, less senior employees should be laid off. The company took the position that the employees were not qualified to bid into other positions because their current positions did not require a great deal of training and other positions at the plant did require specialized training.

The union representative (referred to as the business manager) had worked with an FMCS Commissioner in the past; the management representative had not. At the beginning of the grievance mediation the parties argued vehemently about their positions using both the contract language and the past practices to support the positions they were taking. After a number of hours and several separate caucuses, both parties started discussing options for settling the grievance. They then participated in a joint session because the mediator thought they were close to a resolution.

During the mediator's explanation of the basic agreement, the business manager said, "That is not what I agreed to," and walked out in a huff. The management representative asked the mediator, "Aren't you going to go after him?" The mediator replied, "No, he will be back. He needs some time to think." The business manager and his group came back and, eventually, the parties came to an agreement. In this situation, the business manager was not actually experiencing the fight response; he just needed some time to think. He had probably reached the rational stage, but was not sure the agreement would meet all the requirements of the union's membership.

HOW THE TRIUNE THEORY CAN ASSIST IN RESOLVING DISPUTES

When dealing with most conflicts, the goal is to engage the rational part of the brain when working with individuals so they can work toward solutions. Individuals must set aside the initial emotional reaction to a situation before they can rationally weigh the options for settlement and determine if resolving the conflict is in their best interest. This does not mean the emotional reactions are not there; it merely means they have been set aside for the time being.

Recognizing and Working Through Lizard and Puppy Reactions

The important aspect of the triune brain theory (McLean, 1983) for individuals who are assisting others in working through conflict is the recognition that there are reasons behind how individuals react. By understanding that some reactions are not necessarily calculated but come about instinctively, an individual can assess the reactions in a different light and gage one's own actions accordingly. This understanding will also help us to remain neutral in volatile situations.

To be an effective problem-solver in conflict situations, we need to help the participants move from their initial reactions to the conflict (often flight, fight, or fear) to a place where they feel safe to discuss the situation (puppy thinking) and, hopefully, to think rationally about how the situation can be dealt with. Every situation and participant will need to be approached differently because individuals view situations from their own personal background.

Handling Emotions is Essential to Resolving Disputes

One common denominator of most conflicts is that individuals are emotionally involved. Emotion is defined by *Merriam-Webster* as "a: the affective aspect of consciousness: FEELING; b: a state of feeling; [and] c: a conscious mental reaction (such as anger or fear) subjectively experienced as strong feeling usually directed toward a specific object" ("Emotion," n.d., para. 1–3). One needs to deal with emotions to both understand differing worldviews and determine how the conflict may have arisen in order to move toward resolving the conflict by making informed decisions. According to Carter (2014), "Decision-making and judgement are profoundly affected by emotions. This is because emotion "drives" action—without it the brain is like a car with steering but no power" (p. 169). Another aspect of an individual's emotional state is the level of stress he/she is experiencing. McEwen (1999) asserted that the amygdala and the hippocampus "are key players in the interpretation and response to stress," and that the "perception of stress is critical, because what is stressful to one individual may not be stressful to another" (p. 94). For example, a person who has handled a number of conflict situations in the past may move from the emotional reaction to a dispute to rational thinking more quickly than someone who is less experienced in handling conflicts. This is not always the case; even individuals who deal with conflicts on a regular basis may not be able to think rationally when they are personally involved in the situation or it is one that questions their decisions or actions.

TECHNIQUES FOR ASSISTING INDIVIDUALS WITH RESOLVING DISPUTES

Merely recognizing that emotions may govern an individual's thinking process is not sufficient to assist the parties in reaching an agreement. A neutral participant needs to determine the best method to work through the individual's emotional reaction so all the participants can have a reasoned discussion of how best to resolve the conflict.

Sometimes a Cup of Tea Does Help

British murder mysteries give us a good example of how an action that seems silly can actually make a major difference. When something bad happens in a British murder mystery, the person who witnesses the event or the victim, if they survive an attack, is given a cup of tea. This is the usual response in situations ranging from seeing someone murdered to surviving a bomb attack during a war; the exception is when they are occasionally offered brandy or whisky.

There is evidence that this may, indeed, help someone to calm down. Some of the benefits come from the warmth of the drink while others come from the fact you can't guzzle a hot drink; you have to slow down and let the liquid cool before it is drunk. It may even change the person's disposition toward another. Research indicates individuals "who briefly held a cup of hot (versus iced) coffee judged a target person as having a 'warmer' personality (generous, caring)" (Fleming, 2014, para. 2). Additionally, the caffeine in tea, or coffee, has an effect on the brain. L-Theanine, which is contained in tea, "is an amino acid which is responsible for relaxing the nervous system.... Some studies have suggested the L-Theanine, especially when combined with caffeine, can improve attention and brain function" (Billi UK, 2017, para. 4–5).

The following is an example of how tea helped the mediator assist the parties in conflict management. During a mediation in an equal employment opportunity pre-complaint case, where a woman accused her supervisor of engaging in bullying behavior, the mediator asked the complainant to give an opening statement about her concerns. The mediator realized the complainant was too upset to give the opening statement. The mediator asked the company representative if he would mind if the mediator met with the complainant for a little while without the company representative present. The mediator and the complainant went to the cafeteria and got a cup of tea. While they were drinking tea, the mediator took some time to explain the process to the complainant and let her know there would be no adverse effects from the mediation process. The complainant calmed down and was able to proceed with the mediation. Although the parties were not able to reach an agreement during the mediation, they had a good discussion and were able to set up a system of communication that would avert future misunderstandings. While the discussion concerning the process as well as the reassurance that there would be no negative repercussions from her complaint may have calmed the complainant down enough to proceed with the meeting, the tea did not hurt.

EMOTIONS MAY DETRACT FROM OR ASSIST IN NEGOTIATIONS

In *Beyond Reason: Using Emotions as You Negotiate,* Fisher and Shapiro (2005) discussed the role of emotions in negotiations. According to Fisher and Shapiro (2005), emotions can be "troubling" for a number of reasons:

> *They can divert attention from substantive matters.* If you or the other person gets upset, each of you have to deal with the hassle of emotions.
>
> *They can damage a relationship.* Strong emotions can overshadow your thinking, leaving you at risk of damaging your relationship.
>
> *The can be used to exploit you.* Careful observers of your emotional reaction may learn how much you value proposals, issues, and your relationship with them. They may use this information to exploit you. (p. 7)

Many experienced negotiators attempt to put on their "poker faces" when dealing with the other participants to the negotiations. This is especially true when the parties are in economic negotiations which do not involve an ongoing or personal relationship. However, when the negotiations do involve such issues the approach may backfire by sending the message the personal aspects of the negotiations are unimportant.

On the other hand, emotions can be beneficial to the negotiations process. Fisher and Shapiro (2005) listed three ways:

> *Positive emotions can make it easier to meet substantive interests.* You can try out new ideas without the fear of being taken advantage of.... You are more open to learning about the other party's interests, making a mutually satisfying outcome with your reach. As a result, your agreement is more likely to be stable over time.
>
> *Positive emotions can enhance a relationship.* Positive emotion can provide you with the intrinsic enjoyment that comes from a person-to-person interaction.
>
> *Positive emotion need not increase your risk of being exploited.* Although positive emotion my help you produce a mutually satisfying agreement, there is a danger that you may feel so comfortable that you make unwise concessions or act with overconfidence.... Before you commit to an agreement, check that it satisfies your interests. (p. 8, emphasis in original)

Experienced neutrals understand that most negotiations will include both negative and positive emotions. These may not come from the same person. For example, in grievance meetings the union and the company representatives may have a long-standing relationship during which they have been able to resolve a number of problems. The floor supervisor, who is alleged to have violated the contract, and the grievant may have developed an animosity toward each other due to the nature of the grievance. While the representatives may want to proceed directly to discussing how the grievance can be settled, the floor supervisor and the grievant need some time to vent their anger before they can think about an agreement. If this disparity in attitudes is ignored by the neutral and the representatives are allowed to merely concentrate on an agreement, it may result in the represented individuals perceiving that their interests are not important because the union and the company are colluding with each other.

Inter-party negotiations are part of the neutral's job; this allows the neutral to move the process forward toward resolution. A major factor in doing this effectively is the ability to identify the leadership's emotional state and capitalize on it. If the leader of the group is exhibiting positive emotions then the neutral can build on this to bring the remainder of the group along. This can be accomplished by referring to statements made by the leader and building options based on these statements. If the leader is exhibiting negative emotions then the neutral needs to identify the basis of the emotions and work toward changing the leader's attitude to be more positive. A more positive attitude will provide the neutral with the opportunity to explore options for settlement of the dispute.

Help Participants Understand How Emotions Affect Decisions

Sometimes participants become so involved in their emotions they fail to remember the goals they set for themselves coming into the meeting. Such a situation can be referred to as *not being able to see the forest for the trees.* The neutral's job in this situation is to help the participant remember the end goal and how it can be achieved.

This usually can't be done at the beginning of the meeting; allowing the participants to initially vent their anger, and then implementing a method to calm the parties so they can work through their anger or apprehension is typically first employed. Although most neutrals believe this is important, it does come with some risk. In a discussion on the effects of neuroscience and mediation, Richard Birke (2010) made the following observation:

> Turning then to mediation, one must ask the question whether it makes sense to ask the parties to recapitulate the story that leads to the hard feelings that lead to a lawsuit. There are certainly reasons to be cautious.... However, failure to adequately discuss the underlying emotional aspects of a lawsuit often results in the missed opportunity to discover the underlying interests of the parties. In a case that is driven by a mix of emotions and other tangible damages—for example, a discharge claim—a plaintiff might ask for money to address lost wages but may also be asking for additional money that addresses her anger of the incident, or her fear that she may not be readily employable elsewhere. If these feelings of fear can be explored, it may be possible to address the fears in some way other than purely through financial compensation. (p. 510)

Since the most effective neutrals use the party's interests to develop settlement possibilities, it does seem that some type of statement from the parties is necessary.

Different styles of allowing the parties to work through emotions and prepare for the negotiations process are used by neutrals. The most common is to let the participants vent prior to engaging in the negotiations process. One seasoned FMCS commissioner does this by meeting with the parties separately before a joint meeting; he believes this dissipates some of the anger and the tension the parties may be feeling. Other commissioners start with a joint meeting. In their view, this gives the parties a chance to let the other side know how they feel, and give them the ability to point out the facts and arguments supporting their positions in their own words.

No matter how a neutral decides to gather the facts and hear the participant's initial comments, he/she should be prepared for the "old" brain, either the lizard or the puppy to be in control of the conversation. This may be explained by either the other participant's inability or unwillingness to listen at this point in time (Fisher, Ury, & Patton, 1991), or because the participant may be overwhelmed by the information being provided (Birke, 2010).

The neutral's next decision is to determine how to proceed to the next step; that being how to get the participant's from reacting emotionally to negotiating rationally. Birke (2010) suggested that participants may not be ready immediately to proceed:

> What does this mean for the mediator? Perhaps it means that after a party tells a re-traumatizing tale, they need a substantial cool-down period before they are ready to bargain. The notion that a party should "get it all out" and then they are ready to bargain is accurate to a degree. They are ready to bargain after they get it all out, but not right away. I suggest that after a party experiences the trauma/catharsis of telling their story, it is a very good time for a coffee or lunch break, and it may even be the case in some disputes that it is a good place to end for the day. (p. 511)

Postponing the meeting to another day is not an option in many cases. However, it is usually an option to take a break. This allows the neutral to help the participants view the situation in a different light.

Sometimes the neutral may want to meet with the participants in a different area to disassociate the emotional storytelling from the next discussion. This may be as simple as going outside for a while or moving to a different room. William Ury (2007) suggested the following technique:

> When you find yourself facing a difficult negotiation, you need to step back, collect your wits, and see the situation objectively. Imagine you are negotiating on a stage and then imagine yourself climbing onto a balcony overlooking the stage. The balcony is a metaphor for a mental attitude of detachment. From the balcony you can calmly evaluate the conflict almost as if you were a third party. (pp. 37–38)

As neutrals we can help the participants "go to the balcony" by asking questions like "Tell me what you see about the other side's position that makes sense to you?" or "How do compare your circumstances to comparable ones?" These are normal questions for mediators who want to have the participants evaluate their positions objectively.

The Participants Emotions May Require a Specific Process

Once the participants are in the right frame of mind to negotiate, the neutral needs to decide what type of negotiation process would be most successful for the participants to reach an agreement. Sometimes this is done through a discussion with the participants about how they want to proceed. After a discussion with the participants, the neutral, who is best equipped to make the final decision, will determine the best process to use. Neutrals often have a default style they utilize in their work. Sometimes this style is not the best approach to a specific case. A neutral must be able to revise their default style in order to meet the needs of the participants.

A number of different styles are utilized by neutrals. Although there are a wide variety of names for these processes, three general types will be discussed in this section: problem-solving, interest based/facilitative, and relational. Deutsch, Coleman, and Marcus (2006) provided the following description of the problem-solving process:

> The problem-solving style has long been the dominant mediation approach.... It gives priority to unblocking the parties stalled efforts to reach agreements (the "problem" to be solved) through the mediator's active grappling with the issues in the form of shaping and making proposals and the liberal application of pressure tactics. (p. 743)

The interest based/facilitative process is set out in Fisher et al. (1991) work, *Getting to Yes: Negotiating Agreement Without Giving In.* The basic principle for this type of bargaining is:

> Dealing with a substantive problem and maintaining a good working relationship need not be conflicting goals if the parties are committed and psychologically prepared to treat each separately on its own legitimate merits. Base the relationship on accurate perceptions, clear communication, appropriate emotions, and a forward-looking, purposive outlook. Deal with people problems directly; don't try to solve them with substantive concession. (Fisher et al., 1991, p. 21)

The guiding principles of transformative mediation were set out by Robert A. Baruch Bush and Joseph Folger (2004) in their book *Promise of Mediation: The Transformative Approach to Conflict.* This is the basis for the relational style of mediation. The "relational styles focus less on agreement making and more on opening lines of communication and clarifying underlying feelings and perceptions" (Deutsch et al., 2006, p. 744).

When the participant's reactions dictate that a process change would be beneficial, a neutral should be open to changing the type of process he/

she is using. An example of this is a case involving an equal employment opportunity charge filed by an African-American filed against the postmaster of a U.S. post office (USPS) for discriminating against her because of her race. The charge involved the employee being scheduled every Tuesday, her normal day off, after a federal holiday. The district manager decided that the postmaster did not have to be present because it was simply a question of whether the postmaster had the authority to schedule the employee on Tuesdays after a federal holiday. The USPS utilizes the transformative mediation process; however, the district manager took the attitude that the claim was frivolous so he did not want to spend a lot of time on the issue.

The complainant was very upset about the issue, and started her opening statement by saying she did not want to file the charge but felt like the postmaster had turned against her and was treating her differently than any other employee. She did not understand this change in treatment because, when there was not a floor manager at the facility, she would go to the postmaster with her concerns and they could resolve them. At this point, the mediator suggested that a conference with the district manager and the postmaster may be in order to determine if the postmaster should be involved in the mediation. Since she was in the building, the postmaster joined the meeting. When the postmaster came to the meeting the district manager left. The complainant started her story again. A crucial part of her story was a statement made to her by another employee; the woman told her that the postmaster had made the statement that the complainant would be working Tuesdays all the time in the foreseeable future. The postmaster explained that the complainant had been scheduled for Tuesdays after federal holidays because the facility was understaffed and the day after a federal holiday was always a busy day for the post office. The postmaster expressed concern that the complainant did not come to her with her concerns. In response, the complainant said the postmaster was not as available as she used to be because the postmaster's secretary now required the employees to schedule a time if they wanted to see the postmaster. After about 45 minutes of discussion the complaint was withdrawn and a system for communication between the two women was established.

If the neutral had accepted the premise that the problem was one of scheduling for which a more directive approach would be appropriate, the underlying issues of the complaint would likely have not been resolved. Since the neutral realized the transformative approach was needed, the parties were able to have a productive discussion and resolve the disagreement. This illustrates the necessity for the neutral to be open to changing his/her initial assessment of the process to be used in a particular dispute.

CONCLUSION

Most conflicts contain, at least in part, a person's emotional involvement. Individuals in conflict may exhibit automatic responses to the situation. These reactions are created by the brain functions taking familiar paths which have been set out in the brain due to past experiences in similar situations. Thus, a person facilitating a conversation between two parties may need to utilize a number of techniques to assist the participants with working through their automatic emotional responses, and help the participants look at the problem more rationally in order to resolve the conflict. A neutral can use some of the following techniques to help the parties:

1. Ensure the participants are comfortable with the process and circumstances.
2. Understand that emotions are natural and need to be recognized; they can be both disruptive and beneficial to negotiations.
3. Work toward an understanding that emotions may get in the way of the parties making informed, rational decisions.
4. Utilize an appropriate process for the parties and the situation.

Ultimately, the parties have control of whether they reach an agreement; however, a neutral can help them move toward an agreement by utilizing some of the principles discussed above.

NOTE

1. A number of the examples in this chapter come from work performed by commissioners with the Federal Mediation and Conciliation Service (FMCS). FMCS was established by the Labor-Management Act Relations Act of 1947 (Taft-Hartley Act) 29 U.S.C. § 141-197. The FMCS was "created as an independent agency of the U.S. government. The agency is given the mission of preventing or minimizing the impact labor-management disputes on the free flow of commerce by providing mediation, conciliation and voluntary arbitration" (Federal Mediation and Conciliation Service, n.d., para. 3). The agency works towards developing new initiatives and training commissioners in evolving dispute resolution theories.

REFERENCES

Amthor, F. (2016). *Neuroscience for dummies* (2nd ed.). Hoboken, NY: Wiley.

Billi UK. (2017, October 27). *When you drink tea, how does it affect your brain?* Retrieved from www.billi-uk.com/drink-tea-affect-brain

Birke, R. (2010). Neuroscience and settlement: An examination of scientific innovations and practical applications. *Ohio State Journal of Dispute Resolution, 25*(2), 477–529. Retrieved from https://kb.osu.edu/bitstream/handle/1811/76925/1/OSJDR_V25N2_0477.pdf

Bush, B. R., & Folger, J. P. (2004). *The promise of mediation: The transformative approach to conflict* (2nd ed.). San Francisco, CA: Jossey-Bass.

Carter, R. (2014). *The human brain book* (2nd ed.). New York, NY: DK.

Deutsch, M., Coleman, P., & Marcus, E. (2006). *The handbook of conflict resolution* (2nd ed.). San Francisco, CA: Jossey-Bass.

Emotion. (n.d.). In *Merriam-Webster* online dictionary. Retrieved from https://www.merriam-webster.com/dictionary/emotions?src=search-dict-hed

Federal Mediation and Conciliation Service. (n.d.). *About us, our history.* Retrieved from https://www.fmcs.gov/aboutus/

Fisher, R., & Shapiro, D. (2005). *Beyond reason: Using emotions as you negotiate.* New York, NY: Penguin Group.

Fisher, R., Ury, W., & Patton, B. (1991). *Getting to yes: Negotiating agreement without giving in* (2nd ed.). Boston, MA: Houghton Mifflin Company.

Fleming, A. (2014). A little warmth goes a long way—The science of hot drinks. *The Guardian.* Retrieved from https://www.theguardian.com/lifeandstyle/wordofmouth/2014/oct/28/hot-drinks-science-tasting-notes

Hawaii Naturopathic Retreat. (2017, November 9). *The triune brain.* Retrieved from http://www.hawaiinaturopathicretreat.com/2017/11/change-not-change/the-triune-brain/

Keys, C. (1999). *Mystery light and dark.* London, England: Routledge.

Komninos, A. (2018). The concept of the "triune brain." *Interaction Design Foundation.* Retrieved from https://www.interaction-design.org/literature/article/the-concept-of-the-triune-brain

McEwen, B. (1999). Stress and the brain. In R. Conlan (Ed.), *States of mind: New discoveries about how our brains make us who we are* (pp. 81–120). New York, NY: Wiley.

MacLean, P. D. (1990). *The triune brain in evolution: Role in paleocerebral functions.* New York, NY: Plenum Press

Ury, W. (2007, March). *Getting past no: Negotiating in difficult situations* (Revised ed.). New York, NY: Bantam Books.

CHAPTER 16

CANINES AND CUBICLES

Dogs in the Workplace

David M. Simpson

More and more companies are promoting dog-friendly workplaces and dog-friendly policies (DFPs), ranging from doggie-day care to bring-your-dog to work policies. The corporate trend of canines in the day-to-day workspace is growing and will continue to grow in the near future. We will examine the reasons behind this trend, and the workplace policies that must evolve with it. Emerging research demonstrates positive physiological and psychosocial benefits of the human-canine bond, as well as the net-positive impacts on the workplace environment. These findings provide corporate leadership with a foundation to create DFPs appropriate for their companies, allowing for potential increases in worker happiness and productivity. The chapter concludes by recommending a thoughtful and intentional approach to allowing dogs in the workplace, along with recommendations for implementation and issues to consider when creating DFPs.

From Discord to Harmony, pages 277–288

THE ROLE OF DOGS IN AMERICA

If you thought you were seeing more dogs, even in the workplace, you would be correct. In 2017, more than 89 million dogs lived in households in the United States as pets, compared to 68 million dogs in 2000 (Statista, 2017). With approximately 43 million households, that averages to more than two dogs per household. The pet industry expects we will spend more than $72 billion on our animal companions in 2018 (see Figure 16.1; APPA, 2018). The role of the human–canine relationship has evolved, even as canines, humans, and the society in which they coexist has evolved. In addition to "working dogs" (i.e., those performing tasks in hunting, policing, rescuing, searching, and guiding), we have seen the emergence of physiological assist dogs (those working with sight-impaired, hearing-impaired, mobility needs, or other tasks), dogs assisting with psychological issues (PTSD and social anxiety), and dogs that can alert to cancer, seizures, blood sugar variation, and low blood pressures/fainting. (Assistance Dogs of America, 2019; Lord, Schneider, & Coppinger, 2016). These roles are expanding as we increase our understanding of the intricate relationship between humans and canines. Beyond the working and service aspects, dogs continue to play their largest role as a companion, providing affection and devotion to their human caretakers. We, in turn, are becoming more likely to think of our companion dogs as members of the family.

WHAT'S DRIVING DOG-FRIENDLY POLICIES?

Younger Demographics

Two converging trends are influencing the idea of dogs as a "perk" in the workplace, and framing the expansion of dog-friendly policies (DFPs). Those trends are (a) younger demographics in the workforce, and (b) the competitive hiring marketplace for those younger talented workers. Millennials drive the demographic trend (Kaifi, Nafei, Khanfar, & Kaifi, 2012). Recent generations in the workforce have delayed getting married, buying homes, having children, and other similar life choices due to soaring

General Dogs Statistics

- Number in United States: 89 million
- Average number per household: 2+
- 45% of dogs sleep in owners bed
- Amount spent each year: $72 billion
- 150 distinct dog breeds

Figure 16.1 General dog statistics for the United States.

student debt, employment and market shifts since the 2008 recession, and changes in culture and technology (Levinson, 2010). As a result, millennials (also known as Gen Y) are choosing to have companion pets that serve as a proxy for having a family. In turn, employees who do see their pets as family may feel anxious leaving them at home and seek options to ensure their care during the day (Zilcha-Mano, Mikulincer, & Shaver, 2011).

The "dog-as-family-member" perception has given rise to pet services such as on-demand pet walking, which parallel smartphone apps' ride services (i.e., Uber and Lyft). These dog walking services, such as Wag! and Rover, as well as "doggie day-care" businesses, are rapidly increasing, and provide services to include walks, playtime, pool time, grooming, and other activities. A quick search in most cities will reveal this economic sector of dog care services that have names such as "happy hounds" daycare, "dogtopia," and "camp bow-wow" among many others. Any corporate policy that can ease the concern of a "dog parent" with respect to their pet will be appealing.

Marketplaces and Competitive Hiring Environment

The second trend, competitive hiring in the workforce, ties in closely to the changes in demographics. As younger generations are maturing within the workforce, they are enjoying a post-recession growth period with lower unemployment. As the economy expands and draws from a pool that includes younger employees, the competition for a tech-skilled workforce becomes more intense (Top-Employers Institute, 2019). In this competitive hiring environment, leading edge companies are trying to be proactive in meeting the perceived needs of the younger employees, evidenced by the practices of companies such as Google, Facebook, and others in the high-tech economy. For example, in an article titled "The Top Pet Friendly Offices in Silicon Valley," Penaloza (2015) stated:

> From Zynga's "barking lot" adjacent to their main lobby, to the free-roaming Fidos at Google HQ, dozens of companies in the Bay Area offer perks for employee pets. After all, the future of the New World Order started in San Francisco and the sociological trickle-down effect of the greatest "gold rush" of the digital age is expressed poignantly in the pet policies of these tech titans. (para. 2)

As industrial leaders incorporate dog-friendly workplace policies, there is a trickle-down effect for other companies looking to emulate the success of faster paced, rapid-growth companies. As demonstrated in Figure 16.2, companies of varying size and type are experimenting with dog-friendly workplace environments, and we should expect more growth in the future (Moor, 2018). Figure 16.2 lists the top 30 companies with DFPs currently in place.

Top 30 Companies With Dog-Friendly Policies

Amazon	G5 (real estate marketing)	Kimpton Hotels
Purina	Atlantic Health Systems	Etsy
Hubspot	Tradesy	Zynga
Life is Good	Kurgo (dog accessories)	Advent Software
Big Spaceship	Bissell Homecare, Inc.	Boa Technology
Butler, Shine, Stern	Century Box (manufacturing)	Certified Wildlife Friendly
Clif Bar & Co.	Salesforce (software)	Mars Co. (candy and petfood)
Build-a-Bear	Workday (HR software)	GoDaddy
Activision Blizzard	PetPlan	Ben and Jerry's Ice Cream

Figure 16.2 Companies with dog-friendly policies. *Source:* Adapted from Moor, 2018.

WHAT'S THE PAYOFF FOR COMPANIES AND THE WORKPLACE?

In addition to demographic trends and competitive marketplaces for younger high-tech employees, other factors can positively affect the company's bottom line. Those factors are worker well-being, increased productivity, improved sociability, and, more recently, the idea of canine-assisted mediation as an alternative dispute resolution (ADR) technique.

Worker Well-Being

Current research indicates companion canines have positive health effects from both physiological and psychosocial perspectives (Knight & Edwards, 2008). Company executives may observe market forces leading to more DFPs, but the positive effects on worker's health and morale do much more to influence CEOs and HR departments. Happy, healthy employees are more productive, and higher productivity directly influences the corporate bottom line.

There are several positive physical effects associated with the human–canine bond, which may directly affect productivity, either in the short run or across a longer time span. The two most frequently observed benefits are lower blood pressure and increased physical activity resulting from getting up more frequently and walking the dog (Allen, Blascovich, & Mendes, 2002). A lower stress level also helps maintain lower blood pressure. Barker, Knisely, Barker, Cobb, and Schubert (2012) measured stress levels across workers with their dogs present and those without, and found higher stress levels in those without dogs present. Both humans and dogs benefit from the release of positive hormones that occur when a person is petting a dog for more than a few minutes. Petting a dog continuously for 15 minutes

Positive Health Effects of Dog Ownership

- Lower blood pressure
- Lowered cholesterol
- Reduced anxiety
- Reduced loneliness
- Reduced stress
- Improved outlook
- Increased social interaction
- Higher self-esteem
- Faster recovery from illness
- Increased physical activity
- Better cardiovascular health

Figure 16.3 Improved health effects of dog ownership.

releases serotonin, prolactin, and oxytocin, and lowers the stress hormone cortisol (Weaver, 2004). Figure 16.3 lists additional positive health effects of dog ownership.

Productivity and Morale

Research shows that a dog's presence not only reduces anxiety and stress, but also improves employee satisfaction, task performance, and cognition (Foreman, Glenn, Meade, & Wirth, 2017). With less anxiety and stress, there is also less loneliness and depressive symptoms. The net effect is an overall improvement in employee morale. In terms of productivity, these effects mean employees want to come to work, their health is better, and they are happier. Perhaps one research finding that would stand out to CEOs is that employees take fewer sick days when allowed to bring their dogs to work (Wilkin, Fairlie, & Ezzedeen, 2016). Improved morale decreases time taken off as sick days, which is a direct measure of increased productivity.

An additional bonus to employees are the potential direct cost savings. For those employees that use doggy day care, bringing their dogs to work is a direct benefit due to the elimination of day care expenses. Employees using dog-walking services during their work hours would also find savings. Another potential benefit to employees would be if their employer covered pet health insurance premiums.

Social Interaction

Having dogs present in the workplace leads to increased social interaction and general sociability since others may be inclined to stop and talk to owners about their dogs, or to pet the dog. Research indicates that people who are introverts actually have more interaction with other people, and decreased social anxiety when their dogs are with them. Conversely, people without a dog who encounter someone who does are more inclined to be helpful or interested in engaging with additional interaction (Guéguen & Ciccotti, 2008). Similar research shows increased social interactions with people who have dogs with them, even if the person interacting with them is a stranger (McNicholas & Collis, 2000).

Dogs and ADR

One of the newest additions to dogs in the workplace is the use of canines in mediation and ADR techniques. ADR strategies, as part of a broader conflict management system, have the potential to reduce conflict in the workplace environment and offer a means of decreasing tensions and improving relationships (Thomas, 2002). In a recent article published by the *Harvard Negotiation Law Review*, David Paul (2012) explored the benefit of having dogs present during family law mediation proceedings. Paul found that having a dog in the room helped with the emotional aspects of the mediation, providing a "calming presence." Paul called this "canine assisted mediation (CAM)," and similar findings have demonstrated the positive presence of canines for calming children before domestic abuse trials, and in other therapy-based settings (McQuiston, Burd, & Hayton, 2016). Anecdotally, professional mediators have found that having a dog as a "co-mediator" can be helpful in defusing highly emotional conflict resolution (Benjamin, 2000). The use of CAM has the potential to create a less stressful setting for conflict resolution in nearly any workplace environment.

SOME CHALLENGES (AND SOLUTIONS) TO DOG-FRIENDLY POLICIES

While the positives of DFPs appear to outweigh the negatives, organizations should consider several potential issues prior to implementation. The first issue is allergies. Ten to 20% of the world population has dog and cat allergies (Chan & Leung, 2018). In these instances, DFPs will only be successful if there can be segregation of those with allergies from those without. The organization may even have to go to the extent of installing separate HVAC systems. However, multiple office mates or open cubicle environments could make DFPs difficult.

A second issue is fear. Many individuals fear dogs, either because of a dog attack at some point in their lives, or simply because they were raised in a culture where dogs are not seen as "inside" animals. These feelings, if not responded to, will have an opposite effect on morale, and employees will not see the workplace as improved by the presence of dogs. Strict adherence to nonaggressive dogs and "leashed at all times" clauses in the dog-friendly policy may help.

Other considerations are health and sanitation. Zoonosis is the transmission of animal illnesses to humans, and while there is not tremendous crossover, the transmission of some illnesses from one person to another can occur through the act of multiple people petting the same dog (Parker-Pope, 2009). Dogs would need to be current on their vaccinations and cleared of illnesses, both for their own health and for the health of other dogs that might be in the workplace on a given day. One solution would be to require owners to register their dog with the company and provide documentation of vaccination.

Sanitation may also be a concern. Dogs will inevitably have "accidents." It will be important for organizations to have a "green space" nearby to take care of a dog's bathroom needs. The company may consider creating an interior area for dogs to play or eliminate, particularly on rainy, snowy, or extremely hot days. Multiple stations with cleaning supplies will also be helpful.

A final issue to consider is that not all employees are canine enthusiasts, and would prefer to have another type of animal (i.e., cat, pig, bird, etc.). Company leadership needs to articulate the animal policy to avoid animal confrontations. It is possible that some employees would feel discriminated against for their less positive responses to canines in the workplace. Similarly, if there were an increase in insurance passed along to employees for having dogs present, employees who do not bring dogs to work may see this as a penalty.

IMPLEMENTING DOG FRIENDLY POLICIES

In order to implement a more dog-friendly work environment, companies should consider a step-by-step approach that identifies some of the more important factors that will lead to success. Figure 16.4 lists the nine steps of the process. The first step in creating a dog-friendly workplace would be to survey employees to determine support, existence of allergies, and level of interest. How many employees have dogs? How many employees are interested in having their dogs at work? Careful attention to the responses will help guide the implementation of a dog-friendly policy. Company management can consider a variety of DFPs, ranging from controlled interactions with canines, such as visitation of programmed therapy dog interaction, to unregulated, unlimited "bring your dogs if you like," scenarios. Policies in between those extremes consist of approaches that place restrictions on when and how canines may come to work, through the regulation of days and/or numbers

Dog-Friendly Policies: 9-Step Implementation Process

1. Survey employees
2. Determine level of employee support
3. Assess physical and logistical elements of space
4. Create policy committee
5. Determine level of policy
6. Establish rules and regulations
7. Initiate trial or pilot program
8. Evaluate success and address negatives
9. Implement policy and adjust as needed

Figure 16.4 9-step process for implementing dog-friendly policy.

of dogs. The company's size (in terms of employee numbers) will also help determine the appropriateness, scale, and scope of the policy.

Space Planning

Before implementing a dog-friendly policy, corporate leadership should assess the physical facility and its ability to handle the presence of dogs. The assessment would include determining reasonable access to outside space or the provision of an interior courtyard. The logistics of dog movement in and out of the building also bears consideration, particularly if there is a need for separation of employees with and without allergies. The separation might require a dedicated entrance/exit separate from the main building entrance. If there was inclement weather, there would likely be the need for a "mud room," or an area to dry and clean the dog before proceeding further into the building.

Scale and logistics are also important. If it is a large company and many of the employees wish to bring their dogs, a situation may arise in which too many dogs are in the workplace, and depending on the canines' training and behaviors, could potentially create a chaotic environment. For larger numbers, there may need to be scheduling as to when each employee or section may bring their dog to work. In the case of creating an onsite doggie daycare, owners would need to register their dog and the facility would have to incorporate an upper limit on the number of dogs at any given time as well as hire dedicated pet care staff.

Determine Level of Policy

While there are many benefits to having a dog-friendly work environment, there are other dog-friendly approaches available for implementation if a dog-friendly workplace is not appropriate or feasible for your organization. The first might be adding pet insurance as a benefit, available with health care insurance for the employee. This benefit is increasing in popularity. "According to the Society for Human Resource Management, nearly 9% of organizations reported offering pet health insurance as a voluntary benefit in 2016, representing a 5% increase from 2011" (Gitlen, 2018). The plans vary in coverage and cost, but this rise in coverage offered as a defined benefit shows the private sector responding to employee needs and desires.

There are two other possibilities for canine presence without a full policy. The first is the idea of visitation dogs. Dog visitations are instances where trained dogs (or puppies) come to the workplace specifically to interact with employees on a short-term, nonpermanent basis. These canines can be trained therapy dogs or other dogs trained for visitation and socialization. As a noncorporate example, there are canine organizations who provide dogs and/or puppies to universities during final exams to help students destress (Harder, 2015). Another related example is the use of "comfort dogs" to provide a morale boost to a specific group of people, typically those who have recently experienced a disaster or crisis event. A second example that would be limited in approach would be a trial or pilot program.

Rules and Regulations

Companies should spend time developing rules to regulate the dog-friendly policy. It may be beneficial to create a "pet policy committee" that has representation from dog owners and non-dog owners alike. Some of the obvious rules that a committee might create would be that dogs may not be aggressive to employees or other dogs, must have current vaccinations, and meet established grooming standards for odor and hygiene purposes. Further, those bringing in their dogs could be required to show their canine has earned a "canine good citizen" certificate, indicating a minimum level of behavior and obedience skills. There are also additional levels of obedience training, demonstrated through American Kennel Club trials and the awarding of companion dog (CD) or companion dog excellent (CDX) titles, which may also be required.

Trials or Pilot Programs

If the organization is large, it is advisable that the company try a smaller-scale approach before implementing a full-scale rollout. The trials can be limited in time or scope. The company could try pilot programs implemented in a single unit, department, or division, with later assessment for success and/or lessons learned. Similarly, the company could test different logistical arrangements—whether by specific day or method of sign-up—for a limited number of dogs. If there are too many insurmountable issues, the company can revert to the preexisting no-pet policy. If successful, there would be a general guideline for how to scale the program to the rest of company. Regardless of the scale, consider the following issues for implementation.

OTHER CONSIDERATIONS FOR DOG-FRIENDLY POLICIES

Another issue that may arise is what to do when there is bad behavior on the part of the dog, or the owner. What will be the policy and consequence (e.g., warning or banning) for dogs and owners that display inappropriate workplace behavior? What about policy regarding cleaning up after a canine? Here, too, the company would benefit from a "pet committee" that can create uniform and equitable approaches for handling policy violations.

Risk Management

In a perfect world all dogs would always be on their best behavior; however, the reality is that a dog may react poorly in a specific situation and bite another dog, employee, or client. Companies would need to investigate the need for sufficient liability coverage in those rare circumstances. While bites may be a rare issue, there exists other potential hazards, such as an employee tripping over a leash or having an employee knocked down by an exuberant canine. These are real risks, and one lawsuit would be enough to stop DFPs.

CONCLUSION

If done thoughtfully and with employee support, creating a dog-friendly workplace can have beneficial effects with a more productive and positive workforce. While benefits to individuals are readily apparent, the positive effects on small groups and overall functioning of the company may also be improved. It is very likely that the number of dog owners in the United States will continue to grow, and that demographic and cultural trends will continue to create a demand for dog-friendly work environments. However, if companies decide to pursue dog-friendly workplaces, there are policies and logistical considerations that require address. There is a clear need for more comprehensive research on companies that have long-standing

DFPs as there may be yet unseen or unpredicted consequences. Additional research should focus on the holistic effect of DFPs, the net impact on employee productivity and morale, and the quantifiable role these have in company profitability.

REFERENCES

Allen, K., Blascovich, J., & Mendes, W. (2002, September–October). Cardiovascular reactivity and the presence of pets, friends, and spouses: The truth about cats and dogs. *Psychosomatic Medicine, 64*(5), 727–739.

APPA. (2018). American Pet Products Association. Retrieved from https://www.americanpetproducts.org/press_industrytrends.asp

Assistance Dogs of America. (2019). *Types of assistance dogs.* Retrieved from https://assistancedogregistry.com/types-of-assistance-dogs/

Barker, R. T., Knisely, J. S., Barker, S. B., Cobb, R. K., & Schubert, C. M. (2012). Preliminary investigation of employee's dog presence on stress and organizational perceptions. *International Journal of Workplace Health Management, 5*(1), 15–30.

Benjamin, R. (2000, December). Dogs as conflict mediators. *Mediation News, 19*(1), 10–11.

Chan, S. K., & Leung, D. Y. M. (2018, March). Dog and cat allergies: Current state of diagnostic approaches and challenges. *Allergy, Asthma, & Immunology Research, 10*(2), 97–105.

Foreman, A. M., Glenn, M. K., Meade, B. J., & Wirth, O. (2017). Dogs in the workplace: A review of the benefits and potential challenges. *International Journal of Environmental Research and Public Health, 14*(5), 498. https://doi.org/10.3390/ijerph14050498

Gitlen, J. (2018). More employers are offering pet insurance benefits in 2017. *Lendedu.* Retrieved from https://lendedu.com/blog/more-employers-offering-pet-insurance-benefits

Guéguen, N., & Ciccotti, S. (2008). Domestic dogs as facilitators in social interaction: An evaluation of helping and courtship behaviors. *Anthrozoös, 21*(4), 339–349.

Harder, W. (2015). Puppy power: Law students de-stress during 'dog days of finals.' *University of Kentucky News.* Retrieved from https://uknow.uky.edu/content/puppy-power-law-students-de-stress-during-dog-days-finals

Kaifi, B. A., Nafei, W. A., Khanfar, N. M., & Kaifi, M. M. (2012). A multi-generational workforce: Managing and understanding millennials. *International Journal of Business and Management, 7*(24), 88–93.

Knight, S., & Edwards, V. (2008). In the company of wolves: The physical, social, and psychological benefits of dog ownership. *Journal of Aging and Health, 20*(4), 437–455.

Levinson, A. R. (2010). Millennials and the world of work: An economist's perspective. *Journal of Business and Psychology, 25*(2), 257–264.

Lord, K., Schneider, R. A., & Coppinger, R. (2016). Evolution of working dogs. In J. Serpell (Ed.), *The domestic dog* (2nd ed., pp. 43–64). New York, NY: Cambridge University Press.

McNicholas, J., & Collis, G. M. (2000, December). Dogs as catalysts for social interactions: Robustness of the effect. *British Journal of Psychology, 91*(1), 61–70.

McQuiston, D. E., Burd, K., & Hayton, C. G. (2016, July). Utilizing courthouse dogs and comfort items to assist vulnerable witnesses during trial. *American Psychology- Law Society Newsletter, 41.* Retrieved from https://www.apadivisions.org/division-41/publications/newsletters/news/2016/07/courthouse-dogs

Moor, A. (2018). The 30 most pet-friendly companies in the U.S. *Best Life Online.* Retrieved from http://bestlifeonline.com/30-most-pet-friendly-companies-in-the-united-states/

Parker-Pope, T. (2009, May 11). Therapy dogs may fetch hospital germs. *New York Times.* Retrieved fromhttps://well.blogs.nytimes.com/2009/05/11/therapy-dogs-and-hospital-infections/

Paul, D. (2017). Canine-assisted mediation. *Harvard Negotiation Law Review, 23.* Retrieved from https://www.hnlr.org/wp-content/uploads/sites/22/HNLR-Paul-Final.pdf

Penaloza, S. (2015, December 10). The top pet-friendly offices in Silicon Valley. *Get Leashed Magazine.* Retrieved from https://getleashedmag.com/2015/12/10/the-top-pet-friendly-offices-in-silicon-valley/

Statista. (2017). *Number of dogs in the United States from 2000 to 2017 (in millions).* Retrieved from https://www.statista.com/statistics/198100/dogs-in-the-united-states-since-2000/

Thomas, R. (2002). Conflict management systems: A methodology for addressing the cost of conflict in the workplace. Retrieved from https://www.mediate.com/articles/thomasR.cfm

Top-Employers Institute. (2019). *Millennials are tech savvy. Gen Z's are tech native.* Retrieved from https://www.top-employers.com/en-US/insights/talent-strategy/millennials-are-tech-savvy.-gen-zs-are-tech-native/

Weaver, J. (2004). Puppy love—it's better than you think. *Pet Health.* Retrieved from http://www.nbcnews.com/id/4625213/ns/health-pet_health/t/puppy-love——its-better-you-think/#.W_t2RzhKi70

Wilkin, C. L., Fairlie, P., & Ezzedeen, S. R. (2016). Who let the dogs in? A look at pet friendly workplaces. *International Journal of Workplace Health Management, 9*(1), 96–109.

Zilcha-Mano, S., Mikulincer, M., & Shaver, P. R. (2011). An attachment perspective on human–pet relationships: Conceptualization and assessment of pet attachment orientations. *Journal of Research in Personality, 45*(4), 345–357.

CHAPTER 17

ALTERNATIVE DISPUTE RESOLUTION PROCESSES FOR MANAGERS AND PRACTITIONERS

Gary Boettcher

If you seek out alternative methods to constructively settle your disputes focused on the co-creation of mutually beneficial solutions, your journey will always end with satisfaction and a new friend.

—Gary Boettcher

April 1976 marks the birth of the alternative dispute resolution (ADR) system. More than 200 legal scholars, judges, and leaders of the American Bar Association met at the National Conference on the Causes of Popular Dissatisfaction with the Administration of Justice in what is known as the Pound Conference (Goldberg, Sander, Rogers, & Cole, 2003). The gathering sought to examine and discuss concerns about the fairness and efficacy of the American justice system. The legal system was inundated with litigation, which ultimately bogged down court cases to the point that some took years to reach a judge's bench for adjudication. Arbitration and mediation became the go-to hallmark processes that were meant to ease the load on

From Discord to Harmony, pages 289–315

the judicial system and help disputants amicably and fairly resolve their differences. The idea was to give disputants a greater role in identifying common interests and then for them to collaborate to create durable, mutually beneficial, and satisfying resolutions.

Although the new ADR processes helped to reduce court loads, people were still angry and dissatisfied and often litigated unenforceable parts of an ADR agreement (Goldberg et al., 2003). Practitioners began to understand that neutral third-party intervention often occurred too late in the process to manage deeply negative emotions. Disputants needed a process that provided neutral intervention that helped mitigate current and prevent future intractable disputes. Subsequently, ombuds and facilitation processes began to grow as a profession in North America.

This chapter will explore arbitration, facilitation, mediation, negotiation, and ombudsmanship processes. The author will clearly define each and explain why a manager or practitioner might use or choose to avoid a particular process.

NEUTRAL THIRD-PARTY ARBITRATION AND MEDIATION PROCESSES

What happens when arguing parties just cannot seem to manage emotions and engage in empathic conversations that honor the core-value paradigm (Boettcher, this volume; Schwarz, Davidson, Carlson, & McKinney, 2005)? Impasse. When disputants and/or their respective attorneys are locked in impasse, litigation does not have to be the next step. A neutral third-party ADR process expert can help the parties resolve ungrounded expectations and mitigate disruptive behaviors caused by jaded personality disputes and unmanaged emotions. The neutral manager can help disputing office workers identify issues that block constructive conversations, which may otherwise result in intractable confrontations. For the past 4 decades ADR models, based on a neutral and unbiased third-party process expert, have led parties to co-create solutions in a cooperative conflict environment because mutually participative ADR processes avoid the win–lose dynamic of a legal system that imposes a solution on disputants (Kressel, 2006; Livingood, 2008).

The four impasse-breaking and neutrally led processes are arbitration, facilitation, mediation, and ombudsmanship. Managers can use techniques from all of these neutral-processes to resolve peer-to-peer workplace disputes.

Arbitration

Arbitration is commonly a private dispute-resolution process that can be binding or advisory. Goldberg claims there are five general forms of arbitration.

First, Goldberg claims that commercial arbitration is the oldest form of arbitration in the United States and antedates the American Revolution. Commercial arbitration is used throughout most industries, between consumers and manufacturers, in medical malpractice, family disputes, securities disputes, attorney-client fee disputes, and in many other commercial relationships. Most commercial arbitration rulings are not supported by an arbitrator brief. The neutral creates the remedy without supplying written reasoned decisions for the respective verdict (Goldberg et al., 2003).

Perhaps the second most common form of arbitration is labor arbitration. Labor arbitration occurs most often when organized labor and management have a contract dispute. Arbitrators can also settle peer-to-peer differences within organized labor and between labor and nonlabor members. In labor disputes arbitrators issue written reasoned decisions in the form of a brief that supports the remedy. Written briefs can and do set precedence (Goldberg et al., 2003).

Some states refer specific types of court cases to the arbitration process in lieu of litigation. These *court-ordered* or *court-annexed* arbitration proceedings are generally not voluntary and result in the arbitrator's ruling as final and binding (Goldberg et al., 2003).

Last best-offer, final offer, or baseball-style arbitration occurs when the parties individually present their viewpoint and respective remedy to the arbitrator. The arbitrator then decides which remedy to use to most fairly settle the case. The arbitrator is not allowed to modify either offer and must pick one of the disputant's remedies.

Med-Arb is a blending of mediation and arbitration. The arbitrator will strive to mediate the case, but if the parties cannot create a settlement, the arbitrator will then use the parties' testimony to render a binding decision based on the evidence presented throughout the mediation process.

Binding arbitration requires the arbitrator to adjudicate a decision or remedy based upon the disputants' agreed-upon process; that is, the parties determine the procedural rules instead of a judge. Once the arbitrator and disputants set procedural rules, the arbitrator then listens to presentations and cross-examinations by all the parties and renders a decision based on the information presented.

Arbitration hearings are generally less formal than a courtroom. Additionally, with mutual party agreement, pretrial discovery and the rules of evidence are managed by the arbitrator and are not strictly applied as in a court of law (Goldberg et al., 2003).

Not all arbitrations end with a binding ruling by an arbitrator. Arbitrators can rule in an advisory or evaluative role with the goal of helping the parties achieve a voluntary settlement of their own volition (Goldberg et al., 2003). Parties will agree to an evaluative form of arbitration when one party's perspective may not be grounded in practicality or reality. Once a remedy is offered to the parties, either party may accept the decision or move on to litigation.

When parties seek a neutral (binding or advisory) arbitration process, an odd number of arbitrators recommended by the National Academy of Arbitrators or the American Arbitration Association form a panel of qualified arbitrator candidates. The two parties alternately strike names from the panel until one arbitrator is left to adjudicate. This neutral arbitrator will preside over the entire process. Arbitrators generally retain authority over any future conflict directly related to the case.

Arbitrations are generally less expensive and end quicker than litigation for the following reasons. Typically, based on the process approved by the disputing parties, the rules of proofs and arguments are presented to the arbitrator in a somewhat informal meeting. The arbitrator determines the limits of pretrial discovery; rules of evidence by the courts are not strictly applied; and the rule of law does not precisely guide the process or arbitrator's remedy.

There are limited grounds for overturning an arbitration ruling. In a vast majority of cases, courts are loathed to overturn an arbitrator's ruling if there is no malfeasance, collusion with one of the parties, fraud, or rulings made outside the intended scope of the arbitration. Goldberg also notes that arbitration outcomes are generally more satisfying to disputants than litigation because the counterparts have a say in the outcome.

Other advantages of arbitration are: (a) the arbitrator is often a subject-matter expert, unlike a judge who is bound to declare a verdict based on law; (b) in binding arbitration, because the arbitrator's decision is final and generally cannot be appealed, arbitration is generally quicker and less costly than litigation because there are no appeals that take time and money; (c) the proceedings are commonly private and held outside the purview of the public eye; and (d) the parties, not a judge, decide on a level of procedural informality that can further save time and produce quicker results than litigation (Goldberg et al., 2003). As previously mentioned, the totality of the arbitration process usually results in reduced costs over litigation due to lower fees, a simpler process that requires less time, and a significant reduction in the opportunity for ongoing appeals, which is why parties often select arbitration over litigation (Goldberg et al., 2003).

Facilitation

Facilitators are often inaccurately viewed as meeting monitors or meeting leaders. A neutral facilitator is actually a process or content expert. From the practitioner view Wilkinson (2004) says, "A facilitated session is a highly structured meeting in which the meeting leader (the facilitator) guides the participants through a series of predefined steps to arrive at a result that is created, understood, and accepted by all participants" (p. 23). From an academic-practitioner perspective Schwarz et al. (2005) says, "A *facilitator* is a substantively neutral third party, acceptable to all members of the group, who has no substantive decision-making authority" (p. 27, emphasis in original).

Schwartz (2005) notes that a facilitator can fulfill several roles:

- as a process expert, who is neutral on the content;
- as a consultant, who is an expert in both the process and the subject matter;
- as a coach, who is a process expert and gets involved in the content but leaves decision-making up to the clients;
- as a partnering agent, who helps the clients build dispute-resolution processes to keep a project on task and on time;
- as a trainer, who helps clients develop knowledge and skills; and
- as a formal or informal leader of a group, who manages the process though diagnosis and intervention and manages the structure of the group to meet the goals and objectives of the hiring agent.

Facilitated sessions are appropriate when an issue has been discovered and the clients' needs change, and/or where the solution is not readily apparent and the group wants to collaboratively create a resolution (Schwarz et al., 2005). All neutral facilitators provide a process that empowers the group to find solutions using consensus-based decision-making. Consensus-based outcomes require buy-in from all parties in order for the solution to be successful over time. A facilitation process is usually commissioned before the parties reach impasse.

Facilitators can be attorneys. However, because most facilitated sessions are not about legal issues, facilitators are generally not lawyers, but instead are highly trained process experts or subject matter experts. Some organizations have internal facilitators. Unfortunately, participants usually view internal facilitators as less than neutral because they work for the organization and are often thought to be driving hidden agendas. If neutrality is an issue, organizations generally hire an outside facilitator.

Facilitation is not appropriate when there is no need to create a solution to break impasse, the issue(s) is/are too complex, and/or confidentiality keeps all members from being fully informed in a way that would allow them to collaborate (Schwarz et al., 2005). Most facilitated meetings can be completed within a day unless they are complicated or multi-stepped. For example, strategic-planning facilitations often take multiple days.

In the workplace, when a group or team is behaving with dysfunction, a facilitator can be hired to help the group deconstruct the issues and generate constructive change. A facilitator can also help when groups are competing with each other in an unhealthy or nonproductive manner.

Using highly structured brainstorming sessions, facilitators can help a group or team break through stagnation and create new visions and solutions. Facilitation can be effective with one person (a facilitative coach), a small group or team, and with extremely large groups. Facilitation is suitable for government, academic institutions, the military, organizations, communities, families, and individuals (Schwarz et al., 2005).

No one group has oversight authority for facilitator credentialing. When seeking to hire a facilitator, the hiring agent should thoroughly review the facilitator's education, experience, and training. A facilitator's education, experience, training, and personality should be a fit for the needs of the organization. In other words, a team-building facilitator may not be the best fit for a group that specifically needs a subject matter expert in strategic planning, even though the principles of facilitation are transferable between varying topics.

Mediation

Mediation is a private dispute-resolution process whereby the neutral strives to help the parties identify and resolve issues (Moore, 2003) without bias or preconceived notions (Livingood, 2008). Mediation is generally voluntary and is appropriate for parties that have stopped communicating but want a solution. Many state and commonwealth courts mandate mediation education, yet disputing parties ultimately decide whether they want to continue with the mediation process or resume litigation.

There are several types and styles of mediation (Kressel, 2005; Shonk, 2018; Zumeta, 2019). Common types of mediation are e-mediation, court-mandated, private voluntary, or mediation required by the construct of a contract (Shonk, 2018). The most popular styles of mediation are facilitative, evaluative, transformative, narrative (or storytelling), and restorative justice. In all styles and types of mediation, the mediator manages the process and the parties determine the outcome; that is, unlike arbitration, results are not a binding outcome mandated by the mediator. The disputants are responsible for any negotiated agreement. The most popular styles of mediation each have a specific purpose.

Facilitative mediation, the first form of mediation in the United States, began in volunteer dispute-resolution centers in the late 1960s and early 1970s (Zumeta, 2019). In facilitative mediation, a professional mediator attempts to facilitate discussions that result in a settlement between the parties. The mediator does not suggest solutions but rather helps the parties communicate to understand common interests. The mediator seeks to help make the process easier and more constructive for the disputants. Facilitated mediation is appropriate for most disputes and can generally be resolved in less than a day. This form of mediation is highly applicable for the workplace.

Evaluative mediation is also a voluntary process, where the parties declare their respective perspectives. The disputants make their case and hope the mediator will render an opinion on the legal merits of their case should it proceed to trial. Most evaluative mediators are experienced attorneys or retired judges and are usually experts on the specifics of the laws that apply to the dispute. Evaluative mediation can be costly, but it also serves to ground disputants' expectations and can prevent protracted litigation (Kressel, 2006; Zumeta, 2019). Evaluative mediation is not appropriate for minor disputes and can be time consuming.

In 1994, Bush and Folger published the book *The Promise of Mediation* and made the case that mediation can help the parties make positive changes in a constructive and reparative process—thus transformative mediation was born. It is a form of facilitative mediation where the mediator helps the parties to negotiate a settlement and also repair a broken relationship. For example, two partners may find themselves in a business dispute that is destroying their personal relationship. The transformative mediator will help them settle the dispute and also help the partners transform the broken relationship into a functioning connection whereby they can better manage future change.

Transformative mediation is not a quick fix. During the author's mediation certification process, part of the procedure was to interview other mediators to gain a breadth of mediator perspectives. The author interviewed several mediators with varying backgrounds, but one mediator with 15 years of experience practicing as both a non-attorney and attorney stood out. The mediator's pseudonym is Sue. Sue was so dedicated to the mediation process that after 5 years as a non-attorney mediator, she attended law school, became an attorney, and subsequently built a collaborative law practice based on mediation processes. In other words, Sue did not litigate cases; rather, she used mediation to help the parties create mutually beneficial outcomes and avoided litigation.

During the interview Sue shared a transformative mediation experience that went bad. Two long-term best friends, life-partners, and business owners ran into a business situation that ended in an ugly impasse between them. After a long period of transformative mediation, a solution was co-created and the relationship seemingly restored. The last step in the mediation process was for each party to take their agreement to independent attorneys for review before taking the agreement to the judge for adjudication. Unfortunately, one attorney was a strong advocate for the law and convinced his client to litigate a settlement. At the end of a protracted trial, not only was the business dissolved, the two friends separated, never to see each other again.

Mediation is an opportunity to create solutions that work for both parties. Litigation can and often does end up with 50% of the parties losing, and frequently neither party satisfied (Goldberg et al., 2003).

Transformative mediation is time-consuming and often deeply touches emotions. It is appropriate when peer-to-peer relationships have hurt workplace productivity and the parties have an interest in both a fair settlement and restoration of the relationship because they have to work with each other in the future. Workplace disputants may also benefit from conflict-coaching sessions based on the Jones and Brinkert (2008) or CINERGY™ (Noble, 2012) conflict coaching models reviewed in Boettcher (this volume).

Narrative mediation is arguably a form of transformative mediation. Facts of the case are disclosed in a storytelling form, where the clients' interpretations are woven to construct a collaborative conversation that represents each party's perspective (Winslade & Monk, 2001). Cobb (1994) writes, "Narratives are interactively developed, modified, and contested as disputants elaborate portions of their own and each other's conflict stories" (p. 53). Narrative mediation is a blend of the problem-solving approach and the transformative approach and encompasses empowerment, recognition, and social justice (Hansen, 2003).

Restorative justice through victim–offender mediation is one of the newest forms of mediation and is purposed to serve both the offender and the victim. A specially trained mediator will guide the conversation in a face-to-face meeting between the victim, offenders, and even the community, to discuss the crime, its impact on all parties, and to create or further develop a restitution plan. Umbreit (1998) writes:

> Restorative justice emphasizes the importance of elevating the role of crime victims and community members, holding offenders directly accountable to the people they violate, restoring the emotional and material losses of victims, and providing a range of opportunities for dialogue, negotiation, and problem solving, whenever possible, which can lead to a greater sense of community safety, conflict resolution, and closure for all involved. (p. 1)

Paraphrasing Umbreit would water down the specificity and meaning of Umbreit's perspective. Given today's milieu of diversity sensitivity and root causes of the Me Too movement, restorative justice techniques may be a highly meaningful and useful process to support effective change in organizational cultures. It is the author's experienced opinion that real and satisfying change occurs within organizations when past poor behaviors are brought forward with recognizable transparency and organizational leadership support for the needed change. Restorative justice techniques are also useful for addressing bullying behaviors because the techniques can help both the perpetrator and victims move forward in the organization.

Mediators can be attorneys, educated and trained dispute resolution practitioners, or merely an interested party claiming to be a qualified mediator. In a study on mediator certification, Boettcher (2010) noted, "There is, to date, no universal set of qualifications for mediators, as each program or organization that offers mediation services establishes its own, or the qualifications are established by statute or court rule for the program" (Hill, 1998, p. 1). As of the date of this publication there is no designated organization with oversight for mediation credentialing, such as there is for attorneys via the American Bar Association or doctors via the American Medical Association. Notwithstanding a central oversight agency, mediation as a process can be successful and satisfying for the disputants. Common sense suggests that when disputing parties resolve a conflict with a mutually beneficial agreement, 100% of the parties are winners. If they go through the litigation process, 50% will lose. Arguably, judges' rulings are at least somewhat unsatisfactory for both parties and often result in future litigation because of the losing party's dissatisfaction and opportunity to appeal the lower court ruling (Goldberg et al., 2003).

Unlike arbitration, the mediator does not impose remedies or solutions upon the disputants, but instead strictly manages the process so a fair and effective outcome is both achievable and created by the disputing parties (Goldberg et al., 2003). In fact, in most styles of mediation, the mediator does not even make personal suggestions or recommendations. The mediator must maintain a "neutral" status.

Mediation outcomes become binding only when the parties sign the co-created agreement, thereby forming a legal contract. When mediation fails, a party might turn to litigation or become exhausted by the dispute, give up the claim, and walk away with relationships still broken.

Goldberg et al. (2003) asserts that litigation is biased toward justice and mediation is biased toward bringing harmony. Based on my experience, I often ponder this fair question: "Does mediation water down social justice, or is mediation a form of private justice that uniquely and more effectively serves respective disputants with more satisfying outcomes than litigation?" Metaphorically, is a fence built to keep people in or keep people out? It is my perspective that mediation serves as a gateway to the fence like barriers formed by intractable conflict. Mediation allows the parties to create satisfying outcomes without regard to the limitations of the law—a law-based outcome which is often abstractly applied to the larger population based on a judge's personal interpretation of that law without regard to the desires of the disputants. Simply, there is more constructive value in the parties' collective self-determination than in a judge's decision that has no personal investment in the immediate outcome or the long-term effects on the parties of that legally based decision. Basically, it is always better for disputants to co-create solutions than it is for supervisors to impose a purely manager-based resolution.

Academics and ADR practitioners often argue that mediation has no "teeth" because the mediator has no power to enforce or render a remedy (Goldberg et al., 2003), yet seasoned mediators often help disputants break through the impasse barricade and restart conversations. Managers can use mediator techniques to constructively and effectively settle interoffice and peer-to-peer disputes and, thereby, preserve workplace relationships and productivity. Goldberg et al., (2003) identifies several mediator behaviors that will serve the workplace manager well:

- Encourage the exchange of information, both old and new.
- Help the parties empathize with each other's views.
- Ensure each party understands the perspectives of their counterparts with empathy.
- Help the parties seek grounded and durable solutions.
- Encourage flexibility.
- Have an open-mind and create mutually beneficial solutions.
- Shift the focus from the past to the future.
- When all else fails, invent new options that are mutually beneficial.

Managers should empower their workers to solve peer-to-peer disputes with empathy and objective standards (Boettcher, this volume). Ultimately, workers will enhance their buy-in of a solution and make the solution durable when they are creator-owners of the resolution process.

Ombudsmanship

An ombudsman is "a designated neutral who is appointed or employed by an organization to facilitate the informal resolution of concerns of employees, managers, students and, sometimes, external clients of the organization" (Wesley, 2004, p. 1). The terms ombudsman, ombuds, and ombudsperson are equally interchangeable and are not gender specific. The expression ombudsman is derived from Sweden and literally means "representative." The origins of ombudsman-like work dates to the Qin Dynasty (221 BC) and in modern times is linked to the Swedish Parliamentary Ombudsman by the Instrument of Government of Sweden of 1809 (Park, 2008). Ombudsmanship is embraced around the world, yet it is not a widely known concept in the United States.

Ombudsmen do serve many places, including educational institutions, governments, corporations, hospitals, and news organizations. The three primary roles of ombudsmen are as an organizational ombudsman (a corporate neutral acting internally and/or externally), classical ombudsman (one who deals with government policies and processes), and advocate ombudsman (who represents a medical patient in a hospital; Wesley, 2004). Less commonly known roles of ombudsmen are hybrid ombudsman, executive ombudsman, legislative ombudsman, and media ombudsman.

The standards and functions of the role vary. Although the ombudsman serves much like an arbitrator or mediator in dispute-resolution processes, the ombudsman generally functions independently and reports directly to the organizational CEO or board of directors. The ombudsman generally has no other collateral duties and does not render binding decisions (Goldberg et al., 2003).

The organizational ombudsman is generally a senior-level employee who operates outside of usual corporate hierarchy. The ombudsman office is customarily comprised of highly trained individuals competent in mediation, education and training, conflict-resolution strategies, and dispute-system designs. The ombudsman functions as a coach; should be an active listener; can facilitate discussions acting as a go-between; is a trainer, mediator, and investigator; and recommends changes in policy and procedure to mitigate workplace conflict. Department heads, senior managers, and supervisors of large employee groups may find it useful to select and train an individual in the group to function as an ombudsman to help manage interdepartmental disputes.

Unlike some forms of arbitration, the ombudsman does not generally make binding decisions but acts as a neutral third party with a responsibility to report discrepancies to their immediate supervisor. The ombudsman is an advocate for fairness and equity within the organization, with the primary task of ensuring that all employees are treated with fairness. To protect employee identity, ombudsmen operate with strict confidentiality so personnel do not have to be concerned about retribution. To preserve confidentiality, ombudsman offices are usually located offsite or in a discrete location within the organization (Wesley, 2004).

NEGOTIATION PROCESSES: CHANGE VERSUS NEGOTIATION

When circumstances change and the parties do not want to solve the problem, the incident is termed conflict. When those same parties desire change, yet want to control the change to advantage their respective positions, the process is called negotiation. Simplistically, negotiation is a process used to manage change. Furthermore, Lewicki, Barry, and Saunders (2010) note that bargaining and negotiation are different processes. Bargaining is a win–lose dynamic based on power and rights; whoever has the greatest power or rights generates the greatest leverage to force an advantageous change. The term *negotiation* refers to "win–win situations such as those that occur when parties are trying to find a mutually acceptable solution to a complex conflict" (p. 3).

For the purpose of this chapter negotiation is much more than a mere exchange of money, goods, or sales/purchase agreements. Negotiation is the primary process used to equitably manage conflict between individuals, groups, and organizations and can result in an increase of mutually beneficial tangible and intangible values for the negotiators.

The two common forms of negotiation used to settle disputes are framed as *distributive* negotiation and *interest-based* negotiation (Lewicki et al., 2010; Lum, 2005). This chapter will only cover the basics of these two negotiation concepts, as there are many books and academic papers already written on the topic (Churchman, 1995; Cohen, 2002; Fisher, Ury, & Patton, 1991; Karrass, 1992, 1996; Lewicki et al., 2010; Lum, 2011; Mnookin, Peppet, & Tulumello, 2000; Reardon, 2005; Shackford & Shackford, 2003). The purpose of this section is to provide manager-coaches who have no formal negotiation training, some useful negotiation techniques to help them coach disputing workplace employees to achieve more effective and productive outcomes.

The Distributive Negotiation Strategy

Distributive negotiation, also known as traditional, competitive, positional, or win–lose negotiations, has been prevalent in human society since the beginning of humankind's existence (Lewicki et al., 2010; Shackford & Shackford, 2003). I have a bushel of wheat and you have a hindquarter of meat. I have a bag of coffee beans and you have a bag of corn. You and I haggle over the respective value of our goods and then settle on a method to trade—it is a form of bartering, bargaining, or haggling.

Distributive negotiators focus on anchoring positions and then use power dynamics or rights-based arguments to claim value in any form from the respective counterpart (Fisher et al., 1991; Lewicki et al., 2010). The party with the most power or leverage usually gains the largest relative share of the fixed resource (commonly known in negotiation lingo as a larger slice of the pie).

In distributive bargaining, the goals of the parties are initially at odds—or at least appear that way to some or all of the parties. It is fair to say the parties will treat each other's goals as mutually exclusive objectives. Why? In order for my slice of the pie to grow (to increase my value), one party must take a piece from the opponent's slice of the pie (decrease the counterpart's value). The author defines values, as applied to the negotiation process within the context of this chapter, as tangible or intangible principles or standards, and elements that represents price, costs, worth, monetary value, face issues (ethics, moral, & personal codes), and strategic importance.

From a communication perspective, in a distributive negotiation, information is usually shared when it gives one party a strategic or tactical advantage over the other party—in other words, the information shared increases one's relative leverage/power at the table. Distributive negotiators frequently use misdirection and manipulation (Reardon, 2005) to retain a power or leverage advantage. Savvy negotiators will carefully walk the gray line between outright lying and bad faith bargaining prohibited under U.S. labor law (Churchman, 1995).

Distributive negotiators regularly fill their communication efforts with assertions and defensive rhetoric. The best defense against misdirection, manipulation, and outright bad-faith bargaining is the wise use of effective questions that require objective substantiation by the counterpart. Take no assertion by your counterpart at face value and ask enough questions to objectively validate your counterpart's claims.

In brief, the distributive strategy is confrontational in nature. Central to distributive negotiation communication dialogues are assertions and positional claims that are frequently emotionally intense, and can escalate to bitter hostility. Conflict is resolved through use of power and force. This strategy requires extensive planning, strong execution of hardball tactics, and constant monitoring of the counterpart's actions and reactions (Karrass, 1992, 1996; Lewicki et al., 2010; Reardon, 2005). The negotiations can end with one party feeling bitter about the outcome. Distributive-based agreements are rarely durable over time because one party was forced to acquiesce to the other's power advantage (Karrass, n.d.; Karrass, 1996) leaving the slighted party looking for ways to get even or regain lost value.

The Integrative Negotiation Strategy

Integrative negotiation is vicarious in nature in that each negotiator experiences it differently. The *Integrative* approach is also known as cooperative, collaborative, win–win, mutual gains, problem-solving, and is frequently referred to as either interest-based or *principled* negotiations (Reardon, 2005; Shackford & Shackford, 2003). Lewicki describes integrative negotiations in part as a process where

> the goals of the parties are not mutually exclusive. If one side achieves its goals, the other is not necessarily precluded from achieving its goals. One party's gain is not necessarily at the other party's expense. The fundamental structure of an integrative negotiation situation is such that it allows both sides to achieve their objectives. (pp. 71–72)

The methodology and the attitudes of the parties define the nature of the negotiation strategy. The focus of a principled negotiation process is how the outcome affects *us*, whereas the focus in a distributive negotiation is on how the outcome affects me with little regard to the we aspect. Glaser (2014) refers to this perspective as a *we-centric* form of communication (Boettcher, this volume).

Interest-based negotiators generally ask many questions that seek the understanding of the why (interests) behind the want of positions of their counterparts. They ask questions to gather information and validate understanding. Interest-based negotiators view the opposing party as a *counterpart* instead of an adversary, enemy, or rival. After all, one of the precepts of integrative negotiation is to create a larger pie so all parties fairly reap greater values (Fisher et al., 1991).

The interest-based strategy holds a fundamental underpinning of a free flow of information that promotes innovation, collaboration, and problem-solving conversations, whereby the negotiators reveal their true objectives, interests, and needs (Reardon, 2005). The emphasis is on discovering commonality between the parties and minimizing their respective differences. Rhetorically, "How do we expand the original pie so everyone can enjoy a larger slice in the end?" Integrative negotiators look beyond the tangible dollar or cost of the agreement and instead consider the total tangible and intangible values of the collective agreement. Increasing the size of the pie may mean more than just increasing greenbacks in your pocket.

Shackford says that most integrative negotiators retain a certain attitude of, "As long as the solution does not negatively affect me, I'm not overly concerned about how much it positively affects you." The process invokes an improved relationship between the parties by building open communication and trust among the negotiators. One side will not take advantage over the other because of information gained from an open dialogue between the parties, because to do so would destroy any trust built between the parties and ultimately shut down communication (Lewicki et al., 2010; Reardon, 2005; Shackford & Shackford, 2003).

Fisher suggests a four-step method or model negotiators can use to achieve successful principled negotiation agreements:

- Separate the people from the problem—don't allow the process to become a personality issue.
- Focus on the interests and then on commonalities—do not derail the process because of different perspectives and positions. Seek accurate understanding of the why behind the claim or assertion.
- Invent options—co-create solutions that address the mutual needs/interests of the parties even when there appear to be none. Do so by focusing on common needs and interests. Jointly discover the *why* behind the interest and need. Sometimes folks state a need or want

yet do not really understand why they are making that claim. Learn things by asking a lot of relevant questions.
- Stipulate that *objective criteria* will determine valuations and fair standards.

There is a prevailing myth that principled negotiations are easier, kinder, or gentler than distributive negotiations. Nothing could be further from the truth. Based on the author's experience, integrative negotiations are frequently intense, focused, frustrating, difficult, and challenging. The primary differences between distributive and integrative strategy are a focus on *us* versus *me* and seeking commonalities versus differences. It is easy to fall into the trap of defending your own positions, so work diligently at listening and understanding your counterpart's interests.

Principled negotiations provide an opportunity to create elegant solutions. Shackford stresses that if the parties collaboratively engage in a process that captures the Italian economist Pareto's concept of an elegant solution, a somewhat radical idea for negotiators, negotiated agreements will provide mutual satisfaction. As the parties explore and mull over ideas, value for one party may bubble up with little expense or loss of value to the counterpart. As the parties dive into their respective interests, more latent value is discovered at little expense to either party. Co-creating an elegant Pareto solution requires the parties closely focus on the values gained through mutually beneficial reciprocity (Shackford & Shackford, 2003). An example of the value gained by interest-based Pareto effects in negotiation is depicted in Figure 17.1. The gray area represents total value gain by each negotiator in a distributive solution—where the goal is to divide the pie based on leverage and power. The parties must divide the fixed value of the gray shaded area. If the parties take a deep dive into their respective interests, thereby striving to learn more about each other's needs and interests, and seek to understand why those interests and needs are important, they may be able to capture previously unknown value represented by the area in orange. For example, if two workers are assigned to research, analyze, and evaluate the potential of a new client or product and merely divide the work, the effort may result in an adequate work product valued by the gray shaded area. However, if one worker is excellent at research but struggles with synthesizing a lot of information at one time, and the other peer is poor at research but excellent at analytics and critical evaluations, the two cohorts could divide the tasks based on their respective strengths and produce a higher-quality work product. From a personal perspective, "If I can do something of high value for you with little expense to me, and you can do something of high value for me at little expense to you, and neither effort harms either of us, why should we not engage in the mutually beneficial efforts?" The two cohorts may be able to "make the pie larger" as visualized

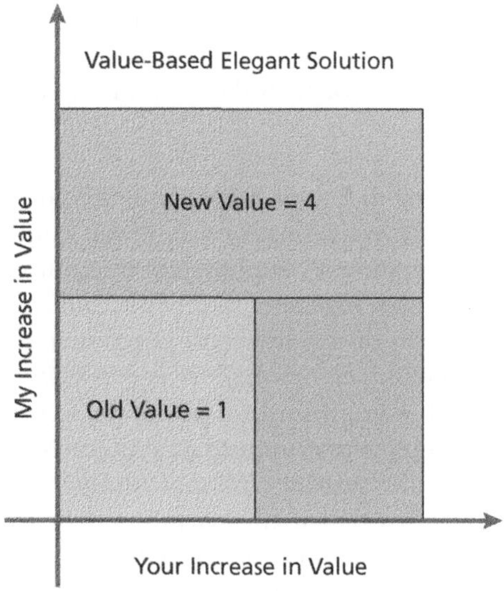

Figure 17.1 Redrawn from Mattford Group class notes by Dr. G. Boettcher.

in the orange shaded area, because the parties took the time to understand each other's needs and abilities.

Often negotiators struggle to create elegant solutions. Too much collaboration may result in negotiators falling into the trap of *groupthink*. Groupthink builds harmony but destroys creativity (Janis, 1971). The skilled negotiator should balance both distributive and principled strategies to optimize creativity in order to generate meaningful value for the collective group. In other words, healthy tension between negotiators is a good thing and will assist the parties as they strive to use creativity to help solve difficult issues.

Also, in a negotiation that does or does not end with a signed agreement, it is helpful to have established a trustful relationship with your counterpart so you can quickly resolve any future issues or opportunities to negotiate. Retaining a transparent and trusting relationship throughout the negotiation process creates future opportunity to collaboratively solve impending problematic issues with proper tension that leads to balanced and fair brainstorming. Constructive problem-solving during implementation will also help establish a solid foundation for the beginning of the next negotiation event.

Negotiation Terms and Timeline

Folks often confuse negotiation strategy with negotiation tactics. Strategy is your overall style, such as distributive strategy, integrative strategy, or mixed strategy; it is your overarching plan to achieve your goals. A negotiation tactic is a specific action you take to achieve a specific goal or purpose. For example, Churchman (1995) identified more than 50 kinds of negotiation tactics that support the distributive strategy. It is important to know these tactics because the best way to counter a tactic is to state: "I see you are using the 'second bite at the apple' tactic. We have already agreed to that provision as a temporary agreement contingent on the whole (TACOW), so let us move on to the next topic unless you want to reallocate the value in our previous agreement." Karrass (1992, 1996), who is often known as the godfather of modern negotiation, and Lum (2011) are also good resources on negotiation tactics.

Note that in Karrass' early years as a negotiating attorney, Karrass was a strong advocate of the distributive and power-based negotiation strategy. As time passed and he witnessed the destructiveness of a pure distributive negotiation disposition, so he began to lobby for a balance of negotiation strategies and advocated for a greater role of the interest-based process so as to achieve more constructive outcomes (Karrass, 1996).

Drawing from my extensive education, experiences, and training, and adapting ideas from various readings over the years, I created the following seven-step timeline model for effective relational negotiations (Boettcher, 2009) depicted in Figure 17.2.

Relational negotiation processing fosters good will toward the parties' ongoing relationship and creates future negotiation value—it is modeled after the integrative negotiation strategy. The positional strategist can also use this model to improve negotiation outcomes. The *plan and organize* phase is perhaps the most important phase. Poor planning can derail the efforts of the most highly skilled negotiators, but proper planning can make even a green negotiator appear to be a skilled and seasoned veteran.

The roadmap of relational negotiation model offers a three-dimensional representation of the negotiation process timeline. Each graphic symbolizes a distinct phase of negotiations as a polychromic event; that is, the seven phases are related and each flows into the others. For example, the

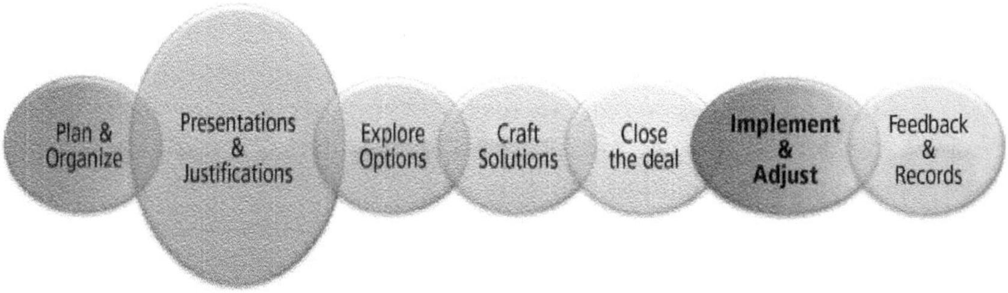

Figure 17.2 Roadmap of relational negotiations.

attitudes developed and exhibited in the *presentation and justification* phase will directly affect the parties' working relationship during other phases of the negotiation process. Or the wielding of power in the *explore options* phase will affect the products created in the *craft solutions* phase.

The overlap of elements depicts the fact that there are no clear lines or moments of transition from one phase to the next. It is possible to be in two phases at the same time. For example, during the organize phase, while the negotiating team members are gathering information and making decisions on the who, what, when, where, and how of the process, those issues overlap with the design of their respective presentation of opening statements, and staging and ordering of proposals. The oval graphic of the presentation and justification phase vertically depicts the potential for markedly different opening positions of the parties. It also portrays the potential jockeying among the parties for relative power balance.

The explore options phase is back in a circular graphic because even if one party has a more powerful position or leverage in the negotiation, in order to brainstorm and create new meaningful options that help both sides, the stronger party must manage that power so as not to create an atmosphere of mistrust that may stymie the next couple of phases. Exploring options should be mutually beneficial to all parties.

Next, the *implement and adjust* phase is in a different shape because it represents how the parties' relationship may be stretched as the actual language, meaning, and product are translated, interpreted, and implemented from the negotiating table to the workplace environment. What *I* said at the negotiation table may not be what *you* understood, which creates potential for the process to breakdown during implementation. Even if what *I* said is what *you* heard, our understanding of the concept we agreed to may be problematic in actual application. So the parties need to continue to negotiate, adjust and adapt, and reformulate the original plan. If the parties have a shared memory of having worked well together, the positive experience will encourage them to re-engage in a principled process to help them craft a new solution for problematic issues that occur during the implementation phase of the negotiated contract.

Forthcoming the author will discuss and define several common negotiation terms: aspiration or opener, goal, reservation, resistance or bottom-line, and walk-away points that apply to the craft solutions and close the deal phases. Additionally, five acronyms useful in any negotiation are BATNA, WATNA, Settlement Zones, ZOPA, and TACOW. The terms and acronyms are aligned with a negotiation timeline.

Within the plan and organize stage, the savvy negotiator will identify aforementioned terms and acronyms and place an objective valuation on each position that forms a respective settlement zone. *Settlement zones* are comprised of an aspiration, a goal, a walk-away point, and a resistance point or bottom line (Lewicki et al., 2010; Lum, 2005). Each negotiator should have a predetermined settlement zone identified before the negotiation discussions begin. Settlement zone points may change as you learn information from your counterpart, and may change even as late as the close the deal phase.

First, an *opener* or *aspiration*, whether it is a single item or a complex and interrelated list of issues, is the highest value one can justifiably and objectively place on the issue or topic (Lewicki et al., 2010). Consider this example: An employee may request a $10 an hour pay raise objectively based on the objective historical average hourly pay rates of other employees in like positions in competing organizations on similar career paths.

The second settlement zone point is a negotiator's *goal*, a rational and more likely attainable target or value. Based on an organization's resources, even though an aspiration of a $10 an hour pay raise is defendable based on the objective valuations of other competing pay rates, a new start-up company or a company struggling with achieving target revenues, may not have the financial resources to match competitor pay rates. The aspiration of $10 an hour pay raise may seem objectively achievable to the employee, yet may not be reasonably viewed by management.

A negotiator should start with a lofty and defendable aspiration, but must be prepared to accept a lesser value as a reasoned and fair goal. In our example case, the employee may set a goal of $5 an hour pay raise.

High aspirations are set for three reasons. First, if you do not ask, your counterpart cannot say yes to your aspiration. Second, high justifiable aspirations allow the employee–negotiator to gracefully make measured concessions toward the logical fair goal of $5 an hour. Third, it is wise for all negotiators to have a reasoned and calculated concession plan so they do not end up making poor emotionally based decisions aimed at merely "getting a deal."

The third point of value in a negotiation settlement zone is the *walk-away* point. This point is a bit tricky because it does not mean that the negotiator walks away with the purpose of ending the negotiation. The walk-away point is a conflict management technique and is usually executed when talks have stalled with the negotiators approaching impending impasse. Walk-away is a time to disengage from table *talk* so the parties can reflect on their respective positions and further reconsider the *why* behind positions presented to counterparts using an in-depth objective review of the stated positions. It is a time for each negotiator to revalidate and confirm their goals based on the most current information obtained during table discussions. Additionally, negotiators should reaffirm the validity of their previously determined BATNA and WATNA defined forthwith.

The final value point of a negotiation settlement zone is the resistance, reservation, or bottom-line—the lowest/highest value at which the negotiator will settle (Lewicki et al., 2010). Generally the resistance point is at the opposite end of a value continuum for respective negotiators. The resistance point is the *most* a buyer will pay for an item and it is the *lowest point* the seller will take for the item.

Once the negotiator has a handle on the potential settlement zones for all parties, the negotiator can then make a best-guess determination of a negotiated ZOPA, or zone of potential agreement (Lewicki et al., 2010; Shackford & Shackford, 2003). Lewicki and Shackford identify the spread between the resistance points as the bargaining range, settlement range, or ZOPA.

For example, in the aforementioned manager–employee negotiation on an increase in hourly pay rates, the employee's aspiration was $10, a goal of $5, and a bottom-line of $3 an hour pay raise. The manager's aspiration could be $2, a goal of $3, and a bottom-line of $4 an hour pay raise. The settlement zone is the difference between the respective parties' resistance points; that is, between $4 (maximum amount manager is willing to commit to a pay raise) and $3 per hour (minimum amount the employee is willing to accept as a pay raise). In this example a negotiated deal is possible, but the parties may end up at an impasse if they become too anchored in defending their respective goals.

This potential ZOPA is exactly that—a *potential*. Even though a common overlap in the settlement zones may exist, many negotiations have gone awry because the negotiators became locked at an impasse and failed to explore ideas and options that would help them achieve success. Too often, negotiators dig in with their positions (wants) and fail to break the impasse boundary that identifies an overlap in their respective settlement zone resistance points. Research indicates that most timed negotiations settle in the last 5 minutes of discussions (Karrass, 1996); thus when you feel exhausted and ready to walk away without agreement, pause, take some time to reflect on your position and the position of your counterpart, and then come back refreshed with a new way of looking at the ongoing dynamic (Karrass, 1996). That is why using a walk-away point becomes important to negotiators. Now, an obvious question presents itself. When and how do negotiators end the discussions and walk away from any future discussion; that is, end negotiations without an agreement?

BATNA is the best alternative to a negotiated agreement and means exactly that (Reardon, 2005). The wise negotiator will know what they are going to do if they fail to reach a negotiated agreement. That singular "best" achievable option is your BATNA (pronounced "bat-nah"). BATNA is established so the negotiator does not enter into an agreement of less value than their predetermined bottom line (resistance point; Lewicki et al., 2010; Reardon, 2005). If the negotiator cannot achieve their bottom line, then walk away and execute the BATNA.

BATNA is often confused as a counteroffer that closes the deal (Reardon, 2005). For example, let us say you are negotiating a pay raise and you decide that if you do not achieve a high enough pay raise noteworthy of your value to the organization, you are going to quit and find another job. Your plan to quit is only a valid BATNA if you actually have a job offer that brings you more total value than your current job. It would not be wise to just quit and hope that you can find another job of equal or greater value. If you wanted a 5% annual raise and the boss will not move off of 3%, counter-offering 3.5% is not your BATNA, it is merely a counter offer.

Logically, cousin to BATNA would be WATNA (worst alternative to a negotiated agreement). Knowing your WATNA helps you keep your emotions in check and your brain engaged in creative thinking. In the above pay raise example, if the boss offered 3% and you walked away in disgust and began to underperform on the job, your boss could demote or fire you, which would be worse than the negotiated offer you snubbed.

BATNA and WATNA can and often change as negotiators communicate and exchange information. Cohen (2002) refers to changing BATNA as dynamic BATNA and cautions the reader to constantly reevaluate the legitimacy of the negotiator's original BATNA. It is wise to always be aware of your BATNA and WATNA and make changes as appropriate. Both concepts will help keep negotiators from agreeing to a poor deal and end a negotiation with buyer's remorse.

Negotiators are challenged by lack of accurate information and must often make a best and reasoned guess about what the counterpart is thinking. The plan and organize phase is the time to complete competent research on your counterpart and his/her organization in order to develop a sound settlement zone and executable BATNA. Negotiators who fail to adequately plan for a negotiation do not know their BATNA, and never really understand what their respective bottom line is, much less their counterpart's bottom line. Failure to set a BATNA and loss of focus on potential ZOPAs, often result in premature concessions and may result in settling for a value well below the original bottom line. Why? No one wants to fail and inexperienced negotiators often have an overwhelming desire to close the deal. This erroneous desire to reach an agreement results in undervalued settlements because of a failure to exercise a planned BATNA. Also, pre-identifying settlement zone value points helps arm the negotiator with knowledge that protects them from making emotional decisions based on fear, ignorance, or poor planning, because they will have confidence in knowing when to walk away from the process and execute their BATNA.

The second common negotiator challenge is figuring out what your counterpart's settlement zone looks like. Every negotiator's goal should be to figure out what is on their counterpart's dream sheet and what their counterpart's bottom line is. Short of the counterpart negotiator honestly disclosing what their bottom line is (that rarely happens), all negotiators can do is make an educated guess after asking a lot of questions and completing thorough research on the counterpart and his/her organization.

Not all negotiations have a positive settlement zone. Sometimes the respective bottom lines do not overlap, and the failed overlap of respective resistance points creates a negative value. For example, the manager's hourly pay rate increase bottom line may be $2 an hour, and the employee's bottom line is $3. This creates a negative $1 per hour differential. The negotiators would then need to create alternative values to settle their differences, or they would each need to execute their respective BATNAs.

TACOW means tentative agreement contingent on whole. Lum (2005) defines a tentative agreement as: "An option agreed to and set aside temporarily to move the decisionmaking [*sic*] process forward. In the end, the whole must be acceptable" (p. 173). Most negotiations are centered on varying goals and concepts/topics. Collectively each concept/issue/topic comprise the totality of an agreement. As the parties agree on each specific concept/topic, it is wise to paper (negotiation slang) or document the specific topic agreement, noting the agreed-upon value specific to the respective topic or issue. In other words, that singular piece of the total agreement is settled and documented as a TACOW and is not modifiable without agreement from both parties.

As an example of the TACOW concept, let us say that an employee is negotiating a pay raise and increased benefits with a manager in accordance with the contract and the two have agreed on a 3%t annual pay raise for the next 3 years. It would be wise to document the pay raise agreement as a TACOW before entering discussions on the next topic—let us say vacation benefits. Next, discussions begin on the next topic of vacation with the discussions on a pay raise settled via a TACOW. The employee currently has 10 days of annual vacation and wants 16 days of vacation in the future. The manager digs in at 12 days and the employee anchors at 16 days. To break the impasse the manager may offer a 2.5% annual pay raise with 15 days of annual vacation thereby using the pay rate change to leverage the negotiation on vacation days. The employee would be correct to declare that the pay rate was established in a TACOW and that the focus should return to vacation days. The two should then focus on objective criteria (what is the normal vacation period within the company and at other like companies) to fairly determine a new vacation period. Of course, the employee always has the right to entertain a change in a TACOW, but should not feel pressured to do so. The employee could also become creative and suggest, "I'll accept a 2.5% pay raise the first year, 2.75% the second year, and 3% the third year if I receive 15 days of vacation the first year and for every quarter in a calendar year I do not use sick leave, I earn another one-half day of vacation for the next year." This example demonstrates the intricacies of a multilevel agreement and the importance of written documentation. TACOW is a technique that protects all parties from other hard-bargaining negotiation tactics and establishes prior agreements in written historical document (Lum, 2005).

Negotiation is the core of all dispute resolution processes and can be constructively managed to resolve any type of dispute. Always strive to be constructive and positive. Keep your emotions in check. Strive to achieve a *we-centric* relationship and then co-create solutions that are both fair and mutually beneficial using Fisher's four-step negotiation model (Fisher et al., 1991; Glaser, 2008).

Attorney or Non-attorney Third-Party Neutrals?

Disputants often ask whether it is necessary or prudent to use attorney-trained neutrals in dispute-resolution settlement processes. It is an excellent question with differing answers depending on the circumstances of the case and ADR process. Based on experience, training, and discussions with my professional peers, the author suggests that in any arbitration, mediation, or mock-trial case where the mediator is acting as an *evaluator*, or negotiation of complex issues (Goldberg et al., 2003), it is usually best to have an attorney or retired judge with expertise in the law on the specific subject at hand preside over the case. However, there are non-attorney subject matter experts that can and will serve disputants well.

From a personal experiential perspective, as a non-attorney mediator for the court system and in private practice, I would often discuss problematic issues that were common in difficult family disputes with an attorney mediator cohort. One day I asked my attorney cohort whether she would use a non-attorney mediator, and she quickly responded "NO!" I was a bit put off and asked her why. Her response was sound: "If my counterpart is an attorney, I know they have been educated and trained and have passed the bar." Her position makes sense because other than court-mandated certifications and mediation association certifications (such as the Academy of Professional Family Mediators), there is no recognized mediator credentialing oversight organization. Nonetheless there are thousands of highly trained, qualified, and professional non-attorney neutrals from all around the world that can serve disputing parties well.

Alternatively, while serving as a high official in a large labor union, I was involved in several precedent-setting arbitrations and mediations. After several years of work, I was approached by a couple of internationally known arbitrators and was asked whether I would be interested in sponsorship to become a National Mediation Board arbitrator. I asked which law schools I should consider attending, and they both said, "Do not go to law school." Their opinion was that attorneys make the worst arbitrators because they are trained to be advocates for the law. Additionally, my attorney-arbitrators noted that it takes new attorney-neutrals too long to learn how to be an effective unbiased third-party neutral. Instead, they suggested I seek out graduate-level dispute-resolution training. Hence, there is a PhD after my name instead of "esquire."

As a court-trained mediator in all four levels of the Virginia judicial system, I spent time training with more than 50 other mediator trainees. Within that group, only three or four were attorneys. Two of the four trainers were attorneys. Most states do not require court mediators to be members of the American Bar Association. Here is what Daiker (2005) concluded:

> Non-lawyer mediators make the mediation process better. Studies and writings overwhelmingly demonstrate that possession of a law degree does not improve the effectiveness of a mediator and may actually hinder mediators who have had legal training. Consequently, not only should programs not require mediators to have a JD, but the mediation profession ought to encourage more non-lawyers to become trained mediators because they bring to the field their own strengths and attributes, many of which are not brought to the field by lawyer mediators. (p. 17)

Simplistically, attorneys are not mediators and mediators are not attorneys—the roles and professions are quite different. Regardless, whether you choose to use an attorney or non-attorney mediator in an arbitration or mediation process, it is prudent to run all written agreements by an attorney so you can make a fully informed choice about the settlement, especially in complex cases (Boettcher, 2007).

In arbitration, most arbitrators recommended by the National Academy of Arbitrators are attorneys or retired judges, while most arbitrators from the American Arbitration Association are non-attorney practitioners with a high degree of education and experience. If you are engaged in a high-value case, and choose not to use an attorney-arbitrator, it is in your best interest to use an attorney to at least review your case. But it is even better if the attorney presents the case for you in the arbitration. It may also be wise to consult with a non-attorney subject-matter expert who specializes in the topic of your case. Attorney arbitrators/mediators are generally not necessary in simple disputes.

CONCLUDING THOUGHTS

In review: All ADR processes are appropriate for workplace disputes. Facilitation is a process most organizations use before the group reaches an impasse. Mediation is used when the parties have hit the impasse wall and need help communicating to create an interest-based solution. Arbitration is generally required when the parties are at an intractable impasse and simply cannot reach an agreement. Arbitration is also usually a settlement process for commercial sales contracts and labor contracts.

From the author's perspective, the core process of all ADR models is negotiation. Negotiation can be power or rights-based where distributive strategies are used to further positions or negotiations can be interest-based where the parties discuss common interests and co-create mutually beneficial solutions based on the "why" behind parties' respective needs (Lewicki et al., 2010). Even when time is limiting a negotiation or one party seems committed to a distributive strategy, academics and practitioners from the Harvard Project on Negotiation (Fisher et al., 1991; Mnookin et al., 2000) recommend that the counterpart continue to engage with interest-based or principled negotiation strategies.

Negotiators should always look for the latent value that is metaphorically often left under the table because the parties failed to be empathetic and understand the *why* behind the *what* people claim they need. Negotiators should strive to take the time to explore in detail the why behind assertions and positions claimed by counterparts. Negotiators who explore the why behind the what better understand the reasoning behind asserted positions and needs, and create more opportunities to generate mutually beneficial forward looking solutions. Negotiators should strive to achieve the Pareto effect and co-create eloquent agreements in order to invent agreements with the highest possible values.

In the workplace, managers should use all available conflict management techniques. If the organization has an ombudsmanship program, use their expertise. If the human resources or legal departments have coaching or mediation services, use the appropriate service. If the manager has a gift of helping others, use the techniques espoused in this chapter.

Always strive to be neutral and act without bias. Mnookin et al. (2000) explains the idea of neutrality through this simple example. Two siblings are arguing over the last piece of cake. Mom walks in during the dispute, and both children turn to mom to settle the dispute. How does she do so while retaining neutrality? Managers should think about this dilemma for a moment and then embrace the solution to guide you in future peer/subordinate disputes. The solution is simple and eloquent—have one child cut the last piece of cake in half and then let the other child choose the half they want to eat. Mom preserved her neutrality and helped the children satisfactorily and fairly solve the problem without bias. Simple and eloquent solutions will bring the greatest satisfaction to the workplace and will preserve relationships and manager neutrality.

ADR process techniques can help the manager bring peace between disputing parties through self-determined and co-created solutions. Justice is obtained when the parties view the solution as fair and mutually beneficial. Harmony is brought back to the office or workplace and results in a workplace atmosphere that better serves workers and customers. Supervisors who eloquently manage conflict by empowering workers to fairly self-determine destructive discord create opportunities for the entire workplace and customer relationship to hum along like a well-tuned clavier. Help your people manage conflict wisely.

NOTES

1. From Shackford, K., & Shackford, J. (2003). *Charting a Wiser Course.* Incline Village, NV: The Mattford Group Press. Adapted and reprinted with permission.
2. From Boettcher, G. W. (2009). *Seven phases of the negotiation process.* From Conflict Management Strategies, Inc. documents. Available from gary@conflictcounts.com. Reprinted with permission.

REFERENCES

Boettcher, G. W. (2007). *Mediation models: Is there a role for non-lawyers in effective mediation?* (Master's thesis). Sullivan University, Louisville, KY. Available from gary@conflictcounts.com

Boettcher, G. W. (2009). *Seven phases of the negotiation process.* From Conflict Management Strategies, Inc. documents. Available from gary@conflictcounts.com

Boettcher, G. W. (2010). *The schism of professionalizing mediation services: An organizational theory perspective of the mediator certification debate* (PhD research). Sullivan University, Louisville, KY. Available from gary@conflictcounts.com

Bush, R. A. B., & Folger, J. P. (1994). *The promise of mediation.* San Francisco, CA: Jossey-Bass.

Churchman, D. (1995). *Negotiation.* Lanham, MD: University Press of America.

Cobb, S. (1994). A narrative perspective on mediation: Toward the materialization of the storytelling metaphor. In J. P. Folger & T. S. Jones (Eds.), *New directions in mediation: Communication research and perspectives* (pp. 48–63). Thousand Oaks, CA: SAGE.

Cohen, S., (2002). *Negotiating skills for managers.* New York, NY: McGraw-Hill.

Daiker, M. (2005). No J. D. required: The critical role and contributions of non-lawyer mediators. *24 Review of Litigation, 499,* 1–17.

Fisher, R., Ury, W., & Patton, B. (1991). *Getting to yes: Negotiating agreement without giving in* (2nd ed.). New York, NY: Penguin Books.

Glaser, J. E. (2014). *Conversational intelligence: How great leaders build trust and get extraordinary results.* Brookline, MA: Bibliomotion.

Goldberg, S., Sander, F., Rogers, N., & Cole, S. (2003). *Dispute resolution: Negotiation, mediation, and other processes* (4th ed.). New York, NY: Aspen.

Hansen, T. (2003). *The narrative approach to mediation.* Retrieved from https://www.mediate.com/articles/hansenT.cfm

Hill, N. J. (1998). Qualification requirements of mediators. *Journal of Dispute Resolution, 37*, 1–17.

Janis, I. L. (1971). Groupthink. *Psychology Today, 5*(6), 43–46.

Jones, T. S., & Brinkert, R. (2008). *Conflict coaching: Conflict management strategies and skills for the individual.* Los Angeles, CA: SAGE.

Karrass, C. (n.d.). Effective negotiating workbook and discussion guide. Beverly Hills, CA: Karrass.

Karrass, C. (1992). *The negotiating game* (revised ed.). New York, NY: Harper Business.

Karrass, C. (1996). *In business as in life—You don't get what you deserve, you get what you negotiate.* Beverly Hills, CA: Stanford St. Press.

Kressel, K. (2006). Mediation revisited. In M. Deutsch, P. T. Coleman, & E. C. Marcus (Eds.), *The handbook of conflict resolution: Theory and practice.* San Francisco, CA: Jossey-Bass.

Lewicki, R. J., Barry, B., & Saunders, D. M. (2010). *Negotiation* (6th ed.). New York, NY: McGraw-Hill Irwin.

Livingood, J. (2008). Addressing bias in conflict and dispute resolution settings. *Dispute Resolution Journal, 62*(4), 52–61.

Lum, G. (2005). *The negotiation fieldbook: Simple strategies to help you negotiate everything* (2nd ed.). New York, NY: McGraw-Hill.

Mnookin, R. H., Peppet, S. R., & Tulumello, A. S. (2000). *Beyond winning: Negotiating to create value in deals and disputes.* London, England: The Belknap Press of Harvard University Press.

Moore, C. W. (2003). *The mediation process: Practical strategies for resolving conflict* (3rd ed.). San Francisco, CA: Jossey-Bass.

Noble, C. (2012). *Conflict management coaching: The Cinergy™ model.* Canada: Cinergy.

Park, S. (2008). Korean preaching, Han, and narrative (American University Studies. Series VII. Theology and Religion). *Asian American Theological Forum, 6*(2). Retrieved from https://aatfweb.org/2014/10/31/korean-preaching-han-and-narrative-american-university-studies-series-vii-theology-and-religion/

Reardon, K. (2005). *Becoming a skilled negotiator.* Hoboken, NJ: Wiley.

Shackford, K., & Shackford, J. (2003). *Charting a wiser course.* Incline Village, Nevada: The Mattford Group Press.

Schwarz, R., Davidson, A., Carlson, P., & McKinney, S. (2005). *The skilled facilitator fieldbook.* San Francisco, CA: Jossey-Bass.

Shonk, K. (2018). *Types of mediation: Choose the type best suited to your conflict.* Retrieved from https://www.pon.harvard.edu/daily/mediation/types-mediation-choose-type-best-suited-conflict/

Umbreit, M. S. (1998). Restorative justice through victim-offender mediation: A multi-site assessment. *Western Criminology Review, 1*(1), 1–28.

Wesley, M. (2004). The compleat ombuds: A spectrum of resolution services. *CPER Journal, 166*(3), 6–12.

Wilkinson, M. (2004). *The secrets of facilitation: The S.M.A.R.T. guide to getting results with groups.* Jossey-Bass: San Francisco.

Winslade, J., & Monk, G. (2001). *Narrative mediation.* San Francisco, CA: Jossey-Bass.

Zumeta, Z. D. (2019). Styles of mediation: Facilitative, evaluative and transformative mediation. Retrieved from https://www.mediate.com/articles/zumeta.cfm#bio

[illegible]

[illegible] Press.

[illegible] (2000). *Narrative Inquiry* [illegible]

[illegible] (2001). [illegible] New York, NY: [illegible]

[illegible] The Falmer Press.

Scarborough, R., [illegible] (2008). *The nuts and bolts of art-based research* (2nd ed.). New York, NY: [illegible]

Shapiro, H. [illegible] (2013). *The discussion of* [illegible] [illegible]

SECTION III

MAKING THE WORKPLACE HUM

CHAPTER 18

FROM DISCORD TO HARMONY

Five Skills for Keeping Your Workplace Humming

LaVena Wilkin

As individuals we have different experiences, values, beliefs, perceptions, and assumptions, and while these differences promote creativity, they can also lead to unproductive conflicts. As a society, we also seem to be more vocal and less tolerant about differences. In our personal and professional relationships we often compete for scarce resources, such as control, money, time, and recognition. On top of that, stir in a little power imbalance, and add a sprinkling of different styles of conflict management or different communication styles. Then, for good measure, consider that in today's world the only constant is change, and the very thought of that can paralyze some people with fear. Mix this all together and you have a society that is bubbling over with conflicted people and situations. When you view organizations as microcosms of society, it is easy to see how unmanaged or mismanaged conflict situations can have a negative impact on organizations and their missions, visions, and employees.

From Discord to Harmony, pages 319–331

SO WHAT?

Conflict happens. It is a naturally occurring part of life. If anyone tells you they do not experience conflicts, please take their pulse to make sure they are living and breathing. We all have conflicts in our lives. We simply cannot escape them; they are inevitable. To live is to experience conflict (Wilkin, 2018). However, it is important to know that no matter what the dictionary says or what you were taught as a child, conflicts are not negative. It is how we deal with conflict situations that determine if the outcomes are productive or destructive. In fact, one of the first paradigm shifts to make is reframing the way we think about conflicts. They are not negative occurrences that need to be avoided at all costs. Nor are they occasions to exert power over others. Rather, conflicts are opportunities. Conflict situations are merely symptoms that something is not working, and they present opportunities to change and improve not only the current situation, but also our own perceptions and circumstances.

Unproductive, mismanaged, or unmanaged conflicts can result in a myriad of negative outcomes for both the individuals involved in the situation and for the organization. From an individual perspective, when we are in a conflict with someone, we often spend a lot of time thinking about the situation, pondering what we can or will do, considering what the other person will do, and talking to somebody else (usually somebody who is not involved) about the state of affairs. Our time and energy are consumed, we can lose sleep, and our emotions spin from anger to fear to indignant and back again. We make decisions based on emotions, not evidence. Unresolved conflict can be exhausting, and it can rob us of our motivation, satisfaction, and joy.

If that is not enough, there are also a myriad of physical ailments associated with the stress of chronic, ongoing conflicts. Individuals who experience prolonged unresolved conflicts report stress-related health issues, such as insomnia, headaches, and skin rashes (NIOSH Working Group, 1999). More serious illnesses, such as stomach disorders and cardiovascular disease, are also linked to worrying about these conflicts (Bjorkqvist, Osterman, & Hjelt-Back, 1994; DeDreu, Van Dierendonck, & Dijkstra, 2004). In addition, employees who are exposed to negative conflicts become less motivated and less satisfied with their jobs (Georgakopoulos, Wilkin, & Kent, 2011). Many express an intention to voluntarily leave their organizations. Absenteeism increases as a result of both stress-related illnesses and the need to take a mental health day to avoid the conflict.

One problem is that most people have never been taught how to deal with conflicts. As young students, we learn to read, write, and do math, but the life skill of conflict management is often left to chance. We learn our conflict styles from our families, and if we grow up avoiders, that is what we tend to do. Likewise, if our families love a good argument, we tend to approach conflict situations as a time to engage in a verbal war of words. When organizational leaders do not have conflict management skills, they often say to conflicted employees "go work it out." However, if people knew what to do they likely would have already worked through the situation and arrived at a productive resolution.

THE COSTS OF UNMANAGED CONFLICT (DISHARMONY)

From an organizational perspective, some costs associated with unresolved, ongoing, negative conflicts include wasted time, loss of skilled employees, lost work time, increased health insurance costs, lawsuits, labor strikes, workplace bullying, and even workplace violence (Freres, 2011). In fact, Freres found that managers spend between 20% and 40% of their work week dealing with conflicts. A 2008 study commissioned by Consulting Psychologists Press (CPP) found that 85% of employees are impacted by workplace conflicts, and the estimated cost of these attempting to manage those conflicts is $359 billion (CPP). With that much time focused on conflict, much of the other work does not get done. In addition, when managers are not trained in conflict management, they can make the situation worse. Turnover ensues, and the most qualified and knowledgeable employees leave because they are the ones who can find other meaningful employment. Not only are organizations left with the more marginal employees, but they also lose institutional knowledge.

Moreover, the stress-induced health-related issues result in higher health care costs for the employer (Dana, 2001). Employees' lack of motivation and satisfaction leads to lower organizational commitment, which spirals into reduced productivity and profitability for the organization (Georgakopoulos et al., 2011). While absenteeism is costly, presenteeism is often a hidden and unpredictable cost. Presenteeism occurs when employees show up but do very little actual work. They are there in body only.

Given the negative consequences of conflict, it is reasonable that most people do not choose to exacerbate these behaviors that escalate conflict situations. They act or react because they do not have the skills to deal with conflict in the workplace. They simply do not know what to do, so they keep doing what they have always done, expecting a different result.

A few years ago, I facilitated a focus group on hiring wherein human resource managers identified conflict management, communication, diversity, negotiation, and leadership as skills most valued by their organizations. One of the participants (a human resource manager at a Fortune 100 company) stated that she estimated that managers spend approximately 30% of their time facilitating conflicts between people or groups, therefore making conflict management skills absolutely necessary for anyone in management. Another participant, who is the human resource director at a regional financial institution, said that in today's market, people will find it very difficult to succeed in a management position without good listening and communication skills.

Additionally, another member of the focus group said people must be able to get along well with others. Teamwork and leadership skills are essential in today's changing work environment. He said, "At one time, we were looking for that shining star. Now, we shun the stars. We are looking for people who can play well together." When asked to choose one skill that they believe would benefit managers and help them develop and work with teams, they unanimously answered "conflict management skills." Moreover, they emphasized that in addition to facilitating conflicts, managers need to learn communication skills that will help them in all types of situations, ranging from disagreements between coworkers to negotiating with labor unions and vendors.

So, what can we do to improve communication skills? How might we become better at conflict management? How can we address the issues in a way that is kind and compassionate? These types of questions formed the basis of my research to better understand skills that are helpful for managing unproductive conflicts in the workplace.

IMPROVING CONFLICT MANAGEMENT SKILLS

Armed with the information that conflict skills are keys for successful managers, I was curious to better understand what specific skills and abilities would be important for managers to learn as part of conflict management training. I conducted a short pilot study to determine this, and my findings are presented below. The framework for developing these skills is built on the precepts of conflict management and transformation, and learning how to employ each of these concepts will help make managers develop more productive ways to interact; they can communicate differently and more effectively, and their workplace relationships can improve.

For interventions to be effective, they must address both the root causes and antecedents of the conflict. Communication and perceptions are at the root of almost every conflict, so these are fundamental components of any conflict management workshop. Additionally, self-awareness, empathy, and emotional intelligence have a positive effect on workplace conflicts. Self-awareness helps people become attuned to their emotions so they understand the motivations behind their actions (Olson, Nelson, & Parayitam, 2005). Likewise, empathy allows people to understand the other person's feelings and view the world through his or her lens. Finally, when people understand the role emotions play in their responses, they are less likely to react to negative situations in a destructive manner.

Although presented separately, the following five precepts, or skills, are not individual steps in a process. In fact, they overlap and build upon one another. For example, we are able to view the world through the other person's lens when we listen to them and value their ideas and experiences and practice emotional intelligence. Each of these actions will lead to a more collaborative process of working together to make decisions and solve problems. The end result will likely be a resolution that respects individuals and individuality, satisfies the true needs of all parties involved, and empowers people to own their emotions, their actions, and their reactions to conflict situations.

Compassionate Listening: The Silence Between the Notes

Music is not made solely by holding down the piano key or by one sound. Rather, it is the silence between the notes that produces the melodious sounds. The same can be said of listening. Being still and listening to the other person produces a sonata of harmony. One of the most powerful tools we have in our toolbox is compassionate listening. As humans, we have a compelling need to be understood and respected, and being a compassionate listener is a clear sign that we understand and respect the speaker's perceptions, ideas, and feelings. Compassionate listening requires us to listen to understand, rather than listen to respond. When we suspend our own ideas and agendas and compassionately listen, we will hear the underlying meaning of the message, rather than the spoken words. Compassionately listening requires us to engage our hearts, not just our minds and ears.

Since many conflicts are rooted in assumptions and perceptions based on personal history, background, or biases, messages are often filtered through those assumptions. If people practice compassionate listening, relationships can be transformed. We have all heard of the Golden Rule, which is treating others the way you want to be treated. Compassionate listening and conflict management takes this a step further to the platinum rule. Treat others the way they want to be treated, not the way you assume they want to be treated. And how do we discover this? We simply ask and listen to what they tell us. Others may not be motivated by the same things we are, so take time to listen to their needs.

Although listening to the other person's perspective does not eliminate the conflict, not listening to them has a greater potential to intensify it. Moreover, when people learn to actively and compassionately listen, they can uncover and address emotions that influence perceptions of the conflict.

Value Differences: Not One Part Harmony

When every musical instrument is a trumpet, we miss out on the beautiful music created by the unique blending of talents from the entire orchestra. The same happens when we do not value differences. Failing to understand, embrace, and appreciate other's thoughts and ideas stunts growth and may increase discord among individuals involved in the conflict.

Our differences extend beyond race, age, gender, or ethnicity. They encompass so much more, including experiences, perceptions, ideas, and values. However, sometimes, we try to change "them" to make them model behaviors we value, rather than appreciating them for who they are and where they are in life. Instead of being intolerant of diverse ideas and experiences, recognize that when we open our heart space and appreciate our differences, we invite healing and harmony into our lives.

Those differences can also mean ways we deal with conflict. Some of the most notable conflict style research was conducted by Kenneth Thomas and Ralph Kilmann in 1974, and the five styles they promote are

- avoiding,
- accommodating,
- collaborating,
- compromising, and
- competing.

Strategies most used by avoiders who deny that a conflict exists are withdrawing from the situation, delaying resolution, and refusing to engage in a courageous conversation about the situation. Typically, avoidance produces a lose–lose outcome because denying conflicts exist does not make them magically go away. Additionally, there is no opportunity for the relationship to grow and evolve, so everyone loses.

Accommodators seek harmony at all costs, even when the result is a lose–win (they lose so others can win). To create this harmony, they say they agree with others, even if they do not; they engage by appeasing and flattering others. Moreover, they would prefer others force an issue so they do not have to promote their ideas.

Collaborating is a conflict style that promotes open, honest, respectful communication. Collaborators gather information, look for alternatives, and welcome diverse ideas. This exchange of ideas builds trust among the parties involved in the conflict. The outcome with this style is a win–win where both parties have at least some of their needs met.

Most people think that compromise is an appropriate conflict management style. I give up something I want, and you do the same. However, therein lies the problem with compromise. Neither person has their needs fulfilled, so the outcome is win some–lose some.

The final style, competing, often uses power, cajoling, and belittling. Competitors see life as a game, and games have a winner and a loser. They want to win at all costs, which makes the other party lose (Kilmann & Thomas, 1978).

The style one uses depends upon the situation and the relationship with the person with whom we have the conflict. However, these various conflict management styles can escalate the problem if we do not understand the predominate style used by the other person. While there is not one best style of conflict management, it is easy to see that the different strategies can negatively impact the outcome. And, when we do not understand why the other person is interacting with us based on a conflict style that is different from ours, it can exacerbate the situation. Understanding and appreciating that different situations call for different styles can alleviate potential negative outcomes.

Valuing differences may also be recognizing the diverse ways we communicate. Some people are direct communicators, and others are more indirect. And, not understanding these differences can wreak havoc in relationships. When my husband and I first started dating, he called to ask me if I wanted to go to dinner. My response was "I had lunch." Looking back, I can see why he was perplexed. What does that even mean? He is quite talented, but he is not a mind reader. But, at that time in my life, and I did not even realize it, I often did not answer questions directly. It took a conscious effort of being mindful to shift how I communicated with him. You see, in his world, his perception was if someone did not answer a question directly, they must be dishonest or hiding something.

Although diversity in organizations improves the quality and longevity of decision-making, it also leads to interpersonal conflicts. Diverse groups are more creative and innovative because they have rich and varied perspectives for collaborative problem-solving; however, these divergent views can also result in aggressive behavior if points of view are not clarified and appreciated. When organizational leaders provide opportunities for exploring differences and sharing experiences, employees may begin to understand and appreciate their diversity. One way to accomplish this understanding and appreciation is by encouraging diversity dialogues. These diversity dialogues increase mutual understanding, clarify misinformation, and stifle the spread of bias. If we open our minds and our hearts to different perspectives, we may discover a wealth of ideas and more creative solutions.

Viewing the World Through the Other Person's Lens: Don't Allow Seeing to Be Believing

Perceptions are the lenses through which we view the world, and sometimes our eyes deceive us. Explaining our perspectives of what we think we see, feel, or experience and then listening to others points of view are important keys that can unlock potential opportunities for satisfying and fulfilling relationships. We also decide how we will react to the conflicts based on our viewpoints. An appropriate reaction can resolve the issue, while inappropriate behavior escalates it. Understanding others perspectives and viewpoints helps us manage conflict before a minor issue spirals out of control.

For example, a few years ago, I stopped by a colleague's office to discuss some ideas about classes I taught. Outside of her office there was a whiteboard with a lot of writing on it, but what caught my eye was "LW Dingbat of the Week." Of course, my initials are LW, and I was quite taken aback. Instead of walking into her office and asking her about this, I turned around and went back to my little corner of the campus. My first emotional reaction was embarrassment—What had I done to deserve that momentous title? My ego was firmly in charge, and my feelings were hurt. Then, I got a little angry. The monkey mind was chattering, "I thought we had a good working relationship. If that is the way she feels, I may not be quite so easy to work with in the future."

But wait! Maybe she was not talking about me. Maybe there is another LW in our system, and that person is the dingbat, not me. I logged into our faculty directory to determine who that other LW was, and lo and behold, there was not another LW. Now my feelings were really hurt, so before I left the office for the day, I sent her an email asking about the statement on the whiteboard. As I pulled into my garage that day, she called. She was apologetic and told me the story of who LW actually was and why that person was publically vilified on the whiteboard. She also said notes like that would never go on the whiteboard again, and that was a positive outcome.

The moral of this story is that I saw with my own eyes a derogatory comment about me. Then, I verified the information by searching for and not finding other LWs in the company directory. My emotions, ego, and monkey mind could have destroyed a very good working relationship that was mutually beneficial for both of us. The conflict management thing to do would have been to not avoid a courageous conversation, and to go into her office and ask about the note. It sounds so passé and rote, but there is no substitute for communication. Open, honest, respectful communication prevents negative outcomes and enhances relationships.

In workshops where I teach conflict management skills, I often use the image in Figure 18.1 which shows both an older and a younger woman.

Figure 18.1 Image of an older/younger woman.

Many times, participants can only see the young woman, while others just see the older one. As we discuss both being in the picture, people tilt their heads as they attempt to find both images. In other words, they shift their focus and begin to look at the world through a different perspective. Even when they cannot see both, I reiterate that their perception does not change the reality. The picture includes a young woman and an older one, and even if they cannot see that, the reality is that they are both there. Do not allow seeing to be believing.

When organizational leaders understand that we construct meanings, perceptions, and responses to conflicts based on social realities, experiences, and cultures, they can develop interventions that help employees clarify the perceptions of the intent of a coworker's behavior, as well as the effect their own behavior may have on others. The end result is reduced negative conflict. In addition, understanding perspectives may stop the escalation of interpersonal conflicts.

As mentioned previously, perceptions may also impact how we deal with and react to workplace conflicts. Many people employ antisocial interpersonal actions against the other person because they perceive incompatible goals, scarce resources, or interference with individual aspirations. Including perspective-taking in the intervention can help employees understand the differences between appropriate and inappropriate behavior, the effect their individual behavior has on others, and the interdependence of employees' interests. Perspective-taking goes a long way in alleviating unproductive workplace conflict.

Emotional Intelligence

The next skill I identified as important to productive conflict management is emotional intelligence. Emotions are a part of life, and employees do not check them at the door when they enter the workplace. Unfortunately, in many organizational cultures it is taboo to express or acknowledge emotions, and as a result, these unacknowledged feelings can create tension and exacerbate conflict. In fact, Jones and Bodtker (2001) suggested that all conflicts are driven by emotions. Rather than ignore the inevitable, recognizing emotions of anger, fear, shame, and sadness can help organizational leaders effectively deal with them, rather than ignore their existence. By becoming aware of and sensitive to the underlying feelings of their coworkers, leaders can make more appropriate responses to potential conflict situations (Caruso & Salovey, 2004).

Emotional intelligence is the ability to monitor your own (and others') feelings and emotions, to discriminate among them, and to use this information to understand motivations and to make decisions (Caruso & Salovey, 2004). Emotionally intelligent individuals are able to recognize their own emotional reactions, as well as decode others' emotions. When emotions are properly managed, constructive communication improves (Jones & Bodtker, 2001); trust, loyalty, and commitment increase (Sheehan, 1999); and conflict management is less painful.

The next time you feel anger, fear, worry, or guilt, notice how your body tenses. You might even feel that knot in the pit of your stomach or an increased heart rate. Likewise, when you feel joy, contentment, calmness, and serenity, notice the physical reactions in your body. We are completely responsible for our emotions, both healthy and toxic ones. No one can make us mad or hurt or afraid or happy or joyful. Since we choose our emotions, it is important for us to be mindful of them, to observe the triggers, to choose to let go of what does not serve us, and to embrace the emotions that help us do what is ours to do.

Self-awareness helps people become attuned to their emotions so they can understand the motivations behind their actions and communications. Likewise, empathy allows people to understand the other person's feelings and view the world through his or her lens. Finally, when people understand the role emotions play in their responses, they are less likely to have negative reactions to change (Olson et al., 2005).

These concepts of conflict management are particularly applicable in today's business environment. Yesterday's hierarchical management style is becoming less effective and less appropriate, and proactive companies are looking for a better way to accomplish their vision and goals. In part, these changes are a result of knowledge workers replacing factory workers. Employees are more educated. Moreover, since organizations are becoming flatter, they have fewer layers of management. More and more teamwork is the way organizational objectives are realized. People are an organization's greatest asset, and the ability to work with people is a key factor in determining the likelihood of being a successful leader.

Collaborative Problem-Solving (A Chorus—Not a Solo)

Finally, collaborative problem-solving is akin to all the band members playing their instruments and singing their parts in such a way that the sounds blend into perfect harmony. Collaborative problem-solving occurs when people work together to identify and resolve their problems. While it sounds simple, one of the most difficult aspects of collaborative problem-solving is to clearly identify the problem. It is impossible to resolve "it," if everyone does not agree on what "it" is. According to Bernstein and Ablon (2011), the most significant phase in collaborative problem-solving is to clearly define the problem by allowing the employees to offer their perceptions before managers expresses their viewpoints.

One thing to be careful about is focusing on the person as the problem. Although some would say a particular person stirs the pot or does not play well in the sandbox, we cannot change the person. So, focus on what can change, which is the problem or the behavior. In their foundational conflict management book, *Getting to Yes: Negotiating Agreement Without Giving In*, Roger Fisher, William Ury, and Bruce Patton call this separating the people from the problem (1991). Most likely, the "people" problems are rooted in perceptions, emotions, or communication.

Another of Fisher, Ury, and Patton's (1991) basic principles is to focus on the interests, not the positions. This can be a difficult concept for people to grasp, and there are many misunderstandings about the differences between interests and positions. Consider this: There are two chefs creating an important dinner. They both need an orange to make their respective dishes perfect. One needs it for the entrée, and the other needs it for the dessert. There is no time to get another orange. What do they do? Some people say "cut it in half." This would be compromise, and both would give up something important. The end result is that neither dish would be perfect. Others say "the entrée is more important than the dessert" (or vice versa). We often do this in conflict situations where we try to decide whose need is greater. The answer is to ask "Why do you need the orange?" You might find the answer is: "I need the pulp for my entrée" or "I need the rind for my dessert." In that case, both chefs get 100% of their needs met. The orange represents positions (what we state we need), and the pulp and the rind represent interests (what we really need). However, we do not know if we do not communicate.

Employees who work in tandem to identify the problem, determine root causes of the situation, generate possible solutions, and select the most appropriate approach to resolve the problem take ownership in the solution. They have buy-in, and there is a sense of accomplishment in being part of the solution.

CONCLUSION

Organizational leaders have many functions, including motivating people, communicating a vision, promoting change, and creating effective interpersonal relationships, and if they are unsuccessful at these, they may be derailed. Since leadership encompasses a myriad of roles, there is not a one-size-fits-all recipe for leadership effectiveness. The skills identified in this chapter provide leaders with a holistic approach to conflict management.

Imagine a workplace where conflicts are viewed as opportunities that inspire us to grow and transform and to realize our full potential. Imagine a workplace where we are compassionate and kind, where we listen to understand, value diversity, and work together to make decisions and resolve problems. Imagine if we practice these more inclusive and collaborative skills as the preferred ways to manage the inevitable conflicts.

Employees who understand their own reactions and learn how to respond to workplace conflict may experience higher levels of job satisfaction, improved self-confidence, less stress, and increased motivation. You cannot change others; you only have the power to change yourself. Therefore, the focus of the intervention is on changing one's own behaviors and reactions to workplace conflict. By openly communicating, respecting one another's ideas, understanding perceptions, and acknowledging feelings and emotions, the conflicted parties may find a resolution that enriches them individually and enhances their relationship. As employees, they are motivated and productive. The outcome is a win–win for both the individual and the organization.

REFERENCES

Bernstein, S., & Ablon, S. (2011). *Collaborative problem solving: An effective approach for managing conflict in the workplace.* Mediate.com. Retrieved from https://www.mediate.com/articles/BernsteinS1.cfm

Bjorkqvist, K., Osterman, K., & Hjelt-Back, M. (1994). Aggression among university employees. *Aggressive Behavior, 20*(3), 173–184.

Caruso, D. R., & Salovey, P. (2004). *The emotionally intelligent manager: How to develop and use the four key emotional skills of leadership.* San Franscisco, CA: Jossey-Bass.

Dana, D. (2001). *Conflict resolution.* New York, NY: McGraw-Hill.

DeDreu, C. K. W., Van Dierendonck, D., & Dijkstra, M. T. M. (2004). Conflict at work and individual well-being. *International Journal of Conflict Management, 15*(1).

Fisher, R., Ury, W. L., & Patton, B. (1991). *Getting to yes: Negotiating agreement without giving in* (2nd ed.). New York, NY: Penguin.

Freres, M. (2013). Financial costs of workplace conflict. *Journal of the International Ombudsman Association, 6*(2), 83–94.

Georgakopoulos, A., Wilkin, L., & Kent, B. (2011). Workplace bullying: A complex problem in contemporary organizations. *International Journal of Business and Social Sciences, 2*(3), 1–20.

Jones, T. S., & Bodtker, A. (2001). Mediating with heart in mind: Addressing emotion in mediation practice. *Negotiation Journal, 17*(3), 217–244. https://doi.org.suscorp.idm.oclc.org/10.1111/j.1571-9979.2001.tb00238.x

Kilmann, R. H., & Thomas, K. W. (1978). Four perspectives on conflict management: An attributional framework for organizing descriptive and normative theory. *Academy of Management Review, 3*(1), 59–68.

NIOSH Working Group. (1999). Stress . . . at Work (The National Institute for Occupational Safety and Health [NIOSH] Publication No. 99-101). Retrieved from https://www.cdc.gov/niosh/docs/99-101/

Olson, B. J., Nelson, D. L., & Parayitam, S. (2006). Managing aggression in organizations: What leaders must know. *Leadership & Organization Development Journal, 27*(5), 384–398.

Sheehan, M. (1999). Workplace bullying: Responding with some emotional intelligence. *International Journal of Manpower, 20*(1/2).

Wilkin, L. (2017). Mediation as a tool for resolving workplace conflicts. In A. Georgakopoulous (Ed.), *The mediation handbook: Theory, research, and practice* (pp. 180–184). New York, NY: Routledge.

CHAPTER 19

HOW TO MANAGE WORKPLACE CONFLICT THROUGH INTELLIGENT CONVERSATIONS AND CONFLICT MANAGEMENT TOOLS

For Executives, Leaders, Managers, and Practitioners

Gary Boettcher

Conflict counts . . . Wisely choose how you will manage your conflict events.
—Gary Boettcher

As social creatures, humans spend a lot of time talking with, to, and at each other. Infants respond to the spoken word and quickly learn to communicate desires, needs, and wants through nonverbal gestures to attain what they want or need. Ironically, given the deep importance of effective

From Discord to Harmony, pages 333–354

communication, other than learning the rules of grammar, few people ever receive formal training about how to communicate in a way that helps them understand the true meanings of words used in everyday conversations. It seems as if people are generally satisfied with superficial dialogue, which is supported by Glaser's (2014) claim that 9 out of 10 conversations miss the mark. Green (2017) also notes that even though words are clearly uttered, the meanings of the words are often misinterpreted. The resultant effect is that poor or failed communication regularly leads to conflicted emotions that ultimately disrupt relationships and lead to inefficient workplace environments (Dana, 2006; Fisher & Shapiro, 2006).

Based on the early studies by Mehrabian and Ferris (1967) and Mehrabian and Wiener (1967), academics and researchers concluded that only 7% of communication is verbal and that nearly 93% of the transfer of intended meaning between people comes from nonverbal cues (Burgoon, Guerrero, & Floyd, 2016). This idea not only defies common sense, it has been proven wrong by other researchers. For example, Birdwhistell and Philpott independently estimated that 66% of verbal exchanges between individuals' interactions are derived from kinetic nonverbal behaviors (Birdwhistell, 1955; Philpott, 1983). But even given this research data, is it realistic, based on our everyday experiences, that words only convey 34% of the meanings in verbal human exchanges? Consider this example. If you see me look at my watch am I saying to you: It is time for you to go. Or, it is time for us to go. Or do I merely want to know what time it is? I sent a message without saying a word, and the person viewing my actions made an un-validated assumption about what my action meant unless they seek any confirming feedback on those assumptions based on how I looked at my watch.

This chapter will focus on Glaser's (2014) theory of Conversational Intelligence® (C-IQ) and tools she uses to improve workplace conflict outcomes by making it easier for everyone to understand the meaning behind the words exchanged between conflicted individuals. Discussions will also explore how the concepts of the dual concerns model (Rahim, 1992) and the Thomas-Kilmann conflict mode instrument (TKI) model can be blended to manage conflict behaviors, achieve positive emotions, and improve communication and feedback between disputants. Leaders and supervisors who are good at managing worker conflict behaviors, emotions, and communication may subsequently see better results in conflict outcomes and workplace productivities. If managers can teach workers how to improve self-management of peer-to-peer conflict events, then managers will be able to spend more time managing organizational activities and achieve higher productivity rates (Dana, 2006). Self-managed conflict events will result in departments humming along with high efficiencies and productivity.

CONVERSATIONAL INTELLIGENCE

Researchers have made tremendous strides in understanding the inter-working brain functions that influence behavior typology (MBTI©), cognitive styles (KAI©), and conversational intelligence (C-IQ®) through cutting-edge brainwave and imaging technology (Glaser, 2014; Kirton, 2003; Myers, McCaulley, Quenk, & Hammer, 2003; Nardi, 2009; Perez, Carreiras, & Dunabeitia, 2017). Glaser's theory on conversational intelligence (C-IQ) is based on her 30 years of experience as an executive coach and her master's degree research on how the brain influences human communication dynamics. Although Glaser (2014) contains little documented research on brain activity during communication processes, the concepts and her mapping tools make sense and prove useful to practitioners. For example, Glaser's research indicates that when two people arrive within 10 to 15 feet of each other, their brain waves begin to sync up, and within 0.7–1.5 seconds their subconsciousness engages and sends signals to the primitive brain to either trust or not trust the counterpart. Glaser's work supports the kinetic pretenses of nonverbal communication but does not assert any specific division of roles that verbal and nonverbal actions play in human communication dynamics. Instead Glaser focuses on building a trusting and co-creative communication relationship that will help the disputants resolve their conflict more productively.

One of Glaser's key claims is that nine out of 10 conversations miss the communicative mark chiefly because individual focus is *I-centric* instead of *we-centric.* C-IQ is a relatively new framework focused on strengthening relationships that results in mutually beneficial success. Glaser emphasizes time and again that human relationships built on trust and transparency will result in improved relationships that yield more meaningful conversations over time. Glaser's agenda is to build on a synergy of *co-creating* mutually beneficial solutions that humanize discussions centric to sharing and discovering in a way that increases understanding that result in better cultures and communities. This mutually beneficial orientation is a notion grounded in common interest negotiations that parallel the Harvard Project on Negotiation's foundational values of interest-based negotiation processes (Fisher, Ury, & Patton 1991). Disputant focus should be on commonalities instead of differences (Fisher et al., 1991; Glaser, 2014). Poorly understood and expressed perspective differences that lack in empathy (Schwarz, 2002) can result in negative emotions, dysfunctional behaviors, and ultimately impasse (Dana, 2006; Fisher & Shapiro, 2006). See Boettcher (this volume) for more information about the concept of value in a dispute.

Lakhani (2005) further claims that in order to fulfill the needs of counterparts, all disputants must strive to understand the counterpart's needs with empathy. That means *you* must hear *your* counterpart's perspective accurately by placing yourself in the counterpart's shoes. Schwarz (2002) describes empathy as compassion where "people temporarily suspend judgement... are concerned for others' and their own good... and appreciate others' and their own suffering" (p. 47). Ultimately, understanding the meaning of another person's words only occurs through accurate and validated conversations (Boettcher, this volume; Glaser, 2014).

Glaser's work was based on the idea that in order to have productive and healthy conversations, participants must have a high degree of trust as the basis of their relationship. Without trust, the risk of damage to identity and emotion via abuse of power is high (Boettcher, this volume). Glaser believed there are three levels of conversation, with Level 3 being the most intimate, trusting, and productive. Glazer's "3 Levels of Communication" are:

- Level 1: *transactional*, where there is merely an exchange of data and information. Generally, folks begin with a distributive strategy (Fisher et al., 1991), where they exchange their current positions about the event or process. This distributive process leads to natural anchoring in Level 2 and makes it difficult for people to move away from their initial positions without losing face or appearing to be weak (Fisher et al., 1991). In Level 1, neurochemical activities influence the release of cortisol, which puts the brain and body in a fight-or-flight mode. People with a competitive conflict style become even more competitive, and those who have avoiding or accommodating conflict styles tend to shrink back and acquiesce (Thomas & Kilmann, 2007).
- Level 2: *positional*, where parties further anchor to a locus and use power to make assertions that defend and persuade others to acknowledge their rights-based position. If both parties are adamant about asserting power and defending their initial positions, conversations become stagnant and focus on the problems and people instead of solutions (Fisher et al., 1991). Seldom do the parties ever discuss the interests behind the positions during Level 2 conversations. In Level 2, instead of asking questions to learn about the *why* behind the counterpart's positions, questions are asked to reinforce *my* perspective and *my* wants, thereby further anchoring and solidifying the positions revealed in Level 1. Disputants may rock back and forth between Level 1 and Level 2 and ultimately find themselves locked in an impasse with raging emotional discourse.
- Level 3: *transformational*, where trust is at the highest level and the parties share empathy, identify common interests, and co-create resolutions/solutions based on mutually beneficial success. In Level 3 the parties share a we-centric attitude and view each other as counterparts instead of opponents or adversaries (Fisher et al., 1991; Glaser, 2014). See Figure 19.1 for a graphical synopsis of the Conversational Intelligence® Matrix based on the *3 Levels of Conversations*.

Glaser strongly believed that understanding brain wave connections between people can help coaches and managers engage in deeper and more meaningful conversations. A comprehensive discussion on how interpersonal brain wave connections works is beyond the scope of this chapter. But some basic forthcoming information can be useful to the manager coach.

The three subcomponents of the human brain important to this discussion are the prefrontal cortex (sometimes referred to as the executive brain), the limbic brain (which includes the amygdala, where our memories and emotions are generated), and the brain stem (the reptilian or primitive brain), where implicit memories, street smarts, and basic life functions are managed (Glaser, 2014). I characterize the functions of the three brains as forward thinking (the executive brain where we create mindful solutions), stuck in the middle (focused on amygdala generated memories of past events), and trapped in the past (when we let our primitive brain drive our thoughts and actions without regard to constructive future possibilities).

The brain creates eight chemicals that influence our behavior, communication efforts, emotions, and physical actions (Glaser, 2014). Glaser makes the following observations about the eight brain-produced chemicals:

- *Adrenaline:* This helps us react to threats with heightened energy and awareness.
- *Cortisol:* Produced by the adrenal glands, cortisol initially mobilizes our energy and enhances memory to help with the decision to be competitive or avoiding. Stress leads to the release of too much cortisol, which can damage the immune system, impair memory, and make it difficult to manage emotions.
- *Noradrenaline:* This cousin to adrenaline helps create a more metered feel of energy and focus. It tends to reduce executive thought because it directs the body to move blood to defensive muscles thereby resulting in less blood in the brain for executive thinking and decision-making.
- *Oxytocin:* This chemical reinforces relationships and is associated with nurturing and bonding. Oxytocin enhances generosity and reduces anxiety while encouraging a social connection. It is a key biochemical element that helps to build a trusting relationship.
- *Dopamine:* This enhances feelings of desire, motivation, curiosity, creativity, focus, and satisfaction of accomplishment. We get a burst of this chemical when affirmed by others. If you want to improve your relationship with another individual, honest and reaffirming comments will certainly help that happen.
- *Endorphins:* Produced by the pituitary glands, endorphins help the limbic brain to cope with fear and pain and maintain a pleasurable state. They enhance a feeling of emotional and social security. Chocolate and exercise seem to increase the generation of endorphins.

- *Serotonin:* This brain chemical is an inhibitory as opposed to excitatory chemical that helps to manage appetite and digestive system, regulates mood, perception of pain, cardiovascular system, and sleep cycles. Practicing gratitude can increase serotonin production and balances our psychological well-being.
- *Gamma-Amino Butyric Acid (GABA):* This inhibitory neurochemical helps to relax our body and emotions. Alternatively, stress inhibits its production and leaves us feeling anxious.

Managers that promote a workplace environment contains opportunity for physical activity, encourages sharing words of affirmation, supports open and honest dialogue between coworkers and customers, and practice expressions of gratitude on a regular basis will enhance the brain's ability to generate more of the positive chemicals that result in stronger and more trusting workplace relationships. Positive workplace environments result in more Level 3 communication activities. Alternatively, an overly restrictive and/or hostile work environment will result in the brain's production of cortisol, which may keep conversations at Level 1 and Level 2 (Glaser, 2014).

Moreover Glaser claims that it is important to recognize that cortisol, a steroid hormone, is produced when we engage in conflict and causes the brain to enter deeper into fight-or-flight modes. Cortisol has a long half-life and often lasts hours in the bloodstream. This is why we cannot immediately calm down and reconfigure our emotions after a dispute. Furthermore, production of the four calming/inhibitory brain generated biochemicals (oxytocin, dopamine, endorphins, and serotonin) do not neutralize the effects of cortisol on a one-to-one basis, but they can somewhat mitigate the fight response (Glaser, 2014). Only time can completely dissipate the full biochemical effects of cortisol.

In an emotional confrontation that elicits a fight response, it is wise to pause the discussions and begin again after cortisol levels in the blood have diminished. Glaser (2014) also recommends implementing *down-regulating* behaviors to mitigate brain production of cortisol—actions that she defines as "minimizing the types of conversations that trigger fear, power plays, uncertainty, a need to be right, and group think" (p. 180). In other words, disputants should purposely choose words that build trust and empower people to build relationships so that the subconscious brain will not automatically release cortisol to fight with the counterpart(s) or flee the conversation, hence a *down-regulation* of the brain's production of cortisol. Instead of engaging in a fight-or-flight mode, the brain will alternatively release four calming/inhibitory chemicals. See Figure 19.1, the Conversational Intelligence Matrix, for a graphical depiction of the three levels of conversation and Figure 19.2, the Conversational Dashboard™ for a list of *up and*

Conversational INTELLIGENCE® for Coaches

CONVERSATIONAL INTELLIGENCE® MATRIX

	LEVEL I	LEVEL II	LEVEL III
	TRANSACTIONAL Exchange Information (TELL / ASK)	**POSITIONAL** Exchange Power (ADVOCATE / INQUIRE)	**TRANSFORMATIONAL** Exchange Energy (SHARE / DISCOVER)
Intention	Confirm what I know	Defend what I/We know	Discover what we don't know
I-WE	I-centric	I & WE-centric	WE-centric
Space	Defines Space	Explores Space	Creates Space
Healthy Mindset	Exchange information. Validate what we know	Persuade & influence others to agree with my point of view. Opportunity to seek win-win solutions	Hold a neutral space to explore uncharted territory. Ask questions for which we have no answers & listen to connect
Unhealthy Mindset/ Blind Spots	**Tell-Sell-Yell Syndrome** Tendency toward telling more than listening or asking	**Addicted to Being Right** Overuse of telling. Tendency to ask questions to persuade.	**All Talk, No Action** Tendency for too much ideation & not enough execution
Interaction Dynamics	Inform	Persuade	Co-create
Listen	Listen to Protect	Listen to Accept or Reject	Listen to Connect
Success	My Success	Explore each other's positions; accept or reject	Co-creating Mutual Success
Trust	Low Trust	Conditional Trust	High Trust
Influence	Not open to Influence	Open to Influence	Open for Co-influence
Power	Informational Power	Positional Power	Personal Power
Skills to Develop	Ability to invite open-ended questions & foster 'give and take'	Ability to share the conversational space with others	Ability to Co-create, Innovate & Transform
Neurochemistry	Cortisol & Oxytocin	Intermittent releases of Cortisol (unhealthy exchange) & Oxytocin (healthy exchange)	Release high levels of Oxytocin & Dopamine; Co-creation & Transformation

CONVERSATIONAL INTELLIGENCE®

Figure 19.1 Conversational Intelligence Matrix® 3 levels of conversation.[1]

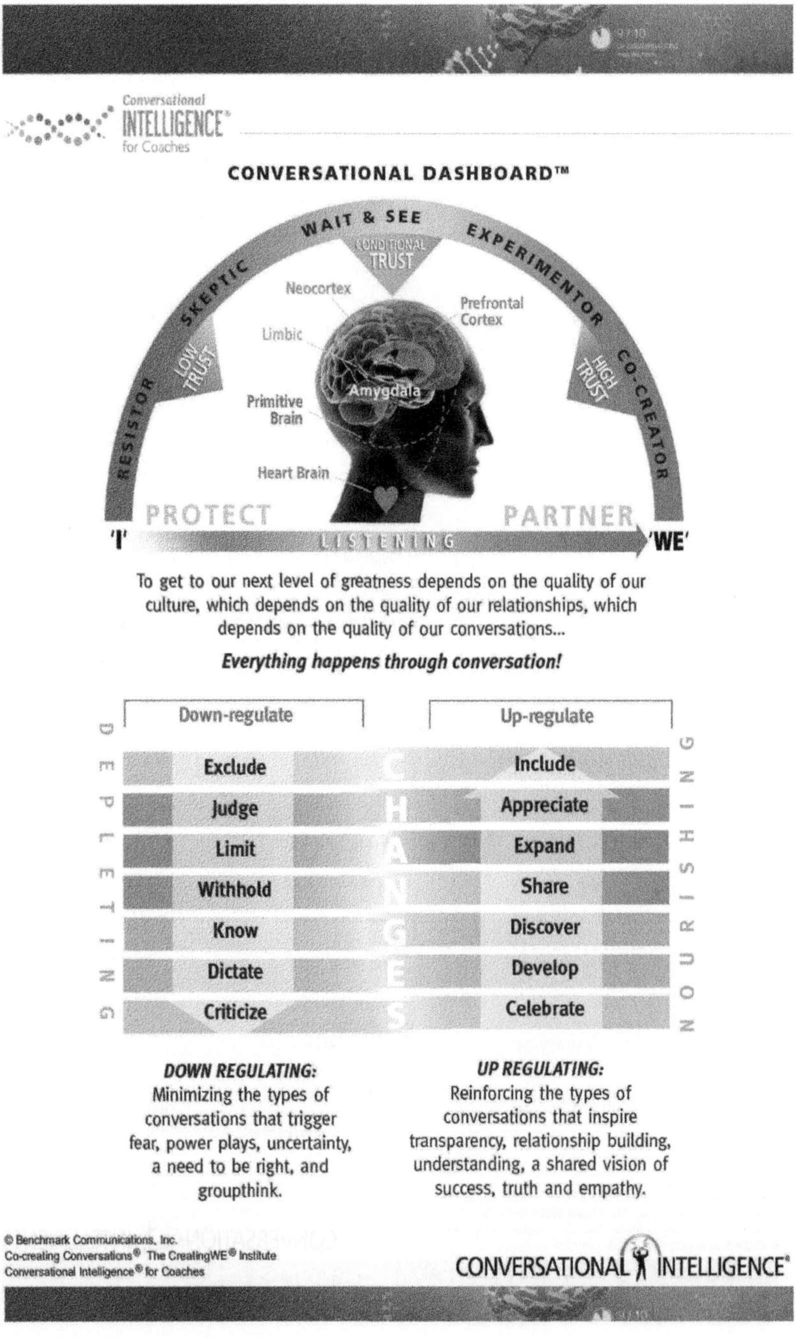

Figure 19.2 Conversational Dashboard™ Neuroscience of WE continuum.[2]

down-regulating behaviors that individuals can choose to purposely engage in to prevent unnecessary brain production of cortisol.

Cortisol can enhance our memories and also distort them (Glaser, 2014). How people make another feel is real. What drives a person to feel a particular way is not always based on complete or accurate facts. Rusk and Miller (1993) claim that people feel feelings before they think thoughts, and those human feelings are responsible for the archetype of our memories. The manager-coach can help the parties achieve satisfactory solutions by appropriate and holistic use of conflict-coaching models and emotion management techniques (see Boettcher, this volume). Throughout the conflict management experience the manager or practitioner should appropriately help workers address negative emotions and help the disputing parties achieve Level 3 conversations through effective use of down-regulating behaviors and dialogue as exhibited in Figure 19.1 and Figure19.2.

HOW TO USE THE CONVERSATIONAL DASHBOARD TOOL

The Conversational Dashboard is a useful conflict-management tool that can help identify a client's current state of mind. The Glaser arch in Figure 19.2 of the Conversational Dashboard identifies two continuums: (a) trust, depicted as low, conditional, or high trust; and (b) participant engagement status, ranging from resisting change to co-creator.

The baseline indicates relational attitude: Is the client focused on self, or is there a balance of concern for the collective relationship? This axis can be addressed as the *I- we-centric* listening continuum; that is, are the clients focused on and engaged in active-listening with empathetic respect for each other's perspectives? Or are they anchored in an attitude of *its all about me?*

Notice that the degree of trust and engagement status both run coincidentally on the arch. Moreover, in the center of the diagram is a pictorial of the brain. The primitive brain is colocated with I-centric resistor-skeptic attitudes of low trust and usually results in release of cortisol as the party tries to determine whether to fight (competitive TKI conflict style) or flee (avoiding TKI conflict style) from the ongoing event. Alternatively, if a party is in a we-centric attitude, they are engaging their executive brain and are willing to participate as an experimentor [see Figure 19.2] and co-creator with high levels of trust. When engaged in a trusting and emotionally balanced attitude the brain generates the five positive chemicals (oxytocin, dopamine, endorphins, serotonin, and GABA) that help us connect, trust, and build strong relationships.

Once disputants see and understand the Conversational Dashboard, they can identify where they think they are on the scales. Generally disputants find themselves with an I-centric attitude espousing words that trigger fear, exert power plays, create uncertainty, and/or maintain an, *I am right and you are wrong* attitude (Glaser, 2014) in an effort to preserve self (see Boettcher, this volume for a discussion on identity). The manager-coach can then help the individual use introspection to determine what it will take to move them to a we-centric behavior pattern with up-regulating actions. Once all parties are engaged in we-centric behavior patterns, trusting relationships can begin to grow.

There are also two columns of behaviors on the Glaser Conversational Dashboard as seen in Figure 19.2 that identify poor conversational behaviors (failure to constructively manage down-regulate techniques that deplete conversations) and positive conversation behaviors (progressive actions that nourish conversations and build trusting relationships). Engaging in the types of conversations characterized in the down-regulate column will probably trigger emotions of fear, uncertainty, and a need to be right that subsequently result in destructive power plays. These kinds of power and rights-based conversations often lead to the release of three brain chemicals (cortisol, adrenaline, and noradrenaline) that make empathic and co-creating conversations nearly impossible. Alternatively, the up-regulate column identifies the constructive behaviors parties should engage in to generate the five brain produced chemicals that stabilize and uplift emotions, which ultimately foster the ability and opportunity to build better relationships. Once educated on the characteristics of up and/or down-regulating behaviors, disputants can proactively choose behaviors that build up relationships and trust so as to achieve higher-valued outcomes (Glaser, 2014).

MANAGING CONFLICT STYLES AND EMOTIONS

Thomas and Kilmann (2007) define conflict as a situation "in which the concerns of two people appear to be incompatible" (p. 7) where a concern is any issue or topic that individuals care about. Another perspective is that conflict is merely competition for a limited resource (Boettcher, this volume). Remember, conflict is neither good nor bad. Thomas claims that conflict is neutral and that how individuals manage the conflict event determines if the conflict event will end poorly or well. Simply, conflict outcomes are the result of how the disputants choose to behave in a conflict event. In conflict events people will react with levels of assertiveness (concern for self) or cooperativeness (concern for others; Thomas, 2007). Disputants can proactively choose to address conflict constructively or if they instead react with unmanaged emotions, they may behave with destructive outcomes that harm relationships and workplace efficiencies.

Fisher and Shapiro (2005) define emotion as "a felt experience" (p. 4) and note that emotions can be either negative or positive. Positive emotions are uplifting and build rapport and send a signal of goodwill and understanding. Negative emotions, such as anger and frustration, are distressing and result in out-of-sync relationships (Fisher & Shapiro, 2005). Unbridled negative emotions can damage a relationship and often lead to an impasse and subsequent actions that hurt all parties.

Dana (2006) writes that people are affected by three kinds of conflict issues: substantive, emotional, and pseudo-substantive.

- Substantive issues are objective concerns or questions that directly affect individuals' self-interests. For example, in a sales department, which salesperson will answer the next call, was a performance review properly conducted, or who will address another agent's client's complaint?
- Emotional issues are usually centered around excessive or loss of power over others and the resultant loss of social status; the need for approval, acceptance, or inclusion by social/work groups; a loss of justice or sense of fairness and equitably; and, a loss of identity (Boettcher, this volume; Dana, 2006).
- Pseudo-substantive issues are usually subconsciously generated and emotionally based and often divert attention away from the objective issue. For example, Sally is a new employee and is a millennial. After 3 months at work, Sally does not understand why she has to work the desk on every Saturday when Sam (a baby boomer with 30 years at the company) never has to work on Saturdays. Sally's anger with Sam is a pseudo-substantive issue because she blames Sam for her having to work Saturdays. The substantive issue is the department policy on working weekends.

The Dual Concerns Model is a common model in conflict resolution pedagogies. This model is based on Mary P. Follett's work where she identified three conflict strategies: (a) domination, (b) compromise, and (c) integration. Thomas (1976) and Rahim (1979) independently further developed Follett's ideas, which eventually became the basis of the dual concerns model (Rahim, 1979) and the Thomas-Kilmann TKI (Thomas and Kilmann, 2007). Fundamentally both models are predicated on the duality relationships between concern for self (assertiveness) and concern for others (empathy). If plotted on a standard two-axis graph, the intersection of the dual-concerns axis plots out 1 of 5 behaviors: avoidance (low concern for self), yielding (accommodating), competition (high concern for self), cooperation, or conciliation (collaboration; Boettcher, 2010; Rahim, 1979; Thomas & Kilmann, 2007).

The Thomas-Kilmann conflict mode assessment (TKI) is based on this fundamental model and predicts one's conflict style. Everyone has a primary and secondary conflict style, but no one style is appropriate for all situations (Thomas & Kilmann, 2007). Each of the five conflict styles is appropriate under specific circumstances. However, in most workplace instances compromising (alternatively cooperative; Boettcher, 2010), and collaborative approaches based on mutually beneficial solutions yield the best results. See website http://www.kilmanndiagnostics.com/overview-thomas-kilmann-conflict-mode-instrument-tki for more information on the TKI conflict-styles concepts.

As depicted in Figure 19.3, simply plotting out where both parties' interests are in regard to assertiveness (concern for self) and empathy (concern for others) can help disputants determine a value-laden conflict management strategy. For example, if a party's primary conflict-style is competing, the party can use Glaser's tools identified in Figure 19.1 and Figure 19.2 to purposely engage in more constructive, cooperative, and collaborative behaviors to achieve higher valued outcomes that build and/or preserves trusting relationships. By implementing Glaser's tools and identifying a need to focus on assertiveness, an individual can purposely choose positive emotions and actions while embracing core values (Schwarz, 2002) to constructively build a solution with another assertive counterpart.

Consider that in a negotiation paradigm (the core process underlying all conflict resolution) of a conflict event the common questions are: "How do I know when to use a distributive strategy versus a principled strategy?"; or "Should I be more competitive or more collaborative?" Just being aware

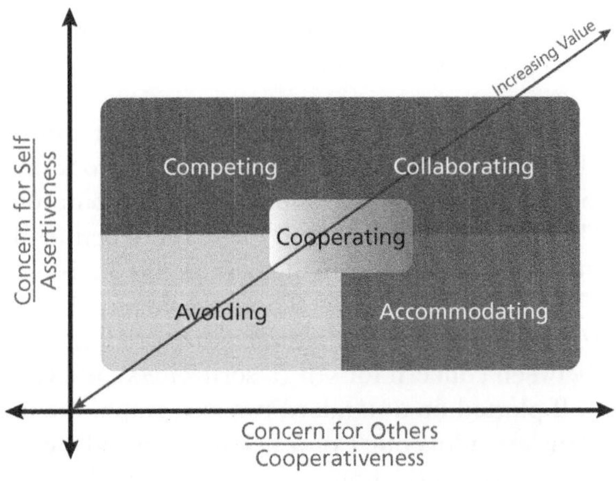

Figure 19.3 Dual concerns and conflict styles: Where do you need to be? *Source:* Adapted from Kilmann Diagnostics 2009–2019 with permission.[3]

of your natural conflict style can help you manage your behavior and emotions to generate higher valued outcomes. For example, if time is critical, a party may not want to nor can it afford to engage in a lengthy collaborative process; therefore, a decision has to be made based on critical time factors to determine if the party must be more assertive (competitive) to move the decision-making process forward due to time constraints. Or can the party take the time to formulate a more collaborative approach to resolve the dispute? Even if the party finds a need to be assertive, be assertive constructively by using Glaser's tools wisely.

In another example of conflict style differences, if the counterpart is avoiding, fails to engage, or is indecisive, in order to move the process forward, a party might have to become less competitive and invite/encourage the counterpart to engage more in a collaborative conflict management process. Ury (2007) even suggests that given your Dual Concerns Model insights, you may need to proactively build the avoider *a golden bridge to which they cannot say no* in order to create a high-valued outcome through a partnered type relationship.

Viewing Figure 19.3, if you have equally balanced moderate concern for self and concern for others, you would land in the cooperative section and would benefit from an interest-based negotiation strategy (Boettcher, this volume). Alternatively, if you had high concern for self and low concern for others based on factors you cannot change, you would rank in the competitive zone and would probably benefit from a *constructively* oriented distributive negotiation strategy. Fisher et al. (1991) suggest that participants always attempt to engage in integrative negotiations and use collaborative processes to settle differences (see Boettcher, this volume). However, as previously mentioned, time constraints or other factors might make extensive interest-based investigations unfeasible. Also, in some simple negotiations it may not be worth the time to negotiate a lengthy principled solution. Nonetheless, to generate the best outcome given a compressed timeline, the parties should strive to use the core values of interest-based negotiations (Fisher et al., 1991) to co-create a fundamentally, mutually beneficial solution so as to avoid counterpart resentment that results in an agreement that will probably fail over time.

Thomas (2009) emphasizes that there is no one best conflict strategy that should be used all the time. Thomas and Kilmann's strategy is to use the conflict style that best fits the particular event. Cooperation and collaboration are key centric attitudes in effectively managing TKI conflict styles with the greatest valued outcomes. However, Glaser (2014) does not like the term collaborate (which means to work with the enemy) and found that using the term *co-create* often motivated clients to generate better solutions. Co-create holds the unspoken inference that all parties have meaningfully

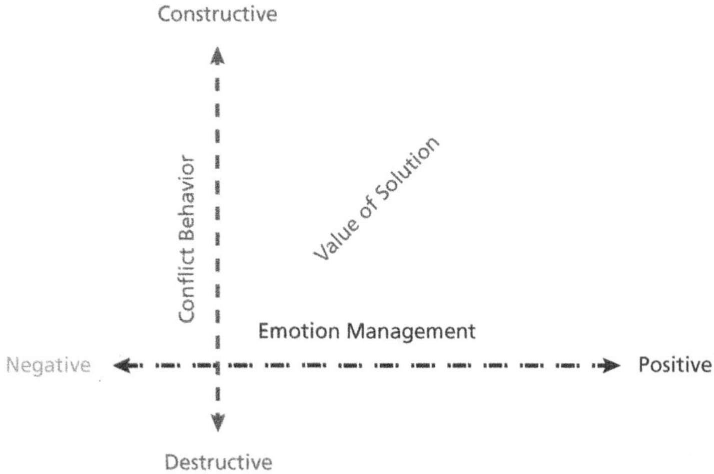

Figure 19.4 Conflict management value of investment: CMVOI. Reprinted with permission.

contributed to the solution-creating process and will ultimately buy into the final outcome to assure durable success (Fisher et al., 1991; Glaser, 2014).

Figure 19.4 is a pictorial of the conflict management value of investment (CMVOI) concept that can help parties better manage the value of conflict outcomes (Boettcher, 2010). Disputants can choose to proactively manage their respective emotions and conflict behavior styles instead of merely reacting to others. If individuals proactively choose to manage conflict with constructive conflict styles and positive emotions, conflict outcomes will almost always result in better outcomes. Managers and practitioners can help employees/clients determine where they are in the current conflict event by plotting out the individual's behaviors and emotions. Are behaviors constructive and emotions positive, or are behaviors and emotions running amuck?

If behaviors and emotions are on a destructive or negative value side of the pictorial, the manager/practitioner can help the parties begin a constructive/positive conversation about what future actions they can take to improve their relationship and subsequently achieve a higher value conflict outcome. Dana (2006) asserts that the problem does not have to be resolved to improve the relationship. Once the *opponents,* who are behaving like adversaries, transform into *counterparts* focused on common interests, with a restored relationship, they can then move forward to *co-create* a solution that meets the mutual needs of the individuals.

CORE VALUES, FEEDBACK, ALTERNATIVE SETTLEMENTS, AND VALIDATION OF THE PROCESS

Armed with the knowledge of conversational intelligence and conflict management diagnosis and intervention strategies, the manager-practitioner can use a variety of tips and techniques to constructively manage conflict events in the workplace. Explicit to every conflict management model should be a clear list of core values (Schwarz, 2002) upon which the parties agree to abide by. Core value agreement is often a valuable step when bringing disputants together for the first time. Core values help anchor contentious conversations in a milieu of fairness, respect, and confidence such that the outcome will address the parties' collective interests in a mutually beneficial way. Conflict management models should contain at least these five core value principles (Boettcher, 2018; Schwarz, 2002):

- All information must be validated on an objective standard. Avoid making un-validated assumptions, inferences, and presumptions (Boettcher, 2018):
  - assumption: something is true;
  - inference: what is stated is an accurate fact; and
  - presumption: something will happen.
- All participants are entitled to make a free and informed choice.
- All parties must make an internal commitment to the group's choice; that is, "You are committed to the decision because it is intrinsically compelling or satisfying, not because you will be rewarded or penalized for making that choice" (Schwarz, 2002, p. 46).
- Everyone must hold an attitude of empathy and compassion for each member in the group. In other words, suspend judgment of alternative views; hold genuine concern for others' circumstances; and appreciate others' conditions (Schwarz, 2002).
- Set process ground rules so that a consensus-based solution can be achieved. A consensus solution is not a first choice that everyone agrees with—rarely can you get there. Consensus means you can live with the decision and personally commit to its success over time (Schwarz, 2002).

MANAGER-COACH AND WORKER FEEDBACK DYNAMICS

Stone and Heen (2015) focus on the science and art of receiving feedback well, even when it is not given well. Sixty-three percent of executives believe that their supervisors do not effectively manage difficult performance evaluations (Stone and Heen, 2015). Not surprisingly, 51% of workers felt their performance reviews were either inaccurate or unfair. Nonetheless, according to Stone and Heen, managers are taught to push feedback on workers persistently, but pushing rarely results in learning.

> In the workplace, treating feedback not just as something to be endured, but something to be actively sought, can have a profound impact. Feedback-seeking behavior—as it's called in the research literature—has been linked to higher job satisfaction, greater creativity on the job, faster adaption in a new organization or role, and lower turnover. And seeking out negative feedback is associated with higher performance ratings. (p. 9)

In Boettcher's discussion on conflict-coaching models (Jones & Brinkert, 2008; Noble, 2012), the importance of identity (saving face), emotion, and power along with the factors that affect our memories as our own reality, which in turn, drives our respective perspectives and behaviors were extensively discussed (Boettcher, this volume). If the supervisor and employee/coachee have a history of poorly received performance feedback interface (bad memories), the manager-coach will be challenged to create a dynamic where the coachee will be open to effective conflict-management feedback. In other words—in such a situation, there is no meaningful conversation between the worker and manager. The worker, client, or disputant may subsequently become entrenched in an I-centric perspective and anchor their behaviors and beliefs such that they cannot "hear" the positive-constructive feedback that would help them achieve greater success or settle a dispute. They become stuck in Level 1 conversations.

If the performance review process is flawed and ineffective, the manager-coach may need to step back and reevaluate it in order to not only improve the review process, but to also help workers obtain an open-minded perspective that will help them constructively engage in future conflict management and dispute resolution processes. The manager-coach must teach workers how to receive feedback well, and employees need to adapt a feedback-seeking attitude in order to capture the full value of constructive feedback (Stone & Heen, 2015).

The transformational power of constructive critique and descriptive feedback is evidenced in Ron Berger's story of *Austin's Butterfly*. First grade students at Anser Charter School in Boise, Idaho, helped Austin (a first grader) draw a penciled sketch of a Tiger Swallowtail butterfly. Austin was shown a detailed scientific picture of the butterfly and was asked to draw a likeness of the butterfly (see Figure 19.5). After the first draft, his teacher and fellow students (his feedback team) gave Austin *specific* critique on Austin's first draft. Based on specific peer-to-peer feedback, Austin tried a second time. Austin subsequently made five different draft sketches of

Figure 19.5 Picture of Austin's scientific butterfly. Reprinted with permission.[4]

the butterfly with the team giving him specific feedback following each new draft. After the fifth draft, Austin and the team were satisfied with the sketch and then asked Austin to add color to the sketch.

Two key factors between feedback giver and receiver made the feedback process successful. First, Austin had a positive attitude, received the feedback critique well, and tried to do better with each draft. Second, the team gave Austin specific and detailed feedback as opposed to making generalized comments. Feedback-seeking behavior (Stone & Heen, 2015) as noted above helped make the experience positive for everyone. The complete series of Austin's sketches are in Figure 19.6 and end with pretty amazing results.

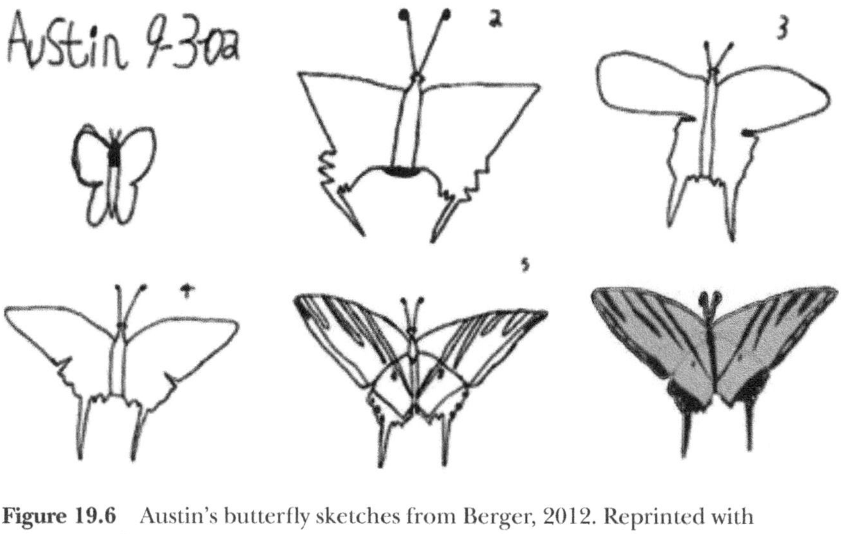

Figure 19.6 Austin's butterfly sketches from Berger, 2012. Reprinted with permission.[5]

CONFLICT, EMOTIONS, ETHICS, MORALS, AND VALUES

In Boettcher (thic volume), conflict was simply defined as "competition for a limited resource." Although this definition is simple and accurate, sometimes the underlying factors driving conflict between two work peers is complicated. Synthesizing Blackard and Gibson (2002), Lipsky, Seeber, and Fincher (2003), and Rahim's (1992) perspectives on organizational conflict, workplace conflict may be more usefully defined as: A process of social interaction whereby individuals and or groups compete for limited common resources, power, and social status, using their own system of beliefs, ethics, morals, values, and cultures. Close examination of this definition may help the manager identify a key factor in a peer-to-peer dispute—the hidden impact of cultural influences. Ease of travel and Internet services have made our world smaller, resulting in blending of cultures and a mix of beliefs, ethics, morals, values, and religious dogmas. Sometimes these factors clash.

Ethics, morals, and values are independent concepts that are inextricably connected. The terms are frequently and erroneously interchanged and are often overlooked and misunderstood in conflict events.

Ethics are broadly applied social standards linked to right and wrong. They grow out of particular philosophies accepted by individual societies. A society is nothing more than an ordered community—a group or subgroup in the workplace, or people in a town, region, or country (Hofstede & Hofstede, 2005). Right and wrong is defined by the respective group. What might be right or acceptable to one may be terribly wrong for another. There are often large differences in the continuums when compared across social, group, or organizational networks (Hofstede & Hofstede, 2005).

Hofstede and Hofstede (2005) define values as the core of culture: culture of an organization, of a nation, of a country, and/or of a population within that country. Values are polarized feelings with dimension: evil versus good, dirty versus clean, dangerous versus safe, and forbidden versus permitted. Hofstede and Hofstede (2005) caution readers not to burden an individual with the values of their respective organizational or social cultures. After all, individuals are individuals and should not be stereotyped or branded by their overarching organizational or social culture.

Morals are individual and personal beliefs tied to a singular person (Hofstede & Hofstede, 2005). So while a culture's core is based on values, the individual's morals determine his or her respective behavior—a behavior influenced by cultural values. An individual may accept cultural and social values, but his or her own personal morals may drive outward behaviors—behaviors substantially different than a cultural norm.

Ethics, morals, and values are separate, yet linked. These concepts are not mutually exclusive and when combined are a challenge to manage well in a multicultural workplace. The manager-coach must explore how ethics, morals, and values are affecting the disputants' relationship, from both a personal and organizational culture perspective.

CONCLUDING THOUGHTS

Intelligent conversations do not just happen. People must strive to not merely understand the words of another through active listening, they must also work diligently to correctly interpret other kinetic factors such as body language, tone, tenor, facial features, and gestures as well as the meaning of the words to everyone involved in the conversation. Intelligent conversations should be multidirectional with all parties consistently seeking feedback to validate assumptions, inferences, presumptions, and understanding, ensuring that they correctly interpreted the other party and that the other party accurately comprehends them.

Glaser (2014) created tools to help people identify where they are in a conflict-conversation process. Understanding where one is on the Conversational Dashboard will then help parties move to the proper level of conversation identified on the Conversational Intelligence Matrix (transactional, positional, or transformational). Proper implementations of C-IQ concepts can lead to more trusting and lasting relationships. Stronger and more transparent relationships can in turn result in higher valued co-created solutions, both now and in the future.

Blended use of the TKI and Dual Concerns Model can help you diagnose and implement the proper conflict style to resolve a dispute. Recognizing where the other party is on the model can also help you respond with empathy (Schwarz, 2002) and use constructive/positive language that may result in co-creation (Glaser, 2014) of better solutions. Additionally, integral to all meaningful conversations is the need for effective feedback processes (Stone & Heen, 2015).

Managers and practitioners must always be aware of and balance the factors of ethics, morals, values, and organizational culture. Finally, the dispute resolution process must continuously honor core values of objective valuation, free and informed choices, empathic perspective sharing, consistent ground rules, and commitment to a consensus based co-created solution (Glaser, 2014; Schwarz, 2002). Commitment to a process with co-created solutions (Glaser, 2014) based on core values will always result in higher-valued outcomes of a positive nature. Constantly strive to use integrative negotiation techniques that lead to mutually beneficial solutions for all the parties (Boettcher, this volume; Fisher et al., 1991). How individuals manage conflict is an emotional and behavioral choice. Conflict counts.

Manage it wisely and effectively with positive emotions and thoughtful constructive behaviors and your organization will hum along in harmony and efficiency.

NOTES

1. From 3 Levels of Conversation© Benchmark Communications, Inc., /The CreatingWE Institute (see Conversational Intelligence Matrix graphic.) All content is derived from Conversational Intelligence and the work of Judith E. Glaser. Conversational intelligence: *How great leaders build trust and get extraordinary results*. Glaser, J. E. (2014), Brookline, MA: Bibliomotion, Inc. Reprinted with permission.
2. From Conversational Dashboard Neuroscience of WE, Benchmark Communications, Inc./The CreatingWE Institute (see Conversational Dashboard graphic.) All content is derived from Conversational Intelligence® and the work of Judith E. Glaser. Conversational intelligence: *How great leaders build trust and get extraordinary results*. Glaser, J. E. (2014), Brookline, MA: Bibliomotion, Inc. Reprinted with permission.
3. Adapted from Kilmann Diagnostics (2019). Copyright© 2009–2019 by Kilmann Diagnostics. All rights reserved. Original figure is available at http://www.kilmanndiagnostics.com/overview-thomas-kilmann-conflict-mode-instrument-tki (Adapted and reprinted with permission).
4. Berger, 2012. Reprinted with permission.
5. Berger, 2012. Reprinted with permission.

REFERENCES

Berger, R. (2012, March). Austin's butterfly. [Video file] Retrieved from https://groveacademy.co.uk/inspiration/butterfly/

Birdwhistell, R. L. (1955). Background to kinesics. *Et cetera, 13*(1), 10–28.

Blackard, K., & Gibson, J. W. (2002). *Capitalizing on conflict: Strategies and practices for turning conflict to synergy in organizations.* Palo Alto, CA: Davies-Black.

Boettcher, G. W. (2010, March). *Understanding communication and conflict to avoid unnecessary impasse.* Presentation to Virginia Mediation Network. Richmond, Virginia.

Boettcher, G. W. (2018, September). *Useful assessments for facilitation.* Presentation to Mid-Atlantic Facilitators Network. GAO Building, Washington D. C.

Burgoon, J. K., Guerrero, L. K., & Floyd, K. (2016). *Nonverbal communication.* New York, NY: Routledge.

Dana, D. (2006). *Managing differences.* Prairie Village, KS: MTI.

Fisher, R., & Shapiro, D. (2006). *Beyond reason: Using emotions as you negotiate.* New York, NY: Viking-Penguin.

Fisher, R., Ury, W., & Patton, B. (1991). *Getting to yes: Negotiating agreement without giving in* (2nd ed.). New York, NY: Penguin Books.

Glaser, J. E. (2014). *Conversational intelligence: How great leaders build trust and get extraordinary results.* Brookline, MA: Bibliomotion.

Green, M. (2017). Speech Acts. In E. N. Zalta (Ed.), *The Stanford encyclopedia of philosophy* (Winter edition). Retrieved from https://plato.stanford.edu/archives/win2017/entries/speech-acts/

Hofstede, G., & Hofstede, G. J. (2005). *Cultures and organizations: Software of the mind.* New York, NY: McGraw-Hill.

Jones, T. S., & Brinkert, R. (2008). *Conflict coaching: Conflict management strategies and skills for the individual.* Los Angeles, CA: SAGE.

Kilmann, R. H. (2009). *Frequently asked questions about the Thomas-Kilmann Conflict Mode Instrument.* Retrieved from http://www.kilmanndiagnostics.com/frequently-asked-questions-about-tki-assessment

Kirton, M. J. (2003). *Adaption-innovation in the context of diversity and change.* New York, NY: Routledge.

Lakhani, D. (2005). *Persuasion: The art of getting what you want.* Hoboken, NJ: Wiley.

Lipsky, D. B., Seeber, R. L., & Fincher, R. D. (2003). *Emerging systems for managing workplace conflict: Lessons from American corporations for managers and dispute resolution professionals.* San Francisco, CA: Jossey-Bass.

Mehrabian, A., & Ferris, S. R. (1967). Inference of attitudes from nonverbal communication in two channels. *Journal of Consulting Psychology, 31*(3), 48–258.

Mehrabian, A., & Wiener, M. (1967). Decoding of inconsistent communications. *Journal of Personality and Social Psychology, 6*(1), 109–114.

Myers, I. B., McCaulley, M. H., Quenk, N. L., & Hammer, A. L. (2003). *MBTI Manual: A guide to the development and use of the Myers-Briggs Type Indicator®* (3rd ed.). Mountain View, CA: CPP.

Nardi, D. (2009). *Neuroscience of personality: Principles of the psyche as a living system.* Retrieved from https://www.pdx.edu/sysc/sites/www.pdx.edu.sysc/files/neuro-systems.pdf

Noble, C. (2012). *Conflict management coaching: The Cinergy™ model.* Toronto, Canada: Cinergy.

Pérez, A., Carreiras, M., & Duñabeitia, J. A. (2017). Brain-to-brain entrainment: EEG interbrain synchronization while speaking and listening. *Scientific Reports,* 7(4190). https://doi.org/10.1038/s41598-017-04464-4

Philpott, J. S. (1983). *The relative contribution to meaning of verbal and nonverbal channels of communication: A meta-analysis.* Unpublished master's thesis, University of Nebraska.

Rahim, M. A. (1979). Managing organizational conflict: A model for diagnosis and intervention. *Psychological Reports, 44*(3), 1323–1344.

Rahim, M. A. (1992). *Managing conflict in organizations* (2nd ed.). Westport, CT: Praeger.

Rusk, T., & Miller, D. P. (1993). *The power of ethical persuasion: From conflict to partnership at work and in private life.* New York, NY: Viking Adult.

Schwarz, R. (2002). The skilled facilitator: A comprehensive resource for consultants, facilitators, managers, trainers, and coaches. San Francisco, CA: Jossey-Bass.

Stone, D., & Heen, S. (2015). *Thanks for the feedback: The science and art of receiving feedback well.* New York, NY: Penguin Books.

Thomas, K. W. (1976). Conflict and conflict management. In M. Dunnette (Ed.), *Handbook of industrial and organizational psychology* (pp. 889–935). Chicago, IL: Rand McNally.

Thomas, K. W. (2008). *Making conflict management a strategic advantage.* Mountain View, CA: CPP.

Thomas, K. W., & Kilmann, R. H. (2007). *Thomas-Kilmann Conflict Mode instrument.* Sunnyvale, CA: CPP.

Ury, W. (2007). *Getting past no: Negotiating in difficult situations.* New York, NY: Bantam.

CHAPTER 20

THE WORK OF EMPLOYEE ENGAGEMENT

Practical Strategies for the Workplace

E. Kobena Osam and Brad Shuck

Few ideas have generated more excitement in recent years with leaders than employee engagement. Everyone wants more of it, yet application, measurement, and practice—not to mention results—can vary widely. What seems to be missing from the conversation is a fundamental understanding of what employee engagement is, how it develops, and how leaders can influence engagement in ways that deeply impact their employees. Indeed, the work of building employee engagement is difficult, and at times, can be severely disconnected from research and practice. What leaders and employees need are practical common-sense strategies, rooted in real world experience and evidence based, for influencing the real work of driving higher levels of employee engagement. Such strategies would provide a generous opportunity to explore practical approaches that impact results and positively influence the lives of those who work in positive transformative ways.

In this chapter on employee engagement, we overview the work of employee engagement for leaders and employees at all levels of an organization.

From Discord to Harmony, pages 355–366

We detail what we mean when we use the term employee engagement and explore what it means to be engaged. Next, we consider the current context of work and how that could impact the way that employee engagement might develop in practice. Last, we offer specific strategies for implementing practices that leaders and employees can use to influence employee engagement, no matter their context, tenure, and level in the organization.

WHAT IS EMPLOYEE ENGAGEMENT?

Employee engagement is a slippery term. Since Gallup first published the Q12 (Harter, Schmidt, & Hayes, 2002), leaders and employees of all walks have chased the engagement idea. Everyone wants more of it. We have, for example, yet to be in a boardroom where a group of leaders have asked us to reduce the levels of engagement of their teams because they were too profitable, too committed, and too successful. No one wants less engagement; when it comes to having engaged employees, more is almost always believed to be better. While every leader we have ever talked with desires higher and higher levels of engagement, few have been able to name exactly what engagement is. For some, they have defined employee engagement as profit. Others have defined employee engagement as commitment or satisfaction, and some have defined engagement as lower turnover. Certainly, we would agree that engagement is related to all of these things, but none of them fully capture what we mean when we say employee engagement.

For instance, engagement and outcomes like job satisfaction seem cut from the same cloth—that is, they appear in practice together, may influence one another, and are closely related, yet there must be some level of distinction. Are engaged employees *always* satisfied employees, and do engaged employees stay with a company forever? Shuck, Osam, Zigarmi, and Nimon (2017) defined employee engagement as "a positive, active, work-related psychological state operationalized by the maintenance, intensity, and direction of cognitive, emotional, and behavioral energy" (p. 269). In their positioning, Shuck, Osam, et al. (2017) suggested that engagement was transformational; that is, the experience of employee engagement elevated the experience of being at work, it defined the positive experience of being mentally and emotionally caught up in work, and being engaged meant working toward a work-related goal with your mind, heart, and body. Engaged employees work with their whole person, and they are all in, they are present, and they are focused.

This differs greatly from being satisfied or committed. Satisfaction, as it is commonly understood, is a state of status quo. An employee who says they are satisfied might say something like, "I am satisfied with my work, and my job. There is no need to change anything." A committed employee might offer, "I am comfortable here; I am committed to this work as long as things remain as they are right now." But what happens when things change—or need to change? What happens when the compensation plan shift, a co-worker leaves, or a new project comes along? What happens when change is necessary to keep the organization viable? How does a company accomplish a bold vision with satiated employees? This is a distinguishing hallmark of employee engagement in light of other workplace outcomes. For many, like satisfaction and commitment, these outcomes are transactional. That is, they rest upon an equal transactional state grounded in an exchange framework—you give to me and then I give to you. Employee engagement, on the other hand, is transformational and grounded in reciprocity—a very powerful, often overlooked principle of psychology. In short, reciprocity suggests that employees (and all human beings for that matter) give freely to those they believe give to them, and that the interaction is not an assumed exchange but a transformation of the relationship. As change occurs, the engaged employee leans in, while the satisfied employee may push away. This is the difference between transaction (exchange) and transformation (engagement).

Some years ago, on his very first day of work, one of the authors of this chapter walked into his office at 9:00 a.m. to meet his new team. A new job. A new team. And, so much possibility for his future. The first person he met when he walked in the door was Vivian. Vivian was the administrative assistant for a large multifaceted complex. Excited to meet a member of his new team and anxious to develop a relationship, he stopped to say good morning. This being Vivian's third boss in so many years, she put her hand up and shared the following:

> This is not a good morning; we are very busy today. I come to work at 8:15 a.m., and I take my lunch at 11:30 a.m.—every day. I go home at 4:30 p.m. Do not ask me to come in early and do not ask me to stay a minute over 4:30 p.m. Those are my hours. Here is a copy of my job description; I will do these things, but do not ask me to do anything outside of my defined role responsibilities that I am not compensated for. If you have any questions, as I said, we are busy, so please . . . make it quick.

For all intents and purposes, Vivian was about as disengaged as they come, at least on the surface. And she made that clear. She was rough, direct, and proved hard to work with over the next few months. She had been seasoned through years and years of being passed along from team to team, and no one had taken the time to get to know her. And now, she did not want to be known or know anyone else, for that matter. Her work was—at least on the surface—not meaningful and unfulfilling. She was borderline insubordinate, and her past had taught her that she could outlast this new manager, just as she had outlasted the last one, and the one before that;

time had taught her that she would be the last person standing. She just needed to stand her ground and stay within policy and procedure.

Vivian's story is one that highlights what it feels like when we are disengaged. It is likely that we have all had a coworker like Vivian (or maybe we have been Vivian); someone who, through the years, had been taught that to survive is to thrive. Just put your head down, survive this one, and move on. Or, the coworker who has constantly pushed away from new projects, evaded responsibility, and is overly negative. You might have even come across the pervasive complainer, who has an opinion about everything in the workplace. Surely, Vivian—and this coworker you are thinking of—cannot possibly be engaged or get to a place where they are positive and active, working through tough projects collaboratively as a part of a team, and who, in the midst of the action, throws their mind, heart, and body at a project. Surely, for someone like Vivian, this is not possible.

This is an important point of distinction. For us, we believe that it is very possible for Vivian to be engaged. As Shuck (2013) suggested, "We refuse to accept that for some, feeling trapped in quiet desperation is the only future possible" (p. 282). Some people believe that employees like Vivian are a lost cause, meaning that that may never experience an abundant work life, while others believes that employees like Vivian are a cancer to be cut out (Kelleher, 2013), blood-sucking vampires (Sheridan, 2017), or workplace prisoners (Hewitt, 2015) as some popular consulting firms have routinely suggested. These, however, are not our positions. Viewing engagement from this position objectifies the idea and experience of employee engagement, and when we objectify something we remove the human element. Employee engagement then becomes devoid of those things that gave it meaning in the first place. When that happens, as Wagner (2015) suggested, employees become resources to be controlled like lumber, coffee beans, and widgets. No one likes to be referred to as a widget or compared to coffee beans. Instead, we believe—and our research shows—that engagement is for everyone. "We believe that human beings who live an engaged life, who can engage authentically and at healthy levels with their work, fundamentally experience life more abundantly" (Shuck, 2013, p. 282). This is the transformation of engagement, and how we both define and understand what it means to be engaged. Even for an employee like Vivian, we believe that engagement is a future she can achieve and experience when the conditions are presented for her to be engaged. Vivian is not broken; she is just reacting reasonably to the rules she has been presented with.

Engagement without context is not possible, and for employee engagement that context is work. Before we go further, to better explore the work of employee engagement and understand how it happens, including the practical utility of engagement in work—for both leaders and employees—we must understand the context in which employee engagement occurs. This enables us to explore how we can influence engagement in subtle and important ways without objectifying the experience. In the next section, we detail the current context of work and what that means for how leaders might influence the ways that employee engagement could develop in practice.

THE CURRENT CONTEXT OF WORK

In order to properly understand employee engagement and how it works, we must understand that it has context and operates within that context (i.e., work and the workplace). This is especially important given the excitement around employee engagement over the past decade, and in our experience, has often led to employers placing an elevated focus on a magical number that provides evidence of employee engagement. A misguided practice to be sure. Not too long ago, one of the authors of this chapter was hired by a Fortune 500 company. He was asked to work at one of the company's multimillion dollar sites, and was tasked with the mandate of facilitating a stronger bond between management and associates by frequently engaging associates on the production floor. To this company, employee engagement was important, and they considered their associates to be engaged if they met or exceeded a certain score on an employee engagement survey administered to all employees once every fiscal year. In order to meet this target, the company decided to introduce the presence of HR on the production floor, and a few months before the survey was deployed, have pizza parties for teams with the highest number of units produced each month. During the author's time there, the company met the targeted engagement score and prided themselves as having an engaged workforce. However, because this author spent a lot of time interacting with associates, he realized that there was more to engagement than just a number, or pizza parties to reward high productivity. It became clear to him that associates wanted more than this; they wanted to feel like their supervisors and managers cared about them and appreciated them, because that would really motivate them to give their all when they came into work. To be clear, pizza parties do not equal engagement, yet that is exactly how most leaders approach improving engagement. You can take out the words "pizza party" and insert whatever activity you like; it is still an objectification that someone could bribe (with a party) or coerce (heightened presence on the floor) higher levels of engagement. It just does not work that way.

There is so much more to employee engagement than a number or a superficial target, and when leaders understand this, they can take appropriate steps to create the kind of workforce that is truly engaged. This experience at the Fortune 500 Company showed that creating a work environment that provides meaning and purpose is a good start to influencing higher levels of employee engagement. This is not to say that having a number or using surveys to measure employee engagement is a bad thing. Data can change the conversation and provide leverage points that focus effort and provide actionable insight. In fact, the most widely used practice to measure engagement is through the use of surveys, and there are numerous instruments backed by strong research (e.g., interested readers might explore the employee engagement scale; Shuck, Adelson, & Reio, 2017). However, through our own extensive research across numerous samples and studies, we have come to realize that engagement surveys tend to produce high scores that suggest inflated levels of engagement, and taking these at face value alone may not get to the core of engagement. As Shuck, Osam, et al. (2017) noted in their definition, employee engagement is a psychological state. If engagement is a state, that means it is dynamic in experience and that it is possible for employees to be engaged one week and, based on their experiences, not the next. To have a state of sustained engagement, companies must do more than seek out a magic number. As much as employees are not coffee beans or lumber, engagement is not a number.

Within the context of work, not all work can be exhilarating and fun all the time. It is not reasonable to expect that every day would be someone's best day. Not all work is rousing, but all work should be dignified. Notwithstanding, there may be elements of a work environment that have high demands and low resources (Demerouti, Bakker, & Fried, 2012) or that are toxic, which may periodically—and consequently—ebb and sap away at engagement. For example, in some industries there are periods where the work volume is high, such as in retail, and these periods are often characterized by longer work hours, higher stress, and so on and may culminate in a work environment that feels disengaging. These types of environments are not likely to foster high levels of employee engagement. We think of these characteristics (e.g., longer hours, increased workload coupled with a lack of support, poor leadership, and work that is not meaningful) as triggers for disengagement. Leaders must be careful to be intentional in their culture building and to work daily to actively mitigate these triggers—not just during periods where work volume is high, but routinely. That is the way to sustained, authentic, and deeply rooted employee engagement.

On the way to creating a work environment that is engaging, we must be careful with adopting practices out of context. Because higher levels of employee engagement are in such high demand, there is great temptation to copy or adopt engagement strategies being used by other employers. We laud honors, like being named to the Best Places to Work annual lists, through award banquets and ceremonies that celebrate the unique practices of the most engaging places of work. What often happens is that we want to know what those leaders who work at the best places are doing differently, and when we found out, we try to emulate their approach. Rarely, however, does that work. Blanket or copycat approaches to creating and sustaining engagement are just not appropriate and often taken out of context. Just like the pizza party example, employees can tell when their leaders truly care about them versus when they are trying to simply meet their objectives. We would encourage leaders to undertake an environmental scan so that they might closely examine their work environment and identify triggers that might lead to disengagement. As an example, if an organization identifies that increased workload is causing employees to disengage and that introducing remote working improves engagement, it would be a mistake for another organization to implement remote working to improve engagement if one of their triggers is a lack of recognition. This is a prime example of objectifying employee engagement and taking practices out of context.

As we close this section, in sum, it is important to highlight that we believe in a work environment where employees of all kinds can immerse themselves in work that is meaningful, and that when it comes to employee engagement, leaders make or break the culture. Being in tune with their employees and taking intentional action to build higher levels of employee engagement is the work of leaders who desire employees who are engaged. Being attentive to cues in the workplace that lessen an employees' desire to fully immerse themselves at work is a critical aspect of creating an engaged workforce, and the role of leadership that cares. Actionable and accurate data can help with this, but leaders and the organizations they work with must do more, go deeper, and develop methods that tease out issues of both opportunity and concern to employees in ways that are authentic and grounded in practice. Employers who do not do this risk being viewed as being fashionable, or only promoting engagement because it is the trendy thing to do, without actually doing anything to substantially create and sustain employee engagement. With this understanding of the context of work in relation to employee engagement, we now turn attention to detailing specific recommendations for building employee engagement that leaders and employees at all levels can implement.

RECOMMENDATIONS: THE TRANSFORMATIVE POWER OF EMPLOYEE ENGAGEMENT

That first morning, Vivian had made it clear that she was busy, and she did not have time to be bothered. Just before heading into his office, the author in question looked directly at Vivian and shared, "It's a great morning and it is so good to meet you; obviously, you have a lot of knowledge and a lot to offer the team." He said it all with a smile. Before turning around, he asked Vivian if she had some time later that day to talk with him about some questions he had, and just like that, the meeting was set. At the prescribed time, Vivian came into the office and sat down, pen and paper ready. Coming out from behind his desk, he invited Vivian to sit at a small table with him and was intentional to share the space by the window with her. He had two simple questions: (a) "How are you doing today?"; and (b) "Is there anything that I can do to be helpful?" Vivian was puzzled. She answered that she was fine and there was nothing that she needed help with. In less than 60 seconds the meeting was over, but the author made the request that they have the same meeting next week, same day and time. The next week came. Same outcomes; 60 seconds in and the meeting was over. This happened for more than 6 weeks. "How are you doing today, and is there anything that I can do to be helpful?" Same questions and same outcomes, until one meeting Vivian shared about a challenging experience that she was having with a coworker and was not sure how to handle it. For 10 minutes they talked about it, and quickly, he sprang into action to help. In the grand scheme of the many things he had to worry about, her problem was perhaps minor and easy to fix. But not to Vivian. It was a huge and burdensome problem; a weight that she no longer had to carry alone. He worked intentionally to partner and help, be supportive, listen, and take great care to make sure she knew her problem was important to him. The next week's meeting came, and they talked for 30 minutes. "Progress," he thought. Same two questions. "How are you doing today, and is there anything that I can do to be helpful?" But this time, a very different outcome. The question is why was the outcome so different?

As we have suggested, no one likes to be a number or to be objectified. For years, the messages that Vivian received from her direct supervisors were that she was just another human resource. She might as well have been a pile of lumber that got moved from one place to the next and so, she responded accordingly—and in our opinion, within reason. Your employees thirst to matter. Vivian desperately wanted to matter. And for years, she did not believe she mattered, until one day, she did. Understandably skeptical, trust was slow to build, but it grew in a cumulative fashion over time. There was no big transformation, no balloons falling out of the ceiling, and certainly no one was showing up on a Best Place to Work survey that year. This, however, is the work of engagement. One human being at a time. Employee engagement is individual and it is a cumulative build. So often, employee engagement is not in the big events, but rather grounded in those things that are equally easy to do and easy not to do. The small interactions that either work for us or they work against us. Other simple actions that, in our experience, have been linked with higher levels of employee engagement include holding doors or elevators open for others, exchanging pleasantries in the hallway, leaving hand written notes of appreciation after a job well done, and brewing the next pot of coffee after taking the last cup in the morning. These are all pedestrian, and we understand that, but that is what makes employee engagement so meaningful and accessible—everyone can do it.

Through a recent research project, our team looked into the behaviors of what we call compassionate leaders. What we found was surprising. Across a sample of more than 1,500 people, who were asked about their direct leaders, their levels of employee engagement, their health, turnover intentions, and effort, participants stated that when leaders treated them with dignity, they were twice as likely to be engaged. In fact, dignity predicted future levels of employee engagement. That is, the more a person said that a leader treated him or her with dignity, the more we could predict the person's level of future engagement. The thing about dignity is that it is not hard to do, and in fact, it is very easy to do. But, at the same time, it is also very easy not to do. We get busy; we have schedules to keep and emails to write, and people get in the way of those things. Dignity is free; it has absolutely no cost except for the time it takes to be intentional about the interactions you are having. The other leader behaviors that we identified included presence, authenticity, accountability, empathy, and integrity. What we learned from this research was that the ways in which employees experienced their leader was very important and directly connected to their experience of employee engagement. None of these behaviors cost any money, and that makes things like dignity a very hard sale. If we told you that we could fix your engagement problems, but it would cost a lot of money, involve big programs, and require large-scale culture change, you might believe us. You might even take that on. The more money we charged, the more validating the program and outcomes, and the better you would feel about all the training and organizational development work going on around you. There would undoubtedly be a lot of meetings with complicated agendas and schedules, work-flow processes, and analysis to look at, and probably some pie charts. In an organization, those artifacts make leaders comfortable.

But when we tell leaders that if they want higher levels of employee engagement they should start with dignity, and then pack our stuff and leave without charging a dime, who would believe that? Certainly, we have been laughed out of our share of boardrooms. The hard truth, however, is that engagement is about believing your voice matters, that your work has meaning, that you add value to your team, and that when you need it, someone will be there to support you. Your coworkers feel the same way. These experiences are so overlooked and so pedestrian that they are hard to even believe, but we know they are true from every relationship we have ever had in our life. Those relationships that give us meaning, that validate our contributions, that tell us we are loved, and that someone is looking out for us—we pull toward those relationships, and the ones that tell us we are resources to be objectified, we push away from those.

We do recognize that organizations and leaders require strategy, and to that end, there are several things we might recommend in addition to treating employees with dignity. First, in order to get the most out of any employee engagement strategy, organizations must have a strategic focus on engagement. By this, we mean that there should be a well thought out plan that is developed by leadership, and that aligns with existing organizational objectives. This requires that leaders understand what engagement means, why it matters, and the conditions necessary to stimulate it, and then blend this knowledge to fashion out an engagement strategy that is authentic. One area that organizations can apply engagement strategy to is leadership development.

We advocate engagement-focused leadership development because the work environment is a significant determinant of employee engagement, and leaders' actions and behaviors influence employees' feelings about their workplace. Managers and supervisors, in a way, regulate employee engagement by influencing emotions and experience. The core piece to engagement-focused leadership development lies in creating leaders that optimize the emotional climate in the workplace. Simply put, if employees feel positively about their leaders (or manager—you can use whatever word you want here), they are more likely to believe that their organization is a great place to work and will go all out in the performance of their duties. Engagement-focused leadership development should include training that focuses on explaining what engagement means, why it is important, and the benefits that arise from employee engagement (e.g., reduced turnover, increased performance). This training should also include teaching leaders to enhance their subordinates' personal capacity such as positive thinking, goal setting, time management, and stress management.

Another practice we recommend is conducting periodic engagement pulse assessments. The engagement pulse assessment should be a lightweight tool that focuses on identifying triggers of disengagement, such as role conflict and turnover intentions. For example, practitioners might just have two questions: (a) "Based on your experience of work over the last 30 days, would you recommend this as a place to work to your friends?"; and (2) "Based on your experience of work over the last 30 days, would you trust our product, service, care, and so on with your family?" This assessment could take a variety of formats such as brief surveys and random sampled interviews, tracking the number of callouts, as well as the number of formal or informal grievance reports—all ways to get a sense of how employees are feeling about the workplace. We emphasize that engagement pulse tests be brief because long assessments tend to wear out employees and could impact the quality of information they provide.

These recommendations represent a top–down approach to engagement that starts with leadership. Organizations that take advantage of any of the top–down strategies we recommended, and combine them with daily acts of kindness that dignify employees, can realize higher levels of employee engagement. As we close this piece, in sum, we have come to understand that all people want is to do meaningful work in organizations that provide a work environment that is supportive, respectful, and positive, and where they feel their leaders and supervisors truly care about them as people and not as just mere employees; this fact remains the same regardless of industry.

Workplaces that reflect these attributes motivate employees to bring their full selves in the performance of their jobs—and this is the very essence of employee engagement. While leaders may have grown used to the idea that creating a positive work environment is an expensive endeavor, it is high time that we dissociate from this idea. Consider the transformative power of treating others with dignity, respect, and kindness, and elevating the experiences that matter. Following these simple guidelines, organizations of all types and sizes can lay the foundation on which to build a more positive work environment that leads to higher levels of engagement.

REFERENCES

Demerouti, E., Bakker, A. B., & Fried, Y. (2012). Work orientations in the job demands-resources model. *Journal of Managerial Psychology, 27*(6), 557–575. https://doi.org/10.1108/02683941211252428

Harter, J. K., Schmidt, F. L., & Hayes, T. L. (2002). Business-unit-level relationship between employee satisfaction, employee engagement, and business outcomes: A meta-analysis. *Journal of Applied Psychology, 87*(2), 268–279. https://doi.org/10.1037/0021-9010.87.2.268

Hewitt, A. (2015). *Actively disengaged and staying: Dealing with prisoners in the workplace.* Retrieved from https://www.hrdive.com/spons/actively-disengaged-and-staying-dealing-with-prisoners-in-the-workplace/429022/

Kelleher, B. (2013). *Employee engagement for dummies.* Hoboken, NJ: Wiley.

Sheridan, K. (2017, March 31). *Employee engagement: The disengaged employee* [Video File]. Retrieved from https://www.youtube.com/watch?v=d3bquNLC30A

Shuck, B. (2013). Invited reaction: Further observations on the relationship between work engagement and performance: A review of empirical literature and a proposed research agenda. *Human Resource Development Review, 12*(3), 277–283. https://doi.org/10.1177/1534484312470804

Shuck, B., Adelson, J. L., & Reio, T. G. (2017). The employee engagement scale: Initial evidence for construct validity and implications for theory and practice. *Human Resource Management, 56*(6), 953–977. https://doi.org/10.1002/hrm.21811

Shuck, B., Osam, K., Zigarmi, D., & Nimon, K. (2017). Definitional and conceptual muddling: Identifying the positionality of employee engagement and defining the construct. *Human Resource Development Review, 16*(3), 263–293. https://doi.org/10.1177/1534484317720622

Wagner, R. (2015). *Widgets: The 12 new rules for managing your employees as if they're real people.* New York, NY: McGraw Hill.

CHAPTER 21

CULTURE BY DESIGN

A Case Study in Transformational Change

Diane Banic

As more and more companies expand their operations domestically and globally, the need to understand their own culture and the culture of other companies becomes paramount. Executives are often confounded by culture because much of it is anchored in unspoken behaviors, mindsets, and social patterns. However, culture is evident in the behaviors of employees, visible in the "way work gets done," and in the daily practices of staff. As a concept, culture can help us better understand hidden and complex aspects of organizational life.

Many leaders let culture go unmanaged, not realizing that if properly managed, culture can help them build organizations that will thrive in even the most difficult times. Organizations are increasingly focused on learning, critical thinking, innovation, and adaptation in response to technological advances and social change. Change can happen quickly, and today's organizations want to be nimble, flexible, and resilient or they may face extinction.

From Discord to Harmony, pages 367–381

As companies expand, recruit, and hire new employees, these individuals enter with pre-existing frameworks for thinking about work and how work gets done as well as expected behaviors and values. Blending them into the existing culture can be planned or left to chance. Some may stay if their values and assumptions fit the new culture; some may leave within a year if the stretch is too much. It takes time for a new culture to evolve, taking as long as ten years after many trials and adjustments. Once one is immersed in studying a culture then there is an understanding of it. Then, you can set the stage for something new to evolve, with new assumptions and new behaviors.

CULTURAL PERSPECTIVE ON ORGANIZATIONS

The concept of organizational culture was in common use in the 1980s. Organizational research originally focused strongly on the surveying of corporate climate, but in the 1980s the organizational climate concept was to some extent replaced by the concept of organizational culture. It was in 1997 that I became involved with transforming corporate culture. I secured a position with a 5,000-employee company led by a CEO who supported change throughout the organization. As a member of the development team, I was tasked with initiating leadership and organizational development. Since companies were just waking up to the concept of organizational culture and culture change, I began to research the topic to understand how to implement change throughout the company I was working with. That is when I attended a workshop on Organizational Culture presented by Dr. Edgar Schein. His model has guided my work with several different companies within various industries.

WHAT IS ORGANIZATIONAL CULTURE?

Organizational culture can be defined as an enduring set of values, beliefs, and assumptions that characterize the organization and its members (Schein, 1984, 1992, 2006, 2010). Dr. Schein has been a leading researcher of the interplay between the individual conscience and the collective consciousness in business and organizations (Senge, Roberts, Ross, Roth, & Smith, 1999). According to Schein's theory (Schein, 1984, 1992, 2010) group members learn patterns of shared basic assumptions as a way to solve problems, and these assumptions are then taught to new members as a correct way to perceive, think, and feel in relation to those problems. Culture regulates organizational behavior or group behavior, and influences individual performance (Schein, 2016). Schein considered organizational

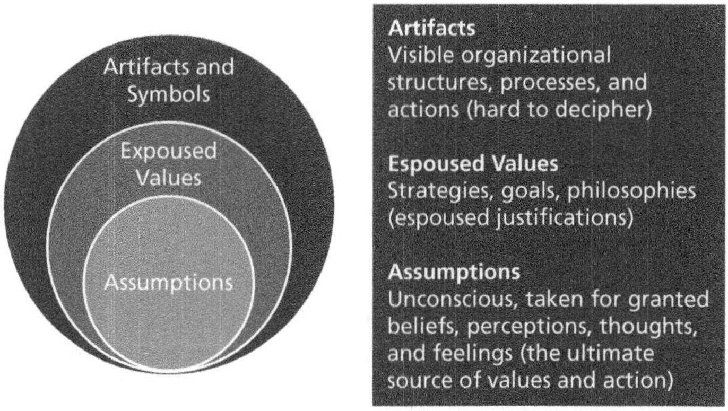

Figure 21.1 Illustration of Schein's (1992) model of organizational culture.

culture to be a three-layered phenomenon which can be examined on different levels. Schein's (1992) model of organizational culture is illustrated in Figure 21.1.

Artifacts and Symbols: Level I

The first level of culture consists of *visible* organizational processes and various artifacts that mark the surface of the organization (Schein, 1984). They are the noticeable fundamentals in the organization such as logos, architecture, structure, processes, and corporate clothing. These are not only visible to the employees, but also visible and recognizable to external visitors.

What are some artifacts in organizations? Dress codes, the general cleanliness of the workplace, various quality systems, information systems, and databases connected with safety and operations (Reason, 1997) are all artifacts. Likewise, cultural artifacts include accident statistics, sick leave, and turnover statistics which are interpreted and used to form conclusions about the deeper characteristics of an organization's culture.

According to Schein (2010), this first level of culture is difficult to interpret because it represents the most superficial cultural phenomena (i.e., only reflections of the true corporate culture). Behavior, which is a cultural artifact, is also influenced by countless factors other than a company's culture (Schein, 2010).

As I reflect on the companies I have worked with, I recall impressions I had as I drove into the parking lot and vividly remember the entrances into the buildings. Some had a uniformed guard at the front desk. As a visitor, I had to wait to be escorted up to the meeting area. The senior leadership team was located on the top floor of the building. I remember the pictures on the walls, seating arrangements, and office layouts. These were all artifacts—observable signals of the organization's way of life. I have found that the best way to make culture "conscious" is to ask new employees: "What details struck you?" and "What procedures and rules were noticeable your first week of work?"

Espoused Values: Level II

The second cultural level in the Schein model consists of the organization's espoused values (Schein, 1984). Values are important and lasting beliefs shared by the members of a culture about what is good or bad, desirable or undesirable. Values have a major influence on an employee's behavior and attitude, and serve as broad guidelines of acceptable behavior within the organization (BusinessDictionary.com). These are apparent in the organization's official objectives, declared norms, rules of conduct, standards, and operating philosophy. Some common business values are fairness, innovation, diversity, inclusion, teamwork, and community involvement.

Espoused values, however, do not always reflect a company's everyday operations. Problems arise when the values of managers are not in line with the basic assumptions of the organization. I've seen this displayed when a manager states to employees, "They (i.e., upper management) said we have to do this." A statement such as this indicates dispersant views between upper and lower levels of management. This can also be noticed when departments unconsciously use words that imply us and them.

It is important to understand what the philosophies are behind the organizational structure and how visible these structures support values. In a Scottish firm I had the pleasure to visit, the only closed doors (which were glass) were meeting rooms. All other work areas were located in the center of the room. There were few assigned desks, with the vice president of the division seated at any open desk that was available. Posted in the lunch room were targets, goals, results, and the values that guide the company. The absence of hierarchy, open communication, and cooperation were evident in the actual layout of the corporate offices. This was in contrast with the organizations I have experienced with private offices and closed doors.

Underlying Assumptions: Level III

Most important in terms of operations is the culture's deepest level; namely, its underlying assumptions (Figure 21.1; Schein, 1984, 2006, 2010, 2016). Basic underlying assumptions are deeply embedded in the organizational culture, and are experienced as self-evident and unconscious behavior. Assumptions are hard to recognize from within the organization precisely because they become unconscious habits.

Underlying assumptions relate to the group's learned solutions to problems and how they adapt. These solutions gradually become self-evident assumptions that cannot be called into question later. You might hear, "That's how we do things around here." Tasks and objectives are implemented and assessed. Solutions to problems have to be found so that members of the organization can function together in an organized and predictable working community (Schein, 2006). Over time, a common language helps to form an identity. I have seen this in the acronyms and "nick names" used in companies for products, procedures, and customers.

Deeper underlying assumptions relate to views of human nature. Are people good or bad, changeable or immutable, proactive or reactive? Should emotions be expressed or suppressed at work? All these assumptions come into play under our consciousness. Douglas McGregor's 1960 book, *The Human Side of Enterprise*, had a profound influence on education practices. McGregor (1960) articulated two beliefs still common today, but rarely talked about. Theory X posits that people are basically lazy, uninterested, and don't want to take responsibility, so management must take the lead and create rules and rewards, and punish those who are inherently bad (McGregor, 1960). Theory Y suggests that humans are complex and basically good and those employees should be trusted and empowered. If someone messes up, the structure or processes are partially at fault. The individual is given a second chance, and the benefit of the doubt.

Recently, a newly hired manager stated in the break room that employees need to be pushed and watched or they will slack off. This is an ingrained belief that "popped out" and caught my attention. Deeper underlying assumptions about human nature are strongly influenced by national and geographical culture. One can assume that the deeper underlying assumptions influence how the members of an organization perceive, think, and feel in matters relating to the organization.

Our lives are made up of what we are taught and what we experience in life. We have background conversations that influence our thinking. This includes but is not limited to assumptions we are aware we are making and background assumptions we do not even know we have. These background conversations help us to make sense of the world and to notice discrepancies and dichotomies. A culture's explanation for events and ideas about what those events mean are running in the background. Often, the meaning of a common view of reality is based on incomplete information. Our acquired knowledge, which comes from our teachers, parents, bosses, colleagues, and our past experiences, helps us make sense of our world. Simply put, we gain perspective of a situation through our lived history. Remembering and looking back are a primary source of meaning. These structures of interpretation are often widely shared, and greatly influence our behavior and the culture of an organization. It becomes evident that underlying assumptions are not static; culture is the creation and recreation of shared reality.

Anyone who has spent time in an organization recognizes that there are inconsistencies and unintended consequences between values, actions, and decisions. Actions are influenced by situation-specific and individual factors (Schein, 2016). Espoused norms and an organization's official rules may, however, be in conflict with every day (artifact level) actions. Thus, they can also be in conflict with the underlying assumptions, which in the end direct these actions. Many organizations espouse teamwork as a theme in the workplace, yet it is often acted out as "my team vs. your team."

Often, competitive goals for one business line or unit versus another may undermine the larger goals set for the total company. Organizations may not necessarily perceive this conflict themselves or they may even actively deny its existence. The challenge is to bring to the surface hidden attitudes that trigger the contradictions. For example, if a company increases sales without also increasing human resources, extended overtime can eventually affect an employee's performance.

Although Schein's theory has been criticized (Deal & Kennedy, 1983), it does cover the central elements of culture well, namely that culture is holistic, partly unconscious, and learned. By reducing uncertainty and ambiguity experienced in an environment, the organization integrates and maintains its capacity to operate. Organizational culture, therefore, is not merely a single new variable which describes organizations or can be examined separately from the other variables that affect an organization's activities, such as the structure, strategy, market orientation, and the technology it uses.

SUB CULTURES

Most leaders of organizations would agree that unity and functionality of the culture is a worthy goal. However, theories about the unity of culture have been undermined by showing that various subcultures are evident in organizations. The *Oxford English Dictionary* defines a subculture as "a cultural group within a larger culture, often having a common set of values, or a common experience, that differs from the majority culture in a way that is significant to them" ("Subculture," n.d.). One type of subculture is a professional subculture. An example is a finance team. Your finance team likely has shared experiences and values related to their professional training and their individual identity as accounting and finance professionals. This experience may be slightly at odds with an organization's dominant culture, such as if it emphasizes innovation and creativity (i.e., "move fast and break things"). As a result, a subculture may arise in the finance team that guides their day-to-day behavior in a manner that better suits their professional values and obligations.

As companies attempt to speed up processes and delivery of products, they are discovering that problems once viewed as communication failures or lack of teamwork are more a function of a breakdown of sub-cultural boundaries. Employees identify with different groups within the organization. These groups can form on the basis of age, gender, education, and department. Subcultures are distinguished from each other, among other things, according to how a group perceives its role in the organization, and the significance of the other subcultures within the company and within society at large.

Subcultures may have their own rituals and traditions that may be quite different than the organization's core values. For example, an organization built around teamwork and sharing information may not mesh with a subculture that thrives on competition and aggressiveness. As already mentioned, I have observed this phenomena developing between departments and work groups. Employees from different functions in a company may think that their functional areas are most important—the ones that drive the organization. Often, competition develops between these silos. I have observed this in the medical field, between pre-operations, surgery, and post-operations, and in manufacturing between sales, engineering, and production. If these subcultures are known but not addressed, they can cause serious challenges for leadership. It manifests in the language spoken, with members implying "we are more important than them." However, when an organization functions as a unit, when all are pulling together for a common goal, magic happens. But, staying in the sweet spot takes cooperation and collaborative leadership.

Jim Collins (2001), in his ground-breaking book *Good to Great,* summed up this matter by stating that cultures are historically developed, socially maintained, and individually interpreted. Every culture, however, has an inbuilt tendency to unify behavior. This happens by creating common norms and a shared social identity. The norms determine how one ought to behave in each situation and role. A new employee infers from the group members the norms that guide actions and behaviors. Is lunch 30 minutes or can I stretch it to 45 minutes? Can I park my car in the front lot or do I need to park on the street? These norms are conscious; many are unconscious (i.e., underlying assumptions). Some members have a more powerful influence than others in forming acceptable norms. I have overheard employees telling a new hire, "Don't work so fast, you'll make the rest of us look bad"; or "The open door policy isn't really open. Keep your head down or you may get it chopped off."

ALIGNING CULTURE AND LEADERSHIP

As a student of organizational culture, I believe that founders have a significant impact on early organizational culture. They play a key role as creators of a culture's underlying assumptions. Over time, norms develop that are consistent with these values. The character and behaviors of top executives can have a strong effect on culture. Groysberg, Lee, Price, and Cheng's (2018) research showed that lack of cultural fit is responsible for up to 68% of new-hire failures at the senior leadership level, and that for individual leaders, cultural fit is as important as capabilities and experience.

Schein and others who study organizational culture believe that cultures begin with leaders who impose their own values and assumptions on a group (Cameron & Quinn, 2011; Schein 2006). If these values and assumptions lead to success in the organization, these assumptions are taken for granted and will be accepted and taught to new members. But if the organization runs into situations that challenge cultural assumptions, leadership needs to step outside the culture and examine their own values (Schein, 2016).

Culture manifests itself in a variety of ways, including leadership behaviors, degree of hierarchy, sense of urgency, communication styles, nonverbal language, people versus task orientation, and even how and if the company takes time to celebrate. In addition, leaders must simultaneously consider culture styles and key organizational and market conditions if they want their culture to help drive performance (Groysberg et al., 2018). Any culture change process must have buy-in from top leadership in order to have successful outcomes.

THE INDIVIDUAL

It is self-evident that culture is made up of individuals that bring with them their own views of life, of work, and how things get done in a company. There are differences in the motives of individuals to do work. Some seek security from an organization while others look for challenges and risks. These individual factors have an influence on how an organization's culture is experienced (Cameron & Quinn, 2011). Social identity is an important source of self-esteem for individuals, and a binding force for the group. Maybe that is why, over the years, logo shirts, caps, and other paraphernalia have been used to represent a binding identity to the outside world. Because one tends to see oneself in a slightly more positive light than reality, this identification with the group also emphasizes those sides of the group which are seen as positive and strong. Culture can blend the intentions of top leaders with the knowledge and experience of all levels of employees.

CULTURAL EVOLUTION—ASSESSING AND CHANGING ORGANIZATIONAL CULTURE: A CASE STUDY

The remainder of this chapter outlines the culture change process carried out at a surgery center/hospital in the Midwest United States. The initiative to assess and create culture came from the very top, a CEO who had a financial and management background and saw the bigger picture. To better serve the needs of patients, referring physicians, and surgeons, the organization enlarged its medical campus, added specialty services, and expanded into the urgent care business line during this project. I had worked with the management team for 2 years prior to this initiative, meeting quarterly with the organization to focus on leadership development, professionalism, and team building. During this project there was minimal turnover of personnel; however, turnover did occur in human resource leadership. Because HR played a key role in planning and implementing the project, each time turnover occurred, the incoming leader had to be brought into the project and brought up to speed quickly.

The blueprint for planning and implementing the culture change effort was divided into data collection, plan development, and implementation phases. As the organization expanded and moved into additional areas of health care, the CEO wanted to design a culture employees could be proud of. He realized that not everything was working well, and he wanted to include all levels of the organization in creating the future culture. Consciously creating corporate culture is one of the most strategic actions leadership can take because the underlying beliefs, values, and norms that define a culture shape strategy. We knew that to be effective, designing the culture must be applied to all levels to support and align everyone. The goal of creating standards is expected to be followed by all.

Data Collection Phase

Even before we began to collect information from all levels of the organization, we devised a strategy/plan to guide the collection of data and involve key members of the organization. In this culture transformation process, we began with an offsite meeting with the management team. We had already initiated team building sessions with this team to begin opening the lines of communication with a focus on insight-oriented leadership development. To assess readiness for change, we asked the question, "Why would you need to change your culture at all?" In this health care setting, the managers identified concrete business challenges that might bring them to a cultural impasse, including:

- loss of patient volume,
- lack of physician commitment,
- poor survey results,
- patient complaints about staff,
- staff complaints about policies or how they are treated,
- physician complaints about staff actions and/or attitudes, and
- desire to create the future.

The Power of Involvement: Why Do We Care About People?

After clarifying purpose with the leadership team, we put together a plan to diagnose culture and determine cultural assets and liabilities. Analysis of key documents, such as organizational structure, gave us a picture of the main recorded artifacts. We wanted to involve as many stakeholder groups as possible in the process, to include leaders, managers, physicians, employees, patients, and patient's families. Through focus groups and interviews with members of these subgroups, we were able to gather relevant information about the current state, and to determine which norms and values to keep and which ones need to be addressed to create the desired future.

In the process, we wanted to know what was working and why. Many times, the employee focus groups touted leadership as a strong positive force and inconsistent policies and procedures as an area of concern. As a way to bring accountability into the groups, we asked individuals what they could do to strengthen what was not working. In the end, a change in culture depends on implementing behaviors in the organization that reinforce the new cultural values and are consistent with them. Unless the change process becomes personalized, individuals are willing to engage in new behaviors, and the managerial competencies demonstrated in the organization are altered, the fundamental culture will not change. Habits are hard to break. Without personal behavior change on the part of the organization's members, culture change would be frustrated.

Once we established the current state, the next challenge was to define the culture two to three years in the future. To accomplish this, we facilitated an imaginary trip into the future. Participants were asked to describe the desired future culture with positive outcomes for employees, patients, and physicians. Rather than engaging in an intellectual discussion, the facilitators moved to a more somatic level of inquiry, asking participants to imagine an ideal culture from their perspective and that of the community at large. What would the organization feel like? What might they observe inside the campus and outside in the community? We wanted the participants to experience through imagery the organization as they thought it could be. The final step was to identify key value to permeate the future organizational culture.

We wanted to obtain data from a variety of stakeholders, not just hospital staff. The structured interviews of patients, their families, and physicians gave us more data from various perspectives, providing an opportunity for themes to emerge that supported or detracted from current values and practices. For physicians, quality care embodied surgery cases that flow smoothly and efficiently, where they have needed supplies, including access to operating facilities. For physicians, they wanted their patients and the patient's families cared for, from pre-admissions testing to discharge. For both patients and physicians, clean and safe surgery and recovery rooms were a minimum requirement for quality care. This data was collected then combined into a feedback report for the company leaders and board of directors.

At this point, we had enough data to move forward with an action plan to close the gap between the current state and future state. This organization's desire was to include as many stakeholders as possible in the cultural transformation process so research was performed to evaluate the culture assessments on the market versus devising our own survey. The Organizational Culture Inventory (OCI) development by Robert A. Cooke, PhD and J. Clayton Lafferty, PhD was our first choice, but was too costly. The OCI measures the attributes of organizational culture (above and beyond company culture, workplace culture, and corporate culture) most closely related to the behavior and performance of members. It reveals what members collectively believe is expected of them and how those behavioral norms influence their engagement and effectiveness.

An additional assessment tool we investigated was the Organizational Culture Assessment Instrument (OCAI) developed by Cameron and Quinn (2011). Based on the competing values framework, the OCIA uses four culture types: clan, adhocracy, market, and/or hierarchy culture. We found that the competing values culture framework didn't have meaning for this organization because the categories or types did not fit this organization. We had to come up with a new, creative plan. After meeting with the CEO and other key leaders, the decision was made to review the information we collected from stakeholders and move into defining behaviors that would reinforce the desired culture. Where a difference arose between the desired and the prevailing culture, scenarios were designed as interventions to define behaviors.

In all my years of work in organizations, I find that it is never easy to change an individual's behavior, let alone change the culture of an organization. When I see articles or books written about how to change, I realize that few companies are willing to do the work required. This is usually due to leadership at the top of the organization departing or new business challenges arising that take precedence so the emphasis on culture is put on the back burner. However, this was not the case with this hospital system.

INDIVIDUAL CHANGE: THE KEY TO CULTURE

When it comes to organizational change, the constraints of the past are built into the change process. There often in a heavy drag or resistance when trying to drive culture change. Transformation is based on the assertion that the future is generated through actions taken in the present moment. The prerequisite is a willingness to identify and surface fundamental beliefs and mental constraints that underpin an organization's competitive success.

Cultural change is a *transformation process*; behavior must be unlearned first before new behavior can be learned in its place. Without personal behavior change on the part of the organization's members, culture change will be frustrated. In the end, a change in culture depends on implementing behaviors in the organization that reinforce the new cultural values and are consistent with them. Individuals have their own inner lives, populated by their beliefs, priorities, values, and fears. These interior elements vary from person to person, directing people to behave differently. Interestingly, most people aren't aware that their choices are based on their beliefs or that their inner dynamics drive what they support, what they do, and what they say. Vip Vyas (2018), a thought partner with Distinctive Performance, stated that from a practical standpoint, the hidden part of the iceberg shows up in the ideas and conversations that are considered safe versus unsafe (http://knowledge.insead.edu).

Habits are hard to break, partly because when habits are well established they become unconscious. If habits are not recognized and understood, they cannot be changed. In his book *The Power of Habit*, Charles Duhigg (2012) brought to bear what Skinner discovered long ago. By putting together a cue, a routine, and a reward, and then cultivating a craving that drives the loop, a new habit is created. Duhigg suggested that you can't extinguish a bad habit; you can only change it by changing the routine. But, most of the time we are unaware of our mechanical nature, the habit, the routine, and the underlying somatic aspects that have occurred for so long. We don't pay attention to what causes it anymore. When consciousness is brought to the habit, it acts as a catalyst to help us understand our own unconscious behavior. I find when coaching managers or employees, they are often unaware of how they affect others. They justify their behavior while pointing out the flaws in others, their leaders, and the organization.

Determine Your Supporters and the Nay-Sayers

When change is introduced to a group of people, there are those who support and those who find all the reasons why the new process, the combination of teams, or the innovative change won't work. Most leaders experience resistance when trying to drive a transformation. Fear can weigh heavily on one's thoughts, and paralyzes actions to support any kind of culture change. The question that is underground and in each person's mind is, "How will this affect me"? If an employee becomes stuck in a pit of fear, he or she will be unable to think or function. Often, the questions feeding the fear are: "Will I lose my job?" and "How will I maintain myself and my family if the company changes course and I am not needed anymore"? Fear also severely hinders creative abilities. When a new leader comes into an organization, those employees who are negative or constantly fearful can feel exceptionally threatened. Keeping employees informed and involved with the culture change, through employee meetings, can relieve the fear and allow more positive responses to the fear. Allowing employees to express their difficult emotions without judgement can move them along the change curve. Employees being heard can go a long way in their adjusting to and supporting a change, a different strategy, or a totally new vision for the company. Fear driven leadership approaches kill the possibility of authentic dialogue within the business.

ENGAGE SENIOR LEADERSHIP TO LOOK INWARD AND OUTWARD

In our work with organizations undertaking cultural transformations, we've found that the best way to achieve the company's aspirations is for leaders to combine looking outward (linking strategy and vision) to genuine self-discovery and self-development. Looking inward allows leaders to examine their own modes of operating—what makes them tick. Those in leadership positions who look at their internal experiences can understand precisely how their motives and inner drives affect how they behave and take action.

Self-awareness is not a given with leaders. Awareness involves perception of a wide range of inner experiences and their impact on behavior. These include current mind-set and beliefs, hopes and fears, and desires and defenses. A pre-requisite for transformation is the willingness to identify and surface fundamental beliefs and mental constraints that underpin a company's competitive success. Guiding questions are: "What can generate a fundamental shift in perspective that can activate imagination?"; "What else is possible?"; and "How can this be adapted?"

While many leaders recognize their tendency to exhibit negative behaviors under pressure, they don't often realize they are displaying these behaviors until well after they have done so. Emotional intelligence (EI) is a process that can be learned. EI is a practice of becoming aware of what is going on inside oneself, and responding versus reacting to internal cues. Learning to alter behavior when one is still capable of affecting the outcome, and not overreacting to events because they are reminiscent of something in the past, develops EI. Staying in the present, in real time, then shifting one's attention to the inner state is accomplished by sensing the body. This takes practice, commitment, and follow-up, usually by an experienced professional. If not observed, the old behavior soon returns. New mental connections strengthen the behavior until it becomes part of a belief system which others can experience and absorb. Learning to look within while transforming an organization's culture tends to accelerate the pace and depth of the change dramatically. Closing the disparity between what the leaders know they should do or say to behave successfully and what they actually do affect those they lead. Developing character, an unfaltering aim, and discipline will pay off and sustain the effort through the dark times. It's a journey. It is a choice.

REFERENCES

Cameron, K., & Quinn, R. E. (2011). *Diagnosing and changing organizational culture: Based on the competing values framework* (3rd ed.). San Francisco, CA: Jossey-Bass.

Collins, J. (2001). *Good to great: Why some companies make the leap and others don't.* New York, NY: Harper Business Books.

Deal, T., & Kennedy, A. (1983). Culture: A new look through old lenses. *The Journal of Applied Behavioral Science, 19*(4), 498–505.

Duhigg, C. (2012). *The power of habit: Why we do what we do in life and business.* New York, NY: Random House.

Groysberg, B., Lee, J., Price, J., & Cheng, J. Y. (2018). The leader's guide to corporate culture. *Harvard Business Review, 96*(1), 44–52.

McGregor, D. (1960). *The human side of enterprise.* New York, NY: McGraw-Hill.

Reason, J. (1997). *Managing the risks of organizational accidents.* Burlington, VT: Ashgate.

Schein, E. H. (1984). Coming to a new awareness of organizational culture. *Sloan Management Review, 25*(2), 3–17.

Schein, E. (1992). *Organizational culture and leadership.* San Francisco, CA: Jossey-Bass.

Schein, E. (1996). Culture: The missing concept in organizational studies. *Administrative Science Quarterly, 41*(2), 229–240.

Schein, E. (2006). *Organizational culture and leadership* (3rd ed.). San Francisco, CA: Josey-Bass.

Schein, E. (2010). *Organizational culture and leadership* (4th ed.). San Francisco, CA: Jossey-Bass.

Schein, E. (2016). *Organizational culture and leadership* (5th ed.). San Francisco, CA: Jossey- Bass.

Senge, P., Roberts, C., Ross, R., Roth, G., & Smith, B. (1999). *The dance of change: The challenge of sustaining momentum in learning organizations.* New York, NY: Random House.

Subculture. (n.d.). In *Oxford English Dictionary.*

Vyas, V. (2018, August 8). *Aim for transformation, not change* (Leadership and Organizations). Retrieved from https://knowledge.insead.edu/blog/insead-blog/aim-for-transformation-not-change-9866

CHAPTER 22

THE EVOLUTION OF ETHICAL LEADERS AND ORGANIZATIONS

Marilyn Faulkenburg

Ethical leadership has become a topic of discussion and focus in many organizations and companies. The definition of ethical leadership has continually been refined. The definition by Brown, Trevino, and Harrison (2005) and Kalshoven, Den Hartog, and De Hoogh (2011) redefined ethical leadership as a multi-dimensional construct that has seven distinct dimensions: fair treatment, power sharing, role clarification, people orientation, integrity, ethical guidance, and concern for sustainability. As the focus becomes more intense, ethical leaders need to establish a positive environment at three levels: individual, the team, and the overall organization (Villanova University, 2015). By focusing on all three levels, the leader is more able to develop a positive and ethical organization overall.

In this chapter, I explain specific examples of ethical and unethical leadership that I have experienced over my 40 year career, and how each of these experiences relate to the levels leaders should be focusing on to create a positive environment. I conclude with some strategies leaders could implement in their quest to develop an ethical organization.

From Discord to Harmony, pages 383–390

FOCUS ON THE INDIVIDUAL

The first level a leader should focus on is the individual, and creating an open line of communication and support with each employee. In order for a leader to develop a strong and successful relationship with an employee, there are key qualities that need to be addressed. One of those qualities is trust. It takes time and effort to build trust, and you can lose this trust within a split second (Goman, 2017). The following things can help build trust: Be an open and effective communicator, don't set up employees to fail, lead by example and demonstrate you can be trusted, and be transparent and show heart (Coveney, 2018). A personal example will help explain the impact of developing an open line of communication and environment of trust:

> I began my career at the young age of 21 after graduating from college, and was given the opportunity to be in a manager role. At this age, I had very little experience in supervising others, but I did have a keen ability to lead others. I was placed in a management training program and in six months I was a manager. I worked for a small chain of discount department stores, and here is where I encountered my first experience with a person who was unethical. I was one of three assistant managers, with one of the managers over operations and two over merchandising. I was a merchandise manager. I had forged a good working relationship with the store manager who acted as a mentor to me. The operations manager was 30 years older than me and had been with the company for ten years. We worked with an outside vendor on disposing of large lots of clearance merchandise that were taking up space in the store. I understood the process on how we were to work with the vendor. However, the outside vendor only seemed to come in when the store manager was not there, and would then work exclusively with the operation manager. I watched this for 3 or 4 months, and I thought it was odd that no other manager was included in the transaction with the vendor. It was totally the discretion of the operations manager as to what price we received for the clearance merchandise. One night, I was closing the store and I had to get something from the operations manager's desk drawer. When I opened the desk drawer, I found a stack of checks from the outside vendor that had never been deposited. I was surprised to find the checks since we had a procedure on how to handle the checks. I thought about what to do with this information for about a week. I knew it was wrong and I knew I had to tell the store manager, but I did not want to get the operations manager in trouble. After thinking about it for a week, I told the store manager what I found and he was very surprised. An investigation ensued. The outcome was the termination of the operations manager. I was also commended by the store manager for coming forth and telling him about the checks and he thanked me. That was my first big world experience with ethics.

I know I would have never decided to tell the store manager about this incident unless he had established an open line of communication and trust with me. By developing an individual relationship with me, the store manager created a positive environment and an overall ethical organization.

FOCUS ON THE TEAM

The next level the leader should focus on is the team. In a team environment, the leader is leading by example. Leadership means that a leader should act ethically at all times, which sets the standard for others to follow. Leaders are in a unique position above their staff, and they should inspire others to do the right thing (Halvorson, 2014). In my career, I have experienced leaders who did not exhibit ethical behavior. Some examples are: promotion of employees who were not as capable as others but were favored by higher management, and termination of employment of individuals who were capable but again not favored by higher management. When the leader led the promotion or the termination, or condoned the decision, he/she was not leading by example. This type of leader behavior can lead to more unethical behavior by those who are not the leader.

If a leader does not lead ethically, then the team members will either follow the leader's example and possibly act unethically, or decide to leave the organization. I experienced unethical behavior that ultimately caused me to make the decision to leave the organization:

> I worked at a large casino and experienced unethical behavior by leaders. The casino had been open for 4 years, and had remained non-union even though it was located by a city with a long history of unions, and after numerous attempts to unionize the casino workers. I had never worked in or with a union and had no experience in this arena. One day, the general manager informed me we were flying on a private jet to Las Vegas to meet with the CEO of the company. The CEO told us there were some new restaurants coming into Las Vegas with high-end chefs and they did not want to work with the unions. They had met with the union and decided the new restaurants could open without the union if the corporation compensated with the headcount in a different location. The CEO decided the headcount would come from the casino 2,000 miles away. They had signed an agreement stating we would no contest the unions and they may organize the workers. This was quite a shock since we had worked hard for 4 years to keep the unions out. The general manager and I were not given a voice in the matter, and we returned to the casino. Upon our return, we explained the agreement to the supervisors and managers. Many were upset and decided to leave the company. We trained the supervisor and managers on exactly what they could and could not do, and the union organization began. There were three unions who were organizing four different areas of casino workers. Usually, there would be four different contracts, but we had only one contract for all unions since one group of workers were opposed to the union and they would not vote for

> the contract. When all were combined into one contract, the union contract would be ratified.
>
> The next big step in the process was writing the union contract. Since I had no experience in writing a union contract, I was sent to Las Vegas for a week to train. An attorney from New York was also sent to help us write the contract. When the attorney showed up, he had on a light blue leisure suit. At the time, I thought it was odd that he was dressed in clothes from the 1960s. Each month that he came back, though, he dressed better and better, and by the last meeting he was in a very expensive silk suit. I think this was very intentional and used to win over the employees. When we began the process of writing the union contract, the skeleton was basically the current policies and procedures. We were to meet and discuss the contract, and an employee representative from each area was present. The night before the meeting, the union representatives, the attorney, and I met. I witnessed a discussion of them deciding what the contract would be and how each of them would act out an argument to make it look like they were not agreeing but they already had decided on the contract. I was taken back by this, but was told that this is the way it is done. The contract negotiations continued for 6 months, and each month the "act" was displayed by the union representatives and attorney. During the time the contract was being negotiated, the casino was bought by a major competitor. This was not a merger, but a complete buyout. When a company is bought by another company, all contracts go with the sale of the company. The employees were not told this. They were told if they ratify the completed union contract, the unions and attorney will ensure that the employees keep their jobs and that the contract will stay in place. The contract was ratified. The ironic part was there were 25 employees laid off the next week due to a change in the process of cashing out customer winnings. The process went coinless and fewer employees were needed. The union contract did not protect their jobs.

There were many unethical things that happened during the unionization process, and I knew then that I would not be with this company for long—I left less than a year later. I knew I was not in a position to change how the company worked with the unions, but I also knew I could not work in that type of environment. The leaders did not act ethically, which led to me and many others leaving the organization.

FOCUS ON THE OVERALL ORGANIZATION

The third area the leader should focus on is the overall organization—building a sense of respect between leaders and employees and valuing each other's opinion. This leads to a healthy environment, and then to an ethical organization (Harned, 2017).

In this area of focus, I have encountered a lack of respect by leaders throughout my career. The lack of respect was displayed by the leader in the form of not listening to or valuing my opinion, lack of transparency, and personal disrespect.

> I taught at a variety of colleges and universities as an adjunct professor, and had the chance to meet with the chancellor of one of the community colleges in my local area. We began to converse about an opportunity at the community college to develop a leadership develop program for local businesses and organizations. I agreed to spearhead the program as this was an opportunity to share my passion for leadership development and impact the leadership talent in the community. When I began to develop the leadership program, I was told this was a service to the community since the community college's role was to be a partner with organizations in the community in workforce development. We did not discuss the profitability of the program except that it needed to break even. The program was developed, and I taught some of the classes offered. The organizations in the community were responsive to the new leadership development program, and the program's attendance was on track as planned. After a year of offering the program, the chancellor began to talk about the program making a profit, and stated that she was not going to continue the program unless this was possible. It appeared that the initial vision of service to the community and breaking even was no longer an option. At the same time, I was approached about taking another position with the college as the vice chancellor of Academic Affairs but I would not have still been over the leadership program. A faculty member was given the responsibility of the leadership program. The pressure continued for the program to turn a larger profit, and we proved to the chancellor the program was turning a profit. However, she said it was not sufficient and discontinued the program. I know decisions are made every day whether programs are continued or not, but this decision was detrimental to organizations in the community and our vision to be a partner in workforce development.

The lack of respect and transparency was evident, and was not only witnessed by me but by many others on the team. This led to an unhealthy team environment and a dysfunctional team. The erosion of a team will continue if the leader does not focus on mutual respect, valuing others' opinions, and displaying honesty and transparency.

Transparency is the key to fostering a culture of trust between leaders and their employees. Employees who are kept in the loop and understand their role in the overarching purpose and goals of the company are, understandably, more likely to put their trust in their employer. By fostering transparency, this will lead to better relationships, engagement, alignment, solutions, and, ultimately, an ethical organization. A reason leaders are not transparent is because they believe they will be viewed as less authoritative or will lose their power, leverage, and gravitas (Llopis, 2012). There are specific ways to promote transparency: tell the truth, encourage people to speak truth to power, reward mavericks, practice having tough conversations, tackle the culture, and share information freely (Leigh, 2017). This example explains the lack of transparency I encountered.

> I used to work as the director of a corporate college (established within a local community college) that focused on workforce development initiatives, which encompassed the development and offering of certification programs and non-credit courses. I took this position because I thought this would allow me to make an impact on workforce development, and envisioned the corporate college as a company within the community college. Throughout my 18 months in the position, I was introduced to a new level of unethical behavior. I had come from a corporate background where I had always been given the tools to do my job, and everything was transparent. I learned very quickly that was not how the community college operated. Since I was responsible for the operation of the corporate college, I wanted to ensure we broke even or turned a profit. I asked every month for the corporate college profit and loss statement, but was never given this information. I did not know until after I left this position that expenses were being dumped into the corporate college in order to shore up other departments, which resulted in the corporate college never showing a profit. This was a lack of transparency and, to me, is one of the most grievous forms of unethical behavior. I was continually told that the corporate college did not make a profit, but I was never given the information to try to impact the outcome. I was highly frustrated in this position, and when I was offered a full-time position at a local university to teach full time in their graduate school, I accepted their offer. When I spoke to the chancellor of the community college about this new opportunity, I was yelled at and told I was ungrateful—she said she could not understand why I would leave the community college. I reminded her that my intent when I entered into higher education was to teach, and then she agreed with my decision. However, she was concerned about how my exit would be perceived by the board of directors so she allowed me to explain my reason for leaving. I do think she was concerned I was going to tell the board about the experience I had in the corporate college.

In creating a healthy organization, the leader needs to focus on mutual respect, valuing others' opinions, and displaying honesty and transparency. Without a healthy organization, it is difficult to develop an ethical organization.

STRATEGIES FOR DEVELOPING AN ETHICAL ORGANIZATION

Throughout my career, I have experienced unethical behavior. I do think all of the behaviors were influenced by the leader. No matter how ethical a company tries to be or how many codes of conduct or ethics that are written, the buck stops with the leader. The leader cannot stop all unethical incidents, but I think they can do the following:

- *Set the stage. Walk the talk.* These are not just words, they have to be actions. If the leader respects work time, then the employees will. If the leader abuses work time, then the employees will. If the leader is deceptive and not transparent, the employees will be the same way. Leading by example creates an environment that fosters productivity (Duggan, 2018; Fine, 2014).
- *Talk about ethical behavior and what is and is not accep*table. If the organization has ethics training on an annual basis, the leader needs to be the first and last presenter. The leader needs to, again, set the stage and tell employees what is expected.
- *The leader needs to be fair and consistent.* If exceptions are made, then they become the baseline for the future. Even though the leader sometimes wants to make exceptions, they need to explain why they cannot. It is not easy, but can be done. All employees need to be treated with respect and dignity, regardless of their position in the organization. This will enable fair and equal opportunity for promotions, and prohibits discrimination (Duggan, 2018).
- *The leader needs to be respected and trusted.* How do you gain respect and trust? The first step is to know your employees on a personal basis. Show the employees you care about them as a person. Open up and let employees get to know you on a personal basis. An organizational leader who is reliable, willing to admit mistakes, and trustworthy gains subordinates' confidence in their leadership—they believe that leaders will keep their promises and will commit to the organization's goals (Duggan, 2018).
- *An ethical leader makes decisions carefully, and communicates in a timely manner.* A leader asks for and accepts input from subordinates, and uses the input in making decisions (Duggan, 2018).
- *Leaders should revisit the organization's code of ethics and/or code of conduct with the management team on an annual basis.* By leading this review, the leader is telling the entire management team that ethics is important.
- *Hire and develop ethical leaders.* I learned more from bad, unethical leaders than I ever learned from ethical leaders. I learned what not to do. I think by ensuring that the right ethical leader is hired and then trained, future leaders will learn from the best and not the worst leaders.

In my opinion, being ethical is a choice. However, I also believe people need to understand expectations and then be led to make ethical decisions. It can be a very slippery slope, but a company and leaders within the company can be ethical. Ethical leaders need to establish a positive environment at three levels: individual, the team, and the overall organization. By focusing on all three levels, the leader will develop a positive and ethical organization overall.

REFERENCES

Brown, M. E., Trevino, L. K., & Harrison, D. A. (2005). Ethical leadership: A social learning perspective for construct development and testing. *Organizational Behavior and Human Decision Process, 97*(2), 117–134. https://doi.org/10.1016/j.obhdp.2005.03.002

Coveney, N. (2018, January 4). *Five simple tips for building trust as a leader.* Retrieved from https://www.forbes.com/sites/forbescoachescouncil/2018/01/04/five-simple-tips-for-building-trust-as-a-leader/#39a6068a59bb

Duggan, T. (2018, April 18). *What are the key elements of ethical leadership in an organization?* Retrieved from https://yourbusiness.azcentral.com/key-elements-ethical-leadership-organization-8819.html

Fine, L. (2014, November 15). *Leading by example: Ethics begins at the top.* Retrieved from http://lawrencefine.com/businessethics/leading-by-example-ethics-begins-at-the-top/

Goman, C. K. (2017, November 27). *How leaders build—and destroy—trust.* Retrieved from https://www.forbes.com/sites/carolkinseygoman/2017/11/27/how-leaders-build-and-destroy-trust/#49c2229c40e5

Halvorson, H. G. (2014). *The most important skill for great leaders? Trustworthiness.* Retrieved from https://99u.adobe.com/articles/32883/the-most-important-skill-for-great-leaders-trustworthiness

Harned, P. J. (2017, December 14). *Lead by example: The many benefits of ethical leadership.* Retrieved from https://boardagenda.com/2017/12/14/benefits-ethical-leadership

Kalshoven, K., Den Hartog, D. N., & De Hoogh, A. H. B. (2011). Ethical leadership at work questionnaire (ELW): Development and validation of a multidimensional measure. *The Leadership Quarterly, 22*(1), 51–69.

Leigh, A. (2017, November 13). *Transparency in business: Time for leaders to fall in love with making it happen.* Retrieved from Ethical Leadership website http://www.ethical-leadership.co.uk/transparency-in-business/

Llopis, G. (2012, September 10). *5 powerful things happen when a leader is transparent.* Retrieved from Forbes website_https://www.forbes.com/sites/glennllopis/2012/09/10/5-powerful-things-happen-when-a-leader-is-transparent/#3ac23fe74a3a

Villanova University. (2015, January 7). *What is ethical leadership?* Retrieved from Villanova University website https://www.villanovau.com/resources/leadership/what-is-ethical-leadership/

CHAPTER 23

IN PURSUIT OF HARMONY

How a Shared Leadership Practice Works as a Conflict Management System

Alexia Georgakopoulos and Barb Allen

Creating harmony in the workplace is a lofty ideal and may even seem beyond reach given the reality of an increasingly diverse and ever-changing workforce, surging competition from around the globe, and relentless change. This new normal creates organizational conditions rife with conflict as competition for scarce resources intensifies, pressure to increase productivity escalates, and demand on people's capabilities expands. Contemporary organizational life is becoming progressively complex as leaders face unprecedented challenges and must be agile in finding innovative approaches to getting things accomplished; yet we are all-too-often operating within inherited conventional structures that are unfit and maladapted for the age in which we live. In fact, according to Manville and Ober (2003), "We're in a knowledge economy, but our managerial and governance systems are stuck in the Industrial Era. It's time for a whole new model (p. 48).

The stage is set for an entirely new way of being in organizations. Step back for a moment and visualize your organization as a complex, learning,

From Discord to Harmony, pages 391–419

self-correcting system practicing streamlined, open collaborative processes that reduce bureaucracy, solve difficult problems, generate innovative solutions, and build trusting and harmonious relationships. This chapter focuses on creating harmony in the workplace, but it cannot be implemented as a special one-off project. Harmony is a natural outcome of organizational systems in place designed to address the multiple needs of everyone in the organization. To attain real harmony, we have to institutionalize some structures that allow issues to be addressed and resolved productively. This chapter is divided into two parts. We first discuss the need to expand our thinking about conflict and leadership that flows to a conversation about the benefits of having a formal conflict management system (CMS) as a productive way to create a harmonious workplace. In part two, we then offer an elegant and artful approach to conflict resolution which ruthlessly dismantles sources of conflict inherent in conventional organizational structures, thereby paving the way for a more unified, cohesive, and harmonious work environment. Finally, we suggest ideas on how to get started in your own organization.

PART ONE: CONFLICT MANAGEMENT SYSTEMS

Expanding Our Ideas of Conflict Management and Leadership

Supporting harmony requires a significant shift in mainstream thinking about both leadership and conflict management in organizational settings. The key to this challenge is our ability to intentionally unlearn what we have learned about conventional leadership and conflict management, opening space in our minds to explore innovative and radically participative forms of leadership and conflict management to competently meet the unprecedented challenges of our time. Progressive leaders in today's thriving organizations are open to learning and in constant pursuit of truth—even if it comes from the janitor. They allow people to grow and develop their capabilities, understanding that—if the proper channels of expression are provided—these nascent capabilities will contribute to realizing the organizational mission. These leaders understand that they cannot possibly have all the answers and solutions to the increasingly complex issues their organizations face—and they don't pretend as if they do. They earnestly seek ways to tap into the latent potentialities of people within their organizations, knowing that the solutions can only be found through the collaborative interaction of diverse people. These leaders know if they design the proper system, the dormant forces within their organization can be unleashed. By intentionally opening our minds to rethink leadership and trying out new ways of behaving as leaders, we set ourselves and our organizations on a trajectory of perpetual evolution—an essential organizational capability in today's competitive landscape. This new path will teach us powerful lessons about ourselves and our impact on others, the workplace, and extend into the wider communities in which we live.

Embracing Conflict as an Opportunity

Conflict is a natural and inevitable fact of life. Anytime you have different people with diverse backgrounds come together, there will naturally be many ways of seeing things and doing things, especially when people are interdependent and must work together (Georgakopoulos, 2017). These clashes of opinions and practices have a tendency to take on destructive forms if there is not a process in place in which people are able to listen to and share with each other constructively and together work through issues. Enlightened leaders who hold harmony in the organization as a deliberative goal, understand that it cannot happen on its own, but that a system must be in place for issues to be worked through in a functional manner. When there is a system in which people are able to speak openly in a safe psychological space, conflict has a functional channel of expression and becomes a beautiful opportunity for creating more unified and resilient relationships when things get rough.

Shifting Our Mind-Sets

Organizations which are riddled with conflict at all levels of the hierarchy, may be the result of leaders who are using by default, an inherited mind-set about how to handle conflict. This conventional leadership mind-set comes in many forms. Ingrained in a hierarchical design comes the prescriptive command-and-control approach in which people with higher status tell people with lower status what to do. A conventional leadership mind-set believes that telling employees what the problem is and then prescribing the solution, is what an effective leader does. This power-over approach is anathema to leaders who use a power-with approach and who believe people are capable of identifying problems, developing solutions, and resolving their own conflicts, given the opportunity in a safe environment. Institutional blindness occurs when some organizational leaders look the other way as the organization is plagued with conflict, imagining that, somehow, their organization is immune to the detrimental consequences of failing to see it, name it, and design a system to address it. Some leaders fear the perception that conflict is a sign of weakness for them personally or for the organization which they represent. Other leaders see resolving conflict effectively as an impossible goal and something they are simply not willing to confront. Either these leaders don't see conflict as an opportunity to improve conditions, or they want to but don't know where to start so it gets pushed aside and nothing is done. Taking any of these stances, sets an apathetic tone in the organization and contributes to systemic dysfunction that permeates the entire organizational culture. From the onset of this chapter, we argue that leaders who want to transform their organizations into more responsive, agile, learning, functional, self-correcting, and unified workplaces must first look at the system that is producing their current results. Dismantling conventional organizational structures that impede communication, interaction, collaboration, creativity, and human connection—all sources of structural conflict by design—make way for functional channels of communication, interaction, and human connection.

This is most effectively accomplished through either formal CMSs or informal inclusive dialogic events in which conflict is not only addressed productively, but in the process something almost magical happens as people from all parts of the organization are invited to give voice and have choice in naming the issues and ultimately shaping the work they do together. An enlightened leader knows people want to give their best and be their best at work when they are respected and have agency over the work they do and influence over the path forward. Inclusive dialogic events communicate respect for all and invite people to work at the top of their intelligence—in all their dazzling diversity—addressing the complex issues they face together. Whether a formal CMS is used or an informal dialogic event, these spaces invite conflict and channel it into productive conversations which have the potential to improve conditions, as struggle begets progress, communication resolves misunderstandings, and continual feedback improves the system. Constructive conflict communication and enhanced interaction often lead to recognition and empowerment paving the way for interactional transformation (Bush & Folger, 2005). And if we can transform the nature of our relationships through dialogue and interaction, then harmony in the workplace has a real chance of being attainable.

Leaders have a choice in the way in which we engage and permit conflict to be addressed. We can draw upon the conventional mind-set using a power-over approach, which is ultimately destructive and disenfranchising, or, we can expand our understanding and believe everyone is capable of leadership and that it is up to us to make space and time for those latent potentialities to emerge. This leadership approach sees conflict as essential to discovering the priority issues and necessary for finding the right solutions moving forward. In this environment, conflict propels us forward and catalyzes both individual and organizational transformation. It is the purposeful structure of a CMS or regularly scheduled dialogic events that send a powerful message to others that their participation is important, they are valued, and their voice counts.

We begin our discussion and emphasize the importance of looking at the system. In an ideal world, CMSs would be designed and integrated in every organization to seamlessly address conflict in a humanistic and unbiased manner as a normal part of organizational life rather than the episodic atypical event scheduled only when it is no longer possible to ignore the consequences of tuning-out conflict. We present a workable and straightforward approach to enable people to lean into conflict with confidence instead of apprehension, with enlightened understanding that encourages engagement rather than avoidance, and with vision that see others as allies and cohorts rather than as competitors and opponents. Having a CMS is a preemptive and proactive approach to conflict and circumvents the default reactive and defensive conventional leadership responses. Designing CMSs may be the key to promoting harmony in the workplace because it offers a pathway to address the invariable tensions that arise within everyday organizational life.

Harmony in the workplace will require change and there is no question that change can be stressful, but we argue that change is necessary if progress is to ensue. When discussing the topic of change management, Seijts (2006) argued, "Change is the only constant. Change is occurring at an ever-accelerating rate. Some people change when they see the light; others change when they feel the heat" (p. 177). We hope this chapter inspires leaders to heed the tides of change and see the light to be preemptive and proactive not only in expecting and initiating change, but in implementing change when it comes to progressive conflict management and leadership.

Understanding Conflict to Support Harmony

The presence of conflict can be very healthy if members of an organization know how to appropriately and responsibly address it. It is in the manner of how we address conflict that is imperative. Intuitively, harmony would appear to be an important goal for leaders, but harmony doesn't happen in a vacuum where there are no intentional and deliberative approaches to support it. Often, the sentiment that harmony is supposed to emerge naturally or automatically is precisely the reason why leaders fail to support harmony in the workplace. Harmony should be purposeful, deliberative, and intentional. In fact, harmony requires an effort and this effort often comes from the people who have power—most often our leaders who have influence to support or squelch it in organizational contexts. Ironically, it is precisely leaders' attitudes about conflict combined with leaders' power, control, and influence in how conflict is handled in their organizations that will ultimately support or impede harmony in the workplace.

Conflict Management Systems and Harmony

We wrote this chapter because together we have decades of experience working with various multinational organizations to address progressive forms of conflict management and leadership. We will illustrate how an integrative CMS approach that includes progressive and state-of-the-art processes in alternative dispute resolution may render excellent alternatives to litigious or biased systems that are all too often observed and established in today's society and organizations. You may be asking at this point, "What exactly is a conflict management system?" According to Georgakopoulos (2017), the term *conflict management systems* is defined as follows:

> A CMS is a strategic system that involves managing conflict and overall aids in preventing, intervening, and resolving conflict. A CMS can establish a grievance or conflict management process for various types of conflict within the organization between its members, or outside the organization with suppliers, vendors, and/or customers. Preventing future conflict or reducing the escalation of conflict can contribute to the health of relationships associated with the organization. This can reduce corporate costs, improve customer satisfaction, strengthen organizational teams, and support business partners. A CMS includes dispute resolution tools, assessments, trainings, and mechanisms to support organizations in effectively addressing conflict from prevention to resolution. (p. 155)

We add an important element to CMS here by adding that it prioritizes people. We firmly argue that if organizations put their people first, they will ultimately have healthy, successful, and thriving organizations. In a recent study, Georgakopoulos and Kelly (2017) found that workplace wellness initiatives were perceived by over a hundred people to facilitate in the resolution and management of conflict which, if ignored, might otherwise lead to workplace bullying, harassment, and violence. The findings of this study suggested that workplace wellness is a system that is interconnected and influenced by physical, psychological, relational, spiritual, financial, environmental, policy, and occupational wellness. Intuitively then with these findings, workplace wellness should serve as a sweet spot for strategically supporting harmony in organizations since it alleviates stress and mitigates conflict in the organization, while it appears to satisfy essential needs of working professionals. A CMS would likely profit considerably by integrating workplace wellness initiatives in its overall design. See Georgakopoulos and Kelly's (2017) study for details of the various forms of workplace wellness initiatives that may be infused into a system to tackle conflict and foster harmony in the workplace.

When we educate organizations about the importance of designing and implementing CMSs, we save organizations millions of dollars in litigation costs related to conflict, but beyond the dollars spent in adversarial forms of conflict resolution, the reputation of the organization, retention of highly trained employees, employee satisfaction, and well-being of employees in the workplace are invaluable and can be better protected with a solid CMS in place. In addition to these benefits, avoiding the psychological and emotional stresses of taking the route of adversarial forms of conflict resolution where there is a lack of control and predictability in the outcomes of the process may make a CMS an exceptional alternative to avoid these problems. Among a host of benefits, the most significant benefit is that a solid CMS in an organization communicates a strong message to the employees and perhaps extends it to those who do business with the organization that there is a concern for individuals when they face conflict circumstances (Georgakopoulos, 2017). Imagine knowing that your organization has provided you with a formal platform to share your voice and concerns during conflict. Instead of blocking, avoiding, or ignoring conflict, this system provides individuals with a channel to address conflict; thus, it is proactively engaging in conflict management. According to Georgakopoulos (2017),

> Disagreements of values, norms, processes, objectives, and goals are all conflict topics that can arise within an organization. Thus, a CMS would seem to alleviate uncertainty and lead to constructive conflict management, especially when members are trained in the management system. (p. 154)

While an entire book can be devoted to this topic, the scope of this chapter prevents us from going into extensive depth and breadth of every type of dispute resolution method to possibly include in an effective CMS; however, we provide a brief overview of a few formidable methods and processes and direct readers to review Georgakopoulos (2017) for additional details and design processes of CMS. In determining the type of dispute resolution approaches or processes that should be selected, organizational leaders should make decisions based on consensus from the stakeholders in the organization as this will promote ownership and buy-in, which will enhance the long-term sustainability of the CMS. According to Constantino and Merchant (1996), there are six principles that are essential elements to the design of a dispute resolution system or CMS as we argue that follows: (a) the process should be interest-focused, (b) the options should be viable and cost effective, (c) alternative options should be proposed in the event that preceding options fail, (d) training/education should be provided prior to implementation with a debrief built-in, (e) cost for methods should follow from low to high cost, and (f) methods should be combined with incentives and reinforcements to enhance their utility and application.

We are in agreement with Constantino and Merchant (1996) who argue that individuals should begin their design with informal conflict management processes in the early stages, and then if these don't work, individuals have the option to apply more formal approaches to address the more challenging disputes. These approaches are often observed on a continuum that moves from informal, interest-based approaches toward formal, rights-based approaches of conflict management. The types of approaches may be illustrated best as shown in Figure 23.1.

A CMS is precisely what it sounds like. It is a system that is designed to address conflict through management approaches, and several popular conflict management approaches are illustrated in Figure 23.1. As one moves from the left toward the right, the more formal approaches give way and the cost associated with these approaches often increases. There tends to be greater self-determination by parties when they themselves control the processes, which rests in the informal approaches, and the cost associated with these approaches often decreases compared to the more formal approaches. This continuum is beneficial for organizational leaders to see what options are available when they are designing a CMS as the resources available in the organization will be an important consideration for feasibility. What is needed for a CMS to be successful?

Step 1: Commitment to Change to Utilize a CMS

There must be a commitment to a CMS with leadership and stakeholders as a part of the design. With the implementation of a CMS, organizational members will change the nature of their organizations and the way they view each other and conflict. However, as you may recall, we argued earlier that change requires effort. Seijts (2006) cautions that organizations have a poor track record in major organizational change initiatives for these reasons:

- lack of sharing the need for change,
- inadequate communication from a coalition for change,
- unclear vision and objectives,
- allowing barriers to impede making the vision a reality,
- insufficient communication of the vision to employees,
- failure to celebrate early successes that generate excitement or confidence,
- premature labeling of change as successful, and
- failure to integrate aspects of change into the corporate culture.

We present these reasons so that leaders may be aware of these impediments and may overcome them in their responses; so change can be possible if the goal is to transform ideas into actions and hopes for peace into actual harmony. Seijts (2006) presented a comprehensive change model that implores leaders to work with experienced change agents to utilize this model as a powerful guide to implement and initiate change that involves

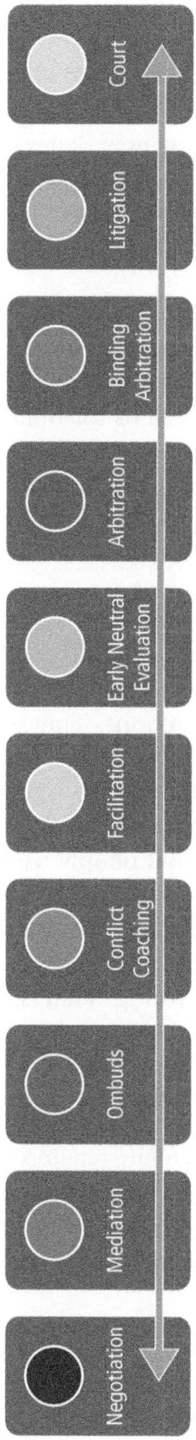

Figure 23.1 Continuum of dispute resolution approaches.

these elements: active consensus, leadership commitment/support, full participation, lack of coercion, appropriate training, time for transition, and sequential steps to take action toward change. These sequential steps to implementation are as follows: "determine desired state, assess readiness of change, initiate change, adopt new behavior and stabilize new behaviors" (p. 178). We encourage leaders to secure a CMS designer who is a change agent facilitator to effectively move the organization through the comprehensive change model sequence.

Step 2: Designing a CMS

Building a CMS requires a blueprint to detail the structure and design of the approaches along with backups that will be implemented. Therefore, just as an architect customizes designs for buildings and structures, a CMS designer is necessary to craft the design for CMSs that will be utilized by organizations that are also feasible for it. It is necessary for organizational leaders to locate quality designers who have extensive experience and expertise with design, implementation, and evaluation of a CMS.

Step 3: A CMS Will Require Training

All people in the organization should be familiar and formally trained in the CMS that is designed specifically for their organization so they understand it and know how it functions. They should know precisely when to call for it or how to handle themselves once they are involved with a conflict. This requires a two-part process—knowledge and action. Argyris (1993) argued that "actionable knowledge is not only relevant to the world of practice; it is the knowledge that people use to create the world" (p. 1). Many of the behaviors we have learned in organizational life refer to actionable knowledge, but they may not have produced effective actions. Argyris (1993) suggested that in order to change the status quo, people must understand that action is tied to learning. That is, Argyris (1993) claimed that

> effective actions are not only stored as rules in actors' heads; it means that their requirements are known publicly, usually in the form of formal and informal policies and routines that are rewarded by organizational cultures. Building policies, routines, and culture requires learning. (pp. 3–4)

A CMS thus requires learning, but also action to pave the way for healthy and constructive interactions that permit harmony to grow.

Step 4: Selecting Neutrals and Conflict Management Service Providers

Selecting professionals who are deemed to be credible, acceptable, and impartial candidates by organizational members will be important. If the selection of professionals is or has the appearance that individuals have been planted for the position by organizational leaders, the process will be perceived as corrupted and people will not trust or benefit from the process.

Step 5: A CMS Must Be Evaluated and Assessed for Its Effectiveness

Evaluation is essential to determine if the CMS, or aspects of it, needs to be modified/amended or changed with alternative approaches with formal appraisals solicited from all stakeholders. Thus, feedback is key in this process, and it will be important to assess harmony as a result of the CMS. Perhaps a pre-assessment and post-assessment of harmony would be an important way to gauge if the CMS is supporting the change in the status quo that is desired. It will be important for leaders with the assistance of a CMS designer to conduct formal evaluations of the CMS to determine what the strengths and limitations of the model in practice are to see what adjustments, improvements, or even replacements appear to be necessary in order to design a CMS that is the best fit for the organization and one that squarely places harmony as a major objective in the conflict management initiative.

It is important for organizational leaders to be familiar with their options when they are committed to building a CMS, but they also need to be aware that their system should be strategically tailored and custom designed for their organizational culture to ensure there is a successful match and fit with the organization, its members, and the nature of conflict. Keyton (2005) devoted an entire book on this topic, and suggested that "organizational culture is a set of artifacts, values, and assumptions that emerge from the interactions of organizational members" (p. 1). She goes on to claim that managers are uniquely interested in organizational culture because it has come to be associated with productivity, efficiency, and effectiveness (Keyton, 2005). Employees, on the other hand, are interested in organizational culture when they are deciding on where to work or when they are determining if they want to stay or leave based on whether they like or dislike the organizational culture. Thus, the CMS is an important component to building a culture of harmony versus a culture of discord, indifference, dysfunction, harassment, bullying, and/or chaos. Along with designing a CMS that is a good fit with the organizational culture, it is essential that there is a recognition that when one approach doesn't work that there will be backups as a part of the design so conflict can be approached by alternative methods until it can ultimately be resolved. Backups are all the options that one can select from in designing their CMS. It is like a menu with a variety of choices and each choice has its strengths and limitations as well as different forms.

An integrative CMS must be envisioned and designed with a big picture in mind for what constitutes the CMS. There are several options in this selection process. Leaders with the commitment of their stakeholders may decide to go step-by-step and move sequentially from informal process to formal processes until the conflict gets resolved or there may be the desire to design a CMS that expedites the process with a three-phase process. For example, the CMS may initially start with the least informal approaches such as negotiation, mediation, or conflict coaching and then progress to an approach like early neutral evaluation or arbitration, which are approaches in the middle of the continuum, to finally binding arbitration or litigation, approaches on the formal end of the continuum, in circumstances when parties are unable to resolve their disputes using earlier approaches. This CMS example recognizes the constraints and challenges (e.g., time, cost, effort, etc.) of moving through all the approaches so it offers a more realistic approach to addressing conflict in two or three major steps, which will likely lead to harmony with resolved conflicts and issues.

PART TWO: DIALOGIC EVENTS AS A CMS

If the idea of implementing a formal CMS in your organization is daunting or simply not practical given the reality of your current situation, the second part of this chapter proposes regularly scheduled dialogic events as an informal and accessible alternative to a formal CMS. The liberating structures problem-solving (LSPS) model (Allen, 2018) was developed to creatively destroy structural sources of organizational conflict that are inherent in a conventional (hierarchical) leadership approach. This section will highlight the challenge of operating from a conventional leadership mind-set, propose a shared leadership approach, list the six dysfunctions of conventional leadership, and outline the LSPS model as a practice of shared leadership. Finally, suggestions on how to start will be offered.

The Real Challenge

Conventional conceptions of leadership place leaders and followers in a dyadic relationship in which one exerts power over the other. Hierarchical authority grants formal leaders the power to make sweeping decisions that significantly impact the work of others. Those with leadership status diagnose the disorders, prescribe the remedies, and impose the solutions upon those with follower status whose job it is to unquestioningly accept the information and execute accordingly. These sources of power are structural in the sense that they reflect the qualities institutionalized within the organization rather than the psychology of particular individuals within the organization (Astley & Sachdeva, 1984). This relationship creates a great burden on the leader to have an all-embracing vision, complete knowledge, a thorough understanding of the issues, and a solid grasp of all the possible solutions to the complex challenges organizations face today. Let's be honest about the challenge. No one person or small group of people are capable of this. Acknowledging this reality helps us engage in a little creative destruction of conventional notions of leadership found in hierarchical organizational structures.

Leadership Re-Imagined

A new way of thinking about leadership is emerging. From this perspective, leadership is not viewed as a set of attributes inherent in particularly gifted individuals, but instead is seen as a set of practices among those engaged together in realizing their choices (Raelin, 2015). This emerging concept of leadership involves various activities, including inviting participation of diverse stakeholders, scanning the environment, mobilizing resources, arranging interactions across new networks, and facilitating reflection that offers feedback (Raelin, 2015, p. 95). This shared leadership practice is employed in the LSPS model. This chapter focuses on bringing the practice of shared leadership to life through dialogic events. Before we describe the LSPS model which is used to design dialogic events, let's discuss the importance of conversations.

Organizations Are Conversations

As people socially interact with each other, reality and truth are constantly created and re-created through conversations and experiences. A shared leadership approach understands organizations as conversations where people, drawing from their individual experiences, make meaning and construct reality together from their collective and emerging stories, narratives, and discussions. Therefore, to change an organization you must change the conversations and narratives that occur within them (Ford & Ford, 2008; Shaw, 2002). If your organization is not creating dedicated space and time to conduct inclusive, participative, dialogic events on a regular basis, your organizational reality is deprived of access to vital information as well as to affirming, unifying, relational experiences that can change your organization's trajectory. This section focuses on the impressive instrumentality of the dialogic event and offers an accessible approach to implementing these generative conversations in your organization, paving the way for transformational change.

This approach to creating harmony in the workplace avoids the blame-the-person form of conflict resolution and, instead, acknowledges and confronts the system that induced the conflict in the first place. Dysfunctional systems seek to maintain the status quo by constructing conflict narratives that personalize systemic conflict. These practices are an attempt to mask or fill in the cracks in the system that are laid bare through conflict and are used as an immunity against insight and change (Cloke, 2001).

The Costs of Conflict Perpetuated by Hierarchy

We all know conflict is costly. Pausing a moment to reflect on the tremendous use of scarce resources of time, energy, money, and human talent that it takes to try to fix the fallout from sparse communication, tense relationships, resistance to change, employee dissatisfaction, organizational silos, low morale, poor productivity, and untapped innovative ideas, helps us visualize just how costly conflict is. Let's take a closer look at the six dysfunctions inherent in hierarchical structures that, if left unchanged, will predictably churn conflict in your organization, rendering harmony an elusive ideal.

Dysfunction 1: Hierarchy Erodes Trusting Relationships and Encourages Bad Behavior

Your organizational chart will give you a good idea of the degree of hierarchy in your organization. These conventional structures produce power inequalities and status differences, authorizing people with higher status the power to make sweeping decisions over the work of others; whose input is viewed as more valuable than subordinates. It perpetuates a system that breeds personal resentments, interdepartmental estrangement, resistance to change, feelings of dissatisfaction and rejection, and reduced morale, trust, and motivation (Krasman, 2014). Furthermore, hierarchy teaches people to be obedient and to disengage, suppressing their own ability to think creatively and solve problems (Pinchot, 1992).

Dysfunction 2: Hierarchy Excludes and Produces Inequality

The formal distribution of titles, functions, and privilege determine who is included and who is excluded. As decisions that identify the issues and the solutions are made by those with leader status, access to diverse and critical information remains buried within people closest to the problems, leaving leaders blind to both serious risks and enticing opportunities (Tett, 2015). This dynamic hinders full understanding of both challenges and sustainable solutions and handicaps organizational progress.

Dysfunction 3: Hierarchy Dominates, Manipulates, and Distorts Communication

First, hierarchy over-simplifies communication from the top to make it more understandable, yet those messages without context force those at the bottom of the hierarchy to guess the actual meaning and they end up relying on speculation and rumors to fill in the blanks (Cloke & Goldsmith, 2002). Second, hierarchy provides no feedback loop for listening going back up the hierarchy (Tourish, 2005). Critical upward feedback is often constrained, misrepresented, or entirely discarded, resulting in information of little value. Finally, gossip, in the form of a colorful behind-the-scenes network that thrives on hearsay, slander, prejudice, and innuendo, naturally develops in hierarchical organizations to fill in the gaps of corporate silence. This informal mode of communication exacerbates the dissemination of inaccurate information, generating a greater probability of conflict.

Dysfunction 4: Hierarchy Stifles Collaboration

Conventional structures divide the organization into silos, encouraging communication within functional areas (Garvin, 1998) but discouraging cross-functional exchange of information (Hersted & Gergen, 2013) which limits people's ability to think holistically about the organization and its purpose (Cloke & Goldsmith, 2001). This structure makes collaboration with other departments burdensome and further advances conditions ripe for misunderstanding and conflict.

Dysfunction 5: Hierarchy Suppresses Creativity and Innovation

A hierarchical design does not allow for distributed actors with diverse talent and experience to contribute to something that emerges without imposing a managerial mastermind (Kornberger, 2017). The over-centralization of functions in a hierarchy reinforces unquestioning conformity, and encourages managers to manipulate employees into obeying rules blindly and shelving their creativity and critical thinking (Cloke & Goldsmith, 2001). Too many bureaucratic rules stymie the emergence of bottom–up, spontaneous processes and are "a quite extraordinary waste of subordinate knowledge" (Blaug, 2007, p. 40).

Dysfunction 6: Hierarchy Impedes Adaptability and Efficiency

Hierarchy impedes the adaptive capacity of the organization to evolve and respond to rapidly changing conditions and is among the most serious of its flaws. Unilateral commands strengthen conformity and reinforce rigid silos that repress organizational responsiveness and adaptive action (Ford, 2012). Organizations cannot afford to resist change or cling to what may have worked in the past, yet hierarchies are designed to reinforce and propagate the status quo, perpetuating inefficiencies (Hersted & Gergen, 2013).

We Have a Choice

It's important to keep in mind hierarchy is a system with an intentional design. If we put our own best design thinking to work, it becomes obvious we can create something much more functional as leaders; however, it requires a fundamental choice about how power is used to resolve conflicts and create a more unified workplace. We can passively accept a power-over approach and adhere to an authoritarian structure that relies upon control and coercion exerted through consolidated hierarchical power or rights; or, we can choose to adopt a power-with approach relying upon democratic structures grounded in collective dialogue and choice exercised through inclusive collaboration of diverse interests; or, some combination of the two (Cloke & Goldsmith, 2001, p. 203).

Our approach to conflict resolution skews hard toward democratic structures that give people voice and choice in shaping their work and inviting people to collectively work at their highest intelligence. Everywhere we go, we witness bright, capable, talented, good-hearted people in all parts of the organization, and recognize how widely distributed leadership is. Everyone is capable of leadership, so how do we as leaders share leadership? What would organizational life be like if we could unleash the latent human potential that lies untapped, waiting to be called into being?

Using the LSPS Model as a Shared Leadership Practice

The underlying assumption to a shared leadership approach is that we are better together. Collectively, we are smarter, more efficient, more creative, and overall better decision makers. Together, we are much more proficient in defining the real issues, discovering root causes, and generating creative and innovative solutions that are more likely to be implemented because everyone has a part in coproducing next steps. As work is shaped together, purpose is clarified, conflicts are resolved, local solutions to sticky challenges are surfaced, relationships are strengthened, and trust is built as people unite in getting important work done. The question every awakened leader must ask is, "How can I creatively destroy those structures that are holding people and this organization back?"

The LSPS model of facilitation (Allen, 2018) is one such way to answer this question. More progressive organizations reduce barriers by sharing more knowledge and providing opportunities to include diverse people from all parts of the organization in the communication, problem-solving, and decision-making processes (Cloke & Goldsmith, 2002; Raelin, 2012; Scharmer & Kaufer, 2013; Stephenson, 2009; Tourish, 2005). In these environments, people can confront each other supportively, rumors are challenged, and there is both greater freedom within and responsibility for the success of the organization (Lipmanowicz & McCandless, 2013). As everyone is pulled into these dialogic processes, less time is spent correcting misinformation, resolving conflicts, and doing damage repair from rumors and gossip (Cloke & Goldsmith, 2002). The LSPS model is precisely designed to pull diverse people into the dialogic group processes of communication, problem-solving, and decision-making using microstructures (described below) that enable qualitatively different kinds of human interaction than are ordinarily found in organizations, giving voice and choice to all participants while unleashing the latent potential within the organization. Liberating structures are at the heart of the LSPS model and are further described.

Liberating Structures—Putting Innovative Power in the Hands of Everyone!

Henri Lipmanowicz and Keith McCandless co-developed what they named liberating structures (LS) to assist groups in navigating more effectively the complexity of organizational life, to break down barriers that hold us back, and to get important work done while at the same time strengthening relationships so crucial to success. Liberating structures are a disruptive innovation that shake up conventional patterns of human interaction by injecting tiny shifts in the way people meet, plan, decide, and relate to one another, and put in the hands of everyone the innovative power once reserved for experts only (Lipmanowicz & McCandless, 2013). Liberating structures level the playing field "so to speak," by designing a safe organizational setting or container where diverse voices are heard and valued; where participation is equalized, making way for full discussion of relevant issues, and opening space for creative solutions co-developed and brought forth by participants who experience the challenges directly.

Learning in Action

Liberating structures are learning in action. The key to building capabilities is actually doing it as opposed to sitting in a classroom learning about it. The limitations of a text-based pedagogy to leadership development become clear when the purpose of leadership development is to improve skills in practice (Fergen & Hersted, 2016). It is, therefore, essential to be immersed in actual practices that expose participants to opportunities for dialogic relationships. Every liberating structure designs experiences with a specific purpose while concurrently building individual capabilities. Liberating structures are methods of a learn-by-doing approach that assist the process of enabling individuals to develop greater capabilities through participation. Most people understand a workshop here or there is unlikely to change behavior overnight; however, as liberating structures are used over a period of time with consistent application of a set of principles, many of these moments build up to a point where evolved practices and mindsets become embodied (Ledwith & Springett, 2010) and transformational change occurs.

A Closer Look at Macrostructures and Microstructures

Structures are everywhere. Whatever transpires in an organization is supported by a structure that directs and guides what is being done. A macrostructure is something that is built or designed for the long-run that cannot be easily changed such as buildings, strategies, policies, and core operating processes (Lipmanowicz & McCandless, 2013). Microstructures, on the other hand, are small structures that are routinely selected to facilitate interactions with others such as office space, meeting rooms, presentations, agendas, questions, and discussions (Lipmanowicz & McCandless, 2013, p. 10). In contrast to macrostructures, microstructures can be changed easily and inexpensively. It is the microstructures that liberating structures tweak to include and engage everyone according to five design elements. These elements are (a) making an invitation, (b) arranging space, (c) distributing participation, (d) configuring groups, and (e) sequencing and allocating time. Full descriptions of the 33+ liberating structures and how to conduct these facilitation processes can be found (free of charge) at http://www.liberatingstructures.com/

Using the LSPS Model to Design a Dialogic Event

The LSPS model intentionally structures more democratic, inclusive, and participative group processes to create conditions for the emergence of latent human potential, closer human connection, new knowledge, innovation, and a fresh way of communicating and interacting as empowered participants lead change together. The LSPS model carefully and intentionally leverages inclusive, participative, group processes that structure equal time among participants sharing with and listening to each other, regardless of where an individual resides on the organizational hierarchy. The space is created to be psychologically safe so that people have one-on-one and small group conversations about the issues they collectively choose to address. At the same time, the problems associated with hierarchical organizations are greatly reduced by structuring systemic sources of conflict out of the processes. As participants work together over time, they practice reflecting collectively, learning from their experiences, and developing organizational adaptive capacity moving forward. By changing the simple microstructures of how people relate to one another, the power dynamic shifts and space clears for transformational change to take place.

Nine Core Principles and Practices Merged With Nine Problem Solving Steps

The model was inspired by seeing the magic of liberating structures in action. The LSPS model is to be used for dialogic events. Liberating structures as elegant and powerful group processes are placed within a framework that advances four core principles and five practices as people progress through problem-solving steps. The four core principles inform the leadership mind-set which, in turn, guides the five core practices. The four core principles are: (a) pursue justice, (b) seek truth, (c) believe in the nobility of everyone, and (d) assume interconnectedness. The five core practices are: (a) create a container for dialogue, (b) address purpose and vision, (c) cultivate unity, (d) build individual capacity, and (e) develop organizational adaptability. The nine problem-solving steps provide the overall direction of the workshops, although the progression of the steps need not be linear. The nine steps include: (a) define the problem, (b) establish criteria for evaluating solutions, (c) identify root causes, (d) generate alternative solutions, (e) evaluate alternative solutions, (f) select the best solutions, (g) develop an action plan, (h) implement the action plan, and (i) evaluate outcomes and the processes (Schwarz, 2002). Designing a dialogic event starts with a mind-set anchored in principles that inform the practice of creating space for meaningful and practical collaboration of diverse participants.

The four core principles are:

- *Pursue Justice.* Justice is a comprehensive principle with many aspects to be considered. The LSPS model is mindful of the three aspects of organizational justice (Psychology Research and Reference, 2018), including distributive justice which refers to people's belief they have received a fair amount of work-related outcomes, procedural justice which is concerned with the fairness of the decision processes (Leventhal, Kanuza, & Fry, 1980), and interactional justice which refers to the quality of interpersonal treatment received by employees (Lee, 2000). When an organization relies upon hierarchical structures that use power to unilaterally define who is included in decision-making, how work is accomplished, and how resources are distributed, it is easy to see how unity would be elusive.
- *Seek Truth.* The dialogic process can be "understood as the collective investigation of reality" giving "due importance to valid empirical information" (Universal House of Justice, 2013, para. 10) while also not raising mere opinion to the status of fact or defining truth as the compromise between opposing interest groups. Dialogic processes must also take into account emotions, intuition, and abstract thinking (Cloke & Goldsmith, 2002) to gain a greater understanding of

the unspoken-yet-very-real nuances that are a significant part of the collective reality. Through inclusive dialogic processes where diverse voices are heard and valued, in which prevailing narratives are challenged and the quest for truth is a constant goal, the collective intelligence of the group has the space and opportunity to emerge.

- *Believe in the Inherent Nobility of Everyone.* The core principle of inherent nobility in every human, placed within the context of an organizational setting, holds implications for designing a work environment that is developmental. Part of the conventional leadership mind-set assumes that some people are more valuable than others which is reified by a hierarchy that constructs inequalities in status, power, and access to organizational resources. A shared leadership mind-set, on the other hand, views every person as highly valuable in their own unique way, all vital to organizational success. Operating from the principle of believing in the nobility of everyone provides the platform to create an organizational culture and experiences that help people achieve their potential. This principle of inherent nobility recognizes that every person belongs and that perhaps it is the organizational structure which has thwarted someone's ability to contribute meaningfully. The LSPS model is designed with a deep respect for all, giving them the space and opportunities to express virtues, develop higher *capabilities, and realize their latent potential.*
- *Assume the Interconnectedness of Everything.* Collective life suffers when any one segment of humanity thinks of its own well-being in isolation from others. The Universal House of Justice (2017) stated that "the welfare of any segment of humanity is inextricably bound up with the welfare of the whole" (para. 2). That "humanity constitutes a single people" is a truth that "claims widespread acceptance today" (Universal House of Justice, 2013, para. 6). Within the organizational context, recognition that what happens in one part of an organization necessarily impacts other parts of the organization either directly or indirectly necessitates this reconceptualization of relationships and the way in which work is accomplished.

The four core principles serve as a guiding constellation in designing group dialogic experiences that include each of the five core practices. Drawing upon the core principles in every activity, the change practitioner is concerned with creating conditions in which shared leadership can emerge. The change practitioner must tend to five core practices within every dialogic experience.

- *Create a Container for Dialogue.* The idea of a "container" is defined as "the intangible yet real spaces in which the potential and possibility of a group can unfold" (Corrigan, 2015, p. 291). This includes tending to both the physical and psychological space in which dialogue occurs.

- *Arrange Physical Settings.* Silently but powerfully, the layout of the room structures the nature of the relationships between participants and either constrains or emancipates possibilities. Because there is very little one-to-all communication using liberating structures and most of the conversations are conducted in dyads, triads, quads, and small groups, the ability for participants to move around easily in different conversations and activities with diverse people is fundamental to this dialogic process. Lecture halls, conference tables, and fixed furniture should be avoided, if at all possible.
- *Create Psychological Safety.* A 2012 study called Project Aristotle focused on Google's quest to find the perfect team, identifying group norms as the key influence on productivity (Duhigg, 2016). The results of the study indicated that two primary group norms contributed to creating a safe psychological environment: (a) members spoke in roughly the same proportion to everyone else, and (b) highly effective team members demonstrated "social sensitivity" which is a reflection of how well group members are attuned to each other through tone of voice, expressions, and nonverbal cues (Duhigg, 2016). To set the stage for transformational conversations, change practitioners must ensure "equality in distribution of conversational turn-taking" (Duhigg, 2016, p. 6) as well as practice checking in with each other emotionally, especially when people seem to be disengaged.

• *Address Purpose and Vision.* Organizations define vision and mission, but often fall short in living up to those statements in the daily work lives of people and becoming a deeper part of organizational culture. Addressing purpose as an ongoing conversation is a critical part of connecting people more deeply to their own purpose and how it ultimately contributes to the larger organizational purpose. Creating space and time to have these vital conversations helps organizations move from a conventional leadership approach that imposes rules and regulations to control others toward a shared leadership approach where people are empowered to draw upon their own sources of motivation.

• *Cultivate Unity.* Unity is not a passive state that simply exists with the absence of conflict. It must be cultivated through persistent action on two organizational fronts: (a) removing structural sources of conflict, and (b) introducing new patterns of interaction and communication. First, working to remove structural sources of conflict is essential to ensuring the system's practices live up to its principles. The simple act of convening a gathering of diverse people who all have equal say in identifying issues and shaping their work together is a form of power-sharing that eliminates or greatly reduces structural sources of conflict (i.e., one-way communication, silos, predefined problem with prescribed solutions). Second, new patterns of interaction and communication are introduced to foster quality relationships which are the key to collaborating and getting things done. "Whether an organization prospers or perishes depends importantly upon the relationships among its participants" (Gergen & Hersted, 2016, p. 179). These relationships are primarily dialogic in character. Scheduling time and space for diverse personal interaction fortifies relationships while tackling tough issues. By intentionally structuring one-on-one and small-group interactions, experiences are created that set the stage for people to connect in meaningful ways as they work together to effect change. Liberating structures largely avoid one-to-all communication making every interaction a structured opportunity for diverse personal connection and trust-building as people get to know each other better through dialogic processes. Liberating structures are designed to include, engage, and listen to diverse perspectives and information. The use of liberating structures cultivates a unifying environment where people are seen, heard, and respected (Lipmanowicz & McCandless, 2013).

- *Build Individual Capacity*. The LSPS model is built upon the premise that leadership occurs as a collective practice rather than from the attributes or behaviors of particular individuals (Raelin, 2016). The question for the change practitioner then becomes, "How do individuals participate in the practice of emerging leadership and ultimately develop individual capabilities in the process?" Gergen and Hersted (2016) asserted that leadership is an emergent outcome of the ongoing patterns of relationship primarily practiced through dialogue. Working through the problem-solving steps within the dialogic approach of the LSPS model, participants are able to develop a wide array of individual capabilities, including but not limited to:
  - critical thinking and analytical skills;
  - emotional intelligence, especially empathy and respect;
  - principle-centered thinking and decision-making;
  - effective communication skills including listening, speaking up, asking for help, and giving help;
  - indispensable collaboration skills with diverse people;
  - open-minded inquiry;
  - essential conflict resolution skills; and
  - imaginative and creative thinking skills.

As people engage in a dialogic practice they inevitably build individual capabilities as they are invited to name challenging issues, address difficult questions, think about paradoxical realities, identify underlying causes, understand diverse perspectives and complexities, listen to others with curiosity and empathy, expand their vision, seriously explore new ideas of what is possible, learn to collaborate on equal footing, make collective decisions, understand their individual role in contributing to the larger organizational mission, and reflect both individually and collectively on their work and group processes.

- *Develop Organizational Adaptability.* Being responsive to quickly changing conditions and resilient when experiencing setbacks is essential in today's hyper-competitive environment. Adaptive firms are more competitive (Long, 2001) and tend to perform better than their peers (Dreyer & Gronhaug, 2004; Tuominen, Rajala, & Moller, 2004). Organizational adaptability refers to an organization's ability to respond quickly to changing conditions within and outside of the organization by adjusting or modifying its way of thinking, its practices, or its course. In other words, an adaptive organization is a learning organization.

The Necessity of Regularly Scheduled Reflective Gatherings

An organization's adaptive capacity is enhanced when the needs and demands of various stakeholders are acknowledged (Heifetz & Laurie, 1997). This starts with including diverse stakeholders in dialogic processes in which important conversations occur and decisions are made; however, simply including diverse stakeholders is not enough. To learn what is happening in the internal and external environment, the organization needs regularly scheduled processes designed to gather information from the various stakeholders. The top–down communication flow of a hierarchically structured organization omits these reflective gatherings, resulting in a slower learning process and ultimately slower adaptability.

The LSPS model builds within it regularly scheduled, continuous cycles of action, reflection, and dialogue in which diverse participants can collectively look back at action taken and, through dialogic processes, discover together what worked well and what did not. The LSPS model is designed to gather information from all parts of the organization in understanding a shared reality and co-creating a path forward. An array of liberating structures is used to design the flow of activities intended to draw out knowledge and insights, expose natural paradoxes of complex situations, and provide the opportunity for collective exploration of new and creative ideas moving forward. Quick cycles of action, reflection, and dialogue with an experimental mind-set that views failure as a natural part of the learning process build organizational adaptive capacity.

Shared Leadership as a Conflict Management System

This section described a more democratic and progressive idea of leadership as a practice and something that emerges when diverse people come together and engage in dialogue. A cultural and organizational transformation is made possible by including people from all parts of the organization to participate in dialogic events where they are able to listen to others and contribute to the collective narrative, and where they are able to have agency in shaping their work and mapping out steps moving forward. Regularly scheduled dialogic events conducted with liberating structures have the power to open people's minds to its undeniable benefits. When time and space are made for listening, learning, and sharing, a collective narrative takes shape as people understand the bigger picture of what is going on in the organization. As people's understanding of their colleagues' work evolves—what they do, as well as their successes and challenges—empathy and understanding are elevated. Additionally, as people are invited to share their unique insights, a very strong message is conveyed that they are valued by leadership. Suddenly, problems become much easier to identify, curiosity is amplified, generative ideas flow more easily, sustainable solutions are surfaced, and stronger bonds and trust between people are realized. When people from all parts of the organization are invited to talk to each other by design, silos get crushed and one-way communication is eradicated. When undiscussables are made safe to talk about, there is little need for gossip and hearsay to fill in the blanks of corporate silence. When people from all departments and from different levels in the organization are given time to engage in meaningful dialogue, the array of diverse ideas is exponentially expanded and paves the way for creative and innovative solutions to previously unsolvable challenges. As people experience the transformative power of liberating structures, they will want more . . . and there is no going back. Expect people to step up and offer to experiment with liberating structures. In this way, people become self-organizing and self-correcting.

Given the irrefutable advantages of a shared leadership approach, we advance it as a powerful CMS that creatively destroys structural sources of conflict. We encourage leaders of organizations of any size to expand their vision of what is actually possible within their own organization, but you may be wondering exactly where to start.

Where Do I Start?

If you are a leader in your organization with authority to institute a formal CMS, we encourage you to have conversations with your employees and learn from them what would be helpful in addressing conflicts that occur in the organization. Too often, we jump ahead and assume we know what people might need or want without asking. Assuredly, you will go farther and faster if you engage in some on-the-ground listening first. You can have one-on-one conversations, conduct focus groups, develop anonymous online surveys, ask direct supervisors, or develop your own creative way to gather information. This data will give you a solid foundation and inform your next steps.

Maybe you don't have formal leadership status in your organization, but you want to try something new. Most transformational organizational changes start from the bottom–up. Therefore, if you have the volition to experiment, we encourage you to just do something! Small actions are *always* better than elaborate yet unadopted plans. We present a progression of ideas for you to consider, wherever you may be comfortable in starting something new:

- *Learn about liberating structures.* Visit the website www.liberatingstructures.com and learn about the 33+ liberating structures that have all of the steps and instructions for you to try out. Remember that learning happens best in action. One of the easiest and most useful structures is called 1-2-4-All. Check it out.
- *Start an ongoing conversation.* Be curious and start asking questions of cohorts. What fabulous insight do you have that you wish others knew? If you were the boss, what is the first thing you would change? What do we need to be talking about as an organization that we are not talking about? You know what you want to know. Start asking and remember to always skew inquiry and responses towards the positive.
- *Practice with a friend.* If you're tired of monotonous one-to-all flow of information during meetings, enlist the support of a cohort and try out one liberating structure in your meetings and watch people become alive and engaged.
- *Design a dialogic event.* Volunteer to design and facilitate a meeting using liberating structures with a friend. Each liberating structure has a specific purpose, and you can select among the menu and design a unique string of liberating structures that can help you have the conversations you need and want to have.
- *Find a liberating structures user group or start your own.* Practicing these innovative facilitation methods with other practitioners is the key to elevating your understanding and honing your skills. Liberating

structures user groups are conducted all over the world, and information on starting a group can be found on the website.

CONCLUSION

This chapter looked at organizational systems as an essential instrument for addressing conflict and ultimately creating a more unified and harmonious workplace. It was divided into two parts: (a) a discussion of the formal CMS and the benefits of institutionalizing it in your organization, and (b) the LSPS model as a shared leadership practice as a more informal approach to conflict resolution that effectively functions as a CMS.

In part one, the ability to change our minds about what we know about conflict management and leaders was proposed as the first step in advancing toward a more harmonious workplace. When we stand in place unflinchingly when conflict arises and choose to see it as an opportunity to have essential conversations that have previously remained unspoken, we open a world of possibilities in creating the kind of work environment that brings out the best in people. A spectrum of CMSs was described as well as the steps involved for implementing a formal CMS.

Part two offered a more informal approach to conflict resolution by proposing regularly scheduled dialogic events. We first presented the challenges and dysfunctions of a conventional leadership mind-set which relies upon hierarchical structures. We suggested that organizations are conversations, so if you want to change the organization you must intentionally change the conversations occurring within it. Dialogic events can effectively function as a CMS. We concluded the chapter by introducing some accessible ideas on where you can get started, regardless of where you may be situated within an organizational hierarchy.

Design Matters

Every result we have in organizations is by design. When we see undesirable results in our organization, it is a function of either a structure that is generating these outcomes or the lack of a structure to effectively intervene in changing the outcomes. Creating, by design, an organizational culture in which people are respected, listened to, valued, given opportunities to develop capabilities, and to interact and contribute to shaping their work and organizational life requires a systemic approach that puts structures such as a CMS or regularly scheduled dialogic events in place. Creating a more harmonious workplace is entirely possible and one step, regardless of how large or small, will move the needle in the direction of harmony. Be bold. Be confident. And take that first step that is entirely within your power.

REFERENCES

Allen, B. (2018). *Leading change together: Reducing organizational structural conflict through a dialogic OD approach using liberating structures* (Doctoral dissertation). Nova Southeastern University, Davie, FL. Retrieved from NSUWorks website: https://nsuworks.nova.edu/shss_dcar_etd/91/

Argyris, C. (1993). *Knowledge for action: A guide to overcoming barriers to organizational change.* San Francisco, CA: Jossey-Bass.

Astley, W. C., & Sachdeva, P. S. (1984). Structural sources of intraorganizational power: A theoretical synthesis. *The Academy of Management Review, 9*(1), 104–113.

Blaug, R. (2007). Cognition in a hierarchy. *Contemporary Political Theory, 6*, 24–44.

Bush, R. A. B., & Folger, J. P. (2005). *The promise of mediation: The transformative approach to conflict.* San Francisco, CA: Jossey-Bass.

Cloke, K. (2001). *Mediating dangerously: The frontiers of conflict resolution.* San Francisco, CA: Jossey-Bass.

Cloke, K., & Goldsmith, J. (2002). *The end of management and the rise of organizational democracy.* San Francisco, CA: Jossey-Bass.

Corrigan, C. (2015). Hosting and holding containers. In G. R. Bushe & R. J. Marshak (Eds.), *Dialogic organization development* (pp. 291–304). Oakland, CA: Berrett-Koehler.

Costantino, C., & Merchant, C. (1996). *Designing CMSs.* San Francisco, CA: Jossey-Bass.

Dreyer, B., & Gronhaug, K. (2004, May). Uncertainty, flexibility, and sustained competitive advantage. *Journal of Business Research, 57*(5), 484–494.

Duhigg, C. (2016, February 28). *What Google learned on its quest to build the perfect team.* Retrieved from https://www.nytimes.com/2016/02/28/magazine/what-google-learned-from-its-quest-to-build-the-perfect-team.html?_r=0

Ford, J. D., & Ford, L. W. (2008). Conversational profiles: A tool for altering the conversational pattern of change managers. *Journal of Applied Behavioral Science, 44*(4), 445–467.

Ford, R. (2012, January–February). Reduce health care costs: Eliminate structural traps. *Physician Executive, 38*(1), 36–40.

Garvin, D. A. (1998). The processes of organization and management. *Sloan Management Review, 39*(4), 33–51.

Georgakopoulous, A. (Ed.). (2017). *The mediation handbook: Research, theory, and practice.* New York, NY: Routledge.

Georgakopoulos, A., & Kelly, M. (2017). Tackling workplace bullying: A scholarship of engagement study of workplace wellness as a system. *International Journal of Workplace Health Management, 10*(6), 450–474.

Gergen, K. J., & Hersted, L. (2016). Developing leadership as dialogic practice. In J. A. Raelin (Ed.), *Leadership-as-practice: Theory and application* (pp. 178–197). New York, NY: Routledge.

Gordon, J. (Ed.). (2007). *The Pfeiffer book of successful conflict management tools.* Hoboken, NJ: Wiley.

Heifetz, R. A., & Laurie, D. L. (1997). The work of leadership. *Harvard Business Review, 36*(4), 844–863.

Hersted, L., & Gergen, K. J. (2013). *Relational leading, practices for dialogically based collaboration.* Chagrin Falls, OH: Taos Institute.

Keyton, J. (2005). *Communication & organizational culture: A key to understanding work experiences.* Thousand Oaks, CA: SAGE.

Kornberger, M. (2017). The visible hand and the crowd: Analyzing organization design in distributed innovation systems. *Strategic Organization, 15*(2), 174–193.

Krasman, J. (2014, June 26). Do my staff trust me? The influence of organizational structure on subordinate perceptions of supervisor trustworthiness. *Leadership and Organizational Development Journal, 35*(5), 470–488.

Ledwith, M., & Springett, J. (2010). *Participatory practice: Community-based action for transformative change.* Bristol, England: The Policy Press.

Lee, H.-R. (2000, April 27). *An empirical study of organizational justice as a mediator of the relationships among leader-member exchange and job satisfaction, organizational commitment and turnover intentions in the lodging industry* (Doctoral dissertation). Virginia Polytechnic Institute and State University, Blacksburg, VA. Retrieved from https://vtechworks.lib.vt.edu/bitstream/handle/10919/27465/dissertation.pdf?sequence=1&isAllowed=y

Leventhal, G. S., Kanuza, J., & Fry, E. R. (1980). Beyond fairness: A theory of allocation preferences. In G. Mikula (Ed.), *Justice and social interaction* (pp. 167–218). New York, NY: Springer-Verlag.

Lipmanowicz, H., & McCandless, K. (2013). *The surprising power of liberating structures: Simple rules to unleash a culture of innovation.* Seattle, WA: Liberating Structures Press.

Long, R. L. (2001). Pay systems and organizational flexibility. *Canadian Journal of Administrative Sciences/Revue Canadienne des Sciences de l'Administration, 18*(1), 25–32.

Manville, B., & Ober, J. (2003). Building empowerment: Building a company of citizens. *Harvard Business Review.* Retrieved from https://eclass.aueb.gr/modules/document/file.php/DET156/SESSION%206%3A%20CORP%20GOV%20MODELS%2C%20CONVERGENCE%20TRENDS/a%20company%20of%20citizens.pdf

Pinchot, E. S. (1992, September). Balance the power. *Executive Excellence, 9*(9), 3–5.

Psychology Research and Reference. (2018, February 15). *Organizational justice.* Retrieved from http://psychology.iresearchnet.com/industrial-organizational-psychology/job-satisfaction/organizational-justice/

Raelin, J. A. (2012). Dialogue and deliberation as expressions of democratic leadership in participatory organizational change. *Journal of Organizational Change Mangement, 25*(1), 7–23.

Raelin, J. A. (2015, Summer). Rethinking leadership. *MIT Sloan Management Review, 56*(4). Retreived from https://sloanreview.mit.edu/article/rethinking-leadership/

Raelin, J. A. (2016). *Leadership-as-practice: theory and application.* New York, NY: Routledge.

Scharmer, O., & Kaufer, K. (2013). *Leading from the emerging future.* San Francisco, CA: Berrett-Koehler.

Schwarz, R. (2002). *The skilled facilitator.* San Francisco, CA: Jossey-Bass.

Seijts, G. H. (2006). *Cases in organizational behavior.* Thousand Oaks, CA: SAGE.

Shaw, P. (2002). *Changing conversations in organizations.* London, England: Routledge.

Stephenson, K. (2009). Neither hierarchy nor network: An argument for heterarchy. *People and Strategy, 32*(1), 4.

Tett, G. (2015). *The silo effect.* New York, NY: Simon & Schuster.

Tourish, D. (2005). Critical upward communication. *Long Range Planning, 38*(5), 485–503.

Tuominen, M., Rajala, A., & Moller, K. (2004, May). How does adaptability drive firm innovativeness? *Journal of Business Research, 57*(5), 494–506.

Universal House of Justice. (2013, March 2). *Non-involvement in partisan politics.* Retrieved from http://universalhouseofjustice.bahai.org/involvement-life-society/20130302_001

Universal House of Justice. (2017, March 1). *Universal House of Justice.* Retrieved from http://universalhouseofjustice.bahai.org/activities-bahai-community/20170301_001

CHAPTER 24

INCORPORATING EVIDENCE-BASED CONFLICT MANAGEMENT INTO ORGANIZATIONAL OMBUDS PRACTICE

Toran Hansen, Lisa Witzler, and Tyler Smith

This chapter examines evidence-based conflict management practice, and illustrates how it is used in an organizational context, specifically by an ombudsman (commonly referred to as an ombuds). This is an enhanced form of practice that should only be attempted when one is familiar with basic ombuds work. Evidence-based practice is new to the field of conflict management but has existed for over 30 years, emerging first in medicine and then being adopted by other helping professions, such as social work. This chapter defines what evidence-based conflict management is, and illustrates both its step-by-step framework and how it is used. After explaining how it is used in general terms, an example of what evidence-based conflict management looks like in ombuds practice is provided in order to give a

From Discord to Harmony, pages 421–443

better sense of how it can be helpful for ombuds and other third parties within organizations. Overall, this chapter provides an overview of how to use the approach in organizational practice.

EVIDENCE-BASED CONFLICT MANAGEMENT

Evidence-based practice (EBP) is a new development in the field of conflict management, but it emerged out of the field of medicine in the 1980s (Rosenthal, 2006). Evidence-based practice was then taken up by other therapeutic fields, such as social work, psychology, and public health in the 1990s (Myers & Thyer, 1997). In the field of social work, for example, EBP came to mean selecting effective interventions to social problems by using, in part, scientific evidence to discover and justify those interventions (Grinnell & Unrau, 2011). This process is termed *clinical decision-making* in the field of social work. Evidence-based practice came about in response to the criticisms that social work research was not frequently used in clinical decision-making, and that the potential effectiveness of social work interventions was not often discussed with social work clients (Gambrill, 2003; Mullen, Bledsoe, & Bellamy 2008). Evidence-based practice came to the field of conflict management in 2017, with Hansen's publication of "Evidence-Based Conflict Management Practice" in the *Journal of Conflict Management* (Hansen, 2017).

Evidence-based conflict management (EBCM) is when third parties access and use scholarly sources (both quantitative and qualitative) in a structured way to better inform conflict parties about their conflict management options, assist them in deciding which ways to address their conflicts, and reveal how conflict management approaches should be carried out and under what circumstances (Hansen, 2017). Evidence-based conflict management should only be used in cases of conflict that involve a third party (i.e., an outside party such as an ombuds), and where there is more than one potential way to address a conflict. For instance, if the only way for an employer to address a request for a raise is to make an administrative decision as to whether or not to give an employee a raise, then it does not typically make sense to spend time looking up scholarly resources to inform the decision about how to address the conflict. However, when a third party is assisting in managing a conflict, and the specific conflict requires a generalist approach where many different processes, models, or techniques could be considered, then consulting with scholarly sources may well prove helpful (Hansen, 2013). In addition, EBCM is ideally used when third parties find conflicts complex and/or unfamiliar. In such instances, discovering evidence supporting the effectiveness of different conflict management processes, models, or techniques under various circumstances can be invaluable.

After understanding what EBCM is, it is important to discuss what it is *not.* Evidence-based practice is not just a third party collecting background information on conflict parties prior to working with them, although this is an important element of successful conflict management practice (Moore, 2003). Evidence-based practice is also not *exclusively* using scientific evidence as a basis for making decisions about the best way to proceed in a conflict (the process termed clinical decision-making in social work). When third parties work with conflict parties in an organization to determine the most suitable form of conflict engagement, they must consider the needs and preferences of the conflict parties, the availability of possible interventions, and the capacities and limitations of the organization, in addition to any scientific evidence (Proctor & Rosen, 2006). Evidence-based practice is also not just using "best practices" to determine conflict processes. Best practices that emerge from conflict management research are referred to as "empirically supported interventions" by EBCM practitioners, and, while they should be considered compatible with EBP, using an empirically supported intervention alone is not considered EBP in and of itself (Mullen et al., 2008). Finally, well-informed third parties, who have a strong background in conflict management scholarship, engage in what is termed "evidence-*informed* practice"; however, having background knowledge alone is not evidence-*based* practice as this involves searching for scientific evidence while applying it to a specific conflict, much like a case study (Mullen & Streiner, 2006).

The structure of EBCM is provided in a step-by-step process, and includes up-to-date evidence from rigorous conflict management research which informs and assists third parties in making decisions with conflict parties about the most helpful ways to address their conflict (Hansen, 2017). This process involves six steps, although the steps do not have to occur in order and third parties may cycle back to revisit previous steps at any time. Hansen (2017) outlines the steps as follows:

Step 1: Interrogating the Conflict—Creating answerable questions to consider in relation to the conflict and conflict management options.

Step 2: Finding and Reviewing Scientific Evidence—Finding the best possible answers to the questions posed in conflict management research.

Step 3: Analyzing the Evidence—Considering the merits of the evidence and consulting with conflict parties about it.

Step 4: Collaborative Decision-Making and Conflict Management Implementation—Working with conflict parties to decide how they want to address the conflict and then implementing any conflict management processes.

Step 5: Monitoring and Evaluating the Conflict Management Processes—Observing conflict management processes with conflict parties to determine their possible intended and unintended consequences, as well as conducting formal evaluation research.

Step 6: Sharing Lessons Learned—Disseminating information about conflict management processes as well as EBCM practice.

These six-steps provide the structure for EBCM practice.

Following the six-steps of EBCM practice, third parties turn a case of conflict into a kind of case study. In a case study, researchers consider a specific conflict in depth in order to better understand it, using various sources of information, different theories, and, frequently, both numerical and non-numerical data (Yin, 2009). Therefore, third parties should consult with a wide range of research when searching for scientific evidence. The scientific evidence itself should come from conflict management research that is often published in scholarly databases and journals, evaluation research, and other reliable sources of scholarly information (such as the International Ombudsman Association and other professional bodies and clearinghouses of information). As conflict management is a relatively new field and there is not always a lot of evidence that definitively demonstrates the effectiveness of one conflict management process over another, the pursuit of scholarly evidence should not be thought of as a search for the best way to address a conflict but rather a search for effective scientifically researched alternative pathways for third parties and conflict parties to consider. Schon (1983) called a similar process the discovery of "generative metaphors" in comparable cases, which helps practitioners make sense of challenges in practice and particular circumstances in order to make sense of ambiguity and open up new possible pathways forward.

In Step 1 of EBCM practice, coming up with answerable questions can prove to be difficult. Questions can be generated using the client oriented practical evidence search model (COPES), which is used to build questions by considering the following components: the types of conflict parties, the types of problems that conflict parties have, possible interventions, and possible outcomes that they might like to achieve, under specific circumstances (Gibbs, 2003). So, for example, if an employee is having a hard time getting along with the male manager that supervises her and goes to an ombuds for assistance, the ombuds, using the COPES model, might ask such questions as:

- What are some common concerns that arise between male managers and female employees that they supervise? (involving types of parties)
- How might women and men perceive workplace conflict differently? (involving a specific type of problem)
- How effective is mediation in dealing with manager–employee conflict? (involving a specific process)
- What are some different approaches to conflict management that have helped in employee–supervisor conflicts? (involving a range of approaches)
- How can employees and their supervisors achieve a productive working relationship? (involving a specific outcome)

These different types of questions would lead the ombuds in different possible directions. In practice, as databases are extremely valuable sources of scholarly information and people that use them employ keyword searches as a means to find scientific evidence (from scholarly journals), it can be quite helpful to convert these "answerable questions" into keywords relating to the conflict parties, their problems, potential conflict management approaches, and possible outcomes, under specific circumstances. These keywords then provide the basis for searching databases.

In Step 2, "Finding and Reviewing Scientific Evidence," typically a third party will then enter the keywords that they developed in step one into a social science database (such as EBSCOHOST or JSTOR) in order to find rigorous scientific research that could inform their work with the conflict parties. In the example outlined above, the ombuds could conduct keyword searches like: "female employee"; "gender" and "workplace conflict"; "employee," "manager," and "relations"; "conflict management" and "supervisor"; and "employee," productive*," and "work* relationship," in various scholarly databases. However, all of these searches are bound to provide too many scholarly articles to efficiently read through, perhaps thousands of sources in some instances. Therefore, practically, it is important to establish boundaries prior to engaging in such a search (e.g., limiting your search to one hour), and to carefully but quickly go through the titles and abstracts to determine which ones might be relevant. The abstracts of articles are particularly helpful in outlining any key findings in scholarly articles as efficiently as possible. Once the third party reaches his or her time limit (e.g., searching for one hour), the third party must then spend some time organizing any key findings that have emerged (again a time limit can be helpful; for example, 30 minutes). With any findings that have yet to be understood, the third party can go back and skim or read through the articles where the findings came from. A summary of the key findings can then be used as an outline to contribute to the discussions with the conflict parties that occur in step four in order to make a collaborative decision about how to proceed.

In Step 3, "Analyzing the Evidence," an EBCM practitioner methodically goes over the outline of findings to consider their utility, given the capabilities of the organization, and the unique circumstances surrounding the conflict. The third party may need to consult with conflict parties at this time to begin weighing the evidence with them, in accordance with their needs. At this point, it is important that the third party go beyond the scientific evidence, including his or her prior experience and wisdom as an important part of the analysis and any discussions with conflict parties. In addition, EBCM practitioners, like ombuds, have to take into account their additional professional constraints, such as their foundational values of: independence, neutrality and impartiality, informality, and confidentiality (Ziegenfuss & O'Rourke, 2010). In Step 4, "Collaborative Decision-Making," third parties then discuss the options that emerged from their analysis in separate meetings with the conflict parties to see how they accord with the parties' preferences, strengths, and values (Otto, Polutta, & Ziegler, 2009). This discussion may necessitate going back and searching databases for additional evidence and information. Once the conflict and its potential management have been sufficiently considered, the parties, in consultation with the third party, make a decision about how to address their conflict. This decision is then implemented.

After implementation, Step 5, "Monitoring and Evaluating Conflict Management Processes," becomes the next step (known as "practice-based research" in EBP). Practice-based research is important to ensure that conflict management processes are as helpful as possible, interventions achieve their intended outcomes, and unintended negative consequences are minimized (Grinnell & Unrau, 2011; Roberts, Yeager, & Regehr, 2006). In order to monitor the effects of conflict management processes, third parties must work with the conflict parties to determine their hoped-for outcomes and provide some mechanism for measuring progress toward them. For instance, in the example above, perhaps the employee would like a working environment that she deems safer and more stable, while the supervisor would like a more compliant employee. The ombuds could then work with the employee to develop a 7-point scale for determining how safe a workplace is and another for how stable it is, while simultaneously working with the supervisor to develop a 7-point scale for determining what employee compliance looks like. Then both parties could record responses on their scales on a daily or weekly basis to determine if their intervention is having their desired impacts. This type of research, called a single-systems research design, can also be used to establish psychological testing for evaluating conflict outcomes; however, this type of testing is often quite burdensome and would need to be administered by someone qualified to use and assess such a research instrument (Hansen, 2013). Formal evaluation research of conflict outcomes or conflict management processes may also be conducted in some organizations, but may not be necessary or plausible in other organizational contexts (Hansen, 2013).

Step 6, "Sharing Lessons Learned," involves disseminating any findings from evaluation research or process insights. Third parties should always regard their cases of conflict as learning opportunities to discuss with their colleagues in conferences and informal discussions, while ensuring the confidentiality of conflict parties. Such knowledge can then be integrated into the conflict management knowledge base (for future EBP), ultimately informing best practices in conflict management (empirically supported interventions) and supporting the creation of practice guidelines and manuals (Mullen et al., 2008). EBCM as a process can also be taught in university programs and training workshops.

Taken together, these six steps constitute EBCM practice. Hansen (2017) suggested that EBCM practice holds a good deal of promise. Hansen (2017) stated that "it is a structured approach that addresses the gap between scholarship and practice, ensures that conflict management practice is grounded in solid research findings, and reduces scholar-practitioner biases" (p. 60). He also asserted that it even provides an additional measure of protection against ineffective or harmful practice (Hansen, 2017). As scholar-practitioners who have used the approach, we also contend that the approach broadens the perspectives of third parties with respect to available conflict management approaches (providing alternative ways of thinking about conflicts and conflict management), provides insights that bring awareness to potential blind spots and areas where third parties lack knowledge, and makes third parties more aware of the potential effectiveness of their work. In these ways, EBP ensures that conflict management scholar-practitioners keep learning and growing as practitioners, much like they do when participating in continuing education opportunities. What follows is a discussion of the ombuds' role in organizations, and an illustration of EBCM practice using actual examples that were taken from ombuds using EBP in a large government agency.

THE ROLE OF THE OMBUDS IN EVIDENCE-BASED CONFLICT MANAGEMENT

The International Ombudsman Association defines an organizational ombuds as "a designated neutral who is appointed or employed by an organization to facilitate the informal resolution of concerns of employees, managers, students, and, sometimes, external clients of the organization" (Wesley, 2004, as cited in International Ombudsman Association, n.d., para. 3). The

International Ombudsman Association outlines the function of an organizational ombuds as: "To work with individuals and groups in an organization to explore and assist them in determining options to help resolve conflicts" and work-related issues or concerns (International Ombudsman Association, n.d., para. 4) and uniquely situated in their organizations to identify and bring systemic concerns to the attention of the organization for resolution (International Ombudsman Association, n.d., para. 4).

Organizational ombuds who practice according to the International Ombudsman Association Standards of Practice and Code of Ethics "operate in a manner to preserve the confidentiality of those seeking services, maintain a neutral/impartial position with respect to the [individuals and] concerns raised, work at an informal level of the organizational system, and are independent of formal organizational structures" (International Ombudsman Association, n.d., para. 5). Ombuds practice in a wide variety of settings, including: government (classical ombuds), nonprofit and for-profit organizations (corporate ombuds), hospitals and prisons (advocate ombuds), and within human-rights organizations (hybrid corporate-advocate ombuds), each with a unique focus and skill set (Ziegenfuss & O'Rourke, 2010).

Ombuds, by nature of their process and philosophy, are open, flexible when considering options, and do not purport to be experts in conflict situations. As illustrated in Figure 24.1, ombuds generally conduct their work in stages, which closely parallel those in EBCM. The stages are as follows: (a) an initial conversation, (b) clarifying roles and expectations, (c) understanding the situation, (d) analyzing, (e) exploring options, and (f) determining next steps. Therefore, ombuds are trained and prepared to use a wide variety of conflict management and resolution processes and methods. Ombuds rarely use prescribed or predetermined interventions, and do not require or instruct parties to take a particular course of action in response to conflict. They are trained to work with individuals and groups to understand the situation, and explore a range of options in order to seek resolution. No two situations are identical. Ombuds approach each situation with a curious, open, and flexible mind.

Ombuds focus on the conflict management process and provide parties with options and information. Evidence-based conflict management fits seamlessly into an ombuds' practice when it is used correctly in an appropriate organization. EBCM allows for the use of empirical research to aid in the processes of exploring a range of options and considering potential interventions (particularly during the "exploring options" and "determining next steps" phases, as described above). By sharing lessons learned, Stage 6 of EPCM, ombuds can contribute to a much-needed body of knowledge about effective conflict management approaches in organizations. These contributions can begin to inform future EBCM ombuds practice and further increase the body of knowledge as more ombuds contribute to the

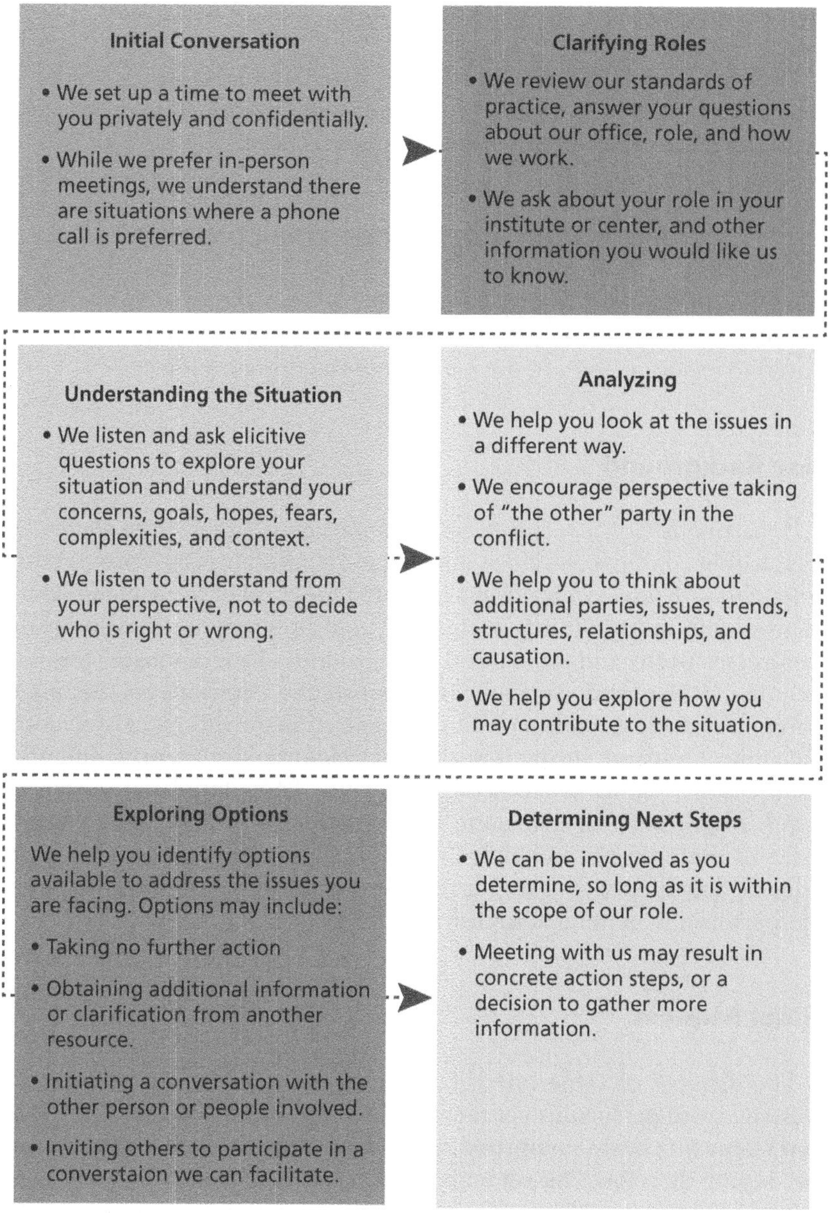

Figure 24.1 A model of ombuds practice. *Source:* Office of the Ombudsman, 2017.

literature. Additionally, ombuds who employ reflective practice through case review (a weekly sharing of cases where ombuds can ask for feedback/ guidance on a particularly difficult case as well as provide lessons learned from individual cases) are, in a way, performing Stage 6 of EBCM (sharing lessons learned).

The next section will offer a case study based upon an ongoing group intervention that addresses intragroup conflict and dynamics, to demonstrate the integration of EBCM into ombuds practice.

CASE STUDY: A DEPARTMENTAL CONFLICT

The following case study is based on an actual case within an organization. Identifying details have been modified (changed to pseudonyms) or removed to ensure privacy of the parties and the organization.

Case Background

Department C is a relatively small department (total of 20 staff members) within a large scientific organization. Department C is a programmatic division with a scientifically diverse staff. One-third of the staff are administrative staff and two-thirds of the staff hold programmatic positions that require scientific and/or clinical backgrounds. Programmatic positions include staff that work directly with scientists and clinicians conducting research to provide guidance on funding and strategic direction of scientific and clinical research through workshops, scientific conferences, and other resources in support of biomedical research. The administrative staff are largely responsible for managing the department's budget, organizing logistics of conferences (including international travel, housing, and meeting space arrangements), answering requests for information from the public, and performing general administrative duties.

Initial Request

The director of Department C came to the ombuds office requesting assistance with personality conflicts between the admin staff and the leadership team, which was comprised of three branch chiefs, the director, and the deputy director. The ombuds office was familiar with Department C from their previous efforts offering executive coaching for the leadership and conflict coaching with staff (see, e.g., Jones & Brinkert [2008] for additional information on conflict coaching), so the first two stages of ombuds practice (initial conversation and clarifying roles) were truncated.

The ombuds intervention team (IT) consisted of four members experienced in organizational development. The initial request made of the team was to provide assistance with resolving concerns and conflicts with the administrative staff within the group. The IT developed an interview protocol and interviewed all members of the leadership team, as well as all administrative staff.

EBCM Step 1

Individual interviews were conducted by IT partners. Two of the IT interviewed all of the leadership team and the other two interviewed the administrative staff. One partner conducted an interview while another took handwritten notes. Notes were transcribed and reviewed by the entire IT. Each member of the IT individually analyzed the data and then met as a team. During multiple sessions, the IT reviewed, discussed, and identified major themes emerging from the data. Themes were written on flipchart paper (one theme to a page), and specific examples demonstrating or elaborating each theme were noted from the data on each flipchart.

The themes identified were: lack of succession planning, lack of communication across branches, structure of meetings, inequities in application of administrative policies (ability to take advantage of telework, backup, etc.), perceived racism, perceived favoritism, and lack of trust and respect.

EBCM Step 2

The data themes were used as the basis for conducting scholarly research for resources to inform the IT's recommendations. The IT conducted research in EBSCOHost online databases using multiple search terms. In order to manage the amount of time spent conducting the research, the research practitioner (RP) limited searches to 90 minutes. 90 minutes was the selected time frame because the IT believed that it would be a reasonable amount of time to conduct fruitful research (one of the criticisms of EBCM is lack of time to conduct research). The following initial research questions identified using the COPES method: "How do we understand lack of trust in organizations?"; "How do we rebuild trust in a group?"; and "What is the impact of unclear roles and responsibilities on a team in conflict?"

Based on the initial themes from the data gathered, the RP developed the following search terms:

1. lack of trust in organizations,
2. lack of trust in leader,
3. lack of trust in the workplace,
4. rebuilding trust in organizations,

5. rebuilding trust in the workplace,
6. unclear roles and responsibilities in the workplace,
7. psychological safety in the workplace,
8. study of impact on organization when intervention fails,
9. how to transition when a leader retires,
10. succession planning in healthcare organizations,
11. micromanagement in the workplace, and
12. conflict between administrative staff and management.

Starting with the "lack of trust in organizations" word search, the RP uncovered articles on lack of trust in leadership. Lack of trust in leadership stimulated additional searches on rebuilding trust in teams. Because the leadership of the division had medical backgrounds, additional search terms were used to identify specific research on succession planning, leadership, and trust themes in medical environments. This led the RP to consider the following question: "How does the director's medical background impact her leadership, organizational, and cultural skills?" It was thought that answering this question could provide insight into the motivations behind some of the director's expectations and behaviors as a manager.

Throughout the 90-minute research period, the search and subsequent search terms evolved based on the articles that were discovered and reviewed, using their abstracts. For example, the search term "lack of trust in organizations" led to "lack of trust in the workplace" to "lack of trust in the leader." Every search did not glean helpful or relevant information. However, each search did build upon previous searches to naturally elicit specific topics not originally identified, which ultimately proved quite useful.

Articles returned for the search term of "trust in organizations" triggered the RP to recall a similar previous case where psychological safety was used as a framework to address group conflict. The characteristics of the leader of Department C reminded the author of the leader of a different department that two of the IT had worked with several years ago. This is an example of how the EBCM process can trigger additional ideas to inform the approach to the conflict (both from scholarly research and as a reminder of previous ombuds' experiences). This kind of holistic approach can be particularly helpful for organizational ombuds, especially since they can be viewed as repositories for organizational knowledge regarding previous conflicts.

The search of "trust in organizations" led to an additional line of inquiry in measuring trust in teams. When the RP met with the IT to present the additional scholarly research found during the search, she presented the idea of measuring the levels of trust within the team at different points throughout the intervention (at the beginning, middle, and after). This suggestion was based on research that the RP found on key elements of successful interventions. One of the more challenging aspects of conflict intervention is measuring success. The IT determined that measuring trust within the group (a predominant theme in the initial data collection) would be a way for the IT and the group to measure progress and success (which is a critical element of Step 5 in EBCM). The IT also believed that this would be relevant for this particular group because of their proclivities for research/data driven measurements of results. The RP performed subsequent research on instruments for measuring trust within groups, and consulted with a colleague with expertise in program evaluation in order to develop a custom-tailored instrument for the conflict intervention.

EBCM Step 3

Once the research was compiled, the IT met to discuss possible intervention strategies to present to the director for consideration. They interrogated the data collected and reviewed the scholarly research. They ultimately developed a series of possible interventions to address the lack of trust within the group by rebuilding trust with the leadership, as well as with staff. They connected the director with an internal group responsible for succession planning throughout the organization for a consultation to develop a plan for the department.

EBCM Step 4

An overview of the findings from the data collection and subsequent recommendations were presented to the director of Department C in a private meeting with the IT. The director had questions about some of the findings, which were answered by providing additional details without revealing the identity of people who contributed information. The key recommendations for potential interventions were: facilitated conversations; skill building on topics such as managing conflict, crucial conversations, and work-related skills; specific facilitated meetings to transition new leadership; trust-building activities (facilitated by the IT); ongoing coaching offered for any member of the group; and a review of organizational structures regarding efficiency and effectiveness. The director approved of all of the recommendations and agreed to present a timeline and plan for interventions to Department C with the IT.

EBCM Step 5

In order to monitor and evaluate progress of the interventions, an instrument was developed for staff to use at designated times throughout the series of interventions, beginning with a baseline measurement prior to any intervention activities. The instrument consisted of a Likert-scale self-evaluation of elements of trust within the department. The survey was delivered via an anonymous online survey tool, and the results were shared with the group to measure progress throughout the interventions.

EBCM Step 6

The RP was able to share the EBCM process with members of the IT who were unfamiliar with the practice. The IT's initial reaction to the use of EBCM reflected the concerns previously raised about time and skills required to conduct scholarly research. To address these concerns, the RP agreed to conduct the research and present a summary of articles and information discovered at the next IT meeting. Members of the IT were also appeased when the RP described the search process (having a time limit, using specific search terms, etc.). A lack of time and resources may continue to be a challenge when conducting EBCM, particularly for novice researchers, as well as those who have assumptions about the difficulty of conducting scholarly research within a specified time limit. In this case, the initial 90-minute search period was only adequate for the RP to explore two of their desired topics. Additional research time was required in this instance because of the complicated nature of the case (involving multiple topics to explore). The fact that this case study involved a group in conflict and a team of intervention specialists may have contributed to the need for additional time required to adequately research all of the topics. Another potential concern that emerged was that, in some contexts, ombuds may not have access to scholarly databases at all.

The intervention plan in this case is ongoing, and the RP plans to conduct additional research prior to conducting some of the interventions in order to inform the structure of the sessions. For example, prior to the session on trust building, the RP plans to conduct another time-limited search on methods for building trust in teams. In this way, EBCM will continue to be a cornerstone of future conflict interventions in this case.

Overall, the IT members all benefited a great deal from using EBCM. The team considered alternative interventions that they would not have otherwise thought of, new mechanisms for measuring the success of interventions, and different ways of thinking about the conflict. All of these insights have added to the IT's organizational repertoire in dealing with this conflict, as well as leading to deeper reflection and professional growth as ombuds, employees, and people within the organization.

Reflections on EBCM

Reflecting back on what was different about using the EBCM in this group case, we can make the following observations:

- The 90-minute time frame kept the research focused and efficient; however, additional research was required for multiple topics uncovered from the initial research (meaning the 90-minute limit was inadequate in this case).
- Scholarly articles and lines of inquiry were revealed that would likely not have been revealed without EBCM.
- Actual instruments for use in measuring intervention success (i.e., improvement in a team's trust score) were identified through EBCM and modified for use with the intervention.

EBCM may be an ideal addition to practice and enhancement for many solo ombuds practitioners as well. The research uncovered during the practice of EBCM adds additional layers to understand the complexity of a case for a solo practitioner who rarely has the benefit of reflection with colleagues regarding cases. Incorporating EBCM into an ombuds' practice strengthens the foundational ombuds' principle of independence by systematically ensuring multiple perspectives are included.

EBCM is not designed to replace but to augment an ombud's natural conflict management style. For example, an ombuds with a preference for a humanistic approach, which is very compassionate, organic, and open to exploring emotional aspects of conflicts, could use EBCM as a means of expanding the range of possible options for addressing a particular conflict. As demonstrated in the group case above, the research evolves organically by topic, and the practitioner follows the data throughout the research session. The ombuds frames the conflict using questions and keywords that match his or her particular style (in this case, focusing on compassion, emotions, and corresponding interventions). In the above example, each subsequent search term evolved organically from the previous search terms. Thus, EBCM can be incorporated into a humanistic style so a practitioner need not choose between the two. If the ombud's style is more compassionate and focused on emotions, and the options generated reflect this style, EBCM could assist the ombuds by either deepening the level of understanding of how this approach could be implemented in a specific case or by broadening the ombuds' outlook to consider other less familiar but compatible options if the research indicates a different approach could yield positive results. It is important to stress that EBCM develops organically out of an ombud's style, which helps deepen and broaden his or her knowledge, thus enhancing the ombud's practice. It should never result in ombuds using approaches to conflict management that they are uncomfortable with.

The receptiveness of conflict parties to EBCM may depend somewhat on the audience within their organization. We acknowledge that the organizations within which we practice have affinities for data and data-driven processes. In other types of organizations, where research and data are less valued, it is possible that EBCM may not be received as well. However, ombuds that work within an organization that is open to but skeptical of EBCM can result in other staff members understanding it and embracing it after they understand what it is. We also acknowledge that our own personal proclivities for research, reflective practice, and EBP make us prime candidates for incorporating EBCM into our practice, while practitioners with other backgrounds *may* have different experiences with EBCM.

CRITERIA FOR EBCM UTILIZATION

The EBCM approach was presented as a sequential process to be completed from start to finish for each case. However, after applying the EBCM approach to ombuds cases, we have discovered that the EBCM approach can be a flexible process, modified and applied based on a variety of case-dependent factors. We have identified five features of cases that may inform whether a practitioner should use EBCM and, if so, how to use it in a particular case. These five features include: the *complexity* of the case, the *novelty* of the issues to the practitioner, the perceived *efficiency* of the EBCM approach, the organizational *culture,* and the perceived *receptiveness* of the parties to the conflict. Additional criteria may also be relevant given the uniqueness of each case, but these five features are common considerations in most cases.

Complexity

As indicated above, ombuds provide a variety of services. The example above illustrated a larger group case with complex characteristics, including multiple layers of issues and challenging group dynamics. In many instances, the characteristics of a case are far less complex with respect to the parties involved and/or the issues at hand. Sometimes, cases involving multiple parties lead to direct intervention by the ombuds (mediation, facilitation, training, etc.), and sometimes they do not (only consultation, coaching, or referral making with the initiating party). Employees often contact the ombuds office because they are simply seeking organizational information (policies, processes, resources, etc.) to assist them in making informed decisions about their situation and the actions that they may take to seek resolution independently. We acknowledge that less complex cases like this may not be appropriate or well-suited for an EBCM approach.

Novelty

It is difficult for ombuds to predict what the next case that "comes through their door" will involve. Ombuds are constantly faced with new and unique issues. A "novel" case means that it presents something very new, unique, or unusual to the individual practitioner. Sometimes the uniqueness comes from the specific conflict dynamics of the case. Some practitioners may consider a case novel if it does not originate from common organizational conflict sources, such as resources, structure, communication, roles, change, power, external pressures, styles, and personalities. Instead, it might involve issues of identity or culture, or perhaps conflict drivers that originate from the technical nature of the organization's work, such as research, education, manufacturing, or business processes. Novelty is subjective. Each practitioner will view cases in a different way based on their own knowledge, experiences, background, training, and familiarity with the organization they are operating in. The EBCM approach may be more fitting for cases that the practitioner designates as novel. In such cases, EBCM helps the practitioner to gain a better knowledge and understanding of the issues at hand, and make more informed decisions about interventions (in collaboration with the parties). Novelty can also be interpreted as the novelty of the position to the individual practitioner. In instances where an ombuds is quite new to the profession, EBCM may prove overwhelming given everything else that he or she must learn. Thus, EBCM is recommended for intermediate to advanced-level practitioners.

Efficiency

How an ombuds perceives the efficiency of EBCM depends largely upon an ombuds' workload and his or her comfort in conducting research. An ombuds' caseload and schedule will determine whether there is time to conduct a research session for a given case and/or use this research to collaborate with the parties to select an appropriate pathway forward. The timeframe put forth by the ombuds to conduct research is ultimately flexible, depending upon his or her time constraints (in the example above, a 90-minute timeframe was proposed). An appropriate time limit is essential so that EBCM does not become overly burdensome and render an ombuds' work inefficient. Considering the time available must also impact the nature of any single-systems research design or evaluation research proposed by the ombuds, both for the ombuds and the conflict parties.

Organizational Culture

The organizational culture within which an ombuds practices may inform the practitioner's decision to share that they are using EBCM and specific information gleaned from EBCM. In our experience in academic and scientific research organizations, many of our cases involve people who generally respond well to the idea of using research to inform practice decisions. In other types of organizations, it may make sense to use EBCM, but not overtly draw attention to it, or avoid using EBCM entirely if there is a general aversion to research.

Receptivity

In addition to the organizational culture, it is important for the practitioner to consider the individual parties' receptivity to the EBCM approach. Some people are more comfortable considering research than others. However, if a conflict party is not open to the idea of EBCM that does not necessarily mean that the ombuds cannot still use research to inform their approach and interventions. The ombuds may want to keep that developmental piece of the approach private, though.

EBCM LIGHT: EVIDENCE-INFORMED PRACTICE

Another use of evidence in ombuds work that we have explored is the concept of evidence-informed practice or what we came to term *EBCM Light*. For cases that may not be complex enough or novel enough to justify the use of full-blown EBCM, such as policy or procedure clarification, practitioners that have a strong background in conflict management scholarship and models may consider them to provide new insights on a case. EBCM Light involves actively dredging up the practitioner's knowledge of specific and proven models and applying them to a specific presenting case. EBCM Light, therefore, blends practitioner wisdom and expertise with previous findings from scholarship or applied models. For example, in the group case described above, the ombuds relied on her knowledge of group dynamics theory and proven models, which guided some of the decision-making. This form of practice could be considered evidence informed conflict management (EICM), where practitioners rely on their own knowledge without seeking new evidence or research. Many ombuds may well use EICM without consciously identifying it as such. For example, when an ombuds researches a policy or draws on knowledge from previous cases, they could be considered practicing EICM. However, EICM is even stronger when knowledge about the process is shared among practitioners, closing the cycle of knowledge by sharing insights with them. Imagine what a great body of knowledge could be created from short reports on how the models that we use are implemented, successes and failures alike.

CASE STUDY: AN INDIVIDUAL CONFLICT

Here we present a case study of an organizational conflict that we faced where EBCM was not used but could've been, which may have led to different outcomes. Thus, this is a real case where EBCM is hypothetically applied. When applying the approach in a hypothetical way, we consider the criteria for using EBCM outlined above and offer three alternative ways that EBCM could be applied in this case. This illustrates how flexible EBCM can be in practice, and how ombuds must use their best judgement in determining how to use it in a specific case. We outline what these three alternative pathways look like below.

Case Background

Aniya, an IT specialist in higher education institution, reached out to the ombuds for some assistance with a difficult workplace conflict. Aniya had been an IT specialist for 7 years. She was very proud of her work and involvement in a critical cyber security initiative for the organization. In fact, about 18-months ago she was promoted to team leader. She struggled taking on the new management responsibilities, but was up for the challenge. Unfortunately, about 9 months ago, Aniya experienced some difficulties in her personal life. As a result, she fell into a state of deep depression. The depression became rather severe. It eventually had a strong impact on her ability to focus while at work. Aniya was making some mistakes when running security tests and missed a few project deadlines. Her supervisor, Camille, grew increasingly frustrated with her lack of attention to detail. In fact, she even issued Aniya a formal letter of expectations, the first step in officially documenting an employee's poor performance. Aniya eventually decided to take an approved medical leave of absence to address her depression. She was on a leave of absence for about four months. During that time, she received counseling and treatment.

Aniya came back to work feeling better and believing that she was ready to return. At the same time, she was feeling worried about her relationship with her supervisor, Camille. The relationship was damaged in the months leading up to her medical leave of absence. What was once a very respectful, supportive, and trusting relationship had now become stressed and increasingly uncomfortable. Aniya did not think Camille understood or even believed the extent of her depression and the impact that it had on her work. She thought Camille was treating this strictly as a performance issue, which meant that Aniya could be demoted from her position as team leader. Aniya was looking for a way to resolve this conflict and ensure her smooth transition back into the workplace.

By the end of the initial meeting, the ombuds obtained permission from Aniya to reach out to her supervisor, Camille. The ombuds scheduled a meeting with Camille to understand her perspective on the situation.

Hypothetical Scenarios

Prior to meeting with Camille, the ombuds could assess the case's appropriateness for EBCM using the criteria for considering the use of the approach.

Hypothetical Application of EBCM: Option A

The EBCM criteria could be applied to this case in the following way:

- *Complexity*: This case has two parties involved.
- *Novelty*: Procedures, regulations, and resources regarding employee health, especially mental health, are constantly evolving in the organization. Thus, additional research on employee health topics specific to the organization would prove useful in this case. Additionally, depending on the ombuds' familiarity with mental health issues and the dynamics of an employee returning to work after a leave of absence, research could be informative for the ombuds.
- *Efficiency*: A modified EBCM approach in this case could easily be incorporated into an ombuds' practice (the authors acknowledge that ombuds have different methods of practice and caseload demands that may impact this criteria).
- *Organizational Culture*: The case takes place in an academic institution. Generally, one could assume that a higher education institution's culture would be open and receptive to the idea of EBCM. At the same time, it is important to note that the specific case takes place in an Information Technology department, which functions more as an administrative department in the organization. The sub-

culture of the Information Technology department may differ from the larger culture of the organization (or academic culture).

- *Receptivity*: Given the technical nature of the work the parties do, combined with the knowledge of the organizational culture, the practitioner could make an assumption that the parties might be open to data-driven options.

EBCM Step 1. After a conversation with Aniya and Camille, the ombuds could take into consideration the background information obtained, and identify the following themes:

- managing employees with mental health issues/depression,
- challenges new managers face,
- stress management in new supervisors,
- returning to work after medical leave (from a manager's perspective and from an employee's perspective), and
- resources for employees with mental health issues.

EBCM Step 2. The themes identified above would be used to identify scholarly and organizational research that could inform options and next steps.

EBCM Step 3. The ombuds could meet with Camille individually, and provide resources or information based on the research conducted. This evidence could inform the decisions for how the ombuds' work with the two parties could proceed. The evidence could also provide the basis for resources that the ombuds could refer Camille to, in addition to working with the ombuds.

EBCM Step 4. The ombuds could meet with both parties individually, and present several options based on the data collected in Step 2. It would then be up to the parties to determine how to proceed with the additional data gleaned from the ombuds' research.

Hypothetical Application of EBCM: Option B

Another application of EBCM in this case might be to gather more information from Camille, the supervisor, prior to using the EBCM approach. The ombuds would then be able to potentially narrow the topics for research. For example, if Camille shares with the ombuds that she is concerned about the organizational-wide impact that Aniya's mistakes are having and that she is concerned that Aniya is overwhelmed with her new supervisory duties and not performing acceptably, the ombuds could modify the search terms in Step 1 and then proceed in a similar manner with Option A's steps 2 through 4.

Hypothetical Application of EBCM: Option C

A third way to incorporate the EBCM approach might be to conduct Option A's Steps 1, 2, and 3 after meeting with Aniya, and again after meeting with Camille. This modified approach might be useful because the ombuds could have researched available resources for an employee in Aniya's situation, as well as resources available to the managers of such employees. The ombuds could then enter a conversation with Camille with an increased knowledge of the resources that would be available to her. The ombuds would also gain additional information about the situation and the relationship from Camille that could inform additional research in Step 2. The ombuds could then proceed through the EBCM model.

CONCLUSION

This chapter provided an outline which illustrates how EBCM in organizations is conducted. EBCM is particularly useful in ombuds work, which often involves complex, unique cases of organizational conflict that require custom-tailored interventions that may be unfamiliar to the ombuds working with the conflict parties. This chapter also specifically outlined the role of the ombuds, followed by an overview of how EBCM was used by a team of ombuds when addressing a complex organizational conflict and a consideration of different ways that it could be applied to another hypothetical case. As can be seen, the EBCM process does not always proceed exactly as the step-by-step framework would indicate, but the cases do illustrate the utility of such an approach and how it can enhance ombuds practice. The twin concerns of having sufficient time and having the requisite research skills to conduct EBCM continue to be ongoing difficulties. However, when those concerns can be reconciled, it is clear that EBCM can be a powerful approach for ombuds when addressing complex and unfamiliar conflicts in order to reduce ambiguity, consider the effectiveness of interventions, provide alternative conflict management approaches, and determine mechanisms for measuring the progress of interventions. Ombuds can then use these insights as points of reflection, and share these lessons with their colleagues (while respecting confidentiality) in order to facilitate the appropriate use of EBCM and to continue to learn from the approach.

REFERENCES

Gambrill, E. (2003). Evidence-based practice: Sea change or the emperor's new clothes? *Journal of Social Work Education, 39*(1), 3–23.

Gibbs, L. E. (2003). *Evidence-based practice for the helping professions: A practical guide with integrated multimedia.* Pacific Grove, CA: Brooks.

Grinnell, R. M., & Unrau, Y. A. (2011). *Social work research and evaluation: Foundations of evidence-based practice* (10th ed.). New York, NY: Oxford University Press.

Hansen, T. (2013). *The generalist approach to conflict resolution: A guidebook.* New York, NY: Lexington Books.

Hansen, T. (2017). Evidence-based conflict management practice. *The Journal of Conflict Management, 5*(1), 43–62.

International Ombudsman Association. (n.d.). *What is an organizational ombudsman?* Retrieved from https://www.ombudsassociation.org/Resources/Frequently-Asked-Questions/What-is-an-Organizational-Ombudsman.aspx

Jones, T., & Brinkert, R. (2008). *Conflict coaching: Conflict management strategies and skills for the individual.* Los Angeles, CA: SAGE.

Moore, C. W. (2003). *The mediation process: Practical strategies for resolving conflict* (3rd ed.). San Francisco, CA: Jossey-Bass.

Mullen, E. J., Bledsoe, S. E., & Bellamy, J. L. (2008). Implementing evidence-based social work practice. *Research on Social Work Practice, 18*(4), 325–338.

Mullen, E. J., & Streiner, D. L. (2006). The evidence for and against evidence-based practice. In K. Yeager & A. R. Roberts (Eds.), *Foundations of evidence based social work practice* (pp. 21–34). New York, NY: Oxford University Press.

Myers, L., & Thyer, B. (1997). Should social work clients have the right to effective treatment? *Social Work, 42*(3), 288–298.

Office of the Ombudsman. (2017). *NIH Office of the Ombudsman Center for Cooperative Resolution: Annual Report 2013–2017.* Retrieved from https://ombudsman.nih.gov/sites/default/files/OmbudsmanAnnualReport2017.pdf

Otto, H. U., Polutta, A., & Ziegler, H. (2009). Reflexive professionalism as a second generation of evidence-based practice: Some considerations on the special issue "What works? Modernizing the knowledge base in social work." *Research on Social Work Practice, 19*(4), 472–478.

Proctor, E. K., & Rosen, A. (2006). Concise standards for developing evidence-based practice guidelines. In K. Yeager & A. R. Roberts (Eds.), *Foundations of evidence based social work practice* (pp. 93–102). New York, NY: Oxford University Press.

Roberts, A. R., Yeager, K., & Regehr, C. (2006). Bridging evidence-based health care and social work. In K. Yeager & A. R. Roberts (Eds.), *Foundations of evidence based social work practice* (pp. 3–20). New York, NY: Oxford University Press.

Rosenthal, R. N. (2006). Overview of evidence-based practices. In K. Yeager & A. R. Roberts (Eds.), *Foundations of evidence based social work practice* (pp. 67–80). New York, NY: Oxford University Press.

Schon, D. A. (1983). *The reflective practitioner: How professionals think in action.* New York, NY: Basic Books.

Wesley, M. (2004). The compleat ombuds: A spectrum of resolution services. *CPER Journal,* 166, 6–12.

Yin, R. K. (2009). *Case study research: Designs and methods* (4th ed.). Thousand Oaks, CA: SAGE.

Ziegenfuss, J. T., & O'Rourke, P. (2010). *The ombudsman handbook: Designing and managing an effective problem-solving program.* Jefferson, NC: McFarland.

CHAPTER 25

WHAT IN THE WORLD IS AN OMBUDSMAN?

Tony Belak and Creighlynn D. Thoele

When a person is troubled or upset due to some workplace incident or decision, where does he or she turn for help, instruction, guidance, or answers? That person may turn to a grievance officer, perhaps a human resources manager, or sometimes a coworker. Almost every workplace has an unofficial ombudsman—that person who listens well and can give some advice or feedback to friends and colleagues. This role is necessary at the workplace since people have an inherent need to be heard and understood. Many seek guidance on how to handle certain issues at the workplace, such as conflict with a coworker or supervisor, while others search for an avenue to voice major concerns about policies, procedures, or egregious behaviors without fear of retaliation. Having an individual who listens and provides sound advice regarding workplace concerns relieves stress and anxiety, and helps to establish more productive employees. Though it is difficult to measure the value of such interactions, one must assume it does have benefit since it repeats daily in the workplace. To harness the benefits of intervention by a knowledgeable and competent person can be extremely valuable to an organization; however, in many cases, there is no one in perceived

From Discord to Harmony, pages 445–467

authority that can render assistance or insight in an informal, meaningful, and non-aligned manner. Enter the *ombudsman.*

While ombudsman is the formal title, most people use the gender-neutral term *ombuds* to refer to a person who receives complaints and questions from individuals concerning the functioning of an entity, works for the resolution of issues, and can make recommendations for the improvement of the general administration of the organization served. These trusted leaders have inherent attributes of active listening and emotional intelligence to be the change agents of the workplace, and serve as internal champions, neutrals, and intermediaries when called upon to be peacemakers.

INTRODUCING THE OMBUDSMAN

Ombudsman is a Swedish word meaning agent or representative, and is recognized internationally as a generic term. King Charles XII of Sweden is most notably credited with establishing the first ombudsman program in the 18th century in an effort to ensure the Swedish officials abided by the laws and properly executed their respective duties and responsibilities (Howard, 2010). The concept of an ombudsman gained in popularity during the 19th and 20th centuries as more governments from around the world began implementing ombudsman programs into their structures, and became popular in the United States in the late 1960s, especially in public entities and government offices. For those interested in a more detailed history of the origin and role of the ombudsman, we recommend Charles L. Howard's (2010) book titled *The Organizational Ombudsman.*

While the original role of the ombuds was to investigate allegations of misconduct and misuse of power by government officials, different types of ombuds emerged when the United States started restructuring the role and responsibilities of ombudsmen offices to meet the needs of nongovernmental entities, specifically universities and corporations. There are three broad types of ombudsman: traditional/classical, organizational, and advocate. Classical ombuds are typically appointed by a legislative body and receive authority through legislative statutes. The primary responsibility of a classical ombuds is to investigate complaints regarding administrative acts of a government entity, and to advocate for fair and just practices rather than for an individual. Organizational ombuds are appointed by organizations to facilitate informal conflict resolution between internal and external stakeholders, to include employees, customers, and suppliers. Organizational ombuds do not participate in formal resolution procedures or investigations, but do advocate for fair and just practices rather than for an individual. An advocate ombuds can be appointed to a private or public organization, but are commonly found in health and long-term care organizations. The primary responsibility of an advocate ombuds is to advocate on behalf of an aggrieved individual or group of individuals. Table 25.1 provides a more detailed comparison of the roles and characteristics of the types of ombudsman.

Though there are variations in the structure and scope of responsibilities between the different types of ombuds offices, the American Bar Association established three essential characteristics for all ombuds: independence, impartiality, and confidentiality (American Bar Association, 2004, p. 2). These three characteristics will be discussed in-depth in the following

TABLE 25.1 Comparing Types of Ombuds

Roles & Characteristics	Organizational	Classical	Advocate
Neutral/impartial in receiving and considering complaints	YES	YES	YES
Independent	YES	YES	YES
Informal channel	YES	YES	YES
Confidentiality	YES	YES	YES
Offers guidance, coaching or options counseling for all levels of hierarchy	YES	YES	YES
Recommends changes to prevent problems from reoccurring	YES	YES	YES
Wide discretion to determine approach to issues or complaints	YES	YES	YES
Provides early warning to decision makers and acts as a proactive change catalyst regarding systemic issues	YES	YES	YES
Spots and communicates trends	YES	YES	YES
May handle matters only from employees, external customers/complainants, or both	YES	YES	NO
Has formal investigative authority	NO	YES	YES
Keeps records of individual cases on behalf of the organization	NO	YES	YES
Keeps non-identifying statistical data	YES	YES	YES
May issue public reports	YES	YES	YES
Mandates changes/makes decisions for the entity	NO	NO	NO
Advocates for individuals	NO	NO	YES
Advocates for fair process	YES	YES	YES

Note: Types of ombudsmen.

Source: Stier, Williams, & Thacker, 2015 (reprinted with permission).

section. The remainder of this chapter focuses on the *organizational ombuds* (OO), and how the OO can add value to your organization and assist in conflict management.

ORGANIZATIONAL OMBUDS: OOS LICENSED TO HEAL

The 1960s was a contentious time in history for the United States due to discontent and conflict surrounding the Vietnam War and the public unrest sparked by the civil rights movement. Thus, when ombudsmen programs gained popularity in state, county, and municipal governments during this time period, scholars began to explore the idea of implementing ombudsmen offices into nongovernmental institutions as a means to mediate disputes and mitigate conflict in other social settings. Colleges and universities quickly adopted the idea of an ombuds, and established the role of the *campus ombudsman* whose primary responsibility was to "mediate between groups of demonstrators and the college/university administration" (Griffin, 1995, para. 4). Throughout the 1960s and 1970s, the responsibilities of the campus ombuds continued to shift away from the traditional ombudsmen role in order to better align with the social dynamics of the time. It was this initial shift in role and responsibilities of the campus ombuds that led to a change in function of the ombudsman in an organizational setting from that of the traditional/classical ombudsmen.

Inspired by the works of Columbia University law professor Walter Gellhorn (Howard, 2010), Isidore Silver published an article in the *Harvard Business Review* advocating the need for *corporate ombudsmen*. According to Silver (1967), organizations are social systems and, as such, should "seek mechanisms to effect employee justice" (p. 78). Silver contended that the role of a corporate ombuds would be to serve as "an embodiment of the corporate conscience" (p. 87), and would work with management to bridge the communication gap between management and employees in an effort to manage and resolve conflict. Based on the work and advocacy of Silver (1967) and others, corporations slowly began to implement ombuds programs into their institutions, which culminated in the formal organization of the Corporate Ombudsman Association in 1985 (Howard, 2010). In today's society, the OOs, comprised of both campus and corporate ombuds, is recognized as an effective and efficient means of dealing with conflict within organizational settings.

Roles and Responsibilities of the Organizational Ombuds

The scope of specific duties and authority of an OO vary slightly between organizations; however, independence, impartiality, and confidentiality are imperative to the successful operation of all OO programs. To be credible and effective, the ombuds office must be independent in its structure, function, and appearance to the highest possible degree within the organization. Independence means that OOs must be free from interference in the legitimate performance of their duties, and unaligned to avoid an appearance of conflict of interest or bias. The OO often reports to and is supported by the chief executive officer or board of directors, but remains independent and, if possible, should not have any other role within the organization.

Impartiality is also a key characteristic of the OO. An ombuds office is designated as a neutral resource, and advocates for fair, just, and equitable resolutions rather than supporting either party. Thus, an OO's responsibilities include developing, evaluating, and discussing options available to aggrieved individuals rather than actively promoting a specific course of action. OOs can also act as negotiators, facilitators, or mediators between parties in order to assist in the conflict resolution process. Though the ombuds office does conduct inquiries in an impartial manner, OOs may become advocates for change where the process demonstrates a need for it.

Confidentiality is crucial to the successful operation of the ombuds office. An OO must not disclose or be required to disclose any information provided in confidence unless with permission or as required by law, such as in cases involving child or elder abuse. This includes any records pertaining to a complaint, inquiry, or investigation maintained by the ombuds office. In many organizations, OOs do not take notes, keep records, or file reports indicating specific cases to ensure the confidentiality of those individuals seeking their guidance and/or assistance. It is important to note that the ombuds office is also an informal resource and, thus, does not join in any formal adjudicative or administrative procedure related to a matter under attention.

Other important roles of an OO are education, identifying complaint patterns and trends, and making recommendations for the resolution of an individual complaint or a systemic problem to those persons who have the authority to act upon them. Figure 25.1 illustrates the areas of involvement an OO can have within an organization, and the kinds of activities necessary for a harmonious workplace.

Due to the nature of the independent, impartial/neutral, confidential, and informal work of the ombuds office, OOs typically do not have a role or engage in formal investigations, serve in any post that might compromise the neutrality of the office, make binding decisions or mandate policies, or create and maintain official records or reports. Formal training in mediation and other conflict resolution processes is invaluable for the OO's work, and membership in the International Ombudsman Association

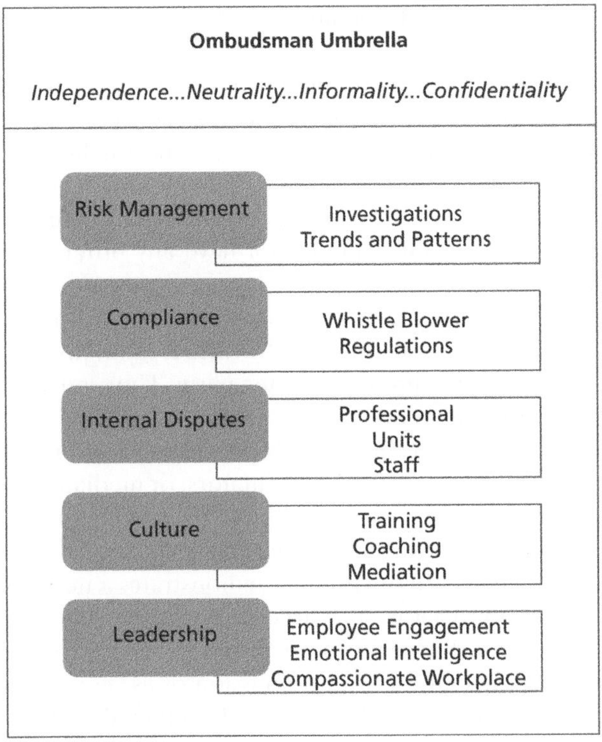

Figure 25.1 Involvement and activities of the Ombudsman.

(www.ombudsassociation.org) is important in order to stay on the cutting edge of critical OO issues and to maintain critical skills.

WHY DOES MY ORGANIZATION NEED AN OMBUDS? THE BENEFITS OF AN OO

Many organizational leaders ask the question: "Why does my organization need an ombuds office?" That is a fair question. With the influx in organizational ethics offices, compliance offices, bolstered human resource departments, and legal counsel services, it would appear that employees have many channels through which to voice grievances, report organizational issues, and seek assistance for resolving conflict within the workplace. While all of these channels do offer valued services to employees, we contend that the introduction of an ombuds office can bring additional benefits to an organization, specifically through positive corporate image, high return on investment (ROI), complementary reporting channel, growth in performance and change management, positive shift in organizational culture, and an anonymous avenue for whistleblowing.

Corporate Image

Corporate image refers to the manner in which an organization presents itself to the public. While organizations want to be perceived as profitable and well organized, they also want to be perceived as valuing their stakeholders, specifically their employees and customers. Addison-Laurie (2017) also stated that organizations that "focus on a humanistic approach to culture portray to its members and to society that its mission is aligned with the mission of its workforce and that the company performs according to these values and beliefs of its members" (p. 6). The OO can play a crucial role in an organization's corporate image. Introducing an ombuds office to the organization indicates that the organization's leaders value their employees' opinions, concerns, and well-being. The ombuds office can also help align the organization's values, beliefs, and mission with those of its employees through recommendations for change based on pattern identification and trend analysis of organizational issues. According to Stephen P. Norman, the corporate governance officer for American Express, "One of the surest ways to prevent brand damage is to identify problematic behavior at its earliest stage... An active ombuds office does that for us, as one of our key channels for helping surface issues" (McBride & Hostetler, 2008, p. 16).

Return on Investment

Every organization examines the cost-to-benefit ratio when considering the introduction of a new asset or program, and the addition of an ombuds office to an organization is no exception. While there are initial and recurring costs to implementing and running an ombuds office, the benefits do outweigh the costs as managing conflict effectively results in low-cost solutions that save time, resources, and relationships. According to John Zinsser, a leading performance metrics expert from Pacifica Human Communications, LLC, organizational ombuds programs have a high ROI, averaging a 14 dollar return per one dollar invested (McBride & Hostetler, 2008). McBride and Hostetler (2008) contended that "while the ombuds function is sometimes dismissed as a 'cost' center, we challenge boards to show comparable ROI results from more conventional 'profit' centers" (p. 17).

Interestingly, the above-stated ROI does not take into account the legal fees that would likely have incurred from employee-initiated litigation had the cases handled by the ombuds office gone directly to formal proceedings. While an OO is not a substitute for a legal or personal representative, the OO can be instrumental during the first stages of conflict. The independent, confidential, and informal actions of the OO to address a complaint, assess its merit, and close the inquiry or investigation without further action can be extremely beneficial to all involved. Most major lawsuits or upheavals in businesses began as small incidents not properly dealt with and allowed to advance into formal claims or controversies. The goal is not only to keep the genie in the bottle, but to respond immediately to those murky signals of disharmony which, invariably, can lead to serious conflict. The OO is involved in risk management by allowing people with a problem to work it out in an early and simple way before it gets out of control and more difficult to manage, which typically leads to expensive formal litigation.

Complementing Formal Channels

One of the past reasons organizations have chosen not to implement an ombuds office is that they already had established ethics offices, compliance offices, and bolstered human resources departments. While all of these offices bring value and benefits to an organization's employees, they are viewed as formal reporting channels and often require employees to identify themselves when reporting any type of organizational issue or concern. An ombuds office is an informal channel so communication between an OO and an employee does not require formal notice to the organization. Many times, employee concerns or grievances can be discussed and resolved without further intervention or involving formal channels. The addition of an ombuds office can also make formal channels more efficient. An OO can direct an employee to the appropriate formal channel and, through guiding and coaching, assist the employee in effectively articulating the issue as well as the outcome he or she seeks. According to McBride and Hostetler (2008), "This saves the formal channels valuable time from addressing or investigating issues that belong elsewhere" (p. 16). Table 25.2 illustrates the differences in roles and responsibilities in issue management between formal channels, hotlines, other formal channels (such as ethics and compliance officers and human resources), and OOs.

Performance and Change Management

Organizational leaders and employees alike can benefit from participating with OOs when disharmony presents, as the benefits of having an ombuds office directly relate to increased productivity, satisfaction, work

TABLE 25.2 Comparison of Organizational Ombuds and Other Formal Channels

Roles and Responsibilities	Formal Channel, Hotline	Other Formal Channels (Ethics, Compliance, HR)*	Informal Ombuds
Configured to be independent of ordinary line and staff management structures and operates as an informal entity reporting to top management and/or board; may report to various board committees	NO	NO	YES
Makes management decisions; Sets and enforces policy	NO	YES	NO
Performs formal investigations, acts an advocate, accepts appeals	NO	YES	NO
Provides a channel to give the organization notice of claims against it	YES	YES	NO
Maintains business records for the organization	YES	YES	NO
Provides internal and external compliance reports for the organization	YES	YES	NO
Accepts anonymous calls; Provides anonymity	LIMITED	LIMITED	YES
Provides data from a neutral viewpoint to the board and senior executives	LIMITED	LIMITED	YES
Acts as proactive change catalyst to help prevent problems	NO	YES	YES
Provides a channel for employees and managers to seek confidential guidance, based on assertion of a privilege under Federal Rule of Evidence 501 and based on the terms under which the ombuds program is made available	NO	NO	YES
Allows employees to maintain control and determine resolution options (except for cases with imminent threat of serious harm)	NO	NO	YES
Provides off-the-record coaching for options to resolve problems, and guidance to get information to the most appropriate channel in a timely manner	NO	NO	YES
Provides guidance and options for all cohorts, throughout the entire organization, on all types of work related issues	NO	NO	YES

* Also includes corporate secretary, legal, line management, audit, security, finance, etc.
Note: Comparison of organizational ombuds and other formal channels.
Source: Adapted from Redmond, Williams & Associates, 2012 (reprinted with permission).

engagement, and employee retention. An OO can be the eyes, ears, and intellect of an enlightened organization that recognizes the value and importance of alert and proactive intervention of common and ordinary complaints, reflected as the value leadership places on the people who work in such a caring environment. An OO provides managers and employees the opportunity to have an active role in the resolution process, and also helps to diffuse hostile feelings and emotions that could lead to inappropriate solutions such as theft or violence.

The office of ombudsmen acts as a change agent for the organization as well. An OO's analysis of patterns or trends in organizational issues can help the chief executive office or board of directors identify "hot spots" within the organization that need managerial intervention or policies and procedure that require change (McBride & Hostetler, 2008). An OO's identification of patterns can help "resolve contentious issues early, and can prevent their recurrence" (McBride & Hostetler, 2008, p. 16).

Organizational Culture

In its broadest sense, culture is a way of life; within an organization, it means the shared attitudes, beliefs, behaviors, and relationships that make up the organization's norms and customs. Organizations are social systems in which people are strongly influenced by the organizational culture. A potent tool for improvement is cultural change with a goal to increase the long-term health and performance of the organization, while enriching the lives of its members. People can affect systems as much as systems affect people, and effective organizational development includes allowing people to influence the systems which influence them. Changing strategies and structures could prove ineffectual or detrimental if the culture remains unaltered. Often, a neutral person like an OO, not plagued with any cultural contagion, can be the tonic to bring about acceptance by recognizing the need for cultural change and identifying the method to allow constructive communication to foster healing and growth. The simple introduction of an ombuds office may act as a catalyst for cultural change as it can be perceived as leadership's effort to foster collaboration and open communication within the organization. The implementation of an ombuds office may also begin to shift the organizational culture toward one of equal opportunity and authentic professional relationships as a primary responsibility of an OO is to advocate for fair and just processes while facilitating direct dialogue between leaders and employees.

Whistleblowing

Though "Sarbanes-Oxley, the NYSE, and NASDAQ mandate that companies provide channels of communication through which employees can act as 'whistleblowers' free from fear of retribution" (McBride & Hostetler, 2008, p. 15), employees still suffer from retaliation. According to the 2013 Global National Business Ethics Survey, 22% of its respondents said that they suffered retaliation after reporting a major organizational issue, with the percentage increasing to 44% in the recent 2018 survey (Volkov, 2018). Corporations have responded to this concern, and publicly committed to shifting their organizations toward a "speak up" culture in order to encourage employees to report major organizational issues that could cause serious harm to employees, customers, stakeholders, or the organization as a whole (Volkov, 2018). Organizations have also created new ethics and compliance offices, hotlines, and other formal channels to give employees multiple avenues to report organizational issues; however, employees are still hesitant to report issues for fear of retaliation. This is likely due to the fact that the above-mentioned channels often require employees to reveal their identity to management when reporting an incident or major organizational issue.

The independence, impartiality, and confidentiality of the ombuds office provides a safe environment for employees to report major organizational issues. In a 2007 National Business Ethics Survey, employees reported that they were three to ten times more likely to report a major organizational issue to an OO than to a hotline (McRitchie, 2011). McBride and Norman (2011) asserted that "because an office of ombudsman provides anonymity, its presence may be one of the most powerful governance tools corporate directors and management have at their disposal today (p. 33). Volkov (2018) also stated that forward-thinking companies may want to examine the idea of introducing an ombuds office into their organizations not only as an avenue for employees to address concerns, but also as a means to build trust between the organization's leaders and its employees. "As the ombudsman gains credibility, employees will increase reporting of concerns with the expectation that they will be heard, investigated, and addressed. This is a vital communications loop that has to be promoted as part of a 'speak up culture'" (Volkov, 2018, para. 11).

LET'S TALK CONFLICT

Conflict is a type of phenomenon, and can occur when two or more people interact in any enterprise or endeavor. Robbins and Judge (2015) described the traditional view of conflict as "a dysfunctional outcome resulting from poor communication, a lack of openness and trust between people, and the failure of managers to be responsive to the needs and aspirations of their employees" (p. 401). We subscribe to the interactionist view wherein functional conflict can lead to creativity and innovation within the group and the organization overall. Regardless of the viewpoint, conflict is a reality in the workplace and cannot be avoided, and, since it occurs naturally, the focus should be how best to deal with it rather than pretend it is not there. Sometimes conflict cannot be seen, but is felt in the form of anxiety, stress, discomfort, suspicion, mistrust, low morale, disharmony, and an emotional malaise in the workplace. If left unresolved, latent conflict could emerge as overt hostility, which greatly increases the risk and cost to the organization if timely, appropriate, and decisive action is not taken.

Conflict is inevitable, but combat is optional. Discord can be felt if not seen among those involved in unmanaged conflict, and, while dissonance can sometimes reveal flaws, more often it brings threat and the instinctual and visceral responses that we know as flight or fight. Table 25.3 illustrates some basic action and behavioral responses to conflict.

An OO can act as the lightning rod for conflict, and is not only available to people in conflict but seeks out those individuals who appear to be involved in disputes or disagreements at work. The objective is to interact early before an interpersonal conflict spreads to other members of the workgroup or escalates to a point that requires formal proceedings. Below is an example of how an OO can help in situations of interpersonal conflict:

TABLE 25.3 Three Basic Responses to Conflict

Avoidance	Problem-Solving	Aggression
Silent, unresolved	Shares feelings and needs	Attacks the other
Withdraws	Asks mutual questions	Interrupts
Allows interruption	Speaks for self	Subordinates others
Allows stereotyping of self	Neither stereotypes or allows stereotyping of self	Stereotypes others
Does not make eye contact	Maintains eye contact	Glares
Exhibits poor posture	Exhibits open posture	Exhibits invasive posture
Withholds information, opinions, and feelings	Discloses information, opinions, and feelings	Conceals information, opinions, and feelings
Listens ineffectively	Listens effectively	Listens selectively
Indecisive	Is able to consider options	Dominating
Apologetic	Investigates interests and needs	Loud, abusive, blaming, and sarcastic
Very little confidence	Confident	Overconfident and acts powerful
Passive	Assertive	Aggressive
Sees conflict as negative	Sees conflict as an opportunity	Sees conflict as a contest
Hides	Cooperates	Competes

> A woman in a 50-person work unit complained of being bullied by another high-level female colleague. The manager of this unit requested training for the entire group on workplace civility and bullying as a means of educating and eradicating such behavior. The OO asked a female colleague, a workplace-bullying expert, to join him in this training. When education alone did not resolve the issue with one party, the OO was able to get both parties to agree to meet at an off-campus site for mediation with their trainers. The colleagues had the opportunity to listen to each other uninterrupted and with emphasis on their underlying motivations and interests. The session was successful, and both renewed their professional relationship even though their interpersonal interactions remained strained but civil. Most importantly, the assumptions and fears each held about the other were dispelled within a healthy and safe environment of a facilitated discussion.

When we believe others view us negatively or in a false light, we may struggle as if breathing oxygen deprived air. The implications are huge since the more we feel devalued the more energy and effort we expend in defending and restoring our value, which allows less energy to generate personal worth. When we express feelings about ourselves, others, the situation in which we are currently in, or just about anything, a new level of dialogue is opened, and we can exchange and share authentic relationship data that could strengthen bonds and build trust. When trust exists in personal and professional relationships, almost everything else is easier and more comfortable to achieve, including problem solving and conflict resolution. When our actions are consistent with our words, trust can be achieved. Because cooperation cannot be compelled, social interactions are valuable as a foundation for confidence or the belief one feels toward another or others to overcome doubt or fear. Empathetic communication links people and performance, forms the basis for common action, generates power to leverage communication to targeted goals, and gives relationships their foundation to empower rewarding and positive exchanges.

There are many examples of how problems are exacerbated if left unattended long enough. We provide one of these examples below, and show how the OO was able to assist with the situation:

> A vice president (VP) and a senior leader in an intellectual technology unit of 150 people had worked together successfully for several years on a series of complicated and difficult projects. During that time, though, the workplace culture either deteriorated or an existing underlying level of toxicity bubbled to the top. Nevertheless, a disturbing level of distrust materialized, and, after a difficult and unsuccessful project, a rift developed between the VP and the senior leader which was further aggravated by a series of anonymous communications. Not only was the level of toxicity growing throughout the unit, but all remnants of trust between the VP and the senior leader dissolved. After private discussions with both parties, the OO determined that each longed

> for the time when their relationship had been one of mutual trust. In recognizing the expressions of loss, bordering on grief, that each expressed, the OO approached each of the individuals separately to ask if they would agree to a facilitated discussion or mediation. They both agreed, and each was able to define not only the effect the loss of trust was having on them personally but how it was affecting their families. These expressions of the here-to-fore concealed pain that each voiced, opened the discussion to a place where both accepted that trust was absent yet realized their assumptions of the other's motives were incorrect. Healing began to take place when their discussion turned to mutually crafting new rules for collaboration and engagement with one other, and hope that these new efforts would forge the pathway to re-establishing trust and mutual respect.

If collaboration is a sharing of responsibilities and resources to achieve a common goal, we do this all the time; however, the extent and quality of those interactions often do not meet our expectations. The shared reality of people at work depends on the structure of their relationships, the culture within their organization (including the subculture of their immediate workplace), and the degree of cooperation, communication, solidarity, and collaboration among them.

Intergroup Conflict

Limited resources and reward structures can foster intergroup conflict by making the differences in goals within a group more apparent. Reorganization of the workplace and integration of services and facilities can also be stressful to some and create negative conflict. Some individuals within the group may have inherent traits or social histories that impact intergroup conflict, but problems with intergroup relations are not usually just caused by the deviate behavior of a few people.

Intergroup conflict causes changes to occur not only within the group in conflict, but also between groups. Differences in perceptions among groups regarding time and status, when coupled with different group goals, can also create serious conflict. Within the groups, members will usually overlook individual differences in an effort to unite against the other side, and with this concerted effort, the focus is on the task. The group can become more efficient and effective at what they do, and members can even become more loyal, closely following group norms; however, problems can occur when the group loses focus of the organization's goals and becomes closed off from other groups. Haughtiness and isolation quickly lead to decreased communication. Communication is the key between interdependent groups, and these situations will have the highest negative consequences from ineffective communication. Miscommunication can be the death knell of any organization.

Conflict within or between groups can be destructive or constructive depending on how the conflict is handled. When an organization is creating a dispute resolution process, there are key factors to success:

1. a critical mass of individuals who are committed to the process,
2. a leadership group who perceive it in their best interest and the best interests of the people they serve,
3. strategic cooperation among historical enemies,
4. realistic and satisfactory outcomes, and
5. a moratorium on hostilities or conflict-seeking behavior.

There are also barriers to success:

1. fear of losing power,
2. unwillingness to negotiate,
3. no perceived benefit,
4. corporate philosophy,
5. top leadership reluctance,
6. lack of knowledge about ADR (alternative dispute resolution), and
7. lack of success stories.

Responsible measures to reduce barriers and encourage a true paradigm shift are training, incentives, marketing, periodic review, case studies, and top management support and participation. Trust leaders, like an OO, trained in mediation and other forms of ADR, are a necessary resource from outside or within the organization. The workplace of the future will have in-house mediation or other conflict management programs to reduce formal claims and act as a risk management business practice.

Workplace Abuse

Clinical psychologists who specialize in workplace trauma have noted that real or perceived abuse of employees is costing billions of dollars, and this type of trauma is emerging as a more crippling and devastating problem than all the other work-related stresses put together. It has been estimated that as many as 20 million Americans face workplace abuse as a daily occurrence; this is one in six workers, and is more common than either racial or sexual harassment (Namie, Christensen, & Phillips, 2014). With all the laws, policies, and regulations to protect workers one may ask how this can be. There are several reasons, but the most prevalent being that behaviors such as mobbing and bullying are often ignored, tolerated, misinterpreted, and even instigated by employees or the organization's management as a deliberate strategy. Several states are considering legislation to address workplace incivility much like hostile work environment; however, this behavior has not yet been identified as a legal cause for action (Duffy & Yamada, 2018).

THE INTEGRATIVE CONFLICT MANAGEMENT MODEL

The integrative conflict management model (ICM2) is a novel and compassionate approach that "treats unhealthy conflict as a thought-borne pathogen—a destructive neurological transaction arising from an experience of power deprivation" (Belak, 2018, p. 403; Cowan, n.d.). Essentially, this approach to conflict management focuses on the nature of power, and provides different methods to help individuals replace unhealthy expressions of power (bullying behavior, taking a victim role, etc.) with expressions of healthy power (listening to others' concerns, a sense of value and belonging within the organization, etc.). The ICM2 is founded on the idea that individuals have unique constructs of reality—how they perceive themselves as a person, their role in their personal and professional environments, and their overall place in this world. An individual's construct of reality is formed through an inimitable combination of beliefs, relationships, social interactions, experiences, genetics, and surroundings, and is constantly changing as it is continually being influenced by family, peers, media, religion, economics, and other elements to which an individual is exposed every day.

Though difficult to fully comprehend, an individual's construct of reality can often be identified and understood through his or her expressions of power. We discuss power as an expression rather than a feeling since expression of power is a significant component of interpersonal relationships whereas an unexpressed feeling is not. This is especially true in bullying behavior. Figure 25.2 provides examples of expressions of healthy power when applied universally and with discernment.

Figure 25.3 provides examples of unhealthy power. These expressions of power produce some degree of negative results, even when applied for good purposes.

According to Belak (2018), if negative conflict is an expression of unhealthy power then helping an individual replace unhealthy power with expressions of healthy power will assist in resolving the negative conflict. The ICM^2 provides several techniques that an OO can use to assist individuals with changing power expressions. One specific technique is referred to as the Five Ps, and is displayed in Figure 25.4. One aspect of the Five Ps model

- Belonging
- Caring
- Compassion
- Confidence
- Consideration
- Cooperation
- Courage
- Courtesy
- Creativity
- Determination
- Diligence
- Enthusiasm
- Excellence
- Flexibility
- Forgiveness
- Friendliness
- Generosity
- Gentleness
- Helpfulness
- Honesty
- Honor
- Hope
- Humility
- Idealism
- Inclusion
- Integrity
- Joyfulness
- Justice
- Kindness
- Love
- Loyalty
- Moderation
- Modesty
- Patience
- Peacefulness
- Perseverance
- Purposefulness
- Reliability
- Respect
- Reverence
- Responsibility
- Self-discipline
- Service
- Tact
- Tenacity
- Thankfulness
- Tolerance
- Trust
- Truthfulness
- Understanding
- Wisdom

Figure 25.2 Examples of healthy power. *Source:* International Center for Compassionate Organizations, n.d.

- Arrogance
- Avarice
- Begrudging
- Boundary Crossing
- Combativeness
- Corruption
- Covetousness
- Cowardice
- Cynicism
- Discourtesy
- Dishonesty
- Disloyalty
- Disorderliness
- Disrespect
- Distrust
- Disunity
- Doubt (baseless)
- Envy
- Excessiveness
- Expediency (Inappropriate)
- Greed
- Harshness
- Hate
- Hopelessness
- Hostility
- Hurtfulness
- Ignorance (applied)
- Impatience*
- Indifference*
- Inflexibility
- Injustice
- Intimidation
- Intolerance
- Irresponsibility
- Joylessness*
- Lying
- Misrepresentation
- Malice
- Miserliness
- Moral Weakness
- Negativity
- Noncommitment*
- Noncooperation*
- Obstruction*
- Pride (false)
- Procrastination
- Purposelessness
- Rigidity
- Sloppiness
- Superstition
- Suspicion*
- Tactlessness
- Thanklessness
- Timidity*
- Uncleanliness
- Unreliability
- Untrustworthiness
- Vacillation
- Wrath

* Constitute negative power when applied pathologically

Figure 25.3 Examples of unhealthy power.

is power swapping. Power swapping consists of openly addressing the issue of unhealthy power with an individual. Another effective yet more conservative approach to handling expressions of unhealthy power is mirroring. Mirroring is the use of deliberate forceful expressions of healthy power in response to unhealthy power. While both approaches can produce positive results, the most effective approach to use in a situation will depend on an individual's unique construct of reality. "By respecting and understanding every unique reality, the ombuds can better provide alternatives, choices, and guidance to assist in meeting the challenges that brought the person to the ombuds" (Belak, 2018, pp. 402–403).

The exercise of compassionate action can also help an OO more effectively serve those suffering. The International Center for Compassionate

Five Ps

1. **Pause:** See if and how *you* are affected by the conflict issue.
2. **Presentation:** Frame those involved as presenting with symptoms, rather than viewing them through a moral (right/wrong) lens. This is at the compassionate heart of the approach.
3. **Power Issue:** Unhealthy conflict emerges from an experience of loss of power. Identify the power issue.
4. **Power Swap:** Support replacing unhealthy conflict (unhealthy power) with healthy power by mirroring positive power that the person possesses but has discounted or failed to see.
5. **Power Infusion:** Assist creating a continuing experience of power (by listening, caring, acknowledging, reframing, illustrating by example, etc.).

Figure 25.4 The ICM2 Five P's protocol. *Source:* Belak, 2018. Reprinted with permission.

Organizations (n.d.) defined compassion as "a feeling of deep sympathy and sorrow for another who is stricken by misfortune, accompanied by a strong desire to alleviate the suffering" (para. 6), and defined compassionate action as taking personal responsibility for alleviating and preventing the suffering of others. The ICM^2 stresses the value of compassion, and informs OOs to use real compassion to better understand, evaluate, and educate those individuals in conflict distress.

THE POWER OF LISTENING

Listening is so basic it is often taken for granted. Listening effectively is to pay attention, take an interest in, care about, take to heart, validate, acknowledge, be moved by, and appreciate the person. It is especially hurtful not to be listened to in those relationships we count on for understanding. The need to be heard is one of the most powerful motive forces in human nature, and how we define and sustain ourselves in conversations with others. That recognition through being listened to is the response from another person that makes our feelings, actions, and intentions meaningful. Who we are and what we say can trigger other people's responses to us. Such responses and our connection to others are vital to our psychological well-being. Being listened to can spell the difference between feeling accepted and feeling isolated. We don't usually stop to examine patterns of misunderstanding in our lives because we are stuck in our own point of view. Misunderstandings can be painful, and when we are hurt we tend to look outside ourselves for explanations. In this linear thinking we often reduce human interactions to a matter of personalities. Attributing other people's lack of understanding to their character can shield us from our own ignorance and passivity. That some people repeat their annoying ways with others does not prove that lack of responsiveness is fixed in character; it only proves that these individuals trigger many people to play out the reciprocal role in their dramas of two-way disharmony (Nichols, 1995).

Few aspects of human experience are as powerful as the longing to be understood. When we think someone listens, we believe we are being taken seriously, that our ideas and feelings are being recognized, and that we have something to contribute. A listener's empathy, which is an understanding of what we are trying to say and showing it, builds a bond of understanding between the listener and the speaker; thus, an OO who displays empathy through understanding and concern is able to connect to the speaker by confirming that the speaker's feelings are recognizable and legitimate. When deeply felt but unexpressed feelings take shape in the words that are shared and come back clarified, the result is a reassuring sense of being understood and a grateful feeling of humanness with the one who understands. If listening strengthens our relationships by cementing our connection with one another, it can also fortify our sense of self. In the presence of a receptive listener, we can clarify what we think and discover what we feel. Accordingly, by giving an account of our experience to someone who listens well, we are better able to understand ourselves, identify our interests and needs, and find resolution. If we cannot change the direction of the wind, we can certainly adjust our sails. An OO can assist in making those adjustments.

THE FENG SHUI OF WORKPLACE CONFLICT

Feng shui is the art of creating an environment that is in harmony with our energetic dreams and goals. In this Asian view of harmony, the goal is not seeing new boundaries but seeing with new eyes, and it is not a blind acceptance of new fads or trendy approaches to old issues. It is a look at what you have and a different view of what it does for you. The contemporary style of feng shui will show how to uncover the roots of concerns in your environment so that you can then develop cures that are personal and specific for you. It asks the question, "How can I use the things I already have in my space to support and enhance the way I live?" Supported by techniques of psychology and contemporary scientific knowledge about how we are affected by the spaces around us, the goal is to build up a space that will support certain needs and goals. The workforce has certain needs and goals as well, so maybe it's time to apply feng shui to the conflicts that plague our offices, factories, and places of employment.

Placing wind chimes, bamboo flutes, red ribbons, bells, or crystals around the office probably won't diminish conflict, but it might decorate the place. The real icons of conflict resolution and harmony within the workplace are respect and communication. To achieve precision and effectiveness in communication, a message must be conveyed, the message must be received, there must be a response, and each message must be understood.

Communication is much more than talking and waiting to talk; yet, in so many workplace conversations we listen just enough to respond, not caring to understand the complete message. If a pattern of such weak communication establishes itself, problems loom on the horizon. Because we don't like to be confused, we often make assumptions or anticipate solutions that serve our needs. Listening without comprehension has many side effects, none of which are positive to the mission of the workplace. The essence of good listening is empathy, and in that climate of better understanding a respect for the other person can be established. Respect can be reflected in trust, openness, and a willingness to share vulnerabilities. We all have weaknesses, even though we sometimes would like to think they are invisible, and, when we display them as a signal of power, we undermine our own authority. Just as the basic tenet of feng shui is the value of influence, inspiring others to move in a direction without them consciously knowing that you are making that encouragement can redistribute the energy of conflict in a way that inspires a positive environment. The power of active listening should not be discounted, for it is an essential leadership trait and critical for maintaining a competitive advantage in the workplace. "Listen or your tongue will keep you deaf" (www.listen.org).

The use of an OO or trust leader to bridge the divide between or among people is a feng shui approach to uncover roots of concern. If an organization's leadership wants to change the corporate culture, bring in an expert to rearrange the things already existing. Organizational culture provides the framework under which work is done and how people are selected, developed, managed, and rewarded. It includes an organization's values, decision-making processes, allocation of resources, division of power, and level of risk allowed and encouraged. To successfully support the strategy and mission of the organization, the culture—with all of its elements—must be aligned with the work process and human resource considerations. Reorganization alone will not ensure success. For culture change to be effective, it must include:

- mobilization of leadership to take ownership of the change,
- creation of new roles and work policies that are aligned with strategic and cultural changes,

- development of human resources strategies to support the cultural change, and
- application of validated behavior science to address the human side of change.

This improved way of dealing with people and their problems should motivate, and even encourage, added change within the workplace. Change can be a good thing if it is done for the right reasons. If you merely want to rearrange the furniture without feng shui, that's your privilege; however, if you want to change the conflict culture you should consider an expert in conflict resolution, such as an OO. With appropriate intervention through informed understanding of the issues raised by all stakeholders, OOs can help resolve matters, preserve relationships, maintain managerial authority, and minimalize the potential for additional problems. Sometimes the distinction between doing the right thing and doing the thing right can be as simple as trusting people to select the proper choice when given the power to choose.

CONCLUSION

Conflict is a normal occurrence in any type of environment as it is a byproduct of individual differences in constructs of reality, perceived power, and unfulfilled psychological needs (such as recognition, respect, control, and affection). Thus, conflict cannot be avoided, but it can be managed and, in many cases, resolved. Organizational ombuds (OOs) provide employees an independent, impartial, confidential, and informal avenue to address conflict within the workplace. OOs show compassion, actively listen, and offer guidance to those individuals seeking assistance with how to handle organizational issues, interpersonal conflicts, or negative behaviors affecting them personally and/or professionally at work. OOs can also use conflict management approaches to resolve negative conflict and assist with changing expressions of unhealthy power to healthy power. Though formal channels do provide employees avenues for reporting organizational issues, the introduction of an ombuds office offers additional benefits to employees and the organization as a whole. A progressive workplace recognizes its people, encourages and builds trust between its leaders and employees, and openly communicates in a respectful fashion. Let an OO help your company realize the power that harmony brings to the mission, people, and culture of an organization.

REFERENCES

Addison-Laurie, E. (2017). *The role of an ombudsman in mitigating conflict* (Doctoral dissertation). Retrieved from https://scholarworks.waldenu.edu/cgi/view content.cgi?article=4686&context=dissertations

American Bar Association. (2004). *Standards for the establishment and operation of ombuds offices* (Report to the House of Delegates, adopted February 4, 2004). Retrieved from https://www.prearesourcecenter.org/sites/default/files/library/abaadoptedbythehouseofdelegatesfeb92004.pdf

Belak, T. (2018). The role of the ombuds in addressing workplace bullying and mobbing. In M. Duffy & D. C. Yamada (Eds.), *Workplace bullying and mobbing in the United States* (pp. 387–412). Santa Barbara, CA: Praeger.

Cowan, A. (n.d.). *The integrative conflict management model.* Retrieved from https://www.compassionate.center/pgs/tracks/ccm/icm2.html

Duffy, M., & Yamada, D. C. (Eds.). (2018). *Workplace bullying and mobbing in the United States.* Santa Barbara, CA: Praeger.

Griffin, T. (1995, February/March). The evolution of the role of ombudsperson on university and college campuses. *The Fourth R, The Newsletter of the Association for Mediation in Education,* 55. Retrieved from http://web.archive.org/web/20080511213601/http://www.campus-adr.org/Main_Library/Articles/Griffin.html

Howard, C. L. (2010). *The organizational ombudsman: Origins, history, and operations—A legal guide.* Chicago, IL: ABA.

International Center for Compassionate Organizations. (n.d.). *Understanding the meaning of compassion.* Retrieved from http://www.compassionate.center/pgs/resources/definitions.html

McBride, J. E., & Hostetler, J. S. (2008, May). Board champions for the ombudsman. *Directors Monthly.* Washington, DC: NACD. Retrieved from http://www.mcbrideassociates.com/auxiliary/Board_Champions_for_the_Ombudsman.pdf

McBride, J. E., & Norman, S. (2011, February). Time for an ombudsman? *Corporate Secretary.* Retrieved from http://www.mcbrideassociates.com/auxiliary/Time_for_an_Ombudsman.pdf

McRitchie, J. (2011, December 13). Review: The organizational ombudsman: Origins, roles, and operations–a legal guide. *Corporate Governance.* Retrieved from https://www.corpgov.net/2011/12/review-the-organizational-ombudsman-origins-roles-and-operations-a-legal-guide/

Namie, G., Christensen, D., & Phillips, D. (2014, April 8). *Workplace bullying: U.S. national prevalence.* Retrieved from http://www.workplacebullying.org/2014-prevalence/

Nichols, P. (1995). *The lost art of listening.* New York, NY: The Guilford Press.

Redmond, Williams, & Associates. (2012). *An informal ombuds program complements and does not duplicate the role of formal channels in a conflict management system.* Prescott, AZ: Author.

Robbins, S. P., & Judge, T. A. (2015). *Organizational behavior* (16th ed.). Boston, MA: Pearson.

Silver, I. (1967, May–June). The corporate ombudsman. *Harvard Business Review, 45*(3), 77–87.

Stier, J., Williams, R., & Thacker, S. (2015, February). *Ombuds offices.* Retrieved from abaombudsday.files.wordpress.com/2018/09/overview-and-comparison-of-ombuds-chart.pdf

Volkov, M. (2018, May 18). *Time for companies to establish an independent corporate ombudsman.* Retrieved from https://www.jdsupra.com/legalnews/time-for-companies-to-establish-an-57545

ABOUT THE CONTRIBUTORS

Barb Allen, PhD, is an independent consultant who works in the field of OD and change management. Barb assists groups in practicing new communication and interaction patterns as they lead change together. Her inclusive participatory approach gives voice to and leverages the diverse talent from all parts of the organization towards creatively solving complex problems. She holds an MBA from the University of Arkansas in Little Rock and a PhD in conflict analysis and resolution with a concentration in organizations from Nova Southeastern University in Ft. Lauderdale, Florida.

Dr. Diane Banic is the founder of Executive Development Resources (EDR). She views leadership as an inside out process of personal growth and learning and takes a holistic approach to her work. As a licensed psychologist and executive coach she serves as a trusted advisor, focusing on enhancing the effectiveness of leaders, teams, and organizations. Allowing success to emerge! Dr. Banic brings a unique mix of skills and talents to her work in leadership. With an academic background in behavior change and practical organizational experience, she partners with senior leaders to align structure, talent, and systems with corporate vision and business goals.

Diane's passion is the development of leaders, to assist them in reaching their highest potential. In various roles over 3 decades, she has gained experience in change management, human resources, leadership development, corporate education, and organizational culture. During her career, she has implemented strategies for successful people integration during mergers and acquisitions and she has been on the ground floor with start-ups.

From Discord to Harmony, pages 469–481

Diane has accumulated a wealth of knowledge and insight which she brings to each assignment.

She serves as a trusted resource and coach who can challenge senior leaders to "do the right thing when it comes to the people side of business." She assists leaders at all levels in exploring ways to work together and create a climate of cooperation among themselves and with their work groups. Her most recent work involves various aspects of organizational effectiveness where she works with senior leaders to navigate the challenges with leading complex organizations. She has served clients in the automotive, transportation, manufacturing, health care, food production, technology, telecommunications, chemical, entertainment, sports, and service industries.

Diane holds a BA in psychology, an MA in organizational development, and a PhD in counseling psychology. She has served on the board for the March of Dimes and the Urban League. She is currently a board member for the Arrow Fund, a member of the Kentucky Psychological Association, the Organizational Development Network, and the American Society for Training and Development. Diane is also actively involved with the thoroughbred horse industry in Kentucky.

Tony Belak, JD, is the former ombudsman at the University of Louisville; associate director of the Center for Conflict Resolution at La Sierra University, Riverside, California; associate director of the International Center for Compassionate Organizations (www.compassionate.center); and the former executive director of the International Center for Collaborative Solutions at Sullivan University, Louisville, Kentucky, where he was also on the faculty of the Master of Science in conflict management program. He is a faculty member of the Department of Urban and Public Affairs at the University of Louisville and associate editor of the online *Journal of Conflict Management* at Sullivan University. He was the senior dispute resolution counsel for the Department of Veterans Affairs and is not only a mediator and arbitrator but also a teacher in basic, advanced, and specialized conflict resolution. He is recognized for his innovation in designing conflict resolution programs within the workplace.

He has taught conflict resolution at the University of Louisville Louis D. Brandeis School of Law, Indiana University Southeast College of Business, and MBA courses and seminars at the Vienna campus of Webster University and Bratislava, Slovakia. He is the first attorney graduate of the George Washington University Interagency Institute for Federal Health Care Executives (1992). He was an original founder of the Louisville Bar Association ADR Committee and served for 8 years on the Kentucky Bar Association ADR Committee and as its chair for 2 years. He is the former Regional Counsel for the Department of Veterans Affairs and was an initial member of the Civil Justice Reform Act Committee for the Western District of

Kentucky, former assistant Commonwealth Attorney, special assistant U.S. Attorney, and president of the Federal Bar Association, Kentucky Chapter. He is a certified mediator and arbitrator with the Financial Industry Regulatory Authority (FINRA); the Kentucky Collaborative Family Network, the U.S. Postal Service REDRESS program; trained as an arbitrator by the American Academy of Matrimonial Lawyers (AAML) and the Federal Mediation and Conciliation Service (FMCS); a mediator/arbitrator with the Southern Indiana Realtors Association, Inc.; and a past member of the Louisville Labor-Management Committee. He also is past two term chair of the Louisville Bar Association ADR/Mediation Section and past president of the Mediation Association of Kentucky, and president of the Kentucky Chapter of the Labor and Employment Relations Association.

Dr. Gary Boettcher is a long-time dispute resolution practitioner. Imbued with wisdom as a third-party neutral from several thousand hours of face-to-face experience within commercial aviation, organized labor, high-level government officials, military settings, and management perspectives, his Conflict Management Strategies, Inc. company focuses on facilitation processes for small and large organizations, both for profit and NPOs. *Intelligent Communication* techniques coupled with conflict management coaching processes are centric to focused facilitations that result in highly effective and satisfactory co-created, consensus-based, and forward-looking solutions. Please address any questions on the chapter or concepts to: ManageConflict@me.com or gary@ConflictCoutns.com

Dr. Kimberly Castle is the owner, director of The Appalachian Peace Center, a mediation, and consulting Center since 2008. She teaches management and conflict management courses for the graduate programs at three universities—University of Pikeville, University of the Cumberlands, and Sullivan University. She specializes in conflict management, mediation, high conflict divorces, and domestic violence. Dr. Castle has authored "Motivation of a Workplace Bully" (2017 Global Business and International Management Conference, Orlando, FL, published in conference paper, Feb. 2017). And she authored (using pen name Twiggy Bean, PhD) *Divorce Bullying—An Epidemic* (Balboa/Hay House Press, 2018). She has written articles for her local newspaper, *The Winchester Sun*, and she writes and hosts various trainings and is available as a keynote speaker for many topics.

Dr. Castle focused her doctoral research on the motivation of a workplace bully and works professionally with perpetrators of bad behaviors in a variety of situations, personal and professional. She conducts seminars and workshops and she teaches the skills to change and motivates clients to seek change. Her philosophy is that "our mistakes do not define us—it is our changes that will be remembered."

Teresa A. Daniel, JD, PhD, serves as the dean of the human resource leadership program at Sullivan University (www.sullivan.edu) based in Louisville, KY, and also teaches in the PhD in management program. An active scholar-practitioner with an emphasis on helping employers develop strategies to address toxic leadership, workplace bullying, and sexual harassment, her growing body of research on these problems has been actively supported by the national Society for Human Resource Management through numerous articles, interviews, and books. Her most recent book is titled *Stop Bullying at Work: Strategies and Tools for HR, Legal, & Risk Management Professionals* (SHRM Books, 2016). She can be reached via e-mail at: tdaniel@sullivan.edu.

Maureen Duffy, PhD, is a workplace consultant to organizations and individuals and a preeminent authority on workplace mobbing behaviors. She is co-author of *Mobbing: Causes, Consequences, and Solutions* and *Overcoming Mobbing: A Recovery Guide for Workplace Aggression and Bullying* and is co-editor of the recently published *Workplace Bullying and Mobbing in the United States, Volumes 1 & 2*. She is also a family therapist who works with targets and their families. Her clinical and consulting work focuses on workplace mobbing and bullying. Maureen has been a frequent featured speaker at national conferences addressing workplace issues.

Dr. Marilyn Faulkenburg is full time faculty in the graduate school at Sullivan University and teaches in the human resource, management, and leadership program at the graduate school. Marilyn holds a BS degree from Purdue University, MA in human resources/management from Webster University, and an EdD in leadership education from Spalding University. She has over 30 years of experience in business and 6 years exclusively in human resources. Marilyn owns MJ Training and Consulting and specializes in emergenetics and other training: ethics in the workplace, team building, leadership, change management, conflict resolution, communications, supervisor training, problem-solving and decision-making, and customer service. Marilyn is also a certified trainer and coach for the John Maxwell group and is CP-SHRM and SCP-SHRM certified.

Prior to joining Sullivan University, Dr. Faulkenburg was the executive director of workforce/economic development at Ivy Tech Community College in Sellersburg. She was responsible for workforce training and development, grants, and the apprenticeship program. Marilyn developed the Ivy Tech Center for Leadership Excellence and facilitated classes in the center. This center focused on leadership development for manager level and above. Prior to this position, Marilyn was the vice chancellor of Academic Affairs at Ivy Tech in Sellersburg and led the academic programs with over 25% in student enrollment. Marilyn has been an adjunct instructor in the School of Business at Ivy Tech Community College, Webster University,

Indiana University Southeast, Ottawa University and Spalding University in the doctoral program.

Marilyn has worked for Target stores and Horseshoe Indiana. At Target, Marilyn was a store team leader and also a district team leader over the operations of multiple stores in southern Indiana and the Louisville metro area. At Horseshoe Indiana, Marilyn was vice president of human resources and managed all aspects of human resources for over 2,200 employees.

Dr. Nancy Geist Giacomini is an independent ombuds, mediator, educator, author, and nationally recognized thought leader advancing integrated conflict management systems with foundations in restorative justice and inclusive excellence. She mediates and facilitates statewide special education disputes for the PA Office for Dispute Resolution and is a subject matter expert and online adjunct faculty for graduate strategic leadership and management courses in conflict, diversity, and human resource management at Sullivan University (KY) and St. Bonaventure University (NY). Dr. Giacomini is an accomplished practitioner certified across a spectrum of process options as a mediator, victim–offender conference facilitator, conflict coach, and grievance/due process administrator. She is an external policy and process review expert and nonprofit board consultant as past president of the Association for Student Conduct Administration (ASCA). Association legacies include creating sustained annual professional development opportunities and curriculums that bridge traditional student conduct practice with conflict resolution and restorative justice initiatives, and building the association's multi-cultural capacity through ongoing diversity responsive strategic planning, inclusive member outreach, and targeted institutional recruitment. Dr. Giacomini founded and chaired the ASCA Community of Practice for Women, served on the Foundation Board and provided transformative leadership as chair of the Executive Director Task Force and member of the Diversity Task Force. Nancy is also a member of the International Ombudsman Association, Association for Conflict Resolution, ACPA-College Student Educators International, and PA Council of Mediators. She contributes scholarship in the field as a published author, *Journal of Conflict Management* (JOCM) editorial board member and dissertation committee member. The second edition of her coedited publication *Reframing Campus Conflict: Student Conduct Practice Through a Social Justice Lens* (Schrage & Giacomini, 2009) is under full collaborative revision for a 10 year anniversary release.

Alexia Georgakopoulos, PhD, is a professor in the Department of Conflict Resolution Studies at Nova Southeastern University and director of the Institute of Conflict Resolution & Communication (ICRCtraining.com), a world-class conflict resolution training and consulting firm. She was featured on NBC's *Today Show* to discuss peace and is the editor of *The Mediation Handbook: Research, Theory, and Practice* published by Routledge.

Dr. Toran Hansen is the director of the graduate program and an associate professor in the Department of Conflict Analysis and Dispute Resolution at Salisbury University. He was previously an assistant professor at Nova Southeastern University's Department of Conflict Analysis and Resolution, in Florida. He earned his PhD in social work from the University of Minnesota and a master's degree in conflict analysis and resolution from Nova Southeastern University. In addition to evidence-based practice, Toran has research interests in restorative, transitional, and social justice; and conflict transformation, peace, and approaches to dialogue. He has written scholarly articles and chapters on a variety of subjects related to these interests including: regenerative justice, victim–offender (humanistic) mediation, truth and reconciliation commissions, critical approaches to conflict resolution, narrative mediation, inter-organizational network facilitation, community organizing in social movements, social capital, holistic peace, and, of course, evidence-based conflict management practice. He is the author of *The Generalist Approach to Conflict Resolution.*

Dr. Bill Hymes finished his surgical training in Houston, Texas and practiced in the Louisville area for 20 years, the vast majority in solo practice. He now does consulting and spends time considering how to make amends for his past transgressions.

Dr. Barbara Lassiter is both an executive coach and a certified personal coach with 11 years' experience working with clients around the world. She has owned multiple businesses and worked across a broad spectrum of industries. Barbara's interest in intimate partner violence and workplace bullying stems from past personal experience with both forms of violence. Dr. Lassiter lives and works in Florida.

Dr. Angela Lewis serves as the corporate operations department director and business director for the Naval Surface Warfare Center (NSWC), Crane Division. She and her staff ensure a mission-ready environment for the command's operations. Her department and staff responsibilities include enterprise level planning, corporate strategy, program office assignments, customer advocacy, human resources, infrastructure, safety, security, congressional and public affairs, information technology, corporate business office services, business and financial management, and property management.

Dr. Lewis began her career at Crane in 1990 where she has held numerous operational, leadership, and management roles. She was an HR practitioner, spent time in the corporate business office, and served as a branch and division manager in multiple organizations. In 2009, Dr. Lewis was named the deputy department director for the Global Deterrence and Defense Department. In this capacity, she provided operational oversight for strategic mission's workload, developed and maintained strong customer relationships, and facilitated strategic and business planning efforts with the department director and division leadership team. The department is responsible for development, acquisition, and sustainment of electronic systems and components in support of defense strategic missions and customers.

In 2012, Dr. Lewis was selected as the command's first female chief of staff. In this position she was recognized as a member of Crane's Executive Leadership Team, and she served as an advisor to the commanding officer and technical director, and their staff. Throughout her career, she has maintained an active role in working on behalf of the Crane workforce. She has been instrumental to the establishment of Crane Division University, and to the facilitation of the organization's hallmark leadership development courses.

Dr. Helen MacLennan is assistant professor of management at Saint Leo University's Tampa, FL and MacDill AFB education centers where she teaches a variety of management and leadership courses at the undergraduate and graduate levels and organizational behavior and applied research at the doctoral level. She also serves as the dissertation committee chair for several Saint Leo University DBA students.

Dr. MacLennan serves as a certified small business mentor for Pinellas County SCORE. She serves on the editorial review board for the *Journal of Conflict Management* and as a reviewer for the *Transnational Journal of Business* and the *International Journal of Doctoral Studies.* Dr. MacLennan also serves as a site evaluator for the Accreditation Council for Business Schools and Programs (ACBSP). She has published research in the *Journal of Conflict Management, International Journal of Doctoral Studies, Journal of Excellence in Business Education, Southeast Case Research Journal, Journal of Transportation Management, International Journal of Diverse Identities,* and the *Journal of the Scholarship of Teaching and Learning.* (LinkedIn: https://www.linkedin.com/in/helenmaclennan/)

Peggy McNeive is the owner of Peggy A. McNeive, LLC., a business providing arbitration, facilitation, and mediation services. Currently, as well as operating her business, she teaches as an adjunct professor for two classes at the University of Missouri-Kansas City School of Law: Mediation and Lawyers and Dispute Resolution. Her website is pamcneive.com.

Ms. McNeive holds a Master of Law in dispute resolution from the University of Missouri-Columbia School of Law, a Juris Doctorate from the University of Missouri-Kansas City School of Law, and a bachelor's degree in general studies from the University of Kansas.

Before she retired from the federal government Ms. McNeive was a commissioner with Federal Mediation and Conciliation Service (FMCS) in the Kansas City, Missouri field office. Prior to joining FMCS, Ms. McNeive was employed by several private law firms, including being a sole practitioner, whose work centered on labor management relations. She also practiced in the area of equal employment opportunity discrimination claims, personal injury, Taft-Hartley pension and health and welfare funds, social security claims, and worker's compensation.

Christina Murtaugh spent the past decade working to build sustainable peace across the globe and integrating these principles into organizational change. Her previous work in international peacebuilding includes: helping lead a multi-project rule of law portfolio in Libya; supporting the development of a new approach to reforming justice and security systems; and facilitating a process to redefine the business model and marketing strategy for peacebuilding education and training. Christina graduated from the University of Kentucky with a BA in political science and economics and from the College of William and Mary with a JD.

Dr. E. Kobena Osam is an assistant professor in organizational leadership and an affiliate faculty member of the master's in public administration program at Northern Kentucky University. His primary research interest is focused on employee engagement, with a specific focus on exploring ways to create, manage, and sustain a happier and healthier workforce. Dr. Osam's additional research interests include corporate social responsibility and performance improvement. He has been published in several journals including *Human Resource Development Review* and *Performance Improvement Quarterly*, and has presented his research at many national and international conferences. Dr. Osam also has consulting experience, specializing in job analysis, job evaluation, and employee relations for clients in the retail, higher education, and manufacturing industries in North America.

Gerry Rooney has a particular expertise in alternative dispute resolution and has been involved in the conduct of hundreds of independent investigations and workplace mediations in both the public and private sector organizations. Gerry has completed investigations into a range of matters including company governance issues, abuse in care, and protected disclosures. However, Gerry's primary investigation experience is in the area of respect and dignity in the workplace including bullying, harassment, and sexual harassment cases.

Gerry was appointed to the panel of external adjudicators at the Workplace Relations Commission in 2015 and he currently hears a range of disputes and complaints as an adjudicator officer.

Gerry has worked as a mediator for over fifteen years. He is a practitioner member and a former president of the Mediators' Institute of Ireland. (2013–2015). Gerry has extensive experience in mediating in all types of workplace and commercial disputes. He is also a certified mediator trainer. Gerry also sits as an external mediator for the Financial Services Ombudsman Bureau. He was a member of the National Audit Panel for the Equality Authority where he has conducted some 30 organizational reviews and action plans across a range of sectors, and has provided training to EQUINET—the European Network of Equality Bodies representing some 33 member organizations from 28 EU countries. Gerry has provided training for workplace investigators and provides training for MII Certified Mediators, including mediation training for the Financial Services Ombudsman Bureau and former Equality Tribunal Equality Officers.

Anthony (Tony) L. Rose has been married to Joie Lanham for 39 years. He has four children and nine grandchildren. Tony has served on the church staff at First Baptist in West Memphis, Tennessee and Arkansas and Porter Memorial Baptist in Lexington, Kentucky. He served as senior pastor at Columbia Baptist Church in Columbia, Kentucky and Sherbrooke Baptist Church in Lake Worth, Florida. Currently, he is the senior pastor at LaGrange Baptist Church in LaGrange, Kentucky, where he has been for 26 years. For the 2014–2015 Southern Baptist Conventions, he was the chairperson of the Mental Health Advisory Group. Tony has a BA in history from Western Kentucky University; a Master of Divinity from Mid-America Baptist Theological Seminary, Memphis, Tennessee; a Master of Science in conflict management from Sullivan University, Louisville, Kentucky; and a Doctorate of Ministry from the Southern Baptist Theological Seminary, Louisville, Kentucky.

Dr. Brad Shuck is associate professor in the College of Education and Human Development at the University of Louisville. His primary areas of research include the application, meaning, and measurement of employee engagement, emerging areas of positive psychology, and leader development. He has given presentations and conducted research in four of the seven continents across the globe. In addition to his academic work, he is routinely cited in U.S.-based international media outlets including *Forbes, The Washington Post,* and *TIME,* as well as international outlets including *Business World Online* and the *Hindu Times.* Shuck was named the 2016 Early Career Scholar by the Academy of Human Resource Development and has received several awards for his applied research, including the AHRD Excellence in Scholarly Practice (2016), the Child-Life Council Research-to-Practice Award (2015), the E F Holton III Outstanding Article of the Year (2013 & 2015), and the Advances in Developing Human Resources Outstanding Issue of the Year (2011). Shuck was recognized as a Faculty

Favorite at UofL in 2012, 2013, 2014, 2015, 2017, and 2018, and named one of the Top Four Faculty Favorites in 2016. Shuck is a Commonwealth Scholar and a member of the Honorable Order of Kentucky Colonels. He holds faculty affiliate status with the Department of Counseling and Human Development (UofL) and has done extensive work with the United States Army Cadet-Command, Ft. Knox, Kentucky.

Dr. David Simpson is the Fifth Third Bank Professor in Community Development at the University of Louisville, and serves as department chair for Urban and Public Affairs. Dr. Simpson was a founding faculty in the creation of the university's Master of Urban Planning degree. Dr. Simpson has directed the Center for Hazards Research since 2003, bringing in over $10 million dollars in external funding. In 2012, Dr. Simpson became chair of the University's Sustainability Council, and has successfully led efforts create undergraduate and graduate degrees in Sustainability. Since 2015, Dr. Simpson has been exploring the relationship of humans and canines, particularly in urban environments. He annually offers a course entitled: "Dogs in Society: Understanding the Human–Canine Relationship." In January 2019, he launched a new research lab, called the "Human–Canine Dynamics Research Lab," which he co-directs with Dr. Sandra Sephton.

Dr. Simpson has served on the National Academies of Science, Disaster Roundtable, and has been a Natural Hazards Research Fellow for the National Science Foundation. Dr. Simpson has been recognized by AAAS as one of the "Next Generation of Leaders in Science and Technology." Dr. Simpson loves to travel, camp, and hike with his family (and dogs!).

Tyler Smith is an associate ombudsman at the National Institutes of Health's Office of the Ombudsman, Center for Cooperative Resolution. He earned a Master of Arts in conflict analysis and dispute resolution from Salisbury University. Smith has trained and worked as a mediator, facilitator, conflict coach, and trainer in community and organizational settings. Prior to joining the NIH community, he spent several years working at The Bosserman Center for Conflict Resolution; a nonprofit organization that fosters local, national, and international peace building through the teaching, training, and research of conflict analysis techniques and skills. Smith is an active member of the International Ombudsman Association (IOA), where he co-chairs a subcommittee of the Research and Assessment Committee, and the Coalition of Federal Ombudsman (COFO). Smith is interested in research related to ombuds practice, the connection between ombuds work and related fields. He is currently working on a research group to understand and measure perceptions of the ombuds role within the organizations they serve. Tyler Smith contributed to this chapter in his personal capacity. The views expressed are his own and do not necessarily represent the views of the National Institutes of Health or the United States Government.

Creighlynn D. Thoele, PhD, serves as branch chief of the Airmen Innovation and Mission Enhancement Division for the United States Air Force's Global Strike Command based out of Barksdale Air Force Base, LA. Drawing from her past experiences as a U.S. Army Human Intelligence Officer, Creighlynn's research efforts focus on explaining the impact of individual and collective behavior on organizational and operational effectiveness. Her growing body of research examines the psychological, generational, and cultural differences that influence employee behaviors and how these differences can create a competitive advantage for an organization. She holds an MBA from Cameron University in Lawton, OK, and a PhD in strategic management from Sullivan University in Louisville, KY.

Dr. Monica Valentine is a human resources practitioner-scholar with expertise in the areas of developing HR policies and procedures, employee relations, diversity management, and training and development. She's held numerous positions with the Commonwealth of Kentucky, where she spent over a decade building infrastructure through technology, compliance, and people. As an HR subject matter expert, Dr. Valentine's consulting portfolio includes working through complex issues with clients and creating sound solutions that address current and future business needs. Upon earning a master's degree in public administration and a terminal degree in strategic management, Dr. Valentine was highly sought after to teach public administration, human resource management, diversity, social equity, and nonprofit administration courses. In 2017, she accepted a tenure-track faculty position with Kentucky State University, her alma mater. Currently, Dr. Valentine directs the Master of Public Administration program, which offers concentrations in human resources management, nonprofit administration, international development, and management information systems. As the first female and minority to hold this position, she projects a progressive message of educational opportunity for all, inspiring women and minorities to pursue both their educational and personal dreams.

Dr. Kyle Werner is the director of the office of engagement for the Naval Surface Warfare Center, Crane Division. With a civil service career of more than two decades, Dr. Werner has held various leadership positions of increasing responsibility throughout his civil service career of more than two decades. In his current position, Dr. Werner serves as NSWC Crane's director of the Office of Engagement. As the director of the Office of Engagement, Dr. Werner is responsible for strategic command initiatives that contribute to advancing the command's robust and rapidly expanding innovation ecosystem, establishing national leadership roles, and promoting meaningful strategic engagements on behalf of NSWC Crane. The Office of Engagement is responsible for coordinating regional and national strategic partnerships that enhance the command's ability to carry out its assigned mission and contribute positively to the quality of life within the region.

Dr. LaVena Wilkin is the director of the PhD and graduate management programs at Sullivan University (www.sullivan.edu), a position she has held since June 2013. Before joining Sullivan University, she spent 26 years in the construction industry, and three of those years she co-owned a commercial masonry sub-contracting company. After selling the construction company in 2001, she came to work full time at Sullivan serving as the associate director of the evening and weekend division. She was also the dean of the College of Business for Sullivan University for 3 years and the dean of Conflict Management programs for 5 years.

LaVena has facilitated workshops on conflict styles, workplace bullying, forgiveness, emotional intelligence, organizational conflict, conflict and change, employee engagement, dealing with difficult people, and the P.E.A.C.E.© model of conflict management. She is also coeditor of a book entitled *Organizational Conflicts: Challenges and Solutions.* She contributed a chapter in the book, *The Mediation Handbook: Theory, Research, and Practice.* Finally, she is the editor for the *Journal of Conflict Management,* a scholarly journal that publishes research in many of the multidisciplinary areas of managing conflicts.

LaVena is the vice president for the leadership council at Unity Church of East Louisville. Additionally, she previously served on the board of directors for the Society for the Prevention and Aggression Among Adolescence (SPAVA). She has an MBA from Sullivan University in Louisville, Kentucky and a PhD in conflict analysis and resolution from Nova Southeastern University in Ft. Lauderdale, Florida. (Her website is: peacefromconflict.com. Her LinkedIn page is: https://www.linkedin.com/in/lavena-wilkin-71104a6/)

Dr. Lisa Witzler is a training specialist in the National Cancer Institute's Office of Workforce Planning and Development. She was previously an associate ombudsman in the National Institutes of Health Office of the Ombudsman/Center for Cooperative Resolution. She earned her PhD in conflict analysis and resolution from Nova Southeastern University and a Master of Arts in dispute resolution from the University of Massachusetts. Prior to joining NIH, Dr. Witzler worked at the program on negotiation at Harvard Law School. She became interested in managing conflict in a scientific research organization during her time at the Broad Institute of MIT and Harvard University where she learned about the unique needs of scientists, post-doctoral research fellows, and administrators. She is a former vice president of the International Ombudsman Association, the leading professional association for organizational ombuds. Her research interests and scholarly publications include the influences on organizational ombuds practice, group development and dynamics, managing group conflict and leadership development. She has spent the majority of her professional career managing conflict within scientific and research organizations and enjoys the unique challenges people in these organizations face. Dr. Witzler contributed to this chapter in her personal capacity. The views expressed are her own and do not necessarily represent the views of the National Institutes of Health or the United States Government.

Dr. Sandy Zehr serves as the director of Congressional & Public Affairs for Naval Surface Warfare Center, Crane Division (NSWC Crane) and is the division manager for the Corporate Communications Division. He was appointed to his present position in 2016. Sandy leads a highly talented workforce focused on planning and protocol, corporate communications, and visual information. His division serves as the principal advisor to NSWC Crane regarding policy decisions, courses of action, and ramifications related to internal and external communication. Prior to joining NSWC Crane, Dr. Zehr spent over 27 years in private sector corporate leadership. During this time, he served as vice president and shareholder for Artistic Media Partners, which was Indiana's largest radio broadcasting corporation. In this role, Sandy was primarily responsible for organizational leadership and operational oversight for part of the organization's portfolio. Sandy joined NSWC Crane as the command advocacy lead in 2011 and was responsible for command-level leadership in the development, planning, and execution of NSWC Crane corporate outreach strategy. In 2015, Sandy was appointed as the division manager for the NSWC Crane Customer Advocacy and Strategy Division. In this role Sandy led NSWC Crane efforts in customer management, customer satisfaction, and corporate strategy development.

Printed and bound by CPI Group (UK) Ltd, Croydon, CR0 4YY

15/09/2026

14962335-0005